Joe Cummings has been involved in South-East Asian studies for many years and was a Peace Corps volunteer in Thailand during the '70s. Since then he has been a translator/interpreter of Thai in San Francisco, a graduate student in Thai language and Asian art history (MA 1981) at the University of California (Berkeley), a columnist for *The Asia Record*, an East-West Center Scholar in Hawaii, a university lecturer in Malaysia, and a bilingual studies consultant in the US and Taiwan. He has also lived or travelled in Burma, Canada, China, Hawaii, Hong Kong, India, Indonesia, Laos, Malaysia, Mexico, Nepal, Singapore, and Western Europe.

Fluent in Thai, Joe has travelled through all 74 of the Kingdom's provinces by bus, air, train, motorcycle, boat, elephant and foot. Joe is also the author of Lonely Planet's *Thai Phrasebook* and a contributor to several other LP titles, including guides on Burma, Laos, Malaysia/Singapore and Indonesia. He occasionally writes for *The San Francisco Examiner*, *Transitions Abroad*, *Great Expeditions*, *Conde Nast's Traveler* and other periodicals.

Lonely Planet Credits

Editors	Katie Cody
	Chris Taylor
Maps	Chris Lee Ack
	Ralph Roob
	David Windle
Cover Design,	
Design & Illustrations	Vicki Beale

Thanks to Gillian Cummings for copy editing; Peter Turner for invaluable help in fathoming the mysteries of Ventura; Tom Smallman and Lyn McGaurr for help with final proofing; Sue Mitra and Peter Turner for editorial guidance; Peter Flavelle and Greg Herriman for additional mapping; Anne Jefree, Margeret Jung and Graham Imeson for additional illustrations; and Dr Deja for the Thai script;.

Acknowledgements – this edition

First, heaps of thanks to the following Thais who assisted along the way: the Jenlapwatt-anakul family, Satit Nillwongse, Chalermlap Ganachara Na Ayuthaya, Kritkamon Sakun, Chalong Anunyapisit, Pradthana Doungmala, Apin Banduwongse, Sapachai Pitaksakorn, Preecha Poolphok phol, Col Somchai Tantemsapya, K Pimol, Tchaisiri Samudavanija, Max and Tiok, Khun Jaruphong, Khun Thanachai, Doonchu Hankham, Suraphon Svetsreni, Khun Phonprapa, Khun Nuantha D, Khun Sansern, the manager of Jansom Thara (sorry I forgot your name); Suthon Namvises, Chanida Thongraksawong, Virawat Wattanayakorn, Suksom Senajai, Ajaan Nirundorn, Suvan Boonthae, and Siriwan Campbell. Most of all I am indebted to M L Chainimit Navarat, whose advice, assistance and friendship have been invaluable throughout the updating of this book.

The Tourist Authority of Thailand and its employees, as usual, were of considerable assistance.

I also owe thanks to these farangs: travelling companion David Sheppard, travelling companion/tireless research assistant Doug Glenn, map assistant Lynne Cummings, David Unkovich, Bill Zabel, Nancy Chandler, Ralph Radtke, Robert Mather, and Don Campbell.

I've tried to name everyone who was of direct assistance but know I've forgotten a few names along the way. Please forgive me if you're not listed and accept my gratitude.

Thanks also to the hundreds of travellers who have taken time to write, especially letter-writers Heather McNeice, Alastair Murray, Doug Hinckley. Isabelle Metayer, Betsy Neidel, Lucas van Wees and Veronique van der Grinten.

Author's Note to Readers
When using the information contained in this guide to find your way around Thailand, keep in mind the Buddhist concept of *anicca* or 'impermanence'. All things in the world of travel especially are in a constant state of flux and Thailand is no exception. What you read here are conceptual snap-shots of single moments in time, filtered through one person's perceptions. They represent the very best of my research efforts at the time

of writing, but were bound to change the second I turned my attention away from research and began writing it all down, a necessary part of the process in getting this book to you. Don't expect to find things to be exactly as described in the text – stay flexible and you'll enjoy yourself more.

A Warning & a Request
Things change – prices go up, schedules change, good places go bad and bad places go bankrupt – nothing stays the same. So if you find things better or worse, recently opened or long since closed, please write and tell us and help make the next edition better.

Your letters will be used to help update future editions and, where possible, important changes will also be included in a Stop Press section in reprints.

All information is greatly appreciated and the best letters will receive a free copy of the next edition, or any other Lonely Planet book of your choice.

Thailand
a travel survival kit

Joe Cummings

Thailand - a travel survival kit
4th edition

Published by
Lonely Planet Publications
Head Office: PO Box 617, Hawthorn, Vic 3122, Australia
US Office: PO Box 2001A, Berkeley, CA 94702, USA

Printed by
Singapore National Printers Ltd, Singapore

Photographs by
Don Campbell (DC), Joe Cummings (JC), Meredith Hunnibell (MH), Ralph Kaminski (RK),
Tracy Maurer (TM), Richard Nebeski (RN), Bill Preston (BP), David Sheppard (DS),
Chris Taylor (CT), Tony Wheeler (TW), Tourist Authority of Thailand (TAT)
Front cover: Buddhas, Chiang Mai (CT)
Back cover: *Mawn Khwan* (TAT)

Cartoons by
Tony Jenkins

Thai script typeset by
Polyprint, Melbourne

First Published
February 1982

This Edition
March 1990

**Although the author and publisher have tried to make the information as
accurate as possible, they accept no responsibility for any loss, injury or
inconvenience sustained by any person using this book.**

National Library of Australia Cataloguing in Publication Data

Cummings, Joe.
Thailand, a travel survival kit.

4th ed.
Includes index.
ISBN 0 86442 080 3.

1. Thailand – Description and travel – 1976 – Guide-books.
1. Title.

915.930444

Contents

Contents

Introduction

Thailand, or Siam as it was called until the 1940s, has never been colonised by a foreign power, while all of its South-East Asian neighbours have undergone European imperialism (or more recently, ideological domination by Communism – which originated in Europe) at one time or another. True, it has suffered periodic invasions on the part of the Burmese and the Khmers and was briefly occupied by the Japanese in WW II, but the kingdom was never externally controlled long enough to dampen the Thais' serious individualism. I say serious because the Thais are so often depicted as fun-loving, happy-go-lucky folk (which they often are), but this quality is something they have worked hard to preserve.

This is not to say that Thailand has not experienced any western influence. Like other Asian countries it has both suffered and benefited from contact with foreign cultures. But the everchanging spirit of Thai culture has remained dominant, even in modern city life. The end result is that Thailand has much to interest the traveller: historic culture, lively arts, exotic islands, nightlife, a tradition of friendliness and hospitality to strangers, and one of the world's most exciting cuisines.

Travel in this tropical country is fairly comfortable and down-to-earth. The rail, bus and air travel network is extensive and every place worth visiting is easily accessible. There are many places worth visiting, many sights to see, a multi-faceted culture to experience and it is all quite affordable by today's international travel standards.

Transliteration

As Thai uses a totally different script to our own, any Thai name has to be transliterated into our script. Transliteration is very often a matter of opinion, and this book, like anything else on Thailand, is bound to be out of step at times. Generally names in this book follow the most common practice or, in the case of hotels, for example, simply copies their Roman script name, no matter what devious process was used to transliterate directly from Thai.

Problems often arise when a name is transliterated differently, even at the same place. 'Thavee', for example, can be Tavi, Thawee, or various other versions. Outside of the International Phonetic Alphabet, there is no 'proper' way to transliterate Thai - only wrong ways. The Thais themselves are incredibly inconsistent in this matter, often using English letters that have no equivalent sound in Thai: Faisal for Phaisan, Bhumiphol for Phumiphon, Vanich for Wanit.

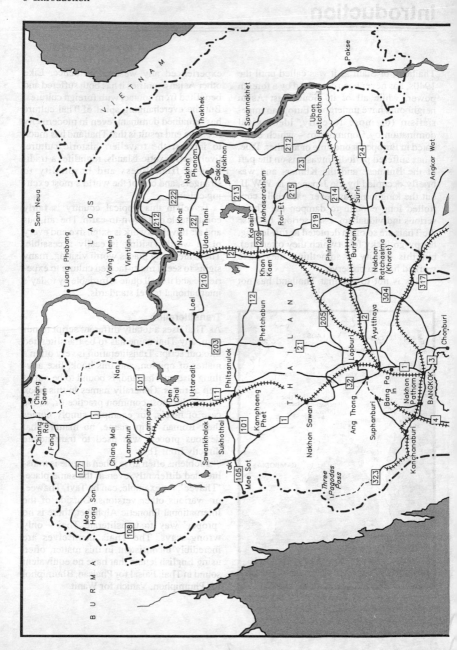

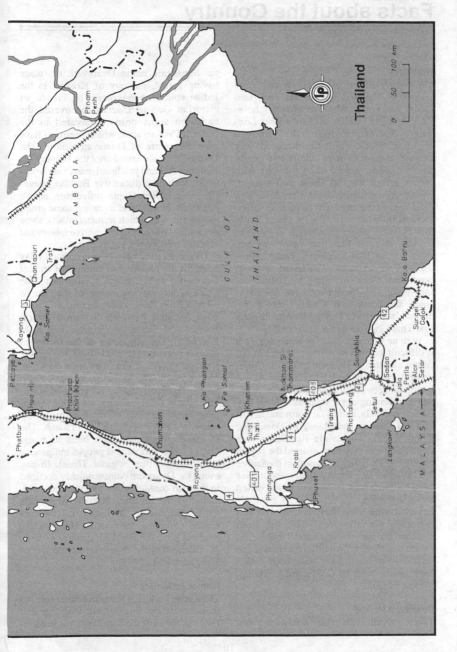

Facts about the Country

HISTORY

The history of the geographical area now known as Thailand reaches far back into 'hoary antiquity'. World-renowned scholar Paul Benedict (author of *Austro-Thai Language & Culture*) found that modern linguistic theory, which ties numerous key items in ancient Chinese culture to an early Thai linguistic group, taken together with recent archaeological finds in Thailand, enable us to establish South-East Asia 'as a focal area in the emergent cultural development of homo sapiens. It now seems likely that the first true agriculturists anywhere, perhaps also the first true metal workers, were Austro-Thai speakers'. These proto-Thais seem to have proliferated all over South-East Asia, including the islands of Indonesia, and some may have settled in south and south-west China, later to 're-migrate' to northern Thailand to establish the first Thai kingdom in the 13th century.

With no written records or chronologies it is difficult to say with certainty what kind of cultures existed in Thailand before the Christian era. However, by the 6th century AD an important network of agricultural communities was thriving as far south as modern-day Pattani and Yala, and as far north and northeast as Lamphun and Muang Fa Daet (near Khon Kaen). Theravada Buddhism was flourishing and may have entered the region during India's Ashokan Period, in the 2nd or 3rd centuries BC, when Indian missionaries were said to have been sent to a land called Suvarnabhumi – 'Land of Gold'. Suvarnabhumi most likely corresponds to a remarkably fertile area stretching from southern Burma, across central Thailand, to eastern Cambodia. Two different cities in the central river basin have long been called Suphanburi, 'City of Gold', and U Thong, 'Cradle of Gold'.

Dvaravati Period

This loose collection of city-states was given the Sanskritic name Dvaravati, or 'place having gates', the city of Krishna in the Indian epic *Mahabharata*. The French art historian George Coedes discovered the name on some coins excavated in the Nakhon Pathom area, which seems to have been the centre of Dvaravati culture. The Dvaravati Period lasted until the 11th or 12th centuries AD and produced many fine works of art, including distinctive Buddha images (showing Indian Gupta influence), stucco reliefs on temples and in caves, some architecture (little of which remains intact), some exquisite terracotta heads, votive tablets and other miscellaneous sculpture.

Dvaravati may have been a cultural relay point for the pre-Angkor cultures of ancient Cambodia and Champa to the east. The Chinese, through the travels of the famous pilgrim Xuan Zang, knew the area as T'o-lo-po-ti, located between Sriksetra (North Burma) and Tsanapura (Sambor Prei Kuk-Kambuja). The ethnology of the Dvaravati peoples is a controversial subject, though the standard decree is that they were Mons or Mon-Khmers. The Mons themselves seem to have been descended from a group of Indian immigrants from Kalinga, an area overlapping the boundaries of the modern Indian states of Orissa and Andhra Pradesh. The Dvaravati Mons may have been an ethnic mix of these people and people indigenous to the region (the original Thais). In any event, the Dvaravati culture quickly declined in the 11th century under the political domination of the invading Khmers who made their headquarters in Lopburi. The area around Lamphun, then called Haripunchai, held out until the late 12th century or later, as evidenced by the Dvaravati architecture of Wat Kukut in Lamphun.

Khmer Influence

The Khmer conquest brought Khmer cultural influence in the form of art, language and religion. Some of the Sanskrit terms in Mon-

10

Thai vocabulary entered the language during the Khmer or Lopburi Period between the 11th and 13th centuries. Monuments from this period located in Kanchanaburi, Lopburi and many locations throughout the northeast, were constructed in the Khmer style and compare favourably with architecture in Angkor. Elements of Brahmanism, Theravada Buddhism and Mahayana Buddhism intermixed as Lopburi became a religious centre, and some of each remain to this day in Thai religious and court ceremonies.

Other Kingdoms

While all this was taking place, a distinctly Thai state called Nan Chao (650 to 1250) was flourishing in what later became Yunnan and Sichuan in China. Nan Chao maintained close relations with imperial China and the two neighbours enjoyed much cultural exchange. The Mongols, under Kublai Khan, conquered Nan Chao in 1253, but long before they came, the Thai peoples began migrating southward, homesteading in and around what is today Laos and northern Thailand. They 'infiltrated' South-East Asia in small groups, assimilating the peoples they encountered. Some Thais became mercenaries for the Khmer armies in the early 12th century, as depicted on the walls of Angkor Wat. The Thais were called 'Syams' by the Khmers, possibly from the Sanskrit *syam* meaning 'swarthy', because of their relatively deeper skin colour. This may have been how the Thai kingdom eventually came to be called Syam or Siam.

Southern Thailand, the upper Malay Peninsula, was under the control of the Srivijaya Empire, the headquarters of which were in Sumatra, between the 8th and 13th centuries. The regional centre for Srivijaya was Chaiya, near the modern town of Surat Thani. Srivijaya art remains can still be seen in Chaiya and its environs.

Sukhothai Period

Several Thai principalities in the Mekong Valley united in the 13th and 14th centuries, and Thai princes took Haripunchai from the Mons to form Lan Na, and the Sukhothai Region from the Khmers, whose Angkor government was declining fast. The Sukhothai Kingdom declared its independence in 1238 and quickly expanded its sphere of influence, taking advantage not only of the declining Khmer power but the weakening Srivijaya domain in the south. Sukhothai is considered by the Siamese to be the first true Thai kingdom. It lasted until it was annexed by Ayuthaya in 1376, by which time a national identity of sorts had been forged.

The second Sukhothai king, Ram Khamheng, organised a writing system which became the basis for modern Thai, and also codified the Thai form of Theravada Buddhism, as borrowed from the Sinhalese. Many Thais today view the Sukhothai Period with sentimental vision, seeing it as a golden age of Thai politics, religion and culture – an egalitarian, noble period when everyone had enough to eat and the kingdom was unconquerable. Under Ram Khamheng, Sukhothai extended as far as Nakhon Si Thammarat in the south, to Vientiane and Luang Prabang in Laos, and to Pegu in southern Burma. For a short time (1448-86) the Sukhothai capital was moved to Phitsanulok.

Ayuthaya Period

The Thai kings of Ayuthaya became very powerful in the 14th and 15th centuries, taking over U Thong and Lopburi, former Khmer strongholds, and moving east in their conquests until Angkor was defeated in 1431. Even though the Khmers were their adversaries in battle, the Ayuthaya kings incorporated Khmer court customs and language. One result of this was that the Thai monarch gained more absolute authority during the Ayuthaya Period and assumed the title *devaraja* (god-king) as opposed to the then-traditional *dhammaraja* (dharmaking).

In the early 16th century Ayuthaya was receiving European visitors, and a Portuguese embassy was established in 1511. The Portuguese were followed by the Dutch in 1605, the English in 1612, the Danes in 1621 and the French in 1662.

In the mid-16th century Ayuthaya and the independent kingdom in Chiang Mai came

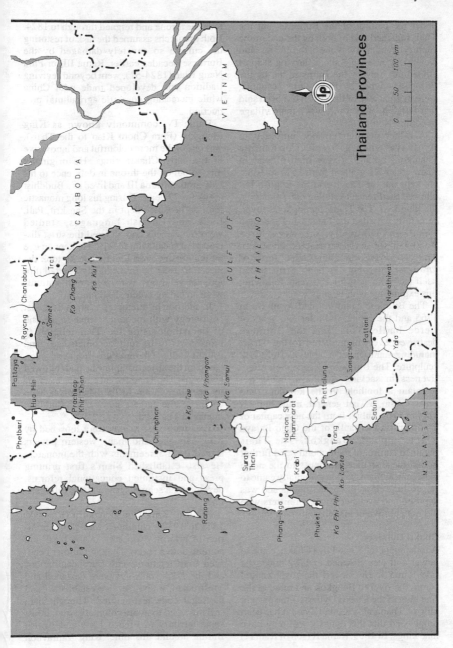

Thailand Provinces

0   50   100 km

under the control of the Burmese, but the Thais regained rule of both by the end of the century. Ayuthaya was one of the greatest and wealthiest cities in Asia, a thriving seaport envied not only by the Burmese but by the Europeans who, by their early accounts, were in great awe of the city. It has been said that London, at the time, was a mere village in comparison.

A rather peculiar episode unfolded in Ayuthaya when a Greek, Constantine Phaulkon, became a very high official in Siam under King Narai from 1675 to 1688. He kept out the Dutch and the English but allowed the French to station 600 soldiers in the kingdom. The Thais, fearing a takeover, forcefully expelled the French and executed Phaulkon. Ironically, the word for a 'foreigner' (of European descent) in modern Thai is *farang*, an abbreviated form of *farangset*, meaning 'French'. Siam sealed itself from the west for 150 years following this experience with farangs.

The Burmese again invaded Ayuthaya in 1765 and the capital fell after two years of fierce battle. This time the Burmese destroyed everything sacred to the Thais, including manuscripts, temples and religious sculpture. The Burmese, despite their effectiveness in sacking Ayuthaya, could not maintain a foothold in the kingdom, and Phya Taksin, a Thai general, made himself king in 1769, ruling from the new capital of Thonburi on the banks of the Chao Phraya River, opposite Bangkok. The Thais regained control of their country and further united the disparate provinces to the north with central Siam. Taksin eventually came to regard himself as the next Buddha and was deposed and executed by his ministers who did not approve of his religious fanaticism.

Chakri Dynasty

Another general, Chao Phya Chakri, came to power and was crowned in 1782 under the title Rama I. He moved the royal capital across the river to Bangkok and ruled as the first king of the Chakri Dynasty – the present king of Thailand is Rama IX and it has been prophesied that this dynasty will only have nine kings. In 1809, Rama II (son of Rama I)

took the throne and reigned through to 1824. Both monarchs assumed the task of restoring the culture so severely damaged by the Burmese decades earlier. Rama III, or Phra Nang Klao (1824-51), went beyond reviving tradition and developed trade with China while increasing domestic agricultural production.

Rama IV, commonly known as King Mongkut (Phra Chom Klao to the Thais), was one of the more colourful and innovative of the early Chakri kings. He originally missed out on the throne in deference to his half-brother Rama III and lived as a Buddhist monk for 27 years. During his long monastic term he became adept in the Sanskrit, Pali, Latin and English languages, studied western sciences and adopted the strict discipline of local Mon monks. He kept an eye on the outside world and when he took the throne in 1851 he immediately courted diplomatic relations with European nations, while avoiding colonialisation.

In addition he attempted to align Buddhist cosmology with modern science to the end of demythologising the Thai religion (a process yet to be fully accomplished), and founded the Thammayut monastic sect, based on the strict discipline he had followed as a monk. The Thammayut remains a minority sect in relation to the Mahanikai, who comprise the largest number of Buddhist monks in Thailand.

Thai trade restrictions were loosened by King Mongkut and many western powers signed trade agreements with the monarch. He also established Siam's first printing press and instituted educational reforms, developing a school system along European lines.

His son, King Chulalongkorn (Rama V, 1868 to 1910), continued Mongkut's tradition of reform, especially in the legal and administrative realm. Thailand further benefited from relations with European nations and the USA; railways were designed and constructed, a civil service established and the legal code restructured. Though Siam still managed to avoid colonialisation, it lost some territory to French Laos and British Burma around this time. King Vajiravudh

(Rama VI, 1910-25), during his rather short reign, introduced compulsory education as well as other educational reforms and further 'westernised' the nation by making the Thai calendar conform to western models.

While Vajiravudh's brother, King Prajadhipok (Rama VII, 1925-35), ruled, a group of Thai students living in Paris became so enamoured of democratic ideology that they mounted a successful coup d'etat against absolute monarchy in Siam. This bloodless revolution led to the development of a constitutional monarchy along British lines, with a mixed military-civilian group in power. Phibul Songkhram, a key military leader in the 1932 coup, maintained an effective position of power from 1938 until the end of WW II. Rama VIII (Ananda Mahidol), a nephew of Rama VII, ascended the throne in 1935 but was assassinated under mysterious circumstances in 1946. His brother Bhumipol Aduldej succeeded him as Rama IX.

Under the influence of Phibul's government, the country's name was officially changed from Siam to Thailand in 1949 – rendered in Thai as *Prathet Thai*. ('Prathet' is derived from the Sanskrit *pradesha* or 'country'; 'thai' is considered to have the connotation of 'free', though in actual usage it simply refers to the Tai races, which are found as far east as Tonkin, as far west as Assam, as far north as south China, and as far south as north Malaysia.)

World War II & Post War

The Japanese outflanked the Allied troops in Malaya and Burma in 1941 and the Phibul government complied with the Japanese in this action by allowing them into the Gulf of Thailand; consequently the Japanese troops occupied Thailand itself. Phibul then declared war on the USA and Great Britain (in 1942) but Seni Pramoj, the Thai ambassador in Washington, refused to deliver the declaration. Phibul resigned in 1944 under pressure from the Thai underground resistance and after V-J Day in 1945, Seni became premier.

In 1946, the year King Ananda was assassinated, Seni and his brother Kukrit were

unseated in a general election and a democratic civilian group took power for a short time, only to be overthrown by Phibul in 1948. In 1951 power was wrested from Phibul by General Sarit Thanarat, who continued the tradition of military dictatorship. However, Phibul somehow retained the actual position of premier until 1957 when Sarit finally had him exiled. Elections that same year forced Sarit to resign, go abroad for 'medical treatment' and then return in 1958 to launch another coup. This time he abolished the constitution, dissolved the parliament and banned all political parties, maintaining effective power until his death in 1963 of cirrhosis. From 1964 to 1973 the Thai nation was ruled by army officers Thanom Kittikachorn and Praphat Charusathien, during which time Thailand allowed the USA to develop several army bases within her borders in support of the American campaign in Vietnam.

Reacting to political repression, 10,000 Thai students publicly demanded a real constitution in June 1973. In October of the same year the military brutally suppressed a large demonstration at Thammasat University in Bangkok, but General Krit Sivara and King Bhumiphol refused to support further bloodshed, forcing Thanom and Praphat to leave Thailand. An elected, constitutional government ruled until October 1976 when students demonstrated again, this time protesting the return of Thanom to Thailand as a monk. Thammasat University again became a battlefield and a new right-wing government was installed with Thanin Kraivichien as premier. This particular incident disillusioned many Thai students and older intellectuals not directly involved, the result being that numerous idealists 'dropped out' of Thai society and joined the insurgents in the forests. In October 1977 another coup ousted Thanin and installed Kriangsak. In 1980 the military-backed position changed hands again, leaving Prem Tinsulanonda at the helm.

If you get the idea that the coup d'etat is popular in Thailand you're on the right track: I've counted 15 successful or attempted coups since 1932 (an average of almost three per decade!), not counting election-forced resignations. There have also been 10 'permanent' constitutions enacted since the first. However, even the successful coups rarely have resulted in drastic change and the Thai commoner will tell you that things *never* change – it depends on how closely you observe politics. On the other hand, it's very difficult to observe Thai politics over the last ten years or so and not recognise some real, functional changes emanating from non-coup sources.

Prem served as prime minister through 1988 and is credited with the political and economic stabilisation of Thailand in the post-Vietnam war years (only one coup attempt in the '80s!). The major accomplishment of the Prem years was a complete dismantling of the Communist Party of Thailand through an effective combination of amnesty programmes (which brought the students back from the forests) and military action. His administration is also considered responsible for a gradual democratisation of Thailand which culminated in the 1988 election of his successor, Chatichai Choonhavan.

It may be difficult for new arrivals to Thailand to appreciate the distance Thailand has come in the last 10 to 15 years. Between 1976 and 1981, freedom of speech and press were rather curtailed in Thailand and there was a strict curfew in Bangkok. Anyone caught in the streets past 1 am risked spending the night in one of Bangkok's mosquito-infested 'detention areas'. Under Prem, the curfew was lifted and dissenting opinions began to be heard publicly more often.

Traditionally every leading political figure in Thailand, including Prem, has had to receive the support of the Thai military, who are generally staunch reactionaries. Considering Thailand's geographic position it was difficult not to understand, to some extent, the fears of this ultra-conservative group. But with Prime Minister Chatichai, who is widely recognised as a particularly 'business-oriented' leader, this has begun to change. Approximately 60% of his Cabinet are former business executives rather than ex-military officers, as compared to 38% in the previous Cabinet.

High-ranking military officers are naturally disappointed with this *coup d'argent* and complain that Thailand is now being run by a plutocracy. Whereas government leadership during the '60s and '70s exploited the threat of invasion from bordering Marxist countries, Chatichai's plan is to incorporate Vietnam, Laos, Cambodia and Burma in a grand economic scheme in which Thailand will serve as broker to the rest of the world. Whether this will come to pass remains to be seen. Without a doubt, however, Thailand is entering a new era in which an inter-relationship between the country's current economic boom and democratisation will be interesting to observe.

GEOGRAPHY

Thailand has an area of 517,000 square km, making it slightly smaller than the state of Texas in the USA, or about the size of France. Its longest north-to-south distance is about 1860 km but its shape makes distances in any other direction a lot less. Its shape on the map has been compared to the head of an elephant, with its trunk extending down the Malay Peninsula, but it looks to me as if someone had squeezed the lower part of the 'boot' of Italy, forcing the volume into the top portion while reducing the bottom. The centre of Thailand, Bangkok, is at about 14° north latitude, putting it on a level with Madras, Manila, Guatemala and Khartoum.

The topography varies and can be divided into four main regions: the fertile centre region, dominated by the Chao Phraya river network; the north-east plateau, the kingdom's poorest region (thanks to 'thin' soil plus occasional droughts and floods), rising some 300 metres above the central plain; northern Thailand, a region of mountains and fertile valleys; and the southern peninsular region, which extends to the Malaysian frontier and is predominantly rainforests. The southern region receives the most annual rainfall and the north-east the least, although the north has less general humidity. Thailand's climate is ruled by monsoons, resulting in three seasons: rainy (June to October); cool and dry (November to February); and hot (March to May). For more information on climate see the Facts for the Visitor chapter.

For administrative purposes, Thailand is divided into 74 *jangwat* or provinces. Each province is subdivided into a number of *amphoe* or districts, which are further subdivided into *tambon* (precincts), and *muu baan* (villages). Municipal zones are called *thetsabaan*. The capital of a province is an *amphoe muang*; it takes the same name as the province of which it is capital.

CLIMATE

Thailand basically has three more or less distinct seasons: hot (March to June); rainy (July to October); and cool and dry (November to February). Some people say the rainy season begins in June, some say it begins in July. However, although 'officially' the rains begin in July, the truth is, it depends on the monsoons in any given year. It rains more and longer in the south, which is subject to two monsoons, so that the wet season effectively lasts through January. The temperature is more even year-round in the south; when it is 35°C in Bangkok it may be only 32°C in Phuket. The hot season is the hottest along the north-east plain, easily reaching 39°C in the daytime and only a few degrees less at night.

Most of Thailand is very humid, the mountains in the north being the exception. The temperature can drop to 13°C at night during the cool season in Chiang Mai and even lower in Mae Hong Son – if you're visiting the north during the cooler months, longsleeved shirts and pullovers would be in order.

In central Thailand it rains most during August and September, though there may be floods in October since the ground has reached full saturation by then. If you are in Bangkok in early October don't be surprised if you find yourself in hip-deep water in certain parts of the city. In 1983, when the floods were reputed to be the worst in 30 years, it was that deep in every part of the city! It rains a little less in the north, August being the peak month. The north-east gets less rain and periodically suffers droughts. In Phuket it rains most in May (for an average

21 out of 30 days) and in October (for an average of 22 out of 30 days), undergoing two monsoons. Generally, travelling in the rainy season is not unpleasant at all, but unpaved roads may close down occasionally.

The best overall time to visit Thailand vis à vis climate would be between November and February – during these months it rains least and is not so hot. See the south during the coolest months, December and January, the north in February when it begins warming up, elsewhere (Bangkok included) in November. Of course, if you can't choose your time so carefully, come anytime, but be prepared to roast in April and to do some wading in October – probably the two worst months weatherwise.

On the other hand, there are more tourists about in December and August. Avoid these months if you want to avoid crowds of *farang* vacationers. The least crowded months are June and September.

OPIUM & THE GOLDEN TRIANGLE

The opium poppy, *Papaver somnniferum*, has been cultivated and its resins extracted for use as a narcotic at least since the time of the early Greek empire. The Chinese were introduced to the drug by Arab traders during the time of Kublai Khan (1279-94). It was so highly valued for its medicinal properties that hill tribe minorities in southern China began cultivating the opium poppy in order to raise money to pay taxes to their Han Chinese rulers. Easy to grow, opium became a way for the nomadic hill tribes to raise what cash they needed in transactions (willing and unwilling) with the lowland world. Many of the hill tribes that migrated to Thailand and Laos in the post WW II era, in order to avoid persecution in Burma and China, took with them their one cash crop, the poppy. The poppy is well suited to hillside cultivation as it flourishes on steep slopes and in nutrient-poor soils.

The opium trade became especially lucrative in South-East Asia during the '60s and early '70s when US armed forces were embroiled in Vietnam. Alfred McCoy's *The Politics of Heroin in Southeast Asia* recounts how contact with the GI market not only expanded the immediate Asian market, but provided outlets to world markets. Before this time the source of most of the world's heroin was the Middle East. Soon everybody wanted in and various parties alternately quarrelled over and cooperated in illegal opium commerce. Most notable were the Nationalist Chinese Army refugees living in northern Burma and northern Thailand, and the Burmese anti-government rebels, in particular the Burmese Communist Party, the Shan States Army and the Shan United Army.

The American CIA eventually became involved in a big way, using profits from heroin runs aboard US aircraft to Vietnam and further afield to finance covert operations throughout Indo-China. This of course led to an increase in the availability of heroin throughout the world, which in turn led to increased production in the remote northern areas of Thailand, Burma and Laos, where there was little government interference. This area came to be known as the 'Golden Triangle' because of local fortunes amassed by the 'opium warlords' – Burmese and Chinese military-businessmen who controlled the movement of opium across three international borders.

As more opium was available, more was consumed and the demand increased along with the profits – so the cycle expanded. As a result, opium cultivation became a full-time job for some hill-tribe groups within the Golden Triangle. Hill economies were destabilised to the point where opium production became a necessary means of survival for thousands of people, including the less nomadic Shan people.

One of the Golden Triangle's most colourful figures is Khun Sa – also known as Chang Chi-fu, also known as Sao Mong Khawn – a half-Chinese, half-Shan opium warlord. He got his start in the '50s and '60s working for the Kuomintang (KMT) – Chiang Kai Shek's Nationalist Chinese troops who had fled to Burma. The KMT were continuing military operations against the Chinese Communists along the Burma-China border, financed by the smuggling of opium (with CIA protection). They employed Khun Sa as one of their prime local supporter/advisors. Khun Sa

broke with the KMT in the early '60s after establishing his own opium-smuggling business, with heroin refineries in northern Thailand.

From that time on, the history of heroin smuggling in the Golden Triangle has been intertwined with the exploits of Khun Sa. In 1966, the Burmese government deputised Khun Sa as head of 'village defence forces' against the Burmese Communist Party (BCP), which was at maximum strength at this time and fully involved in opium trade. Khun Sa cleverly used his government backing to consolidate power and build up his own militia by developing the Shan United Army (SUA), an anti-government insurgent group heavily involved in opium throughout the Golden Triangle in competition with the BCP and KMT.

When the KMT attempted an 'embargo' on SUA opium trade by blocking caravan routes into Thailand and Laos, Khun Sa initiated what has come to be known as the Opium War of 1967 and thwarted the embargo. However the KMT managed to chase Khun Sa, along with a contingent of SUA troops running an opium caravan

routed for Thailand, into Laos, where Burmese officials arrested Khun Sa and the Laotian government seized the opium. Khun Sa escaped Burmese custody by means of a carefully planned combination of extortion and bribery in 1975 and returned to take command of the SUA. About the same time, the Burmese government broke KMT control of opium trafficking and Khun Sa stepped in to become the prime opium warlord in the Triangle, working from his headquarters in Ban Hin Taek, Chiang Rai Province, Thailand. Coincidentally, US forces pulled out of Indo-China at this time so there was no longer any competition from CIA conduits in Laos. Ironically since then, the primary law enforcement conflict has been between US-backed Thai forces and the SUA.

Whenever they receive a large financial contribution from the USA Drug Enforcement Agency (DEA), Thai army rangers sweep northern Thailand from Tak to Chiang Rai and Mae Hong Son, destroying poppy fields and heroin refineries but rarely making arrests. One recent sweep, a US$800,000 operation in December 1985, accomplished the destruction of 40 square km or 25,000 rai (one rai is equal to 1600 square metres) of poppy fields in Chiang Mai, Chiang Rai, Mae Hong Son, Tak and Nan. Hill-tribe and Shan cultivators, at the bottom of the profit scale, stood by helplessly while their primary means of livelihood was hacked to the ground. A crop substitution programme, developed by the Thai royal family in 1959 (a year earlier cultivation of the opium poppy for profit had been made illegal), has generally been recognised as an almost complete failure. Success has only occurred in selected areas where crop substitution is accompanied by a concentrated effort to indoctrinate hill tribes into mainstream Thai culture.

In the late '70s and early '80s, the SUA continued to buy opium from the BCP, Shan and hill-tribe cultivators in Burma and Thailand, transporting and selling the product to ethnic Chinese syndicates in Thailand who control access to world markets. SUA strength has been estimated at between 1500 and 8000 regulars, putting it on a par with the BCP and the Karen National Union, Burma's two largest insurgent groups (among the 25 different groups operating in 1983).

A turning point in Khun Sa's fortunes occurred in 1982 and 1983 when the Thais launched a full-scale attack on his Ban Hin Taek stronghold, forcing Khun Sa to flee to the mountains of the Kok River Valley across the border in Burma, where he lives in a fortified network of underground tunnels. This led to the breaking up of opium and heroin production in the Mae Salong – Ban Hin Taek area.

The area is now undergoing heavy 'pacification' or Thai nationalisation. At great expense to the Thai government, tea, coffee, corn and Chinese herbs are now grown where opium once thrived. Whether this particular project is successful or not is another question but the government's strategy seems to be one of isolating and then pushing pockets of the opium trade out of Thailand and into Burma and Laos, where it continues uninterrupted.

The Laotian People's Revolutionary Party (LPRP), Laos' ruling group, is currently taking advantage of Thai government actions in northern Thailand to encourage an increase in opium production in Laos. They are effectively capturing some share of the market vacated by the SUA in Thailand. If the Burmese government steps up efforts to suppress poppy cultivation in Burma, as the Thai government has done in Thailand, Laos may in fact be in a position to corner the market, as it's the only government in the region with an official tolerance towards opium production. Smuggling routes for Laotian opium and heroin cross the Thai border at several points throughout the north and north-east, including the provinces of Chiang Mai, Chiang Rai, Nan, Loei, Nong Khai and Nakhon Phanom.

The cycle continues with power being transferred from warlord to warlord while the hill-tribe and Shan cultivators continue as unwilling pawns in the game. The planting of the poppy and the sale of its collected resins has never been a simple moral issue. The cultivators who have been farming poppies for centuries and heroin addicts have both been exploited by governments and crime syndicates who trade in opium for the advancement of their own power. This leads to the obvious conclusion that opium production in the Golden Triangle must be dealt with as a political, social, cultural and economic problem and not simply as a conventional law-enforcement matter.

So far a one-sided approach has only resulted in the unthinking destruction of minority culture and economy in the Golden Triangle area, rather than an end to the opium and heroin problem. Meanwhile, opium cultivation continues in Thailand in hidden valleys not frequented by the Thai armed forces. Any hill-tribe settlement may legally plant opium poppies for its own consumption. Small plots of land are 'leased' by opium merchants who have allowed heroin production to decentralise in order for poppy resin collection to appear legal.

ECONOMY

During the '80s, Thailand maintained a steady GNP growth rate which by 1987 exceeded 10% per annum. Suddenly Thailand has found itself on the threshold of attaining the exclusive rank of NIC or 'newly industrialised country', which experts forecast will be fulfilled within the next five to ten years. Soon, they say, Thailand will be joining Asia's 'little dragons', also known as the Four Tigers – South Korea, Taiwan, Hong Kong and Singapore – in becoming a leader in the Pacific Rim economic boom.

By 1992, it is expected that more than half of Thailand's labour force will be engaged in the manufacturing and industrial sectors. Currently, about 66% of Thai labour is engaged in agriculture, 10% each in commerce and services, and 8% in manufacturing. Thailand's major exports are rice, tapioca, sugar, rubber, maize, tin, cement, pineapple, tuna, textiles and electronics. Manufactured goods have become an increasingly important source of foreign exchange earnings and now account for 60% of all Thailand's exports.

In 1987, tourism became the leading earner of foreign exchange, out-distancing even Thailand's largest single export, tex-

tiles. Nearly five million tourists spent 57 billion baht (over US$2 billion) in 1988. The government economic strategy remains focused, however, on export-led growth through the development of light industries such as textiles and electronics, backed by rich reserves of natural resources and a large, inexpensive labour force. Observers predict that such a broad-based economy will make Thailand a major economic competitor in Asia in the long term. Thailand also has the lowest foreign debt in South-East Asia, just 20% of the gross domestic product.

Average per capita income by the end of the '80s was US$880 per year. Regional inequities, however, mean that local averages range from US$300 in the north-east to US$2300 in Bangkok. The current inflation rate is about 4% per annum. Travellers should keep this in mind when referring to prices in this edition, which are based on 1989 information. As in most countries, prices continue to rise.

The north-east of Thailand has the lowest inflation rate and cost of living. This region is poorer than the rest of the country and doesn't get as much tourism; it therefore offers excellent value for the traveller and is in dire need of your travel dollar. Handwoven textiles and farming remain the primary means of livelihood in this area. In the south, fishing, tin mining and rubber production keep the local economy fairly stable. Central Thailand grows fruit (especially pineapple), sugar cane and rice for export, and supports most of the ever-increasing industry (textiles, food processing and cement). North Thailand produces mountain or dry rice (as opposed to 'water-rice', the bulk of the crop produced in Thailand) for domestic use, maize, tea, various fruits and flowers, and is very dependent on tourism. Teak and other lumber was once a major product of the north, but since early 1989 all logging has been banned in Thailand in order to prevent further deforestation.

Some say that Thailand is growing faster than its infrastructure can handle. Incoming ships have to wait a week before they can get a berth at busy Khlong Toey port. Two new seaports along the eastern seaboard and one on the southern peninsula are expected to be completed in the early '90s, but even these may be inadequate to cope with projected demand. Transport and telecommunications systems are in dire need of upgrading.

One of the biggest dilemmas facing the economic planners is whether to acquire a larger foreign debt in order to finance the development of an infrastructure which is capable of handling continued high growth, or whether to allow growth to slow while the infrastructure catches up. Continued rapid growth will probably result in a disproportionate development of the more relatively industrialised central and southern regions, leaving the agricultural north and north-east behind.

Advocates of a slow-growth approach hope for better distribution of wealth around the country through a combination of agribusiness projects and welfare programmes that would bring a higher standard of living to poor rural areas. This makes good sense when one considers the relative differences between Thailand and the Four Tigers (eg the proportion of rural to urban dwellers and the high fertility of the land).

Tourism

According to the statistics of the Tourist Authority of Thailand, the country is currently averaging about five million tourist arrivals per year, up from 2.8 million in 1986 and 2.2 million in 1983. Figures are expected to continue to rise for at least the next few years.

In 1987, when total arrivals hit 3.5 million, nearly two-thirds of the visitors came from East Asia and the Pacific, with Malaysians leading the way at around 765,000, followed by the Japanese (341,000), Singaporeans (240,000), and Taiwanese (195,000). Europeans as a whole made up 794,320 of the total, with Britons at the top (184,000), West Germans second (148,000), and the French third (132,000). The Americas, including Canada and all Latin American countries, totalled about 292,000, made up primarily of Yanks (236,000) and Canadians (44,000). South Asians chalked up around 217,000

while Australians totalled 111,000 and the Middle East sent roughly 118,000.

The prize for longest average length of stay goes to Germans and Scandinavians. The average for West Germans was 12 nights, followed by the Swiss (11.1), Austrians (10.5), Swedes (10.26), Danes (10.22), Norwegians (10) and Fins (9.9). In contrast, the average stay for Australians was only 8.2 nights, Britons 7.5 nights, Americans 6.6 and the Japanese 4.2.

Surprisingly, the biggest spenders were the Taiwanese, who averaged a daily per capita expenditure of 3331B, followed closely by the Japanese at 3268B. Scandinavians spent an average of 2916B per day/person, US visitors 2744B, Italians 2251B, Canadians 2220B, Britons 2185B, French 2119B, Australians 2205B, Swiss 1903B, and the frugal West Germans 1511B.

POPULATION

The population of Thailand is about 53 million and currently growing at a rate of 1.5% per annum (as opposed to 3% twenty years ago and 2.5% in 1979), thanks to Khun Mechai's nationwide family planning campaign. This does not include the recent influx of Lao, Cambodian and Vietnamese refugees. About 75% of the citizenry are ethnic Thais, 14% are Chinese, and the remaining 11% include Malays, the Yumbri (Mrabri), Semang, Moken ('sea gypsies'), Lawa, Kui, Karen, Meo, Yao, Akha, Lahu, Lisu tribes (the latter six are the true hill tribes; for more information see the Hill Tribe section of the North chapter), Khmers and Mons. A small number of Europeans and other non-Asians live in Bangkok and Chiang Mai.

The literacy rate of Thailand is approximately 85% and increasing, and the average life expectancy is 61 – in both respects Thailand is a leader in the region. Thailand as a whole has a relatively youthful population; only about 12% are older than 50.

Bangkok is by far the largest city in the kingdom, with a population of nearly six million (over 10% of the total population) – too many for the scope of its public services and what little 'city planning' exists. Khorat (Nakhon Ratchasima) is the second largest city but does not have nearly such a big population – just over 200,000. Third is Chiang Mai with a population of around 150,000. All other towns in Thailand have well below 100,000, with few over 40,000.

CULTURE & ARTS
Sculpture & Architecture
The following scheme is the standard one used to categorise historical styles of Thai art, principally sculpture and architecture (since very little painting prior to the 19th century has survived).

Dvaravati style	6th to 11th century
Srivijaya style	8th to 13th century
Lopburi style	11th to 14th century
U Thong style	12th to 15th century
Sukhothai style	13th to 15th century
Chiang Saen style	12th to 20th century
Ayuthaya style	15th to late 18th century
Bangkok style	late 18th century to present

A good way to acquaint yourself with these styles, if you are interested, is to visit the National Museum in Bangkok, where works from each of these periods are on display. Then as you travel upcountry and view old monuments and sculpture you'll know what you're seeing, as well as what to look for.

In 1981, the Thai government made restoration of nine key archaeological sites part of their 5th National and Economic Development Plan (1982-86). As a result, the Fine Arts Department, under the Ministry of Education, has developed nine Historical Parks (*Uthayaan Prawatisaat*):

Sukhothai Historical Park in Sukhothai Province; Phra Nakhon Si Ayuthaya Historical Park in Ayuthaya Province; Phanom Rung Historical Park in Buriram Province; Si Thep Historical Park in Phetchabun Province; Phra Nakhon Khiri Historical Park in Phetburi Province; Si Satchanalai Historical Park in Sukhothai Province; Phimai Historical Park in Nakhon Ratchasima Province; Muang Singh Historical Park in Kanchanaburi Province; Kamphaeng Phet Historical Park in Kamphaeng Phet Province.

These Parks are administered by the Fine Arts Department to guard against theft and vandalism and to protect tourists from bandits at more remote sites. In 1988 they even managed to get the famous Phra Narai lintel returned to Prasat Phanom Rung from the Art Institute of Chicago Museum.

Additional areas of historical interest for art and architecture are Thonburi, Lamphun, Nakhorn Pathom, Nan, Ratburi, Lopburi, Chaiya, Sawankhaloke, Chiang Mai, Phitsanuloke, Chiang Saen and Nakhon Si Thammarat. Some of the monuments at these sites have also been restored by the Fine Arts Department and/or by local interests. For more detail on the historical sites, see the relevant regional sections in this book.

Some recommended books are *Arts of Thailand* by A B Griswold and *A Concise History of Buddhist Art in Siam* by Reginald Le May. Several good English-language books on various aspects of Thai art are for sale at the National Museums around Thailand (particularly at the Bangkok National Museum) and at the Muang Boran office on Ratchadamnoen Rd in Bangkok.

For information about the export of antiques or objects of art from Thailand, see the Customs section in the Facts for the Visitor chapter.

Spirit Houses
Every Thai house or building has to have a spirit house to go with it – a place for the spirits of the site, or Phra Phum, to live in. Without this vital structure you're likely to have the spirits living in the house with you and that can cause all sorts of trouble. Spirit houses look rather like a birdhouse-sized Thai temple mounted on a pedestal. At least your average spirit house does – a big hotel may have a spirit house as big as an average house.

How do you ensure that the spirits take up residence in your spirit house rather than in the main house with you? Mainly by making the spirit house a better place to live than the main house. Most important, it should have the best location and should not be shaded by the main house. Thus the spirit house's position has to be planned from the very beginning. The spirit house has to be installed with due ceremony and if your own house is improved or enlarged then the spirit house should be as well.

Music

From a western perspective, traditional Thai music is some of the most bizarre on the planet and is an acquired taste for most of us. It is well worth the effort! The classical, central Thai music is spicy, like Thai food, and features an incredible array of textures and subtleties, hair-raising tempos and pastoral melodies. The classical orchestra is called the *piphat* and can include as few as five players or more than 20.

Among the more common instruments is the *pi*, a woodwind instrument which has a reed mouthpiece and is heard prominently at Thai boxing matches. The pi is a relative of a similar Indian instrument, as is the *pin*, a banjo-like string instrument descended from the Indian *vina*. A bowed instrument similar to ones played in China and Japan is aptly called the *saw*. The *ranaat ek* is the wooden percussion instrument resembling the western xylophone. An instrument of tuned gongs arranged in a semi-circle is the *gong wong yai*. There are also several different kinds of drums, some played with the hands, some with sticks.

The piphat ensemble was originally developed to accompany classical dance-drama (*khon*) and shadow theatre (*nang*) but can be heard in straightforward performance these days, in temple fairs as well as concerts. One reason classical Thai music may sound strange to the western ear is that it does not use a tempered scale as we have been accustomed to hearing since Bach's time. The standard scale does feature an eight-note octave but it is arranged in seven full intervals, with no 'semi-tones'.

In the north and north-east several types of reed instruments with multiple bamboo pipes, functioning basically like a mouth-organ, are popular. Chief among these is the *khaen*, which originated in Laos and when played by an adept musician sounds like a rhythmic, churning calliope. The funky *luuk thung*, or 'country' style, which originated in the north-east has become a favourite throughout the country.

Popular Thai music has borrowed much from western music but still retains a distinct flavour of its own, despite the fact that modern Thai musicians play electric guitars, saxophones, drum kits, electronic keyboards, and so on. Although Bangkok bar bands can play fair imitations of everything from Hank Williams to Olivia Newton-John, there is a growing preference among Thais for a blend of Thai and international styles. The best example of this is Thailand's famous rock group, Carabao. Carabao is by far the most popular musical group in Thailand at this writing and has even scored hits in Malaysia, Singapore, Indonesia, and the Philippines with songs like 'Made in Thailand' (only the chorus is in English). This band and others have crafted an exciting fusion of Thai classical and luuk thung forms with heavy metal. Cassette tapes of Thai music are readily available throughout the country in department stores, cassette shops and street vendors. The average price for a Thai music cassette is 50 to 60B. Western tapes are cheaper (about 30B each) if bootlegged, but the days of pirate tapes in Thailand are numbered now that the US music industry is enforcing on international copyright laws.

If you're interested in learning how to play traditional Thai instruments, contact the Bangkok YMCA (tel 286-1542 or 286-2580) to enquire about their weekly classes taught by Mr Pranai Navarat.

Some recommended books are *The Traditional Music of Thailand* by David Morton and *Thai Music* by Phra Chen Duriyanga.

RELIGION

About 95% of the Thai citizenry are Theravada Buddhists. The Thais themselves frequently call their religion *Lankavamsa* (Sinhalese lineage) Buddhism because Siam originally received Buddhism during the Sukhothai Period from Sri Lanka. Strictly speaking, Theravada refers to only the earliest forms of Buddhism practised during the Ashokan and immediate post-Ashokan periods in South Asia. The early Dvaravati and pre-Dvaravati forms of Buddhism are not the same as that which has existed in Siamese territories since the 13th century.

Since the Sukhothai Period Thailand has maintained an unbroken canonical tradition and 'pure' ordination lineage, the only country among the Theravadin (using Theravada in its doctrinal sense) countries to do so. Ironically, when the ordination lineage in Sri Lanka broke down during the 18th century under Dutch persecution, it was Siam that restored the Sangha (Buddhist brotherhood) there. To this day the major sect in Sri Lanka is called *Siamopalivamsa* (Siam-Upali lineage, Upali being the name of the Siamese monk who led the expedition to Ceylon), or simply *Siam Nikaya* (the Siamese sect).

Basically, the Theravada school of Buddhism is an earlier and, according to its followers, less corrupted form of Buddhism than the Mahayana schools found in East Asia or in the Himalayan lands. The Theravada (teaching of the elders) school is also called the 'southern' school since it took the southern route from India, its place of origin, through South-East Asia (Burma, Thailand, Laos and Cambodia in this case), while the 'northern' school proceeded north into Nepal, Tibet, China, Korea, Mongolia, Vietnam and Japan. Because the Theravada school tried to preserve or limit the Buddhist doctrines to only those canons codified in the early Buddhist era, the Mahayana school gave Theravada Buddhism the name Hinayana, or the 'lesser vehicle'. They considered themselves Mahayana, the 'great vehicle', because they built upon the earlier teachings, 'expanding' the doctrine in such a way as to respond more to the needs of lay people, or so it is claimed.

Theravada or Hinayana doctrine stresses the three principal aspects of existence: *dukkha* (suffering, unsatisfactoriness, disease); *anicca* (impermanence, transience of all things); and *anatta* (non-substantiality or non-essentiality of reality – no permanent 'soul'). These concepts, when 'discovered' by Siddhartha Gautama in the 6th century BC, were in direct contrast to the Hindu belief in an eternal, blissful Self or *Paramatman*, hence Buddhism was originally a 'heresy' against India's Brahmanic religion.

Gautama, an Indian prince-turned-ascetic, subjected himself to many years of severe austerities to arrive at this vision of the world and was given the title Buddha, 'the enlightened' or 'the awakened'. Gautama Buddha spoke of four noble truths which had the power to liberate any human being who could realise them. These four noble truths are:

1. The truth of suffering – 'Existence is suffering'.
2. The truth of the cause of suffering – 'Suffering is caused by desire'.
3. The truth of the cessation of suffering – 'Eliminate the cause of suffering (desire) and suffering will cease to arise'.
4. The truth of the path – 'The eight-fold path is the way to eliminate desire/extinguish suffering'.

The Eightfold Path (atthangika-magga), which if followed will put an end to suffering, consists of (1) right understanding, (2) right mindedness (or 'right thought'), (3) right speech, (4) right bodily conduct, (5) right livelihood, (6) right effort, (7) right attentiveness and (8) right concentration. These eight limbs belong to three different 'pillars' of practice: morality or sila (3 to 5); concentration or samadhi (7 and 8); and wisdom or panna (1 and 2). Some Buddhists believe the path – called the Middle Way, since ideally it avoids both extreme austerity and extreme sensuality – is to be taken in successive stages, while others say the pillars and/or limbs are interdependent.

The ultimate end of Theravada Buddhism is nibbana (Sanskrit: nirvana), which literally means the extinction of all desire and thus of all suffering (dukkha). Effectively it is an end, not only to suffering and action (karma), but also to the cycle of rebirths that is existence. In reality, most Thai Buddhists aim for rebirth in a 'better' existence rather than the supramundane goal of nibbana, which is highly misunderstood by Asians as well as westerners.

Many Thais express the feeling that they are somehow unworthy of nibbana. By feeding monks, giving donations to temples and performing regular worship at the local wat (temple) they hope to improve their lot, acquiring enough merit (Pali: puñña; Thai:

bun) to prevent or at least lessen the number of rebirths. The making of merit (tham bun) is an important social and religious activity in Thailand. The concept of reincarnation is almost universally accepted in Thailand, even by non-Buddhists, and the Buddhist theory of karma is well-expressed in the Thai proverb tham dii, dai dii; tham chua, dai chua – 'do good and receive good; do evil and receive evil'.

The Triratna, or Triple Gems, highly respected by Thai Buddhists, include the Buddha, the Dhamma (the teachings) and the Sangha (the Buddhist brotherhood). Each is quite visible in Thailand. The Buddha, in his myriad and omnipresent sculptural forms, is found on a high shelf in the lowliest roadside restaurants as well as in the lounges of expensive Bangkok hotels. The Dhamma is chanted morning and evening in every wat and taught to every Thai citizen in primary school. The Sangha is seen everywhere in the presence of orange-robed monks, especially in the early morning hours when they perform their alms-rounds, in what has almost become a travel-guide cliche in motion. Socially, every Thai male is expected to become a monk for a short period in his life, optimally between the time he finishes school and the time he starts a career or marries. Men or boys under 20 years of age may enter the Sangha as novices – this is not unusual since a family earns great merit when one of its sons takes robe and bowl. Traditionally the length of time spent in the wat is three months, during the Buddhist lent (phansaa) which begins in July and coincides with the rainy season. However, nowadays men may spend as little as a week or 15 days to accrue merit as monks. There are about 32,000 monasteries in Thailand and 200,000 monks; many of these monks ordain for a lifetime. Of these a large percentage become scholars and teachers, while some specialise in healing and/or folk magic.

The Sangha is divided into two sects, the Mahanikai and the Thammayut. The latter is a minority sect (one Thammayut to 35 Mahanikai) begun by King Mongkut and patterned after an early Mon form of monastic discipline which he had practised as a monk (*bhikkhu*). Generally, discipline for Thammayut monks is stricter. For example, they eat only once a day, before midday and must eat only what is in their alms-bowls, whereas Mahanikais eat twice before noon and may accept side dishes. Thammayut monks are expected to attain proficiency in meditation as well as Buddhist scholarship or scripture study; the Mahanikai monks typically 'specialise' in one or the other.

An increasing number of foreigners come to Thailand to be ordained as Buddhist monks, especially to study with the famed meditation masters of the forest wats in north-east Thailand (see the Meditation Study section).

There is a Buddhist bookshop selling English-language books across the street from the north entrance to Wat Bovornives in Bangkok.

If you wish to find out more about Buddhism you can contact the World Fellowship of Buddhists (tel 251-1188), 33 Sukhumvit Rd (between Soi 1 and Soi 3). There's an English meditation class here on Wednesday evenings, all are welcome.

Recommended books about Buddhism in Thailand include the following titles:

Buddhism in Transition by Donald K Swearer, the Westminster Press, 1970 (Philadelphia)
Buddhism in the Modern World ed by Heinrich Dumoulin, MacMillan Publishing, 1976 (New York)
Buddhism, Imperialism, and War by Trevor Ling, D. Reidel Publishing, 1980 (Dordrecht)
World Conqueror and World Renouncer by Stanley Tambiah, Cambridge University Press, 1976 (Cambridge)
Living Buddhist Masters by Jack Kornfield, Buddhist Publication Society, 1989 (Kandy)
Buddhism Explained by Phra Khantipalo, Mahamakut Rajavidyalaya Press, 1973 (Bangkok)
Buddhism in Thailand: Its Past and Present by K. Kusalasaya, Buddhist Publication Society, 1965 (Kandy)

General books about Buddhism include:

What the Buddha Taught by Walpola Rahula,Motilal Banarsidass, 1971 (Delhi)
The Central Conception of Buddhism by Th Stcherbatsky, Motilal Banarsidass, 1974 (Delhi)
Buddhist Dictionary by Mahathera Nyanatiloka, Island Hermitage Publications, 1950 (Dodanduwa)

Meditation Study in Thailand

Thailand has long been a popular place for Western students of Buddhism, particularly those interested in a system of meditation known as *vipassana* (wi-pat-sa-naa), a Pali word which roughly translated means 'insight'. Foreigners who come to Thailand to study vipassana can choose among dozens of temples and study centres which specialise in these teachings. Teaching methods vary from place to place but the general emphasis is on learning to observe mind-body processes from moment-to-moment. Thai language is usually the medium of instruction but several places also provide instruction in English.

Information on some of the more popular meditation-oriented temples and centres is given in the relevant sections. Instruction and accommodation are free of charge at temples, though donations are expected. Short-term students will find that two-month tourist visas are ample for most courses of study. Long-term students may want to consider a three or six-month non-immigrant visa. A few westerners are ordained as monks in order to take full advantage of the monastic environment. Monks are generally (but not always) allowed to stay in Thailand as long as they remain in robes. For a detailed look at vipassana study in Thailand, including visa and ordination procedures, read *Guide to the Meditation Temples of Thailand* (Wayfarer Books, PO Box 5927, Concord, California 94524, USA).

Minority Religions

A small percentage of Thais and most of the Malays in the south, amounting to about 4% of the total population, are followers of

Islam. Another 1% are Confucianists, Taoists, Mahayana Buddhists, Christians and Hindus. Muslim mosques (in the south) and Chinese temples are both common enough that you will probably come across some in your travels in Thailand. Before entering *any* temple, sanctuary or mosque you must remove your shoes, and in a mosque your head must be covered.

HOLIDAYS & FESTIVALS

The number and frequency of festivals and fairs in Thailand is incredible – there always seems to be something going on, but especially during the cool season between November and February.

10 to 12 January
Chaiyaphum Elephant Round-up – a rather recently established event that focuses on re-enactment of medieval elephant-back warfare. Much smaller and less touristy than the Surin round-up in November.

24 to 31 January
Don Chedi Memorial Fair – commemorates the victory of King Naresuan of Ayuthaya over Burmese invaders in 1592. The highlight of the fair is dramatised elephant-back duelling. At the Don Chedi memorial in Suphanburi Province.

1st week of February
Flower Festival in Chiang Mai – colourful floats and parades exhibiting Chiang Mai's cultivated flora.

February
Magha Puja (Makkha Buchaa) – held on the full moon of the third lunar month to commemorate the preaching of the Buddha to 1250 enlightened monks who came to hear him 'without prior summons'. A public holiday throughout the country culminating in a candle-lit circumambulation of the main chapel at every *wat*.

1st week of March
Barred Ground Dove Fair – large dove-singing contest held in Yala that attracts dove-lovers from all over Thailand, Malaysia, Singapore and Indonesia.

14 to 21 March
Phra Buddhabaht Fair – annual pilgrimage to the Temple of the Holy Footprint at Saraburi, 236 km north-north-east of Bangkok. Quite an affair, with music, outdoor drama and many other festivities. The shrine is worth visiting even in the 'off-season', if you're in the area.

6 April
Chakri Day – public holiday commemorating the founder of the Chakri Dynasty, Rama I.

13 to 15 April
Songkran Festival – the New Year's celebration of the lunar year in Thailand. Buddha images are 'bathed', monks and elders receive the respect of younger Thais by the sprinkling of water over their hands and a lot of water is tossed about for fun. Songkran generally gives everyone a chance to release their frustrations and literally cool off during the peak of the hot season. Hide out in your room or expect to be soaked; the latter is a lot more fun.

13 April
Phanom Rung Festival – a newly-established festival to commemorate the restoration of this impressive Angkor-style temple. Involves a daytime procession to Khao Phanom Rung and spectacular sound-and-light shows at night. Be prepared for very hot weather.

5 May
Coronation Day – public holiday. The King and Queen preside at a ceremony at Wat Phra Kaew in Bangkok, commemorating their 1946 coronation.

May (Full Moon)
Visakha Puja (Wisakha Buchaa) – falls on the 15th day of the waxing moon in the 6th lunar month, which is considered the date of the Buddha's birth, enlightenment and *parinibbana*, or passing away. Activities are centred around the wat, with candle-lit processions, much chanting and sermonising, etc. A public holiday.

2nd week of May
Royal Ploughing Ceremony – to kick off the official rice-planting season, the King participates in this Brahman ritual at Sanam Luang (the large field across from Wat Phra Kaew) in Bangkok. Thousands of Thais gather to watch, and traffic in this part of the city reaches a standstill.

2nd week of May
Rocket Festival – all over the north-east, villagers craft large skyrockets of bamboo which they then fire into the sky to bring rain for rice fields. This festival is best celebrated in the town of Yasothon, but also good in Ubon and Nong Khai.

Mid-July
Asanha Puja – full moon is a must for this holiday, too, commemorating the first sermon preached by the Buddha. A public holiday.

Mid to late July
Khao Phansaa (beginning of Buddhist 'lent') – the traditional time of year for young men to enter the monkhood for the rainy season and for all monks to station themselves in a single monastery for the three months. A good time to observe a Buddhist ordination. This is a public holiday.

Mid to late July
Candle Festival – in the north-east they celebrate Khao Phansaa by carving huge candles and

parading them on floats in the streets. This festival is best celebrated in Ubon.

12 August

Queen's birthday – this is a public holiday. Ratchadamnoen Avenue and the Grand Palace are festooned with coloured lights.

September

Thailand International Swan-Boat Races – takes place on the Chao Phraya River in Bangkok near the Rama IX Bridge.

September

Narathiwat Fair – an annual week-long festival celebrating local culture with boat races, dove-singing contests, handicraft displays, traditional southern Thai music and dance. The King and Queen almost always attend.

Late September to early October

Vegetarian Festival – a nine-day celebration in Trang and Phuket during which devout Chinese Buddhists eat only vegetarian food. There are also various ceremonies at Chinese temples and merit-making processions that bring to mind Hindu Thaipusam in its exhibition of self-mortification.

Mid-October to mid-November

Thawt Kathin – a one-month period at the end of 'lent' during which new monastic robes and requisites are offered to the Sangha.

23 October

Chulalongkorn Day – a public holiday in commemoration of King Chulalongkorn (Rama V).

November

Loi Krathong – on the proper full-moon night, small lotus-shaped baskets or boats made of banana leaves containing flowers, incense, candles and a coin are floated on Thai rivers, lakes and canals. This is a peculiarly Thai festival that probably originated in Sukhothai and is best celebrated in the north. In Chiang Mai, residents also launch hot-air paper balloons into the sky. At the National Historical Park in Sukhothai, there is an impressive sound and light show.

Third weekend in November

Surin Annual Elephant Round-up – pretty touristy these days, but no more so than the 'running of the bulls' in Pamplona, Spain.

Late November to early December

River Kwai Bridge Week – sound and light shows every night at the Death Railway bridge in Kanchanaburi, plus historical exhibitions and vintage train rides.

5 December

King's birthday – this is a public holiday, which is celebrated with some fervour in Bangkok.

31 December to 1 January

New Year's Day – a rather recent public holiday in deference to the western calendar.

Note: The official year in Thailand is reckoned from 543 BC, the beginning of the Buddhist Era, so that 1990 AD is 2533 BE.

NATIONAL PARKS

Despite Thailand's rich diversity of flora and fauna, it has only been in recent years that most of the 53 national parks have been established. The majority of the parks are well-maintained by the Forestry Department, but a few have allowed rampant tourism growth to threaten the natural environment, most notably on the islands of Ko Samet and Ko Phi Phi. In 1989, all logging was banned in Thailand so that it is now illegal to sell timber felled in the country – this should help to curb illegal logging operations in the interior.

A number of national parks are easily accessible for visitors. There is usually somewhere to stay, and sometimes meals are provided, but it's a good idea to take your own sleeping bag or mat, and basic camping gear is useful if there is not much accommodation. You should also take a torch (flashlight), rain gear, insect repellent, a water container and a small medical kit.

Most parks charge a small fee to visit. Advance bookings for accommodation are advisable at the more popular parks, especially on holidays and weekends. Most national park bungalows are around 500 to 1000B a night (unless otherwise noted) depending on size, but will sleep five to ten people. A few parks also have *reuan thaew*, or long- houses, where rooms are around 150 to 200B for two. Some have tents for rent for 50 to 60B a night. Finally, if you bring your own tent it's only 5B per person – almost every park has at least one camping area.

In Bangkok the reservations office is at the National Parks Division of the Forestry Department (tel 579-4842, 579-0529), Phahonyothin Rd, Bang Khen (north from Siam Square). Bookings from Bangkok must be paid in advance.

Below are some remarks on twenty of the more notable national parks.

Khao Yai เขาใหญ่

This is the oldest national park in Thailand

and one of the world's best, covering 2168 square km. It has some of Asia's largest remaining areas of rainforest and is rich in wildlife, with elephants, tigers, deers, gibbons and other large mammals. There are over 500 km of hiking trails and visitors' facilities are very good.

Accommodation can be arranged with the Tourism Authority of Thailand, but may be expensive. Forestry bungalows (there are 19) are 500 to 1000B and there are camping areas. The coolest months are December and January.

The park is 205 km north-east of Bangkok. Take a bus to Pak Chong from the Northern Bus Terminal (or a train from Krung Thep station). From Pak Chong a large truck with seats in the back leaves at 12 noon on weekdays, 10.30 am on weekends (15B).

Erawan, Sai Yok & Sinakharin
เอราวัณ, ไทรโยค และ ศรีนครินทร์

These three parks form one main complex, north-west of Kanchanaburi. Large mammals and many birds can be found in this region. There are Forestry bungalows at all the parks, as well as a range of private accommodation. The best time to visit is from November to February.

Erawan is best known for its waterfall and the spectacular Phrathat Cave. Buses run daily from Kanchanaburi to the market near the park; from there it's two km – hire a minibus, hitch or walk. Try to avoid weekends.

Sinakarin is also noted for its waterfall. To reach the park, continue on the dirt road north from the Erawan headquarters, or hire a boat at Tha Kradan 24 km past the junction to Sinakarin Dam, for a 1½-hour ride.

Sai Yok is between Erawan and the Burmese border. It has the world's smallest mammal – a bat weighing just two grams, discovered in 1973.

From Kanchanaburi, daily buses going north on Highway 323 pass the park entrance and from there it is about one km.

Khao Chamao-Khao Wong
เขาชะเมา, เขาวง

This park of only 83 square km has an abun-dance of wildlife for which it is a refuge from the habitat destruction caused by the forestry industry in surrounding areas.

From Rayong, take a minibus to Ban Khao Din, where minibuses to the park are available. The best time is from November to February. There are seven bungalows and camping areas in the park.

Khao Sam Roi Yot เขาสามร้อยยอด

This offers a large variety of easily accessible attractions. It is on the east coast, north of Prachuap Khiri Khan and consists of a series of striking limestone hills rising from the sea. Wildlife includes the serow, a goat-antelope that lives on the limestone crags, and monkeys, porcupines and leopards.

From Bangkok take a bus to Pranburi, from there you can hitch a ride; trucks go the 35 km to the park headquarters several times daily. The best time to go is from November to February. There are five bungalows and camping areas.

Doi Suthep-Pui ดอยสุเทพ-ดอยปุย

Doi Suthep-Pui only became a national park in 1981. In spite of the heavy human use which has displaced the larger animals, some trails off the side of the road to the summit offer pleasant walking after a visit to the famous Wat Phrathat. This is described in more detail in the North Thailand chapter.

Doi Inthanon ดอยอินทนนท์

Doi Inthanon is Thailand's highest mountain (2565 metres). Off the new 47-km road to the summit there are many trails to explore and several impressive waterfalls.

From Chiang Mai take a minibus to Chom Tong, then a *songthaew*. Ask for Doi Inthanon and say you want to get off at km 31. From the park headquarters there is plenty of traffic for hitching. There are five bungalows and camping areas. Accommodation is also available in hill-tribe villages.

Doi Khuntan ดอยขุนตาล

In this seldom visited park, the trail to the summit of Doi Khuntan (1273 metres) offers great views and a good chance of seeing large mammals, including black bear, serow, tiger and sambar.

The only access is by the Chiang Mai to Lamphun train to Khuntan station (one to two hours); the train makes only a quick stop, so be careful not to miss it (watch for the tunnel near the station). Weekdays are the best time to go; try to arrive by noon to reach the bungalows (2½ km above the headquarters) before dark. There are eleven bungalows ranging from 200 to 1200B. The best time to go is from November to February.

Ram Khamhaeng รามคำแหง

The mountains here are famous as the birthplace of the Thai nation over 700 years ago. One notable animal seen here is the scaly pangolin, a strange anteater the size of a small dog. Plan to spend at least two days here and camp on the summit of Khao Luang.

From Sukhothai take a bus to Kamphaeng Phet and get off after 22 km at a police post opposite a hospital sign. From there it's 16 km by unsealed road to the park; hitching is usually the best way to reach the headquarters. The best time to go is from November to February.

Thung Salaeng Luang ทุ่งแสลงหลวง

This is Thailand's third largest park (1262 square km), spread across parts of Phitsanulok and Phetchabun provinces. The topography here is characterised by rugged mountains and grassy valleys and is said to be a habitat for wild elephants, tigers, boars, deer, and various large birds.

The park is about 50 km from Lom Sak off the Lom Sak to Phetchabun highway. There are four bungalows, long-houses and tents for rent.

Lansang ลานสาง

This small park (104 square km) in Tak Province is a popular local recreation spot, with a large hill-tribe centre on the west side. Several trails meander to waterfalls. It's a pleasant stopover along the Bangkok to Chiang Mai highway.

From Chiang Mai get out at Tak and take a bus for Mae Sot; the park headquarters is reached after 18 km. The best time to go is

November to January. There is one bungalow and a camping area.

Nam Nao น้ำหนาว

One of Thailand's most beautiful and valuable parks, covering nearly 1000 square km in Chaiyaphum and Phetchabun provinces. Rumours of rhinoceros persist (last seen 1971) and the bizarre fur-coated Sumatran rhinoceros may survive here.

From Sukhothai take a bus to Chum Phae; the park headquarters is 55 km from Lom Sak. Daily buses run through the park from Lom Sak or Khon Kaen. The best time to go is from November to February. There are nine bungalows and camping areas.

Phu Kradung ภูกระดึง

Phu Kradung is a bell-shaped mountain in the north-eastern province of Loei about 1500 metres above sea level. The top of the mountain is a large plateau with a network of marked trails and government-owned cabins. The weather is always cool on top hence the flora is more like what you see in temperate zones.

The park is best visited between mid-October and mid-June, before the rains set in and flood the trails. Phu Kradung also should be avoided during school vacations unless you like crowds.

There are daily buses from Loei for the 75 km trip to Phu Kradung.

Kaeng Krachan แก่งกระจาน

Kaeng Krachan is Thailand's largest national park, spreading over 2900 square km or nearly half of Phetburi Province. In addition to semi-tropical rainforest you'll also find areas of savannah-like grasslands, mountains, steep cliffs, caves, waterfalls, long-distance hiking trails and two rivers, the Phetburi and the Pranburi, which are suitable for rafting. The large reservoir above the Kaeng Krachan Dam is stocked with fish. Animals living in Kaeng Krachan include wild elephants, deer, tigers, bears, boars, gaurs and wild cattle.

Kaeng Krachan is about 60 km from Phetburi off Route 3175. The Route 3175 turn-off is at Tha Yang on Highway 4. There is no regular transport to the park, but you can hitch or charter a pick-up. There are six bungalows for 600 to 700B, a camping area, and a private floating resort. The park is best seen from November to June.

Thaleban   ทะเลบัน
Thailand's southernmost park (101 square km) borders Malaysia. The beautiful, unspoilt forests support a great variety of wildlife and there are good trails too.

The park headquarters is only two km from the border. It is about 90 km south of Hat Yai; coming from Malaysia it's about 75 km from Alor Star. The best time to go is from December to March. There are ten bungalows.

Tarutao   ตะรุเตา
The 51 islands off the south-west coast offer beaches, coral reefs and rainforest. Turtles nest on Ko Adang from around September to December. The park headquarters on Ko Tarutao includes an outdoor museum, an aquarium and turtle-rearing ponds. There is a store selling basics, and snorkelling gear can be hired.

Share taxis run from Hat Yai to the pier at Pak Bara. The best time is from November to April. For more detailed information see the Tarutao section in the South Thailand chapter.

Hat Nai Yang   หาดในยาง
This is a marine park protecting the north-west portion of Phuket Island. Turtles nest here from around November to February. There are facilities for day visitors; bring your own snorkelling gear if you can.

The park headquarters is 1½ km from Phuket Airport. From Phuket Town minibuses can be hired at the central market for the 32-km ride to Hat Nai Yang. There are several bungalows and tents for rent. The best time to go is from September to December.

Khao Sok   เขาสก
Khao Sok is a 646-square-km park in Surat Thani Province that features thick rainforest, waterfalls, limestone cliffs and a lake formed by the Chiaw Lan Dam.

The park is located 1½ km off Route 401 between Takua Pa and Surat Thani at km 109. There is a camping area and private bungalows.

Ao Phang-Nga   อ่าวพังงา
The forested limestone pillars of Ao Phang-Nga, made famous by the James Bond film *Man with the Golden Gun* are the major attraction. The park is 96 km from Phuket Town and nine km from Phang-Nga Town where a minibus can be hired at the market. Alternatively, organise a day tour from Phuket. There are no bungalows but camping is allowed. This park is best seen early in the morning before the hordes of package tour boats start arriving from Phuket.

Khao Laem Ya – Mu Ko Samet
เขาแหลมหญ้า – หมู่เกาะเสม็ด
Officially declared a national park in 1981, the Ko Samet group and Laem Ya have only recently had a park headquarters installed (1985). The main islands of the Ko Samet group are Samet, Chan, Makham, Kruai, Plai Tin, Kut and Thalu. Laem Ya is opposite Samet on the mainland, south-west of Ban Pho. There are many places to stay along the mainland sections of the park, as well as on Ko Samet, while the other islands may be visited on day trips from Ko Samet. Admission to the National Park is 5B. Unfortunately, Ko Samet itself is beginning to suffer as growth on this island continues unchecked.

Noppharat Thara – Phi Phi
นพรัตน์ธารา – พี.พี.
This park consists of several islands in offshore Krabi Province along with a long stretch of beaches from Noppharat Thara to Phranang. There is good snorkelling and beachcombing. For more detail see the section on Krabi in the South Thailand chapter. There are five national parks' bungalows, camping areas, and many private bungalows. Ko Phi Phi, one of Thailand's most beautiful islands, is a bit overcrowded

during the high season (from December to March).

LANGUAGE

During your travels in Thailand, meeting and getting to know Thai people can be a very rewarding experience. I would particularly urge travellers, young and old, to make the effort to meet Thai college and university students. Thai students are, by and large, eager to meet their peers from other countries. They will often know some English, so communication is not as difficult as it may be with merchants, civil servants, etc, plus they are generally willing to teach you useful Thai words and phrases.

Learning some Thai is indispensable for travelling in the kingdom; naturally, the more language you pick up, the closer you get to Thailand's culture and people. Foreigners who speak Thai are so rare in Thailand that it doesn't take much to impress most Thais with a few words in their own language. Don't let laughter at your linguistic attempts discourage you; this amusement is an expression of their appreciation.

Thai is one of the oldest languages in East and South-East Asia; according to linguist/anthropologist Paul Benedict it may even pre-date Chinese, at least in its prototypical form. Many of the so-called 'loan words' thought to be borrowed from Chinese by the Thais actually have an Austro-Thai origin. At any rate, Chinese and Thai have many similarities, since both are monosyllabic tonal languages.

In Thai the meaning of a single syllable may be altered by means of five different tones (in standard central Thai): level or mid tone, low tone, falling tone, high tone and rising tone. Consequently, the syllable *mai*, for example, can mean, depending on the tone, 'new', 'burn', 'wood', 'not?' or 'not'. This makes it rather tricky to learn at first, for those of us who come from more or less non-tonal-language traditions. Even when we 'know' what the correct tone in Thai should be, our tendency to denote emotion, verbal stress, the interrogative, etc, through tone modulation, often interferes with speaking the correct tone. So the first rule in learning to speak Thai is to divorce emotions from your speech, at least until you have learned the Thai way to express them without changing essential tone value.

The Thai script, a fairly recent development in comparison with the spoken language (King Ram Khamheng introduced the script in 1283), consists of 44 consonants (but only 21 separate sounds) and 48 vowel and diphthong possibilities (32 separate signs) and is of Sanskrit origin. Written Thai proceeds from left to right, though vowel signs may be written before, above, below, 'around' (before, above *and* after), *or* after consonants, depending on the sign. Though learning the alphabet is not difficult, the writing system itself is fairly complex, so unless you are planning a lengthy stay in Thailand it should perhaps be foregone in favour of learning to actually speak the language. Where possible, place names occurring in headings are given in Thai script as well as in Roman script, so that you can at least 'read' the names of destinations at a pinch, or point to them if necessary.

The following is a brief attempt to explain the tones. The only way to really understand the differences is by listening to a native or fluent non-native speaker. The range of all five tones is relative to each speaker's vocal range so there is no fixed 'pitch' intrinsic to the language.

The level or mid tone is pronounced 'flat', at the relative middle of the speaker's vocal range. Example: *dii* means good.

The low tone is 'flat' like the mid tone, but pronounced at the relative *bottom* of one's vocal range. It is low, level and with no inflection. Example: *baat* means Baht (the Thai currency).

The falling tone is pronounced as if you were emphasising a word, or calling someone's name from afar. Example: *mai* means 'no' or 'not'.

The high tone is usually the most difficult for westerners. It is pronounced near the relative top of the vocal range, as level as possible. Example: *nii* means 'this'.

The rising tone sounds like the inflection English speakers generally give to a question

– 'You like soup?' Example: *saam* means 'three'.

On a visual curve the tones might look like this:

| Mid | Low | Falling | High | Rising |

Words in Thai that appear to have more than one syllable are usually compounds made up of two or more word units, each with its own tone. They may be words taken directly from Sanskrit or Pali, in which case each syllable must still have its own tone. Sometimes the tone of the first syllable is not as important as that of the last, so for these I am omitting the tone mark.

Here is a guide to the phonetic system which has been used in the Language and Food sections, as well as throughout the book when transcribing directly from Thai. It is based on the Royal Thai General System of transcription (RTGS), except that it distinguishes between vowels of short and long duration (eg 'i' and 'ii'; 'a' and 'aa'; 'e' and 'eh'; 'o' and 'oh'), between 'o' and 'aw' (both would be 'o' in the RTGS) and between 'ch' and 'j' (both 'ch' in the RTGS).

Consonants

th	as the 't' in 'tea'
ph	as the 'p' in 'put' (never as the 'ph' in 'phone')
kh	as the 'k' in 'kite'
k	similar to 'g' in 'good', or k in 'cuckoo' but unaspirated and unvoiced
t	as the 't' in 'forty' – unaspirated (no accompanying puff of air); similar to 'd' but unvoiced
p	as the 'p' in 'stopper', unvoiced, unaspirated (not like the 'p' in 'put')
ng	as the 'ng' in 'sing'; used as an initial consonant in Thai - practice by saying 'sing' without the 'si'
r	similar to the 'r' in 'run' but flapped (tongue touches palate) - in everyday speech often pronounced like 'l'

All the remaining consonants correspond closely to their English counterparts.

Vowels

i	as the 'i' in 'it'
ii	as the 'ee' in 'feet'
ai	as the 'i' in 'pipe'
aa	as the 'a' in 'father'
a	half as long as *aa*
ae	as the 'a' in 'bat' or 'tab'
e	as the 'e' in 'hen'
eh	as the 'a' in 'hate'
oe	as the 'u' in 'hut' but more closed
u	as the 'u' in 'flute'
uu	as the 'oo' in 'food', longer than *u*
eu	as the 'eu' in French 'deux', or the 'i' in 'sir'
ao	as the 'ow' in 'now'
aw	as the 'aw' in 'jaw'
o	as the 'o' in 'bone'; exception *ko*, pronounced 'kaw'
oh	as the 'o' in 'toe'
eua	diphthong, or combination, of *eu* and *a*
ia	as 'ee-ya', or as the 'ie' in French *rien*
ua	as the 'ou' in 'tour'
uay	as the 'ewy' in 'Dewey'
iu	as the 'ew' in 'yew'
iaw	as the 'io' in 'Rio' or Italian *mio* or *dio*

There are several other vowel combinations that are relatively rare.

Words & Phrases

When being polite the speaker ends their sentence with *khrap* (for men) or *kha* (for women). It is the gender of the *speaker* that is being expressed here; it is also the common way to answer 'yes' to a question or show agreement.

Greetings & Civilities

greetings/hello
sawàt-dii (khráp/kha)
สวัสดี (ครับ / ค่ะ)

How are you?
pen yangai?
เป็นอย่างไร?

I'm fine
sabàay dii
สบายดี

thank you
khàwp khun
ขอบคุณ

Small Talk

you
khun (for peers)
คุณ

thâan (for elders, people in authority)
ท่าน

I
phǒm (for men) *diichǎn* (for women)
ผม   ดิฉัน

What is your name?
khun chêu arai?
คุณชื่ออะไร?

My name is ....
phǒm chêu .... (men),
ผมชื่อ...(ผู้ชาย)
diichǎn chêu .... (women)
ดิฉันชื่อ...(ผู้หญิง)

Do you have ....?
mii .... *mǎi?*
มีไหม?

Do you have noodles?
mii kǔaythiǎw mǎi?
มีก๋วยเตี๋ยวไหม?

I/you/he/she/it does not have
mâi mii
ไม่มี

no
mâi châi
ไม่ใช่

no?
mǎi? or châi mǎi?
ไหม หรือ ใช่ไหม?

when?
mêu-arai?
เมื่อไหร่?

It doesn't matter.
mâi pen rai
ไม่เป็นไร

What is this?
nîi arai?
นี่อะไร?

What do you call this in Thai?
nîi phaasǎa thai rîak wâa arai?
นี่ภาษาไทยเรียกว่าอะไร?

I understand.
khâo jai
เข้าใจ

Do you understand?
khâo jai mǎi?
เข้าใจไหม?

I don't understand.
mâi khâo jai
ไม่เข้าใจ

a little
nít nàwy
นิดหน่อย

Some Verbs

go
pai
ไป

will go
jà pai
จะไป

come
maa
มา

will come
jà maa
จะมา

(I) like ....
châwp ....
ชอบ

(I) do not like ....
mâi châwp ....
ไม่ชอบ

(I) would like (+ verb) ....
yàak jà ....
อยากจะ...

(I) would not like ....
mâi yàak jà ....
ไม่อยากจะ...

(I) would like to eat ....
yàak jà thaan ....
อยากจะทาน...

(I) would like ....(+ noun)
yàak dâi ....
อยากได้...

Getting Around

I would like a ticket.
yàak dâi tǔa
อยากได้ตั๋ว

I would like to go ....
yàak jà pai ....
อยากจะไป.

Where is (the) ....?
.... *yùu thîi nǎi*
อยู่ที่ไหน?

motorcycle
rót moh-toe-sai
รถมอเตอร์ไซ

train
rót fai
รถไฟ

bus
rót meh
รถเมล์

car
rót yon
รถยนต์

hotel
rohng raem
โรงแรม

station
sathǎanii
สถานี

post office
praisanii
ไปรษณีย์

restaurant
ràan aahǎan
ร้านอาหาร

hospital
rohng phayaabaan
โรงพยาบาล

airport
sanǎam bin
สนามบิน

market
talàat
ตลาด

beach
hat or *hàat*
หาด

Accommodation

food (rice)
khâo
ข้าว

bathroom
hâwng nám
ห้องน้ำ

toilet
hâwng sûam
ห้องส้วม

room
hâwng
ห้อง

hot
ráwn
ร้อน

cold
nǎo
หนาว

bath/shower
aàp nám
อาบน้ำ

towel
phâa chét tua
ผ้าเช็ดตัว

Shopping

How much?
thâo rai?
เท่าไร?

How much is this?
níi thâo rai? (or *kìi bàat?*)
นี่เท่าไร (หรือ) กี่บาท?

too expensive
phaeng pai
แพงไป

cheap, inexpensive
thùuk
ถูก

Emergencies

(I) need a doctor.
tâwng-kaan mǎw
ต้องการหมอ

Time

today
wan níi
วันนี้

tomorrow
phrûng níi
พรุ่งนี้

yesterday
mêua waan
เมื่อวาน

Numbers

1	nèung	หนึ่ง
2	sǎwng	สอง
3	sǎam	สาม
4	sìi	สี่
5	hâa	ห้า
6	hòk	หก
7	jèt	เจ็ด
8	pàet	แปด
9	kâo	เก้า
10	sìp	สิบ
11	sìp-èt	สิบเอ็ด
12	sìp-sǎwng	สิบสอง
13	sìp-sǎam	สิบสาม
14	sìp-sìi	สิบสี่
20	yîi-sìp	ยี่สิบ
21	yîi-sìp-et	ยี่สิบเอ็ด
22	yîi-sìp-sǎwng	ยี่สิบสอง
23	yîi-sìp-sǎam	ยี่สิบสาม
30	sǎam-sìp	สามสิบ
40	sìi-sìp	สี่สิบ
50	hâa-sìp	ห้าสิบ
100	nèung ráwy	หนึ่งร้อย
200	sǎwng ráwy	สองร้อย
300	sǎam ráwy	สามร้อย
1000	nèung phan	หนึ่งพัน
10,000	nèung mèun	หนึ่งหมื่น
100,000	nèung sǎen	หนึ่งแสน
1,000,000	láan	ล้าน
billion	phan láan	พันล้าน

Your first attempts to speak the language will probably meet with mixed success, but keep trying. When learning new words/phrases, listen closely to the way the Thais themselves use the various tones – you'll catch on quickly.

For expanding your travel vocabulary, I recommend *Robertson's Practical English-Thai Dictionary* since it has a phonetic guide to pronunciation, with tones and is compact in size. Published by Charles E Tuttle Co, Suido 1-chome, 2-6, Bunkyo-ku, Tokyo, it may be difficult to find.

For more serious language-learners there is Mary Haas' *Thai-English Student's Dictionary* and George McFarland's *Thai-English Dictionary* (the cream of the crop), both published by Stanford University Press, Stanford, California.

For a more complete selection of phrases and basic vocabulary and grammar for travel in Thailand, see Lonely Planet's *Thai Phrasebook*.

Thai Language Study

Several language schools in Bangkok and Chiang Mai offer courses for foreigners in Thai language. Tuition fees average around 250B per hour. Some places will let you trade English lessons for Thai lessons, or if not you can usually teach English on the side to offset tuition costs. There are three recommended schools in Bangkok:

Union Language School (tel 233-4482) 109 Surawong Rd.
Generally recognised as the best and most rigorous course. Employs a balance of structure-oriented and communication-oriented methodologies.

AUA (American University Alumni) Language Center (tel 252-8170) 179 Rajadamri Rd.
AUA runs one of the largest English language teaching institutes in the world so this is a good place to meet Thai students. On the other hand, farangs who study Thai here complain that there's not enough interaction in class because of an emphasis on the so-called 'Natural Approach', which focuses on the teacher rather than the student. AUA also has a branch in Chiang Mai.

Nisa Thai Language School (tel 286-9323) 27 Sathon Tai Rd.
This school has a fairly good reputation, though teachers may be less qualified than at Union or AUA language schools. In addition to all the usual levels, Nisa offers a course in preparing for the *Baw Hok* or Grade 6 examination, a must for anyone wishing to work in the public school system.

Other Courses Chulalongkorn University, the most prestigious university in Thailand, has recently begun offering an intensive Thai studies course called 'Perspectives on Thailand'. The programme runs four weeks and includes classes in Thai language, culture, history, politics, and economics. Classes meet six hours a day, six days a week (Saturday is usually a field trip) and are offered twice a year, January to February and July to August. Students who have taken the course say they have found the quality of instruction excellent. Tuition is US$1000.

Room and board on campus are available though it's much less expensive to live off-campus. For further information write to Perspectives on Thailand, 7th floor, Sasin Graduate Institute of Business Administration, Chulalongkorn University, Bangkok.

The YMCA's *Siri Pattana Thai Language School* (tel 286-1936), 13 Sathon Tai Rd, gives Thai language lessons as well as preparation for the Baw Hok exam.

Facts for the Visitor

VISAS

Transit visas cost around US$5, tourist visas cost US$10 and three passport photos must accompany applications. The actual fee depends on the country in which you arrange your visa, eg in Penang a tourist visa is M$30. A transit visa is valid for 30 days, a tourist visa for 60 days. People arriving in Thailand without a visa may be granted a 15-day stay, no extension allowed, with proof of onward ticket and sufficient funds. Non-immigrant visas are good for 90 days, must be applied for in your home country, cost around US$15 and are not difficult to get if you can offer a good reason for your visit.

Travellers with New Zealand passports may enter Thailand as visitors for up to 90 days without a visa – or so says the latest report from Thai Immigration in Bangkok. You had better confirm this in writing in advance at a Thai embassy or consulate – it almost seems too good to be true.

Thailand does not issue 'multiple-entry' visas. If you want a visa that enables you to leave the country and then return, the best you can do is to obtain a visa permitting two entries, and this will cost double the single-entry visa. For example, a two-entry three-month non-immigrant visa will cost US$30 and will allow you six months in the country, as long as you cross the Malaysian border (or any other border with immigration facilities) by the end of your first three months. The second half of your visa is validated as soon as you re-cross the Thai border, so there is no need to go to a Thai embassy/consulate abroad. All visas acquired in advance of entry are valid for 90 days from the date of issue.

If you overstay your visa, the practice at Bangkok International Airport now seems to be to fine you 100B per day of your overstay.

Embassies

Bangkok is a good place to collect visas for westward journeys, and most countries are represented by an embassy. For more information see the Embassy section in the Bangkok chapter.

Visa Extensions

Tourist visas may be extended at the discretion of Thai Immigration. The Bangkok office (tel 286-9176) is on Soi Suan Phlu, Sathon Tai Road, but you can apply at any immigration office in the country – every provincial capital has one. The usual fee for extension of a tourist visa (up to one month) is 500B. Bring along two photos and two copies each of the photo and visa pages of your passport. Extension of the 15-day transit visa is only allowed if you hold a passport from a country that has no Thai embassy. The 30-day transit visa cannot be extended for any reason.

Re-entry Visas

If you need a re-entry visa for an out-and-back trip to Burma or the like, apply at the Immigration Office on Soi Suan Phlu. Cost is 300B.

A traveller's comments:

If you fail to get your passport stamped on arrival, as has happened to people arriving by long-tail boat at Satun in the south of Thailand, you can take your sorry story to the Immigration Office in Bangkok and after filling out countless forms and showing a ticket out of the country you might get away without being fined.

Working Holidays

If you want to stay longer, a non-immigrant visa is the one to get. Extending it is very much up to how the officials feel about you – if they like you then they will. Money doesn't come in to it. An Australian teaching English in Thailand recounted how he had to collect various signatures and go through various interviews which resulted in a 'provisional' extension. Back in his province he then had to report to the local office every 10 days for the next three months until his actual extension came through. 'Extensions needn't be expensive', he reported, 'you just have to say nice things and smile to a lot of people'. Becoming a monk doesn't necessarily mean you'll get a longer visa either – again it depends on whom you see and how they feel about you.

CUSTOMS

Like most countries, Thailand prohibits the import of illegal drugs, firearms and ammunition (unless registered in advance with the Police Department) and pornographic media. 'A reasonable amount of clothing for personal use, toiletries and professional instruments' are allowed in duty-free, as are one still or one movie/video camera with five rolls of still film or three rolls of movie film or videotape. Up to 200 cigarettes can be brought into the country without paying duty, or for other smoking materials up to 250 grams total. One litre of wine or spirits is allowed in duty-free.

Electronic goods like personal stereos, calculators and computers can be a problem if the customs officials have reason to believe you're bringing them in for resale. As long as you don't carry more than one of each, you should be OK. Occasionally, customs will require you to leave a hefty deposit for big-ticket items (eg a laptop computer or midi-component stereo) which is refunded when you leave the country with the item in question. If you make the mistake of saying you're just passing through and don't plan to use the item while in Thailand, they may ask you to leave it with the Customs Department until you depart the country.

Upon leaving Thailand, you must obtain an export licence for any antiques or objects of art you want to take with you. An antique is any 'archaic movable property whether produced by man or by nature, any part of ancient structure, human skeleton or animal carcass, which by its age or characteristic of production or historical evidence is useful in the field of art, history or archaeology'. An object of art is a 'thing produced by craftsmanship and appreciated as being valuable in the field of art'. Obviously these are very sweeping definitions, so if in doubt go to the Department of Fine Arts for inspection and licensing.

Application can be made by submitting two front-view photos of the object(s) (no more than five objects to a photo) and a photocopy of your passport, along with the object(s) in question, to one of three locations in Thailand: the National Museum in Bangkok, the Chiang Mai National Museum, or the Songkhla National Museum. You need to allow three to five days for the application and inspection process to be completed.

Thailand has special regulations for taking a Buddha or other deity image (or any part thereof) out of the country. These require not only a licence from the Fine Arts Department but a permit from the Ministry of Commerce as well. The one exception to this are the small Buddha images (*phra phim*) that are meant to be worn on a chain around the neck; these may be exported without a licence as long as the reported purpose is religious.

MONEY

US$1	=	26 Baht
A$1	=	20 Baht
UK£1	=	40 Baht
S$1	=	13 Baht
DM1	=	14 Baht

Thai Currency

There are 100 satang in 1 baht; coins include 25 satang and 50 satang pieces and baht in 1B and 5B coins. Older coins exhibit Thai numerals only, while newer coins have Thai and Roman numerals. At this writing, 1B coins come in three sizes: only the middle size works in public pay phones! Likewise, 5B coins also come in three sizes; a large one with a Thai numeral only and two smaller coins that have Thai and Roman numerals (one of the smaller 5B coins has nine inset edges along the circumference). Eventually Thailand will be phasing out the older coins, but in the meantime it's confusing when trying to count out change.

Paper currency comes in denominations of 10B (brown), 20B (green), 50B (blue), 100B (red) and 500B (purple) denominations. Fortunately for newcomers to Thailand, numerals are printed in their western as well as Thai forms. Notes are also scaled according to the amount; the larger the denomination, the larger the note. Large denominations like 500B bills can be hard to change in small towns, but banks will always change them.

Twenty-five satang equals one 'saleng' in colloquial Thai, so if you're quoted a price of six saleng in the market, say, for a small bunch of bananas or a bag of peanuts, this means 1½B.

Changing Money

There is no black market money exchange for baht, so there is no reason to bring in any Thai currency. Banks or legal money-changers offer the best exchange rate within the country. The baht is firmly attached to the American dollar and is as stable.

Exchange rates are given in the *Bangkok Post* everyday. For buying baht, US dollars are the most readily acceptable currency and travellers' cheques get better rates than cash. Since banks charge 8B commission and duty for each travellers' cheque cashed, you will save on commissions if you use larger cheque denominations (a US$50 cheque will only cost 8B while five US$10 cheques will cost 40B). Note that you can't exchange Indonesian rupiah or Nepalese rupees into Thai currency. Bangkok is a good place to

buy Indian and Nepalese rupees, however, as well as Burmese kyat, if you're going to any of these countries. Rates are comparable with black market rates in each of these countries.

Visa credit card holders can get cash advances of up to US$200 per day through some branches of the Thai Farmers Bank and some Thai Commercial Banks (and also at the night-time exchange windows in well-touristed spots like Banglamphu, Chiang Mai and Ko Samui). If you try to use a Visa card (very common in the south, even at the smaller hotels) at upcountry hotels, the staff may try to tell you that only Visa cards issued by the Thai Farmers Bank are acceptable. With a little patience, you should be able to make them understand that the Thai Farmers Bank will pay the hotel and that your bank will pay the Thai Farmers Bank – that any Visa card issued anywhere in the world is indeed acceptable.

American Express card holders can also get advances, but only in travellers' cheques. The Amex agent is SEA Tours, Suite 414, Siam Center, 965 Rama I Rd. Many shops and hotels that take Visa also accept Master-Card. A few hotels will charge an extra 3% for using credit cards.

Travellers can rent safety deposit boxes at the Safety Deposit Centre, 3rd floor Chan Issara Tower, 942/81 Rama IV Rd (near the Silom Rd intersection) for 150B a month

plus 2000B refundable key deposit. Open from 10 am to 7 pm, Monday to Friday, 10 am to 6pm Saturday, Sunday and public holidays. A few banks will rent safety deposit boxes as well, but generally you need to open an account with them first.

Exchange Control

Legally any traveller arriving in Thailand must have at least the following amounts of money in cash, travellers' cheques, bank draft, or letter of credit, according to visa category:

Non-immigrant visa: US$500 per person or US$1000 per family

Tourist visa: US$250 per person or US$500 per family

Transit visa or no visa: US$125 per person or US$250 per family

This may be checked if you arrive on a one-way ticket or if you look as if you're at 'the end of the road'.

There are also limits on the maximum amounts of Thai currency you may bring in or take out of the country without special authorisation. No more than 2000B per person or 4000B per family is to be brought into the country and no more than 500B per person or 1000B per family is to be taken out.

Although there are no limits on the amount of foreign (non-Thai) currency that can be brought into the country, anything over US$10,000 or its equivalent in another currency must be declared to Customs on arrival in Thailand. A failure to declare the excess can result in confiscation.

It's legal to open a foreign currency account at any commercial bank in Thailand. As long as the funds originate from abroad, there are no restrictions on maintenance or withdrawal of the funds.

Finally, anyone who receives income while in Thailand or who stays in Thailand beyond a cumulative 90 days within one calendar year must obtain a tax clearance certificate from the Revenue Department before they'll be permitted to leave the country. The Bangkok office (tel 281-5777) of the Revenue Department is on Chakka-pong Rd not far from the Democracy Monument. There are also Revenue Department offices in every provincial capital.

COSTS

Food and accommodation outside Bangkok is generally quite inexpensive and even in Bangkok it's fairly low, especially considering the value vis à vis other countries in South and South-East Asia.

Outside Bangkok, budget travellers should be able to get by on 200B per day if they really keep watch on their expenses. This estimate includes basic accommodation, food, non-alcoholic beverages and local transport, but not souvenirs, tours or vehicle hire. Add another 40 to 45B per day for every beer you drink. Expenses vary, of course, from place to place; where there are high concentrations of budget travellers, accommodation tends to be cheaper and food more expensive. With experience, you can travel in Thailand for even less, if you live like a Thai of modest means and learn to speak the language. Average low-to-middle income Thais certainly don't spend 200B a day when travelling in their own country.

In Bangkok there's almost no limit to the amount you *could* spend, but if you live frugally, avoid the tourist ghettos and ride the public bus system you could get by on the same or just a bit more. Where you stay in Bangkok is of primary concern, as accommodation there has generally become a good deal more expensive than upcountry accommodation since the tourist boom of 1987. Typically, the traveller spends well over 150B per day in Bangkok just for accommodation – this is generally the absolute minimum for air-con (in a shared double room). On the other hand, if you can do without air-con, accommodation can be found in Bangkok for as little as 40B per person. But the noise, heat and pollution in Bangkok may drive many budget travellers to seek more comfort than they might otherwise need upcountry.

Food is somewhat more expensive in Bangkok than in the provinces. However, in Thonburi (Bangkok's 'left bank'), where I lived for some time, many dishes are often *cheaper* than they are upcountry, due to the availability of fresh ingredients. This is also true for the working-class districts on the Bangkok side, like Makkasan. Bangkok is the typical 'primate city' cited by sociologists, meaning that most goods produced by the country as a whole end up in Bangkok. The glaring exception is western food, which Bangkok has more of than anywhere else in the kingdom but charges the most for it. Eat only Thai and Chinese food if you're trying to spend as little as possible. After all, why go to Thailand to eat steak and potatoes?

Good bargaining, which takes practice, is another way to cut costs. Anything bought in a market should be bargained for, as well as accommodation. Some more specific suggestions concerning costs can be found in the Accommodation and Things to Buy sections of this chapter.

Transportation between cities and within them is very reasonable; again, bargaining (when hiring a vehicle) can save you a lot of baht. See the Getting Around chapter.

TIPPING

Tipping is not a normal practice in Thailand, although they're getting used to it in expensive hotels and restaurants. Elsewhere don't bother. In taxis where you have to bargain the fare, it certainly isn't necessary.

TOURIST INFORMATION

The Tourist Authority of Thailand (TAT) has several offices within the country and others overseas.

Local Tourist Offices

Bangkok
    4 Ratchadamnoen Nok Avenue, Bangkok 10100 (tel 282-1143/7)

Chiang Mai
    135 Praisani Rd, Chiang Mai 50000 (tel (053) 235334)

Hat Yai/Songkhla
    1/1 Soi 2, Niphat Uthit 3 Rd, Hat Yai 90110 (tel (074) 243747, 245986)

Kanchanaburi
    Saengchuto Rd, Kanchanaburi 71000 (tel (034) 511200)

Khorat (Nakhon Ratchasima)
    2102-2104 Mittaphap Rd, Nakhon Ratchasima 30000 (tel (044) 243427)

Pattaya
    382/1 Chai Hat Rd, Pattaya Beach, Chonburi 20260 (tel (038) 428750)

Phitsanulok
    209/7-8 Surasi Trade Center, Boromtrailokanat Rd, Phitsanulok 65000 (tel (055) 252742)

Phuket
    73-75 Phuket Rd, Phuket 83000 (tel (076) 212213)

Surat Thani
    5 Talat Mai Rd, Ban Don, Surat Thani 84000 (tel (077) 282828)

Overseas Offices

Australia
    12th Floor, Exchange Bldg, 56 Pitt St, Sydney NSW 2000 (tel 277540/9) @SMHI = France
    Office National de Tourisme de Thailande, 90 Ave des Champs Elysees, 75008 Paris, France (tel 4562-8656)

Hong Kong
    Rm 401, Fairmont House, 8 Cotton Tree Drive, Central, Hong Kong (tel 5-868-0732)

Japan
    Hibiya Mitsui Bldg, 1-2 Yurakucho 1-chome, Chiyoda-ku, Tokyo 100 (tel (03) 580-6776)

Singapore
    c/o Royal Thai Embassy, 370 Orchard Rd 0923 (tel 2357694)

UK 9 Stafford Ct, London WIX 3FE (tel (01) 499 7670/9)

USA
    5 World Trade Center, Suite 2449, New York, NY 10048 (tel (212) 432-0433)
    3440 Wilshire Boulevard, Suite 1101, Los Angeles, California, 90010 (tel (213) 382-2353)

West Germany
    4th floor Bethmann Strasse, 58/IV D-6000 Frankfurt/M 1 (tel (069) 295704/804)

GENERAL INFORMATION
Post

Thailand has a very efficient postal service and within the country it's also very cheap. Bangkok's GPO on Charoen Krung (New) Road is open from 8 am to 8 pm Monday to Friday and from 9 am to 1 pm weekends and holidays. There is a telephone and telegram service 24 hours a day. Outside of Bangkok, most post offices close at 4.30 pm on weekdays and only the larger ones are open a half day on Saturday.

The poste restante service is also very reliable, though during high tourist months (December and August) you may have to wait in line at the Bangkok GPO. There is a fee of 1B for every piece of mail collected. As with many Asian countries, confusion at poste restantes is most likely to arise over given names and surnames. Ask people who are writing to you to print your surname clearly and to underline it. If you're certain a letter should be waiting for you and it cannot be found, it's always wise to check it hasn't been filed under your given name. You can take poste restante at almost any post office in Thailand now.

The American Express office, Suite 414, Siam Center, Rama IV Rd, will also take mail on behalf of AMEX cardholders. The hours are from 8.30 am to 12 midday and 1 pm to 4 pm, Monday to Friday.

Postal Rates Airmail letters weighing 10 grams or less cost 13B to Europe and Australia/New Zealand, 15B to the Americas.

Aerograms cost 8.5B and postcards are 8B to Europe/Australia/New Zealand, 9B to the Americas.

Parcels shipped by surface post vary from 174B for 1 kg up to 800B for weights of up to 15 kg.

Telephone

The telephone system in Thailand is quite efficient and from Bangkok you can usually direct dial most major centres with little difficulty. The opposite may not always apply, and in smaller centres it's often best to go to the local telephone office (usually located at the central post office) and make calls from there. You can make international long-distance calls from government telephone offices or from large hotels; it is always cheaper to call abroad from a telephone office. There are also private long-distance telephone offices but these are not for international calls, only for calls within Thailand.

There are two kinds of public pay phones in Thailand, 'red' and 'blue'. The red phones are for local city calls and the blue are for long-distance (within Thailand) calls. Local calls from pay phones cost 1B. Although there are three different 1B coins in general circulation, only the middle-sized coin fits the coin slots.

Electricity

Electric current is 220 volts, 50 cycles.

Time

Thai time is seven hours ahead of GMT (London). Thus 12 noon in Bangkok is 3 pm in Sydney, 1 pm in Perth, 5 am in London, 1 am in New York and 10 pm the previous day in Los Angeles.

Business Hours

Most government offices are open from 8.30 am to 4.30 pm, Monday to Friday, but closed from 12 noon to 1 pm for lunch. Banks are open from 8.30 am to 3.30 pm Monday to Friday, but in Bangkok in particular several banks have special foreign exchange offices which are open longer hours (generally until 8 pm) and every day of the week.

Businesses usually operate between 8.30 am to 5 pm, Monday to Friday and sometimes Saturday morning as well. Larger shops usually open from 10 am to 6.30 or 7 pm but smaller shops may open earlier and close later.

Weights & Measures

Dimensions and weight are usually expressed using the metric system in Thailand. The exception is land measure, which is often quoted using the traditional Thai system of waa, ngaan and rai. Old-timers in the provinces will occasionally use the traditional Thai system of weights and measures in speech, as will boat-builders, carpenters and other craftsmen when talking about their work. Here are some conversions to use for such occasions:

1 square waa = 4 square metres
1 ngaan (100 square waa) = 400 square metres
1 Rai (4 ngaan) = 1600 square metres
1 baht = 15 grams
1 taleung* (4 baht) = 60 grams
1 chang (20 taleung) = 1.2 kg
1 haap (50 chang) = 60 kg
1 niu = 2 cm
1 kheup (12 niu) = 25 cm
1 sawk (2 kheup) = 50 cm
1 waa (4 sawk) = 2 metres
1 sen (20 waa) = 40 metres
1 yoht (400 sen) = 16 km

*also tamleung

MEDIA
Newspapers
There are two English-language newspapers published daily in Thailand and distributed in most provincial capitals throughout the country: the Bangkok Post (morning) and the Nation (afternoon). The Post is the better of the two papers and is in fact regarded by many journalists as the best English daily in South-East Asia.

The Singapore edition of the International Herald Tribune is widely available in Bangkok, Chiang Mai and heavily touristed areas like Pattaya and Phuket.

Radio
Bangkok's national public radio station (Sathani Withayu Haeng Prathet Thai)

broadcasts English-language programmes over the FM frequency 97 MHz from 6 am to 11 pm. Most of the programmes comprise of local, national and international news, sports, business and special news-related features. There is some music on the channel between 9 and 11.15 am, interspersed with hourly English-news broadcasts. For up-to-date news reports this is the station to listen to. An 'Official New Bulletin' (national news sponsored by the government) is broadcast at 7 am, 12.30 and 7 pm.

FM 107 is another public radio station and is affiliated with Radio Thailand and Channel 9 on Thai public television. They broadcast Radio Thailand news bulletins at the same hours as Radio Thailand (7 am, 12.30 pm and 7 pm). At 7.30 pm, FM 107 provides the English-language soundtrack for local and world satellite news on television Channel 9 while FM 104.5 does the same for Channels 3 and 7. Between 5 am to 2 am daily, FM 107 features some surprisingly good music programmes with British, Thai and American disc jockeys.

Chulalongkorn University broadcasts classical music at FM 101.5 MHz from 9.30 to 11.30 pm nightly. A schedule of the evening's programmes can be found in the Nation and Bangkok Post newspapers. The Voice of America, BBC World Service, Radio Canada and Radio Australia all have English and Thai-language broadcasts over short-wave radio. The radio frequencies and schedules, which change hourly, also appear in the Post and the Nation.

Television
There are five television networks in Bangkok. Channel 9 is the national public television station and broadcasts from 6 am until midnight. Channel 3 is privately owned and is on the air from 4 pm until midnight. Channel 5 is a military network (the only one to operate during coups) and broadcasts from 4 pm to midnight. Channel 7 is military-owned but broadcast time is leased to private companies; hours of operation are from 4 pm to midnight. Channel 11 is run by the Ministry of Education and features educational programmes from 5.30 am until midnight,

including TV correspondence classes from Ramkhamhaeng and Sukhothai Thammathirat Open Universities.

Upcountry cities will generally receive only two networks, Channel 9 and a local private network with restricted hours.

HEALTH
Pre-Departure Preparations
Travel Insurance As when travelling anywhere in the world a good travel insurance policy is a very wise idea. A motorcycle accident can make an expensive and nasty end to your travels. 'After paying the hospital bills, damage to the bike I hit and goodwill contribution to the local police,' wrote one traveller, 'I wished I had been insured'.

If you undergo medical treatment in Thailand, be sure to collect all receipts and copies of the medical report, in English if possible, for your insurance company.

Medical Kit For basic first aid, I recommend carrying the following:

Large self-adhesive bandages and band-aids to help protect ordinary cuts or wounds from infection
Butterfly closures for cuts that won't close on their own
Anti-bacterial ointment and powder to treat or prevent infection of wounds
Immodium, Lomotil, or Pattardium to mitigate the symptoms of diarrhoea
Antibiotic eye ointment for all-too-common eye infections
Scissors, tweezers & a thermometer
Aspirin/acetaminophen/paracetamol for headaches, fever
Rehydration mixture for treatment of severe diarrhoea
Insect repellent, sun block, suntan lotion, chap stick and water purification tablets

The best book I've seen on health maintenance in Asia is Dirk Schroeder's *Staying Healthy in Asia, Africa, and Latin America* (Stanford, California: Volunteers in Asia, 1988). In fact, you might want to make this handy little book part of your first aid kit as it clearly describes symptoms and recommended treatment for illnesses common in Thailand (and elsewhere in Asia).

When seriously ill or injured, you should seek medical attention from a qualified

doctor, clinic or hospital if at all possible; employ self-treatment only as a last resort.

Health Preparations Make sure you're healthy before you start travelling, and if you are embarking on a long trip make sure your teeth are OK. If you wear glasses bring a spare pair and your prescription. Losing your glasses can be a real problem, although in many places you can get new spectacles made up quickly, cheaply and competently.

If you require a particular medication, take an adequate supply as it may not be available locally. Take the prescription, with the generic rather than the brand name, which may be unavailable, as it will make getting replacements easier. It's a wise idea to have the prescription with you to show you legally use the medication, it's surprising how often over-the-counter drugs from one place are illegal without a prescription or even banned in another.

Immunisations
There are no health requirements for Thailand in terms of required vaccinations unless you are coming from an infected area. Travellers should have a cholera immunisation prior to arriving and a tetanus booster would be a good idea as well in case you injure yourself while travelling. You should also check if vaccinations are required by any countries you are going to after visiting Thailand. A Japanese encephalitis vaccination is a good idea for those who think they may be at moderate or high risk while in Thailand (see the Japanese encephalitis section for more information). Your doctor may also recommend booster shots against measles or polio.

Plan ahead for getting your vaccinations since some of them require an initial shot followed by a booster while some vaccinations should not be given together.

Basic Rules
Care in what you eat and drink is the most important health rule; stomach upsets are the most likely travel health problem, but the majority of these upsets will be relatively minor. Don't become paranoid - trying the

local food is part of the experience of travel after all.

The number one rule is *don't drink the water*, and that includes ice. If you don't know for certain that water is safe always assume the worst. Reputable brands of bottled water or soft drinks are generally fine, although in some places refilled bottles are not unknown. Take care with fruit juice, particularly if water may have been added. Milk should be treated with suspicion as it is often unpasteurised. Boiled milk is fine if it is kept hygienically and yoghurt is always good. Tea or coffee should also be OK since the water should be boiled.

Salads and fruit should be washed with purified water or peeled where possible. Ice cream is usually OK if it is a reputable brand name, but beware of ice cream from street vendors and ice cream that has melted and been refrozen. Thoroughly cooked food is safest, but not if it has been left to cool or if it has been reheated. Take great care with shellfish or fish and avoid undercooked meat.

If a place looks clean and well run and the vendor also looks clean and healthy then the food is probably safe. In general, places that are packed with travellers or locals will be fine, empty restaurants are questionable.

Nutrition If you're travelling hard and fast and therefore missing meals, or if you simply lose your appetite, you can soon start to lose weight and place your health at risk.

Make sure your diet is well balanced. Eggs, tofu, beans, lentils and nuts are all safe ways to get protein. Fruit you can peel (bananas, oranges or mandarins for example) are always safe and a good source of vitamins. Try to eat plenty of grains (rice) and bread. Remember that although food is generally safer if it is cooked well, overcooked food loses much of its nutritional value. If the food is insufficient it's a good idea to take vitamin and iron pills.

Make sure you drink enough, don't rely on feeling thirsty to indicate when you should drink. Not needing to urinate or very dark yellow urine is a danger sign. Always carry a water bottle with you on long trips. Excessive sweating can lead to loss of salt and therefore muscle cramping. Salt tablets are not a good idea as a preventative but in places where salt is not used much, adding additional salt to food can help.

Food & Water As with any Asian country, care should be taken in consuming food or drink. Besides malaria, really serious diseases are not too common in Thailand.

Thai soft drinks are safe to drink, as is the weak Chinese tea served in most restaurants. Most ice is produced under hygienic conditions and is therefore theoretically safe. During transit to the local restaurant, however, conditions are not so hygienic (you may see blocks of ice being dragged along the street), but it's very difficult to resist in the hot season. In rural areas, villagers mostly drink collected rainwater. Most travellers can drink this without problems, but some people can't tolerate it. It is best to buy fruit that you can peel and slice yourself (cheaper, too), but most fare at food stalls is reasonably safe.

Water Purification The simplest way of purifying water is to thoroughly boil it. Technically this means for 10 minutes, something which happens very rarely! Remember that at high altitudes water boils at a lower temperature, so germs are less likely to be killed.

Simple filtering will not remove all dangerous organisms, so if you cannot boil water it should be treated chemically. Chlorine tablets (puritabs, steritabs or other brand names) will kill many, but not all pathogens. Iodine is very effective in purifying water and is available in tablet form (such as Potable Aqua), but follow the directions carefully and remember that too much iodine can be harmful.

If you can't find tablets, tincture of iodine (2%) or iodine crystals can be used. Two drops of tincture of iodine per litre or quart of clear water is the recommended doseage, and the water should then be left to stand for 30 minutes. Iodine crystals can also be used to purify water, but this is a more complicated process as you have to first prepare a saturated iodine solution. Iodine loses its effectiveness if exposed to air or damp so keep it in a tightly sealed container. Flavoured powder will disguise the taste of treated water and is a good idea if you are travelling with children.

Health A normal body temperature is 98.6°F or 37°C, more than 2°C higher is a 'high' fever. A normal adult pulse rate is 60 to 80 per minute (children 80 to 100, babies 100 to 140). You should know how to take a temperature and a pulse rate. As a general rule the pulse increases about 20 beats per minute for each °C rise in fever.

Respiration rate (breathing) is also an indicator of illness. Count the number of breaths per minute, between 12 and 20 is normal for adults and older children (up to 30 for younger children, 40 for babies). People with a high fever or serious respiratory illness (like pneumonia) breathe more quickly than normal. More than 40 shallow breaths a minute usually means pneumonia.

Many health problems can be avoided by taking care of yourself. Wash your hands frequently, it's quite easy to contaminate your own food. Clean your teeth with purified water rather than straight from the tap. Avoid climatic extremes, keep out of the sun when it's hot. Avoid potential diseases by dressing sensibly. You can get worm infections through bare feet, or dangerous coral cuts by walking over coral without shoes. You can avoid insect bites by covering bare skin when insects are around, by screening windows or beds or by using insect repellents. Seek local advice; if you're told the water is unsafe due to jellyfish, etc, don't go in. In situations were there is no information, discretion is the better part of valour.

Medical Problems & Treatment
Potential medical problems can be broken down into several areas. First there are the climatic and geographical considerations – problems caused by extremes of temperature, altitude or motion. Then there are diseases and illnesses caused by insanitation, insect bites or stings, animal or human contact. Simple cuts, bites or scratches can also cause problems.

Self diagnosis and treatment can be risky, wherever possible seek qualified help. An embassy or consulate can usually advise a good place to go. So can five-star hotels, although they often recommend doctors with five-star prices. This is when that medical insurance really comes in useful! In some places standards of medical attention are so low that for some ailments the best advice is to get on a plane and go somewhere else.

Climatic & Geographical Considerations
Sunburn In the tropics you can get sunburnt surprisingly quickly even through cloud. Use a sunscreen and take extra care to cover areas which don't normally see sun – your feet for example. A hat provides added protection and use zinc cream or some other barrier cream for your nose and lips. Calamine lotion is good for mild sunburn.

Prickly Heat Prickly heat is an itchy rash caused by excessive perspiration trapped under the skin. It usually strikes people who have just arrived in a hot climate whose pores have not yet opened sufficiently to cope with greater sweating. Keeping cool by bathing often, using a mild talcum powder, or even by resorting to air-con may help until you acclimatise.

Heat Exhaustion Dehydration or salt deficiency can cause heat exhaustion. Take time to acclimatise to high temperatures and make sure you get sufficient liquids. Salt deficiency is characterised by fatigue, lethargy, headaches, giddiness and muscle cramps and in this case salt tablets may help. Vomiting or diarrhoea can deplete your liquid and salt levels. Anhidrotic heat exhaustion, caused by an inability to sweat, is quite rare and unlike the other forms of heat exhaustion is likely to strike people who have been in a hot climate for some time, rather than newcomers.

Heat Stroke This serious, sometimes fatal, condition can occur if the body's heat regulating mechanism breaks down and the body temperature rises to dangerous levels. Long, continuous periods of exposure to high temperatures can leave you vulnerable to heat stroke and you should avoid excessive alcohol or strenuous activity when you first arrive in a hot climate.

The symptoms are feeling unwell, not sweating very much or at all, high body temperature (39 to 41°C). Where sweating has ceased the skin becomes flushed and red. Severe, throbbing headaches and lack of coordination will also occur and the sufferer may be confused or aggressive. Eventually the victim will become delirious or convulse. Hospitalisation is essential, but meanwhile get the victim out of the sun, remove clothing and cover them with a wet sheet or towel and then fan them continually.

Fungal Infections Hot-weather fungal infections are most likely to occur on the scalp, between the toes or fingers (athlete's foot), in the groin (jock itch or crotch rot) and ringworm on the body. You get ringworm (which is a fungal infection, not a worm) from infected animals or by walking on damp areas, like shower floors.

To prevent fungal infections, wear loose, comfortable clothes, avoid artificial fibres, wash frequently and dry carefully. If you do get an infection, wash the infected area daily with a disinfectant or medicated soap and water and rinse and dry well. Apply an anti-fungal powder like the widely available Tinaderm. Try to expose the infected area to air or sunlight as much as possible and wash all towels and underwear in hot water and change them often.

Motion Sickness Eating lightly before and during a trip will reduce the chances of motion sickness. If you are prone to motion sickness, try to find a place that minimises disturbance – near the wing on aircraft, close to midships on boats, near the centre on buses. Fresh air usually helps; reading or cigarette smoke doesn't. Commercial anti-motion-sickness preparations, which can cause drowsiness, have to be taken before the trip commences; when you're feeling sick it's too late. Ginger is a natural preventative and is available in capsule form.

Diseases of Insanitation

Diarrhoea Traveller's diarrhoea, which can be caused by viruses, bacteria, food poisoning, stress, or simply a change in diet, may strike some visitors who stay for any length of time outside Bangkok, but usually subsides within a few days. A few rushed toilet trips with no other symptoms is not indicative of a serious problem. Moderate diarrhoea, involving half a dozen loose movements in a day, is more of a nuisance.

Dehydration is the main danger with any diarrhoea, particularly for children, so fluid replenishment is the number one treatment. Weak black tea with a little sugar, flat soft drinks diluted with water or soda water are all good. With severe diarrhoea a rehydrating solution is necessary to replace minerals and salts. You should stick to a bland diet (rice or noodle soups are good) and cut out all alcohol and caffeine as you recover.

Lomotil or Imodium can be used to bring relief from the symptoms of diarrhoea, although they do not actually cure them. Only use these drugs if absolutely necessary: if you *must* travel for example. For children, Imodium is preferable. Do not use these drugs if you have a high fever or are severely dehydrated. Antibiotics can be very useful in treating severe diarrhoea, especially if it is accompanied by nausea, vomiting, stomach cramps or mild fever. Three days treatment should be sufficient and an improvement should occur within 24 hours.

If these don't help and/or your stools contain substantial blood and mucus, you may have amoebic dysentery, which can be serious if left untreated – in this case you should see a doctor.

Giardia This intestinal parasite is present in contaminated water and the symptoms are stomach cramps, nausea, bloated stomach, watery, foul-smelling diarrhoea and frequent gas. Giardia can appear several weeks after you have been exposed to the parasite, the symptoms may disappear for a few days and then return; this can go on for several weeks. Metronidazole known as Flagyl is the recommended drug, but should only be taken under medical supervision - antibiotics are no use.

Dysentery This serious illness is caused by contaminated food or water and is characterised by severe diarrhoea, often with blood or mucus in the stool. There are two kinds of dysentery. Bacillary dysentery is characterised by a high fever and rapid development; headache, vomiting and stomach pains are also symptoms. It generally does not last longer than a week, but it is highly contagious.

Amoebic dysentery is more gradual in developing, has no fever or vomiting but is a more serious illness. It is not a self-limiting disease but will persist until treated and can recur and cause long term damage.

A stool test is necessary with dysentery, but if no medical care is available tetracycline is the prescribed treatment for bacillary dysentery, metronidazole for amoebic dysentery.

Cholera Cholera vaccination is not very effective, but outbreaks of cholera are generally widely reported so you can avoid such areas. The disease is characterised by a sudden onset of acute diarrhoea with 'rice water' stools, vomiting, muscular cramps and extreme weakness. If you contract cholera you need medical help, but treat for dehydration (which can be extreme) and, if there is an appreciable delay in getting to hospital, begin taking tetracycline. This drug should not be given to young children or pregnant women and it should not be used past its expiry date.

Viral Gastroenteritis This is not caused by bacteria but, as the name suggests, a virus and is characterised by stomach cramps, diarrhoea, sometimes vomiting, sometimes a slight fever. All you can do is rest and drink lots of fluids.

Hepatitis Hepatitis A is the most common form of this disease and is spread by contaminated food or water. The symptoms are fever, chills, headache, fatigue, feelings of weakness and aches and pains, followed by loss of appetite, nausea, vomiting abdominal pain, dark urine, light coloured faeces, jaundiced skin and the whites of the eyes may turn yellow. In some case you may feel unwell, tired, have no appetite, experience aches and pains and the jaundiced effect. You should seek medical advice, but in general there is not much you can do apart from rest, drink lots of fluids, eat lightly and avoid fatty foods. People who have had hepatitis must forego alcohol for six months after the illness, as hepatitis attacks the liver and it needs that amount of time to recover.

Hepatitis B, which used to be called serum hepatitis, is spread through sexual contact, especially male homosexual activity, through skin penetration, for example dirty needles and blood transfusions. Avoid having your ears pierced, tattoos done or injections where you have doubts about the sanitary conditions. The symptoms and treatment of type B are much the same as type A but gamma globulin as a prophylaxis is only effective against type A.

Typhoid Typhoid Fever is another gut infection that travels the fecal-oral route, ie contaminated water and food are responsible. Vaccination against typhoid is not totally effective and it is one of the most dangerous infections, so medical help must be sought.

The early symptoms are like so many others, you may feel like you have a bad cold or flu on the way, with a headache, sore throat and fever which rises a little each day until it is around 40°C or more. The pulse is often slow for the amount of fever present and gets slower as the fever rises, unlike a normal fever where the pulse increases. There may also be vomiting, diarrhoea or constipation.

In the second week the high fever and slow pulse continue and a few pink spots may appear on the body, along with trembling, delirium, weakness, weight loss and dehydration. If there are no further complications, the fever and symptoms will slowly go during the third week. However you must get medical help before this as common complications are pneumonia (acute infection of the lungs) or peritonitis (burst appendix) and typhoid is very infectious.

The victim's fever should be treated by keeping them cool and dehydration should also be watched for. Chloramphenicol is the recommended antibiotic but there are fewer side effects with ampicillin.

Worms These parasites are most common in rural, tropical areas and a stool test when you return home is not a bad idea. They can be present on unwashed vegetables or in undercooked meat and you can pick them up through your skin by walking in bare feet. Infestations may not show up for some time, and although they are generally not serious, if left untreated they can cause severe health problems. A stool test is necessary to pinpoint the problem and medication is often available over the counter.

Diseases Spread by People & Animals

Tetanus This potentially fatal disease is found in undeveloped tropical areas and is difficult to treat but is preventable with immunisation. Tetanus occurs when a wound becomes infected by a germ which lives in the faeces of animals or people, so clean all cuts, punctures or animal bites. Tetanus is known as lockjaw and the first symptom may be discomfort in swallowing, stiffening of the jaw and neck, then painful convulsions of the jaw and whole body.

Rabies Rabies is found in many countries and is caused by a bite or scratch from an infected animal. Dogs are a noted carrier. Any bite, scratch or even lick from a mammal should be cleaned immediately and thoroughly. Scrub with soap and running water, then clean with an alcohol solution. If there is any possibility that the animal is infected, medical help should be sought immediately. Even if the animal is not rabid, all bites should be treated seriously as they can become infected or can result in tetanus. A rabies vaccination is now available and should be considered if you are in a high risk category, eg cave explorers (bat bites) or people working with animals.

Sexually Transmitted Diseases Sexual contact with an infected sexual partner spreads these diseases and while abstinence is the only 100% preventative, use of a condom is also effective. Gonorrhea and syphillis are the most common of these diseases and sores, blisters or rashes around the genitals, discharges or pain when urinating are common symptoms. Symptoms may be less marked or not observed at all in women. The symptoms of syphillis eventually disappear completely but the disease continues and can cause severe problems in later years. Treatment of gonorrhoea and syphillis is by antibiotics.

There are numerous other sexually transmitted diseases for most of which effective treatment is available. There is no cure for herpes and there is also currently no cure for AIDS, which is most commonly spread through male homosexual activity, but is becoming more common amongst heterosexuals in Thailand. Abstinence or the use of condoms are the most effective preventatives.

AIDS can also be spread through infected blood transfusions or by dirty needles – vaccinations, acupuncture and tattooing can potentially be as dangerous as intravenous drug use if the equipment is not clean.

Insect-Borne Diseases

Malaria Ask 10 doctors around the world about malaria prevention and you may get 10 different opinions. Malaria, a mosquito-carried disease, is on the increase all over Asia and unfortunately most of the strains in Thailand are chloroquine-resistant, including the deadly *Plasmodium falciparum*. Hence, taking a malaria prophylactic may have little effect as a preventive and will most certainly contribute to an increase in resistance to these drugs, which are also used in the treatment of the disease.

There is much controversy surrounding the use of certain malarial prophylactics, in particular Fansidar. Before leaving, it is wise to get in contact with an infectious diseases hospital or other relevant government health body in your country to find out the latest information regarding malarial prophylactics. Armed with this information, consult a general practitioner for a prescription if you decide to take chemical suppressants. Factors such as your length of stay and the areas you plan to visit are relevant in prescribing antimalarials. All commonly prescribed malarial suppressants (eg chloroquine) have the potential to cause side effects. In particular, persons allergic to sulphonamides should not take Fansidar.

In fact, the use of Fansidar as a prophylactic has been associated with severe and, in some cases, fatal reactions among travellers who have used the drug in multiple doses (ie two to five doses of Fansidar). For this reason there is now a move by many medical authorities away from the prescription of Fansidar as a malarial prophylactic, even for those travelling in areas where the disease is chloroquine-resistant. Although the incidence of severe reaction is not high, lack of information about the drug suggests that other malarial prophylactics should be used before considering Fansidar.

Further information can be found in the article, *Revised Recommendations For Preventing Malaria in Travellers to Areas with Chloroquine-Resistant Plasmodium falciparum*, (published by the Center for Disease Control (CDC) Atlanta Georgia, April 12 1985, Volume 34/No 14).

Most recently the CDC reports that various strains of malaria in Thailand are now chloroquine *and* Fansidar-resistant. Instead they are recommending a daily dose of 100 mg doxycycline (doxycycline is also said to prevent or suppress bacillary dysentery).

Rather than load up on drugs that may do you more harm than good, you can take a few other simple precautions that can greatly reduce your chances of contracting any kind of malaria. First of all, apply a good mosquito repellent to skin and clothes whenever and wherever mossies are about. The best repellents are those which contain more than 30% DEET (N,N-diethyl-metatoluamide) – for maximum protection, use a 100% DEET preparation if you can find it. A fairly good mosquito repellent called Skeetolene is sold in Thailand (manufactured by the British Dispensary in Bangkok). For those with an allergy or aversion to synthetic repellents, citronella makes a good substitute. Mosquito coils (*yaa kan yung baep jut*) do an excellent job of repelling mosquitoes in your room and

are readily available in Thailand. Day mosquitoes do not carry malaria, so it is only in the night that you have to worry – peak biting hours are a few hours after dusk and a few hours before dawn.

According to the Malaria Centre Region II in Chiang Mai, there is virtually no risk of malaria in urban areas. Since malaria-carrying mosquitoes (*Anopheles*) only bite from early evening to early morning, you should sleep under a mosquito net (if possible) when in rural areas, even if you see only a few mosquitoes. If you are outside during the biting hours, use an insect repellent. Even in a malarial area, not every mosquito is carrying the parasite responsible for the disease. Hence, the most important thing is to prevent as many of the critters from biting you as possible, to lessen the odds that you will be 'injected' by one carrying the parasite.

Once the parasites are in your bloodstream, they are carried to your liver where they reproduce. Days, weeks, or even months later (some experts say it can take as long as a year or more in certain cases), the parasites will enter the bloodstream again from the liver and this is when the symptoms first occur. Symptoms generally begin with chills and headache, followed by a high fever that lasts several hours. This may be accompanied by nausea, diarrhoea and more intense headaches. After a period of sweating the fever may subside and other symptoms go into remission. Of course, a severe flu attack could produce similar symptoms. That is why if you do develop a high fever and think you may have been exposed to the disease, it is imperative you get a blood check for malaria. Virtually any clinic or hospital in Thailand can administer this simple test.

Early treatment is usually successful in ridding the victim of the disease for good. If untreated or improperly treated, the symptoms will keep returning in cycles as the parasites move from liver to bloodstream and back.

Like many other tropical diseases, malaria is frequently mis-diagnosed in western countries. If you should develop the symptoms after a return to your home country, be sure to seek medical attention immediately and inform your doctor that you may have been exposed to malaria.

Dengue Fever In some areas of Thailand there is a risk, albeit low, of contracting dengue fever via mosquito transmission. This time it's a day variety (*Aedes*) you have to worry about. Like malaria, dengue fever seems to be on the increase throughout tropical Asia in recent years. Dengue is found in urban as well as rural areas, especially in areas of human habitation (often indoors) where there is standing water.

Unlike malaria, dengue fever is caused by a virus and there is no chemical prophylactic or vaccination against it. In Thailand there are some six strains of dengue and once you've had one you develop an immunity specific to that strain. The symptoms come on suddenly and include high fever, severe headache and heavy joint and muscle pain (hence its older name 'breakbone fever'), followed a few days later by a rash that spreads from the torso to the arms, legs and face. Various risk factors such as age, immunity and viral strain may mitigate these symptoms so that they are less severe or last only a few days. Even when the basic symptoms are short-lived, it can take several weeks to fully recover from the resultant weakness.

In rare cases dengue may develop into a more severe condition known as dengue haemorrhagic fever (DHF), which is fatal. DHF is most common among Asian children under 15 who are undergoing a second dengue infection, so the risk for DHF for most international travellers is very low.

The best way to prevent dengue, as with malaria, is to take care not to be bitten by mosquitoes. The only treatment for it is bed rest, constant rehydration and acetaminophen (Tylenol, Panadol).

Japanese Encephalitis A few years ago this viral disease was practically unheard of. Although long endemic to tropical Asia (as well as China, Korea, Japan and eastern USSR), there have been recent rainy season epidemics in north Thailand and Vietnam which increase the risk for travellers. A night-biting mosquito (*Culex*) is the carrier for JE and the risk is said to be greatest in rural zones near areas where pigs are raised or rice is grown, since pigs and certain wild birds, whose habitat may include rice fields, serve as reservoirs for the virus.

Persons who may be at risk of contracting JE in Thailand are those who will be spending long periods of time in rural areas during the rainy season (July to October). If you belong to this group, you may want to get a Japanese encephalitis vaccination. At this writing, the vaccine is only produced in Japan but is available in most Asian capitals. Check with the government health service in your home country before you leave to see if it's available; if not, arrange to be vaccinated in Bangkok, Hong Kong or Singapore, where the vaccine is easy to find.

Timing is important in taking the vaccine; you must receive at least two doses seven to 10 days apart. The USA Center for Disease Control recommends a third dose 21 to 30 days after the first for improved immunity. Immunity lasts about a year at which point it's necessary to get a booster shot, then it's every four years after that.

The symptoms of Japanese encephalitis are sudden fever, chills and headache, followed by vomiting and delirium, a strong aversion to bright light, and sore joints and muscles. Advanced cases may result in convulsions and coma. Estimates of the fatality rate for JE range from 5% to 60%.

As with other mosquito-borne diseases, the best way to prevent JE (outside of the vaccine) is to avoid being bitten.

Cuts, Bites & Stings

Cuts & Scratches In hot, humid climates like that of Thailand throughout most of the year, even small wounds can become infected easily. Always keep cuts and scrapes scrupulously clean, especially those on the lower extremities, and you can avoid unnecessary trips to the doctor. If a small wound does become infected, clean it regularly with sterilised water and bandage it with an antibiotic balm or powder. If it's serious, you may have to take a course of antibiotic medication. If the infection is on the legs or feet, stay prone as much as possible until the infection subsides.

Many people who spend lengthy periods of time on the beaches, particularly Ko Samui, end up with infected coral cuts on their feet. Coral formations break the skin and coral particles enter the wound – these cuts are very difficult to keep clean when you're in and out of the water all the time. If a cut becomes infected, stay out of the water until it clears up. Light shoes designed for water sports, eg Nike's 'Aqua Socks', provide effective protection against coral as well as sea urchins.

Snake Bite To minimise your chances of being bitten always wear boots, socks and long trousers when walking through undergrowth where snakes may be present. Don't put your hands into holes and crevices and be careful when collecting firewood.

Snake bites do not cause instantaneous death and anti-venenes are usually available. Keep the victim calm and still, wrap the bitten limb tightly, as you would for a sprained ankle, and then attach a splint to immobilise it. Then seek medical help, if possible with the dead snake for identification. Don't attempt to catch the snake if there is any remote possibility of being bitten again. Tourniquets and sucking out the poison are now comprehensively discredited.

Jellyfish Local advice is the best way of avoiding contact with these sea creatures with their stinging tentacles.

Bedbugs & Lice Bedbugs live in various places, particularly dirty mattresses and bedding. Spots of blood on bedclothes or on the wall around the bed can be read as a suggestion to find another hotel. Bedbugs leave itchy bites in neat rows. Calamine lotion may help.

Lice cause itching and discomfort and make themselves at home in your hair (head lice), your clothing (body lice) or in your pubic hair (crabs). They get to you by direct contact with infected people or through the sharing of combs, clothing and the like. Powder or shampoo treatment will kill the lice, and infected clothing should then be washed in very hot water.

Leeches & Ticks Leeches may be present in damp rainforest conditions and attach themselves to your skin to suck your blood. Trekkers often get them on their legs or in their boots. Salt or a lighted cigarette end will make them fall off. Do not pull them off as the bite is then more likely to become infected. An insect repellent may keep them away.

Vaseline, alcohol or oil will persuade a tick to let go. You should always check your body if you have been walking through a tick-infested area as they can spread typhus.

Women's Health

Gynaecological Problems Poor diet, lowered resistance due to the use of antibiotics for stomach upsets and even contraceptive pills can lead to vaginal infections when travelling in hot climates. Keeping the genital area clean, wearing cotton underwear and skirts or loose-fitting trousers will help to prevent infections.

Yeast infections, characterised by a rash, itch and discharge can be treated with a vinegar or even lemon juice douche or with yoghurt. Nystatin suppositories are the usual medical prescription. Trichomonas is a more serious infection with a discharge and a burning sensation when urinating. Male sexual partners must also be treated and if a vinegar-water douche is not effective medical attention should be sought. Flagyl is the prescribed drug.

Pregnancy Most miscarriages occur during the first three months of pregnancy so this is the most risky time to travel. The last three months should also be spent within reasonable distance of good medical care as quite serious problems can develop at this time. Pregnant women should avoid all unnecessary medication, but vaccinations and malarial prophylactics should still be taken where possible. Additional care should be taken to prevent illness and particular attention should be paid to diet and nutrition.

Hospitals

There are several good hospitals in Bangkok and Chiang Mai:

Bangkok:
Bangkok Christian Hospital (tel 233-6981/9), 124 Silom Rd
Bangkok Adventist Hospital (tel 281-1422), 430 Phitsanuloke Rd
Samrong General Hospital (tel 393-2131/5), Soi 78, Sukhumvit Rd
Samitivej Hospital (tel 392-0010/9), 133 Soi 49, Sukhumvit Rd

Chiang Mai:
McCormick Hospital (tel 241107), Nawarat Rd
Ariyawongse Clinic, Changmoi Rd
Chiang Mai Hospital, Suan Dawk Rd
Malaria Center, 18 Boonruangjit Rd

Al-Anon

Members of Alcoholics Anonymous who want to contact the Bangkok Group or others who are interested in AA services can call 253-0305 from 7 am to 7 pm or 253-8422 from 7 pm to 7 am for information.

DANGERS & ANNOYANCES

Since the 1920s and 1930s several insurgent groups have operated in Thailand – the Communist Party of Thailand (CPT) with its tactical force, the People's Liberation Army of Thailand (PLAT) in rural areas all over Thailand, as well as Malay separatists and Muslim revolutionaries in the extreme south. These groups have been mainly involved in propaganda activity, village infiltration and occasional clashes with Thai government troops. Very rarely have they had any encounters with foreign travellers. Aside from sporadic terrorist bombings – mostly in railway stations in the south and sometimes at upcountry festivals – 'innocent' people have not been involved in the insurgent activity.

In 1976, the official government estimate of the number of active guerrillas in Thailand was 10,000. By the end of the '70s however, many CPT followers had surrendered under the government amnesty programme. In the '80s new military strategies, as well as political measures, reduced the number to around two to three thousand. In the south, traditionally a hot spot, communist forces have been all but limited to Camp 508 in a relatively inaccessible area along the Surat Thani-Nakhon Si Thammarat provincial border.

In the north and north-east, the government claims that armed resistance has been virtually eliminated and this appears to be verified by independent sources as well as my own recent travel experience through former CPT strongholds. Part of the reason for the CPT's severely curtailed influence stems from the 1979 split between the CPT and the Chinese Communist Party over policy differences regarding Indochinese revolution – CPT cadres used to get training in Kunming, China. New highways in previously remote provinces such as Nan and Loei have contributed to improved communications, stability and central (Bangkok) control. This means that routes in these provinces closed to foreigners in the '70s are now open for travel, eg Phitsanuloke to Loei via Nakhon Thai. Within the next two years or so, travellers should be able to travel from Nan to Loei by bus, and from Chiang Rai to Nan via Chiang Muan. A new road between Phattalung and Hat Yai has cut travel time between those two cities considerably.

Whether this signals a long-lasting trend or not is difficult to say. Battles are between government and anti-government forces. As long as you are not directly associated with either side there is little danger in travelling through guerrilla territory. Most observers do not expect Communist guerrilla activity to flare again anytime in the foreseeable future. This seems especially true in the light of the great economic strides Thailand has made during the last decade, which have simply made Marxism a less compelling alternative for most of the population.

Border Areas

Probably the most sensitive areas in Thailand now are the border areas. Most dangerous is the Thai-Cambodian border area, especially since the Vietnamese-backed Heng Samrin regime has instituted its 'K-5' plan to seal the border with heavy armament, land mines and booby traps. Most but not all of the latter are planted inside Cambodian territory, so it is imperative that you stay away from this border. The armed guards, booby traps and mines make it impossible to safely visit the Phra Viharn ruins just inside Cambodia near Ubon. Anyway, you would probably be stopped by Thai troops at Kantharalak on approach.

The Thai-Lao border is not nearly as dangerous, but you should avoid walking along the Maekhong River at night, as this is when Thai and Lao troops occasionally trade fire. During the last three years, relations between Laos and Thailand have improved considerably and it is very likely that tourists will soon be allowed to cross overland between the two countries. The Australian government has even promised to build a bridge over the Maekhong River from Nong Khai Province. As with Cambodia, it is not a good idea to try and cross into Laos illegally – you might very well be accused of espionage and end up in prison or worse.

The Burmese border is fairly safe in most places, but there is occasional shelling between Mae Sot and Mae Sarieng coming from Burmese troops in pursuit of Karen rebels. The rebels are trying to maintain an independent nation called Kawthoolei along the border with Thailand. If you cross and are captured by the Burmese, you will automatically be suspected of supporting the Karen. If you are captured by the Karen you will probably be released, though they may demand money.

In the Three Pagodas Pass area, there is also occasional fighting between the Karen and Mon armies, who are competing for control over the smuggling trade between Burma and Thailand. And along the Burmese-Thai border in northern Mae Hong Son and Chiang Rai provinces, the presence of Shan and KMT armies make this area dangerous if you attempt to travel near opium trade border crossings – obviously these are not signposted, so take care anywhere along the border in this area.

The Betong area of Yala Province on the Thai-Malaysian border was until recently the tactical headquarters for the armed Communist Party of Malaya (CPM). Thai and Malaysian government troops occasionally clashed with the insurgents, who from time to time hijacked trucks along the Yala-Betong road. But in December 1989, in exchange for amnesty, the CPM agreed 'to terminate all armed activities' and to respect the laws of Thailand and Malaysia. Nevertheless, for a year or two, until things cool down, travellers are advised to take care when travelling outside Betong, especially at night.

Precautions

Although Thailand is in no way a dangerous country to visit if you stay away from the hot spots mentioned above, it's wise to be a little cautious in general, particularly if you're a solo woman traveller. In that case take special care on arrival at Bangkok Airport, particularly at night. Don't take one of Bangkok's often very unofficial taxis by yourself – better the THAI bus, or even the public bus. Women in particular, but men also, should ensure their rooms are securely locked and bolted at night. Inspect cheap rooms with thin walls for strategic peepholes. Take care with the police, reported several women travellers

Take caution when leaving valuables in hotel safes. Many travellers have reported unpleasant experiences with leaving valuables in Chiang Mai guest houses while trekking. On return to their home countries, they received huge credit-card bills for purchases (usually jewellery) charged to their cards in Bangkok while the cards had, supposedly, been secure in the hotel or guest-house safe! Organised gangs in Bangkok specialise in arranging stolen credit card purchases – in some cases they pay 'down and out' foreigners to fake the signatures. Make sure you obtain an itemised receipt for property left with hotels or guest houses – note the exact quantity of travellers' cheques and all other valuables. You might consider taking your credit cards with you if you go trekking – if they're stolen on the trail at least the bandits won't be able to use them.

On trains and buses, particularly in the

south, beware of friendly strangers offering cigarettes, drinks or sweets (candy). Several travellers have reported waking up with a headache sometime later to find their valuables have disappeared. One letter reported how a would be druggist considerably overdid it with what looked like a machine-wrapped, made-in-England Cadbury's chocolate. His girlfriend spat it out immediately, he woke up nine hours later in hospital having required emergency resuscitation after his breathing nearly stopped. This happened on the Surat Thani to Phuket bus.

Travellers have also encountered drugged food or drink from friendly strangers in bars and from prostitutes in their own hotel rooms. Thais are also occasional victims, especially at the Moh Chit Bus Terminal and Chatuchak Park, where young girls are drugged and sold to brothels. Conclusion – don't accept gifts from strangers.

Keep zippered luggage secured with small locks, especially while travelling on buses and trains. This will not only keep out most sneak thieves, but prevent con artists posing as police from planting contraband drugs in your luggage. That may sound paranoid, but it happens.

With this edition I'm forced to add a warning about the possibility of armed robbery, which appears to be on the increase in remote areas of Thailand.

In 1988, two UK women were robbed and killed on the island of Ko Chang in Trat Province while hiking across the island at night. Another woman was attacked and killed near Tham Lot in Mae Hong Son Province the previous year while hiking alone and I've heard a similar report from Ko Tarutao. A lone male motorcyclist was shot several times (he survived) on the road to Sangkhlaburi in Kanchanaburi Province in '87 and another man was shot on Ko Samui while walking back to his bungalow at night. Two boats carrying tourists on the Kok River in Chiang Rai were attacked by armed bandits the same year. A male New Zealander lagged behind his trekking group in Mae Hong Son and was shot dead during a robbery attempt.

Approximately eight million people trav-

elled through Thailand in 1987 and 1988 and these are the only incidents of extreme violence I've heard of, so the risk of armed robbery should be considered fairly low. On the other hand, the clear message here is that the safest practice in remote areas is not to go out alone at night and, if trekking in north Thailand, always walk in groups. More information on hill trekking is given in the North Thailand chapter.

FILM & PHOTOGRAPHY

Print film is fairly inexpensive and widely available throughout Thailand. Slide films, especially Kodachrome, can be hard to find outside Bangkok and Chiang Mai, so be sure to stock up before heading upcountry. Film-processing is generally quite good in the larger cities in Thailand and also quite inexpensive. Kodachrome must be sent out of the country for processing, so it can take up to two weeks to get it back.

Pack some silica gel with your camera to prevent mould growing on the inside of your lenses. A polarising filter could be useful to cut down on tropical glare at certain times of day, particularly around water or highly polished glazed-tile work. Hill-tribe people in some of the more-visited areas expect money if you photograph them, while certain Karen and Akha will not allow you to point a camera at them. Use discretion when photographing villagers anywhere in Thailand as a camera can be a very intimidating instrument. You may feel better leaving your camera behind when visiting certain areas.

ACCOMMODATION

Places to stay are abundant, varied and reasonably priced in Thailand.

Guest Houses, Hostels & YMCA/YWCA's

Guest houses are generally the cheapest accommodation in Thailand and are found in most areas where travellers go in central, north and south Thailand, and are spreading slowly to the east and north-east as well. Guest houses vary quite a bit in facilities and are particularly popular in Bangkok and Chiang Mai where stiff competition keeps rates low. Some are especially good value, while others are mere flophouses. Many serve food, although there tends to be a bland sameness to meals in guest houses wherever you are in Thailand.

There is a Thai Youth Hostels Association (25/2 Phitsanulok Rd, Sisao Theves, Dusit, Bangkok 10300) with member hostels in Bangkok (one), Chiang Mai (three), Chiang Rai (one), Phitsanulok (one), Kanchanaburi (one), Ko Phi Phi (one) and Rayong (one). Thai Youth Hostels range in price from 30B for a dorm bed to 150B for a room and there are discounts for International Youth Hostel Federation (IYHF) cardholders. Most Thai hostels offer inexpensive meals and are a source of reliable travel information.

YMCA/YWCAs cost a bit more than guest houses and hostels (average 200B and above) and sometimes more than local hotels, but are generally good value. There are Ys in many provincial capitals.

Chinese-Thai Hotels

The standard Thai hotels, often run by Chinese-Thai families, are the easiest accommodation to come by and generally have very reasonable rates (average 50 to 80B for rooms without bath and air-con, or 80 to 150B with bath). They may be located on the main street of town and/or near bus and railway stations.

The most economical hotels to stay in are those without air-con; typical rooms are clean and include a double bed and a ceiling fan. Some have attached Thai-style bathrooms (this will cost a little more). Rates may or may not be posted; if not, they may be increased for the farang, so it is worthwhile bargaining. It is best to have a look around before agreeing to check in, to make sure the room *is* clean, that the fan and lights work, etc. If there is any problem request another room or a good discount. If possible, always choose a room off the street and away from the front lounge to cut down on ambient noise.

Some of these hotels may double as brothels; the perpetual traffic in and out can be a bit noisy but is generally bearable. The best (cheapest) hotels have Thai or Chinese names posted in the scripts of both languages

(newer hotels may have the name in Romanised script as well), but you will learn how to find and identify them with experience. Many of these hotels have restaurants downstairs; if they don't, there are usually restaurants and noodle shops nearby.

National Park Accommodation/Camping

Thailand has 53 national parks and nine historical parks. All but 10 of the national parks have bungalows for rent that sleep as many as 10 people for rates of 300 to 1000B, depending on the park and the size of the bungalow. Camping is allowed in all but four of the national parks (Nam Tok Phliu in Chantaburi Province, Doi Suthep-Pui in Chiang Mai Province, Hat Chao Mai in Trang Province and Thap Laan in Prachinburi Province) for only 5B per person per night. A few parks also have *ruan thaew* or long houses, where rooms are around 150 to 200B for two, and/or tents on platforms for 50 to 60B a night. For further detail see the National Parks section in the Facts about the Country chapter.

A few of the historical parks have bungalows with rates comparable to those in the national parks, mostly for use by visiting archaeologists.

Universities/Schools

College and university campuses may be able to provide inexpensive accommodation during the summer vacation (March to June). There are universities in Chiang Mai, Nakhon Pathom, Khon Kaen, Mahasarakham and Songkhla. Outside Bangkok there are also teachers' colleges (*withayalai khruu*) in every provincial capital which may offer accommodation during the summer vacation.

Tourist Class & Luxury Hotels

These are found only in the main tourist destinations: Bangkok, Chiang Mai, Chiang Rai, Pattaya, Ko Samui, Songkhla, Phuket and Hat Yai. Prices start at around 400B outside Bangkok and Chiang Mai and proceed to 1000B or more – genuine-tourist class hotels in Bangkok start at 500B or so and go to 2000B for standard rooms, and up to 5000B for a suite. These will all have air-con, western-style toilets and restaurants. Added to room charges will be a 11% government tax, and some hotels will include an additional service charge of 8% to 10%.

The Oriental in Bangkok, rated as the number one hotel in the world by several executive travel publications, starts at 3100B for a standard single and tops off at 20,000B for a deluxe suite.

Temples

If you are a Buddhist or can make a good show of it, you may be able to stay overnight in some temples for a small donation. Facilities are very basic though and early rising is expected. They are usually for men only, unless the wat has a place for lay women to stay. See the section on Meditation Study in the Facts about the Country chapter for information on wats in Thailand that will accommodate long-term lay students.

Bathing in Thailand

Upcountry the typical Thai bathroom consists of a tall earthen water jar fed by a spigot and a plastic or metal bowl. You bathe by scooping water out of the water jar and sluicing it over the body. It's very refreshing during the hot and rainy seasons, but takes a little stamina during the cool season if you're not used to it. If the 'bathroom' has no walls, or if you are bathing at a public well or spring in an area where there are no bathrooms, you should bathe while wearing the *phaakhamaa* or *phaasin*; bathing nude would offend the Thais.

CONDUCT

The TAT put out a useful hand-out on do's and don'ts in Thailand, starting with the warning that the monarchy is held in considerable respect in Thailand (they are) and visitors should be respectful too. One of Thailand's leading intellectuals, Sulak Sivarak, was arrested in the early '80s for lese-majesty when he called the king 'the skipper' (a passing reference to his fondness for sailing).

Correct behaviour in temples entails several guidelines, the most important of which is to dress neatly and take your shoes off when you enter the inner compound or buildings. At the temple on Doi Suthep near Chiang Mai you can see a whole snapshot photo gallery of 'inappropriately dressed' visitors. Buddha images are sacred objects, don't pose in front of them for pictures and definitely do not clamber upon them.

Thais greet each other not with a hand shake but with a prayer-like palms-together gesture known as a *wai*. If someone wais you, you should wai back (unless wai-ed by a child). The feet are the lowest part of the body (spiritually as well as physically) so don't point your feet at people or point at things with your feet. In the same context, the head is regarded as the highest part of the body, so don't touch Thais on the head either. Thais are often addressed by their first name with the honorific *Khun* or a title preceding it.

Beach attire is not considered appropriate for trips into town and is especially counterproductive if worn to government offices (eg when applying for a visa extension). As in most parts of Asia, anger and emotions are rarely displayed and generally get you nowhere. In any argument or dispute, remember the paramount rule is to keep your cool.

Nudity on Beaches

Regardless of what the Thais may (or may not) have been accustomed to centuries ago, they are quite offended by public nudity today. Bathing nude at beaches in Thailand is illegal. If you are at a truly deserted beach and are sure no Thais may come along, there's nothing stopping you – however, at most beaches travellers should wear suitable attire. Likewise, topless bathing for females is frowned upon in most places except on heavily touristed islands like Phuket, Samui, Samet and Phangan. Many Thais say that nudity on the beaches is what bothers them most about foreign travellers. These Thais take nudity as a sign of disrespect on the part of the travellers for the locals, rather than as a libertarian symbol or modern custom. Thais are extremely modest in this respect (despite racy billboards in Bangkok) and it should not be the traveller's intention to 'reform' them.

FOOD

Some people take to the food in Thailand immediately while others don't; Thai dishes can be pungent and spicy – a lot of garlic and chillies are used, especially *phrik khii nuu*, or 'mouse-shit peppers' (these are the small torpedo-shaped devils which can be pushed aside if you are timid about red-hot curries). Almost all Thai food is cooked with fresh ingredients, including vegetables, poultry, pork and some beef. Plenty of lime juice, lemon grass and fresh coriander leaf are added to give the food its characteristic tang, and fish sauce (generally made from anchovies) or shrimp paste to make it salty. Rice is eaten with most meals.

Other common seasonings include 'laos' root (*khaa*), black pepper, ground peanuts (more often a condiment), tamarind juice (*nam makhaam*), ginger (*khing*) and coconut milk (*kati*). The Thais eat a lot of what could be called Chinese food, which is generally, but not always, less spicy. In the north and north-east 'sticky', or glutinous rice, is common and is traditionally eaten with the hands.

Where to Eat

Restaurants or food stalls outside Bangkok usually do not have menus, so it is worthwhile memorising a standard 'repertoire' of dishes. Most provinces have their own local specialities in addition to the standards and you might try asking for 'whatever is good', allowing the proprietors to choose for you. Of course, you might get stuck with a large bill this way, but with a little practice in Thai social relations you may get some very pleasant results.

The most economical places to eat and the most dependable, are noodle shops and night markets. Most towns and villages have at least one night market and several noodle shops. The night market(s) in Chiang Mai have a slight reputation for overcharging (especially for large parties), but on the other hand I have never been over-charged for food anywhere in Thailand. It helps if you speak Thai as much as possible. Curry shops are generally open for breakfast and lunch, and are also a very cheap source for nutritious food.

What to Eat

Thai food is served with a variety of condiments, including ground red pepper (*phrik bon*), ground peanuts (*thua*), vinegar with sliced chillies (*nam som phrik*), fish sauce with chillies (*nam plaa phrik*), a spicy red sauce called *nam phrik si raachaa* (from Si Racha, of course) and any number of other special sauces for particular dishes. Soy sauce (*nam sii-yu*) can be requested, though this is normally used as a condiment for Chinese food only.

Except for the 'rice plates' and noodle dishes, Thai meals are usually ordered family-style, which is to say that two or more people order together, sharing different dishes. Traditionally, the party orders one of each kind of dish, eg one chicken, one fish, one soup, etc. One dish is generally large enough for two people. One or two extras may be ordered for a large party. If you come to eat at a Thai restaurant alone and order one of these 'entrees', you had better be hungry or know enough Thai to order a small portion. This latter alternative is not really too acceptable socially; Thais generally consider eating alone in a restaurant unusual – but then as a farang you're an exception anyway.

A cheaper alternative is to order dishes 'over rice' or *raat khao*. Curry (*kaeng*) over rice is called *khao kaeng*; in a standard curry shop khao kaeng is only 7 to 10B a plate.

Thais eat with a fork and spoon, except for noodles which are eaten with spoon and chopsticks (*ta-kiap*) and sticky rice, which is rolled into balls and eaten with hands, along with the food accompanying it.

The following list gives standard dishes in Thai script with a transliterated pronunciation guide, using the system outlined in the Language section and an English translation and description.

Beverages
khrêuang dèum
เครื่องดื่ม

plain water
nám plào
น้ำเปล่า

boiled water
nám tôm
น้ำต้ม

ice
nám khǎeng
น้ำแข็ง

weak Chinese tea
nám cha
น้ำชา

hot water
nám ráwn
น้ำร้อน

cold water
nám yen
น้ำเย็น

Chinese tea
cha jiin
ชาจีน

iced Thai tea with milk & sugar
cha yen
ชาเย็น

iced Thai tea with sugar only
cha dam yen
ชาดำเย็น

no sugar (command)
mâi sài nám-taan
ไม่ใส่น้ำตาล

hot Thai tea with sugar
cha dam ráwn
ชาดำร้อน

hot Thai tea with milk & sugar
cha ráwn
ชาร้อน

hot coffee with milk & sugar
kaafae ráwn
กาแฟร้อน

iced coffee with sugar, no milk
oh-líeng
โอเลี้ยง

Ovaltine
oh-wantin
โอวันติน

orange soda
nám sôm
น้ำส้ม

plain milk
nom jeùt
นมจืด

yoghurt
nom prîaw
นมเปรี้ยว

beer
bia
เบียร์

iced lime juice with sugar (usually with salt too)
nám manao
น้ำมะนาว

no salt (command)
mâi sài kleua
ไม่ใส่เกลือ

rice whisky
mâe khǒng (brandname)
แม่โขง

soda water
nám soh-daa
น้ำโซดา

Curries
kaeng
แกง

hot Thai chicken curry
kaeng phèt kài
แกงเผ็ดไก่

rich, spicy curry with chicken/beef
kaeng mát-sa-man kài/néua
แกงมัสมั่นไก่ / เนื้อ

mild, Indian-style curry with chicken
kaeng kari kài
แกงกะหรี่ไก่

hot & sour fish & vegetable soup
kaeng sôm
แกงส้ม

'green' curry, made with fish/chicken/beef
kaeng khǐaw-wǎan plaa/kài/néua
แกงเขียวหวาน

savoury curry with chicken/beef
kaeng phanaeng kai/néua
แกงพะแนงไก่ / เนื้อ

beef curry
kaeng néua
แกงเนื้อ

catfish curry
kaeng plaa dùk
แกงปลาดุก

Soups
súp
ซุป

mild soup with vegetables & pork
kaeng jèut
แกงจืด

mild soup with vegetables, pork & bean curd
kaeng jèut tâu-hûu
แกงจืดเต้าหู้

soup with chicken, 'Laos', & coconut
tôm khàa kaì
ต้มข่าไก่

prawn & lemon grass soup with mushrooms
tôm yam kûng
ต้มยำกุ้ง

fish ball soup
kaeng jèut lûuk chín
แกงจืดลูกชิ้น

rice soup with fish/chicken/shrip
khâo tôm plaa/ kài/kûng
ข้าวต้มปลา / ไก่ / กุ้ง

Egg
khài
ไข่

hard-boiled egg
khài tôm
ไข่ต้ม

fried egg
khài dao
ไข่ดาว

plain omelette
khài jiaw
ไข่เจียว

omelette stuffed with vegetables & pork
khài yát sài
ไข่ยัดไส้

scrambled egg
khài kuan
ไข่กวน

Rice Dishes
khâo râat nâa
ข้าวราดหน้า

fried rice with pork/chicken/shrimp
khâo phàt mǔu/kài/kûng
ข้าวผัดหมู / ไก่ / กุ้ง

boned, sliced chicken with marinated rice
khâo man kài
ข้าวมันไก่

chicken with sauce over rice
khâo nâa kài
ข้าวหน้าไก่

roast duck over rice
khâo nâa pèt
ข้าวหน้าเป็ด

'red'pork with rice
khâo mǔu daeng
ข้าวหมูแดง

curry over rice
khâo kaeng
ข้าวแกง

Noodles
kuǎytiǎw/ba-mìi
ก๋วยเตี๋ยว / บะหมี่

wide rice noodle soup with vegetables & meat
kǔaytiǎw nám
ก๋วยเตี๋ยวน้ำ

wide rice noodles with vegetables & meat
kǔaytiǎw hâeng
ก๋วยเตี๋ยวแห้ง

wide rice noodles with gravy
râat nâa
ราดหน้า

thin rice noodles fried with tofu, vegetables, egg & peanuts
phàt thai
ผัดไทย

fried thin noodles with soy sauce
phàt siyú
ผัดซีอิ๊ว

wheat noodles in broth, with vegetables & meat
ba-mìi nám
บะหมี่น้ำ

wheat noodles with vegetables & meat
ba-mìi hâeng
บะหมี่แห้ง

Seafood
aahǎan thaleh
อาหารทะเล

sweet & sour fish
plaa prîaw wǎan
ปลาเปรี้ยวหวาน

steamed crab
puu nèung
ปูนึ่ง

steamed crab claws
kaam puu nèung
ก้ามปูนึ่ง

shark fin soup
hǔu chalǎam
หูฉลาม

crisp-fried fish
plaa tâwt
ปลาทอด

fried prawns
kûng tâwt
กุ้งทอด

batter-fried prawns
kûng chúp bâeng tâwt
กุ้งชุบแป้งทอด

grilled prawns
kûng phǎo
กุ้งเผา

steamed fish
plaa nèung
ปลานึ่ง

grilled fish
plaa phǎo
ปลาเผา

whole fish cooked in ginger, onions, soy sauce
plaa jiǎn
ปลาเจี๋ยน

cellophane noodles baked with crab
wún-sên òp puu
วุ้นเส้นอบปู

spicy fried squid
plaa mèuk phàt phèt
ปลาหมึกผัดเผ็ด

roast squid
plaa mèuk yâng
ปลาหมึกย่าง

oysters fried in egg batter
hǎwy thâwt
หอยทอด

squid
plaa mèuk
ปลาหมึก

shrimp
kûng
กุ้ง

fish
plaa
ปลา

Miscellaneous

stir-fried vegetables
phàt phàk lǎi yàng
ผัดผักหลายอย่าง

morning-glory vine fried in garlic & bean sauce
phàk bûng phàt
ผักบุ้งผัด

spring rolls
paw-piá
ปอเปี๊ยะ

beef in oyster sauce
néua phàt nám-man hǎwy
เนื้อผัดน้ำมันหอย

duck soup
pèt tǔn
เป็ดตุ๋น

roast duck
pèt yâng
เป็ดย่าง

chicken fried in holy basil
kài phàt bai ka-phrao
ไก่ผัดใบกะเพรา

roast chicken
kài yâng
ไก่ย่าง

chicken fried with chillies
kài phàt phrík
ไก่ผัดพริก

fried chicken
kài tâwt
ไก่ทอด

'satay' or skewers of barbequed meat, sold on street
saté
สะเต๊ะ

spicy green papaya salad (speciality of the north-east)
sôm tam
ส้มตำ

noodles with fish curry
nám yaa
น้ำยา

chicken with vegetable & peanut sauce
phrá raam long sǒng kài
พระรามลงสรงไก่

chicken fried with cashews
kài phàt mét má-mûang
ไก่ผัดเม็ดมะม่วง

prawns fried with chillies
kûng phàt phrík phǎo
กุ้งผัดพริกเผา

chicken fried with ginger
kài phàt khǐng
ไก่ผัดขิง

fried wonton
kiáw kràwp
เกี้ยวกรอบ

cellophane noodle salad
yam wún sên
ยำวุ้นเส้น

spicy beef salad
lâap néua
ลาบเนื้อ

hot & sour grilled beef salad
yam néua
ยำเนื้อ

chicken with bean sprouts
kài sàp tùa ngâwk
ไก่สับถั่วงอก

fried fish cakes with cucumber sauce
tâwt man plaa
ทอดมันปลา

Sweets
khǎwng wǎan
ของหวาน

Thai custard
sǎngkha-yǎa
สังขยา

coconut custard
sǎngkha-yǎa maphráo
สังขยามะพร้าว

sweet shredded egg yolk
fǎwy thawng
ฝอยทอง

egg custard
màw kaeng
หม้อแกง

banana in coconut milk
klûay bùat chii
กล้วยบวชชี

'Indian -style' banana, fried
klûay khàek
กล้วยแขก

sweet palm kernels
lûuk taan chêuam
ลูกตาลเชื่อม

Thai jelly with coconut cream
ta-kôh
ตะโก้

sticky rice with coconut cream
khâo nǐaw daeng
ข้าวเหนียวแดง

sticky rice in coconut cream & ripe mango
khâo nǐaw ma mûang
ข้าวเหนียวมะม่วง

Fruit
phǒn-la-mái
ผลไม้

mandarin orange
sôm
ส้ม(แมนดาริน)

watermelon
taeng moh
แตงโม

mangosteen
mang-khút
มังคุด

rambutan
ngáw
เงาะ

rose-apple
chom-phûu
ชมพู่

banana (there are over 20 varieties)
klûay
กล้วย

pineapple
sàp-parót
สับปะรด

'sapota'
lamút
ละมุด

'rambeh', sweet, apricot-like
mafai
มะไฟ

mango, several varieties & seasons
ma-mûang
มะม่วง

durian, held in high esteem by the Thais, but most Westerners dislike this fruit. There are several varieties, so keep trying
thurian
ทุเรียน

pomelo
sôm oh
ส้มโอ

longan
lam yai
ลำไย

papaya
málákaw
มะละกอ

custard-apple
náwy nàa
น้อยหน่า

Some Useful Food Words

Men use *phǒm* for 'I' ; women use *dii-chǎn*
ผม   ดิฉัน

I eat only vegetarian food.
Phǒm/dii-chǎn kin jeh.
ผม / ดิฉัน กินเจ.

I can't eat pork.
Phǒm/dii-chǎn kin mǔu mâi dâi.
ผม/ดิฉัน กินหมูไม่ได้

I can't eat beef.
Phǒm/dii-chǎn kin néua mâi dâi.
ผม/ดิฉัน กินเนื้อไม่ได้

(I) don't like it hot & spicy.
Mâi châwp phèt.
ไม่ชอบเผ็ด

(I) like it hot & spicy.
Châwp phèt.
ชอบเผ็ด

(I) can eat Thai food.
Kin aahǎan thai pen.
กินอาหารไทยเป็น

What do you have that's special?
Mii a-rai phí-sèt?
มีอะไรพิเศษ.(?)

I didn't order this.
Nîi phǒm/dii-chǎn mâi dâi sàng.
นี่ผม/ดิฉัน ไม่ได้สั่ง

Do you have ....?
Mii .... mǎi?
มี...ไหม?

ALCOHOL

Drinking in Thailand can be quite expensive in relation to the cost of other consumer activities in the country. The Thai government has placed increasingly heavy taxes on liquor and beer, so that now about 30B out of the 40B to 45B that you pay for a large beer is tax. Whether this is an effort to raise more tax revenue (the result has been a sharp decrease in the consumption of alcoholic beverages for perhaps a net decrease in revenue) or to discourage consumption (if that's the case it works), drinking can wreak havoc with your budget. One large bottle (630 ml) of Singha beer costs more than half the minimum daily wage of a Bangkok worker (73B) as of 1987.

Beer

Four brands of beer are brewed in Thailand: Singha, Khun Phaen, Amarit and Kloster. Singha is by far the most common beer in Thailand, with Kloster a close second. Khun Phaen and Amarit are hard to find, though Khun Phaen is worth asking for since it costs about 5 to 10B less per bottle than Singha and tastes almost exactly the same (I can't tell the difference). Amarit is also fairly similar, perhaps a little less bitter, with no price difference. Kloster is quite a bit lighter in taste than Singha and generally costs 5B more, but it is a good-tasting brew. Boon Rawd Breweries, makers of Singha, have introduced a new lighter beer called Singha Gold in an effort to compete with Kloster, which is becoming increasingly popular in Thailand. At this writing the Gold only comes in small bottles; most people seem to prefer either Kloster or regular Singha to Singha Gold, which is a little on the bland side.

Spirits

Rice whisky is a big favourite in Thailand and somewhat more affordable than beer for the average Thai. It has a sharp, sweet taste not unlike rum, with an alcoholic content of 35%. The two major liquor manufacturers are Suramaharas Co and the Surathip Group. The first produces the famous Mekong (pronounced Mae-khong) and Kwangthong brands, the second the Hong (swan) labels such as Hong Thong, Hong Ngoen, Hong Yok, Hong Tho, etc. Mekong and Kwangthong cost around 90 to 95B for a large bottle (called *klom* in Thai) or 50 to 55B for the flask-sized bottle (called *baen*). An even smaller bottle, the *kok*, is occasionally

Top: Rooftops, Chiang Mai (CT)
Left: Ko Faan, Big Buddha Beach (RK)
Right: Thai monk (CT)

Top: Fruit vendor, Kanchanaburi (JC)
Bottom: Varieties of rice (DS)

available for 25 to 30B. The Hong brands are considerably less expensive.

In March of 1986, the two liquor giants met and formed a common board of directors to try to end the fierce competition brought about when a government tax increase in 1985 led to a 40% drop in Thai whisky sales. This may result in an increase in whiskey prices but probably also in better distribution – Mekong and Kwangthong have generally not been available in regions where the Hong labels are marketed and vice versa. A third company, Pramuanphon Distillery in Nakhon Pathom, has recently begun marketing a line of cut-rate rice whisky under three labels: Maew Thong (Gold Cat), Sing Chao Phraya (Chao Phraya Lion) and Singharat (Lion-King).

One company in Thailand produces a true rum, that is, a distilled liquor made from sugar cane, called Sang Som. Alcohol content is 40% and the stock is supposedly aged, drawn from the leftovers of a rum called Tara that was popular in the '70s. Sang Som costs several baht more than the rice whiskeys, but for those who find Mekong and the like unpalatable, it is an alternative worth trying.

A cheaper alternative is *lao khao*, or 'white liquor', of which there are two broad categories: legal and contraband. The legal kind is generally made from sticky rice and is produced for regional consumption. Like Mekong and its competitors, it is 35% alcohol, but sells for 40 to 45B per klom, or roughly half the price. The taste is sweet and raw and much more aromatic than the amber stuff – no amount of mixer will disguise the distinctive taste.

The illegal kinds are made from various agricultural products including sugar palm, coconut milk, sugar cane, taro and rice. Alcohol content may vary from as little as 10% to 12% to as much as 95%. Generally this *lao theuan* (jungle liquor) is weaker in the south and stronger in the north and northeast. This is the choice of the many Thais who can't afford to pay the heavy government liquor taxes; prices vary but 10B worth of the stronger concoctions will intoxicate three or four people. These types of homebrew or moonshine are generally taken straight with pure water as a chaser. In smaller towns, almost every garage-type restaurant (except, of course, Muslim restaurants) keeps some under the counter for sale. Sometimes roots and herbs are

added to jungle liquor to enhance flavour and colour.

Herbal Liquors

Currently herbal liquors are fashionable throughout the country and can be found at road-side vendors, small pubs and in a few guest houses. These liquors are made by soaking various herbs, roots, seeds, fruit and bark in lao khao to produce a range of concoctions called *yaa dong*. Many of the yaa dong preparations are purported to have specific health-enhancing qualities. Some of them taste fabulous while others are rank. One well-known herbal liquor pub just outside Bangkok is Pak Kraya Chok (Beggars Union) near Wat Phra Si Mahathat in Bangkhen.

BOOKS & BOOKSHOPS

The best bookshops in Bangkok are Asia Books, on Sukhumvit Rd near Soi 15, and DK Books on Surawong Rd near the infamous Patpong Rd area. Asia and DK also have smaller branches in some of the larger tourist hotels in Bangkok and street branches in well-touristed towns like Chiang Mai and Phuket.

In Chiang Mai, Suriwong Book Centre on Si Donchai Rd is also very good. All of these bookshops specialise in English-language publications and offer a wide variety of fiction and periodicals as well as books on Asia.

Guidebooks

Two travel guides with some good stuff on history, culture, art, etc are *Nagel's Encyclopedia-Guide to Thailand*, an expensive little book published in Switzerland and *Guide to Thailand* by Achille Clarac, edited and translated by Michael Smithies.

The *Insight Guide to Thailand* (Apa Productions, Singapore) is beautifully presented and well-written although it's a little hefty to carry around as a travel guide – a worthy item for travel guide collectors at any rate.

If you can get hold of a copy of *Hudson's Guide to Chiang Mai & the North* you'll learn a lot about this area that is unknown to the average traveller. Much of the informa-

tion is out of date (since the book is long out of print) but it makes interesting reading and has one of the best Thai phrase sections ever published – 218 phrases *with* tone marks. (Phrase sections without tone marks are next to worthless.) In 1987, Roy Hudson published the minuscule *Hudson's Guide to Mae Hong Son* which you may come across in the north.

Recently a number of locally produced Thai guidebooks have emerged. *The Shell Guide to Thailand* is basically a directory of hotels, restaurants and service stations but provides many useful addresses and phone numbers and has some good maps.

If this is your first trip to Asia, you might want to have a look at *Before You Go to Asia* by John McCarroll (Laurel Publications, San Francisco). This book weighs the pros and cons of going on your own versus going with a tour group (the author comes out strongly in favour of going on your own) and lists references for further information on Asian travel.

Hill Tribes

If you are interested in detailed info on hill tribes, get *The Hill Tribes of Northern Thailand* by Gordon Young (Monograph No 1, The Siam Society). Young was born of third-generation Christian missionaries among Lahu people, speaks several tribal dialects and is even an honorary Lahu chieftain with the highest Lahu title, the 'Supreme Hunter'. The monograph covers 16 tribes, including descriptions, photographs, tables and maps.

From the Hands of the Hills by Margaret Campbell also has lots of beautiful pictures. The recently published *Peoples of the Golden Triangle* by Elaine and Paul Lewis is also very good, very photo-oriented and expensive.

General Books

Additional serious reading is: *The Indianized States of South-East Asia* by George Coedes – a classic work on South-East Asian history; *The Thai Peoples* by Erik Seidenfaden; *Siam in Crisis* by Sulak Sivaraksa, one of Thailand's leading intellectuals (available at

DK Books in Bangkok) and *Political Conflict in Thailand: Reform, Reaction, Revolution* by David Morrell and Chai-anan Samudavanija, probably the single best book available on modern Thai politics.

Culture Shock! Thailand & How to Survive It by Robert and Nanthapa Cooper is an interesting outline on getting along with the Thai way of life. *Letters from Thailand* by Botan (translated by Susan Fulop) can also be recommended for its insights into traditional Thai culture. *Cooking Thai Food in American Kitchens* by Malulee Pinsuvana is 'great because it has pictures and diagrams so you can identify your meals'!

For insights into rural life in Thailand, the books of Pira Sudham are unparalleled. Sudham is a Thai author who was born to a poor family in north-east Thailand and has written *Siamese Drama, Monsoon Country* and *People of Esarn (Isaan)*. These books are not translations – Sudham writes in English in order to reach a worldwide audience. These titles are fairly easy to find in Bangkok but can be difficult overseas – the publisher is Siam Media International, GPO Box 1534, Bangkok 10501.

For books on Buddhism and Buddhism in Thailand, see the Religion section of the Facts about the Country chapter.

MAPS

The *Latest Tour's Guide to Bangkok & Thailand* has a bus map of Bangkok on one side and a fair map of Thailand on the other, and is usually priced at around 30B. The bus map is quite necessary if you intend to spend much time in Bangkok and want to use the very economical bus system. It is available at most bookshops in Bangkok which carry English-language materials. A better map of the country is published by APA Productions which costs around US$7, also available at many Bangkok bookshops, as well as overseas.

Even better is the four-map set issued by Thailand's Department of Highways. For 65B you get a very detailed road map of the central, northern, north-eastern and southern regions. The maps include information on 'roads not under control by the Highway Department'; for example, many of the roads you may travel on in the Golden Triangle. Bookstores sometimes sell this set for 200B, including a mailing tube, but the Highway Department on Si Ayuthaya Rd and the Bangkok Tourist Authority of Thailand office on Ratchadamnoen Nok offer the set at the lower price. The mailing tube is not worth 135B.

Recently DK Books has published a 44-page bilingual road atlas called *Thailand Highway Map* that has cut the highway department maps to a more manageable size and includes dozens of city maps, driving distances and lots of travel and sightseeing information.

The Highway Department maps are more than adequate for most people. At DK Books in Chiang Mai, however, you can also purchase Thai military maps, which focus on areas no larger than the *amphoe* (local district), complete with elevations and contour lines. These may be of use to the solo trekker, but cost 60B upwards per map. DK also publishes special maps for hill-tribe trekkers. See the section on Hill Tribe Treks in the North Thailand chapter.

There are also Nancy Chandler's very useful city maps of Bangkok and Chiang Mai, which are actually more than just maps. Her colourful maps serve as up-to-date and informative guides, spotlighting local sights, noting local markets and their wares, outlining local transport and even recommending restaurants.

THINGS TO BUY

There are a lot of good bargains awaiting you in Thailand if you have the space to carry them back. Always haggle to get the best price, except in department stores.

Fabrics

Fabric is possibly the best all-round buy in Thailand. Thai silk is considered the best in the world and can be purchased cheaply in the north-east where it is made or, more easily, in Bangkok. Excellent and reasonably priced tailor shops can make your choice of fabric into almost any pattern. A silk suit should cost around 2500 to 4000B.

Cottons are also a good deal – common items like the phaakhamaa, which is reputed to have over a hundred uses in Thailand and the phaasin, the slightly larger female equivalent, make great tablecloths and curtains. Good ready-made cotton shirts are available, such as the *maw hawm* or Thai work shirt and the *kuay haeng* (Chinese-style shirt) – see the sections on Pasang in the north and Ko Yaw in the south for where to see cotton-weaving.

In recent years, cotton-weaving has become very popular in the north-east and there are fabulous finds in Nong Khai, Roi-Et, Khon Kaen and Mahasarakham. The *mawn khwan*, a hard, triangle-shaped pillow made in the north-east, makes a good souvenir and comes in many sizes. The north-east is also famous for its *mat-mii* cloth, thick cotton fabric woven from tie-dyed threads.

Fairly nice batik (*pa-te*) is available in the south in patterns that are more similar to batik found in Malaysia than in Indonesia.

Shoulder Bags

Thai shoulder bags are generally quite well made. The *yaam* comes in many varieties,

some woven by hill tribes, others by Thai cottage industry. The best are made by the Lahu hill-tribes, whom the Thais call 'Musoe'. The weaving is more skilful and the bags tend to last longer than those made by other tribes. For an extra large size *yaam*, the Karen-made bag is a good choice – easy to find in the Mae Hong Son area.

Overall, Chiang Mai has the best selection of standard shoulder bags, but Bangkok has the best prices – try the Indian district, Pahurat, for these as well as anything else made of cloth. Roi-Et and Mahasarakham in the north-east are also good hunting grounds for locally made shoulder bags. Prices range from 45B for a cheaply made bag to 100B for something special.

Antiques

Real antiques cannot be taken out of Thailand without a permit from the Department of Fine Arts. No Buddha image, new or old, may be exported without permission – refer to Fine Arts again, or, in some cases, the Department of Religious Affairs, under the Ministry of Education. Too many private

collectors smuggling and hoarding Siamese art (Buddhas in particular) around the world have led to strict controls. See the section on Customs in this chapter for more information on the export of art objects and antiques.

Chinese and Thai antiques are sold in Chinatown in an area called Wang Burapha the streets with Chinese 'gates' over the entrance. Some antiques (and many fakes) are sold at the Weekend Market, Chatuchak Park. Objects for sale in the tourist antique shops are fantastically overpriced, as can be expected.

Jewellery

Thailand is one of the world's largest exporters of gems and ornaments, rivalled only by India and Sri Lanka. The biggest importers of Thai jewellery are the US, Japan and Switzerland. One of the results of the remarkable growth of the gem industry – in Thailand the gem trade has increased nearly 10% every year for the last decade – is that the prices are rising rapidly.

If you know what you are doing you can make some really good buys in both unset gems and finished jewellery. Gold ornaments are sold at a good rate as labour costs are low. The best bargains in gems are jade, rubies and sapphires. Buy from reputable dealers only, unless you're a gemologist. Be wary of special 'deals' that are one-day only or which set you up as a 'courier' in which you're promised big money. Many travellers end up losing big. Shop around and don't be hasty.

The biggest gem centres are Kanchanaburi, Mae Sot and Chantaburi – these areas are where the Bangkok dealers go to buy their stones. The Asian Institute of Gemological Sciences (tel 233-8388), 4th Floor Rama Jewelry Bldg, 987 Silom Rd, offers short-term courses in gemology as well as tours of gem mines for those interested.

Hill-Tribe Crafts

Interesting embroidery, clothing, bags and jewellery from the north can be bought in Bangkok at Narayan Phand, Lan Luang Rd, at the Queen's Hillcrafts Foundation, in the Sapatum Palace compound behind the Siam

Centre, and at various tourist shops around town.

The International School of Bangkok, on Soi Ruam Chai (Soi 15) off Sukhumvit Rd, has regular hill-tribe craft sales, often featuring good selections, and the prices are good. These are usually held once a month but check with the school to find out the latest schedule.

In Chiang Mai there are shops selling handicrafts all along Thapae Rd and there is a shop sponsored by missionaries near Prince Royal College. There is a branch of the Queen's Hillcrafts Foundation in Chiang Rai. It is worthwhile to shop around for the best prices and bargain. The all-round best buys on northern hill-tribe crafts are at the Chiang Mai night bazaar.

Lacquerware

Thailand produces some good Burmese-style lacquerware and sells some of the Burmese stuff itself, along the northern Burmese border. Try Mae Sot, Mae Sariang and Mae Sai for the best buys.

Fake or Pirated Goods

In Bangkok, Chiang Mai and all the various tourist centres, there is black market street trade in fake designer goods; particularly Lacoste (crocodile) and Ralph Lauren polo shirts and Rolex, Dunhill and Cartier watches. No one pretends they're the real thing, at least not the vendors themselves. The European manufacturers are applying heavy pressure to the Asian governments involved to get this stuff off the street so it may not be around much longer.

Pre-recorded cassette tapes are another slightly illegal bargain in Thailand. The tapes are 'pirated', that is, no royalties are paid to the copyright owners. Average price is 30 to 35B per cassette. Word has it that these will soon disappear from the streets, too, under pressure from the US music industry.

Other Goods

Bangkok is famous the world over for its street markets – Pratunam, Chatuchak Park, Khlong Toey, Sampheng (Chinatown), Banglamphu and many more – where you'll find things you never imagined you wanted but once you see can't do without. Even if you don't want to spend any money, they're great places to wander around.

For top-end shopping, the two main centres in Bangkok are the area around the Oriental Hotel off Charoen Krung (New) Road and the relatively new River City shopping complex on the river next to the Royal Orchid Sheraton Hotel. Thailand's two big department store chains, Robinson and Central, have several branches in Bangkok as well as in the larger towns.

WHAT TO BRING
Bring as little as possible – one medium-size shoulder bag or backpack should do it. Pack light, wash-and-wear, natural-fabric clothes, unless you're going to be in the north in the cool season, in which case you should have a pullover. Pick up a phaakhamaa (short Thai-style sarong for men) or a phaasin (a longer sarong for women) to wear in your room, on the beach, or when bathing outdoors. These can be bought at any local market (different patterns/colours in different parts of the country) and the vendors will show you how to tie them.

The phaakhamaa/phaasin is a very handy item, it can be used to sleep on or as a light bedspread, as a make-shift 'shopping bag', as a turban-scarf to keep off the sun and absorb perspiration, as a towel, as a small hammock and as a device with which to climb coconut palms – to name just a few of its many functions. (It is not considered proper street attire, however.)

Sunglasses are a must for most people and can be bought cheaply in Bangkok. Slip-on shoes or sandals are highly recommended – besides being cooler than tie shoes, they are easily removed before entering a Thai home or temple. A small torch (flashlight) is a good idea, as it makes it easier to find your way back to your bungalow at night if you are staying at the beach or at a government guest house. A couple of other handy things are a compass and a fits-all sink plug. Sunscreen and mosquito repellent (though not 100% DEET – see the Health section) can be pur-

chased in Thailand, as can toothpaste, soap and most other toiletries.

If you plan to spend a great deal of time in one or more of Thailand's beach areas, you might want to bring your own snorkel and mask (see the Snorkelling & Scuba Diving section in the Facts about the Country chapter). This would save on having to rent such gear and would also assure a proper fit. Shoes designed for water sports, eg Nike's 'Aqua Socks', are great for wearing in the water whether you're diving or not. They protect your feet from coral cuts, which easily become infected.

SNORKELLING & SCUBA DIVING
Thailand's two coastlines and countless islands are popular among divers for their mild waters and colourful marine life. The biggest diving centre is Pattaya, probably because it's less than two hours drive from Bangkok. There are several islands with reefs within a short boat ride from Pattaya and the little town is packed with dive shops. Phuket is the second biggest jumping-off point and has the advantage of offering the largest variety of places to choose from – small offshore islands less than an hour away, Ao Phang-Nga (a one to two-hour boat ride) with its unusual rock formations and clear green waters and the world-famous Similan and Surin islands (about four hours away by fast boat).

The up-and-coming area is Chumphon Province, just north of Surat Thani, where there are a dozen or so islands with undisturbed reefs. Most dive shops rent equipment at reasonable rates and some also offer basic instruction and qualification for first-timers.

All of these places have areas that are suitable for snorkellers as well as scuba divers, since many reefs are no deeper than two metres. Masks, fins and snorkels are readily available for rent not only at dive centres but also through guest houses located in beach areas. If you're particular about the quality and condition of the equipment you use, however, you might be better off bringing your own mask and snorkel – some of the stuff for rent is second-rate. And people with large heads may have difficulty finding masks that fit since most of the masks are made or imported for Thai heads.

Some established diving centres are:

Pattaya

Dave's Diver's Den (tel 423-3864), North Pattaya

Max's Dive Shop (tel 428321), Nipa Lodge Hotel, North Pattaya Rd

Seafari Sports Center (tel 428126/7), Royal Garden Beach Resort, South Pattaya

The Reef Dive Shop (tel 428459), Soi 7, Chaihat Rd

Pattaya International Diving Center (tel 433325/9), Soi Chaiyasit, Beach Rd

Steven Dive Shop (tel 428459), 579 Beach Rd

Phuket

Phuket International Diving Center (tel 321106), Coral Beach Hotel, Patong Beach

Loan Island Resort (tel 211253, Bangkok reservations tel 314-5332), Ao Chalong

Sun & Sand Tour (tel 211901/3; Bangkok reservations tel 260-1022/7), Pearl Hotel, Phuket Town

Andaman Divers, (tel 321155), 83/8 Thawiwong Rd, Patong Beach

Chumphon

Chumphon Cabana (tel 511885; Bangkok reservations tel 224-1884), Thung Wua Lan Beach

Pornsawan Home (tel 521031, Bangkok reservations tel 427-1360), Paknam

Bangkok

Thai Diving Center (tel 258-3662), 44/1 Sukhumvit Rd, Soi 21

Sea Frog Thai Co (tel 235-9438), 397/1 Soi Siri Chulasewok, Silom Rd

GOLF

Golfing in Thailand? It's not my sport, but golf addicts can get a fix at any of nearly 50 courses in Thailand. Green fees range from 90 to 300B (except for the Navatanee, which is 300B weekdays, 750B weekends), depending on day of the week and quality of the course. Caddy fees are 50 to 150B (caddies are often women) and clubs can be

rented for 150 to 300B. Here are a few courses that accept non-members:

Bangkok

Navatanee Golf Course, 5679 metres, par 72. Top-rated Robert Trent Jones-designed course. Also has gymnasium and swimming pool – 22 Mu 1, Sukhaphiban 2 Rd, Bangkapi, Bangkok (reservations tel 374-7077)

Railway Training Centre Golf Course, 6052 metres, par 72. Thailand's first 36-hole course, fairly flat, near the airport. Also has swimming pool and tennis courts.

Vibhavadi Rangsit Rd, Bangkhen, Bangkok (reservations tel 271-0130).

Rose Garden Golf Course, 5856 metres, par 72. One of Thailand's most beautiful courses, tight fairways.

Rose Garden Resort, Highway 4 (reservations 253-0295).

Royal Dusit Golf Course, 4476 metres, par 66. Centrally located at the Royal Turf Club in the centre of Bangkok. Closed on race days. Phitsanulok Rd (reservations tel 281-4320).

Outside Bangkok

Phlu Ta Luang Golf Course, 6188 metres, par 72. Thailand's 2nd longest, part of the Sattahip Royal Navy base. This is a tough course. Sattahip, Chonburi (about 30 km south of Pattaya) (reservations (02) 466-1180).

Khao Yai Golf Course, 9 holes, 2712 metres, par 36. This course has high elevation and cool weather. Khao Yai National Park, Khorat (contact TAT for reservations).

Royal Hua Hin Golf Course, 6055 metres, par 72. Oldest course in Thailand (founded 1924), this course features rolling hills. Hua Hin, Prachuap Khiri Khan (reservations tel (032) 511099).

Phuket Golf & Country Club, 5818 metres, par 72. Newly opened, hilly. Off main road between Phuket Town and Patong Beach (reservations tel (076) 213388).

Tong Yai Golf Course, 9 holes. Easy course, low fees. Samila Hotel, Songkhla (reservations tel (074) 311310).

Lanna Golf Course, 6528 metres, par 72. Thailand's longest play, medium difficulty, cool December to January. Highway 107, Chiang Mai (reservations tel (053) 221-911).

Getting There

AIR

The expense of getting to Bangkok per air km varies quite a bit depending on your point of departure. However, you can take heart in the fact that Bangkok is one of the cheapest cities in the world to fly out of, due to the Thai government's loose restrictions on air fares and the close competition between airlines and travel agencies. The result is that with a little shopping around, you can come up with some real bargains. If you can find a cheap one-way ticket to Bangkok, take it, because you are virtually guaranteed to find one of equal or lesser cost for the return trip once you get there.

From most places around the world your best bet will be budget, excursion or promotional fares – when enquiring from airlines ask for the various fares in that order. Each carries its own set of restrictions and it's up to you to decide which set works best in your case. Fares are going up and down with regularity these days, but in general they are cheaper from September through to April than during the rest of the year.

Fares listed here should serve as a guideline – don't count on them staying this way for long (they may go down!).

To/From Australia

Regular one-way economy fare from Australia to Bangkok is A\$1600 from Sydney or Melbourne, A\$1333 from Perth. There are one-way and return advance purchase fares which must be booked and paid for 21 days in advance. Two seasons apply to advance purchase tickets, the peak is 10 December to 10 January, all the rest of the year is off-peak.

One-way advance-purchase fares are A\$831 from Sydney or Melbourne (A\$984 peak), A\$609 from Perth (A\$722 peak). The return excursion fares are around A\$1000 from Sydney or Melbourne (A\$1200 peak), A\$860 from Perth (A\$935 peak). Through travel agents specialising in discount tickets you should be able to knock a bit off these

fares, although you will still need to book in advance.

To/From Europe

London 'bucket shops' will have tickets to Bangkok available for around £180 one-way or £360 return. It's also easy to stop-over in Bangkok between London and Australia, with fares for around £380 to the Australian east coast. Good travel agents to try for these sorts of fares are Trailfinders on Earls Court Rd or STA on Old Brompton Rd. Or you can simply check the travel ads in *Time Out* or the *News & Travel Magazine*.

To/From North America

If you can fly from the West Coast, you can get some great deals through the many bucket shops (who discount tickets by taking a cut in commissions) and consolidators (agencies that buy airline seats in bulk) operating in Los Angeles and San Francisco. One of the oldest and most established of these is *Overseas Tours* (formerly OC Tours) at 475 El Camino Real, Room 206, Millbrae, CA 94030. Toll-free from outside California is now (tel (800) 227-5988), inside California, (tel (800) 323-8777). Overseas Tours is a Chinese-operated corporation which mainly serves the heavy Asian traffic between San Francisco and the Far East. They put out a yearly booklet listing their various fares – give them a call and they'll send it to you. Overseas Tours' return (round-trip) air fares to Bangkok from any of 12 different West Coast cities start at US\$640. Another good discounter in the San Francisco area is Omi Tours.

While the airways themselves can rarely match the prices of the discounters, they are worth checking if only to get benchmark prices to use for comparison. Tickets bought directly from the airlines may have fewer restrictions and/or less strict cancellation policies than those bought from discounters as well (though this is not always true).

Cheapest from the West Coast are: Thai Airways International (THAI), China Airlines, Korean Airlines, Pan Am and CP Air. Each of these has a budget and/or 'super Apex' fare that costs around US$900 to US$1100 round-trip from Los Angeles, San Francisco or Seattle. THAI is the most overbooked of these airlines from December to March and June to August and hence their flights during these months may entail schedule delays (if you're lucky enough to get a seat at all). Several of these airlines also fly out of New York, Dallas, Chicago and Atlanta – add another US$100 to US$200 to their lowest fares.

To/From Asia

There are regular flights to Bangkok from every major city in Asia and it's not so tricky dealing with inter Asia flights as most airlines offer about the same fares. Here is a sample of current estimated fares:

Singapore to Bangkok	US$140
Hong Kong to Bangkok	US$160-200*
Kuala Lumpur to Bangkok	US$120
Taipei to Bangkok	US$240
Calcutta to Bangkok	US$135
Kathmandu to Bangkok	US$190
Colombo to Bangkok	US$190-240*
New Delhi to Bangkok	US$190
Manila to Bangkok	US$240

*varies according to airline

ASEAN Promotional Fares (round-trip from any city, eg a Bangkok/Manila/Jakarta fare is good for Manila/Jakarta/Bangkok/Manila, or Jakarta/Bangkok/Manila/Jakarta, or Bangkok/Manila/Jakarta/Bangkok):

Bangkok/Manila/Jakarta	US$505
Bangkok/Singapore/Manila	US$420
Bangkok/Jakarta/Brunei	US$395
Bangkok/Manila/Brunei/Jakarta/	
Singapore/Kuala Lumpur	US$560

Tickets in Bangkok

Although other Asian centres are now competitive with Bangkok for buying discounted airline tickets, this is still a good place for

shopping around. Note, however, that some Bangkok travel agents have a shocking reputation. Taking money and then delaying or not coming through with the tickets, providing tickets with very limited time life or severe use restrictions are all part of the racket. There are a lot of perfectly honest agents, but beware of the rogues.

Some typical fares being quoted out of Bangkok include:

Around Asia

Calcutta	3510B
Colombo	4966B
Delhi	4940B
Kathmandu	4784B
Rangoon	2470B
Paro (Bhutan)	7770B
Kuala Lumpur	120B
Penang	2600B
Singapore	3500B
Hong Kong	4160B
Jakarta	4560B

Australia & New Zealand

Sydney or Melbourne	9250B
Darwin or Perth	8372B
Auckland	11,700B

Europe

Athens, Amsterdam, Rome, Paris, London,	
Frankfurt	8250B

USA

San Francisco/Los Angeles	10,250B
via Australia	18,200B
New York	12,500B

Booking Problems

During the past couple of years the booking of flights in and out of Bangkok during the high season (December to March) has become increasingly difficult. This is of course due in part to increased demand for seats but is also due to a continuing attempt by THAI to maintain a semimonopoly on international as well as domestic air traffic in Thailand. In spite of the fact that almost every seat on every flight during the high season is booked, and many of their own flights are overbooked and flying under heavy delays, the government-owned THAI has refused to allow additional airlines permission to add much-needed service through Bangkok. In addition, THAI has refused to join a regional computer-reservation system called Abacus that is used by Singapore Airlines and Cathay Pacific to boost reservations efficiency.

This same attitude has so far also precluded any other Thailand-based airlines from flying domestically, though this may change if Bangkok Airways (owned by Sahakol Air) ever receives permission to fly to destinations in the south and north-east not served by THAI.

Departure Tax

Airport departure tax is 200B for international flights and 20B for domestic. There is no longer a tax exemption for passengers in transit. See the Airport section in the Bangkok chapter for more details.

OVERLAND

Trains, buses and taxis enter Thailand from Malaysia at the western point of entry, Padang Besar, or either of two eastern crossings at Sungai Kolok and Tak Bai. There is also limited public transport via much less-frequented Betong, near the centre of the Thai-Malaysian border. See the Getting There & Away section of the Southern Thailand chapter for train fares between Bangkok and Singapore, Bangkok and Butterworth, etc. The crossing at Sungai Kolok is scheduled to be replaced or superseded eventually by the new crossing at Tak Bai in Narathiwat Province, which shortens the road link between Thailand and Malaysia by at least 60 km. Tak Bai was opened in September 1987 and has a boat jetty and ferry dock for boat service across the Kolok River, as well as customs and immigration offices. So far both continue in full operation – it's hard to conceive of Sungai Kolok closing, since it has long been a significant shopping and entertainment destination for Malaysian tourists.

There is currently no land passage between Burma and Thailand (legally) and likewise Cambodia and Laos, although we can look for Laos to open in the near future at the Vientiane crossing.

BOAT

Frequent boats go between Perlis (Kuala Perlis) in Malaysia (departure point for Langkawi Island) and Satun, Thailand. The trip takes about one to 1½ hours and costs M$4 or 30B. Be sure to go to the Immigration Office in Satun to have your passport stamped – there is no office at the pier itself.

Getting Around

AIR

Domestic air services in Thailand are now operated by Thai Airways International (THAI) (there is no longer a separate Thai Airways for domestic flights) and cover 23 airports throughout Thailand. On certain southern routes, domestic flights through Hat Yai continue on to Penang, Kuala Lumpur, Singapore and Bandar Seri Begawan.

THAI operate Boeing 737s on all their main domestic routes, but they also have Avro 748s on some smaller routes and to the more remote locations, particularly in the north and north-east, there are small Shorts 330s and 360s. Some of the fares to these remote locations are subsidised.

The accompanying chart shows some of the fares on more popular routes. Where routes are operated by 737s and by Avro 748s or Shorts 330s and 360s the 737 fares will be higher. Note that through fares are generally less than the combination fares – Chiang Rai to Bangkok, for example, is less than the addition of Chiang Rai to Chiang Mai and Chiang Mai to Bangkok fares. This does not always apply to international fares however. It's much cheaper to fly from Bangkok to Penang via Phuket or Hat Yai than direct, for example.

THAI no longer has a run between Udon Thani and Ubon Ratchathani although there are flights between Khorat and Khon Kaen.

THAI Offices

Bangkok
Head Office, 89 Vibhavadi Rangsit Rd (tel (02) 513-0121)
485 Silom Rd (tel (02) 234-3100, 233-3810 for reservations)
6 Larn Luang Rd (tel (02) 288-0090, 280-0070/80 for reservations)
Bangkok International Airport, Don Muang (tel (02) 523-8271/3, 523-6121)
45 Anuwong Rd, Yaowarat (tel (02) 224-9602/8)
Asia Hotel, 296 Phayathai Rd (tel (02) 215-2020/1)
4th floor, Charn Issara Tower (tel (02) 236-7884/5)

Chiang Mai
240 Prapokklao Rd (tel (053) 211541, 211420, 211044/7)
183/3 Changklan Rd (tel (053) 234150, 235462, 233559/60)
Chiang Rai
870 Phahonyothin Rd (tel (054) 711179, 713663)
Hat Yai
166/4 Niphat Utit 2 Rd (tel (074) 245851, 246165, 243711, 233433)
190/6 Niphat Uthit 2 Rd (tel (074) 231272, 232392)
Khon Kaen
183/6 Maliwan Rd (tel (043) 236523, 239011, 238835)
Lampang
314 Sanambin Rd (tel (054) 217078, 218199)
Loei
191/1 Charoenrat Rd (tel (042) 812344, 812355)
Mae Hong Son
71 Singhanatbamrung Rd (tel (053) 611297, 611194)
Mae Sot
76/1 Prasatwitthi Rd (tel (055) 531730, 531440)
Nakhon Ratchasima
14 Manat Rd (tel (044) 257211/5)
Nakhon Si Thammarat
1612 Ratchadamnoen Rd (tel (075) 342491)
Nan
34 Mahaprom Rd (tel 710377, 710498)
Narathiwat
324-326 Phuphaphakdi Rd (tel (073) 511161, 512178)
Nong Khai
453 Prachak Rd (tel (042) 411530)
Pattani
9 Preeda Rd (tel (073) 349149)
Pattaya
Royal Cliff Beach Hotel (tel (038) 419286/7)
Phitsanulok
209/26-28 Bromtrailokanat Rd (tel (055) 258020, 251671)
Phrae
42-44 Rasdamnern Rd (tel (054) 511123)
Phuket
78 Ranong Rd (tel (076) 211195, 212499, 212946)
41/33 Montri Rd (tel (076) 212400, 212644, 212880)
Sakon Nakhon
1446/73 Yuwapattana Rd (tel (042) 712259)
Songkhla
2 Soi 4 Saiburi Rd (tel (074) 311012)

Surat Thani
    3/27-28 Karoonrat Rd (tel 273710, 273355)
Trang
    31/1 Viseskul Rd (tel (075) 218066)
Ubon
    929/9 Chayanggoon Rd (tel (045) 254431,
    255894)
Udon
    60 Makkang Rd (tel (tel 221004, 243222)

In early 1986, a privately owned domestic airline began operations in indirect competition with THAI. The newcomer was Bangkok Airways and they had four daily flights along the Bangkok to Khorat and Bangkok to Surin routes, along with occasional flights between Bangkok and Krabi. Eventually, they had plans to fly between Bangkok and Ko Samui when the Samui Airport was completed. Within a year, however, all Bangkok Airways flights were suspended due to political friction with THAI, the government carrier. Then in January 1989 Sahakol Air, owners of Bangkok Airways, announced it would resume flights in April of that year, this time from Bangkok to Ko Samui, from Ko Samui to Phuket and Hat Yai, and from Bangkok to Ranong and Krabi routes. The company has as yet to decide whether to resume service to the north-east. Check with any travel agent in Bangkok to see if this venture is off the ground.

Bangkok Airways fares are competitive with THAI's but the company is small and it remains to be seen whether or not it will survive to become a serious contender. At the moment it's like Mekong and Hong Thong whisky, each concentrating on a different share of the market.

The Ko Samui Airport is privately owned by a group of Thai investors who are mostly medical doctors, financiers and retired military. They may allow landing rights for charter flights from Malaysia and Singapore in addition to domestic traffic.

BUS
Government Bus
Several different types of buses ply the roads of Thailand. The cheapest and slowest are the ordinary government-run buses. For some

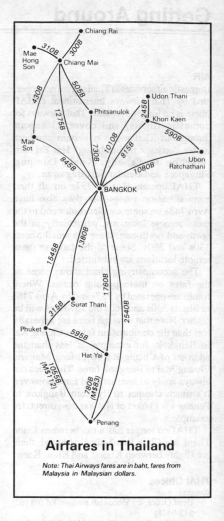

Airfares in Thailand

Note: Thai Airways fares are in baht, fares from
Malaysia in Malaysian dollars.

destinations – smaller towns – these are your only choice. The faster, more comfortable, government-run 'tour buses' (rot thua or rot ae), usually with air-con, only run between certain major cities. If these are available to your destination, they are your very best choice since they don't cost that much more than the ordinary stop-in-every-town buses. The government bus company is called Baw Kaw Saw as an abbreviation for Borisat

Khon Song – literally the Transportation Company. Every city and town in Thailand linked by bus transportation has a Baw Kaw Saw-designated terminal, even if it's just a patch of dirt by the side of the road.

Private Bus

Charter buses are available between Bangkok and major tourist destinations: Chiang Mai, Surat, Hat Yai, Pattaya and a few others. These are called 'tour' buses although there is no tour involved. To Chiang Mai, for example, there are several companies running buses out of Bangkok every day. These can be booked through most hotels or any travel agency. Fares may vary a little bit from company to company but usually not by more than a few baht. However, fare differences between the government and private bus companies can be substantial. Using Surat Thani as an example, the state-run buses from the Southern Bus Terminals are 125B for ordinary bus, 250B air-con, while the private companies charge up to 300B. On the other hand, air-con buses to Phuket are all the same price, 299B (ordinary bus is 165B).

As a result of passenger complaints concerning delayed or non-existent departures, poor baggage service, theft etc, all buses in Thailand are required to be licensed by Baw Kaw Saw, which now oversees all bus operations.

There are also private buses running between major destinations within the various regions, eg Nakhon Si Thammarat to Hat Yai in the south, and Chiang Mai to Sukhothai in the north. New companies are cropping up all the time. The numbers did seem to peak in the early '80s, but are now somewhat stabilised. Where once there were at least 10 different companies running buses to Phuket, at this writing there are only four – that is, fewer companies are running more buses. On some routes they use minivans, eg Surat to Krabi and Tak to Mae Sot.

The tour buses are somewhat more comfortable than the state buses, if you don't mind narrow seats and a hair-raising ride. The trick the tour companies use to make their buses seem more comfortable is to make you think you're not on a bus, by turning up the air-con until your knees knock, handing out pillows and blankets and serving free soft drinks. On overnight journeys the buses usually stop somewhere en route and passengers are awakened to dismount the bus for a free meal of fried rice or rice soup. A few companies even treat you to a meal before a long overnighter. In general, food service seems to be getting better on the long overnight trips.

A new innovation are the 'VIP' buses that have fewer seats so that each seat reclines more – sometimes these are called 'sleepers'. For small-to-medium-sized people they are more comfortable, but if you're big you may find yourself squashed when the person in front of you leans back.

Safety The main trouble with the tour buses is that statistically, they seem to meet with a lot of accidents. Head-on collisions with trucks, and turnovers as they round bad curves are probably due to the inexperience of the drivers on a particular route. This in turn is probably a result of the companies opening and folding so frequently and because they try hard to make good time – tickets are sold on a reputation for speed to Thais.

As fares are higher than the government-run buses, they attract a better-heeled clientele among the Thais, as well as foreign tourists. One result is that a tour bus loaded with money or the promise of money is a temptation for upcountry bandits. Hence tour buses occasionally get robbed by bands of thieves, but these incidents have become increasingly rare due to increased security in the provinces under the Prem and Chatichai administrations.

The most dangerous route now seems to be the road between Surat and Phuket, though this is more so because of the old drugged food/drink/cigarette trick than because of armed robbery. (See the Precautions section in the Facts for the Visitor chapter for details.) In an effort to prevent this menace, which began to increase rapidly during the early '80s, Thai police now board tour buses plying the southern roads at unan-

nounced intervals, taking photos and video-
tapes of the passengers and asking for IDs.
Reported druggings are now on the decrease.
Another dangerous area is in Yala Province
between Yala and Betong on the Malaysian
border, where the Communist Party of
Malaysia insurgents and Thai Muslim separatists occasionally hijack public vehicles.

Large-scale robberies never occur on the
ordinary buses, very rarely on the state-run
air-con buses and rarely on the trains. The
Southern train route is the most dangerous.
Accidents are not unknown to happen on
the state-run buses, so the train still comes
out the safest means of transport in Thailand.

Now that you've decided not to go to
Thailand after all, let me point out that robberies and accidents are relatively infrequent
(though more frequent than they should be)
considering the number of buses taken daily,
and I've never been on a bus that's suffered
either mishap – the odds are on your side.
Travellers to Thailand should know the risk
of tour bus travel against the apparent con-
venience, especially when there are
alternatives. Some travellers really like the
tour buses though, so the private companies
will continue to do good business.

Keep an eye on your bags when riding
buses – thievery by stealth is still the most
popular form of robbery in Thailand (emi-
nently preferable to the forceful variety in my

opinion), though again the risks are not that
great – just be aware. The place you are most
likely to be 'touched' is on the crowded buses
in Bangkok. Razor artists abound, particularly on the buses in the vicinity of the
Hualamphong Railway Station. These dex-
terous thieves specialise in slashing your
knapsack, shoulder bag or even your
trousers' pockets with a sharp razor and slipping your valuables out unnoticed. Hold
your bag in front of you, under your attention, and carry money in a front shirt pocket,
preferably (as the Thais do) maintaining a
tactile and visual sensitivity to these areas if
the bus is packed shoulder to shoulder. Seasoned travellers don't need this advice as the
same precautions are useful all over the
world – the trick is to be relaxed but aware,
not tense.

TRAIN

The railway network in Thailand, run by the
Thai government, is surprisingly good. After
travelling several thousand km by train and
bus, I have to say that the train wins hands
down as the best form of public transport in
the kingdom. It is not possible to take the
train everywhere in Thailand, but if it were
that's how I'd go. If you travel 3rd class, it is
often the cheapest way to cover a long distance; by 2nd class it's about the same as a
'tour bus' but much safer and more comfortable. The trains take a bit longer than a

WARNING

While travelling by bus or train, do not accept foods, drinks or sweets
from strangers no matter how friendly they may seem. You might be
drugged or robbed of your belongings.

Tourist Police
509 Vorachak Road
Bangkok
Tel 221-6206/10

Tourist Assistance Centre
Tourism Authority of Thailand
Ratchadamnoen Nok Avenue, Bangkok
Tel 282-8129, 281-5051

Thailand
Railways

chartered bus but, on overnight trips especially, it is worth the extra time it takes.

The trains offer many advantages; there is more space, more room to breathe and stretch out – even in 3rd class, than there is on the best buses. The windows are big and usually open, so that there is no glass between you and the scenery – good for taking photos – and more to see. The scenery itself is always better along the rail routes compared to the scenery along Thai highways – the trains regularly pass small villages, farmland, old temples, etc. Decent, reasonably priced food is available and served at your seat or in the dining car. The pitch-and-roll of the railway cars is much easier on the bones, muscles and nervous system than the quick stops and starts, the harrowing turns and the pot-hole jolts endured on buses. The train is safer in terms of both accidents en route and robberies. Last, but certainly not least, you meet a lot more interesting people on the trains, or so it seems to me.

For those who plan to travel extensively by train in Thailand, the State Railway of Thailand has announced that, as of 23 October 1989, a Visit Thailand Rail Pass will

be available for 'holders of international passports'. The pass allows 20 days of travel at 1500B for a Blue Pass (2nd and 3rd class, supplementary charges not included), or 3000B for a Red Pass (2nd & 3rd class, all supplementary charges included).

Lines

There are four main rail lines; the Northern, Southern, North-Eastern and Eastern routes. There are several side routes, notably between Nakhon Pathom and Nam Tok (stopping in Kanchanaburi) in the west central region, another between Tung Song and Kan Tang (stopping in Trang) in the south, and between Hat Yai and Songkhla in the south. The Southern line splits at Hat Yai, one route going to Sungai Kolok in Malaysia, through Yala, one route going to Padang Besar in the west, also on the Malaysian border. Within the next few years, there will probably be a line extending from Kiriratnikom to Phuket in the south, establishing a rail link between Surat Thani and Phuket.

Classes

The State Railway of Thailand operates passenger trains in three classes – 1st, 2nd and 3rd – but these can vary considerably amongst themselves depending on whether you're on an ordinary, rapid, or express train. A typical 3rd-class car consists of two rows of bench seats divided into facing pairs. Each bench seat is designed to seat two or three passengers, but on a crowded upcountry line nobody seems to care about design considerations. On a rapid train (which carries 2nd and 3rd-class cars only), 3rd-class seats are padded and reasonably comfortable for shorter trips. On ordinary trains, 3rd-class seats are usually made of wooden slats, and are not recommended for more than a couple of hours at a time. An ordinary train is much slower than a rapid train, naturally. Express trains do not carry 3rd-class cars at all (except for the Special Express 19/20 between Bangkok and Sungai Kolok). Commuter trains in the Bangkok area are all 3rd class and the cars resemble modern subway or rapid transit trains, with plastic seats and ceiling loops for standees.

In a 2nd-class chair car, seating arrangements are similar to those on a bus – pairs of padded seats all facing toward the front of the train. Usually the seats can be adjusted to a reclining angle, and for some people this is good enough for overnight trips. In a 2nd-class sleeping car, you'll find two rows of facing seat pairs; each pair is separated from the next by a dividing wall. A table folds down between each pair and at night the seats convert into two fold-down berths, one over the other. Curtains provide a modicum of privacy and the berths are fairly comfortable, with fresh linen for every trip. A toilet stall is located at one end of the car and washing basins at the other. Second-class cars are found only on rapid and express trains; some routes offer air-con 2nd class as well as ordinary 2nd class.

First-class cars provide private cabins for singles or couples. Each private cabin has individually controlled air-con, an electric fan, a fold-down washing basin and mirror, a small table and a long bench seat (or two in a double cabin) that converts into a bed. Drinking water and towels are provided free of charge. First-class cars are available only on express and special express trains.

In dining cars and in 2nd and 1st-class cars, there are usually two menus available, a 'Special Food' menu with prices at 50 to 60B per dish (generally given to tourists) and a cheaper, more extensive menu at 15 to 20B per dish. If you want the latter but are handed the expensive menu, ask for the *menuu thammadaa* or ordinary menu. The food is basically the same on both menus but the 'special'-menu items get a fancier presentation.

Bookings

The disadvantage of travelling by train, in addition to the time factor mentioned above, is that they can be difficult to book. This is especially true around holiday time, eg the middle of April approaching Songkran festival, since a lot of Thais prefer the train, too. Trains out of Bangkok should be booked as far in advance as possible – a week minimum

for such popular routes as the Northern (to Chiang Mai) and Southern (to Hat Yai) lines, especially if you want a sleeper. For the North-Eastern and Eastern lines a few days will suffice.

To book tickets in advance go to Hualamphong Station in Bangkok, walk through the front of the station house and go straight to the back right-hand corner where a sign says 'Advance Booking'. The other ticket windows, on the left-hand side of the station, are for same-day purchases, mostly 3rd class. In the Advance Booking office you will receive a numbered reservation form, white for the Southern line, green for North, North-Eastern and Eastern. Then proceed into the ticketing room, taking the blank reservation form to the appropriate counter when your number is called. A clerk will fill out the appropriate forms for you, according to available space on the train you want. This done, you take the filled-out form to the desk indicated by the clerk, separate your numbered stub from the form and spindle the form on the nail standing upright on that desk. Then you must wait until your number is called (most likely in Thai, so keep an eye on the numbers around you), at which point the agent at the desk will give you your ticket and collect the money. It's not as bad as it sounds, but takes some time.

Note that buying a return ticket does not necessarily guarantee you a seat on the way back, it only means you do not have to buy a ticket for the return. If you want a guaranteed seat reservation it's best to make that reservation for the return immediately upon arrival at your destination.

Booking trains back to Bangkok is generally not as difficult as booking trains out of Bangkok; however, some stations can be quite difficult, eg, buying a ticket from Surat Thani to Bangkok.

Tickets between any stations in Thailand can be purchased at Hualamphong Station (tel 223-3762), the main railway station in Bangkok. You can also make advance bookings at Don Muang Station, across from Bangkok International Airport. Ticket offices for the State Railway of Thailand are open from 8.30 am to 6 pm on weekdays,

8.30 am to 12 noon on weekends and public holidays.

Train tickets can also be purchased at certain travel agencies in Bangkok, such as Airland on Phloenchit Rd or at the Viengthai Hotel in Banglamphu (see the Travel Agents section in the Bangkok chapter). It is much simpler to book trains through these agencies than to book them at the station.

Charges & Surcharges

There is a 30B surcharge for Express trains (*rot duan*) and 20B for Rapid trains (*rot raew*). These trains are somewhat faster than the ordinary trains, as they make fewer stops. On the Northern line during the daytime there is a 50B surcharge for 2nd-class chairs in air-con cars. For the Special Express (*rot duan phiset*) that runs between Bangkok and Singapore there is a 50B surcharge.

The charge for 2nd-class sleeping berths is 70B for an upper berth and 100B for a lower berth. The difference is that there is a window next to the lower berth and a little more headroom. The upper berth is still quite comfortable. For 2nd-class sleepers with air-con add 100B per ticket. No sleepers are available in 3rd class.

On the north and north-eastern lines, all 1st-class cabins are air-con and a two-bed cabin costs 250B per person while a single-bed cabin is 350B. On the southern line, air-con 1st class is the same but there are also a few ordinary 1st-class rooms available, all with two beds, for 150B per person.

Train fares in Thailand continue to increase regularly, so train travel is not quite the bargain it once was, especially considering that the charge for 2nd-class berths is as high as the cost of most hotel rooms outside Bangkok. You can figure on 500 km costing around 180B in 2nd class (not counting surcharges for rapid/express service), twice that in 1st class, less than half in 3rd. Note that the fares given in this guidebook are guaranteed to the end of 1989 only. Surprisingly, fares had hardly changed since the 1987 edition, in spite of an overall inflation rate in Thailand of about 5%. Relative to fare trends over the last 12 years, this is unusual and I think they're due for an increase. Although the government continues to subsidise train travel to a some extent, I predict that fares will be taking a significant jump in the next two to three years, say around 10% to 15%.

Station Services

The main railway stations in Bangkok (Hualamphong), Phitsanuloke, Chiang Mai and Hat Yai have baggage storage services. The rates and hours of operation vary from station to station. At Hualamphong Station the hours are from 4 am to 10.30 pm and left luggage costs 5B per piece the first day, 10B per piece per day thereafter.

All stations in provincial capitals have restaurants or cafeterias as well as various snack vendors. These stations also offer an advance booking service for rail travel anywhere in Thailand. Hat Yai Station is the only one with a hotel attached, but there are usually hotels within walking distance of other major stations.

The Hualamphong Station has a travel agency where other kinds of transport can be booked. This station also has a post office that's open from 7.30 am to 5.30 pm Monday to Friday, 9 am to 12 noon Saturdays and holidays, and closed Sundays.

Information Accurate up-to-date information on train travel is available at the Rail Travel Aids counter in Hualamphong Station. There you can pick up timetables or ask questions about fares and scheduling – one person behind the counter usually speaks a little English. There are two types of time-tables available: a condensed English timetable with fares, schedules and routes for rapid and express trains on the four trunk lines; and complete, separate Thai timetables for each trunk line, with side lines as well. These latter timetables give fares and schedules for all trains, ordinary, rapid and express.

LOCAL TRANSPORT

The Bangkok Getting Around section has more information on various forms of local transport.

Bus

In most larger provincial capitals, there are extensive local bus services, generally operating with very low fares (2 to 4B).

Taxi

Many regional centres have taxi services but, as in Bangkok itself, although there may well be meters they're never used. Establishing the fare before departure is essential. Try and get an idea from a third party what the fare should be and be prepared to bargain. In general fares are reasonably low.

Samlor

Samlor means three (*sam*) wheels (*lor*, pronounced 'law') and that's just what they are – three-wheeled vehicles. There are two types of samlors, motorised and non-motorised. You'll find motorised samlors throughout the country. They're small utility vehicles, powered by a horrendously noisy two-stroke engine – if the noise and vibration doesn't get you the pollution will. These samlors are often known as *tuk-tuks* from the noise they make. The non-motorised version, on the other hand, are bicycle rickshaws, just like you find, in various forms, all over Asia. There are no bicycle samlors in Bangkok but you will find them elsewhere in the country. In either form of samlor the fare must be established, by bargaining if necessary, before departure.

Songthaew

'Songthaew' means two rows – they're small pickup trucks with two rows of bench seats down the sides, very similar to an Indonesian *bemo* and akin to a Filipino *jeepney*. Songthaews sometimes operate fixed routes, just like a bus, but they may also run a share taxi type of service or even be booked individually just like a regular taxi.

Boat

As any flight over Thailand will reveal, there is plenty of water down there and you'll probably have opportunities to get out on it from time to time. The true Thai river transport is the 'long-tail boat', so called because the propeller is driven by a long extension off the end of the engine. The engine, which can run all the way from a small marine engine to a large car engine, is mounted on gimbals and the whole engine is swivelled to steer the boat. They can travel at a phenomenal speed.

Car & Motorcycle Rental

Cars can be rented in Bangkok, Chiang Mai, Phuket and Hat Yai. Check with travel agencies or large hotels for rental locations. Motorcycles are for rent in these towns as well as many smaller tourist centres like Krabi, Ko Samui, Ko Phangan, Mae Sai, Chiang Saen, Nong Khai, etc (see Motorcycle Trekking). Rental rates vary considerably from one agency to another and from city to city. Since there is a glut of motorcycles for rent in Chiang Mai these days, they can be rented there for as little as 80B per day. A substantial deposit is usually required to rent a car; motorcycle rental usually requires that you leave your passport. Bicycles can also be hired in some locations, particularly Chiang Mai, where they are an ideal form of transport. One traveller wrote in with this warning though, carefully note the condition of the bike before hiring, if it breaks down you are responsible and parts can be very expensive.

THAI RIVER TAXI

MOTORCYCLE TREKKING

Motorcycle travel is becoming a popular way to get around Thailand, especially in the north. Dozens of places along the guest house circuit, including many guest houses themselves, have set up shop with no more than a couple of motorbikes for rent. It is also possible to buy a new or used motorbike and sell it before you leave the country – a good used 125cc bike costs around 20,000B. While motorcycle trekking is undoubtedly one of the best ways to see Thailand, it is also undoubtedly one of the easiest ways to cut your travels short, permanently. You can also run up very large repair and/or hospital bills in the blink of an eye. However, with proper safety precautions and driving conduct adapted to local standards, you can see parts of Thailand inaccessible by other modes of transport and still make it home in one piece. Some guidelines to keep in mind:

1) If you've never driven a motorcycle before, stick to the smaller 80 to 100cc step-through bikes with automatic clutches. If you're an experienced rider but have never done off-the-road driving, take it slow the first few days.

2) Always check a machine over thoroughly before you take it out. Look at the tyres to see if they still have tread, look for oil leaks, test the brakes. You may be held liable for any problems that weren't duly noted before your departure. Newer bikes cost more than clunkers, but are generally safer and more reliable. Street bikes are more comfortable and ride more smoothly on paved roads than dirt bikes; it's silly to rent an expensive dirt bike like the Honda MTX 125 if most of your riding is going to be along decent roads. An MTX 125 uses twice the fuel of a Honda Wing with the same engine size, thus lowering your cruising range in areas where roadside pumps are scarce (the Wing gives you about 300 km per tank while an MTX gets about half that).

3) Wear protective clothing and a helmet (most rental places will provide a helmet with the bike if asked). Without a helmet, a minor slide on gravel can develop into a quick concussion. Long pants, long-sleeved shirts and shoes are highly recommended as protection against sunburn and as a second skin if you fall. If your helmet doesn't have a visor, then wear goggles, glasses or sunglasses to keep bugs, dust and other debris out of your eyes. It is practically suicidal to ride on Thailand's highways without taking these minimum precautions for protecting your body. Gloves are also a good idea – to prevent blisters from holding on to the twist-grips for long periods of time.

4) For distances of over 100 km or so, take along an extra supply of motor oil and, if riding a two-stroke machine like the MTX, two-stroke engine oil. On long trips, oil burns fast.

5) Never ride alone in remote areas, especially at night. There have been incidents where farang bikers have been shot or harassed while riding alone, mostly in remote rural areas. When riding in pairs or groups, stay spread out so you'll have room to manoeuvre or brake suddenly if necessary.

6) In Thailand the de facto right of way is determined by the size of the vehicle which puts the motorcycle pretty low in the pecking order. Don't fight it and keep clear of trucks and buses.

7) Distribute whatever weight you're carrying on the bike as evenly as possible across the frame. Too much weight at the back of the bike makes the front end less easy to control and prone to rising up suddenly on bumps and inclines.

8) Get insurance with the motorcycle if at all possible. The more reputable motorcycle rental places insure all their bikes; some will do it for an extra charge. Without insurance you're responsible for anything that happens to the bike. If an accident results in a total loss, or if the bike is somehow lost or stolen, you can be out 25,000B plus. Health insurance is also a good idea – get it before you leave home and check the conditions in regard to motorcycle riding.

Bangkok

There is a lot to see and do in Bangkok (population 6,000,000) if you can tolerate the traffic, noise, heat (in the hot season), floods (in the rainy season) and somewhat polluted air. The city is incredibly urbanised, but beneath its modern veneer lies an unmistakable Thai-ness. To say that Bangkok is not Thailand, as has been superciliously claimed by some, is like saying that New York is not America, Paris is not France, or London not England.

The capital of Thailand was established at Bangkok in 1782 by the first king of the Chakri Dynasty, Rama I. The name Bangkok means 'place of olives' (not the European variety) and refers to the original site which is only a very small part of what is today called Bangkok by foreigners. The official Thai name is Krungthepmahanakhorn-bowornrattanakosinmahintarayuthayamah-adilokpopnopparatratchathaniburiromudo-mratchaniwetmahasathan, quite a tongue-twister. Fortunately it is shortened to Krung Thep, 'city of angels', in everyday usage. Metropolitan Krung Thep includes Thonburi, the older part of the city (and predecessor to Bangkok as the capital), which is across the Chao Phraya River to the west.

Bangkok caters to diverse interests: there are temples, museums and other historic sites for those interested in traditional Thai culture; an endless variety of good restaurants, clubs, international culture and social events; movies in several different languages and a modern art institute for those seeking contemporary Krung Thep. As the dean of ex-pat authors in Thailand, William Warren, has said, 'The gift Bangkok offers me is the assurance I will never be bored'.

Information

Tourist Offices The TAT (Tourist Authority of Thailand) has a desk in the arrivals area at Bangkok Airport. Their main office (tel 282-1143) is at Ratchadamnoen Nok Ave. The TAT produces the usual selection of colourful brochures, but they're also one of the best tourist offices in Asia for putting out useful hard facts on plain but quite invaluable duplicated sheets. The TAT also maintains a Tourist Assistance Centre (tel 235-4987/8, 234-5364/6, 215-6977) for matters relating to theft or other such mishaps that is open from 8 am to midnight. The paramilitary arm of the TAT, the Tourist Police, can be quite effective in dealing with such matters, particularly 'unethical' business practices (which sometimes turn out to be cultural misunderstandings).

Post The GPO is on Charoen Krung (New) Rd. The poste restante counter opens from 8 am to 8 pm, Monday to Friday and from 8 am to 1 pm, Saturday and Sunday. They charge 1B for each letter you collect and they're very efficient. There's also a packaging service at the post office where they'll wrap parcels for you for about 20B. You can also send letters or parcels from the adjacent Central Telegraph Office after the GPO is shut.

Money Major Thai banks have currency exchange offices in many areas of Bangkok which are open 8.30 am to 8 pm every day of the year. You'll find them located in several places along Sukhumvit, Nana Nua, Khao San, Patpong, Surawong, Ratchadamri, Rama IV, Rama I, Silom and Charoen Krung (New) Rds. If you're after currency for other countries in Asia, check with the money changers along Charoen Krung (New) Rd near the GPO.

Bookshops Bangkok has many good bookshops, possibly the best selection in South-East Asia. If you're looking for second-hand books on Asia, check out Chalermnit Books on Keson (Gaysorn) Rd, near the Le Meridian President Hotel off Ploenchit Rd. They have many titles in

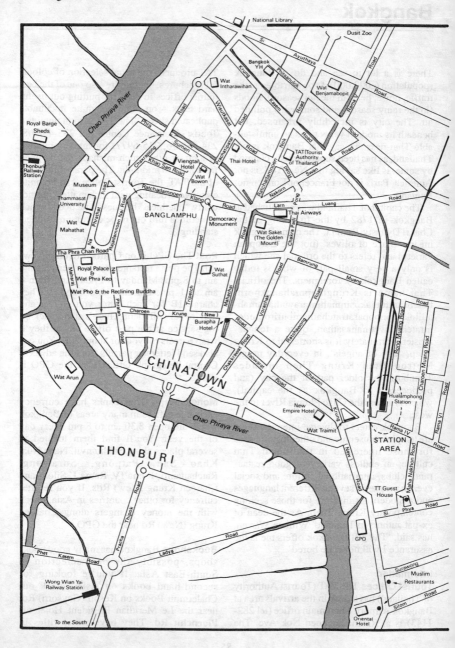

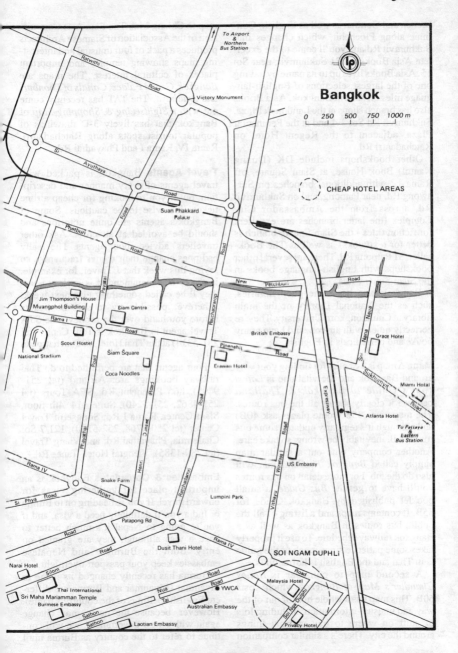

To Airport
& Northern
Bus Station

Bangkok

0   250   500   750 1000 m

CHEAP HOTEL AREAS

Ratwithi Road

Victory Monument

Si Ayuthaya Road

Road

Foei Road

Suan Phakkard
Palace

Phetbun Road

New Petchburi Road

Jim Thompson's House
Muangphol Building

Payathai Road

Siam Centre

Rama I

Rama I Road

Ratchaprarop

Siam Square

British Embassy

Pinenehil Road

Scout Hostel

Erawan Hotel

National Stadium

Coca Noodles

Grace Hotel

Sri Nena Nena

Sukhumvit Road

Miami Hotel

Atlanta Hotel

To Pattaya
& Eastern
Bus Station

Rama IV

Payavithi Road

Convent Road

Henri Road

Ratchadamri Road

Expressway

US Embassy

Vithayu (Wireless) Road

Snake Farm

Si Phya Road

Road

Lumpini Park

Patapong Rd

Rama IV

Dusit Thani Hotel

SOI NGAM DUPHLi

Narai Hotel

Silom Road

Thai International

Sri Maha Mariamman Temple

Burmese Embassy

Sathon Road

Sathon Road

Laotian Embassy

YWCA

Nua Road

Tai Road

Australian Embassy

Malaysia Hotel

Soi Ngam Duphli

Privacy Hotel

French and German as well as English. Continue along Ploenchit, which changes into Sukhumvit Rd and you'll come to the excellent Asia Books at 221 Sukhumvit, near Soi 15. Asia Books lives up to its name by having one of the largest selections of English-language titles on Asia in Bangkok. Asia Books also has branch shops at the Landmark Plaza, Sukhumvit Rd Soi 3-4 and at the Peninsular Plaza, adjacent to the Regent Hotel on Ratchadamri Rd.

Other bookshops include DK (Duang Kamol) Book House, at Siam Square, off Rama 1, with additional branches on Surawong Rd, near Patpong, and on Sukhumvit Rd, across from the Ambassador City Complex (the latter branches are excellent for fiction titles - the Siam Square branch is better for textbooks) as well as The Bookseller, 81 Patpong Rd. There are several other bookshops with English-language books in the Siam Square area.

Bangkok also has some good libraries, such as the National Library or the main library at Chulalongkorn University. They're perfectly quiet, with air-con, and have many books and periodicals in English.

Maps A map is essential for finding your way around Bangkok and the vital one is *Latest Tour's Guide to Bangkok & Thailand* because it clearly shows all the bus routes. The map costs 35B (some places ask 40B) and although it's regularly updated some bus routes will inevitably be wrong, so take care. Another company puts out a similar map simply called *Bangkok Thailand* that will also do the job. For more detail on bus routes you'll have to get the *Bus Guide*, a small booklet published by Bangkok Guide for 35B. It contains maps and a listing of all the public bus routes in Bangkok as well as a Bangkok railway schedule. To use it properly takes some patience since much of the guide is in Thai and the English is horrendous.

A second map to consider is *Nancy Chandler's Map of Bangkok* which costs 60B. This map has a whole host of out of the way and unusual information, including lots of stuff on where to buy unusual things around the city. There's a similar companion map to Chiang Mai. The Fine Arts Commission of the Association of Siamese Architects produces a pack of four unusual and interesting maps showing temples and important places of cultural interest. The maps are *Bangkok*, *Grand Palace*, *Canals of Thonburi* and *Ayuthaya*. The TAT has recently come out with a *Sightseeing & Shopping Map* of Bangkok that has lively 3-D drawings of popular tourist spots along Ratchadamri, Rama IV, Rama I and Phayathai Rds.

Travel Agents Bangkok is packed with travel agents of every manner and description, but if you're looking for cheap airline tickets it's wise to be cautious. Some of Bangkok's agents are quite notorious and should be avoided at all costs. Ask other travellers' advice about agents. The really bad ones change their names frequently, so saying this week that J Travel, for example, is not to be recommended is useless when they'll be called something else next week. Wherever possible try to see the tickets before you hand over the money. The STA Travel agent in Bangkok is Tour Centre (tel 281-5314) at the Thai Hotel, 78 Prachatipatai Rd.

Four agents that are permitted to do Thai railway bookings are: Airland (tel 251-9495), 866 Ploenchit Rd; SEA Tours (tel 251-4862, 251-5240), Suite 414, 4th floor, Siam Center, Rama I Rd; Songserm Travel Center (tel 250-0768, 252-5190), 121/7 Soi Chalermia, Phayathai Rd; and Viang Travel (tel 280-1385), Viengtai Hotel, Tanee Rd.

Embassies & Consulates Bangkok is an important place for gathering visas for onward travel. If you're heading on to Burma or India you'll definitely need a visa, and if you're going to Nepal it's much better to have a visa although they are granted on entry. Both the Burmese and Nepalese embassies keep your passport overnight.

Burma has recently changed its name to Myanmar (Myanmar and Burma are different English spellings of the country's name). However, because the name may change again with a new government, we will continue to refer to the country as Burma until we're sure the name change is permanent. It is now possible to get a 14-day visa to Burma, although not as an independent traveller.

Addresses of some of the Bangkok embassies and consulates include:

Argentina
20/85 Soi 49 Sukhumvit Rd (tel 259-0401/2)

Australia
37 Sathon Tai Rd (tel 287-2680)

Austria
14 Soi Nantha, Sathon Tai Rd (tel 286-3011, 286-3019)

Bangladesh
8 Soi 63 Sukhumvit Rd (tel 391 8069/70)

Belgium
44 Soi Phiphat, Silom Rd (tel 236-0150, 233-9370)

Brazil
Maneeya Center Building, 9th floor, 518/5 Ploenchit Rd (tel 252-6043, 252-6023)

Brunei
26/50 Orakarn Building, Soi Chitlom, Ploenchit Rd (tel 250- 1483/4)

Bulgaria
11 Soi Lumpetch, Huamak, Bangkapi (tel 314-3056)

Britain
1031 Wireless Rd (tel 253-0191/9)

Burma
132 Sathon Nua Rd (tel 233-2237, 234-4698)

Canada
138 Silom Rd (tel 234-1561/8)

Chile
15 Soi 61 Sukhumvit Rd (tel 391-8443)

China
57 Ratchadaphisek Rd (tel 245 7030/49)

Czechoslovakia
197/1 Silom Rd (tel 234-1922, 233-4535)

Denmark
10 Soi Attakanprasit, Sathon Tai Rd (tel 286-3930, 286-3942/4)

Dominican Consulate
92/6 Changwattana Rd, Laksi, Bangkhen (tel 579-1130, 521-0737)

Egypt
49 Soi Ruam Rudi, Ploenchit Rd (tel 252-6139, 253-0161)

European Communities Commission Delegation for South-East Asia
9th & 10th floor, Thai Military Bank Building, Phayathai Rd (tel 282-1452)

Finland
16th floor, Amarin Tower, 500 Ploenchit Rd (tel 256-9306/9)

France
35 Customs House Lane, Charoen Krung Rd (tel 234-0950/6)

Germany (West)
9 Sathon Tai Rd (tel 286-4223/7, 213-2331/6)

Greek Consulate
3rd floor, President Tour Building, 412/8-9 Siam Square Soi 6, Rama I Rd (tel 251-5111)

Hungary
28 Soi Sukchai, Sukhumvit Rd (tel 391-2002/3)

India
46 Soi Prasanmit, Sukhumvit Rd (tel 258-0300/6)

Indonesia
600 to 602 Phetburi Rd (tel 252-3135/40)

Iran
602 Sukhumvit Rd (between Soi 22 and 24) (tel 259-0611/3)

Iraq
47 Pradipat Rd (tel 278-5335/8)

Ireland
205 United Flour Mill Building, Ratchawong Rd (tel 223-0876)

Israel
31 Soi Langsuan, Ploenchit Rd (tel 252-3131/4)

Italy
399 Nang Linchi Rd (tel 286-4844/6)

Japan
1674 New Phetburi Rd (tel 252-6151/9)

Jordanian Consulate
47 Soi 63 Sukhumvit Rd (tel 391-7142)

Korea (South)
Sathon Thani Building, 90 Sathon Neua Rd (tel 234-0723/6)

Korean Consulate (North)
81 Soi Ari 7, Phahonyothin Rd (tel 278-5118)

Laos
193 Sathon Tai Rd (tel 286-0010)

Malaysia
35 Sathon Tai Rd (tel 286-1390/2)

Nepal
189 Soi Phuengsuk (Soi 71), Sukhumvit Rd (tel 391-7240)

Netherlands
106 Wireless Rd (tel 252-6103/5)

New Zealand
93 Wireless Rd (tel 251-8165)

Norway
Chokchai Building, 690 Sukhumvit Rd (tel 258-0531/3)

Oman Consulate
134/1-2 Silom Rd (tel 235-8868/9)

Pakistan
31 Soi Nana Neua, Sukhumvit Rd (tel 253-0288/9)

Philippines
760 Sukhumvit Rd (tel 259-0139/0)

Peruvian Consulate
Louis T Leonowens Building, 723 Si Phaya Rd (tel 233-5910/7 ext 25)

Poland
61 Soi 23, Sukhumvit Rd (tel 258-4112/3)

Portugal
    26 Bush Lane, Si Phaya Rd (tel 233-7610)
Romania
    39 Soi 10, Sukhumvit Rd (tel 252-8515, 251-2242/3)
Saudi Arabia
    Sathon Thani Building, 90 Sathon Tai Rd (tel 235-0875/8)
Singapore
    129 Sathon Tai Rd (tel 286-2111, 286-1434)
Spain
    104 Wireless Rd (tel 252-6112)
Sri Lanka
    48/3 Soi 1, Sukhumvit Rd (tel 251-2789)
Sweden
    11th floor, Boonmitr Building, 138 Silom Rd (tel 234-3891, 233-0295)
Switzerland
    35 Wireless Rd (tel 252-8992/4, 253-0156/60)
Taiwan visa office
    Chiengnuan Building, 140 Wireless Rd (tel 251-9274/6)
Turkey
    153/2 Soi Mahadlekluang 1, Rajdamri Rd (tel 251-2987/8)
USA
    95 Wireless Rd (tel 252-5040/9)
USSR
    108 Sathon Neua Rd, (tel 234-9824, 234-2012, 235-5599)
Vietnam
    83/1 Wireless Rd (tel 251-7201/3, 251-5835/8)
Yugoslavia
    28 Soi 61, Sukhumvit Rd (tel 391-9090/1)

Orientation

The east side of the river, Bangkok proper, can be divided into two by the main north-south rail line. The portion between the river and the railway is old Bangkok where most of the older temples and the original palace is located, as well as the Chinese and Indian districts. That part of the city east of the railway, which covers more than twice as much area as the old districts, is 'new' Bangkok. This latter part can be divided again into the business and tourist district wedged between Charoen Krung (New) Rd and Rama IV Rd and the sprawling residential and tourist district stretching along Sukhumvit and Phetburi Extension (New Phetburi) Rds.

This leaves the hard-to-classify areas below Sathon Tai Rd (which includes Khlong Toey, Bangkok's main port) and the area above Rama IV Rd between the railway

and Withayu Rd, which comprises an infinite variety of businesses, several movie theatres, civil service offices, the shopping area of Siam Square, Chulalongkorn University and the National Stadium. The areas along the east bank of the Chao Phraya River are undergoing a surge of redevelopment and many new buildings, particularly hotels, are going up.

Temples

There are over 400 wats or temple-monasteries in Bangkok. Some of the most interesting are listed, though you may easily discover others on your own. Shoes should be removed before entering the main chapel (*bot*) in any temple compound. Since the wat is a sacred place to Thai Buddhists, visitors should dress and behave decently for their visit.

Wat Phra Kaew & Grand Palace Also called the Temple of the Emerald Buddha, this wat adjoins the Grand Palace on common ground which was consecrated in 1782, the first year of Bangkok rule. Together they have been added to by the different Thai monarchs and consequently feature several different types of architecture, most of it in the Bangkok or Ratanakosin style. The wat is a very colourful place, with extensive murals depicting scenes from the Ramakien, the Thai version of the Indian epic *Ramayana*, along the inside walls of the compound. Originally painted during Rama III's reign (1824-50), the mural has undergone more than one restoration, including a major one finished in time for the 1982 Bangkok/Chakri Dynasty bicentennial.

The so-called Emerald Buddha, 60 cm to 75 cm high (depending on how it is measured), is actually made of a type of jasper or perhaps nephrite, a type of jade, depending on whom you believe. A definite aura of mystery surrounds the image, enhanced by the fact that it cannot be examined closely – it sits in a glass case, on a pedestal high above the heads of worshippers – and photography within the bot is forbidden. Its mystery further adds to the occult significance of the image which is considered the 'talisman' of the Thai kingdom, the legitimator of Thai sovereignty.

It is not known for certain where the image originated or who sculpted it but it first appeared on record in 15th century Chiang Rai; stylistically it seems to be from the Chiang Saen Period. It is said that the image was covered with plaster and gold leaf at that time and located in Chiang Rai's own Wat Phra Kaew (literally 'temple of the jewel holy image'). While being transported elsewhere after a storm had damaged the *chedi* (in which the image had been kept), the image supposedly lost its plaster covering in a fall. It next appeared in Lampang where it enjoyed a 32-year stay (again at a Wat Phra Kaew) until it was brought to Wat Chedi Luang in Chiang Mai.

Laotian invaders took the image from Chiang Mai in the mid-16th century and brought it to Luang Phabang in Laos. Later it was moved to Wiang Chan (Vientiane) and when the Thai king, Taksin, waged war against Laos 200 years later the image was taken back to the Thai capital of Thonburi by General Chakri, who later succeeded Taksin as Rama I, the founder of the Chakri Dynasty. Rama I had the Emerald Buddha moved to the new Thai capital in Bangkok and had two royal robes made for it, one to be worn in the hot season and one for the rainy season. Rama III added another to the wardrobe – to be worn in the cool season. The three robes are still solemnly changed at the beginning of each season by the king himself.

The palace itself is only used by the king on certain ceremonial occasions (eg Coronation Day), as his residence is now Chitlada Palace in the northern part of the city. The Grand Palace was the headquarters for an attempted coup by General San Chitpatima in April 1981.

Admission to Wat Phra Kaew is 100B and hours are from 8.30 to 11.30 am and 1 to 3.30 pm. The admission fee includes tickets for entry to the Royal Thai Decorations and Coins Pavilion (on the same grounds) and to Vimanmek, 'the world's largest golden teakwood mansion'. Vimanmek is near the Dusit Zoo next to the National Assembly.

If you wear shorts you may be refused admission into the Wat Phra Kaew/Grand Palace grounds.

Wat Mahathat A very old monastery, Wat Mahathat is worth a visit as it is right across the street from Wat Phra Kaew, on the west side of Sanam Luang. This wat is a national centre for the Mahanikai monastic sect and houses one of Bangkok's two Buddhist universities. Check out the pigeons in the courtyard behind the main temple.

The temple is officially open to visitors from 9 am to 5 pm every day and on *wan phra* – Buddhist holy days (the full and new moons every fortnight). There is an open-air market which features traditional Thai herbal medicine.

Those interested in learning about Buddhist meditation, or vipassana, should contact the monks in Section 5 within the temple compound. English language instruction is usually available.

Wat Pho (Wat Phra Jetuphon) A long list of superlatives for this one: the oldest and largest wat in Bangkok, it features the largest reclining Buddha and the largest collection of Buddha images in Thailand and was the earliest centre for public education. As a temple site Wat Pho dates back supposedly to the 16th century, but its current history really begins in 1781 with the renovation of the original monastery.

Narrow Jetuphon Rd divides the grounds in two, with each portion surrounded by huge whitewashed walls. The most interesting portion is the northern compound, which includes a very large bot enclosed by a gallery of Buddha images and four *wihans*, four large chedis, commemorating the first four Chakri kings, 91 smaller chedis, an old *tripitaka* library, a sermon-hall, the large wihan which houses the reclining Buddha and a school building for classes in *abhidhamma* (Buddhist philosophy), plus several less important structures. A massage school of sorts convenes in the afternoons at the east end of the compound.

The tremendous reclining Buddha, 46-metres long and 15-metres high, illustrates the passing of the Buddha into nirvana. The figure is modelled out of plaster around a brick core and finished in gold leaf. Mother-of-pearl inlay ornaments the eyes and feet of the colossal image, the feet displaying 108 different auspicious *laksanas* or characteristics of a Buddha. The images on display in the four wihans surrounding the main bot in the eastern part of the compound are interesting. Particularly beautiful are the Phra Jinnarat and Phra Jinachi Buddhas, in the west and south chapels, both from Sukhothai. The galleries extending between the four chapels feature no less than 394 gilded Buddha images.

The temple rubbings for sale at Wat Pho and elsewhere in Thailand come from the reliefs, carved in marble and obtained from the ruins of Ayuthaya, sculpted in the base of the large bot. The rubbings are no longer taken directly from the panels but are rubbed from cement casts of the panels made years ago.

The reclining Buddha image can be seen from 8 am to 5 pm daily; admission is 10B. The ticket booth is closed from 12 noon to 1 pm.

Wat Traimit The 'Temple of the Golden Buddha' is where Yaowarat Rd and Charoen Krung Rd intersect, near the Hualamphong Station. The attraction at this old wat is, of course, the impressive three-metre tall, 5½ tonne solid-gold Buddha image, which gleams like no other gold artefact I've ever seen.

Sculpted in the graceful Sukhothai style, the image was 'rediscovered' some 30 years ago beneath a stucco or plaster exterior when it fell from a crane while being moved to a new building within the temple compound. It has been theorised that the covering was added to protect it from 'marauding hordes' either during the late Sukhothai Period or later in Ayuthaya when the city was under siege by the Burmese. The temple itself is said to date to the early 13th century.

The golden image can be seen every day from 9 am to 5 pm, and admission is 10B.

Wat Arun The 'Temple of Dawn' is named after the Indian god of dawn, Aruna. It appears in all the tourist brochures and is located on the Thonburi side of the Chao Phraya River. The tall, 82-metre *prang* was constructed during the first half of the 19th century by Rama II and Rama III. It is composed of a brick core with a plaster covering embedded with a mosaic of broken Chinese porcelain. The present wat is built on the site of Wat Chang, which was the palace and royal temple of King Taksin when Thonburi was the Thai capital; hence, it was the last home of the Emerald Buddha before Rama I brought it across the river to Bangkok.

The temple looks more impressive from the river than it does up close, though the peaceful wat grounds make a very nice retreat from the hustle and bustle of Bangkok. The main tower can be climbed by means of steep stairs to over half its height and provides a fine view of Thonburi and the river.

Wat Arun is open daily; the admission fee is 5B. To reach Wat Arun from the Bangkok side, catch a river taxi going downriver from the pier at Na Phra Lan Rd (near Wat Phra Kaew) or the one at Thai Wang Rd (near Wat Pho) and it will stop at the Wat Arun landing.

Wat Benchamabophit On Si Ayuthaya and Rama V Rds, this wat of white Carrara marble (hence its tourist name 'the Marble Temple') was built at the turn of the century under Chulalongkorn (Rama V).

The large bot at Wat Ben is a prime example of modern Thai architecture. The courtyard behind the bot exhibits 53 Buddha images, most of which are copies of famous images and styles from all over Thailand and other Buddhist countries – an education in itself if you're interested in Buddhist iconography.

Admission is 10B and the wat is open daily.

Wat Saket Saket is an undistinguished temple except for the Golden Mount (Phu Khao Thong) on the west side of the grounds which provides a good view of Bangkok rooftops. The artificial hill was created when a large chedi under construction by Rama III collapsed because the soft soil beneath would not support it. The resulting mud-and-brick hill was left to sprout weeds until Rama IV built a small chedi on its crest.

Later his son, Rama V, added to the structure and housed a Buddha relic from India (given to him by the British government) in the chedi. The concrete walls were added during WW II to prevent the hill from eroding. Every November there is a big festival on the grounds of Wat Saket, which includes a candle-lit procession up the Golden Mount.

Admission to Wat Saket is free except for the final approach to the summit of the Golden Mount, which costs 5B.

Wat Rajanadda Across Mahachai Rd from Wat Saket and behind the Chalerm Thai movie theatre, this temple dates from the mid-19th century. It was built under Rama III and is an unusual specimen, possibly influenced by Burmese models. There is a well-known amulet market here selling all sizes, shapes and styles of Buddhist amulets or magic charms, (called *phra phim* in Thai) which feature not only images of the Buddha, but famous Thai monks and Indian deities.

This is an expensive place to purchase a charm, but a good place to look; these images are purported to protect the wearer from physical harm though some act as 'love charms'. Those amulets that are considered to be particularly powerful tend to cost thousands of baht and are worn by soldiers, taxi drivers and other Thai believers working in high-risk professions.

Wat Bowonniwet (Bovornives) Wat Bowon, on Phra Sumen Rd, is the national headquarters for the Thammayut monastic sect, the minority sect in relation to Mahanikai. King Mongkut, founder of the Thammayuts, began a royal tradition by residing here as a monk – in fact he was the abbot of Wat Bowon for several years. Bangkok's second Buddhist university, Mahamakut University, is housed here and there is an English-language Buddhist bookshop across the street from the main entrance to the wat.

Lak Muang Shrine
The 'City Pillar' is across the street from the east wall of Wat Phra Kaew, at the south end of Sanam Luang. This shrine encloses a wooden pillar erected by Rama I to represent the founding of the new Bangkok capital. The spirit of the pillar is considered the city's guardian deity and receives the daily supplications of countless Thai worshippers, some of whom commission classical Thai dancers to perform at the shrine. Some of the offerings include severed pigs' heads with sticks of incense sprouting from their foreheads.

Other Temples & Shrines
Wat Intarawihan, on Wisut Kasat Rd, near its junction with Samsen Rd just north of Banglamphu, is marked by its enormous modern-style standing Buddha 32 metres high. Entry to Wat In is by donation. Check out the hollowed-out air-con stupa with a lifelike image of Luang Paw Toh.

At Sao Ching-Cha, the 'giant swing', a spectacular Brahmin festival in honour of the Hindu god Shiva, used to take place each year until it was stopped during the reign of Rama VII. The giant swing is a block south of the Democracy Monument. Nearby is Wat Suthat with interesting Buddha images and panels illustrating incidents in the Buddha's life.

At the corner by what used to be the Erawan Hotel (now torn down and due to reopen in 1991 as the Grand Hyatt Erawan) is a small Brahmin shrine, San Phra Prom, which attracts a steady stream of worshippers. Many of them make an offering by commissioning the musicians and dancers who are always on hand to make an impromptu performance. There's a similar Brahmin shrine at Wat Khaek by the Narai Hotel. Another hotel shrine worth seeing is the lingam (phallus) shrine at the Hilton International in Nai Loet Park off Wireless Rd. Clusters of carved stone and wooden lingam receive a steady stream of worshippers - mostly young women seeking fertility.

There are also numerous temples on the Thonburi side of the river which are comparatively untouristed. See the *Canals of Thonburi* map for more information. They include Wat Kanlayanimit with its towering Buddha statue and, outside, the biggest bronze bell in Thailand. Wat Phailom on the banks of the Chao Phraya in Pathumthani Province is noted for the tens of thousands of open-billed storks that nest in the temple area from December to June.

East of Bangkok, on Sukhumvit Soi 101, is the enormous chedi at Wat Thammamongkhon, which is 95 metres high and contains a lift so you can ride to the top. The chedi is said to contain a hair of the Buddha presented to Thailand by the Sangharaja (head of a Theravada monastic order) of Bangladesh. The official grand opening ceremonies for the chedi will begin in 1993.

National Museum

On Na Phrathat Rd, west side of Sanam Luang, the National Museum is said to be the largest museum in South-East Asia, and it is an excellent place to learn something about Thai art before heading upcountry. All periods and styles are represented from Dvaravati to Ratanakosin and English-language literature is available.

Free English tours of the museum are given on Tuesdays (Thai culture), Wednesdays (Buddhism) and Thursdays (Thai art), beginning at 9.30 am. These guided tours are excellent value and numerous people have written to recommend them. The tours in German have been recommended.

The museum is open from 9 am to 12 noon and 1 to 4 pm every day except Mondays and Fridays; admission is 30B.

Royal Barges

The royal barges are fantastically ornamented boats used in ceremonial processions on the river. The largest is 50 metres long and requires a rowing crew of 54 men. The barges are kept in sheds on the Thonburi side of the river. They're on Khlong Bangkok Noi, near the Phra Pin Klao Bridge. *Suphanahong*, the king's personal barge, is the most important of the boats.

The barge shed is open daily from 8.30 am to 4.30 pm and admission is 10B. To get there, take a ferry to the Noi Station pier, then walk down the street parallel to the tracks

until you come to a bridge over the khlong (canal). Follow the bridge to a wooden walkway that leads to the barge sheds. You can also get there by taking a khlong taxi (5B) up the canal and getting off near the bridge.

Jim Thompson's House

Even though it sounds corny when described, this is a great place to visit, because of its authentic Thai residential architecture. Located at the end of an undistinguished soi next to Khlong San Saep, the premises once belonged to the American silk entrepreneur Jim Thompson, who deserves most of the credit for the current worldwide popularity of Thai silk. Thompson disappeared in the Cameron Highlands of west Malaysia under quite mysterious circumstances in 1967 and has never been heard from since. On display in the main house is his splendid, small Asian art collection as well as his personal belongings.

The Legendary American – The Remarkable Career & Strange Disappearance of Jim Thompson by William Warren (Houghton Mifflin Co, Boston, 1970) is an excellent book on Thompson, his career, residence and intriguing disappearance. In Thailand, it has been republished for distribution in Asia as *Jim Thompson: The Legendary American of Thailand* (Jim Thompson Thai Silk Co, Bangkok).

The house, on Soi Kasem San 2, Rama I Rd, is open Monday to Saturday from 9 am to 4.30 pm. Admission is 100B (proceeds go to Bangkok's School for the Blind) but you may wander around the grounds for free. Students get in for 40B. The rather sleazy khlong at the end of the soi is one of Bangkok's most lively.

Wang Suan Phakkard (Phakat)

The 'Lettuce Farm Palace' is a collection of five traditional wooden Thai houses – containing a varied collection of art, antiques and furnishings – in a beautiful garden with a pavilion. Special exhibitions include seashells and Ban Chiang pottery. In the noise and confusion of Bangkok, the gardens are a peaceful oasis complete with ducks and swans and a semi-enclosed garden reminiscent of Japanese gardens.

The palace is open daily except Sundays from 9 am to 4 pm and admission is 50B (students 30B). It's on Si Ayuthaya Rd, quite close to the Victory Monument.

Vimanmek Teak Mansion (Phra Thi Nang Wimanmek)

This beautiful L-shaped, three-storey mansion built of golden teak was the home of King Rama V in the early 1900s. The building contains 81 rooms and is said to be the world's largest golden teak building. Teak was once one of Thailand's greatest natural resources (it has since all but disappeared) and makes an especially good wood for building houses because it's so durable. A special oil contained in the wood makes teak resistant to heavy rain and hot sun and also repels insects. A solid piece of teak can easily last 1000 years.

The interior of the mansion contains various personal effects of the king and a number of art objects. There are English-language tours every half-hour between 11.15 am and 3 pm.

Vimanmek is open from 9.30 am to 4 pm daily and admission is 50B for adults, 20B for children. Note that it's free if you've already been to the Grand Palace/Wat Phra Kaew and kept the entry ticket for Vimanmek. Vimanmek is located off U-Thong Nai Rd (between Si Ayuthaya and Ratwithi Rds) next to the National Assembly, across from the west side of the Dusit Zoo.

Chinatown (Sampeng)

Off Yaowarat and Ratchawong Rds, Bangkok's Chinatown comprises a confusing and crowded array of jewellery, hardware, wholesale food, automotive and fabric shops, as well as dozens of other small businesses. It's a good place to shop since goods here are cheaper than almost anywhere else in Bangkok and the Chinese proprietors like to bargain. Chinese and Thai antiques in various grades of age and authenticity are available in the so-called Thieves Market or Nakhon Kasem, but it's better for browsing than buying these days.

Pahurat

At the edge of Chinatown, around the intersection of Pahurat and Chakraphet Rds, is a small but thriving Indian district, generally called Pahurat. Here dozens of Indian-owned shops sell all kinds of fabric and clothes. This is the best place in the city to bargain for such items, especially silk. The selection is unbelievable, and Thai shoulder bags (yaams) sold here are the cheapest in Bangkok, perhaps in Thailand.

Behind the more obvious store fronts along these streets, in the 'bowels' of the blocks, is a seemingly endless Indian bazaar selling not only fabric, but household items, food and other necessities. There are some good, reasonably priced Indian restaurants in this area, too, and a Sikh temple off Chakraphet Rd.

National Theatre – National Gallery

This is on Na Phrathat and Chao Fa Rds. Check here if you are interested in Thai classical drama, *lakhon*. Performances are usually excellent and admission fees very reasonable, around 40B depending on the seating. Attendance at a *khon* performance (masked dance-drama based on stories from the Ramakien) is highly recommended. On the last Friday of every month, there are special public exhibitions of Thai classical dance-drama at 5 pm. Contact the National Theatre at 221 5861 for details and for other current programming.

Opposite the theatre is the National Arts Gallery which displays traditional and contemporary art. It's closed Mondays and Fridays, open from 9 am to 12 noon and 1 to 4 pm on other days. Admission is 20B.

Ancient City

The Ancient City (Muang Boran) covers over 80 hectares and presents outstanding scaled-down facsimiles of many of the kingdom's most famous monuments. For students of Thai architecture, it's worth a day's visit (it takes an entire day to cover the area). The owner is Bangkok's largest Mercedes Benz dealer, who has an avid interest in Thai art.

The Ancient City Co (tel 226-1226/7) also

puts out a lavish bilingual periodical devoted to Thai art and architecture called *Muang Boran*. It is edited by some of Thailand's leading art historians. The Ancient City is in Samut Prakarn, 33 km from Bangkok along the Sukhumvit Highway. Admission to the site is 270B. The fare to the Samut Prakan terminal by public bus No 25 is 3B; from there get a songthaew to Muang Boran for 2B. Transportation can be also arranged through the Bangkok office at 78 Democracy Monument Circle, Ratchadamnoen Ave.

In the same area there is a Crocodile Farm, where you can even see crocodile wrestling! The crocodile farm is open from 8 am to 6 pm daily - the reptiles get their dinner between 5 and 6 pm. Admission is 80B. There are over 30,000 crocs here, as well as elephants, monkeys, and snakes.

Thai Boxing

Muay Thai, or Thai boxing, can be seen at two boxing stadiums, Lumpini (on Rama IV Rd near South Sathon Rd) and Ratchadamnoen (on Ratchadamnoen Nok Rd, next to the TAT office). Admission fees vary according to seating: the cheapest seats in Bangkok are now around 140B and ringside seats cost 500B or more. Mondays, Wednesdays, Thursdays and Sundays, the boxing is at Ratchadamnoen and Tuesdays, Fridays and Saturdays it's at Lumpini. The Ratchadamnoen matches begin at 6 pm, except for the Sunday shows which start at 5 pm, while the Lumpini matches all begin at 6.20 pm. Aficionados say the best-matched bouts are reserved for Tuesday nights at Lumpini and Thursday nights at Ratchadamnoen.

Almost anything goes in this martial sport, both in the ring and in the stands. If you don't mind the violence (in the ring) a Thai boxing match is worth attending for the pure spectacle – the wild musical accompaniment, the ceremonial beginning of each match and the frenzied betting around the stadium. The restaurants on the north side of the stadium are well-known for their delicious kai yang and other north-eastern dishes.

Thai boxing is also telecast on Channel 7 every Sunday afternoon; if you're wondering where everyone is, they're probably inside watching the national sport.

Most of what is known about the early history of Thai boxing comes from the Burmese accounts of warfare between Burma and Thailand during the 15th and 16th centuries. The earliest reference (1411 AD) mentions a ferocious style of unarmed combat that decided the fate of Thai kings. A later description tells how Nai Khanom Tom, Thailand's first famous boxer and a prisoner of war in Burma, gained his freedom by roundly defeating a dozen Burmese warriors before the Burmese court. To this day, many martial art aficionados consider the Siamese style the ultimate in hand-to-hand fighting. Hong Kong, China, Singapore, Taiwan, Korea, Japan, the United States, Holland, Germany and France have all sent their best and none of the challengers have been able to defeat top-ranked Thai boxers. On one famous occasion, Hong Kong's top five Kung Fu masters were dispatched in less than six and a half minutes cumulative total, all knock-outs.

King Naresuan the Great (1555 to 1605) was supposed to have been a top-notch boxer himself. He made Muay Thai a required part of military training for all Thai soldiers. Later another Thai king, Phra Chao Seua ('the Tiger King') further promoted Thai boxing as a national sport by encouraging prize fights and the development of training camps in the early 18th century. There are accounts of massive wagers and bouts to the finish during this time. Phra Chao Seua is said to have been an incognito participant in many of the matches during the early part of his reign. Combatants' fists were wrapped in thick horsehide for maximum impact with minimum knuckle damage. They also used cotton soaked in glue and ground glass and later hemp. Tree bark and seashells were used to protect the groin from lethal kicks.

The high incidence of death and physical injury led the Thai government to institute a ban on muay thai in the 1920s, but in the '30s, the sport was revived under a modern set of regulations based on the international Queensbury Rules. Bouts were limited to five rounds of three minutes duration each with a two-minute break in between. Contestants had to wear international-style gloves and trunks (always either in red or blue) and their feet were taped but no shoes worn. There are 16 weight divisions in Thai boxing, from mini-flyweight to heavyweight, with the best fighters said to be in the welterweight division (67 kg maximum). As in international-style boxing, matches take place on a 7.3 metre square canvas-covered floor with rope retainers supported by four padded posts, rather than the traditional dirt circle. In spite of these concessions to safety, today, all surfaces of the body are still considered fair targets and any part of the body may be used to strike an opponent, except the head. Common blows include high kicks to the neck, elbow thrust to the face and head, knee hooks to the ribs and

Top: Brahma shrine at the Erawan Hotel, Bangkok (JC)
Left: Wat Arun, Temple of the Dawn, Bangkok (TW)
Right: Pratunam, Bangkok (JC)

Top: Wat Phra Keo, Bangkok (JC)
Left: Wat Saket, The Golden Mount, Bangkok (JC)
Right: Wat Indrawihan, Bangkok (TW)

low crescent kicks to the calf. A contestant may even grasp an opponent's head between his hands and pull it down to meet an upward knee thrust. Punching is considered the weakest of all blows and kicking merely a way to 'soften up' one's opponent; it is the knee and elbow strikes that are decisive in most matches.

The training of a Thai boxer and particularly the relationship between boxer and trainer is highly ritualised. When a boxer is considered ready for the ring, he is given a new name by his trainer, usually with the name of the training camp as his surname. For the public, the relationship is perhaps best expressed in the *ram muay* or 'boxing dance' that takes place before every match. The ram muay ceremony usually lasts about five minutes and expresses obeisance to the fighter's guru (*khru*), as well as to the guardian spirit of Thai boxing. This is done through a series of gestures and body movements performed in rhythm to the ringside musical accompaniment of Thai oboe (*pii*) and percussion. Each boxer works out his own dance, in conjunction with his trainer and in accordance with the style of his particular camp. The woven headbands and armbands worn into the ring by fighters are sacred ornaments which bestow blessings and divine protection; the headband is removed after the ram muay ceremony, but the armband, which actually contains a small Buddha image, is worn throughout the match. After the bout begins, the fighters continue to bob and weave in rhythm until the action begins to heat up. The musicians continue to play throughout the match and the volume and tempo of the music rise and fall along with the events in the ring.

As Thai boxing has become more popular among westerners (both spectators and participants) there is an increasing number of bouts staged for tourists in places like Pattaya, Phuket and Ko Samui. In these, the action may be genuine but the judging below par. Nonetheless, there are dozens of authentic matches taking place every day of the year at the major Bangkok stadiums and in the provinces and these are easily sought out.

Even more westerners will probably take up Thai boxing after the release of the new Jean-Claude Van Damme martial arts flick, *The Kick Boxer*, which was recently filmed on location in Thailand. Those interested in training at a muay thai camp might try the PB Boxing Gym on Khao San Rd in Bangkok (behind PB Guest House) or the Sityodthong-Payakarun Boxing Camp in Naklua, north of Pattaya. Be forewarned, though, that the training is gruelling and features full-contact sparring.

Thai Classical Dancing

If you are not able to catch a free performance at the Lak Muang or Erawan Hotel shrines or one at the National Theatre, there are several restaurants and hotels that specialise in performances for tourists. Admission charges range from 150B to 300B and include a sumptuous Thai meal as well as martial art and sword-fighting demonstrations. One of the better places is the Baan Thai on Soi 32 (Soi Baan Thai) Sukhumvit Rd – the food is very good and is served in a traditional manner with diners seated at low tables. If you're looking for a splurge this might be it. Phiman Thai Theatre Restaurant (tel 258-7866), 46 Soi 49, Sukhumvit Rd, has also been recommended.

The historic Oriental Hotel, on Charoen Krung Rd, offers dance/martial art performances (the Kodak Siam Show) in the riverside garden every Sunday and Thursday at 11 am for 80B.

Floating Markets

Travellers who have been to the Thonburi floating market on Khlong Dao Kanong in recent years are divided in their opinions as to whether the trip is worth the early rising

to get there by 7 to 7.30 am. There are still plenty of boats out there, selling fresh produce and ready-to-eat foods, but there may be as many boatloads of tourists, not to mention lots of tourist shops.

If you're set on going it might be best to take one of the floating market tours that leave from the Oriental Pier (Soi Oriental) or Tha Phra Chan beside Thammasat University – your only alternative is to hire a boat of your own (at the Oriental Pier) to go up Khlong Dao Kanong and that can be quite expensive these days. Khlong Dao Kanong is located in south Thonburi, across the river from the terminus of Charoen Krung Rd, below Krung Thep Bridge. Floating market tours cost from 50B up but the cheapest tours probably only give you 20 minutes or so at the market. Be prepared for a very touristy experience.

There is a more lively and less commercial floating market on Khlong Damnoen Saduak in Rajburi Province, 104 km south-west of Bangkok, between Nakhorn Pathom and Samut Songkhram. You can get buses from the Southern Bus Terminal on Charansanitwong Rd in Thonburi to Damnoen Saduak starting at 5 am. See the Nakhon Pathom section in the Central Thailand chapter for more details.

At Khlong Bang Khu Wiang in Thonburi there is a small floating market between 4 and 7 am. Boats to the Khu Wiang Market (*talaat nam khuu wiang*) leave from the Tha Chang pier near Wat Phra Kaew every morning between 6.15 and 8 am.

Weekend Market

In 1982 the Weekend Market moved from Sanam Luang, near Wat Phra Kaew, to keep the grounds clear for Bangkok's bicentennial celebration. The market is now at Chatuchak Park, off Phahonyothin Rd, just above the Saphan Khwai district in north Bangkok, across from the Northern Bus Terminal. Aircon bus Nos 3, 9, 10 and 13 all pass the market – just get off before the Northern Bus Terminal. A dozen other ordinary city buses also pass the market.

Like the old weekend market at Sanam Luang, the new one is the Disneyland of

markets. Everything is sold here, from live chickens and snakes to opium pipes and herbal remedies. Thai clothing such as the phaakhamaa (sarong for men) and the phaasin (sarong for women), *kang kaeng jiin* (Chinese pants) and *seua maw hawm* (blue cotton farmer's shirt) are good buys. Best bargains of all are household goods like pots and pans, dishes, drinking glasses, etc. If you're moving to Thailand for an extended period, this is the place to pick up stuff for your kitchen. There is plenty of interesting and tasty food for sale if you're feeling hungry. Don't forget to try out your bargaining skills. The market is in operation all day Saturday and Sunday.

Other Markets

Atok Market, just across Kamphaeng Phet Rd from the new Weekend Market, is open every day of the week with a selection similar to the Weekend Market, including flowers and potted plants. Klong Toey Market, under the super highway at the intersection of Rama IV and Narong Rds in the Khlong Toey district, is possibly the cheapest all-purpose market in Bangkok (best on Wednesdays). Pratunam Market, at the intersection of Phetburi and Ratchaprarop Rds, runs every day and is very crowded, but has great deals in new, cheap clothing. There is good eating here, too.

Samyan Market is at the north-west corner of the intersection of Rama IV and Phayathai Rds, near Chulalongkorn University. It has all the usual stuff, but is worth a special trip for the tasty and cheap seafood restaurants along the first soi on the right off Phayathai Rd above Rama IV.

Shopping Centres

Bangkok has many large and small shopping centres. Central and Robinson department stores have branches in the Sukhumvit and Silom areas and have all the usual stuff – designer clothes, western cosmetics – plus supermarkets and Thai delis, cassette tapes, fabrics and other local products that might be of interest to some travellers. The Oriental (Soi Oriental, Charoen Krung Road) and River City (near the Royal Orchid Sheraton, off Charoen Krung Road and Si Phraya Rd) shopping complexes are for high-end consumer goods. They're expensive but do have some unique merchandise.

Along Ploenchit and Sukhumvit Rds you'll find many newer department stores and shopping centres, including Sogo and Landmark Plaza, but these Tokyo clones tend to be expensive and not that exciting.

One of the most varied shopping centres to wander around in is the Mah Boon Krong (MBK) centre near Siam Square. It's all aircon, but there are many little shops as well as flashy department stores. Bargains can be found here if you look.

Pasteur Institute – Snake Farm

At the Pasteur Institute, Rama IV Rd, venomous snakes are milked daily at 11 am and 2 pm (11 am only on weekends and holidays) to make snake bite antidotes which are distributed throughout the country. Feeding time is 3 pm. This will be boring to some, exciting to others. You can also get common vaccinations such as cholera, typhoid and smallpox here.

The 'farm' is open from 8.30 am to 4 pm daily, admission is 80B.

Siam Society

At 131 Sol Asoke, Sukhumvit 21, are the publishers of the renowned *Journal of the Siam Society* and valiant preservers of traditional Thai culture. The Society headquarters is a good place to visit for those with a serious interest in Thailand – a reference library is open to visitors and Siam Society monographs are for sale. Almost anything you'd want to know about Thailand (outside the political sphere, since the society is sponsored by the royal family) can be researched here. An ethnological museum of sorts, exhibiting Thai folk art is located on the Siam Society grounds in the Kamthieng House. Ban Kamthieng is open Tuesday to Saturday from 9 am to 12 midday and 1 to 5 pm. Admission is 25B.

Other Attractions

The Dusit Zoo (Khao Din Wana) may be of interest to zoo enthusiasts. It's big and quite

pleasant. The collection of animals is not extremely interesting, but they do have white elephants and it's a nice place to get away from the noise of the city and observe how the Thais amuse themselves – by eating mainly. Food is very good and cheap at the zoo! Entry to the zoo is 10B.

Bangkok has a host of artificial tourist attractions including Timland (Thailand in Miniature), an example of the 'see the whole country in half an hour' park which every South-East Asian country seems to have. The Rose Garden Country Resort is south of Bangkok on the Thachin River and includes a Thai cultural village. Admission to the garden area is 10B, another 140B for the 3 pm performances in the cultural village. The garden is open from 8 am to 6 pm daily.

Bangkok also has a science museum and a planetarium, both on Sukhumvit Rd. At Meen Buri, Siam Park is a huge recreational park with pools, water slides, a wave pool and the like. Highly recommended for a splash. Admission is 100B; get there via bus No 27.

River & Canal Trips

Bangkok to Nonthaburi You can observe urban river life from the water for 1½ hours for only 7B by climbing aboard a Chao Phraya River Express boat at Tha Wat Ratchasingkhon, just north of the Krung Thep Bridge. If you want to ride the entire length of the express route all the way to Nonthaburi, this is where you must begin. Ordinary buses Nos 1, 22, 75 and air-con bus No 4 go by this pier. Or you could board at any other express boat pier in Bangkok for a shorter ride to Nonthaburi (eg 20 minutes from Tha Phayap, first stop north of the Krung Thon Bridge, or 30 minutes from Tha Phra Athit in Banglamphu). Express boats run about every 15 minutes from 6 am to 6 pm daily. See the River Transport section in Getting Around for more information on the Chao Phraya express boat service.

Khlong Bangkok Noi Another good boat trip is the Bangkok Noi canal taxi route which leaves from Tha Phra Chan next to Thammasat University. The fare is only a few baht and the further up Khlong Bangkok Noi you go, the better the scenery gets – teak houses on stilts, old wats, plenty of greenery – as if you were upcountry, and in a sense you are.

Other Canals From Tha Tien pier near Wat Pho, get a canal taxi to Khlong Mon (leaving every half-hour) for 4B for more typical canal scenery, including orchid farms. From the Tha Phibun Songkram pier in Nonthaburi you can get a boat taxi up picturesque Khlong Om and see durian plantations. Boats leave every 15 minutes. It is possible to go as far from Bangkok as Suphanburi and Ratburi (Ratchaburi) by boat, though this may involve many boat connections. Beware of 'agents' who will try to put you on the boat and rake off an extra commission. Before travelling by boat, establish the price – you can't bargain when you're in the middle of the river!

Finally, if you're really a canal freak, I suggest you lay out 150B for *50 Trips Through Siam's Canals* by Geo-Ch Veran (translated from French into English by Sarah Bennett, 1979, Editions Duang Kamol). The book contains 25 detailed maps and clear instructions on how to take the various trips – some of which are very time consuming.

River Cruises A dozen or more companies in Bangkok run regular dinner cruises along the Chao Phraya for rates ranging from 30B to 500B per person, depending on how far they go and whether dinner is included with the fare. Most require advance phone reservations. The following cruises cost from 400 to 500B per person, including dinner:

Oriental Hotel (tel 236-0400/9)
  Oriental Pier to Nonthaburi, Wednesdays only
Loy Nava Co (tel 437-4932/7329)
  River City Pier to Wasukri Pier, daily
Thasaneeya Nava (tel 437-4932)
  River City Pier to Wasukri Pier, daily
Dinner Cruise Co (tel 234-5599)
  River City Pier to Krung Thon Bridge, daily

The following cruises cost from 25 to 40B per person, plus dinner as ordered:

Ban Khun Luang Restaurant (tel 243-3235)
  Ban Khun Luang Restaurant to Oriental Hotel, Thursday, Friday, Saturday
Yok-Yor Restaurant (tel 281-1829)
  Wisut Kasat Pier to Menam Hotel, daily
Khanap Nam Restaurant (tel 433-6611)
  Krung Thon Bridge to Sathon Bridge, daily
River Sight-Seeing, Ltd (tel 437-4047)
  River City Pier to Nonthaburi, daily
Riverside Co (tel 4249848)
  Krung Thon Bridge to Rama IX Bridge, daily

There are also longer day and overnight cruises on the river. The Chao Phraya River Express Boat Co (tel 222-5330, 225-3002/3) does a tour starting from Tha Maharat at 8 am and returning at 5.30 pm that includes visits to the Thai Folk Arts & Handicrafts Centre, Bang Pa In Palace in Ayuthaya, and Wat Pailom bird sanctuary. The price is a very reasonable 140B per person, not including lunch, which you arrange on your own in Bang Pa In.

The Oriental Hotel's luxurious all-air-con Oriental Queen (236-0400/9) also does a cruise to Bang Pa In that leaves at 8 am and returns at 5 pm. The Oriental Queen cruise costs 770B including lunch. Note that neither of the above cruises really allows enough time to see Ayuthaya properly, so if that's your primary intention, don't go.

Asia Voyages (tel 235-4100/4) has recently launched the Mekhala, a restored teak rice barge that has been transformed into a six-cabin cruiser. The Mekhala leaves Bangkok in the afternoon on Saturday, Monday and Thursday (or from Ayuthaya on Sunday, Tuesday, and Friday) and heads upriver toward Ayuthaya (or downriver toward Bangkok). In the evening it anchors at Wat Praket where a candle-lit dinner is served. The next morning passengers offer food to the monks from the wat, and then the barge moves on to Bang Pa In. After a tour of the Summer Palace, a long-tail boat takes passengers on for a tour of the ruins of Ayuthaya. The return to Bangkok is by air-con bus. The cost is 2800B per person double occupancy and includes all meals, accommodation, admission fees in Ayuthaya and transfers from your hotel.

Places to Stay – bottom end & middle

There is really quite a variety of places to stay in Bangkok, only some are harder to find than others. Your choice actually depends on what part of the city you want to be in – the tourist ghettos of Sukhumvit Rd and Silom-Surawong Rds, the 'world traveller' ghetto of Banglamphu (north of Ratchadamnoen Klang), the Siam Square area, Chinatown, or the old traveller centre on/off Soi Ngam Duphli around the Malaysia Hotel off Rama IV.

Chinatown/Hualamphong and Banglamphu are the best all-round areas for seeing the real Bangkok and are the cheapest districts for eating and sleeping. The Siam Square area is also well located, in that it's more or less in the centre of Bangkok – this, coupled with the good selection of city buses that pass through the Rama I and Phayathai Rd intersection, makes even more of the city accessible. In addition, Siam Square has a good bookshop, several banks, cheap foodstalls and excellent middle-range restaurants, travel agencies and three movie theatres. Don't confuse Siam Square with the Siam Centre across the street, a large air-con shopping complex for foreigners and rich Thais.

Central Banglamphu If you're really on a tight budget head for Khao San Rd, near the Democracy Monument, parallel to Ratchadamnoen Klang Rd – ordinary buses Nos 17, 44, 56 and 59 will get you there, also a No 11 air-con bus. This is becoming much more the main travellers' centre these days and new guest houses are springing up continuously and radiating in all directions.

A landmark here, although it's in a much higher price bracket (500B up), is the big *Viengtai Hotel*. About 20 years ago, this was one of the three main cheapies in Bangkok, before the advent of guest houses (the other two were the Malaysia Hotel and the Thai Song Greet).

Rates elsewhere in Banglamphu are generally the lowest in Bangkok and although some of the places are basic, a few are excellent value if you can pay just a bit more. At the bottom end, rooms are quite small and the walls dividing them are thin – in fact most are indistinguishable from one another. Some have small attached cafes with limited menus. Bathrooms are always down the hall or out the back somewhere. The least expensive rooms are 40/70B a single/double, though these are hard to come by due to the hordes of people seeking them out. In the high season (pretty much every month except June and September), you'd better take the first vacant bed you come across. The best time of day to find a vacancy is around 9 to 10 am. At night during the peak months, December to March, Khao San Rd is bursting with life.

One of the Banglamphu originals, the *VS Guest House* has two locations, at 136 Tanao Rd (an alley off Khao San Rd) and 1/3 Prachatipatai Rd, near the Thai Hotel. Both hotels have rooms for 40B per person or 70B for doubles, which are dark and not particularly clean, but adequate. Close to the first VS on Tanao is the *Harn Guest House*, another small but slightly nicer place for 60 to 100B.

Entering Khao San from the east, one of the first places you'll come to on the left is *Chada Guest House*, with nice digs for 80 to 100B. Next on the left is *CH Guest House* (they're big on initials here) that is decent value for 40 to 80B. They also do a 180B tour bus ticket to Chiang Mai that includes two free nights at the Khao San Guest House in Chiang Mai (but you don't have to stay at CH to buy the ticket). Just beyond CH on the same side of the street is the relatively new *Grand Guest House* where clean doubles are 100B – there are no singles available.

Make a left at the first little soi and you'll find three long-running guest houses: the *Marco Polo Guest House* (also called 160 Guest House) for 40 to 80B; the *Good Luck Guest House* at 50 to 80B; and the best of the three, *VIP Guest House* (tel 282-5090), where all rooms are 80B. On the right side of Khao San Rd, opposite the VIP soi, are two not-so-clean places that each charge 60 to 100B, the *PR 215 Guest House* and the *Nat Guest House* – if you have an alternative to these, you might want to take it. Continuing

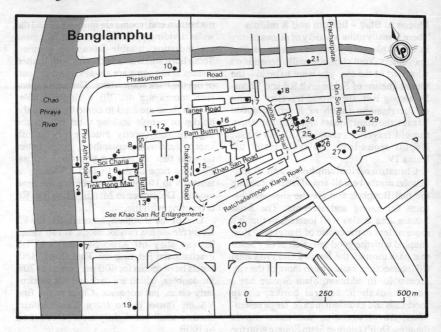

Banglamphu

1   Phra Athit Pier (for Chao Phraya
    Express)
2   UNICEF
3   Beer & Peachy Guest House
4   New Siam Guest House
5   Ngam Pit & Apple Guest House
6   Rose Garden & Golf Guest House
7   Wang Ngar Restaurant
8   Merry V Guest House
9   Mango Guest House
10 Siam Commercial Bank
11 Chusri Guest House
12 Tum I/Haircut Guest House
13 Apple Guest House
14 Wat Chana Songkhram

15 Chana Songkhram Police Station
16 Viengtai Hotel
17 Post Office
18 Wat Bowonniwet
19 National Museum
20 Royal Hotel
21 Bovorn-Nivet Youth Hostel
22 Nice Guest House
23 Central Guest House
24 New Privacy Guest House
25 Post Office
26 Sweety Guest House
27 Democracy Guest House
28 Vijit Restaurant
29 Prasuri Guest House

westward along Khao San, turn right at the next soi and you'll find the old *Charoendee Hotel* where large rooms with character go for 120B. This used to be a favourite but seems to have gone sadly downhill and is ill-kept with negligible service. It's fairly quiet though, since it's off the street.

Across Khao San Rd and down an alley are two of the first guest houses to appear in Banglamphu years ago. The *Bonny Guest House* (tel 281-9877) costs 40/50/80B for dorm/single/double beds, and is fairly clean and friendly. The *Top (also Tum) Guest House* (tel 281-9954) is next door to the

Bonny guest house and owned by the same family. Rates are 60/80/120B for single/double/triple rooms. The newer *Dior Guest House* down the same soi has small rooms for 50/100B.

On the north side of Khao San nearby are two older Chinese hotels set back off the road. The *Khaosan Palace Hotel (New Si Phranakhorn Hotel)* (tel 282-0578), 139 Khao San Rd, has seen better days and rooms cost from 150B with ceiling fan and attached bath. This hotel is undergoing a name change. Practically next door to New Si Phranakhorn Hotel is the *New Nith Charoen Suke Hotel* (tel 281-9872) with similar rates and rooms to the Si Phranakhorn but slightly better service.

The next alley on the right heading west along Khao San winds through the block toward Ram Buttri Rd and leads to several cramped places that nonetheless manage to fill up. The names change from time to time; at this writing the guest houses here were named *Doll, Suneeporn, Pro, Lek* and *AT*. All feature small luggage-crammed lobbies with staircases leading to rooms layered on several floors and which cost around 60 to 100B. I would avoid this alley altogether unless there's no other choice – it's simply too crowded and closed in.

On the other side of the street at 74 Khao San Rd is *PB Guest House*, at the back of the snooker hall. Mr Lu, the proprietor, speaks pretty good English and is very helpful to travellers. It costs 80B for a room with two beds or 40B in a 20-bed dorm. You can get cheap Thai food here (also western breakfasts). His wife, Varapin, runs the PB Thai Boxing Gym and some of the boxers stay at the guest house. This has a definite sporting atmosphere – it's not for everybody. Across from PB are two adequate newer places, the *Buddy Guest House* where singles/doubles are 60/100B or 120B for a larger room with a window overlooking the street, and *Lek Guest House* (tel 281-2775) which also has fairly good-size rooms for 80 to 100B. Don't confuse this Lek with the Lek mentioned earlier.

Next along the same side of Khao San are *Mama's Guest House* and the *Hello Restau-*

rant & Guest House (tel 281-8579). Mam's is 80 to 100B, nothing special, but the Hello is well run and has one of the better restaurants on Khao San Rd. Good-size, clean rooms at Hello are 60/100B single/double or 160B with air-con. The air-con rooms have windows overlooking the street. Hello has another restaurant and guest house further down Khao San on the other side with similar conditions and rates.

Between this latter Hello Guest House and the Chakrapong Rd intersection, you'll find the *PR* and *NS* guest houses with similar rates to the Hello. The NS has doubles overlooking the street for 100B. Across the street the newer *Sitdhi Guest House & Restaurant* is similar to the Hello but singles are 50B. The *Ploy Guest House* is right on the corner of Khao San and Chakrapong Rds, above a coffee house/nightclub. Rooms are clean and large and go for 80/120/160 a single/double/triple.

North from here on Chakrapong Rd you'll find several more guest houses which catch the overflow from Khao San Rd, including an alley with *Chuanpis, Chakrapong* and *J* guest houses and further north the *Siam Guest House*, all in the 60 to 100B range. By the time you arrive, book in hand, there will probably be several more guest houses on and off Chakrapong, as local businesses change over to accommodation.

There are several guest houses clustered in the alleys east of Tanao Rd. In general, rooms are bigger here than at places on Khao San. *Central Guest House* (tel 282-0667) is just off Tanao Rd on Trok Bowonrangsi (*trok* means alley) – look for the rather inconspicuous signs. It's a very pleasant guest house, with clean, quiet rooms for 40B per person. There are some more spacious doubles for 100B. *Nice Guest House*, nearby, is the same price and not bad either. The *New Privacy Guest House* is fair, but perhaps overpriced at 100 to 150B for what you get.

Further south off Trok Bowonrangsi is *59 Guest House* which has a variety of accommodation at 40B dorm, 50 to 60B single and 80 to 100B for large doubles. Around the corner on a small road parallel to Ratchadamnoen Klang is *Sweety Guest*

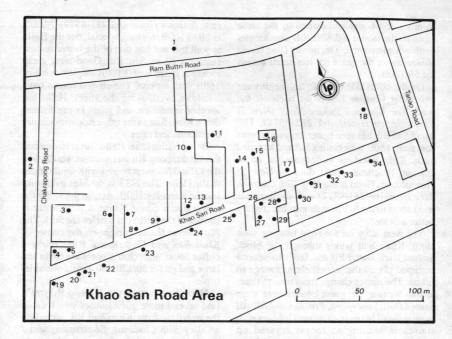

Ram Buttri Road

Tanao Road

Chakrapong Road

Khao San Road

Khao San Road Area

0   50   100 m

1	Viengtai Hotel
2	Wat Chana Songkhram
3	Chana Songkhram Police Station
4	Siam Guest House
5	Chuanpis, Chakrapong & J Guest House
6	Wally Guest House
7	Chart & Hello Guest House
8	Hello Restaurant
9	Mama's Guest House
10	Student Guest House & several others
11	Dolls Guest House & several others
12	Lek Guest House
13	Buddy Guest House
14	Khao San Palace Hotel
15	New Nith Charoen Hotel
16	Charoendee Hotel
17	PR215 & Nat Guest House
18	Harn & VS Guest House
19	Ploy Guest House
20	NS Guest House
21	PR Guest House
22	Hello Restaurant
23	VC Guest House
24	PB Guest House
25	Popular Cafes
26	Bonny & Top Guest House
27	Dior Guest House
28	Marco Polo/160 Guest House
29	Good Luck Guest House
30	VIP Guest House
31	Rit's Cafe & Ice Guest House
32	Grand Guest House
33	CH Guest House
34	Chada Guest House

House (tel 281-6756) with good rooms for 40B per person, right opposite a post office. They have a roof terrace for lounging and hanging clothes. If you follow this road straight through, away from Tanao Rd, you'll run into Din So Rd. Cross Din So, walk away from the traffic circle and you'll see a sign for *Prasuri Guest House* (tel 280-1428), recommended by several readers. It's down Soi Phra Suri on the right and has pleasant, clean rooms for 120/140/210B a single/double/triple and a good noticeboard.

Up on Phra Sumen Rd, near to where Din So Rd becomes Prachatipatai Rd, is the new *Bovorn-Nivet Youth Hostel* (tel 281-6387) which is located over a clinic. Large clean rooms with fan are 70 to 120B, or 170B with air-con. Just north of Phra Sumen Rd (cross Khlong Banglamphu) is *Noi Guest House* (tel 282-2898), affiliated with Noi Guest House of Chiang Mai fame. It's on the 4th floor of an apartment building at 52/9 Soi Ban Phan Thom and gets a breeze most of the time.

Further north-east on a soi off Prachatipatai Rd, near Wat Makut, is a branch of the Bonny Guest House called *James' Guest House* (tel 280-0362). Clean doubles here are only 80B. Another good find is the *River Guest House* (tel 280 0876), which is at 18/1 Soi Wat Samphraya, off Chakrapong Rd near the river and the Wat Samphraya boat landing, north of Phra Sumen Rd; rooms are 60 to 100B. A comfortable middle-range hotel in this area is the *Trang Hotel* (tel 282-2141), 99/8 Wisut Kasat Rd, where rooms start at 400B.

Guest houses are multiplying all over this area and you can walk down just about any street or soi in the Chakrapong-Khao San-Tanao Rd area in Banglamphu and stumble on new guest houses. During the height of the tourist season it may be difficult to find a bed, but keep trying because there seems to be no end to the ingenuity and enterprise of the folks in Banglamphu.

West Banglamphu Several newer guest houses are found on sois between Chakrapong Rd and the Chao Phraya River, putting them within walking distance of the Phra Athit Pier where you can catch express boats down or up the river. This area is also convenient to the Bangkok Noi Railway Station across the river, the National Museum and the National Theatre. West of Chakrapong at 61/1 Soi Ram Buttri is *Chusri Guest House* (tel 282-9948) and *Tum 1 Guest House* (also on Ram Buttri; look for the 'Haircut' sign), both of which have adequate rooms for 40B per person but are nothing

special. Round the corner to the left on the right side of Soi Ram Buttri is the newer *Merry V Guest House* with 60 to 100B rooms. A reader has also recommended *My House* (tel 282-9623) at 37 Soi Ram Buttri, which has nice rooms with windows for 100B, without windows 80B.

Turn right on Soi Chana Songkhram and head west and you'll come to the very nice *New Siam Guest House* (tel 282-4554) where good, quiet rooms are 60 to 100B. Continue on toward the river and you'll hit Phra Athit Rd. On the east side of Phra Athit Rd are *Beer Guest House* and *Peachy Guest House*, which are more like small hotels than family-type guest houses. The Beer is basic but airy, and rooms go for 70 to 100B. Peachy (tel 281-6471) has a pleasant garden restaurant and rooms for 75/120B, or 320B with air-con.

Parallel to Soi Chana on Trok Rong Mai, off Phra Athit Rd, are a few semi-old timers. Most have only two-bed rooms. The *Apple Guest House* (tel 281-6838), 10/1 Trok Rong Mai may not look like much, but it's very popular at 40B per person. Sometimes they put people up in the corridor for 20B if it's really full. The family who run it are helpful, there's a notice board, good food and a garden to sit in. There's also an *Apple Guest House II* out on Soi Ram Buttri close by, which one traveller recommended as being better. The *Ngam Pit Guest House*, 28/2 Trok Rong Mai is also pretty good; it serves food, and costs the same as the Apple.

The *Rose Garden Guest House* (formerly Roof Garden Guest House) (tel 281-8366), 28/6 Trok Rong Mai has very clean doubles for 80B with a fan and shared bath. The rooms are a bit box-like and bare though. On the roof you can get an aerial view of Bangkok and the Chao Phraya River. The *Golf Guest House* next door offers similar accommodation for 40/50/100B a dorm/single/double.

Around Banglamphu – National Library The area north of Banglamphu near the National Library is becoming another little travellers enclave. Heading north up Samsen Rd (the extension of Chakrapong Rd) from

Khao San Rd, you'll come to *TV Guest House* (tel 282-7451) at 7 Soi Phra Sawat, just off Samsen Rd to the right (east). It's good value at 40B for a dorm bed or 80B for a double in this clean and modern guest house.

Continue another km or so to the place where Phitsanulok Rd dead ends on Samsen and where Si Ayuthaya Rd crosses Samsen. Just beyond this junction is the National Library. At 71 Si Ayuthaya on the river side of Samsen Rd is the very popular *Sawatdee* (tel 282-5349), a friendly family-run guest house. It's very basic but clean and well kept, the rooms have fans and it's fairly quiet. Dorm beds are 40B, singles are 50B and 60B, doubles 80B. There's a good market right across the road. Near the Sawatdee is the equally popular *Shanti (Santi) Lodge* (tel 281-2497) where rooms are 55/110B.

Bangkok International Youth Hostel (tel 282-0950) is in the same neighbourhood at 25/2 Phitsanuloke Rd. Dorm beds are 35B, rooms with bath are 120 to 150B. Add a 10B surcharge if you don't have a IYHF card.

Soi Ngam Duphli This area, off Rama IV Rd where the Malaysia, Boston Inn, and Privacy Hotels are located, is where most budget travellers used to come on their first trip to Bangkok. These hotels are not cheap or even good value any more, but other places have opened up in the vicinity with lower rates (60 to 200B range). The entrance to this soi is on Rama IV Rd, near the intersection with Sathon Tai Rd, within walking distance of the imposing Dusit Thani Hotel and Lumpini Park. As a travellers' centre Soi Ngam Duphli is falling from favour as it has simply become too expensive for many backpackers.

If, however, you have a lot of visa collection and airline ticket business to do then it's definitely worth considering Soi Ngam Duphli. It's close to many of the embassies and the main airline office area (Silom Rd). Banglamphu is a good 45-minute bus ride from the area.

The following buses pass by the entrance to Soi Ngam Duphli along Rama IV Rd:

ordinary bus Nos 4, 13, 22, 45, 47, 74, 109 and 115, plus air-con bus No 7.

The *Malaysia Hotel* (tel 286-3582/7263) at 54 Soi Ngam Duphli was once Bangkok's most famous travellers' hotel. In 1975 you could get an air-con room here for 79B. It's 120 air-con standard/superior rooms now go for 312 to 396B for a single, 362 to 426B for a twin, 450 to 500B for a triple and all rooms have hot water. The Malaysia has a swimming pool which may be used by visitors for 50B per day. The notice board which used to be full of the most amazing information and misinformation from all over Asia is now strictly second rate. In fact the Malaysia seems to be making a conscious effort to distance itself from the travellers' market. It's been jazzed up a bit – the lobby area has noisy video game machines – and a backpack is starting to look rather out of place. A big sign out the front advertises 'Day-Off International Club – Paradise for Everyone – You'll Never Be Alone Again', which gives you an idea what kind of clientele the Malaysia is trying to lure these days.

The *Privacy Hotel* (tel 286-2339, 286-8811) is also fully air-con and costs 230B for a double. Many 'short-time' residents here give the place a sleazy kind of feel, but it's actually quieter than the Malaysia, and less of a 'scene'. It's across the road to the south of the Malaysia. In the other direction from the Malaysia is the *LA Hotel* (the English sign just says 'Hotel'), a bit better value if you don't need air-con but also on the short-time circuit – 180B for large rooms with bath and fan.

The *Boston Inn* is on Soi Si Bamphen, off Soi Ngam Duphli. Decaying rooms are 170/190B a single/double with fan and bath; there are no longer any air-con rooms or dorm here. Unlike the Malaysia, the Boston Inn seems to have made an effort to downgrade its facilities and service and is no longer recommended. Almost anywhere is better than here.

Also on Soi Ngam Duphli is the rather commercial-looking *Sweet House Complex* (tel 286-5774) where rooms are 60/70/100B without bath depending on the size of the room. For 140B you can get a room with attached bath and for 250B there are a couple of rooms with air-con and bath. Further south down Ngam Duphli toward the Malaysia is an alley on the left with *Anna* and *Lee 2 Guest House* (there are also a Lee 1 and Lee 3 elsewhere in the area) guest houses. Both have rooms with shared bath starting at 80B; Lee is the better value all round.

Turn left (east) on Soi Si Bamphen and before you arrive at the Boston Inn is an alley to the right. On the left corner of the alley is the *TTO Guest House* and a bit further down on the right is *RSC Guest House*. RSC is forgettable and overpriced, but TTO has adequate rooms with fan for 80B, or 100B air-con (cheapest air-con room in Bangkok), and shared bath. Across Soi Si Bamphen from here is another alley where *Home Sweet Home Guest House* is located. It's a friendly place with rooms for 60/80/100B a single/double/triple. Further down Si Bamphen past the Boston Inn is another alley on the right with a guest house on either corner, *My Place* and *Sabai House*. Both have bar/restaurants on the bottom floor with rooms upstairs that go for 60 to 80B. My Place has the better rooms but the bar can be rather noisy. Down this same alley on the right is *Freddy 3 Guest*

House (tel 287-1665) with basic but clean accommodation (like the other two Freddys) for 80 to 100B.

Make a left at the next soi down Si Bamphen, then a right at the first opportunity and you'll end up in a cul-de-sac with three very good guest houses. *Madam Guest House* has a legion of loyal followers for its 60B rooms and friendly service. Next door, the *Lee 3 Guest House*, the best of the Lee guest houses, is also quite pleasant and has large rooms for 100B up. The *Sala Thai Daily Mansion* (tel 287-1436) is at the end of the alley and has large, very clean rooms for 100 to 150B, plus a nice sitting area downstairs.

Back out on Soi Si Bamphen going east are four more guest houses (maybe more by now) starting with *Lee 1 Guest House* (80B up), *Kit's Youth Center* (100 to 150B), *Welcome Guest House* (90B) and *Freddy 2* (tel 286-7826) (80 to 100B). All four are very similar and feature medium-size rooms and shared baths.

If you're wondering about the original *Freddy Guest House* (tel 286-6722), it's still down Soi Ngam Duphli past the Privacy Hotel on the left in a building with maze-like

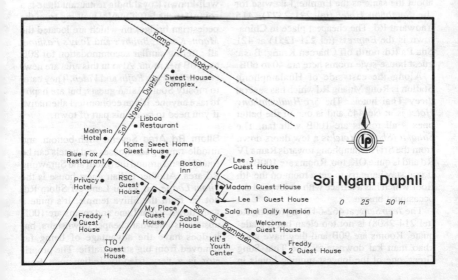

Soi Ngam Duphli

passageways. Freddy 1 has a choice of rooms without bath for 60 to 70B or rooms with attached bath for 120 to 130B.

Chinatown-Hualamphong This area is central and colourful although rather noisy. There are numerous cheap hotels but it's not a travellers' centre like Soi Ngam Duphli or Banglamphu. Watch your pockets and bag around the Hualamphong area, both on the street and on the bus. The cream of the razor artists operate here as the railway passengers make good pickings.

The *New Empire Hotel* (tel 234-6990/6) is at 572 Yaowarat Rd, near the intersection with Charoen Krung (New) Rd, a short walk from Wat Traimit. Doubles are 190B – a bit noisy but a great location if you like China-town. Air-con rooms with hot water are available for 250B. The New Empire has a swimming pool and is a favourite among Thais from the southern region.

Other Chinatown hotels of this calibre, most without English signs out front, can be found along Yaowarat, Chakraphet and Ratchawong Rds. The *Burapha Hotel* (tel 221-3545/9), at the intersection of Chakraphet and Charoen Krung Rds, on the edge of Chinatown, is not too bad with rates about the same as the Empire. Likewise for the *Somboon Hotel* (tel 221-2327), 415 Yaowarat Rd. The cheapest place in China-town is the *Empress* (tel 221-1251) at 421 Sua Pa Rd, north off Charoen Krung. Basic guest house-style rooms here are 40 to 60B.

Along the east side of Hualamphong Station is Rong Muang Rd which has several dicey Thai hotels. The *Sri Hualamphong Hotel* is at No 445 and is one of the better ones – all rooms are 100B with fan. The *Sahakit (Shakij) Hotel* is a few doors down from the Sri Hualamphong towards Rama IV Rd and is quite OK, too. Rooms are 100B up; if you stay here, try to get a room on the 4th floor which has a terrace with a view and the occasional breeze.

The *Jeep Seng*, at 462-64 Rong Muang Rd (tel 214-2808) is not too clean but it's ade-quate. Rooms are 90B and they have good khao man kai downstairs. The Thai Song Greet, one of the longest-running hotels in

this area and a rock bottom travellers' favour-ite for many years, has now disappeared.

Out towards the front of the station, after Rong Muang Rd makes a sharp curve, is the *Station Hotel*, a classic third-world dive. A room with torn curtains, dim sheets and crusty attached bath costs an astounding 120B. What's more astounding is that it seems to be nearly full all the time!

Many travellers have written to recom-mend a guest house near Hualamphong called *TT Guest House* (tel 236-3053). From the station, cross Rama IV Rd, walk left down Rama IV, then right on Mahanakhorn and look for signs to TT. It's about 10-minute walk, at 138 Soi Wat Mahaphruttharam, off Mahanakhorn Rd. It's a bit difficult to find as it's in a little alley but if you follow the signs it's worth the effort as it's very clean and friendly with singles/doubles for 60/100B. They also run a 'left luggage service' which is cheaper than the one at the airport and they also have a laundry service.

There are also several guest houses in the 'India-town' area of Pahurat, on or off Chakraphet Rd. On Chakraphet is the *Amarin Guest House*, with a sign in English, Thai, Hindi and Arabic. Rooms are 80B up and fairly clean. Further down towards the well-known Royal India restaurant there is a soi (off to the left if you're walking from the pedestrian bridge) on which are located the *Moon*, *Kamal*, *Bobby's* and *Tony's Fashion*, all offering similar accommodation for 80B to 100B per room. Also in this area are new-comers *US Pop*, *Rajin* and *Video*. They cater to mostly South Asian guests, but are happy to take anyone. It's an economical alternative if you need to be in this part of town.

Silom Rd Area Several high-bottom and middle-range guest houses and hotels can be found in and around the Silom and Surawong Rd area. Another Indian guest house is the *Silom Lodge*, on Vaithi Lane off Silom Rd, not far from the Shiva temple. It's quite a walk down Vaithi Lane and rooms are 100B upstairs, somewhat cheaper downstairs, but it does have the advantage of being far removed from big street traffic. The propri-etor is a very friendly Indian man from

Madras (a retired gem dealer) and his kitchen serves delicious south Indian food.

The *Suriwong Hotel* (tel 233-3223/5) is in a soi parallel to Patpong 1 Rd, off Surawong Rd. All rooms have air-con and hot water and go for 350B up. Nearby, out on Surawong Rd is old-timer *Rose Hotel* (tel 233-7695/7); comfortable air-con rooms here are 500B and usually full, but there are some bungalows out the back with cheaper rooms that may be available.

On the south side of Silom Rd is Soi Suksavitthaya (Suksa Witthaya), where two good middle-range places are located. First is *Niagara Hotel* (tel 233-5783/4) at 26 Soi Suksavitthaya, where clean air-con rooms with hot water and telephone are 300B, fan rooms under 200B. Further on at 37 Soi Suksavitthaya is *Sathon Inn* (tel 234-4110) which is similar but all air-con.

Also off Silom is *Bangkok Christian Guest House* (tel 233-6303) at 123 Sala Daeng Soi 2, Convent Rd. It has very nice fan-cooled rooms for 380B including breakfast; air-con rooms cost as much as 660B, also with breakfast. Nearby at 3 Convent Rd is the *Swiss Guest House* (tel 234-1107) where clean, comfortable air-con rooms are 300 to 600B depending on the size of the room.

On the river near the Royal Orchid Sheraton are a couple of decent middle-range guest houses. One worth mentioning is the *Riverview Guest House* (tel 234-5429) at Soi Wanit 2. Clean rooms are 300B with fan, 500B with air-con (some have river views). It can be quite difficult to locate even though it's only about 200 metres from the Sheraton. If you call from the Sheraton River City shopping complex, someone from the guest house will pick you up.

Siam Square Area There are several good places in this central area. Unfortunately, several have raised their rates sharply in response to high occupancy in the last couple of years. One place that has not changed its rates is the *Scout Hostel* on Rama I Rd, next to the National Stadium. Dorm beds are still only 30B per night here.

There are several middle-range places on or near Soi Kasem San I, off Rama I Rd near Jim Thompson's house and the National Stadium. The *Muangphol (Muangphon) Building* on the corner of Soi Kasem San 1 and Rama I Rd (931/8 Rama I Rd) has doubles for 380B. It's good value for the discriminating traveller who can afford it – with air-con, restaurant downstairs, friendly staff and good service. Bathrooms have hot water and western-style toilets, both of which function well. The *Star Hotel* is at 36/1, at the end of Soi Kasem San 1. The Star is a classic sort of mid-60s Thai hotel, with fairly clean, comfortable, air-con rooms with bath for 300 to 500B a double, depending on the room. The *Reno Hotel* is between the Muangphol Building and the Star on Soi Kasem 1 and costs 400/450B for single/double rooms; it has similar facilities to the Muangphol.

A new addition to Soi Kasem San I is the friendly and pleasant *A-One Inn* (tel 215-3029) at No 25/12-15, across the street and down a bit from the Reno. Air-con doubles with bath and hot water range from 300B. Also new on this soi is the *Pranee Building*, which has one entrance next to the Muangphol and another on Rama I Rd. Fan-cooled rooms with private bath are 250 to 300B; air-con rooms with hot water start at 350B. The Pranee also does some long term rentals at reasonable rates. Travellers have also recommended the *Krit Thai Mansion* (215-3042), 931/1 Rama I Rd (across from the National Stadium). For 800 to 1000B the facilities include air-con, hot water, private bath, telephone, colour TV, fridge and free newspapers in the lobby. The coffee shop downstairs is open 24 hours.

Sukhumvit Area Nothing much can be said for this area – staying here puts you in the newest part of Bangkok and the furthest from the old Bangkok near the river. Buses take longer to get here and taxis to or from Sukhumvit Rd cost more since it is known as a residential area for farangs. The majority of the hotels in this area are in the middle price range, well above the more basic bottom-end places.

The *Atlanta Hotel* at Soi 2 (Soi Phasak),

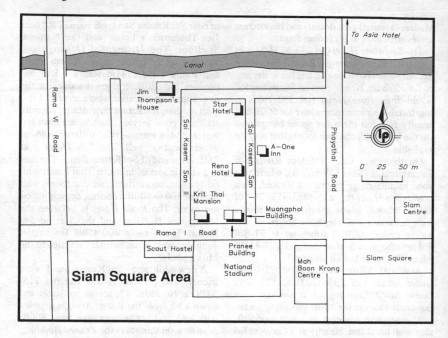

To Asia Hotel

Canal

Rama VI Road

Jim Thompson's House

Star Hotel

Soi Kasem San

A-One Inn

Reno Hotel

Soi Kasem San I

Phayathai Road

0 25 50 m

Krit Thai Mansion

Muangphol Building

Siam Centre

Rama I Road

Pranee Building

Scout Hostel

National Stadium

Mah Boon Krong Centre

Siam Square

Siam Square Area

Sukhumvit Rd has undergone several improvements during recent years in the areas of cleanliness and service. Rooms are now fairly clean and maid service regular. Rooms with shared bath and fan cost 150/200B a single/double. A few rooms have private baths for 50B extra. Small singles with fan and shared bath are available for 120B. Air-con rooms are 250/300/350B a single/double/triple.

The *Miami Hotel* (tel 252 5140/4759/ 5036), Soi 13, Sukhumvit has become a favourite among Arab tourists (rivalling the Rajah, Nana and Grace Hotels on Soi 3), who are driving the prices up. Rooms with fan and bath are 165 to 210B single, 220 to 280B double and 372B triple. For air-con add 100B to each category. The new wing has deluxe air-con singles/doubles for 380/450B. It's comfortable, clean and has a swimming pool.

The *Crown Hotel* (tel 258-0318), at Soi 29, Sukhumvit, costs 196B for a 'budget' room, 219B for a 'deluxe', 296B for a 'super deluxe'. All rooms have air-con and private

bath and the hotel has a swimming pool. Sounds like a good deal but unfortunately standards are slipping here. The *Golden Palace Hotel*, at 15 Soi 1, Sukhumvit, has a swimming pool, is well situated and costs 280 to 340B for a double with air-con and bath. The clientele here are mostly middle-class tourists 'on a budget', but the Golden Palace, too, has seen better days. The *Golden Gate* at 22/1 Sukhumvit Soi 2 is better, with large, clean air-con doubles for 350B, including breakfast.

At Soi 4 (Soi Nana Tai) in Nana Plaza there are two places offering air-con carpeted rooms with hot water, *Nana Guest House* (200B) and *Royal Siam Guest House* (300B). The atmosphere is rather wild, as these two are located amidst a three-storey array of recently established Patpong-type bars. This obviously appeals to some, as rooms are often full. A recent letter recommended *Mermaids Rest* (tel 253-3648) on Soi 8, fan and air-con rooms are 125 to 450B and there are two swimming pools. Another place that has been recommended is the *Ruamchit Mansion*, 1-15 Soi 15, Sukhumvit. Rooms range from 120 to 450B and there is hot water, fridge, air-con or fans, communal kitchen and a supermarket just below. The cheapest hotel on Sukhumvit this side of Phrakhanong, between Soi 25 and Soi 27, has no name, just a chalkboard out the front that reads, in Thai, 'Temporary Use – 50B; All Night – 110B'. Use your own discretion.

The *Squeeze Inn* at Soi 29 is fairly economical for the Sukhumvit area – 95 to 150B for a room with fan.

Pratunam Area Most of the hotels in Pratunam (the area around the Ratchaprarop and Phetburi Rds intersection) have rooms starting at around 1000B, eg the Indra, Florida, Bangkok Palace (see Places to Stay – top end). However, there are a couple of budget places in Pratunam, so if you want to stay close to the fabulous Pratunam markets you don't necessarily have to spend a lot on a hotel. *Mouse Guest House* (tel 252-9702) is near a former US Peace Corps office at 4-6 Soi Somprasong 1, Phetburi Rd and is a favoured transit house among volunteer workers in Thailand. Clean and spacious rooms cost from 130 to 200B with fan. The *Opera Hotel* (tel 252-4031), 16 Soi Somprasong 1, is nearby and features air-con doubles with hot water for 360 to 600B. The Opera also has a swimming pool and coffee shop. Behind the Indra Regent Hotel/Shopping Mall are several Arab/Pakistani guest houses with rates under 300B for air-con rooms, including the pleasant *Aangan Guest House*, which has an Arab/Pakistani/North Indian restaurant downstairs.

The Ys Bangkok has a YMCA and YWCA. The *YMCA* (tel 286-5134/5, 286-5971/3) is at 27 Sathon Tai Rd and has air-con rooms ranging from 600B singles to 1400B doubles. The *YWCA* (tel 286-1936) is at 13 Sathon Tai Rd and has cheaper fan-cooled singles for 290B, air-con doubles for 600B or 100B for a dorm bed. There is also a new *Youth Hostel* at 25/2 Phitsanulok Rd (tel 282-0950, 281-0361).

Places to Stay – top end
Bangkok has all sorts of tourist hotels from the straightforward package places to some of Asia's classic hotels. The riverside *Oriental* is one of the most famous hotels in Asia, right up there with the Raffles in Singapore. What's more it's also rated as one of the very best hotels in the world, as well as being just about the most expensive in Bangkok. It's worth wandering in if only to see the string quartet playing in the lobby! Nowadays it's looking more modern and less classic. The *Bangkok Peninsula* is a close rival to the Oriental in price. Besides the Oriental, the two oldest hotels in the city are the *Erawan Hotel* and the *Royal*. The Erawan was torn down and is currently being rebuilt, but the Royal is still going strong on the corner of Ratchadamnoen Ave and Atsadang Rd near the Democracy Monument and its 24-hour coffee shop is a favourite local rendezvous.

Other well-known hotels include the big *Dusit Thani* at the north end of Silom Rd, the *Airport Hotel* (directly across from the airport) and the *Montien*, perhaps the most Thai of the luxury hotels. The *Central Plaza Bangkok* is also out towards the airport. There's no single area for top-end hotels although you'll find quite a few of them around the Siam Square area, along the parallel Surawong/Silom Rds and along the river while many of the cheaper 'international standard' places are scattered along Sukhumvit Rd.

In the last couple of years, luxury-class hotels in Bangkok have raised their rates more than any other class of hotel in Thailand, ruthlessly capitalising on the over-90% occupancy rates that have occurred since 1987. The government is making an effort to convince such hotels that this practice will be self-defeating in the long term; meanwhile, the top-end places continue to increase tariffs at a rapid pace. New top-end hotel construction may relieve some of the demand for rooms in this range and bring rates down in the future.

Most of the hotels listed will add 10% service charge plus 8.25% tax to hotel bills on departure. The following hotels cost from 500 to 1000B a night:

Baron Hotel (tel 246-4525), 544 Soi Huaykwang Ratchadaphisek Rd, 155 rooms, singles/doubles 400/600B

Century Hotel (tel 245-3271/3), 9 Rajaprarob (Ratchaprarop) Rd, 96 rooms, singles/doubles 540/660B

Continental Hotel (tel 278-1596/8), 971/16 Phahonyothin Rd, 122 rooms, singles/doubles 550 to 605B /695 to 750B

Federal Hotel (tel 253-0175), 27 Sukhumvit Rd, 93 rooms, singles/doubles 400 to 500B/500 to 1200B

Florida Hotel (tel 245-3221/4, 245-1816/9), 43 Phayathai Square, Phayathai Rd, 107 rooms, singles/doubles 500/600B

Fortuna Hotel (tel 251-5121), 19 Sukhumvit Rd, 110 rooms, singles/doubles 450/515B

Golden Dragon (tel 588-4414/5), 20/21 Ngarm Wongvarn Rd, 114 rooms, singles/doubles 600/710B

Golden Horse Hotel (tel 281-6909), 5/1 Damrongrak Rd, 130 rooms, singles/doubles 700/800B

Grace Hotel (tel 252 9170/3), 12 Nana North (Soi 3), Sukhumvit Rd, 550 rooms, singles/doubles 675/822B

Liberty Hotel (tel 271-0880), 215 Sapan Kwai Pratipat Rd, 209 rooms, singles/doubles 400 to 540B/500 to 850B

Miramar Hotel (tel 222-4191), 777 Mahachai Rd, 150 rooms, singles/doubles 450 to 600B

Nana Hotel (tel 250- 1210/9, 250-1380/9), 4 Nana Tai, Sukhumvit Rd, 224 rooms, singles/doubles 550 to 650B/590 to 770B

New Trocadero Hotel (tel 234-8920/9), 34 Surawong Rd, 140 rooms, singles/doubles 610 to 777B/699 to 888B

Park Hotel (tel 252-5110/3), 6 Soi 7, Sukhumvit Rd, 128 rooms, singles/doubles 666/825B

Rajah Hotel (tel 252-5102/9), 18 Soi 4, Sukhumvit Rd, 450 rooms, singles/doubles 980/1050B

Rex Hotel (tel 259-0106), 762/1 Sukhumvit Rd Soi 32, 131 rooms, singles/doubles 500 to 728B/600 to 728B

Royal Hotel (tel 222-9111/20), 2 Ratchadamnoen Klang Ave, 138 rooms, singles/doubles 506/570B

Siam Hotel (tel 252-5081), 1777 Phetburi Rd, 120 rooms, singles/doubles 666/766B

Thai Hotel (tel 282-2833), 78 Prachatipatai Rd, 100 rooms, singles/doubles 520/620B

Victory Hotel (tel 233-9060), 322 Silom Rd, 125 rooms, singles/doubles 580/680 to 850B

Viengtai Hotel (tel 281-5788), 42 Tanee Rd, 240 rooms, singles/doubles 520/620B

The following hotels cost over 1000B a night:

Airport Hotel (tel 566-1020), opposite Don Muang Airport, 300 rooms, singles/doubles 1900/2000B
Ambassador Hotel (tel 254-0444), Soi 11, Sukhumvit Rd, 1050 rooms, singles/doubles 1200 to 2000B/1200 to 2200B

Asia Hotel (tel 215-0808), 296 Phaya Thai Rd, 640 rooms, singles/doubles 1600 to 1800B/1800 to 2000B

Bangkok Center Hotel (tel 235-1780/1799), 328 Rama IV Rd, 225 rooms, singles/doubles 800 to 1200B/900 to 1300B

Bangkok Palace Hotel (tel 253-0500), 1091/336 New Phetburi Rd, 650 rooms, singles/doubles 1200 to 1300B/1400 to 1500B

Dusit Thani Hotel (tel 233-1130), Rama IV Rd, 560 rooms, singles/doubles 2340 to 2600B/2730 to 3640B

Hilton International Bangkok (tel 253-0123, 253-6740), Nai Lert Park, Wireless Rd, 398 rooms, singles/doubles 2270 to 2700B/2380 to 2810B

Central Plaza Bangkok (tel 541-1234), 1695 Phahonyothin Rd, 600 rooms, singles/doubles 1700 to 2500B/2000 to 2900B

Impala Hotel (tel 258-8612/6), Soi 24, Sukhumvit Rd, 220 rooms, singles/doubles 1000 to 1200B/1200 to 1400B

Imperial Hotel (tel 254-0023), Wireless Rd, 400 rooms, singles/doubles 2210/2470B

Indra Regent (tel 251-1111, 252-1111), Rajaprarob (Ratchaprarop) Rd, 500 rooms, singles/doubles 1000 to 2500B/2300 to 2700B

The Landmark (tel 254-0404), 138 Sukhumvit Rd, 415 rooms, singles/doubles 1900 to 2200B/2000 to 2400B

Le Meridian President (tel 253-0444), 135/26 Gaysorn Rd, 1500 to 2000B/1800 to 2500B

Mandarin Hotel (tel 233-4980/9), 662 Rama IV Rd, 343 rooms, singles/doubles 1250 to 1600B/1400 to 1800B

Hotel Manhattan (tel 252-7141/9), Soi 15, Sukhumvit Rd, 206 rooms, singles/doubles 1050 to 1200B/1200 to 2000B

Manohra Hotel (tel 234-5070), 412 Surawong Rd, 250 rooms, singles/doubles 900 to 1200B/1300 to 1400B

The Menam (tel 289-1148/9), 2074 Charoen Krung Rd, Yannawa, 727 rooms, singles/doubles 1500 to 1900B/1700 to 2100B

Montien Hotel (tel 234-8060), 54 Surawong Rd, 600 rooms, singles/doubles 1800 to 2200B/2200 to 3300B

Narai Hotel (tel 233-3350), 222 Silom Rd, 500 rooms, singles/doubles 1400B/1600B

The Oriental Bangkok (tel 236-0400/39), 48 Oriental Ave, 394 rooms, singles/doubles 3800 to 4300B/4000 to 4700B

The Regent of Bangkok (tel 251-6127), 155 Rajadamri (Ratchadamri) Rd, 410 rooms, singles/doubles 3000B

Rama Gardens Hotel (tel 579-5400), 9/9 Vibhavadi-Rangsit Highway, Bangkhen, 369 rooms, singles/doubles 1300 to 1500B/1450 to 1850B

Rama Tower (Holiday Inn Bangkok) (tel 234-1010), 981 Silom Rd, 518 rooms, singles/doubles 1300 to 1700B/1400 to 1800B

The Royal Orchid Sheraton (tel 234-5599), 2 Capt Bush Lane, Siphaya Rd, 780 rooms, singles/doubles 1900 to 2300B/2100 to 2600B

The Royal River (tel 433-0300), 670/805 Charan Sanitwong Rd, Thonburi, singles/doubles 1400B
Shangri-La Hotel (tel 236-7777), 89 Soi Wat Suan Phlu, Charoen Krung Rd, singles/doubles 3400B
Siam Inter-Continental Hotel (tel 253-0355), 967 Rama I Rd, 400 rooms, singles/doubles 2400 to 2800B/2600 to 3000B
Silom Plaza (tel 236 8441), 320 Silom Rd, singles/doubles 1200 to 1900B/1300 to 2100B
Tawana Ramada (tel 236-0361), 80 Surawong Rd, singles/doubles 1700 to 2000B/1800 to 2100B
Windsor Hotel (tel 258-0160), 3 Soi 20, Sukhumvit Rd, 212 rooms, singles/doubles 1000 to 1200B/1100 to 1300B

Places to Eat
Banglamphu & Democracy Monument
There are lots of cheap eating establishments in Banglamphu – many of the guest houses on Khao San Rd have cafes open to the street. The typical menu here has a few Thai and Chinese standards plus a variety of traveller favourites like fruit salads, muesli and yoghurt. The *Hello Restaurants* (there are two on Khao San) are generally reliable. For more authentic (and cheaper) Thai food check out the next street north of Khao San, Ram Buttri Rd. Here there are several open-air restaurants serving excellent Thai food at low prices. At the Tanao Rd end of Ram Buttri is the small *Ta-Yai Restaurant*, which specialises in southern Thai food – great curries.

There are a few good, inexpensive restaurants and food stalls along Phra Athit Rd near Trok Rong Mai – *Taew* across from the alley entrance is very good. Good curry and rice is available for 7B at the outdoor dining hall at Thammasat University nearby; open for lunch only. Good north-eastern food is served at restaurants next door to the boxing stadium on Ratchadamnoen Nok Rd, near the TAT office. There is a decent floating restaurant serving seafood at the Samphraya Pier in Banglamphu called *Yok Yor*. Especially good at Yok Yor is the *haw mok*. They have an English menu. The New World Shopping Center, three blocks north of Khao San, has a food centre on one of its upper floors that has a good selection at very reasonable prices.

At the Democracy Monument Circle, Ratchadamnoen Klang Ave, are a few air-con Thai restaurants, including the *Vijit* and the *Sorn Daeng*, which have fairly inexpensive prices considering the service and facilities. At lunchtime on weekdays they're crowded with local government office workers. Both stay open until 11 pm or so. One of the best restaurants in Bangkok is just off Khao Rd between Ratwithi and Sukhothai Rd, above the Krungthon Bridge near the river – *Baan Khun Luang*. The lunch buffet is especially good value here – 80B for all you can eat from an unbelievable selection.

If you cross Chao Fa Rd from Phra Athit Rd, going towards the National Theatre, you may pass *Wang Ngar*, an excellent Thai seafood restaurant built over the water. Ordering a la carte, a large meal for two would cost about 400B here. For those in the mood for continental food, *Kanit's* at 68 Tee Thong Rd (just south of the Sao Ching Cha 'swing' across from Wat Suthat) is another worthwhile semi-splurge. The lasagne and pizza are probably the best you can find in this part of Bangkok.

Soi Ngam Duphli
This area has several world-traveller hangouts, for example the *Lisboa* and *Blue Fox* are both air-con and slightly expensive since they cater for such western tastes as toast and scrambled eggs. Better are the open-air restaurants on Soi Si Bamphen (near the Boston Inn) which are cheap to moderate in price, have English menus and decent food – mostly Thai and Chinese. In this area, the curry shops out on Rama IV are best for cheap nutrition –10B for curry and rice – check the ones near the pedestrian bridge. Also cheap eats can be had across Rama IV in the daily market, look for a cluster of umbrellas. *Robinson's Department Store* has been recommended by one traveller as being the best fast food place in Bangkok. It's at the northern end of Silom Rd, at the junction with Rama IV, next to the Dairy Queen.

Siam Square
Excellent foodstalls can be found in the alleys between Siam Square sois – khao man kai or other rice-plates, plus tea, for 8 to 10B. The big noodle restaurant on Henri Dunant Rd, called *Coca Garden* (open

from 10.30 am to 10.30 pm), is good for Chinese-style sukiyaki. The *Uptown* (open from 9 am to 11 pm) on Soi 5 offers Thai, Chinese, Japanese and European food at low prices.

The Mah Boon Krong Food Centre, on the 7th floor of the shopping centre directly across from Siam Square on Phayathai Rd (top floor of Tokyu Department Store), has dishes from all over Thailand, including vegetarian dishes, at prices averaging 20B per plate. The food is good and the place is air-conditioned. They also serve farang food. The centre is open from 7 am to 10 pm.

At the end of Soi Lang Suan, near Lumpini Park, there is a large Thai-Chinese seafood restaurant called *Nguan Lee* that is very good and not expensive.

Last and certainly not least, this area has seen an epidemic of American-style fast food eateries in recent years. Siam Square has *Mister Donut*, *Dunkin Donuts*, *Pizza Hut*, *A&W Root Beer* and *Kentucky Fried Chicken*. The Sogo Department Store on Ploenchit Rd has a *McDonald's*. Prices are close to what you would pay in the United States.

Vegetarian The *Whole Earth Restaurant* is on Lang Suan Rd, off Rama I Rd and more or less equidistant from the Siam Centre, Sukhumvit and Silom Rds. It's a good Thai and Indian vegetarian restaurant, but is a bit pricey if you're on a tight budget. Another Thai veggie restaurant is *Prakai* in the new Fuji Hotel on Surawong Rd. The Bangkok Adventist Hospital cafeteria (430 Phitsanulok Rd) also serves inexpensive veggie fare. Across from Chatuchak Park (the Weekend Market) look for a sign reading 'Vegetarian' in green letters and you'll find a small Thai veggie restaurant with great food for only 5 to 10B per dish. All the Indian restaurants in town have vegetarian selections on their menus.

Sukhumvit Rd On Sukhumvit Rd, try the *Yong Lee Restaurant* at Soi 15, near Asia Books. Excellent Thai and Chinese food and good service at reasonable prices has made Yong Lee a favourite among Thai and farang residents alike.

The bottom floor of the Ambassador Hotel between Soi 11 and 13 has a good food mall. It offers several varieties of Thai, Chinese, Vietnamese, Japanese, Muslim and vegetarian food. *Cabbages & Condoms* (open from 11 am to 10 pm) at No 10 Soi 12 is run by the Planned Parenthood Association of Thailand and offers not only a great selection of condoms, but great Thai food at very reasonable prices as well. The tom khaa kai (chicken-coconut soup) is particularly tasty here. The *Mandalay* (open from 11 am to 2 pm and 6 pm to 10.30 pm) at 75/5 Soi 11 is the only Burmese restaurant in town but it isn't cheap.

The famous *Djit Pochana* (open from 10.30 am to 10.30 pm) has a second branch on Soi 20 and is one of the best value restaurants in town for traditional Thai dishes. The all-you-can-eat lunch buffet is 80B. This central section of Sukhumvit Rd is loaded with medium- priced Thai restaurants which feature modern decor but real Thai food. The *Baitarl* (Bai-Taan), at 3 Soi 33, is another very good place for traditional Thai food (though a little more expensive) as is *Fuang Fah* (not as expensive) across the street.

For nouvelle Thai cuisine, try the *Lemongrass* (open from 11 am to 2 pm and 6 pm to 11 pm) at 5/21 Soi 24, which has an atmospheric setting in an old Thai house decorated with antiques. The food is exceptional (try the *yam pet*, 'Thai-style duck salad').

Another hidden gem down Sukhumvit Rd is *Laicram* (Laikhram) at Soi 49/4, 11/1 Sukhumvit Rd, near Samitiwet Hospital. To get there take a bus up Sukhumvit Rd to Soi 49, walk down the soi until it appears to end, bear left and then take the next right, heading towards the hospital (you are still on Soi 49 actually). Across from the hospital go right down Soi 49/4 – the restaurant will be on the left. This is a fairly long walk, so you may want to take a tuk-tuk from the mouth of Soi 49 for 10 to 15B. The food here is authentic gourmet Thai, but not outrageously priced. One of the house specialities is *haw mok hawy*, a thick fish curry steamed with mussels inside the shell – exquisite. Somtam, spicy green papaya salad, is also excellent here, as is *khao man*, rice cooked with coconut milk and *bai toei* or pandanus leaf. Hours are from 10 am to 9 pm Monday to Saturday, 10 am to 3 pm Sunday.

There are many restaurants around the major hotels on Sukhumvit Rd with Thai-Chinese-European-American menus, most of average quality and average prices, like the *Number One Restaurant*. These are good if you're not used to Thai food. *Dusita Restaurant*, 135/7-8 Gaysorn Rd, near the President Hotel, has been recommended for having good Thai food, cheap prices and 'a traditional atmosphere'.

Several rather expensive West European restaurants (Swiss, French, German, etc) are also found on touristy Sukhumvit Rd. *Crown Pizza*, round the corner from the Crown Hotel, between Soi 29 and 31 has been recommended – it's open fairly late and is air-con. *By Otto*, between Soi 12 and 14, is one of the most popular German restaurants in town and has a comfortable bar. A few medium to expensive Indian-Pakistani-Middle Eastern restaurants are cropping up on Soi 3 (Soi Nana Neua), including *Akbar's, Al Hamra, Al Helabi, Nana Fondue* and *Shaharazad*.

There are three food centres on Sukhumvit Rd; the latest eating fashion among young Thais. All are good places to initiate oneself into Thai cuisine, or to pick up inexpensive, good-tasting Thai food in fairly hygienic surroundings.

The first is the *Gaysorn Food Mall* next to Le Meridian President Hotel, located on Ploenchit Rd (which turns into Sukhumvit Rd a few blocks east) between Ratchadamri Rd and Soi Chit Lom. The second is the *Ma-Chim Food Centre*, underneath the Din Daeng superhighway entrance/exit near Soi 1 Sukhumvit. Third is the *Ambassador City Food Centre* at Soi 11, in the Ambassador Hotel complex. All are about the same in price and quality, though the Ambassador seems to have a better selection than the others (the best food centre in town is probably Mah Boon Krong Centre near Siam Square). Dishes average around 15 to 20B

and there are photographs of the foods which are labelled in English and Thai, making it even easier to know what you are ordering. One buys coupons upon entry rather than paying the cooks. Any unused coupons may be returned for a refund.

Victory Monument There are a couple of large but good Thai-Chinese restaurants near the Victory Monument at the intersection of Ratwithi and Phayathai Rds. Especially recommended is *Nguan Lee* on the north-west corner which is a good place for beer and Maekhong whisky with *kap klaem* – finger food for drinkers. For Thai food, *Pun Sip (Pan Sip)* (open from 9.30 am to 6 pm) is worth a visit to the north-east corner of the traffic circle. One of the oldest restaurants in Bangkok, it has wood panelling, teak floors and great food at reasonable prices. The *Achara* is another good inexpensive Thai restaurant, at the intersection of Phahonyothin Rd and Soi Ari, north of the Victory Monument area.

Indian Restaurants The best Indian restaurant in town, frequented almost exclusively by Indian residents, is the *Royal India* at 392/1 Chakraphet Rd in Pahurat, the Indian fabric district. It is very crowded at lunch time, so it might be better to go there after the standard lunch hour or at night. The place has very good dahl, curries, Indian breads, raita and lassi, etc for both vegetarian and non-vegetarian eaters at quite reasonable prices. It is definitely better value than the *Muslim Restaurant* on Charoen Krung (New) Rd, which costs more and has watery curries but has been a travellers' standby.

The *ATM Shopping Center* on Chakraphet near the pedestrian bridge has a food centre on the top floor that features several Indian vendors. The Indian food here is cheap and tasty and there's quite a good selection. Running alongside the ATM building on Soi ATM are several small teahouses with very inexpensive Indian food, including lots of fresh chapatis and Indian tea.

The *Moti Mahal Restaurant* at the old Chartered Bank near the Swan Hotel has good Muslim Indian food, great yoghurt and reasonable prices. *Himali Cha-Cha*, 1229/11 Charoen Krung (New) Rd, also does a north Indian cuisine quite nicely, but prices are medium high.

For south Indian food (*dosa, idli, vada,* etc), try the *Silom Lodge* at 92/1 Vaithy (or Vaithi) Lane, off Silom Rd near the Narai Hotel. It is worth the long walk down Vaithi Lane for the delicious coconut *chatni.* Another place serving South Indian (in addition to North Indian) food is the basic *Simla Cafe* at 382 Soi Tat Mai (opposite Borneo & Co) off Silom Rd, behind the Victory Hotel, not far from Charoen Krung (New) Rd.

Patpong & Silom Rd On Patpong Rd the *Thai Room*, a Thai,Chinese,Mexican,Farang place, is favoured by Thai-farang couples, Peace Corps volunteers and off-duty barmaids. The decor's not much, but prices are reasonable. If you crave German or Japanese food, there are plenty of places serving these cuisines on and around Patpong Rd. *Bobby's Arms*, an Aussie-Brit pub, has good fish & chips.

In the Samyan area at the intersection of Rama IV and Phayathai Rd are several good seafood restaurants. Especially recommended is *Somboon* (open from 11 am to midnight) on Soi Chula 60, where the crab curry is the best in town.

Out on Silom Rd, look for the inexpensive *Charuvan*, 70-72 Silom Rd, a glassed-in Thai restaurant with two rooms, one with air-con, one *au naturel* (sweaty in the hot season). It has very good low-priced Thai food with discounted beer. Across the street are a *Mister Donut* and *Kentucky Fried Chicken*.

The area to the east of Silom Rd off Convent and Sala Daeng Rds is a Thai gourmets' enclave. Most of the restaurants tucked away here are very good but a meal for two will cost 600 to 800B. One that's a bit lower in price, but not in quality is *Rang Peung* ('Honeycomb') at 37 Soi 2, Saladaeng Rd. The menu combines several different regional Thai cuisines and has especially tasty *yam* or Thai-style salads. Two can eat well for 150B. The *Alliance Française* at 29 Sathon Tai Rd has a small French cafe that's open from 7 am until 8 pm.

At the other end of Silom Rd, across from the Narai Hotel, is a south Indian (Tamil) temple near which street vendors sell various Indian snacks. Around the corner of Silom on Charoen Krung (New) Rd is the Muslim Restaurant, already mentioned. Better but more expensive North Indian food is available at the *Himali Cha Cha* nearby. Also off Silom Rd are two restaurants serving south Indian-style food.

Pratunam Pratunam, the market district at the intersection of Phetburi and Ratchaprarop Rds, down from the Indra Regent, is a good hunting ground for Thai food. Check out the night markets behind Ratchaprarop Rd storefronts near the Phetburi Rd overpass and in the little sois near this intersection. These are all great places to eat real Thai food and see 'pure' (non-western) urban Thai culture.

The Pratunam markets are open, with corrugated tin roofs high above the tables and rustic kitchens, all bathed in fluorescent light. The market on the east side of Ratchaprarop Rd is more like a series of connected tents – one speciality here is a tangy fish stomach soup, *kaphaw plaa.* Four people can eat a large meal, drinking beer or rice whisky and nibbling away for hours and only spend around 150B to 200B (cheaper if it's rice whisky rather than beer). Night markets in Bangkok, as elsewhere in Thailand, have no menus so you had better have your Thai in shape before venturing out for an evening – or better, get a Thai friend to accompany you.

For a slightly up-market splurge in the Pratunam area, you might try the *Krua Khunluang* on Soi 33, Phetburi Rd. The restaurant is run by three women from Buriram so there are some *isaan* or north-eastern Thai dishes on the menu like *laap* (spicy meat salad with mint leaves) and somtam, but no English menu.

Expensive Places The *Siam Intercontinental Hotel* has an all-you-can-eat buffet of well-prepared Thai food, including your choice of seafood steamed on the spot. The buffet costs 100B and is open from 12 midday to 2.30 pm, Monday to Friday only, in the *Talay Thong* restaurant. The *Oriental Hotel* does a 'marvellous buffet lunch for 370B, a real touch of class for the weary traveller'. The Terrace Restaurant here is also very good, and has one of the best sunset views in Bangkok.

Tumpnakthai Restaurant, 131 Ratchadapisek Rd, is one of several large outdoor restaurants built over boggy areas of Bangkok's Din Daeng district north of Phetburi Rd. But this one just happens to be billed as the largest outdoor restaurant in the world! It's built on 10 acres of land and water and can serve up to 3000 diners at once. The menu exceeds 250 items and includes Thai, Chinese Japanese, and European food. All orders are computer-coordinated and some of the waiters glide by on roller skates.

The pinnacle of Thai cuisine in Bangkok, according to Thai gourmets who can afford it (though it is not very expensive by European standards), is served at *Bussaracum Restaurant* (pronounced 'boot-sa-ra-kam') at 35 Soi Phipat off Convent Rd. Bussaracum specialises in Royal Thai cuisine, meaning they use recipes that were created for the Royal Court in days past; these recipes were kept secret from 'commoners' until late this century. Every dish is supposedly prepared only when ordered, from all-fresh ingredients and freshly ground spices. The menu is in Thai and English and anything you order is usually near-perfect, like the service. Live classical Thai music, played at a subdued volume, is provided as well. A fancy place, recommended for a splurge. Two can eat for 600 to 800B.

Dinner Cruises There are a number of companies that run cruises during which you eat dinner. Prices range from 30 to 500B per person depending on how far they go and whether dinner is included in the fare. See the River Cruise section for more information.

Ice Cream There are several Sala Foremost Ice Cream shops in Bangkok – one at Siam Square, one on Ploenchit Rd, a couple on Charoen Krung, one on Ratchaprarop Rd in Pratunam - they're springing up everywhere. There is good ice cream and other delicacies at *Pan Pan*; there's one on Sukhumvit at Soi 33 and another near the Siam Society.

Entertainment

Nightlife Bangkok is loaded with bars, coffee shops, nightclubs and massage parlours left over from the days when the City of Angels was an R&R stop for GIs serving in Vietnam. By and large these throwbacks are seedy, expensive and cater to men only. Then there is the new breed of S&S (sex & sin) bar, some merely refurbished R&R digs, that are more modest, classy and welcome females and couples. Not everybody's cup of tea, but they do a good business.

All the major hotels have flashy nightclubs too, which are less seedy but more expensive. Many feature live music – rock, country & western, Thai pop music and jazz, the latter usually played by good Filipino bands. Hotels catering to tourists and businesspeople have rather dated-looking discos. You'll find up-to-date recorded music in the smaller neighbourhood bars and megadiscos.

Bars The girlie bars are concentrated along Sukhumvit Rd from Soi 21 on out; off Sukhumvit on Soi Nana (including the infamous *Grace Hotel*, now an all-Arab spot); and in the world-famous Patpong Rd area, between Silom and Surawong Rds. Wherever you go prices are about the same; beers are usually 40 to 50B. Patpong (named for the Chinese millionaire, Phat Phong, who owns practically everything on Patpong Rds I and II) has calmed down a bit over the years. These days it has kind of an open-air market feel as several of the newer bars are literally on the street and vendors set up shop in the evening hawking everything from roast squid to fake designer watches. The downstairs clubs with names like *King's Castle* and *Pussy Galore* feature 'go-go dancing' while upstairs the real raunch is kept behind closed doors. Don't believe the touts on the street who say the upstairs shows are for free: after the show, a huge bill arrives.

Another hold-over from the R&R days is *Soi Cowboy* (off Sukhumvit between Soi 21 and 23), which still gets pretty wild some nights. Then there's a new bar area located in Nana Plaza off Soi 4 (Soi Nana Tai) Sukhumvit Rd. One bar here, *Woodstock*, plays some of the better recorded music in town over a decent sound system and they don't seem to mind if you come and just listen either, ie the girls keep a low profile. *Asian Intrigue*, in the same complex, has floor shows involving snakes and other interesting scenarios, designed for a wider appeal than the raunchy upstairs shows on Patpong. Nana Plaza comes complete with its own guest houses in the same complex.

Soi Tantawan and Thaniya Rd, on either side of and parallel to Patpong Rds I and II, feature expensive Japanese-style hostess bars (which non-Japanese are usually barred from entering) as well as a handful of gay bars with names like Mandate and Golden

ADAM&EVE BAR – Patpong Rd.

Cock that feature male go-go dancers and 'bar boys'. Transvestite cabarets are big in Bangkok and several are found in this area. *Calypso Cabaret* (tel 258-8987/6819) at 688 Sukhumvit Rd between Soi 24 and 26, has the largest regularly performing transvestite troupe in town, with nightly shows at 8 and 9.45 pm.

Trendy among Bangkok Thais these days is a new kind of bar which strives for a more sophisticated atmosphere, with good service and choice music played at a volume that doesn't discourage conversation. The Thais call them pubs but they bear little resemblance to any traditional English pub. Some are 'theme' bars, conceived around a particular aesthetic. Soi Lang Suan off Ploenchit Rd has several, including favourites *Brown Sugar* and *Old West*. Soi 33 off Sukhumvit Rd has a string of bars named for European artists: *Vincent Van Gogh, Ea Manet Club, Renoir Club 1841*. You get the idea.

Jazz Clubs On Surawong Rd near Patpong is the *Red Elephant Pub & Restaurant* where you can hear live jazz nightly in a Thai setting. The *Saxophone Pub Restaurant* at 3/8 Victory Monument, Phayathai Rd (south-east of the Victory Monument Circle), offers live jazz and blues nightly and on Sundays they have an open jam session. Other places with regular live jazz include *The Glass* at Sukhumvit Soi 11 and *Round Midnight Pub & Restaurant*, 106/2 Soi Lang Suan.

Mega-Discos Bangkok has several huge high-tech discos that hold up to 5000 people each and feature mega-watt sound systems, giant-screen video and the latest in light-show technology. The clientele for these dance palaces is mostly an agro crowd of young, well-heeled Thais experimenting with life styles of conspicuous affluence and excess, plus the occasional Bangkok celebrity. The most 'in' disco is the *Paradise* on Arun Amarin Rd in Thonburi. Another biggie is *Nasa* at 999 Ramkhamhaeng Rd, which features a sci-fi theme. Similar in scope is the *Galaxy* on Rama IV Rd, from which WBA world boxing champions

Khaosai Galaxy and his brother Khaokor have taken their surname. Cover charges at these discos are 150 to 200B and this usually includes a drink or two.

Massage Parlours Massage parlours have been a Bangkok attraction for many years now, though the Tourist Authority of Thailand tries to discourage the city's reputation in this respect. Massage as a healing art is a tradition that is centuries old in Thailand and it is possible to get a really legitimate massage in Bangkok – despite the commercialisation of recent years. That many of the massage parlours also deal in prostitution is well known; less well known is the fact that many (but by no means all) of the girls working in the parlours are bonded labour they are not there by choice. It takes a pretty sexist male not to be saddened by the sight of 50 girls/women behind a glass wall with numbers pinned to their dresses. Should male travellers avail themselves of more than a massage and come down with something they hadn't paid for, there are plenty of VD clinics located along Ploenchit Rd. There is a definite AIDS presence in Thailand, so condom use is imperative not only in Bangkok but anywhere in Thailand.

Traditional Massage Traditional Thai massage, also called 'ancient' massage, is now widely available in Bangkok as an alternative to the red-light massage parlours. One of the best places to experience a traditional massage is at Wat Pho, Bangkok's oldest temple. Massage here costs 120B per hour or 80B for a half-hour. They also teach a 30-hour course in Thai massage which can be attended three hours per day for 10 days or two hours for 15 days. Tuition for the course is 3000B. You must also pay the regular 10B per day admission fee for Wat Pho whether you are a student or massagee.

Other places to get traditional Thai massage in Bangkok include *Buathip Thai Massage* (tel 255-1045), 4/13 Soi 5 Sukhumvit Rd, and *Marble House* (tel 235-3519) 37/18-19 Soi Surawong Plaza. Fees for traditional Thai massage should be no more than 150B per hour, though some

places have a 1½-hour minimum. Be aware that not every place that advertises traditional or ancient massage can offer a really good one; sometimes the only thing 'ancient' about the pommelling is the age of the masseuse. Thai aficionados say that the best massages are given by blind masseurs.

Theatre & Cinema Dozens of movie theatres around town show Thai, Chinese, Indian and occasionally western movies. The majority of films shown are comedies and shoot-em-ups, with the occasional drama slipping through. These theatres are air-con and quite comfortable, with reasonable rates. All movies in Thai theatres are preceded by the Thai national anthem along with projected pictures of King Bhumiphol and other members of the royal family. Everyone in the theatre stands quietly for the duration of the anthem (written by the king, incidentally) in respect for the monarch.

Film snobs may prefer the weekly or twice weekly offerings at Bangkok's foreign cultural clubs:

Alliance Francais
    29 Sathon Tai Rd (tel 286-3841)
American University Alumni
    179 Rajadamri Rd (tel 252-7067/9)
British Council
    428 Siam Square, Rama I Rd (tel 252-6136/8)
Goethe Institut Bangkok
    18/1 Soi Attakanprasit, Sathon Tai Rd (tel 286-9002/9)

French and German films that are screened at the cultural clubs are almost always subtitled in English. Admission is sometimes free, sometimes 30 to 40B. Films of all types are listed in the daily *Bangkok Post* – look for other cultural events in the paper, too, occasionally there are classical music performances, rock concerts, Asian music/theatre ensembles on tour, art shows, international buffets, etc. Boredom should not be a problem in Bangkok, at least not for a short-term visit; however, save some money for your upcountry trip!

Thai Cooking Schools
More and more travellers are coming to Thai-

land just to learn how to cook. While passing through Mae Sai recently, I met a young English chef who was seeking out new cooking secrets. His reputation in England was in part due to his use of Thai ingredients and cooking methods in his own 'nouvelle' cuisine. You, too, can amaze your friends back home after attending a course in Thai cuisine at one of the following places:

Oriental Hotel Cooking School
> Soi Oriental, Charoen Krung (New) Rd (tel 236-0400/39)

UFM Food Centre
> Sukhumvit 33/1 (tel 259-0620/33) 593/29-39

Modern Housewife Centre
> 45/6-7 Sethsiri Rd (tel 279-2832/4)

Bussaracum Restaurant
> 35 Soi Phiphat 2, Convent Rd (tel 235-8915)

Religious Services
More than one reader has written to point out that not everyone who comes to Thailand is either an atheist or a Buddhist. For those seeking houses of worship in the Judaeo-Christian-Muslim tradition:

Catholic
> Assumption Cathedral , 23 Oriental Lane, Charoen Krung (New) Rd(tel 234-8556)
> Holy Redeemer Church , 123/19 Soi Ruam Rudi (behind US Embassy)(tel 253-0505)

Protestant
> Calvary Baptist Church , 88 Soi 2, Sukhumvit Rd (tel 234-3634)
> International Church , 67 Soi 19, Sukhumvit Rd (tel 252-0353)

Seventh Day Adventist
> Bangkok Ekamai Church , 57 Soi Charoenchai, Ekamai Rd (tel 391-3593)
> Bangkok Chinese Church , 1325 Rama IV Rd (tel 215-4529)

Jewish
> Jewish Association of Thailand , 121/3 Soi 22, Sukhumvit Rd (tel 258-2195)

Muslim
> Haroon Mosque, Charoen Krung (New) Rd, near GPO
> Darool Aman Mosque, Phetburi Rd, near Ratthewi Circle

Getting There & Away
Air Bangkok is a major centre for international flights throughout Asia, and Bangkok's airport is a busy one. Bangkok is also a major centre for buying discounted airline tickets (see the Getting There chapter for details), but be warned that the Bangkok travel agency business has more than a few crooked operators. Domestic flights operated by THAI also fan out from Bangkok all over the country. Addresses of airlines offices in Bangkok are:

Aeroflot
> 7 Silom Rd (tel 233-6965/7)

Air France
> 942/51 Rama IV Rd (tel 234-1330/9, reservations 234-9477)

Air India
> Amarin Tower, Ploenchit Rd (tel 256-9614/8, reservations 256-9614/8)

Air Lanka
> 942/34-5 Rama IV Rd (tel 236-4981, 235-4982)

Alitalia
> 138 Silom Rd (tel 233-4000/4)

American Airlines
> 518/2 Ploenchit Rd (tel 251-1393)

Bangkok Airways
> Sahakol Air Co, 144 Sukhumvit Rd (tel 253-4014)

Bangladesh Biman
> Chongkolnee Building, 56 Surawong Rd (tel 235-7643/4, 234-0300/9),

British Airways
> Chan Issara Tower, Rama IV Rd (tel 236-8655/8)

Burma Airways
> 208 Surawong Rd (tel 234-9692, 233-3052)

CAAC Airline
> 134/1-2 Silom Rd (235-6510/1, 235-8159)

Canadian Airlines International
> 518/5 Ploenchit (251-4521, 254-8376)

Cathay Pacific Airways
> Chan Issara Tower, Rama IV Rd (tel 235-4330, reservations 233-6105/9)

China Airlines
> Peninsula Plaza, Rajadamri Rd (tel 253-5733, reservations 253-4438)

Delta Air Lines
> Dusit Thani Building, Rama IV Rd (tel 233-8530/2)

Druk Air, see Thai Airways International

Egyptair
> 120 Silom Rd (tel 233-7599, reservations 233-7601/3)

Finnair
> 518/2 Ploenchit Rd (tel 251-5445, reservations 251-5012)

Garuda Indonesia
> 944/19 Rama IV Rd (tel 233-0981/2, reservations 233-3873)

Gulf Air
Panuni Building, Ploenchit Rd (tel 254-7931/40)
Iraqi Airways
ASC Building, Silom Rd (tel 235-5950/5)
Japan Air Lines
33/33-4 Wall Street Tower, Surawong Rd (tel 234-9111, reservations 233-2420)
KLM Royal Dutch Airlines
2 Patpong Rd (tel 235-5150/4, 235-5155/9)
Korean Air
Dusit Thani Building, Silom Rd (tel 234-9283/9)
Kuwait Airways
159 Rajadamri Rd (tel 523-6993)
Lao Aviation
56 Chongkolnee Building, Surawong Rd (tel 233-7950, reservations 234-0300)
Lufthansa
331/1-3 Silom Rd (tel 234-1350)
Malaysian Airlines System
98-102 Surawong Rd (tel 236-5871, reservations 236-4705/9)
Northwest Airlines
Silom Plaza, 491/39 Silom Rd (tel 253-4822)
Landmark Plaza, 138 Sukhumvit Rd (253-4822/4423)
Peninsula Plaza, 153 Rajadamri Rd (tel 253-4822, 253-4423/5)
Pakistan International Airlines
52 Surawong Rd (tel 234-2961)
Pan American World Airways
965 Rama I Rd (tel 252-2128/30)
Philippine Airlines
Chongkolnee Building, 56 Surawong Rd (tel 233-2350/2),
Qantas
Chan Issara Tower, 942/51 Rama IV Rd (tel 236-9193/6, reservations 236-0102)
Royal Brunei Airlines
c/o Thai Airways International, 485 Silom Rd, (tel 234 3100/9)
Royal Jordanian Airline
Yada Building, Silom Rd (tel 236-0030)
Royal Nepal Airlines
1/4 Convent Rd (tel 233-3921/4)
SAS – (Scandinavian Airlines System)
412 Rama I Rd (tel 252-4181, reservations 253-8333)
Sabena Belgian World Airlines
109 Surawong Rd (tel 233-2020)
Saudi Arabian Airlines
Ground Floor, CCT Building, 109 Surawong Rd (tel 236-9400/3)
Singapore Airlines
12 Floor, Silom Center Building, 2 Silom Rd (tel 236-0303, reservations 236-0440)
Swissair
1 Silom Rd (tel 233-2930/4, reservations 233-2935/8)
Tarom Romanian Air Transport
Zuellig Building, 1-7 Silom Rd (tel 235-2668/9)

Thai Airways International (also agent for Druk Air)
89 Vibhavadi Rangsit Rd (tel 513-0121, reservations 233-3810)
485 Silom Rd (tel 234-3100/19)
6 Larn Luang Rd (tel 288-0090, 280-0070/80)
Asia Hotel, 296 Phayathai Rd (tel (02) 215-2020/4)
United Airlines
183 Rajadamri Rd (tel 253-0559)

Bus Bangkok is the centre for bus services that fan out all over the kingdom. There are basically three types of long-distance buses. First there are the ordinary public buses, then the public air-con buses. These both go from the main bus stations (from separate but adjacent terminals at each station), leave regularly and provide a good service to all the centres. Third choice is the many private air-con services which leave from various offices and hotels all over the city and provide a deluxe service for those people for whom simple air-con isn't enough!

There are three main public bus stations. The Northern/North-Eastern Bus Terminal (tel ordinary 279-6621/5, air-con 391-3310) is on Phahonyothin Rd on the way up to the airport. Lots of city buses heading north go by it. It's also commonly called the Moh Chit Station (*sathaanii maw chit*). Buses depart from here to Chiang Mai and other northern towns, Khorat and other destinations in the north-east, as well as to Ayuthaya, Lopburi and other places close to Bangkok but north of the city. Buses to Aranyaprathet also go from here, not from the Eastern Bus Terminal as you might expect.

The Eastern Bus Terminal (tel ordinary 392-2391, air-con 391-3310), the departure point for buses to Pattaya, Rayong, Chantaburi and other points east, is a long way out along Sukhumvit Rd, at Soi 40 (Soi Ekamai) opposite Soi 63. Most folks call it the Ekamai Station (*sathaanii ek-amai*).

The Southern Bus Terminal (tel ordinary 411-0511, air-con 411-4978/9) for buses south to Phuket, Surat Thani and closer centres to the west like Nakhon Pathom and Kanchanaburi, is across the river in Thonburi. It's on Charan Sanitwong Rd, near the Bangkok Noi (or Thonburi) Railway Station.

Don't forget that the air-con buses and ordinary buses leave from separate terminals at each of the three bus stations. All stations have left-luggage facilities and small restaurants.

When travelling on night buses take care of your belongings. One couple wrote to say that all of their travellers cheques (US$650) were stolen on the night bus from Chiang Mai to Bangkok. The tourist police and Amex were very helpful and they received US$500 back from Amex on the same day.

See the Getting Around chapter for more details on bus travel in Thailand.

Train Bangkok is the terminus for rail services to the south, north and north-east. There are two main railway stations. The big Hualamphong Station on Rama IV Rd handles services to the north, north-east and some of the services to the south. The Thonburi or Bangkok Noi Station handles most services to the south. If you're heading south make certain which station your train departs from.

Getting Around
Getting around in Bangkok may be difficult at first for the uninitiated but once you're familiar with the bus system the whole city is accessible. Bangkok was once called the Venice of the East, but the canal system is fast disappearing to give way to more road construction – with 10% of Thailand's population living in the capital, water transportation, with a few exceptions, is a thing of the past. Many of the smaller canals that do remain are hopelessly polluted and would probably have been filled in by now if it weren't for their important drainage function. Larger canals, especially on the Thonburi side, remain important commercial arteries.

Bus You can save a lot of money in Bangkok by sticking to the public buses, which are 2B for any journey under 10 km on the ordinary (not air-con) buses or 5B for the first 8 km on the air-con lines. The fare on ordinary buses is 3B for longer trips (eg from Chulalongkorn University to King

Mongkut's Institute of Technology in Thonburi on bus No 21) and as high as 15B for air-con buses (eg from Silom Rd to Don Muang Airport on air-con bus No 4). The air-con buses are not only cooler, but are usually less crowded (all bets are off during rush hours).

To do any serious bus riding you'll need a Bangkok bus map – the easiest to read is the *Latest Tour's Guide to Bangkok & Thailand* (put out by Suwannachai), or Thaveeholcharoen's *Bangkok Thailand Bus Map*, both of which also have a decent map of the whole country on the flip sides. The bus numbers are clearly marked in red, air-con buses in larger types (green on the latter map). Don't expect the routes to be 100% correct, a few will have changed since the maps last came out, but they'll get you where you're going most of the time. These maps usually retail for 35B or sometimes 40B. A more complete 113-page *Bus Guide* is available in some bookshops and newsstands for 35B, but it's not as easy to use as the bus maps.

Taxis Taxis in Bangkok may have meters but the drivers do not use them. In this respect Bangkok is one of the last hold-outs in South-East Asia; Kuala Lumpur, Singapore and even Jakarta taxis now use meters, but not Bangkok. Thais say this is because both drivers and passengers distrust meters. At any rate, the fare must be decided before you

a tuk-tuk, BANGKOK

get in the cab unless you really want to 'get taken for a ride'. Fares to most places within central Bangkok should be around 50B – add 10B or so if it's rush hour or after midnight. Short distances should be under 50B – Siam Square to Silom Rd, for example, should be 40B in relatively light traffic.

To get these fares you must bargain well. There is an over-supply of taxis in Bangkok so just wave a driver on if he won't meet a reasonable fare and flag down another cab. It gets easier with practice and better results are obtained if you speak some Thai. Petrol prices are high in Thailand and they are increasing. About 90% of Bangkok taxis have switched over from gasoline fuel to LP gas in recent years. Most cabs are now air-conditioned, so fares continue to rise. Better to take a bus if you are really counting baht, save the taxi for when you're in a genuine hurry. During rush hours taxi drivers can be especially bad tempered (like everybody else on the road at that time). If they only had working meters, tempers would cool down, as they could relax and let the meter tick away.

Tuk-tuks These three-wheeled taxis, which sound like power saws gone berserk, are only good for very short distances. For longer distances they may charge more than the four-wheel variety and there have been some instances of tuk-tuk drivers robbing their passengers at night. Bangkok residents often talk of the tuk-tuks as a nuisance, even a menace, to their already suffering environment. Some have even been trying to enact a ban on tuk-tuks. A few years ago the city supposedly forbade the further production of any new three-wheel taxis, but every time I go to Bangkok I see hordes of brand new ones. It's a bit of a moral dilemma actually, since the tuk-tuk drivers are usually poor north-easterners who can't afford to rent the quieter, less polluting Japanese auto-taxis.

In heavy traffic, tuk-tuks are usually faster than taxis since they're more able to weave in and out between cars and trucks. This is the main advantage to taking a tuk-tuk for short hops, besides the lower fare (say 25 to 30B for what might be 40B in a taxi). On the

down side, they're not air-conditioned and you have to breathe all that lead-soaked air which is naturally thickest in the middle of Bangkok's wide avenues. They're also more dangerous since they easily flip when braking into a fast curve.

Finally, tuk-tuk drivers tend to speak less English than taxi drivers, so many new arrivals have a hard time getting their destinations across to them. Lately travellers have been complaining that tuk-tuk drivers have deliberately taken them to the wrong destination in an attempt to collect commissions from certain restaurants or silk shops. Other folks never seem to have a problem with tuk-tuks and swear by them, so experiences do vary.

River Transport Although Bangkok's canals (khlongs) are disappearing there is still plenty of transport along and across the Chao Phraya River and up adjoining canals. River transport is one of the nicest ways of getting around Bangkok as well as, quite often, being much faster than any road-based alternatives. For a start you get a quite different view of the city; secondly, it's far less hassling than tangling with the polluted, noisy, traffic-crowded streets. Just try getting from Banglamphu to the GPO as fast by road.

First step in using river transport successfully is to know your boats. The main ones you'll want to use are the rapid Chao Phraya Express Boats (*reua duan*), a sort of river bus service. They cost 3, 5 or 7B depending on the distance you travel and follow a regular route up and down the river. They do not necessarily stop at every landing if there are no people there or no one wants to get off. You buy your tickets on the boat. The Chao Phraya Express is a big, long boat with a number on the roof.

Chao Phya express river taxi

Main stops of the
Chao Phraya Express

1 Oriental Hotel
2 Wat Muang Khae
3 Si Phraya
4 Ratchawong – for Chinatown
5 Saphan Phut, Memorial Bridge
6 Rachini
7 Tha Tien – for Wat Pho
8 Tha Chang – for Grand Palace
9 Maharat – for Thammasat University
10 Phrannok
11 Rot Fai – Bangkok Noi Railway Station
12 Phra Athit – for Khao San Rd Guest Houses
13 Wat Daowadung
14 Wat Samphraya
15 Wisut Kasat – for Wat Intarawihan
16 Thewet – for National Librart & Sawatdee Guest House

The boat does not stop at every landing if there are no passengers.

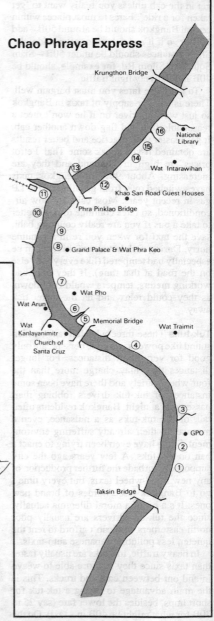

Chao Phraya Express

Krungthon Bridge

National Library

Wat Intarawihan

Khao San Road Guest Houses

Phra Pinklao Bridge

Grand Palace & Wat Phra Keo

Wat Pho

Wat Arun

Memorial Bridge

Wat Traimit

Wat Kanlayanimitr
Church of Santa Cruz

Wat Traimit

GPO

Taksin Bridge

From the main Chao Phraya stops and also from almost every other jetty there are slower cross-river ferries (*reua kham fak*) which simply shuttle back and forth across the river. The standard fares are either 50 satang or 1B and you usually pay this at the entrance to the jetty. Be careful, there will probably be a pay window at the jetty and also a straight through aisle for people taking other boats:

Ferry to cross Chao Phya River

Finally there are the long-tail taxis (*reua hang yao*) which operate a share-taxi system off the main river and up the smaller khlongs. Fares usually start from around 4B – you've really got to know where you're going on these. There are also river taxis where you really do take the whole boat – find them at certain jetties, like the Oriental Hotel and charter them for trips to the floating market or other attractions. Bargain hard.

Long-tailed taxis

Cars & Motorcycles Cars and motorcycles can easily be rented in Bangkok if you can afford it and have steel nerves. Rates are around 600B per day for a car, much less for a motorcycle, not including insurance. An International Driver's Permit and passport are required.

For cross-country trips of some duration, you might consider buying a new or used motorcycle and reselling it when you leave – this can end up being cheaper than renting, especially if you buy a good used bike. See the Motorcycle Trekking section in the Getting Around chapter for more detail.

Here are the names and addresses of a few car rental companies:

Avis Rent-a-Car
    10/1 Sathon Neua Rd (tel 233-0397)
Champion Car Rent
    1422/57 New Phetburi Rd (tel 252-2344)
Grand Car Rent
    144/3-4 Silom Rd (tel 234-9956, 234-6867)
Hertz
    987 Ploenchit Rd (tel 235-6251/4)
    1620 New Phetburi Rd (tel 251-7475)
Highway Car Rent
    6/2 Rama IV Rd (tel 234-9145/6, 235-7657/8, 235-7746/7)
Inter Car Rent
    45 Sukhumvit Rd, near Soi 3 (tel 251-4910, 252-9223)
Klong Toey Car Rent
    1921 Rama IV Rd (tel 250-1141/1361/1930)
Krung Thai Car Rent
    233-5 Asoke-Din Daeng Rd (tel 246-0089, 246-1525/7)
Petchburee Car Rent
    23171 New Phetburi Rd (tel 318-1753/1874)
Royal Car Rent
    67 Sathon Tai Rd (tel 286-3636/6632)
Siam Car Rent
    45-49 Sukhumvit Rd (tel 251-1850)

Silver Rent-a-Car
    402 Sukhumvit Rd (tel 258-2018/2379)
Super Car Rent
    Soi 7-9, 131/2 Sukhumvit Rd (tel 253-7678/9)
Thongchai Car Rent
    1448/1 New Phetburi Rd (tel 254-5700/1, 253-7678/9)

There are several more car rental agencies along Witthayu Rd and New Phetburi Rd. Some auto rent places rent motorcycles, too, but you're better off renting or leasing a bike at a place that specialises in motorcycles. Here are three motorcycle rental places:

Chusak Yont Shop
    1400 New Phetburi Rd (tel 251-9225)
SSK Co
    35/33 Ladprao Rd (tel 514-1290)
Visit Laochaiwat
    1 Soi Prommit, Suthisan Rd (tel 278-1348)
Hurricane Ltd
    Klong Tan (tel 314-6087)

Bangkok International Airport
The main international airport is in Don Muang district, approximately 25 km north of Bangkok. You have several choices of transport modes from the airport to city ranging from 2B to 300B in cost.

Taxi The taxis which wait near the arrival area of the airport are now airport-regulated. You buy a ticket from a booth at one end of the arrival hall (to the left as you leave customs) for 180B and give this to the driver. Two, three, or even four passengers (if they don't have much luggage) can split the fare. A few touts from the old taxi mafia that used to prowl the arrival area are still around and may approach you with fares of around 150B. Their taxis have white and black plates and are not licensed to carry passengers, hence you have less legal recourse in the event of an incident than if you take a licensed taxi (yellow and black plates).

If you really want to save the 30B, go upstairs to the departure area and get an incoming city taxi, one that has just dropped passengers off. These will usually take you to Bangkok for 100 to 150B. Airport officials frown on this practice, however, and you may be hassled.

Taxis flagged down on the highway in front of the airport are cheaper – 80 to 100B. THAI offers an airport limousine service for 300B, which is just a glorified air-con taxi service really.

Going to the airport from the city, taxis will ask an outrageous amount but will usually go for 150B or so (up to 200B if your bargaining is weak or there aren't many taxis around – but the standard fare is 150B), not too bad if you're looking for the fastest way out, or have a few other travellers with whom to share the fare.

THAI Bus Thai Airways International has an airport bus that goes to their city terminal at the Asia Hotel for 60B per person. The Asia Hotel is in a good central location on Phayathai Rd between Phetburi and Rama I Rds. From here a tuk-tuk to accommodation in the Siam Square area should be 25B or less. If you're not carrying much, you could also walk there in around 20 minutes. Or walk north to Phetburi Rd and get ordinary bus Nos 2, 45, 60 or air-con bus No 11 to Banglamphu. To other areas of the city, however, you might as well get a direct taxi since the THAI bus fare plus tuk-tuk or taxi fare to, say, Soi Ngam Duphli would approach the 180B direct taxi fare. This bus is in service from 7 am until 9 pm.

THAI also has a minibus service to major hotels (and minor ones if the driver feels like it) for 100B per person. There are direct air-con buses to Pattaya from the airport twice daily at 11 am and 9 pm; the fare is 180B one way.

There is a free THAI shuttle between the international and domestic terminals every half-hour.

Public Bus Cheapest of all are the public buses which stop on the highway to Bangkok, out front. The ordinary No 29 bus is only 2B, but often crowded – it comes straight down Phahonyothin Rd after entering the city limits. This road soon turns into Phayathai Rd, meanwhile passing Phetburi Rd (where you'll want to get off to change buses if you're going to the Democracy Monument area), Rama I Rd (for buses out

to Sukhumvit, or to walk to Soi Kasem San I for Muangphol Lodging, Reno Hotel, etc) and finally turning right on Rama IV Rd to go to the Hualamphong district. You'll want to go the opposite way on Rama IV for the Malaysia, Boston Inn, etc. Bus No 59 goes straight to the Democracy Monument area from the airport.

The air-con public bus No 4 can also be boarded at the airport for 15B to most destinations in Bangkok. It costs less if you're getting off in north Bangkok (say, for the Liberty Hotel in Saphan Khwai district), though this must be established before you pay the fare. Unless you're really strapped for baht, it's worth the extra 12B for the air-con and almost guaranteed seating on the No 4, especially in the hot season, since the trip downtown by bus can take an hour or more.

The No 4 bus does a route parallel to the No 29 – down Mitthaphap Rd to Ratchaprarop and Rajadamri Rds, crossing Phetburi, Rama I, Ploenchit and Rama IV Rds, then down Silom, left on Charoen Krung, and across the river to Thonburi. You ought to have some kind of map of Bangkok before attempting the buses so you'll know approximately where to get off. The air-con No 13 also goes to Bangkok from the airport, coming down Phahonyothin Rd (like No 29), turning left at the Victory Monument to Ratchaprarop Rd, then south to Ploenchit Rd, where it goes east out Sukhumvit Rd all the way to Bang Na.

The air-con bus No 10 terminates at the Southern Bus Terminal in Thonburi, where you can get buses direct to Kanchanaburi and points south. There is now an air-con bus No 29 that goes to Hualamphong Station along the same basic route as the regular bus No 29.

Air-con buses run from 5 am until 8 or 8.30 pm. Ordinary buses run until 10 pm.

Train You can also get into Bangkok from the airport by train. Just leave the airport building, cross the highway via the pedestrian bridge, turn left and walk about 100 metres towards Bangkok. Directly opposite the big Airport Hotel is the small Don Muang

Railway Station from where trains depart regularly to Bangkok. The 3rd-class fare is 5B on the ordinary and commuter trains. If you happen to get on a rapid or express train you'll have to pay a 20B or 30B surcharge. There are trains every 15 to 30 minutes between 6.25 am and 10 pm and it take 45 minutes to reach Hualamphong. In the opposite direction trains run frequently between 7.05 am and 10 pm. You can also ride trains between Hualamphong and Makkasan, which is north of Phetburi Rd near the intersection of Ratchaprarop and Si Ayuthaya Rds, not far from the Indra and Bangkok Palace Hotels. There are no direct trains between Don Muang and Makkasan; you have to change in Hualamphong. The trip only takes 15 minutes but there are just 11 trains per day, between 6.15 am and 6 pm.

Departure Tax Airport departure tax is 200B for international flights, 20B for domestic. Don't complain: the Thais have to pay a 2000B departure tax when they leave the country.

Airport Facilities Over the last 10 years, Don Muang Airport has undergone a US$200 million redevelopment, including a new international terminal that is one of the most modern and convenient in Asia. One major problem that remains is the very slow immigration lines in the upstairs arrival hall. Despite a long row of impressive-looking immigration counters, there never seem to be enough clerks on duty, even at peak arrival times. Baggage claim, however, is usually quick and efficient (of course they have plenty of time to get it right while you're inching along through immigration).

The customs area now has a green lane for passengers with nothing to declare – just walk on through if you're one of these and hand your customs form to one of the clerks by the exit. Baggage trolleys are free for use inside the terminal.

On the 4th floor of the international terminal is the Rajthanee Food Mall, a small cafeteria area where you can choose among Thai, Chinese and European dishes at fairly reasonable prices. Next door is the larger THAI restaurant with more expensive fare. On the 2nd level above the arrival area is a coffee shop, and there is also a small snack bar in the waiting area of the ground floor.

The airport has the usual bank, post office, left luggage facilities and a tourist information counter in the arrival area. The hotel counter here makes reservations for THA (Thai Hotel Association) members. This doesn't go below the Miami-Malaysia standard of hotel. The Thai Military Bank at the airport gives a good rate of exchange.

If you leave the airport building area and cross the freeway on the pedestrian bridge you'll find yourself in the Don Muang town area where there are all sorts of shops, a market, lots of small restaurants and food stalls, even a wat, all within a hundred metres or so of the airport. For someone who is desperate for a place to stay but can't afford the Airport Hotel (US$60 to $100), the only choice at this writing is the rather dismal *Bamboo Guest House* (tel 531-3506), several hundred metres north of the terminal, where dank rooms are 120B. They claim that if you call they'll pick you up at the airport. The place is overrun with dogs so it's recommended only as a last resort. The Airport Hotel also has 'Special Ministay' daytime rates (8 am to 6 pm) for stays of up to a maximum of three hours for 350/400B a single/double, including tax and service. Longer daytime rates are available on request (tel 566-1020, 566-1021).

The Thai government has plans to open another international airport about 17 km east of Bangkok at Nong Ngu Hao. This additional airport is expected to be completed by 1996 and will be named Raja Deva (Racha Thewa).

Central Thailand

Officially speaking, Central Thailand is made up of 25 provinces, stretching as far north as Nakhon Sawan, south to Prachuap Khiri Khan, west to Kanchanaburi and east to Trat. Because of the rain-fed network of rivers and canals in the central region, this is the most fertile part of Thailand, supporting vast fields of rice and sugar cane, pineapples and other fruit, sugar cane and cassava.

Linguistically, the people of Central Thailand share a common dialect which is considered 'Standard Thai' simply because Bangkok happens to be in the middle of it. High concentrations of Chinese are found throughout the central provinces since this is where a large number of Chinese immigrants started out as farmers and merchants. There are also significant numbers of Mon in Pathum Thani, Burmese to the west, and Lao and Khmer to the east, for obvious reasons.

Many places in Central Thailand can be visited in day trips from Bangkok but in most cases they make better stepping stones to places further afield. You can, for example, pause in Ayuthaya on the way north to Chiang Mai, or in Nakhon Pathom if you're heading south.

Ayuthaya Province

AYUTHAYA TOWN เมือง อยุธยา

Approximately 86 km north of Bangkok, Ayuthaya (population 56,000) was the Thai capital from 1350 to 1767 and by all accounts it was a splendid city. Prior to 1350, when the capital was moved here from U Thong, it was a Khmer outpost. The city was named for Ayodhya, the home of Rama in the Indian epic Ramayana, which is Sanskrit for 'unassailable' or 'undefeatable'. Its full Thai name is Phra Nakhon Si Ayuthaya, the 'Sacred City of Ayodhya'.

Thirty-three kings of various Siamese dynasties reigned in Ayuthaya until it was conquered by the Burmese. During its heyday, Thai culture and international commerce flourished in the kingdom – the Ayuthaya Period has so far been the apex of Thai history – and Ayuthaya was courted by Dutch, Portuguese, French, English, Chinese and Japanese merchants. All visitors claimed it to be the most illustrious city they had ever seen.

The present-day city is located at the confluence of three rivers, the Chao Phraya, the Pa Sak and the smaller Lopburi. A wide canal joins them and makes a complete circle around the town. Long-tail boats can be rented from the boat landing across from Chandra Kasem (Chan Kasem) Palace for a tour around the river/canal; several of the old wat ruins (Wat Panan Choeng, Wat Phuttaisawan, Wat Kasatthirat and Wat Chai Wattanaram) may be glimpsed at from the canal, as well as a picturesque view of river life. Apart from the historic ruins and museums, Ayuthaya is not particularly interesting, but it is one of three cities in Thailand known for their 'gangster' activity.

Many of the ruins now collect a 10 to 20B admission fee during civil service hours (8 am to 4.30 pm).

The MM Swimming Pool at 21/25 Phaton Rd near the police station admits visitors from 8 am to 9 pm for 30B per day.

National Museum

There are two museums, the main one being the Chao Sam Phraya Museum, which is near the intersection of Rotchana Rd (Ayuthaya's main street, connecting with the highway to Bangkok) and Si Sanphet Rd, opposite the town hall near the centre of town. It is open from 9 am to 12 noon and 1 pm to 4 pm, Wednesday to Sunday and entry is 10B.

The second, Chan Kasem Palace (*Phra Ratchawong Chan Kasem*), is a museum piece itself, built by the 17th king of Ayuthaya – Maha Thammarat – for his son

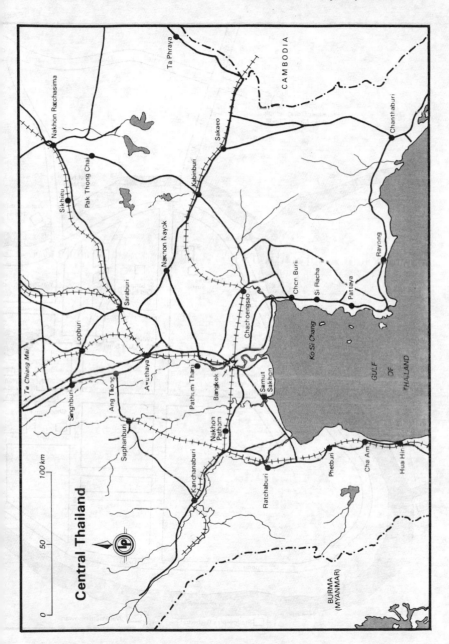

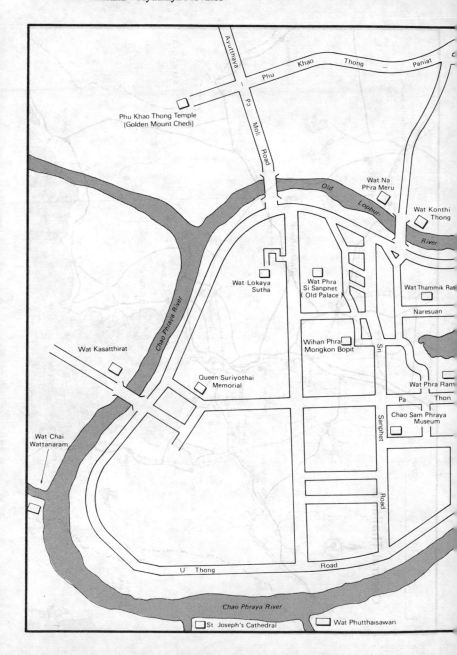

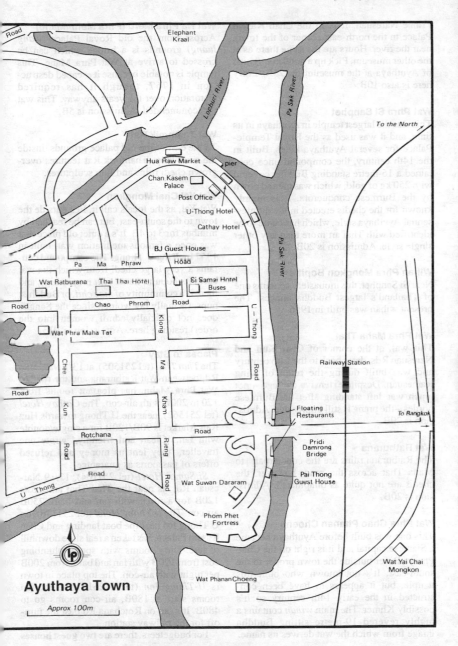

Ayuthaya Town

Approx 100m

Prince Naresuan. It is in the Chan Kasem Palace in the north-east corner of the town, near the river. Hours are the same there as at the other museum. Pick up a good map/guide of Ayuthaya at the museum for 25B. Entry here is also 10B.

Wat Phra Si Sanphet
This was the largest temple in Ayuthaya in its time, and it was used as the Royal Temple-Palace for several Ayuthaya kings. Built in the 14th century, the compound once contained a 16-metre standing Buddha covered with 250 kg of gold, which was melted down by the Burmese conquerors. It is mainly known for the chedis erected in the quintessential Ayuthaya style, which has come to be identified with Thai art more than any other single style. Admission is 20B.

Wihan Phra Mongkon Bopit
Near Si Sanphet, this monastery contains one of Thailand's largest Buddha images. The present wihan was built in 1956.

Wat Phra Maha That
This wat, at the corner of Chee Kun and Naresuan Rds, dates back to the 14th century and was built during the reign of King Ramesuan. Despite extensive damage – not much was left standing after the Burmese hordes – the prang is still impressive. Admission is 20B.

Wat Ratburana
The Ratburana ruins are the counterpart to Maha That across the road, however, the chedis are not quite as dilapidated. Admission is 20B.

Wat Phra Chao Phanan Choeng
This one was built before Ayuthaya became a Siamese capital and it is right on the Chao Phraya River outside the town proper to the south-east. It's not known who built this temple, but it appears to have been constructed in the early 14th century so it's possibly Khmer. The main *wihan* contains a highly revered 19-metre sitting Buddha image from which the wat derives its name.

Wat Na Phra Meru (Phra Mehn/Mane)
Across from the old Royal Palace *(wang luang)* grounds is a bridge which can be crossed to arrive at Wat Phra Mane. This temple is notable because it escaped destruction in 1767, though it has required restoration over the years anyway. This wat is recommended. Admission is 5B.

Wat Thammik Rat
To the east of the old palace grounds, inside the river loop, Thammik Rat features overgrown chedi ruins and lion sculptures.

Wat Yai Chai Mongkon
Wat Yai, as the locals call it, lies outside the town to the south-east, but can be reached by minibus for 3 to 4B. It's a quiet old place that was once a famous meditation wat, built in 1357 by King U Thong. The compound contains a very large chedi from which the wat takes its popular name (*yai* means big), and there is a community of *mae chii*, or Buddhist nuns, (actually lay women since the Sangha does not officially admit women into the order) residing here. Admission is 10B.

Places to Stay
The *Thai Thai* (tel 251505), at 13/1 Naresuan Rd, between Wat Ratburana and the road to Wat Phra Mehn, has pleasant rooms from 120 to 200B with air-con. The *Cathay Hotel* (tel 251562), near the U Thong towards Hua Raw Market is 90B/120B for a single/double with fan. 'Clean and friendly,' wrote one traveller, 'they lent us money and refused offers of passports as guarantee'.

Si Samai Hotel (tel 251104), 12/19 Naresuan Rd, is near the Thai Thai and costs 120B for a room with fan and bath, 250B air-con. The *U Thong Hotel* (tel 251136), on U Thong Rd near the boat landing and Chan Kasem Palace, has taken a real slide downhill of late. Dirty rooms with spotty plumbing cost from 100B with fan and bath, from 200B per night with air-con. The top place in town is *U-Thong Inn* (tel 242618), where fan rooms start at 180B, air-con rooms go to 480B. It's out on Rotchana Rd past the turn-off for the railway station.

For budgeteers, there are two guest houses

in Ayuthaya to choose from. The *Pai Thong Guest House* (tel 241830) is right on the river within walking distance of the railway station. The couple who own the home are helpful and friendly. Food is served and boats can be hired from the back of the house for river tours. Large, clean rooms are 60B with fan and shared bath. To get there from the railway station, cross the river and turn left at the road at the other end of the bridge, then walk about 75 metres until you see a sign for Pai Thong on your left. A tuk-tuk will bring you here from the station for 10B. The couple at Pai Thong do not pay tuk-tuk drivers commissions so if a driver says the Pai Thong is full, make sure you see for yourself.

The *BJ Guest House* (tel 251512) is down a soi off Naresuan Rd near the bus terminal and the Si Samai Hotel. There are 12 rooms here, some with one large bed, others with two twin beds. Rates are 50/80B a single/double. There is a small restaurant downstairs.

Places to Eat

The best places to eat are the Hua Raw market, on the river near Chan Kasem Palace, and the Chao Phrom market, on Chao Phrom Rd east of Wat Ratburana. There are quite a few restaurants on the main road into Ayuthaya, Rotchana Rd, and there are three floating restaurants on the Pa Sak River, one on either side of the Pridi Damrong Bridge on the west bank and one on the east bank north of the bridge. Food is fairly expensive and not all that good at two of them, but the *Phae Krung Kao* has a good reputation – it's the one on the south side of the bridge on the west bank.

Getting There & Away

Bus Daily buses leave from the Northern Bus Terminal in Bangkok every 10 minutes between 5 am and 7 pm. The fare is 17B and the trip takes 1½ hours.

Train Trains to Ayuthaya leave Bangkok's Hualamphong Station every hour or two between 4.30 am and 10 pm. The 3rd-class fare is 15B for the 1½ hour trip (plus rapid/express charges if it's not an ordinary

train); it's hardly worth taking a more expensive seat for this short trip. Train schedules are available at the information booth at Hualamphong Station.

Boat Boats to Ayuthaya leave Bangkok from Tha Tien Pier near Thammasat daily at about 10 am, but the trip is rather long going upriver. Better to take the boat back from Ayuthaya – about three hours or so. Check at the landing near Chan Kasem Palace in Ayuthaya for the current charter rates. A typical round-trip charter fare for a long-tail boat from Bangkok to Ayuthaya to Bangkok would be 1200B. You can get a water taxi from Ayuthaya to Bang Pa In for around 250B. There's a tour boat operating from the Oriental Hotel to Ayuthaya for 760B. You can go by bus or boat and return by the opposite mode of transport. Lunch is included on this deluxe tour.

Getting Around

Minibuses from the railway station to any point in Ayuthaya should be 5 to 10B. You can hire a samlor or songthaew by the hour to explore the ruins. It's also interesting to hire a boat from the palace pier (or Pai Thong Guest House) to do a circular tour of the island to see some of the less accessible ruins. Ayuthaya covers a surprisingly large area – it's not a place where you walk around. A boat can be hired for around 200B an hour and will take up to eight passengers.

During the 10 days leading to the Songkran Festival in mid April, there is a sound & light show with fireworks over the ruins. Every day between 10.30 am and 1.30 pm the local government runs boat tours from the U Thong pier for 50B per person.

BANG PA IN บางปะอิน

Twenty km south of Ayuthaya is Bang Pa In, which has a curious collection of palace buildings in a wide variety of architectural styles. It's a nice boat trip from Ayuthaya, although in itself it's not particularly noteworthy. The palace is open from 8.30 am to 12 noon and 1 pm to 4 pm daily, except Mondays. Admission is 10B.

Palace Buildings

The postcard stereotype here is a pretty little Thai pavilion in the centre of a small lake by the palace entrance. Inside the palace grounds, the Chinese-style Wehat Chamrun Palace is the only building open to visitors. The Withun Thatsana building looks like a lighthouse with balconies. It was built to give a fine view over gardens and lakes. There are various other buildings, towers and memorials in the grounds plus an interesting example of topiary where the bushes have been trimmed into the shape of a small herd of elephants.

Wat Niwet Thamaprawat

Across the river and south from the palace grounds this unusual wat looks much more like a gothic Christian church than anything from Thailand. It was built by Rama V (Chulalongkorn). You get to the wat by crossing the river in a small trolley-like cable car. The crossing is free.

Getting There & Away

Bang Pa In can be reached by minibus (really a large songthaew) truck rather than a bus from Ayuthaya's Chao Phrom market, Chao Phrom Rd, for 6B. From Bangkok there are buses every half-hour or so from the Northern Bus Terminal and the fare is 14B. You can also reach Bang Pa In by train or by boat from Bangkok, or by boat from Ayuthaya.

The Chao Phraya Express Boat Co does a tour every Sunday from the Maharat pier in Bangkok that goes to Wat Pailom in Patum Thani as well as Bang Pa In. The trip leaves from Bangkok at 8.30 am and returns at 5.30 pm. The price is 140B not including lunch, which you arrange on your own in Bang Pa In.

Lopburi Province

LOPBURI TOWN เมือง ลพบุรี

Exactly 154 km north of Bangkok, the town of Lopburi (population 39,000) has been inhabited since at least the Dvaravati Period (6th to 11th centuries AD) when it was called

Lavo. Nearly all traces of Lavo culture have been erased by Khmer and Thai inhabitants since the 10th century, but many Dvaravati artefacts found in Lopburi can be seen in the Lopburi National Museum. Ruins and statuary in Lopburi span 12 centuries.

The Khmers extended their Angkor empire in the 10th century to include Lavo. It was during this century that they built the Prang Khaek (Hindu Shrine), San Phra Kan (Kala Shrine) and Prang Sam Yot (Three-Spired Shrine) – the current symbol of Lopburi Province which appears on the back of the 500B note - as well as the impressive prang at Wat Phra Sri Ratana Mahathat.

Power over Lopburi was wrested from the Khmers in the 13th century as the Sukhothai Kingdom to the north grew stronger, but the Khmer cultural influence remained to some extent throughout the Ayuthaya Period. King Narai fortified Lopburi in the mid-17th century to serve as a second capital when the kingdom of Ayuthaya was threatened by a Dutch naval blockade. Narai's palace in Lopburi was constructed in 1665 and he died there in 1688.

The new town of Lopburi was begun in 1940. It is some distance east of the old fortified town and is centred around two large traffic circles. There is really nothing of interest in the new section, so you should try to stay at a hotel in the old town. All the historical sites in Lopburi can be visited on foot in a day or two.

Phra Narai Ratchaniwet

King Narai's palace is probably the best place to begin a tour of Lopburi. After King Narai's death in 1688, the palace was used only by King Phetracha (Narai's successor) for his coronation ceremony and it was then abandoned until King Mongkut ordered restoration in the mid-19th century.

The palace took 12 years to build (1665-77). French architects contributed to the design and Khmer influence was still strong in central Thailand at that time. It's hardly surprising then that the palace exhibits an unusual blend of Khmer and European style – but it works.

The main gate into the palace, Pratu

Phayakkha, is off Sorasak Rd, opposite the Asia Lopburi Hotel. The grounds are well kept, planted with trees and shrubbery and serve as a kind of town park for local children and young lovers. Immediately on the left as you enter are the remains of the king's elephant stables, with the palace water reservoir in the foreground. In the adjacent quadrangle to the left is the royal reception hall and the Phra Chao Hao, which probably served as a wihan for a valued Buddha image. Passing through more stables, one comes to the south-west quadrangle with the Suttha Sawan pavilion in the centre. The north-west quadrangle contains many ruined buildings which were once an audience hall, various *sala* and residence quarters for the king's harem.

The Lopburi National Museum is located here in three separate buildings. Two of the museum buildings house an excellent collection of Lopburi Period sculpture, as well as an assortment of Khmer, Dvaravati, U Thong and Ayuthaya art. The third building features traditional farm implements and dioramas of farm life. *A Guide to Ancient Monuments in Lopburi* by M C Subhadradis Diskul, Thailand's leading art historian, is available from the counter on the 2nd floor of the museum. Admission into the museum is 10B; it is open Wednesday to Sunday, from 9 am to 12 pm and 1 to 4 pm.

Wat Phra Si Ratana Mahathat

Directly across from the railway station, this very large 12th-century Khmer wat is currently undergoing restoration by the Fine Arts Department. A very tall laterite prang still stands and features a few intact lintels, as well as some ornate stucco. A large wihan added by King Narai also displays a ruined elegance. Several chedis and smaller prangs dot the grounds – some almost completely restored, some a little worse for wear – and there are a few ruined parts of Buddha images laying about. Admission is 20B.

Wat Nakhon Kosa

This wat is just north of the railway station, near San Phra Kan. It was built by the Khmers in the 12th century and may origi-

nally have been a Hindu shrine. U Thong and Lopburi images found at the temple (now in the Lopburi Museum) are thought to have been added later. There's not much left of this wat, though the foliage growing on the brick ruins makes an interesting image. However, half-hearted attempts to restore it with modern materials and motifs detract from the overall effect. A recent excavation has uncovered a larger base below the monument.

Wat Indra & Wat Racha

Wat Indra is across the street from Wat Nakhon Kosa. Practically nothing is known of its history and it is now merely a pile of brick rubble. Wat Racha, off Phra Ya Jamkat Rd, is another pile of bricks with little known history.

Wat Sao Thong Thong

This wat is north-west of the palace centre, behind the central market. The buildings here are in pretty poor shape. The wihan and large seated Buddha are from the Ayuthaya Period; King Narai restored the wihan, changing the windows to an incongruous but intriguing Gothic style so that it could be used as a Christian chapel. Niches along the inside walls contain Lopburi style *naga* Buddhas.

Chao Phraya Wichayen (Constantine Phaulkon Residence)

Across the street north-east of Wat Sao Thong Thong, King Narai built this eclectic Thai-European palace as a residence for foreign ambassadors, of whom the Greek Constantine Phaulkon was the most famous. Phaulkon became one of King Narai's principal advisers and was eventually a royal minister. In 1688, as Narai lay dying, Phaulkon was assassinated by Luang Sorasak, who wanted all the power of Narai's throne for himself. Admission is 20B.

San Phra Kan (Kala Shrine)

Across the railway tracks to the north of Wat Nakhon Kosa, this unimpressive shrine contains a crude gold-leaf laden image of Kala, the Hindu god of time and death. A virtual sea of monkeys surrounds the shrine, falling

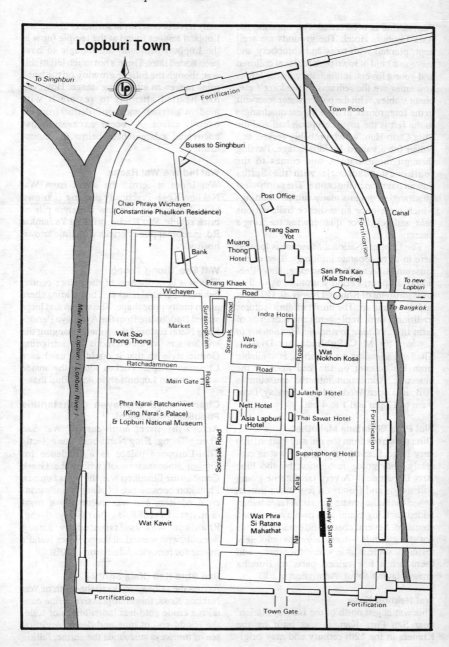

Lopburi Town

To Singhburi

Fortification

Town Pond

Buses to Singhburi

Post Office

Canal

Fortification

Chao Phraya Wichayen
(Constantine Phaulkon Residence)

Bank

Prang Sam
Yot

Muang
Thong
Hotel

San Phra Kan
(Kala Shrine)

To new
Lopburi

Prang Khaek

Wichayen   Road

To Bangkok

Market

Surasongkram Road

Sorasak Road

Indra Hotel

Wat
Indra

Wat Sao
Thong Thong

Wat
Nokhon Kosa

Ratchadamnoen

Road

Main Gate

Road

Road

Julathip Hotel

Mae Nam Lopburi / Lopburi River

Phra Narai Ratchaniwet
(King Narai's Palace)
& Lopburi National Museum

Nett Hotel

Asia Lapburi
Hotel

Thai Sawat Hotel

Suparaphong Hotel

Sorasak Road

Kala

Na

Fortification

Wat Kawit

Wat Phra
Si Ratana
Mahathat

Railway Station

Fortification

Fortification

Town Gate

out of the tamarind trees and scurrying along the steps leading to the sanctuary. They are getting fat on hand-outs.

Prang Sam Yot

Opposite the Kala shrine, near the Muang Thong Hotel, this shrine represents classic Khmer-Lopburi style and is another Hindu-turned-Buddhist temple. Originally the three prangs symbolised the Hindu *trimurti* of Shiva, Vishnu and Brahma. Now two of them contain ruined Lopburi-style Buddha images. Some Khmer lintels can still be made out and some appear unfinished.

A rather uninteresting U Thong/Ayuthaya imitation Buddha image sits in the brick sanctuary in front of the linked prangs. At the back, facing the Muang Thong Hotel, are a couple of crudely restored images, probably once Lopburi style. The grounds allotted to Prang Sam Yot by the town are rather small and make the structure difficult to photograph. The grounds are virtually surrounded by modern buildings as well. The best view of the monument would probably be from one of the upper floors of the Muang Thong. The monument is lit up at night.

Music & Dance

For those interested in Thai classical music and dance, there is a fine arts college (Withayalai Kalasilpa Lopburi) on Pha Ya Jamkat Rd, not far from the palace. Here you can watch young dancers practising the rudiments of classical dance with live musical accompaniment.

Places to Stay

Lopburi can be visited as a day trip en route to the north, but if you want to stay overnight there are a number of hotels you can try.

Asia Lopburi Hotel (tel 411892), on the corner of Sorasak and Phra Yam Jamkat Rds and overlooking King Narai's palace, is clean, comfortable, has good service and two Chinese restaurants downstairs. Rooms are 120B with fan and bath.

Muang Thong Hotel (tel 411036), across from Prang Sam Yot, has noisy but adequate rooms for 100B with fan and bath. Rooms without bath are also available for 60B.

The *Indra* on Na Kala Rd is across from Wat Nakhon Kosa and costs 70B for just passable rooms with fan and bath. Also on Na Kala Rd, the *Julathip Hotel* is near the Indra but closer to the railway station, and has no English sign. This one is 60B with fan and bath – ask to see a room first. Also on Na Kala Rd, the *Suparaphong Hotel* is not far from Wat Phra Sri Ratana Mahathat and the railway station. This costs 70B and is much the same as the Julathip and Indra hotels.

A few shops down from Julathip on the same street is the *Thai Sawat* which, at 50B per room, is Lopburi's cheapest.

The *Nett Hotel* (tel 411738) at 17/1-2 Ratchadamnoen Rd is actually on a soi between Ratchadamnoen and Phra Yam Jamkat Rds, parallel to Sorasak Rd. It's 90B up for clean, quiet rooms with fan and bath.

You can also pay a visit to the *Travellers Drop in Centre* at 34 Wichayen Rd, Soi 3 Maung. Here travellers can meet Thais at the informal English classes held here three times daily. After the class, the students go with travellers and share a meal in a restaurant. They also run a small Guest House for travellers – there are two double rooms; the cost is 50B for one person or 60B to 70B for two.

Behind the bus station in the new part of the town is the *Srisawat*. The rooms here are grubby and cost 90B, but the Chinese owners are friendly. However, it's not recommended unless you have to be in the new town or arrive late at night by bus.

There are so many hotels along Na Kala Rd that bargaining should be possible. Ask if they have a 'cheaper room'. The Thai for this is *Mii hawng tuuk kwaa mai?*

Places to Eat

Several Chinese restaurants operate along Na Kala Rd, parallel to the railway, especially near the Julathip and Thai Sawat hotels. The food is good but they tend to overcharge a bit. Restaurants on the side streets of Ratchadamnoen and Phra Yam Jamkat Rds can be better value. The Chinese-Thai restaurant next to the Asia Lopburi Hotel on Sorasak Rd, across from the main gate to King Narai's palace, makes excellent tom yam kung (shrimp-lemon grass soup), kai phat bai kaphrao (chicken fried in holy basil) and *kuaytiaw raat naa* (fried rice noodles with vegetables and sauce). There are also plenty of cheap curry vendors down the alleys and along the smaller streets in old Lopburi.

The market off Ratchadamnoen and Surasongkhram Rds (just north of the palace) is a great place to pick up food to eat in your hotel room – kai thawt or kai yang (fried or roast chicken) with sticky rice, haw mok (fish and coconut curry steamed in banana leaves), kluay khaek ('Indian-style' fried bananas), a wide selection of fruits, satay, *khao kriap* (crispy rice cakes), thawt man plaa (fried fish cakes) and other delights.

Getting There & Away
Bus Buses leave for Lopburi every 10 minutes from Ayuthaya, or, if you're coming from Bangkok, about every 20 minutes (5.21 am to 8.29 pm) from the Northern Terminal. It's a three-hour ride which costs 32B, or 60B air-con.

Lopburi can also be reached from the west via Kanchanaburi or Suphanburi. If you're coming from Kanchanaburi, you'll have to take a bus first to Suphanburi from the Kan Bus Station. The trip lasts two hours, costs 21B, and has great scenery all the way. In Suphanburi, get off the bus along the town's main drag, Malimaen Rd (has English signs), at the intersection which has an English sign pointing to Sri Prachan. This is also where you catch the bus to Singhburi or Ang Thong, across the river from Lopburi, and a necessary stop.

The Suphanburi to Singhburi leg lasts about 2½ hours for 20B and the scenery gets even better – you'll pass many old, traditional Thai wooden houses (late Ayuthaya style), countless cool rice paddies and small wats of all descriptions. Finally, at the Singhburi Bus Station, catch one of the frequent buses to Lopburi for 7B – takes about 30 minutes. An alternative to the Suphanburi to Singhburi route is to take a bus to Ang Thong (10B) and then a share taxi (15B) or bus (13B) to Lopburi. This is a little faster but not quite as scenic.

From the north-east, Lopburi can be reached via Khorat for 40B.

Train Ordinary trains depart Hualamphong Station, heading north, every hour or so between 4.30 am and 8 pm and take only 20 to 30 minutes longer to reach Lopburi than the Rapid or Express. Only two ordinary trains, the 7.05 am and the 8.30 am, have 2nd-class seats; the rest are 3rd class only. Rapid trains leave at 6.40 am, 3, 8 and 10 pm and take about 2½ hours to reach Lopburi. Only the Express train, which leaves Bangkok every day at 6 pm, has 1st-class seats. Fares are 111B in 1st class, 57B in 2nd class and 28B in 3rd, not including surcharges for Rapid or Express trains.

There are also regular trains from Ayuthaya to Lopburi which take about one hour and cost 13B in 3rd class. It is possible to leave Bangkok or Ayuthaya in the morning, have a look around Lopburi during the day (leaving your bags in the Lopburi Railway Station) and then carry on to Chiang Mai on one of the night trains (departure times are at 5.27, 8.20 pm and 12.22 am).

Getting Around
Samlors will go anywhere in Lopburi for 5 to 10B.

Ang Thong & Saraburi Provinces

ANG THONG TOWN เมือง อ่างทอง
There are some places of interest outside small Ang Thong (population 10,000), between Lopburi and Suphanburi, including Wat Pa Mok with its 22-metre-long reclining Buddha. The village of Ban Phae is famous for the crafting of Thai drums or *klawng*. Ban Phae is behind the Pa Mok Market on the banks for the Chao Phraya River.

Places to Stay
Rooms cost from 80B in the *Bua Luang* (tel 611116) on Ayuthaya Rd. The *Ang Thong Hotel & Bungalows* (tel 611767/8) at 19 Ang

Thong Rd is 90B up in the hotel, 80B in the bungalows.

Getting There & Away

A bus from the Northern Bus Terminal in Bangkok costs 25B.

SARABURI TOWN เมือง สระบุรี

There's nothing of interest in Saraburi Town (population 56,000) itself, but between Lopburi and here you can turn off to the Phra Buddhabat (Phra Phutthabaht). This small and delicately beautiful shrine houses a revered Buddha footprint. Like all genuine Buddha footprints, it is massive and identified by its 108 auspicious distinguishing marks. Twice yearly, in early February and in the middle of March, Phra Buddhabat is the focus of a colourful pilgrimage festival.

Also outside of Saraburi Town is Krabawk Cave Monastery (Samnak Song Tham Krabawk), a famous opium and heroin detoxification centre. Originally begun by Mae-chii Mian, a Buddhist nun, the controversial programme has been administered by Luang Phaw Chamrun Panchan since 1959. The programme employs a combination of herbal treatment, counselling, and Dhamma to cure addicts and claims a 70% success rate. Thousands of addicts have come to Tham Krabawk to seek treatment, which begins with a rigorous 10-day session involving the ingestion of emetic herbs to purify the body of intoxicants. In 1975, Phra Chamrun was awarded the Magsaysay Prize for his work. Visitors are welcome at the centre.

Places to Stay

Try the *Thanin* (100B) or the *Suk San* (60 to 120B) at Amphoe Phra Buddha Baht. In Saraburi there's the *Kiaw An* (tel 211656) on Phahonyothin Rd where rooms with fan cost from 100B, or from 200B with air-con. Other hotels include the slightly cheaper *Saraburi* (tel 211646, 211500) opposite the bus stand or the *Saen Suk* (tel 211104) on Phahonyothin Rd.

Getting There & Away

Ordinary buses from Bangkok's Northern Bus Terminal cost 28B to Saraburi.

Songthaews from Saraburi to Phra Buddhabit or Tham Krabawk cost around 5B per person.

Suphanburi Province

SUPHANBURI TOWN เมือง สุพรรณบุรี

Almost 70 km north-east of Kanchanaburi, Suphanburi (population 25,000) is a very old Thai town that may have had some connection with the semi-mythical *Suvarnabhumi* mentioned in early Buddhist writings. During the Dvaravati Period (6th to 10th centuries) it was called 'Muang Thawarawadi Si Suphannaphumi'. Today the town is a prosperous, typical central Thai town with a high proportion of Chinese among the population. There are some noteworthy Ayuthaya Period chedis and one Khmer prang. If you're passing through Suphan on a trip from Kanchanaburi to Lopburi, you might want to stop off for a couple of hours, see the sights, eat and rest.

Entering Suphan from the direction of Kan, you'll see Wat Palelai on the right at the town limits. Several of the buildings are old, originally built during the U Thong Period, and the bot is very distinctive because of its extremely high whitewashed walls. Looking inside, you'll realise the building was designed that way in order to house the gigantic late U Thong or early Ayuthaya-style seated Buddha image inside. Exotic-looking goats roam the grounds of this semiabandoned wat.

Further in towards the town centre, on the left side of Malimaen Rd, is Wat Phra Si Ratana Mahathat (this must be the most popular name for wats in Thailand), set back off the road a bit. This quiet wat features a fine Lopburi-style Khmer prang on which much of the stucco is still intact. There is a staircase inside the prang leading to a small chamber in the top.

Two other wats this side of the new town, Wat Phra Rup and Wat Chum, have venerable old Ayuthaya chedis.

Don Chedi

Seven km west past Suphanburi off Route

324 on the way to Kanchanaburi is the road to Don Chedi, a very famous battle site and early war memorial. It was here that King Naresuan, then a prince, defeated the Prince of Burma on elephant back in the late 16th century. In doing so he freed Ayuthaya from domination by the Pegu Kingdom.

The chedi or pagoda itself was built during Naresuan's lifetime but was neglected in the centuries afterwards. By the reign of King Rama V (Chulalongkorn) at the beginning of this century, its location had been forgotten. Rama V began a search for the site but it wasn't until three years after his death in 1913 that Prince Damrong, an accomplished archaeologist, rediscovered the chedi in Suphanburi Province.

The chedi was restored in 1955 and the area developed as a national historic site. Every year during the week of January 25 (Thai Armed Forces Day), there is a week-long Don Chedi Monument Fair which features a full costume re-enactment of the elephant battle that took place four centuries ago.

During the fair there are regular buses to Don Chedi from Suphanburi, the nearest place to stay. Transportation from Bangkok can also be arranged through the bigger travel agencies in Bangkok.

Places to Stay

The *King Pho Sai* (tel 511412) at 678 Nen Kaew Rd has rooms from 100B or from 200B with air-con. Other similarly priced hotels are the *KAT* (tel 511619, 511639) at 433 Phra Phanwasa and the *Suk San* (tel 511668) at 1145 Nang Phim Rd. The *Wanchai*, 309-10 Phra Phanwasa Rd, is a Chinese hotel with rooms for 80B.

Getting There & Away

See the Getting There information in the Lopburi section. A bus from the Northern Bus Terminal in Bangkok costs 47B.

KHAO YAI NATIONAL PARK
อุทยานแห่งชาติ เขาใหญ่

Technically speaking, Khao Yai is in north-eastern Thailand, but it's a short trip from Bangkok so I'm including it with central

Thailand. This is a huge (2168 square km) and beautiful park with good walks. You can get a rather inaccurate trail map from the park headquarters. It's easy to get lost on the longer trails so it's advisable to hire a guide. The charge will be 100B per day no matter how many people go. The guide is liable to ask for a tip. If you do plan to go walking, it is a good idea to take boots as leeches can be a problem – although apparently mosquito repellent does help to keep leeches away.

The trailhead and park headquarters are about 4 km from the Khao Yai Hotel. A school bus stops near the hotel at 7 am and will give hikers a lift to the trailhead for free.

Places to Stay

The *Khao Yai Hotel* operates 30 bungalows, 18 motel rooms and several dormitories. The motel rooms are 555B for two beds, 666B with a sitting room, and 777B with four beds - all with bath. It's near the bus station in Pak Chong. Bungalows range from 888B for four beds to 1443B for 10 beds. Dormitory accommodation is available for 80B. Groups can also hire cottages from the headquarters, for 500B or more for six to 15 people. There are also camping areas where you can pitch a tent for 5B per person per night.

Food at the hotel restaurant ranges from 20B for rice soup to 90B for fried chicken with chips, salad, bread or rice, fruit and coffee.

Getting There & Away

Take a bus from the Northern Bus Station to Pak Chong, from where you can hitch or take a songthaew to the park gates. A park car will take you from there. The Khao Yai Hotel runs one bus a day in each direction between Pak Chong and Khao Yai during the week. It leaves Khao Yai at 7 am and returns from Pak Chong at 5 pm. On weekends there should be plenty of public songthaews. The fare is 20B to Khao Yai, 15B from Khao Yai. You may also be able to take a direct bus from Bangkok at certain times of year – enquire at the Northern Bus Station.

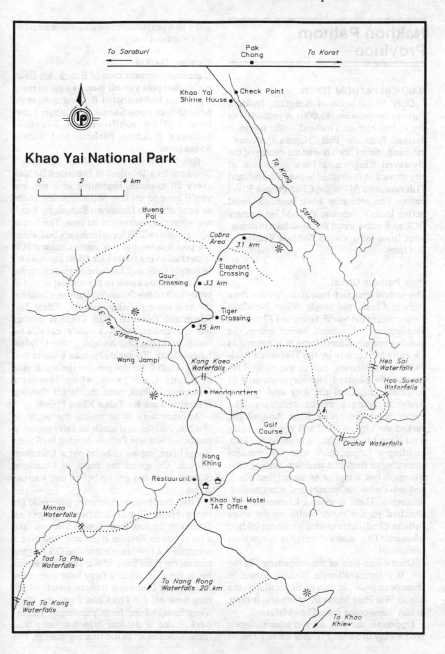

Khao Yai National Park

0   2   4 km

To Saraburi

Pak Chong

To Korat

Khao Yai Shrine House

Check Point

Ta Kong Stream

Bueng Pai

Cobra Area

31 km

Elephant Crossing

Gaur Crossing

33 km

Tiger Crossing

35 km

E Tow Stream

Wang Jampi

Kong Kaeo Waterfalls

Heo Sai Waterfalls

Heo Suwat Waterfalls

Headquarters

Orchid Waterfalls

Golf Course

Nong Khing

Restaurant

Khao Yai Motel
TAT Office

Manaa Waterfalls

Tad Ta Phu Waterfalls

Tad Ta Kong Waterfalls

To Nang Rong Waterfalls 20 km

To Khao Khiew

Nakhon Pathom Province

NAKHON PATHOM TOWN นครปฐม

Only 56 km west of Bangkok, Nakhon
Pathom (population 45,000) is regarded as
the oldest city in Thailand – the name is
derived from the Pali 'Nagara Pathama',
meaning 'First City'. It was the centre of the
Dvaravati Kingdom, a loose collection of
city states that flourished between the 6th and
11th centuries AD in the Chao Phraya River
valley. The area may have been inhabited
before India's Ashokan Period (3rd century
BC), as it is theorised that Buddhist missionaries from India visited Nakhon Pathom at
that time.

Phra Pathom Chedi

The central attraction here is the famous Phra
Pathom Chedi, the single tallest Buddhist
monument in the world, rising to 127 metres.
The original monument, buried within the
massive orange-glazed dome, was erected in
the early 6th century by the Theravada Buddhists of Dvaravati, but in the early 11th
century the Khmer King Suryavarman I of
Angkor conquered the city and built a
Brahman prang over the sanctuary. The
Pagan Burmese, under King Anuruddha,
sacked the city in 1057 and it was in ruins
until King Mongkut had it restored in 1860,
building a larger chedi over the remains
according to Buddhist tradition, adding four
wihans, a bot, a replica of the original chedi
and assorted salas, prangs and other embel-
lishments. There is even a Chinese temple
attached to the outer walls of the Phra
Pathom Chedi, next to which outdoor lakhon
(classical Thai dance-drama) is sometimes
performed.

On the east side of the monument, in the
bot, is a Dvaravati-style Buddha seated in
'European pose', ie, in a chair, similar to the
one in Wat Phra Mehn in Ayuthaya. It may,
in fact, have come from Phra Mehn.

Opposite the bot is a museum, open
Wednesday to Sunday from 9 am to 12 noon
and 1 to 4 pm, which contains some interesting Dvaravati sculpture.

Floating Market

If the commercialisation of Bangkok's floating market puts you off there is a much more
lively and less touristed floating market on
Khlong Damnoen Saduak in Ratburi Province, 104 km south-west of Bangkok,
between Nakhon Pathom and Samut
Songkhram.

Bus No 78 goes direct from Bangkok's
Southern Bus Terminal to Damnoen Saduak
every 20 minutes, beginning at 6 am, but
you'll have to get one of the first few buses
so as to arrive in Damnoen Saduak by 8 or 9
am when the market's at its best. The fare is
40B air-con or 25B for an ordinary bus. From
the pier nearest the bus station, take a 10B
water taxi to the talaat nam (floating market)
or simply walk east from the station along the
canal until you come to the market area. On
either side of the Damnoen Saduak Canal are
the two most popular markets, Talaat Ton
Khem and Talaat Hia Kui. There is another
less crowded market on a smaller canal, a bit
south of Damnoen Saduak, called Talaat
Khun Phitak. To get there, take a water taxi
going south from the pier on the south side
of Thong Lang canal, which intersects
Damnoen Saduak near the larger floating
market and ask for Talaat Khun Phitak.

Another way is to spend the night in
Nakhon Pathom and catch an early morning
bus out of Nakhon Pathom headed for Samut
Songkhram, asking to be let out at Damnoen
Saduak. Or spend the night in Damnoen
Saduak itself and get up before any tourists
arrive.

From the opposite direction, you could get
there from Samut Sakhon. To get to
Damnoen Saduak from Samut Sakhon, take
a local bus to Kratum Baen and then take a
songthaew a few km north to the Tha Angton
pier on the right bank of the Tha Chin River.
From the pier, catch a ferry boat across the
river to the Damnoen Saduak canal, which
runs west off the Tha Chin. From the Bang
Yang lock, where ferry passengers disembark, take a 30-km trip by *hang yao*
(long-tailed boat) to the floating market. The

fare is 16B and includes a boat change half-way at Ban Phaew – worth it for what is one of Thailand's most beautiful stretches of waterway.

Other Attractions
Beside the chedi, the other foci of the town are Silpakorn University, west of the chedi off Phetkasem Highway, and Sanam Chan, adjacent to the University. Sanam Chan, formerly the grounds for Rama VI's palace, is a pleasant park with a canal passing through it. The somewhat run-down palace still stands in the park but entrance is not permitted.

Places to Stay
Near the west side of the Phra Pathom Chedi, next to a furniture store, is the *Mitsamphan*. It's 80B for a clean room with fan and bath.

The *Mittaowan* (*Mit Thawon*), is on the right as you walk towards the chedi from the railway station. This costs 90B for a room with fan and bath, or 160B for one with air-con.

The *Mitphaisan* (tel 242422) – the English sign reads, incorrectly, 'Mitfaisal' – is further down the alley to the right from Mittaowan. Rooms here are 100B for fan and bath and 200B with air-con. All three of the 'Mit' hotels are owned by the same family. Price differences reflect differences in cleanliness and service. I'd recommend Mittaowan.

West of the chedi, several blocks beyond Mitsamphan, is the *Siam Hotel*, but the staff here are unfriendly and it costs 140B for a room with fan and bath, or up to 360B for air-con.

Places to Eat
Nakhon Pathom has an excellent fruit market along the road between the railway station and the Phra Pathom Chedi. The *khao lam* (sticky rice and coconut steamed in a bamboo joint) sold here is reputed to be the best in Thailand. There are many good restaurants in this area and they are cheap too.

A very good Chinese restaurant, *Ha Seng*, is on the south side of the road which intersects the road from the train station to the chedi. Turn right if walking from the chedi and walk about 20 metres.

Getting There & Away
Bus Buses for Nakhon Pathom leave the Southern Bus Terminal in Bangkok every 10 minutes from 5 am to 9 pm; the fare is 13B for the one-hour trip. Air-con buses are 24B and leave the air-con Southern Bus Terminal about every 30 minutes between 7 am and 10.30 pm.

Buses to Kanchanaburi leave throughout the day from the left side (coming from the Nakhon Pathom Railway Station) of the Phra Pathom Chedi – get bus No 81.

Train Ordinary trains (3rd class only) leave the Bangkok Noi Railway Station daily at 8 am and 1.50 pm, arriving in Nakhon Pathom at 9.18 am and 2.51 pm. The 3rd-class fare is 11B.

There are also ordinary trains to Nakhon Pathom from the Hualamphong Station at 9 am; the 3rd-class fare is 14B and the train arrives at 10.29 am. Second class (28B) is available only on rapid and express trains, but it's not worth taking rapid or express trains; travel time for this distance is the same but you'd have to pay the rapid or express surcharges (in addition to the 2nd-class fare) which cost more than the ordinary 3rd-class fares alone.

Kanchanaburi Province

KANCHANABURI TOWN เมือง กาญจนบุรี
Kanchanaburi (population 33,000) is 130 km west of Bangkok in the slightly elevated valley of the Mae Klang River amidst hills and sugar cane plantations. It was originally established by Rama I as a first line of defence against the Burmese who might use the old invasion route through the Three Pagodas Pass on the Thai-Burmese border. It's still a popular smuggling route into Burma today.

During WW II, the Japanese occupation in Thailand used Allied prisoners of war to build the infamous Death Railway along this same invasion route, in reverse, along the Khwae Noi River to the pass. Thousands and thousands of prisoners died as a result of

Kanchanaburi Province

brutal treatment by their captors, a story chronicled by Boulle's book *The Bridge Over the River Kwai* and popularised by a movie based on the same. The bridge is still there to be seen (still in use, in fact) and so are the graves of the Allied soldiers. The river is actually spelled and pronounced Khwae, like 'quack' without the '-ck'.

The town itself has a charming atmosphere and is a great place to hang out for a while. The weather here is slightly cooler than in Bangkok and the evenings are especially pleasant. Although Kan (as the locals call it; also Kan'buri) gets enough tourists to warrant its own tourist office, not many

western visitors make it here – most tourists are Hong Kong/Singapore Chinese or Japanese who blaze through on air-con buses, hitting the River Khwae Bridge, the cemetery on Saengchuto Rd, the Rama River Kwai Hotel, and then they're off to the nearby sapphire mines or one of the big waterfalls before heading north to Chiang Mai or back to Bangkok.

Information

The TAT office is on Saengchuto Rd on the right as you enter town before the police station. They have a free map of the town and province though they may try to sell you a

Top: Three Pagodas Pass, Kanchanaburi (JC)
Bottom: Pattaya Beach (JC)

Top: Wat Phra Maha That, Ayuthaya (TW)
Left: Wat Si Ratana Maha That, Sukhothai (JC)
Right: Phra Pathom Chedi, Nakhon Pathom (TAT)

more colourful map with the same information for 10B.

The GPO on Saengchuto Rd was closed for renovations in 1989 and it was not known when it would reopen. There is a small post office on Lak Muang Rd towards the river, close to the town pillar.

Death Railway Bridge

The so-called Bridge over the River Khwae may be of interest to war historians but really looks quite ordinary. It spans the Khwae Yai River, a tributary of the Mae Klong River, a couple of km north of town – 'Khwae Yai' literally translates as 'large tributary'. It is the story behind the bridge that is dramatic. The materials for the bridge were brought from Java by the Imperial Japanese Army during their occupation of Thailand. In 1945 the bridge was bombed several times and was only rebuilt after the war – the curved portions of the bridge are original. The first version of the bridge, completed in February 1943, was all wood. In April of the same year a second bridge of steel was constructed.

It is estimated that 16,000 POWs died while building the 'Death Railway' to Burma, of which the bridge was only a small part. The strategic objective of the railway was to secure an alternative supply route for the Japanese conquest of Burma and other Asian countries to the west. Construction on the railway began on September 16, 1942 at existing terminals in Thanbyuzayat, Burma and Nong Pladuk, Thailand. Japanese engineers at the time estimated that it would take five years to link Thailand and Burma by rail but the Japanese army forced the POWs to complete the 415-km railway, of which roughly two-thirds ran through Thailand, in 16 months. The rails were finally joined 37 km south of Three Pagodas Pass. Much of the railway was built in difficult terrain that required high bridges and deep mountain cuttings. The River Khwae bridge was in use for 20 months before the Allies bombed it in '45.

Although the statistics of the number of POWs who died during the Japanese occupation is horrifying, the figures for the labourers, many from Thailand, Burma,

Malaysia and Indonesia, are even worse. It is thought that in total 90 to 100,000 coolies died in the area.

Train nuts may enjoy the 'railway museum' in front of the bridge, with engines which were used during WW II on display. Every year during the first week of December there is a nightly light & sound show at the bridge, commemorating the Allied attack on the Death Railway in 1945. It's a pretty big scene, with the sounds of bombers and explosions, fantastic bursts of light, etc. The town gets a lot of Thai tourists during this week, so book early if you want to witness this spectacle.

There are a couple of large outdoor restaurants near the bridge, on the river, but these are for tour groups that arrive en masse throughout the day. If you're hungry, better to eat with the tour bus and songthaew drivers in the little noodle places at the head of Pak Phraek Rd.

The best way to get to the bridge from town is to catch a songthaew along Pak Phraek Rd (parallel to Saengchuto Rd towards the river) heading north. If you're standing at the River Kwai Hotel, just cross Saengchuto Rd, walk to the right, turn left at the first street and walk until you come to Pak Phraek Rd. The regular songthaews are 3B and stop at the bridge. It's about four km from the centre of town.

Allied War Cemeteries

There are two cemeteries containing the remains of Allied POWs who died in captivity during WW II; one is north of town off Saengchuto Rd, just before the railway station, and the other is across the Mae Klong River west of town, a few km down the Khwae Noi (little tributary) River.

The Kanchanaburi War Cemetery is better cared for, with green lawns and healthy flowers. It's usually a cool spot on a hot Kanchanaburi day. To get there, catch a songthaew anywhere along Saengchuto Rd going north – the fare is 3B. Jump off at the English sign in front of the cemetery on the left, or ask to be let off at the *susaan* (Thai for cemetery). Just before the cemetery on the same side of the road is a very colourful

Chinese cemetery with burial mounds and inscribed tombstones.

To get to the other cemetery, the Chung Kai Allied War Cemetery, take a 2B ferry boat from the pier at the west end of Lak Muang Rd across the Mae Klong, then follow the curving road through picturesque corn and sugar cane fields until you reach the cemetery on your left. This is a fairly long walk, but the scenery along the way is pleasant. Thai border police frequent this half-paved, half-gravel road and may offer rides to or from the pier.

Like the more visited cemetery north of town, the Chung Kai Cemetery burial plaques carry the names, military insignia and short epitaphs for Dutch, British, French and Australian soldiers.

Very near the Chung Kai Cemetery is a dirt path that leads to Wat Tham Khao Pun, one of Kanchanaburi's many cave temples. The path is approximately one km long and passes through thick forest with a few wooden houses along the way.

JEATH War Museum

This odd museum at Wat Chaichumphon is worth visiting just to sit on the cool banks of the Mae Klong. Phra Maha Tomson Tongproh, a Thai monk who devotes much energy to promoting the museum, speaks some English and can not only answer questions about the exhibits, but can supply information about what to see around Kanchanaburi and how best to get there. If you show him this book, he'll give you a 5B discount off the usual 20B admission. The museum itself consists of a replica example of the bamboo-atap huts used to house Allied POWs in the Kanchanaburi area during the Japanese occupation. The long huts contain various photographs taken during the war, drawings and paintings by POWs, maps, weapons and other war memorabilia. According to Phra Tomson, the acronym JEATH represents the fated meeting of Japan, England, Australia/America, Thailand and Holland at Kanchanaburi during WW II.

The War Museum is at the end of Wisuttharangsi (Visutrangsi) Rd, near the

TAT office, next to the main compound of Wat Chaichumphon. If you're coming from Saengchuto Rd, you'll pass the Nita Guest House on the left.

Lak Muang Shrine

Like many other older Thai cities, Kanchanaburi has a *lak muang*, or town pillar/phallus, enclosed in a shrine at what was originally the town centre. Kanchanaburi's lak muang is appropriately located on Lak Muang Rd, which intersects Saengchuto Rd two blocks north of the TAT office.

The bulbous-tipped pillar is covered with gold leaf and is much worshipped. Unlike Bangkok's lak muang you can get as close to this pillar as you like – no curtain.

Within sight of the pillar, towards the river, stands Kanchanaburi's original city gate.

Wat Tham Mongkorn Thong

The 'Cave Temple of the Golden Dragon' is well known because of the 'Floating Nun' – a 70-plus year old mae chii who meditates while floating on her back in a pool of water. If you are lucky you might see her as she seems to be doing this less frequently nowadays (try a Sunday). Thais come from all over Thailand to see her float and to receive her blessings which she bestows by whistling onto the top of a devotee's head. A sizeable contingent of young Thai nuns stay here under the old nun's tutelage.

A long and steep series of steps with dragon-sculpted handrails lead up the craggy mountainside behind the main bot to a complex of limestone caves. Follow the string of light bulbs through the front cave and you'll come out above the wat with a view of the valley and mountains below. One section of the cave requires crawling or duck-walking, so wear appropriate clothing. Bats squeak away above your head and the smell of guano permeates the air.

In front of the caves sits a Chinese hermit with a long white beard who prepares and sells ancient Chinese herbal remedies. He won't allow his picture to be taken.

Another cave wat is off this same road about one or two km from Wat Tham Mongkorn Thong towards the pier. It can be seen on a limestone outcropping back from the road some 500 metres or so. The name is Wat Tham Khao Laem. The cave is less impressive than that at Wat Tham Mongkorn Thong, but there are some interesting old temple buildings on the grounds.

Getting There & Away Heading towards Bangkok down Saengchuto Rd from the TAT office, turn right on Chukkadon Rd (marked in English – about half-way between TAT and the GPO), or take a samlor (5B) from the town centre to Tha Chukkadon Pier at the end of Chukkadon Rd. Cross the Mae Klong by ferry (2B per pedestrian) and follow the road on the other side three or four km until you see the wat on the left.

If you can, cross the river with someone who has a car, jeep, truck or motorcycle who can drop you off at Wat Tham Mongkorn Thong; if you pay the driver's ferry crossing (20B per vehicle), they will be glad to take you right to the wat, as there is only one road leading from the river to the villages west of Kanchanaburi. There is no charge for people riding in or on a motor vehicle. The road to Wat Tham is long and dusty so hitching a ride is advisable. Rather infrequent buses (actually large songthaews) also cross the river here and stop at the wat – 4B per person. Recently a bridge was constructed at this junction, so there may be public transport directly past Wat Tham.

The road to the wat passes sugar cane fields, karst formations, wooden houses, cattle and rock quarries.

Waterfalls

There are seven major waterfalls in Kanchanaburi Province, all north of the capital. They are Erawan, Pha Lan, Traitrung, Khao Pang, Sai Yok, Pha That and Huay Khamin. Of these, the three most worth visiting – if you're looking for grandeur and swimming potential – are the Erawan Falls are the easiest to get to from Kanchanaburi Town, while Sai Yok and Huay Khamin are best visited only if you are able to spend the night in the vicinity of the falls. They are too far

for a comfortable day trip from Kanchanaburi.

Any of the waterfalls described here could be visited by motorcycle. Many of the guest houses in town will rent bikes – offer 150B per day for a 80 to 100cc bike, more for a dirt bike.

Erawan Falls The first bus to Erawan leaves the Kanchanburi bus station at 8 am, takes 1½ to two hours and costs 17B per person. Ask for *rot thammada pai nam tok erawan* (ordinary bus going to Erawan Falls). Take this first bus, as Erawan takes a full day to appreciate and the last bus back to Kanchanaburi leaves Erawan at 4 pm.

The bus station/market at Erawan is a good 1½ km from the Erawan National Park which contains the falls. Once in the park, you'll have to walk two km from the trail entrance to the end of seven levels of waterfalls. The trails weave in and out of the numerous pools and falls, sometimes running alongside the water, sometimes leading across footbridges, splitting in different directions. Wear good walking shoes or sneakers. Also bring a bathing suit as several of the pools beneath the waterfalls are great for swimming.

There are food stalls near the park entrance and at the bus station/market, outside the park. The peak crowds at Erawan come in mid-April around Songkran time. The waterfalls here, as elsewhere in Kanchanaburi, are best visited during the rainy season or in the first two months of the cool season, when the pools are full and the waterfalls most impressive. There is now a bamboo dormitory at Erawan where you can spend the night for 10B or get a room for 50B.

Huay Khamin Falls These waterfalls are about 25 km north of Erawan. To get there, take a bus to Si Sawat, either from Kanchanaburi Town or from Erawan. The fare from Erawan should be about 10B; from Kanchanaburi it will be about 27B.

Huay Khamin (Turmeric Stream) has what are probably Kanchanaburi Province's most powerful waterfalls and the pools under

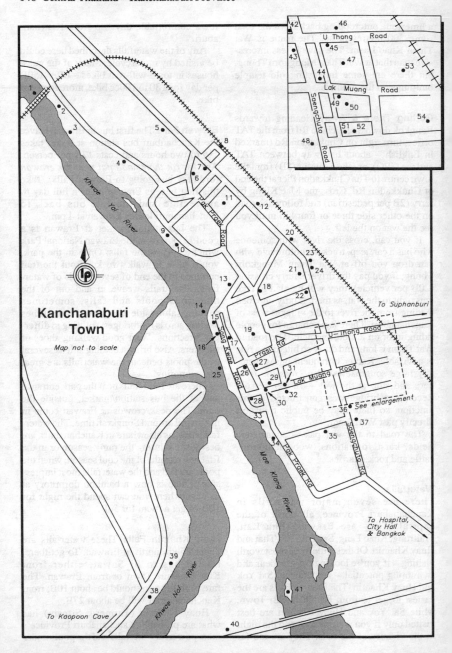

Kanchanaburi
Town

Map not to scale

the waterfalls are large and deep. This is an excellent place for swimming.

Sai Yok Falls About 100 km north-west of Kanchanaburi Town, Sai Yok is well-known for the overnight raft trips that leave from here along the Khwae Noi River, which the waterfalls empty directly into. The trips are not cheap, but those who have gone say they're worth the money. There is fishing and swimming as well as jungle scenery and wildlife. It was near here that the famous Russian roulette scenes in the movie *The Deer Hunter* were filmed.

Near Sai Yok are the Daowadung Caves (20 minutes north by boat) and Hin Dat Hot Springs (40 minutes further north by boat). The hot springs (*baw nam rawn*) are looked after by a Buddhist monastery, so only men are permitted to bathe there.

Sai Yok can be reached by direct bus from Kanchanaburi for 23B and the trip takes a little over an hour. You can also get there by boarding a bus bound for Thong Pha Phum. Tell the driver you're going to Sai Yok and he'll let you off at the road to the falls, on the left side of Route 323. From there you can get local transport to Sai Yok. This method takes about two hours in all and costs about the same as the direct bus. You can also charter boats that can take up to 20 people to Sai Yok for about 400B.

Raft Trips

The number of small-time enterprises offering raft trips up and down the Mae Klong River and its various tributaries in Kanchanaburi Province continues to multiply. The typical raft is a large affair with a two-storey shelter that will carry 15 to 20 people. Average cost for a two-day trip from one of the piers in Kanchanaburi Town is 2000 to 2500B for the whole raft, or roughly 100 to 160B per person. Such a trip would include stops Hat Tha Aw, Wat Tham Mongkorn Thong, Khao Boon Cave and the Chung Kai Allied War Cemetery, plus all meals and one night's accommodation on the raft. Drinks are usually extra. Add more nights and/or go further afield and the cost can escalate quite a bit. It is possible to

<table><tbody>
<tr><td>1</td><td>Bridge on the River Kwai</td></tr>
<tr><td>2</td><td>Japanese War Memorial</td></tr>
<tr><td>3</td><td>Bamboo Guest House</td></tr>
<tr><td>4</td><td>UT Guest House</td></tr>
<tr><td>5</td><td>Petrol Stations</td></tr>
<tr><td>6</td><td>Si Muangkan Hotel</td></tr>
<tr><td>7</td><td>Rung Rung Bungalows</td></tr>
<tr><td>8</td><td>Railway Station</td></tr>
<tr><td>9</td><td>VN Guest House</td></tr>
<tr><td>10</td><td>River Guest House</td></tr>
<tr><td>11</td><td>Kanchanaburi War Cemetery</td></tr>
<tr><td>12</td><td>Luxury Hotel</td></tr>
<tr><td>13</td><td>Songthaews to bridge</td></tr>
<tr><td>14</td><td>Nitaya Raft House</td></tr>
<tr><td>15</td><td>Sam's Place</td></tr>
<tr><td>16</td><td>Supakornchai Raft</td></tr>
<tr><td>17</td><td>PG Guest House</td></tr>
<tr><td>18</td><td>Ni-Dar Guest House</td></tr>
<tr><td>19</td><td>Markets</td></tr>
<tr><td>20</td><td>Sabai-Jit Restaurant</td></tr>
<tr><td>21</td><td>Prasopsuk Bungalow</td></tr>
<tr><td>22</td><td>Issan Restaurant</td></tr>
<tr><td>23</td><td>River Kwai Hotel 1</td></tr>
<tr><td>24</td><td>River Kwai Hotel 2</td></tr>
<tr><td>25</td><td>Floating Restaurants</td></tr>
<tr><td>26</td><td>VS Guest House</td></tr>
<tr><td>27</td><td>Aree Bakery</td></tr>
<tr><td>28</td><td>Ferry Pier</td></tr>
<tr><td>29</td><td>Post Office</td></tr>
<tr><td>30</td><td>Town Gate of Kanchanaburi</td></tr>
<tr><td>31</td><td>City Pillar Shrine</td></tr>
<tr><td>32</td><td>Municipal Office</td></tr>
<tr><td>33</td><td>Nita Raft House</td></tr>
<tr><td>34</td><td>War Museum</td></tr>
<tr><td>35</td><td>Nita Guest House</td></tr>
<tr><td>36</td><td>TAT</td></tr>
<tr><td>37</td><td>Thai Seree Hotel</td></tr>
<tr><td>38</td><td>Wat Tham Kao Pun</td></tr>
<tr><td>39</td><td>Chung Kai Allied War Cemetery</td></tr>
<tr><td>40</td><td>Wat Tham Mangkon Thong</td></tr>
<tr><td>41</td><td>Kasem Island Resort</td></tr>
<tr><td>42</td><td>Chinese Restaurant</td></tr>
<tr><td>43</td><td>Taxi Stand</td></tr>
<tr><td>44</td><td>Thai Military Bank</td></tr>
<tr><td>45</td><td>Bangkok Bank</td></tr>
<tr><td>46</td><td>Telephone Centre</td></tr>
<tr><td>47</td><td>Market</td></tr>
<tr><td>48</td><td>Police Station</td></tr>
<tr><td>49</td><td>Thai Farmers Bank</td></tr>
<tr><td>50</td><td>Market</td></tr>
<tr><td>51</td><td>BT Guest House</td></tr>
<tr><td>52</td><td>Bus Station</td></tr>
<tr><td>53</td><td>Movie Theatre</td></tr>
<tr><td>54</td><td>Movie Theatre</td></tr>
</tbody></table>

arrange trips all the way to Sai Yok Falls, for example.

Enquire at any guest house, the Sunya Rux Restaurant, the TAT or at the main pier at the end of Lak Muang Rd on the river about raft trips. Perhaps the best trips are arranged by groups of travellers who get together and plan their own raft excursions with one of the raft operators. I expect that in the future Kanchanaburi raft trips will join Chiang Mai hill-tribe treks as one of Thailand's big attractions.

Other Attractions

Across the road from Nitaya Raft House is a

place where *li-khe* or Thai folk dance-drama is occasionally performed.

Places to Stay – bottom end

Kanchanaburi has numerous places to stay in every price range but especially in the guest house category. On Visutrangsi Rd, on the way to the JEATH War Museum, is *Nita Guest House* (tel 511300), a friendly place that is a long-time favourite among travellers. Rates are 35/50/70B for a dorm/ single/ double. Sleeping areas are spacious and there is plenty of room to lounge about elsewhere in the compound. They also serve food and can help arrange raft trips, waterfall outings, etc. Down on the riverside at the River Khwae and Khwae Noi junction is another branch, the *Nita Raft House*, where singles/ doubles with mosquito net are 40/50B.

Another nice guest house is the *UT Guest House*, which is near the River Khwae Bridge at 25/25 Mae Nam Khwae Rd. A samlor from the railway station should be about 10B; from the bus station it should be 20B. UT charges 50B per person in large two-bed rooms. The *PG Guest House* at 277/303 Pak Phraek Rd has been recommended by a couple of readers and is 40B per person. Also on Pak Phraek Rd, near the Aree Bakery, is the cut-above-the-rest *VS Guest House* with rooms at 50 to 80B. Another one on this road but well-off the river is the newly-opened *Ni-dar Guest House* with the cheapest rooms in town at 40 to 60B.

If you want to stay out near the Bridge, the *Bamboo Guest House* (tel 512532) at 3-5 Soi Vietnam, on the river about a km before the Japanese War Memorial off Pattana Rd (continuation of Mae Nam Khwae Rd) has rooms for 50B per person. The owner is very friendly and the setting is nice – good value. *BT Travel* (tel 511967) is near the bus station and TAT on Kanchanaburi Rd and has dorm beds for 30B, as well as adequate rooms for 50 to 80B.

You can also stay on the river in a raft house (or over the river in the case of bungalows built on piers) for 25 to 40B per person. Two popular places of this sort are the *River Guest House* and the *VN Guest House* where small, basic rooms are 40 to 70B. Both are in the same vicinity on the river, not far from the railway station. The *Nitaya Raft House* further south along the river near Wat Neua is cheaper at 25B per person. Other places come and go but they're all pretty similar.

Places to Stay – middle

There are two River Kwai (Khwae) Hotels in Kanchanaburi, one next to the other on Saengchuto Rd. The *River Kwai*, 284/4-6 Saengchuto Rd, (tel 511269) has air-con rooms starting at 545B, while the *River Kwai 2*, 284/3 Saengchuto, (tel 511565) has adequate fan-cooled rooms with bath starting at 90B. The Kwai 2 keeps a monkey and an *iihen* (palm civet – a cat-racoon-monkey type of creature) in the lobby for your entertainment. Don't bother with the larger River Kwai Hotel, as it's very over priced for the quality of room offered.

One of the better places in this price range is the new *VL Guest House* across the street from the River Kwai hotels. A clean, spacious room with fan and bath is 100B single or double. Larger rooms holding four to eight persons go for 50B per person. A double with air-con and hot water is 250B. The VL has a small dining area downstairs and they rent bicycles (20B per day) and motorcycles (200B up). One hopes this hotel will stay clean and efficient beyond the first year.

Prasopsuk Bungalows (tel 511777) at 677 Saengchuto Rd is across from the River Kwai hotels. These are good 90B bungalows, off the road a bit, with a friendly staff, restaurant and night club – a Thai scene at night. *Wang Thong Bungalows*, 60/3 Saengchuto Rd (tel 511046) and *Boon Yang Bungalows* offer similar rooms for 90B up. In case you haven't figured this out on your own, 'bungalows' (not the beach kind) are the upcountry equivalent of Bangkok's 'short-time' hotels. They're off the road for the same reason that their Bangkok equivalents have heavy curtains over the carports: so that it will be difficult to spot license plate numbers. Still, they function well as tourist hotels too.

Other hotels in town include the *Si Muang Kan* (tel 511609), at 313/1-3 Saengchuto Rd

(the north end) with clean rooms with fan and bath for 100B or with air-con for 170B and the *Thai Seri Hotel* at the south end of the same road, near the Visutrangsi Rd intersection and the TAT office, somewhat dilapidated but adequate rooms for 70B up.

The *Luxury Hotel* (tel 511168) at 284/1-5 Saengchuto Rd is a couple of blocks north of the River Kwai hotels, and not as centrally located, but good value. Clean rooms with fan and bath start at 70B.

If you want to stay on the river but don't want to sleep on a mat, try *Sam's Place*, near the Nitaya Raft House and all the floating restaurants. The owner is a local guy called Sam who spent 10 years in the US and speaks excellent English. His raft complex is tastefully designed and very reasonably priced for what you get. A room with fan and private bath is 100B for a single or double. For 200B you can get a room with air-con, plus an extra sitting room with a fridge. He's also building a budget section where fan-cooled rooms will be 50B with shared bath. The raft has a small coffee shop. Sam had just opened in February 1989 but says he plans to sponsor raft trips upriver as well as van trips to Sangkhlaburi in the future.

Very near Sam's Place is *Supakornchai Raft* which is similar in scope but not quite as nice. Rooms here are 150B for a room with a large bed or 200B for two beds; both kinds of rooms come with fan and bath.

Perhaps the last word in comfort is *Kasem Island Resort* (tel 511603, Bangkok reservations 391-6672), which is on an island in the middle of the Mae Klong River just a couple of hundred metres from Tha Chukkadon Pier. The tastefully designed thatched cottages and house-rafts are cool, clean, quiet and go for 500B. Four people can rent a house-raft for 800B a night and eight people can for 1600B. There are facilities for swimming, fishing and rafting as well as an outdoor bar and restaurant. The Resort has an office near Tha Chukkadon Pier where you can arrange for a free shuttle boat out to the island.

In the vicinity of the bridge are several river resorts of varying quality. On the river before the bridge is the *River Kwai Resort* (tel 511313), where rustic bungalows on the riverbank are 350B for two, a floating bungalow for two is 450B, and a two-bedroom floating bungalow for four is 700B. Just above the bridge a couple of km before the turn-off for Highway 323, are two more river resorts: *Prasopsuk Garden Resort* (tel 513215, Bangkok reservations 215-4497) with air-con townhouse double rooms for 400B, air-con bungalows for two at 600B, and large bungalows for 10 persons at 1000B per night; and *River Kwai Lodge* (tel 513657, Bangkok reservations 250-0928) where a large room for two is 600B with fan and bath or 700B with air-con.

Places to Stay - top end
Out of Town The River Kwai Farm, a resort that attempts to duplicate for tourists the natural simplicity of jungle life, is 38 km south-west of Kanchanaburi at Ban Kao. The bamboo bungalows are without electricity and the daily rate, including three meals a day, is 450B per person. This is where Bangkok yuppies come to clear out their lungs. Reservations can be made through River Kwai Farm (tel 234-7435), 68/2 Sathon Neua Rd, Bangkok, or through the private tour agency on Saengchuto Rd just north of the TAT office.

The *River Kwai Village* is a 60-room air-con resort 70 km from Kanchanaburi, near Nam Tok, on the Khwae Noi River; they also have a few raft-houses. Accommodation (count on 650 to 800B) can be booked through their office in Bangkok, 1054/4 Phetburi Rd (tel 251-7522/7828) or through any Kanchanaburi travel agency. Other top-end raft-house type accommodation is in the Sai Yok Falls National Park area: *River Kwai Rafts* (Bangkok tel 280-3365) costs 600B per person including all meals; and *River Kwai Jungle Rafts* (Bangkok tel 392-3641) costs 500B per person with meals.

On the River Khwae towards Si Sawat and the Si Nakarin Dam are *Kwai Yai River Hut* (Bangkok tel 392-3286) at 1100B per person including meals and *Kwai Yai Island Resort* (tel 511261, Bangkok reservations 521-2389), at 450 to 500B per person. These can also probably be booked in Kanchanaburi through one of the travel agencies near the bus station. There are several other raft-houses and bungalow operations along the River Khwae and near Sai Yok Falls on the Khwae Noi.

Places to Eat
The greatest proliferation of inexpensive restaurants in Kanchanaburi is along the north end of Saengchuto Rd near the River Kwai hotels. From here south, to where U Thong Rd crosses Saengchuto, are many good Chinese, Thai and isaan-style restaurants. As elsewhere in Thailand, the best are generally the most crowded.

One of the most popular is *Esan* (English spelling), which has good kai yang, khao niaw, somtam, etc, as well as other Thai and local specialities. The kai yang is grilled right out front and served with two sauces – the usual sweet and sour *nam jim kai* and the salt-garlic-fish sauce or roast red pepper sauce, *nam phrik phao*. The menu here is extensive and includes aahaan baa ('forest food') which is popular all over Kanchanaburi Province, characterised by very, very spicy curries without coconut milk and seafood specialities such as haw mok (serpent-fish curry steamed in banana leaves) and *po taek* (literally, 'broken fishtrap'), a gourmet clay-pot soup of crab claws, clams, shrimp, squid and other seafood. Esan also serves good appetisers or drinking food (called kap klaem in Thai), like fried cashews/peanuts, fried potatoes, *yam*, etc.

Unfortunately, the great jukebox full of north-eastern Thai pop that used to be in this place seems to have disappeared. The beer is ice-cold and an English menu is available, although it's not as complete as the Thai-language menu, which sits under a roll of toilet paper on each table. A whole roast chicken for 50B, half a kg of sticky rice for 15B (10B worth is probably more than enough rice), somtam for 10B, and you have a feast for three to four people. On the negative side, the service at Esan can be a little indifferent these days. Apparently, the restaurant became so successful that the original cook/owner split for Bangkok to pursue his dream career as an actor.

The Chinese restaurant on the north-west

corner of U Thong and Saengchuto (look for the old marble-topped tables) has good noodles. In the early mornings some of the smaller, older food stalls on the east side of Saengchuto serve pathong-ko (Chinese 'doughnuts') with hot sweet Thai tea (cha rawn) and clear tea (nam cha) as a chaser – 8B will get you through the morning. As usual, the pathong-ko disappears by 9 am.

A traveller-oriented restaurant, on Saengchuto Rd, is the *Sunya Rux*, near the River Kwai hotels, but the quality here seems to have slipped and they don't serve Thais. Good, inexpensive eating can also be found in the markets along Prasit Rd and between U Thong and Lak Muang Rd east of Saengchuto.

The *Sabai-jit* restaurant has moved north of the River Kwai Hotel from its original spot just south of the hotel. They have an English menu. Beer and Maekhong whiskey are sold here at quite competitive prices and the food is consistently good. Other Thai and Chinese dishes are served apart from those listed on the English menu. If you see someone eating something not listed, point.

A restaurant called *Art & Beer* across from the railway station sells large bottles of Singha beer for only 40B. They also feature unusual dishes like beer-marinated beef and phat thai without the noodles.

Down on the river there are several large floating restaurants where the quality of the food varies but it's hard not to enjoy the atmosphere. Most of them are pretty good according to locals, but if you go, don't expect western food or large portions – if you know what to order, you could have a very nice meal here. Recommended are the *Thong Nathii* and the *Phae Kan*. Across from the floating restaurants, along the road, are several smaller food stalls where you can eat cheaply and which open shop in the evenings. This is a festive and prosperous town and people seem to eat out a lot.

Getting There & Away

Bus Buses leave Bangkok from the Southern Bus Terminal on Charan Sanitwong Rd in Thonburi every 20 minutes daily (beginning at 5 am, last bus at 6.30 pm) for Kanchan-aburi. The trip takes about three hours and costs 28B. Buses back to Bangkok leave Kanchanaburi between 5.10 am and 6.30 pm.

Air-con buses leave Bangkok's Southern AC Bus Terminal hourly from 6 am to 9.30 pm for 53B. These same buses depart Kanchanaburi for Bangkok from opposite the police station on Saengchuto Rd, not from the bus station. Air-con buses only take about two hours to reach Bangkok. First bus out is at 5.30 am; the last one to Bangkok leaves at 7 pm. You can also take a share taxi from Saengchuto Rd to Bangkok for 45B per person, five people minimum. These taxis will make drops at Khao San Rd or in the Pahurat district.

There are frequent buses throughout the day from nearby Nakhon Pathom. Bus No 81 leaves from the east side of the Phra Pathom Chedi, costs 16B, and takes about 1½ hours.

Train Ordinary trains leave Bangkok Noi Station at 8 am and 1.50 pm, arriving at 10.31 am and 4.28 pm. Only 3rd-class seats are available and the fare is 28B. Trains return to Bangkok from Kanchanaburi at 8.04 am and 2.30 pm and arrive at Bangkok Noi Station at 10.50 am and 5.10 pm.

You can also take the train from the Kanchanaburi station out to the River Khwae Bridge – a three-minute ride for 1B. There is one train only at 10.31 am (No 171).

The same train goes on to the end of the railway line at Nam Tok, which is very near Sai Yok Falls. You can catch the train in Kanchanaburi at 10.31 am or at the bridge at 10.36 am; the fare is the same, 17B. Nam Tok is eight km from Khao Pang Falls and 18 km from Hellfire Pass and the River Khwae Village. Two other trains also make the trip to Nam Tok daily, leaving Kanchanaburi at 6 am and 4.28 pm. The trip to Nam Tok takes about two hours. Coming back from Nam Tok, there are trains at 6.05 am, 12.35 pm and 3.15 pm. The early morning trains between Kanchanaburi and Nam Tok (6 and 6.05 am) do not run on weekends and holidays.

Excursion Train There is a special tourist train from Hualamphong Station on weekends and holidays which departs Bangkok at 6.15 am and returns at 7.30 pm. The fare is 60B for adults, 33B for children round-trip. It includes a 40-minute stop in Nakhon Pathom to see the Phra Pathom Chedi, 30 minutes at the Bridge over the River Khwae, a three-hour stop at Nam Tok for lunch, a 2B minibus to Khao Pang Falls and 45 minutes at the Kanchanaburi War Cemetery, before returning to Bangkok. This ticket should be booked in advance although it's worth trying on the day even if you're told it's full. Ordinary train tickets to Kanchanaburi can be booked the day of departure.

Getting Around
Prices are very reasonable in Kanchanaburi, especially for food and accommodation, if you are your own tour guide – don't even consider letting a samlor driver show you around, they want big money. The town is not very big, so getting around is easy. A samlor to anywhere in Kanchanaburi should be 5 to 10B for one person. Songthaews run up and down Saengchuto Rd for 3B per passenger.

Motorcycles can be rented at some guest houses and at the Suzuki dealer near the bus station. Expect to pay about 150B per day, though they may ask for more. Motorcycles can be taken across the river by ferry for a few baht.

AROUND KANCHANABURI
Prasat Muang Singh Historical Park
อุทยานแห่งประวัติศาสตร์ ปราสาท เมืองสิงห์
About 40 km from Kanchanaburi Town are the remains of an important 13th-century Khmer outpost of the Angkor Empire called Muang Singh (Lion City). Located on a bend in the Khwae Noi River, the recently restored city ruins cover 460 rai (73.6 hectares) and were declared a historical park under the administration of the Department of Fine Arts in 1987. Originally this location may have been chosen by the Khmers as a relay point for the trade along the Khwae Noi River.

All of the Muang Singh shrines are constructed of laterite bricks and are situated in a huge grassy compound surrounded by layers of laterite ramparts. Sections of the ramparts show seven additional layers of earthen walls, suggesting cosmological symbolism in the city plan. Evidence of a sophisticated water system has also been discovered amid the ramparts and moats.

The town encompasses four groups of ruins, though only two groups have been excavated and are visible. In the centre of the complex is the principal shrine, Prasat Muang Singh, which faces east (toward Angkor). Walls that surround the shrine have gates in each of the cardinal directions. A sculpture of Avalokitesvara sits on the inside of the northern wall and establishes Muang Singh as a Mahayana Buddhist centre.

To the north-east of the main *prasat* are the remains of a smaller shrine whose original contents and purpose is unknown. Near the main entrance to the complex at the north gate is a small outdoor museum which contains various sculptures of Mahayana Buddhist deities and stucco decorations from the shrines.

Clear evidence that this area was inhabited before the arrival of the Khmers can be seen in another small museum to the south of the complex next to the river. The shed-like building contains a couple of prehistoric human skeletons which were found in the area, and that's it. A more complete exhibit of local neolithic remains are on exhibit at the Ban Kao Museum (see below).

Entry to the Historical Park is 20B and it's open daily from 8 am to 4 pm.

Ban Kao Neolithic Museum
พิพิธภัณฑ์ บ้านเก่า

During the construction of the 'Death' Railway along the Khwae Noi River, a Dutch POW named Van Heekeren uncovered neolithic remains in the village of Ban Kao (Old Town), which is about 7 km south-east of Muang Singh. After the war, a Thai-Danish team retraced Heekeren's discovery and announced that Ban Kao was a major neolithic burial site. Archaeological evidence suggests that this area may have been inhabited as far back as 10,000 years ago.

A small but well-designed museum, displaying 3000 to 4000-year-old artefacts from the excavation of Ban Kao, has been established near the site. Objects are labelled and include a good variety of early pottery and other utensils as well as human skeletons. Hours are from 8 am to 4.30 pm, Wednesday to Sunday.

Places to Stay Guest bungalows are available for rent near the south gate of the Prasat Muang Singh Historical Park for 500B. There are a couple of small restaurants at the north gate.

The *River Khwae Farm* is 3½ km from the Ban Kao (Tha Kilen) railway station. Bungalows and raft-houses here start at 450B, including all meals.

Getting There & Away Ban Kao and Muang Singh are best reached by rail from Kanchanaburi via Ban Kao (Tha Kilen) Station, which is only one km south of Muang Singh. Walk west towards the river and follow the signs to Muang Singh. Trains leave Kanchanaburi daily at 6 am and 10.31 am, arriving in Tha Kilen in about an hour. The fare is 10B. To get to Ban Kao, you may have to walk or hitch 6 km south along the road that follows the Khwae Noi River, though the occasional songthaew passes along this road, too.

If you have your own transportation, Ban Kao and/or Muang Singh would make convenient rest stops on the way to Hellfire Pass or Sangkhlaburi.

Chaloem Rattanakosin (Tham Than Lot) National Park
อุทยานแห่งชาติ เฉลิมรัตนโกสินทร์ (ถ้ำ ธารลอด)

This national park, 97 km north of Kanchanaburi Town, is of interest to speleologists because of two caves, Than Lot Yai and Than Lot Noi, and to naturalists for its waterfalls and natural forests. Three waterfalls - Trai Trang, Than Ngun and Than Thong - are within easy hiking distance of bungalows and camp ground. Bungalows rent from 500 to 1000B per night and sleep five to 12 people. Pitch your own tent for 5B per person.

To get to Chaloem Rattanakosin, take a bus from Kanchanaburi to Ban Nong Preu for around 30B (a two to three-hour trip) and then try for a songthaew to the park. Most visitors arrive by car, jeep or motorcycle.

Hellfire Pass/Burma-Thailand Railway Memorial

In 1988, the Australian-Thai Chamber of Commerce completed the first phase of the

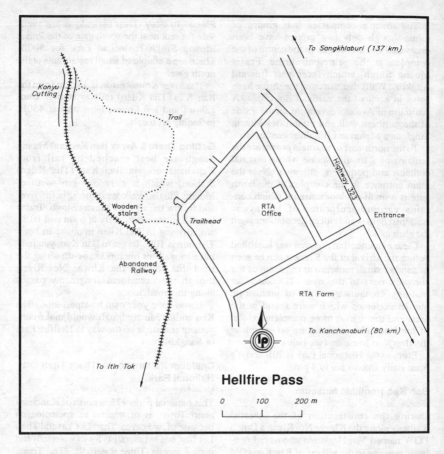

Hellfire Pass

0   100   200 m

To Sangkhlaburi (137 km)

To Kanchanaburi (80 km)

To Itin Tok

Konyu Cutting

Trail

Wooden stairs

Trailhead

Abandoned Railway

RTA Office

RTA Farm

Highway 323

Entrance

Hellfire Pass Memorial Project. The purpose of the project is to honour the Allied prisoners of war and Asian conscripts who died while constructing some of the most difficult stretches of the Burma-Thailand 'Death' Railway, 80 km north-west of Kanchanaburi Town. 'Hellfire Pass' was the name the POWs gave to the largest of a 1000-metre series of mountain cuttings through soil and solid rock, which were accomplished with minimal equipment (3½-kilo hammers, picks, shovels, steel tap drills, cane baskets for removing dirt and rock, and dynamite for blasting). The original crew of 400 Australian POWs was later augmented with 600 additional Australian and British prisoners, who worked round the clock in 12 to 18-hour shifts for 12 weeks. The prisoners called it Hellfire Pass because of the way the largest cutting at Konyu looked at night by torch light. By the time the cuttings were finished, 70% of the POW crew had died and were buried in the nearby Konyu cemetery.

The memorial consists of a trail that follows the railway remains through the Konyu cutting, then winds up and around the pass for an overhead view. At the far end of the cutting is a memorial plaque fastened to solid stone that commemorates the death of the Allied prisoners. There are actually seven cuttings in the area spread over 3½ km – four smaller cuttings and three large. The Australian-Thai Chamber of Commerce also have plans to clear a path to the Hin Tok trestle bridge south-east of the Konyu cutting. This bridge was called the 'Pack of Cards' by the prisoners because it collapsed three times during construction. Eventually some of the track may be restored to exhibit rolling stock from the WW II era.

Access to Hellfire Pass is via the Royal Thai Army Farm on Highway 323, between Kanchanaburi and Thong Pha Phum. Proceeding north-west along Highway 323, the farm is 80 km from Kanchanaburi, 18 km from the Nam Tok Railway Terminus, and 11 km from the River Kwai Village Hotel. Once you arrive at the RTA Farm, you take one of the dirt roads on either side of the RTA offices about 100 metres around to the posted trailhead. From the trailhead, it's about 340 metres up and down a steep walkway and along the rail-bed to the pass. After walking through the Pass and viewing the plaque, you can follow another trail/walkway on the right to get a view of the cutting from above. Then you can either double back the way you came or continue on this trail until it wraps around and meets the trailhead.

Any Kanchanaburi to Thong Pha Phum or Kanchanaburi to Sangkhlaburi bus will pass the RTA farm, but you'll have to let the bus crew know where you want to get off – ask for the *suan thahaan* (Army farm). If you're driving, just remember that the farm is about 80 km from Kanchanaburi and look for the English signs announcing Hellfire Pass on Highway 323.

SANGKHLABURI TO THREE PAGODAS PASS

Three Pagodas Pass (*Chedi Sam Ong*), was one of the terminals of the 'Death' Railway in WW II and is a major smuggling point for the Thai-Burmese black market trade today. It's wild place that the TAT and the Thai government would rather you'd forget about (much like Mae Salong in the north some years ago). But you can go there, either by public transport or on a rented motorcycle. It's an all-day journey and will require that

you spend at least one night in Sangkhlaburi, which is a somewhat interesting off-the-track destination in itself. The distance between Kanchanaburi and Sangkhlaburi alone is about 200 km, so if you take a motorcycle it is imperative that you fill up before you leave Kanchanaburi and stop for petrol again in Thong Pha Phum, the last town before Sangkhlaburi.

The paved highway used to end in Thong Pha Phum, but now the road from Thong Pha Phum to Sangkhla is paved as well. The road between Sangkhla and Three Pagodas is still unpaved and very dusty (or muddy, if you're foolish enough to go there during the rainy season). The best time to go is during the mid-to-late part of the cool season (January to February). During the rainy season nearly the whole of Sangkhlaburi is under water and travel is difficult.

The road between Kanchanaburi and Thong Pha Phum passes mostly through flat terrain interrupted by the occasional limestone outcropping. This is sugar-cane country and if you're travelling by motorcycle during harvest times you'll have to contend with huge cane trucks, overloaded with cut cane, which strew pieces of cane and dust in their wake – take extra care. Cassava is also heavily cultivated here but the cassava trucks aren't such a nuisance.

The road between Thong Pha Phum and Sangkhlaburi is one of the most beautiful in Thailand, winding through limestone mountains and along the huge lake created by the Khao Laem hydroelectric dam near Sangkhla. In spite of the fact that the road surface is in good condition during the dry season, steep grades and sharp curves make this a fairly dangerous journey – on my last trip through here I saw two major accidents.

Sangkhlaburi สังขละบุรี

This small but important Kanchanaburi outpost is inhabited by a mixture of Burman, Karen, Mon and Thai, but is mostly Karen and Mon. Hundreds of former residents of Burma have moved to the Sangkhla area during the last year or two because of the fighting in the Three Pagodas area between the Karen and Mon insurgent armies and between the Burmese government forces and the Karen. These Burmese have fled into Thailand not only to avoid fire-fights but to escape being press-ganged as porters for the Burmese army.

There's not much to do in Sangkhla except explore the small markets for Burmese handicrafts such as checked cotton blankets, *longyi* (Burmese sarongs) and cheroots. One local sight worth seeing, though, is Wat Wang Wiwekaram, also called Wat Mon since most of the monks here are Mon. This wat is about three km north of the town towards the reservoir. A tall and much revered stupa, Chedi Luang Phaw Utama, is the centrepiece of the wat and is currently under renovation. The original chedi is actually located some distance behind the tall one and is 300 to 400 years old. The newer one is built in the style of the Mahabodhi stupa in Bodhgaya, India. From the edge of the monastery grounds is a view of the tremendous lake and three rivers that feed into it.

The distance between Kanchanaburi and Sangkhlaburi is about 217 km.

Three Pagodas Pass เจดีย์พระปรางค์สามยอด

The road to Three Pagodas Pass begins four

km before you reach Sangkhla off Highway 323. At this intersection is a police checkpoint where you may have to stop for minor interrogation, depending on recent events in the Three Pagodas Pass area. If the police allow you to proceed, it's 18 km along a very dusty (or very muddy) road to the pass. Along the way you'll pass a couple of villages entirely inhabited by Mon or Karen; you may also notice the Three Pagodas Pass headquarters for the All Burma Students Democratic Front (ABSDF), where self-exiled Rangoon students have set up an opposition movement with the intention of ousting the Ne Win government from Burma.

The pagodas themselves are rather small, but it is the semi-forbidden atmosphere of this black market outpost that draws a few intrepid travellers. Control of the Burmese side of the border vacillates between the Karen National Union and the Mon Liberation Front, since Three Pagodas is one of several 'toll gates' along the Thai-Burmese border where insurgent armies collect a 5% tax on all merchandise which passes. These ethnic groups use the funds to finance armed resistance against the Burmese Government,

which has recently increased efforts to regain control of the border area. The Karen also conduct a huge multi-million dollar business in illegal mining and logging, the products of which are smuggled into Thailand by the truckload under cover of the night. Not without the palms-up cooperation of the Thai police, of course. Pressure for control of these border points has increased since the Thai Government enacted a ban on all logging in Thailand in 1989, which has of course led to an increase in teak smuggling.

In late 1988, heavy fighting broke out between the Karen and the Mon for control of the 'toll gate' here. Since this is the only place for hundreds of km in either direction where a border crossing is geographically convenient, this is where the Mon army (who traditionally have controlled this area) have customarily collected the 5% tax on smuggling. The Karen insurgents do the same at other points north along the Thai-Burmese border. Burmese Government pressure on the Karen further north led to a conflict between the Karen and the Mon over Three Pagodas trade and the village on the Burmese side was virtually burnt to the ground in the 1988 skirmishes. This means that, at the time of writing anyway, the village is no longer much of an attraction unless you want to see burnt buildings. On the Thai side of the pass is an army camp and a resort that doesn't seem to get many guests.

Places to Stay

Sangkhlaburi has one hotel, the *Sri Daeng Hotel*, which is on the southern edge of town near an army camp. Rooms are 100B and are fairly comfortable. A couple of km north of Sangkhlaburi on the way to Wat Mon, right on the Songkalia River where it meets the lake, is *Songkalia River Huts* (tel (024) 427-4936). A two-room floating bungalow that will sleep up to 10 people costs 300B per night.

Out on the lake are several other more expensive raft-houses, including the *Runtee Palace* (Bangkok reservations 251-7552) where bungalows are 900 to 1500B with meals.

If you get stuck in Thong Pha Phum, the best value is *Somjai Neuk Hotel*, on the left side of the town's main street off the highway (an English sign reads 'Hotel'). Rooms are clean, cost 80B with bath, and there's a shaded courtyard in the centre. They also have air-con rooms for 180B. *Si Thong Pha Phum Bungalows* further down the road has large private bungalows for 70B, but is located next to a noisy primary school.

At Three Pagodas Pass, the only place to stay is at *Three Pagodas Pass Resort* (tel 511079, Bangkok reservations 412-4159), where large bungalows start at 300B. That is, if it's still open; in 1989 it wasn't getting much business.

In Thong Pha Phum there are several small restaurants and noodle stands in the vicinity of the Somjai Neuk Hotel. The Sri Daeng Hotel in Sangkhlaburi has a restaurant downstairs and there are three or four other places to eat down the street. Locals say the best food is at the *No Name Restaurant* (Raan Aahaan Noh Nehm!) in Sangkhlaburi.

Getting There & Away

Buses leave the Kanchanaburi Bus Terminal for Thong Pha Phum every half-hour from 7 am until 6 pm. The fare is 35B and the trip takes about three hours. Buses to Sangkhlaburi leave at 6.45, 9, 10.45 am and 1.15 pm and take four to six hours, depending on how many mishaps occur on the Thong Pha Phum to Sangkhlaburi road.

If you go by motorcycle, you can count on about five hours to cover the 217 km from Kanchanaburi to Sangkhlaburi, counting three or four short rest stops. Or make it an all-day trip and stop off in Ban Kao, Muang Singh, and Hellfire Pass. Be warned, however, that this is not a trip for an inexperienced rider. The Thong Pha Phum to Sangkhlaburi section of the journey (about 70 km) requires sharp reflexes and previous experience on mountain roads. This is also not a motorcycle trip to do alone as stretches of the highway are practically deserted – it's tough to get help if you need it and easy to attract the attention of would-be bandits.

To get to Three Pagodas Pass, you have to take a road running off Highway 323 four km before Sangkhlaburi. In the mornings and evenings, there is usually a songthaew or two going to the Pass from Sangkhlaburi, which will stop in the Karen and Mon villages along the way. You'll find very little English spoken out this way and in fact you may hear as much Burmese, Karen and Mon as Thai.

Chonburi Province

SI RACHA ศรีราชา
About 105 km from Bangkok on the east coast of the Gulf of Thailand is the small town of Si Racha (population 23,000), home of spicy Si Racha sauce (*nam phrik sii raachaa*). Some of Thailand's best seafood, especially the local oysters, is served here accompanied by this sauce. The motor samlors in this fishing town and on Ko Si Chang are unlike those seen anywhere else – huge motorcycles with a side-cars at the rear.

On Ko Loi, a small rocky island which is connected to the mainland by a long jetty,

there is a Thai-Chinese Buddhist temple. Further off shore is a large island called Ko Si Chang, flanked by two smaller islands - Kham Yai to the north and Khang Kao to the south. As this provides a natural shelter from the wind and sea, it is used by large incoming freighters as a harbour. Smaller boats transport goods to the Chao Phraya delta some 50 km away.

Places to Stay
Best places to stay in Si Racha are the hotels built on piers over the waterfront. Three of them are very similar in price and quality: *Siriwattana* and *Siwichai*, across from Tessaban 1 Rd and the Bangkok Bank; and *Samchai*, on Soi 10, across from Surasakdi 1 Rd. All have rooms from 100B up and the Samchai has some air-con rooms as well. The Siriwattana seems to be the cleanest and the service is very good. All three are open and breezy, with outdoor tables where you can bring food in the evening from nearby markets.

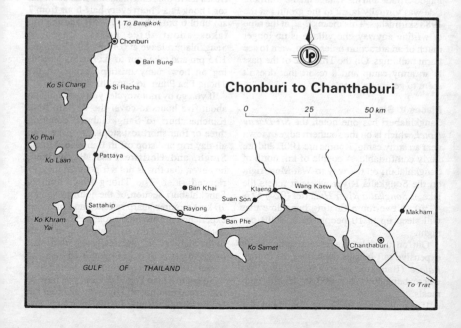

Chonburi to Chanthaburi

To Bangkok
Chonburi
Ban Bung
Ko Si Chang
Si Racha
Ko Phai
Ko Laan
Pattaya
Ban Khai
Sattahip
Rayong
Suan Son
Klaeng
Wang Kaew
Makham
Ban Phe
Ko Khram Yai
Ko Samet
Chanthaburi
GULF OF THAILAND
To Trat

0   25   50 km

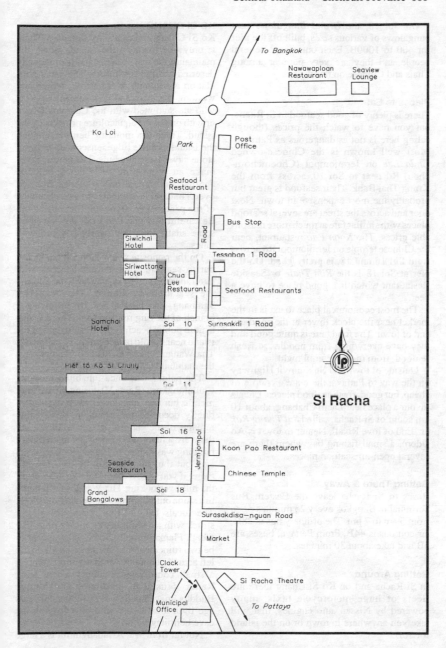

On Soi 18, the *Grand Bungalows* rent bungalows of various sizes, built off the pier for 400 to 1000B. Each one sleeps several people and they are very popular among Thais and Chinese on holidays

Places to Eat
There is plenty of good seafood in Si Racha, but you have to watch the prices (though eating here is not as dangerous as Pattaya). Most well known is the Chinese-owned *Chua Lee* on Jermjompol (Choemchom-phon) Rd next to Soi 10, across from the Krung Thai Bank. Their seafood is great but probably the most expensive in town. Next door and across the street are several seafood places with similar fare at much more reason-able prices. The *Koon Pao* restaurant, near the Chinese temple on Jermjompol Rd across from Soi 16 and 18, is pretty good. On the pier at Soi 18 is the *Rim Thale* or Seaside Restaurant which is a good place to have a beer.

The most economical place to eat is in the market near the clock tower at the southern end of town. The food here is quite good and they have everything from noodles to fresh seafood, from morning until night.

Outside of town, off Sukhumvit Highway on the way to Pattaya, there are a couple of cheap, but good, fresh seafood places. Locals favour a place near Laem Chabang, about 10 km south of Si Racha, called *Sut Thang Rak* or 'End of love Road'. Nearer to town is Ao Udom, a small fishing bay where there are several open-air seafood places.

Getting There & Away
Buses to Si Racha leave the Eastern Bus Terminal in Bangkok every 25 minutes or so from 5 am to 7 pm. The ordinary bus is 28B, air-con bus is 44B. From Pattaya, buses are 5B and take about 30 minutes.

Getting Around
In Si Racha and on Ko Si Chang there are fleets of huge motorcycle taxis, many powered by Nissan auto engines, that will take you anywhere in town or on the island for 10B.

KO SI CHANG เกาะสีชัง
Ko Si Chang makes a nifty getaway. There is only one town on the island, facing the mainland; the rest of the island is practically deserted and fun to explore. The small pop-ulation is made up of fisherfolk, retired and working mariners and government workers who are stationed with the Customs Office or with one of the aquaculture projects on the island. There is a monastic hermitage along the island's centre ridge, ensconced in lime-stone caves and palm huts. The hermit caves make an interesting visit but should be approached with respect – monks from all over Thailand come here to take advantage of the peaceful environment for meditation. Be careful that you don't fall down a lime-stone shaft; some are nearly covered with vines.

On the opposite side of the island, facing out to sea, are some decent beaches with good snorkelling – take care with the tide and the sea urchins, though. The best, Hat Tampang, can be reached by following a branch of the ring road on foot. There is also a more public beach at the western end of the island near the old palace grounds, called Hat Tha Wang. Thai residents and visitors from the mainland come here for picnics.

The palace was once inhabited by King Chulalongkorn (Rama V) during the summer months but was abandoned when the French briefly occupied the island in 1893. Little remains of the various palace buildings, but there are a few ruins to see. The main palace building was moved to Bangkok many years ago, but the stairs leading up to it are still there; if you follow these stairs to the crest of the hill overlooking Tha Wang, you'll come to a stone outcropping wrapped in holy cloth. The locals call it 'Bell Rock' because if struck with a rock or heavy stick it rings like a bell. Flanking the rock are what appear to be two ruined chedis. The large chedi on the left actually contains Atsadangnimit Temple, a small consecrated chamber where King Rama V used to meditate. The unique Buddha image inside was fashioned 50 years ago by a local monk who now lives in the cave hermitage.

Not far from Wat Atsadangnimit is a large

limestone cave called Tham Saowapha which appears to plunge deep into the island. If you have a torch, the cave might be worth exploring.

To the east of town, high on the hill overlooking the sea, is a large and much-frequented Chinese temple. During Chinese New Year in February, the island is overrun with Chinese visitors from the mainland. This is one of Thailand's most interesting Chinese temples, with shrine-caves, several different temple levels and a good view of Si Chang and the ocean. It's a long and steep climb from the road below.

Places to Stay
There are three hotels now on Ko Si Chang, two without an English (or Thai) sign out front and one called the *Tiewpai Guest House*. All are located toward the southern end of town (turn left after disembarking on the pier), on the way to Hat Tha Wang. The first two, on the left side of the road are 100B per room, less for stays of a week or more. Both have good facilities but the *Tiewpai Guest House* also has dorm beds for 40B. Then a little further on the right is another hotel with one-bed rooms for 120B, and two-bed rooms for 150B. They're clean and off the street a bit, so are probably quieter than the other two places.

You can also camp anywhere on the island without any hassle.

Places to Eat
The town has several small restaurants, nothing special, but with all the Thai and Chinese standards.

Getting There & Away
Boats to Ko Si Chang leave regularly throughout the day from a pier in Si Racha at the end of Soi 14, Jermjompol Rd. The fare is 20B each way; the first boat leaves about 9 am and the last at 6.30 pm. Last boat back to Si Racha from Si Chang is at 4.30 pm.

Getting Around
There are fleets of huge motorcycle taxis that will take you anywhere in town for 10B. You

can also get a complete tour of the island for 70 to 80B.

PATTAYA TOWN พัทยา
On the road through Pattaya Town (population 48,000), before Pattaya Beach, the bus passes a number of prosperous sign-making businesses. Upon arrival at Pattaya Beach, the reason for their prosperity is immediately apparent – the place is lit up like Hollywood Blvd at night. Most non-tourists will find Pattaya lacking in culture as well as good taste, since the whole place seems designed to attract the worst kind of western tourist. Budget travellers, in particular, would do well to preclude it from their itineraries. Pattaya Beach is not such a great beach to begin with and its biggest businesses, water sports and street sex, have driven prices for food and accommodation beyond Bangkok levels.

All in all, it's a great place for a sailor on leave, I suppose. Pattaya, in fact, got its start as a resort when there was an American base at nearby Sattahip – nowadays there are still plenty of sailors about, both Thai and American. Food (especially seafood) is great here, as claimed, but generally way over-priced by national (but not international) standards. That part of South Pattaya known as 'the village' attracts a large number of *ka toeys*, Thai transvestites, who pose as hookers and ply their trade among the droves of well-heeled European tourists. Germans and Scandinavians lead the pack. Incidentally, the easiest way to tell a ka-toey is by the Adam's apple – a scarf covering the neck is a dead give-away.

The one thing the Pattaya area has going for it is diving centres (see Snorkelling & Scuba Diving in the Facts about the Country chapter). There are four or five nice islands off Pattaya's shore, expensive to get to, but if you're a snorkelling or scuba enthusiast, equipment can be booked at any of the several diving shops/schools at Pattaya Beach. Ko Laan, the most popular of the offshore islands, even has places to stay.

For beach enthusiasts, if you can't get to one of the better beaches in South Thailand, the best in the Pattaya area is probably Hat

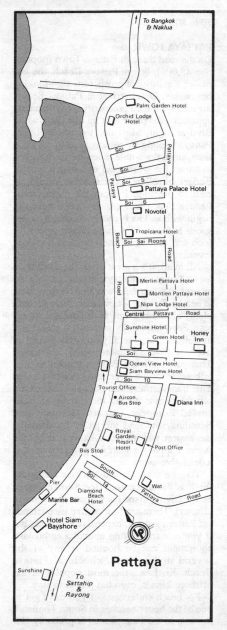

Pattaya

Jomtien (Jawmthian), a couple of km south of Pattaya. Here the water is clean and you're well away from the noisy Pattaya bar scene.

Hat Naklua, north of Pattaya, is also quiet and fairly tastefully developed. Jomtien and Naklua are where visiting families tend to stay, as Pattaya/South Pattaya is pretty much given over to single male tourists or couples on package tours. The glitziest digs are in North Pattaya and Cliff beaches (between South Pattaya and Jomtien).

Information

To give you an idea of how expensive Pattaya is, TAT lists two categories of accommodation: over 800B, and under 800B. 'Best seafood restaurants' are estimated to cost 800B for a meal for two including tax and service, but not including drinks. 'Economy places' are estimated at 200B for two and suggested restaurants in this category include *Mr Donut* and *Pizza Hut*. Don't say you weren't warned.

Waterskiing costs 800 to 1000B per hour including equipment, boat and driver. Parasailing is 250B a shot (about 10 to 15 minutes) and windsurfing 150 to 200B an hour. Diving is actually quite reasonable: about 1500B a dive for boat, equipment and underwater guide.

The Pattaya TAT office is at the mid-point of Pattaya Beach Rd. They keep an up-to-date list of accommodation in the Pattaya area and are very helpful.

The telephone area code for Pattaya is (038). There is a post office in South Pattaya on, where else, Soi Pattaya.

Nightlife

Eating, drinking and making merry are the big pastimes once the sun goes down. Making merry in Pattaya, aside from the professional sex scene, means everything from hanging out in a video bar to dancing all night at the *Marine Bar & Disco* in South Pattaya. Actually, one of the best things to do in the evening is just to stroll down Beach Rd and check out the amazing variety of bars – there's one for every proclivity, including a couple of outdoor Thai boxing bars featuring local talent. Truly the Garden of Earthly Delights, in the most Boschean sense.

Places to Stay – bottom end

The number of places to stay in Naklua, Pattaya and Jomtien is mind-boggling: 142 places classified as hotels; 83 guest houses; and 31 bungalows. The total number of rooms available is over 13,000! Ten more hotels were under construction in 1989.

The average hotel ranges from 350 to 2000B and for guest houses the range is 100 to 300B. The cheapest places in town are the guest houses in South Pattaya along Pattaya 2 Rd, the street parallel to Pattaya Beach Rd. Most are clustered near sois 10, 11 and 12. The *Honey House* (tel 424396) on Soi Honey Inn has 80B rooms, making it Pattaya's lowest price accommodation. The *Uthumphorn*, opposite Soi 10 on Pattaya 2, has 150B rooms, as do the nearby *Wangthong*, the *Supin Guest House* on Soi 10, *Winsand Guest House* on Soi 13 and the *Pattaya View Inn* on Soi Post Office.

Also on Pattaya 2 Rd, the *Diana Inn* (tel 429675) has nearly immaculate rooms with fan and bath (with hot water) for 175B, plus a pool with bar service – this is still Pattaya's best deal. They also have more expensive air-con rooms from 275B.

On Pattaya Sois 11 and 12, the *Pattaya 11* and the *Pattaya 12* have decent fan rooms for 120 and 150B respectively and air-con rooms for 250B. On Soi 13, the *Malibu Guest House* has 250B air-con rooms that include breakfast. The rest of the many guest houses on Soi 13 are in the 200 to 300B range, but rooms are usually cramped and without windows.

A German reader wrote to say 'Our impression of Pattaya wasn't as bad as yours' and recommended a place called *Garden Villa* on Naklua Rd (north Pattaya). It costs 200B for a double, is owned by Germans and has 'traditional German food and customs'. Another place that has been recommended is *In de Welkom*; doubles with fan/air-con cost 220/280B and air-con singles cost 250B.

The cheapest place in Naklua, north of Pattaya, is *LT Guest House* (tel 422969), which has a number of fan rooms for 80B.

In Jomtien Beach, the bottom end consists of the popular *Freddie's Place* (tel 422396) at 250/350B for fan/air-con, *Kitti* with 100B fan rooms, *SK Villa Inn* at 200/250B fan/air-con, and *Sunlight* with 250B air-con rooms.

Places to Stay – middle

Good middle-range places can be found in Naklua, North Pattaya and Jomtien. The *Garden Lodge* (429109), just off Naklua Rd, has air-con rooms for 300B, a clean pool, good service, and an open-air breakfast buffet. *Pattaya Lodge* (tel 428014) is further off Naklua Rd, right on the beach. Air-con

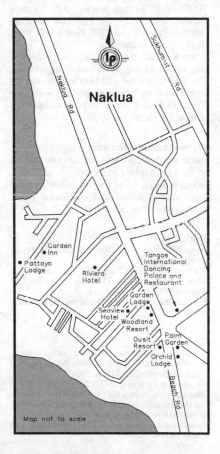

Naklua

Garden Inn

Pattaya Lodge

Riviera Hotel

Tangos International Dancing Palace and Restaurant

Garden Lodge

Seaview Hotel

Woodland Resort

Dusit Resort

Palm Garden

Orchid Lodge

Map not to scale

rooms here are 450B. The *Riviera* (tel 429230) is between the road and the beach and has air-con rooms for 250 to 350B.

Peaceful Jomtien Beach has mostly middle-range 'condotel' places ranging in price from 500 to 700B. The *Jomtien Bayview* (tel 425889) and *Visit House* (tel 426331) have air-con rooms for 300B to 400B. The *Silver Sand* (tel 231010) and *Surf House* (tel 231158) each have air-con rooms for 400 to 450B. The *Marine Beach* (tel 231177) and *Sea Breeze* (tel 231057) are just a bit more expensive at 500 to 750B per air-con room. Jomtien also has several more expensive places that rent bungalows in the 1000 to 2000B range (see top end – Jomtien Beach). Eventually, the high-rise development of Pattaya and Cliff Beach will most likely spread to Jomtien.

On Ko Laan there are only two places to stay at this writing, both mid-to-high range. The *Island Inn* (tel 428444) has fan-cooled rooms with bath for 200 to 500B while the *Ko Laan Resort* (tel 245606) has more up-market fan rooms for 700B.

Places to Stay – top end

Pattaya is really a resort for package tourists so the vast majority of its accommodation is in this bracket. All of the hotels listed below have air-con rooms and swimming pools (unless otherwise noted).

Naklua
Prima Villa Hotel (tel 429398), Naklua Soi 18, 91 rooms, 500 to 600B
Sea View (tel 429317), Naklua Rd, 159 rooms, 968B
Wong Amat Hotel (tel 428118/20), Naklua Rd, 207 rooms, 1300B up
Woodland Resort (tel 421707), Naklua Rd, 80 rooms, 1000B

North Pattaya
Beach View (tel 422660), 104 rooms, 545 to 978B
The Merlin Pattaya (tel 428755/9), Beach Rd, 360 rooms, singles/doubles 1452 to 1694B
The Montien Pattaya (tel 428155/6) Beach Rd,.320 rooms, singles/doubles 1997 to 18,040B
The Orchid Lodge (tel 428175), Beach Rd, 236 rooms, singles/doubles 1452 to 2662B
Pattaya Palace Hotel (tel 428319), Beach Rd, 261 rooms, 1400 to 1600B

Regent Marina Hotel (tel 428015, 429298), North Pattaya Rd, 208 rooms, 750 to 1200B

Central & South Pattaya
Diamond Beach Hotel (tel 428071, 429885/6), Pattaya South, 120 rooms, 835B
Golden Beach Hotel, (tel 428891), 519/29 Pattaya 2nd Rd, 450 to 700B
Nipa Lodge (tel 428321), Beach Rd, 150 rooms, singles/doubles 600 to 2070B
Ocean View Hotel (tel 428434), Beach Rd, 111 rooms, 1160B
Royal Garden Resort (tel 428126/7, 428122), Beach Rd, 154 rooms, 800B up
Hotel Siam Bayshore (tel 428679/80), South Pattaya Rd, 270 rooms, 1300 to 5000B
Siam Bayview Hotel (tel 428728), Beach Rd, 302 rooms, 1300B up

Hat Cliff ('On the Mountain')
Asia Pattaya Beach Hotel (tel 428602/6), Cliff Rd, 314 rooms, 1690 to 6600B
Cosy Beach (tel 429344), Cliff Rd, no pool, 62 rooms, 450 to 787B
Island View (tel 422816), 150 rooms, 850 to 2500B
Pattaya Park Beach (tel 423000/4), 29 rooms, 1210B

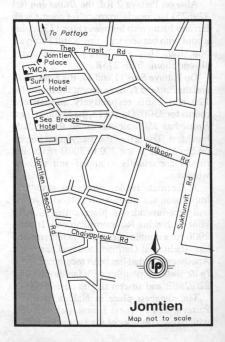

Jomtien
Map not to scale

Royal Cliff Beach Hotel (tel 428344, 428613/6), Cliff Rd, 600 rooms, 2178 to 6050B

Wonderland (tel 428772), 50 rooms, 600 to 1400B

Hat Jomtien

Amnuaythip Villa (tel 429220), 14 bungalows, 1200 to 1800B

Ban Suan (tel 428762), nine bungalows, 1400 (fan) to 2500B (air-con)

Coral Inn (tel 231283), 40 rooms, 600 to 800B

Jomtien Chalet (tel 231205), 36 bungalows, 900 to 1400B

Jomtien Palace (tel 429149), 140 rooms, 1200 to 1800B

Sala Jomtien (tel 231074), 12 bungalows, 1300 to 2100B

Seaview Villa (tel 422766, seven bungalows, 1000 to 3000B, no air-con

Places to Eat

Most food in Pattaya is expensive, but good Thai food is available in shops along Pattaya's back street (Pattaya No 2 Rd), away from the beach. Also look for cheap rooms to rent here. The front signs outside the many snack bars reveal that bratwurst mit brot is far more readily available than khao phat.

Arabs and South Asians are coming to Pattaya in droves these days, so there are an increasing number of Indian-Pakistani-Middle Eastern restaurants in town, some with fairly moderate prices.

The best seafood restaurants are in South Pattaya, where you pick out the sea creatures yourself and are charged by weight. Prices are sky-high.

Getting There & Away

Ordinary non-air-con buses from Bangkok cost 29B one way and leave at 30-minute intervals from 6 am to 8 pm daily. Tour buses from the same station (Eastern Bus Terminal) leave at similar intervals for 53B (or round-trip 96B) between 6 am and 6 pm. Several hotels and travel agencies in Bangkok also run thrice-daily air-con tour buses to Pattaya for around 100B.

From Si Racha you can grab a public bus on the Sukhumvit Highway to Pattaya for 10B.

Finally, if you've just flown into Bangkok International Airport and need to get to Pattaya right away, there are airport minibuses that go directly to Pattaya at 9 am,

12 noon and 7 pm daily for 180B one way. In the reverse direction, the THAI minibus leaves from Alcazar Unity in Pattaya at 6.30 am, 1 pm and 7.30 pm. Song Asawin Co also runs an hourly bus to Bangkok International from Pattaya's Regent Marina Hotel from 7 am until 7 pm for 100B one way.

Getting Around

Songthaews cruise up and down Pattaya Beach and Pattaya 2 Rds frequently – just hop on and when you get out pay 5B. If you go to Naklua it's 10B. Don't ask the fare first as the driver may interpret this to mean you want to charter the vehicle. To get to Jomtien you will have to charter a songthaew and the fare should be about 40B.

The ferry to Ko Laan takes 40 minutes and costs a steep 100B. For 250B the ferry service will throw in lunch.

Motorcycles rent for about 150B per day up to 100cc; a 125cc will cost 200 to 250B and you'll even see a few 750cc to 1000cc machines for hire for 500B. Jeeps go for 300 to 500B per day and cars start at 800B depending on size and model. All rentals in Pattaya are on a 24-hour basis.

AROUND PATTAYA TOWN

Further south, and then east, from Pattaya are more beaches and more resorts. In fact, the more posh places may in the future be restructuring themselves in favour of more middle class tourists and conventioneers.

In Bang Saray, *Bang Saray Villa* (tel 436070) has 19 air-con bungalows for 300B while the *Bang Saray Fishing Inn* and the similar *Ban Saray Fishing Lodge* (tel 436757) are small hotels with 500B air-con rooms. *Nong Nooch Village* (tel 429373) has a choice of rooms or bungalows ranging from 300 to 2500B.

There are still some good seafood restaurants for local Thais in Bang Saray – something Pattaya hasn't seen for years.

Still further south is Sattahip, a vacation spot for the Thai military – some of the best beaches in the area are reserved for their use. There are several Thai navy and air force bases in the vicinity.

Rayong Province

RAYONG TOWN เมือง ระยอง

Rayong Town (population 42,000) is 220 km from Bangkok by the old highway (Route 3) or 185 km on Route 36. The province produces fine fruit (especially durian and pineapple) and nam plaa (fish sauce). Rayong Town itself is not really worth visiting but nearby beaches are fair and Ko Samet is beginning to attract travellers in search of a new Ko Samui. Except for Ko Samet, this area has not received many foreign visitors yet, although it has been popular with Thai tourists for several years now.

The beaches are all near Ban Phe, a seaside town a few km south-east of the provincial capital (this is also the departure point for Ko Samet). If sun and sand are what you've come to Rayong for, head straight for Ban Phe. Then pick out a beach or board a boat bound for Samet.

Another much smaller island nearby is Ko Saket, which is a 20-minute boat ride from the beach of Hat Sai Thong (turn south off Highway 3 at Km 208).

The Suan Son Pine Park, five km further down the highway from Ban Phe, is a popular place for Thai picnickers and has white sand beaches as well.

Suan Wang Kaew is 11 km south of Ban Phe and has more beaches and rather expensive bungalows. Ko Talu, across from Wang Kaew, is said to be a good diving area – the proprietors of Suan Wang Kaew, a private park, can arrange boats and gear. Other resort areas along the Rayong coast include Laem Mae Phim and Hat Mae Ram Pheung.

Khao Cha-mao National Park is inland about 17 km north of Km 274 off Highway 3. Though covering less than 85 square km, the park is famous for limestone mountains, caves, high cliffs, dense forest, waterfalls, and freshwater swimming and fishing. The park service here rents bungalows, longhouses and tents.

Many more resort-type places are popping up along Rayong's coastline. Bangkok developers envisage a string of Thai resorts all the way to Trat along the eastern seaboard, banking on the increasing income and leisure time of Bangkok Thais.

Places to Stay & Eat

Rayong There are three hotels near the bus station off Sukhumvit Highway. The *Rayong*, at 65/3 Sukhumvit and the *Otani*, at 69 Sukhumvit, both have rooms from 100B. The latter has some air-con rooms for 300B as well. The *Tawan Ok*, at 52/3 Sukhumvit, has fan-cooled rooms for 90B without bath, 150B with bath.

For cheap eating check the market near the Thetsabanteung movie theatre or the noodle shop on Taksin Rd next to Wat Lum Mahachaichunphon. There is a very good open-air restaurant along the river belonging to the Fishermen's Association (*Samaakhom Pramong* in Thai).

Ban Phe There are two hotels in Ban Phe, both near the central market. The new *Nuan Napa* has rooms from 150B with fan and bath, while the *Queen* has rooms for 80B (no bath), 100B with bath and 150B air-con.

The *Thale Thawng* restaurant, where the tour bus from Bangkok stops, has good Thai seafood dishes – especially recommended is the *kuaytiaw thaleh*, a seafood noodle soup for 10B. The shop across the street is a good place to stock up on food, mosquito coils, etc to take to Ko Samet. You'll most likely be spending some time in this spot, waiting either for the boat to leave the nearby pier for Ko Samet or for the bus to arrive from Bangkok.

Ko Saket *Ko Saket Phet* (Bangkok reservations tel 271-2750) has 15 bungalows and 10 'tourist houses' for 300 to 1500B.

Getting There & Away

See the Getting There & Away section for Ko Samet for details on transport to/from Rayong.

KO SAMET เกาะเสม็ด

Formerly Ko Kaew Phitsadan ('vast jewel isle' – a reference to the abundant white sand), this island became known as Ko

Samet or 'cajeput isle' after the cajeput tree which grows in abundance here and which is very highly valued as firewood throughout South-East Asia. Locally, the *samet* tree is also used in boat-building. In the early '80s, the 131-square-km Ko Samet began receiving its first visitors interested in more than cajeput trees and sand – young Thais in search of a retreat from city life. At that time there were only about 40 houses on the island, built by fishermen and Ban Phe locals.

Rayong and Bangkok speculators saw the sudden interest in Ko Samet as a chance to cash in on an up-and-coming Phuket and began buying up land along the beaches. No one bothered with the fact that Ko Samet, along with Laem Ya and other nearby islands were part of a national park (one of seven marine parks now in Thailand) and had been since 1981.

When farangs started coming to Ko Samet in greater and greater numbers, spurred on by rumours that Ko Samet was similar to Ko Samui '10 years ago' (one always seems to miss it by a decade, eh?), the Park Service stepped in and built a visitors' office on the island, ordered that all bungalows be moved back behind the tree-line and started charging a 5B admission into the park.

Other rather recent changes have included the introduction of several more vehicles to the island, more frequent boat services from Ban Phe and a much improved water situation. Ko Samet is a very dry island (which makes it an excellent place to visit during the rainy season). Before they started trucking water to the bungalows you had to bathe at sometimes muddy wells. Now most of the bungalow places have proper Thai-style bathrooms and as a result, Ko Samet is a much more comfortable and convenient place to visit, though it may be in danger of becoming overcrowded, like other formerly idyllic isles in Thailand. For now, the bungalows are spread thinly over most of the island with the north-east coast the most crowded area. The beaches really are lovely, with the whitest, squeakiest sand in Thailand. There is even a little surf occasionally (best months are December to January). However, I still

think the accommodation on Samui and Phangan islands is better overall value, though of course it's much more expensive and time-consuming to reach from Bangkok.

In spite of the fact that Ko Samet is supposedly under the protection of the national park service, on my last trip to Ko Samet I was appalled at the runaway growth in the Na Dan and Hat Sai Kaew areas. Piles of rubbish and construction materials have

Ko Samet

really taken away from the island's charm at the northern end. Once you get away from this end of the island, however, things start looking a bit better.

Ko Samet can be very crowded during Thai public holidays: early November (Loy Kratong); 5 December (King's birthday); 31 December to 1 January (New Year); mid-to-late February (Chinese New Year). During these times there are people sleeping on the floors of beach restaurants, on the beach, everywhere. And because of the peak farang tourist seasons (August and December to January) it's so crowded in general that you might consider staying away entirely during these months.

Information

Near Na Dan are several small travel agencies that can arrange long distance phone calls. Citizen Express, between Na Dan and Hat Sai Kaew, can arrange international telephone service, as well as bus and train reservations – they even do air ticketing.

An excellent guide to the history, flora and fauna of Ko Samet is Alan A Alan's 88-page *Samet*, published by Asia Books. Instead of writing a straight-ahead guidebook, Alan has woven the information into an amusing fictional travelogue involving two Swedish twins on their first trip to the island.

Camping Since this is a national park, camping is allowed on any of the beaches, in spite of signs to the contrary posted by certain unscrupulous bungalow owners. In fact, this is a great island to camp on because it hardly ever rains. There is plenty of room; most of the island is uninhabited and tourism is pretty much restricted to the north-eastern beaches, at least so far.

Malaria on Ko Samet A few years ago if you entered the park from the north end of the island near the village, you'd see a large English-language sign warning visitors that Ko Samet was highly malarious. The sign is gone now but the island still has a bit of malaria. If you're taking malarial prophylactics you have little to worry about. If not, take a little extra care in avoiding being bitten by

mosquitoes at night. Malaria is not that easy to contract, even in malarious areas, unless you allow the mosquitoes open season on your flesh. It's largely a numbers game – you're not likely to get malaria from just a couple of bites (that's what the experts say anyway), so make sure you use repellent and mosquito nets at night.

The locals claim that the danger of malaria on Ko Samet is highly exaggerated, but once when I was here, an Argentinean fellow came down with it and was taken to a hospital on the mainland. He had been on Ko Samet for a month.

There is a public health clinic on the island, located halfway between the village harbour and the park entrance. Go there for a blood test if you develop a fever while on Ko Samet, or for any other urgent health problems such as attacks from poisonous sea creatures or snakes.

Boat Trips & Windsurfing Several bungalows on the island can arrange boat trips to nearby reefs and uninhabited islands. At Ao Phutsa and Naga Beach (Ao Hin Khok) are a couple of windsurfing equipment rental places that do boat trips as well. Chan's Windsurfing, on Naga Beach, puts together day trips to Ko Thalu, Ko Kuti, etc, for 150B per person, including food and beverages (10 people minimum). They also rent sailboards at reasonable hourly rates with or without instruction.

Places to Stay

The two most developed (over-developed) beaches are Hat Sai Kaew and Ao Wong Deuan. All of the other spots are still rather peaceful. Every bungalow operation on the island has at least one restaurant and most now have running water and electricity.

Places to Stay – east coast

Hat Sai Kaew Samet's prettiest beach, 'Diamond Sand', is a km or so long and 25 to 30 metres wide. The bungalows here happen to be the most commercial on the island, with video in the restaurants at night and lots of lights. They're all very similar and offer a range of accommodation from 50B (in the low season) for simple huts without fan or bath up to 400 to 500B for one with fan, mosquito net and private bath. All face the beach and most have outdoor restaurants serving a variety of seafood. Like elsewhere in Thailand, the daily rate for accommodation can soar suddenly with demand. The more scrupulous places don't hike rates by much, though.

White Sand, 50 to 200B
Ploy Talay, 150 to 500B
VK Villa, 80 to 350B
Saikaew Villa, 50 to 200B
Diamond, 50 to 400B
Seaview, 50 to 200B
Toy, 100 to 200B
Yaka, 100 to 500B
Jit Preecha, 100 to 300B

Ao Hin Khok The beach here is about half the size of Sai Kaew but nearly as pretty – the rocks that give the beach its name add a certain character. Hin Khok is separated from Sai Kaew by a rocky point mounted by a mermaid statue, a representation of the mermaid that carried the mythical Phra Aphaimani to Ko Samet in the Thai epic of the same name. Two of Samet's original bungalow operations still reign here, *Naga* and *Odds Little Hut* (formerly *Nui's*). Both offer simple bungalows set on a hill overlooking the sea for 60 to 80B and 70 to 100B respectively. The restaurant at Naga sells great bread (which is distributed to several other bungalows on the island) and pastries, baked under the supervision of Englishwoman Sue Wil. Odds restaurant is also quite good.

Further down the beach you may see what looks like a Thai 'gathering of the tribes' – a colourful outpost presided over by Chawalee, a free-spirited Thai woman, who has lived on this beach since long before the bungalows came.

Ao Phai Around the next headland is another shallow bay with *Ao Phai Inn* and *Sea Breeze*, where bungalows are 70 to 80B up, and the newer *Silver Sand* and *Sunset (Samet) Villa*, with bungalows for 150B up.

Ao Phutsa After Ao Phai, the remaining beaches south are separated from one another by steep headlands. To get from one to the next, you have a choice of negotiating rocky paths over the hilly points or walking east to the main road that goes along the centre of the island, then cutting back on side roads to each beach. This is also where the cross-island trail to Ao Phrao starts.

On Ao Phutsa, also known as Ao Thap Thim, you'll find *Phutsa Beach*, where basic huts are 50 to 100B, and the larger *Tub Tim*, where nicer huts are 70 to 300B; the more expensive huts come with fans and bath.

Ao Nuan If you blink, you'll miss this one. Huts at *Ao Nuan* are 70 to 300B.

Ao Cho (Chaw) This bay has its own pier and can be reached directly from Ban Phe on the boat *White Shark*. *Lung Wang* has bungalows starting at 80B. The nicely designed *Tantawan* huts start at 150B.

Ao Wong Deun (Deuan) This area is now mostly given over to more expensive resort-type bungalows. The cheaper bungalows that were here a few years ago have nearly all disappeared and those that remain can't be recommended. It's a little crowded with buildings and people now, but if you want a 300B bungalow, complete with running water and flushing toilet, the best of the lot is *Wong Deun Resort* with huts at 300B. *Wong Deun Villa* is similar but all air-con, ranging from 400 to 2500B. Three boats go back and forth between Ao Wong Deun and Ban Phe – the *Malibu, Seahorse*, and *Wong Deun Villa*.

Ao Thian This is better known by its English name, Candlelight Beach. Far removed from the more active beaches to the north, this is the place to come for a little extra solitude, though the bungalow operations here, *Sangthian Beach* and *Lung Dam* are no great shakes. Food, I'm told, is a definite minus here too. You can bring your own from the village on the northern tip of the island. Rates are 50B up.

Other Bays You really have to be determined to get away from it all to go further south on the east coast of Samet – not a bad idea. None of the bungalows down here have running water – instead you must rely on rainwater from traditional ceramic water jars. Ao Wai is about a km from Ao Thian but can be reached by the boat *Phra Aphai* from Ban Phe. There's only one bungalow operation here, *Sametville*, and rooms are 250 to 500B including all meals. Most bookings are done in Bangkok, but you can try your luck by contacting someone at the Phra Aphai at the Ban Phe Pier.

Ao Kiu also has only one place to stay at this writing, the *Ao Kiu*. Huts are 50 to 500B. The beach here is fairly long and because so few people use it, quite clean. Just a bit further is rocky Ao Karang, where rustic *Pakarang* charges 100B per hut (no electricity). Good coral in this area.

Places to Stay – west coast

Hat Ao Phrao 'Coconut Bay Beach' is the only beach on the west side of the island. There are nice sunset views. At the north end of the beach is *Ao Phra Resort* where huts start at 70B and tents go for 50B. Next down is *Rattana* with huts for 50 to 100B. In the middle of the beach is *Dhom* with nice huts built on the hillside for 100 to 500B. At the south end near the cross-island trail is *SK Hut* where small bungalows are 50B, larger ones up to 500B.

Na Dan Area

To the west of Samet's main pier is a long beach called Ao Wiang Wan where several rather characterless bungalows are set up in straight lines facing the mainland. Here you get neither sunrise (maybe a little) nor sunset. The cheapest place is *SK Bungalows* where accommodation is from 50 to 250B. There are several other places with rates in the 150 to 400B range.

All kinds of construction is going on between Na Dan and Hat Sai Kaew, mostly shop/houses but possibly new bungalows as well.

Getting There & Away

Many Khao San Rd agencies in Bangkok do round-trip transport to Ko Samet including boat for around 220B. This is more expensive than doing it on your own, but for travellers who don't plan to go anywhere else on the east coast it's convenient.

For those who want the flexibility and/or economy of arranging their own travel, the way to go is to bus to Ban Phe in Rayong Province, then catch a boat out to Ko Samet. There are regular buses to Rayong throughout the day from the Eastern Bus Terminal but if your destination is Ban Phe (for Ko Samet), you'd do better to take one of the direct Ban Phe buses, which only cost 1B more; a songthaew to Ban Phe from Rayong is 10B. The Bangkok to Rayong bus is 69B, to Ban Phe 70B. You can also get a return (round-trip) ticket to Ban Phe for 120B, a

saving of 20B. The company that runs the Ban Phe bus, DD Tours, has a reputation for crummy service, often overbooking on the trip back to Bangkok. They also like to put all the farangs in the back of the bus, regardless of reserved seat numbers. Your only alternative is the ordinary non-air-con bus to Rayong (38B) and then local bus to Ban Phe.

Boats to Ko Samet leave the Ban Phe Pier at regular intervals throughout the day starting at around 8 am. How frequently they depart mostly depends on whether they have enough passengers and/or cargo to make the trip profitable, so there are more frequent boats in the high season, December to March. Still, there are always at least three or four boats a day going to Na Dan and Ao Wong Deuan.

For Hat Sai Kaew, Ao Hin Khok, Ao Phai and Ao Phutsa, take the regular Na Dan ferry for 20B. From Na Dan you can either walk to these beaches (10 to 15 minutes) or take one of the trucks that go round the island – if there are several passengers, the fare should be 10B per person to anywhere between Na Dan and Ao Cho. The boat *White Shark* also goes directly to Ao Cho from Ban Phe for 20B – have a look around the Ban Phe Pier to see if it's available.

The *Seahorse*, *Malibu* and *Wong Deuan Villa* all go to Ao Wong Deuan for 20B. There's no jetty here, so passengers are pulled to shore on a raft. You can also get a truck-taxi here from Na Dan, but the fare could be as high as 40B if you're alone. For Ao Thian, you should get either the *White Shark* to Ao Cho or one of the Ao Wong Deuan boats.

The *Phra Aphai* makes direct trips to Ao Wai for 30B. For Ao Kiu or Ao Karang, get the *Thep Chonthaleh* (30B).

For Ao Phrao, you can taxi from Na Dan or possibly get a direct boat from Ban Phe for 20B. The boat generally operates from December to May but with the increase in passengers this service may soon go all-year round.

If you arrive in Ban Phe at night and need a boat to Samet, you can usually charter a one-way trip at the Ban Phe pier for 250 to 300B (to Na Dan)

Getting Around

If you take the boat from Ban Phe to the village harbour (Na Dan), you can easily walk to Hat Sai Kaew, Ao Phai or Ao Cho (Ao Thap Thim). Don't believe the taxi operators who say these beaches are a long distance away. If you're going further down the island, or have a lot of luggage, you can take the taxi (a truck or a three-wheeled affair with a trailer) as far as Ao Wong Deuan. This will cost 20B per person for six to eight people, or 10B apiece to Ao Cho (or anywhere between Na Dan and Ao Cho). If they don't have enough people to fill the vehicle, they either won't go or passengers will have to pay more. There are trails from Ao Wong Deuan all the way to the southern tip of the island, and a few cross-island trails as well. Taxis will make trips to Ao Phrao when the road isn't too muddy.

Chanthaburi Province

CHANTHABURI TOWN เมือง จันทบุรี

Situated 330 km from Bangkok, the 'City of the Moon' is a busy gem mining centre, particularly noted for its sapphires and rubies. Chanthaburi (population 37,000) is also renowned for tropical fruit (rambutan, durian, langsat and mangosteen) and rice noodles – Chanthaburi noodles are in fact exported all over the world. A significant proportion of the population are Vietnamese Christians who fled religious persecution in Vietnam years ago. Because of the Vietnamese-French influence, the town has some interesting shop/house architecture, particularly along the river.

The French-style cathedral here is the largest in Thailand. Originally a small missionary chapel was built on this site in 1711. Four reconstructions took place between 1712 and 1906, when the building finally took its current form. The cathedral is 60 metres long and 20 metres wide.

King Taksin Park is a large public park with gazebos and an artificial lake near the centre of town – nice for an evening stroll.

The gem dealers in town are mostly along

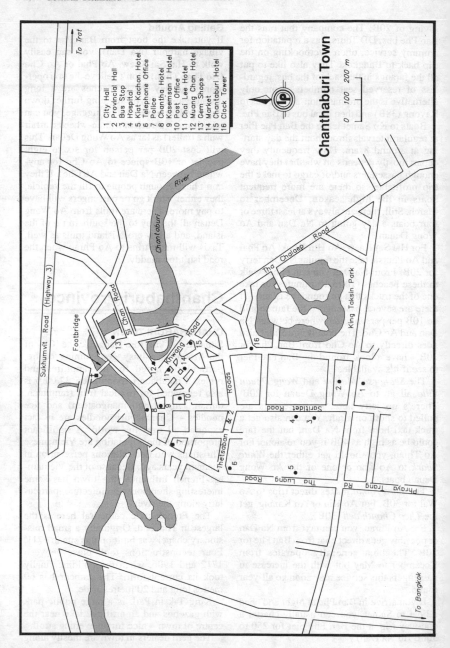

Chanthaburi Town

0   100   200 m

To Trat

River

Chanthaburi

Sukhumvit Road (Highway 3)

Footbridge

Si Chan Road

Khwang Road

Tha Chalaep Road

King Taksin Park

Saritidet Road

Thetsaban 1 & 2 Roads

Tha Luang Road

Phraya Trang Rd

To Bangkok

1 City Hall
2 Provincial Hall
3 Bus Stop
4 Hospital
5 Kiat Kachon Hotel
6 Telephone Office
7 Police
8 Chantha Hotel
9 Kasemsan I Hotel
10 Post Office
11 Chai Lee Hotel
12 Muang Chan Hotel
13 Gem Shops
14 Market
15 Chanthaburi Hotel
16 Clock Tower

Trok Kachang off Si Chan Rd in the south-east quarter. All day long buyers and sellers haggle over little piles of blue and red stones. During the first week of June every year there is a gems festival and Chanthaburi can get very crowded.

Two small national parks are within an hour's drive of Chanthaburi Town. Khao Khitchakut National Park is about 28 km north-east of town off Highway 3249 and is known for Krathing Falls, while Khao Sabap National Park is only about 14 km south-east off Highway 3 and has Phliu Falls. Khao Sabap has a few park bungalows for rent while Khao Khitchakut has bungalows as well as a camp ground.

A few km north of town off Highway 3249 is Khao Phloi Waen, 'Sapphire-Ring Mountain', which is only 150 metres high but features a Sri Lankan-style chedi on top, built during the reign of King Mongkut. Tunnels dug into the side of the hill were once gem-mining shafts.

Wat Khao Sukim is 16 km north of Chanthaburi off Highway 3322 and is a well-known meditation centre.

Places to Stay

The *Kasemsan I Hotel* (tel 312340), 98/1 Benchamarachutit Rd has large, clean rooms from 120B or from 200B with air-con. Down by the river on Rim Nam Rd is the cheaper *Chantha Hotel* with rooms without bath for 60B, rooms with bath for 120B. Some of the rooms have a view of the river.

In the municipal market area is the *Kasemsan II* on Rong Muang Rd with the same rates as Kasemsan I but a little noisier due to the location. The nearby *Chai Lee Hotel* on Khwang Rd is similarly priced again, but not as good. In the same area, the *Chanthaburi Hotel* on Tha Chala Rd is OK at 120 to 200B.

On Si Chan Rd find *Muang Chan Hotel* with adequate rooms in the 120 to 160B range. Out on Tha Luang Rd in the north end of town, away from everything, is the *Kiat Khachon (Kiatkachorn) Hotel* (tel 311212), with rooms from 120 to 200B.

Places to Eat

For those famous Chanthaburi noodles, head for the Chinese-Vietnamese part of town along the Chanthaburi River and you'll see all kinds of variations on the basic rice noodle theme, including delicious crab-fried noodles. On Trok Kachang near the gem stalls is a place serving good *khao mok kai*, a southern Thai chicken biryani. The *Chanthon Phochana* restaurant beneath the Kasemsan I Hotel has a good variety of Thai and Chinese dishes. At the south-east corner of King Taksin Park are a couple of outdoor ice cream parlours that also serve a few standard Thai dishes.

Getting There & Away

From Bangkok, air-con buses cost 103B; regular buses 56B. From Rayong it's 20B. There are also buses between Khorat and Chanthaburi now via Sa Kaew and Kabinburi. The trip takes four to five hours and passes through good mountain scenery. The total fare is about 55B.

Trat Province

About 400 km from Bangkok, the province of Trat borders Cambodia (formerly Kampuchea). As in Chantaburi, gem-mining is an important occupation. Gem markets (*talaat phloi*) are open daily at the Huu Thung market in Bo Rai district between 7 and 10 am and at the Khlong Yo Market in the same district between 1 and 3 pm. Bo Rai is about 40 km north of Trat Town on Highway 3389. Another market is open all day in Khao Saming district only 20 km north-west of Trat. Sapphires and rubies are good buys if (and only if) you know what you're buying.

The other big industry in Trat is the smuggling of consumer goods between Cambodia and Trat. For this reason, travelling alone along the border or in the offshore islands which serve as conduits for sea smuggling requires caution. Two farang women (UK and New Zealand citizens) were killed on Ko Chang in 1988 by bandits. More and more people are discovering the beaches and islands of Trat, however, and as the locals and the police begin to see the benefits of hospitality to outsiders, security will undoubtedly improve.

One relatively safe spot at which to observe the border trade is at the Thai-Cambodian market in Khlong Yai, near the end of Highway 318 south. An estimated 10 million baht changes hands in the markets of Khlong Yai daily.

As Highway 318 goes east and then south from Trat Town on the way to Khlong Yai District, the province thins to a narrow sliver between the Gulf of Thailand and Cambodia. Along this sliver are a number of little-known beaches, including Hat Sai Si Ngoen, Hat Sai Kaew, Hat Thap Thim and Hat Ban Cheun. Ban Cheun has a few bungalows, but there is no accommodation at the other beaches at this writing.

At Km 70, off Highway 318, is a Jut Chom Wiw or 'View-admiring point' where you can get a panorama of the surrounding area.

TRAT TOWN เมือง ตราด

The provincial capital of Trat (population

Trat Province

Top: Wat Mahathat, Sukhothai (DC)
Left: Wat Sri Chum, Sukhothai (BP)
Right: Sukhothai (DC)

Top: Fortune telling in Nakhon Pathom (JC)
Bottom: Bang Pa In (TW)

13,000) has nothing much to offer except as a jumping off point for the Ko Chang island group. The locals are friendly, however, and there are certainly worse places to spend a few days.

You can get info on Ko Chang National Park at the park headquarters in Laem Ngop, a small town 20 km south-west of Trat. This is also where you get boats to Ko Chang. *Laem* means cape; *ngop* is the traditional Khmer rice farmer's hat.

Places to Stay

Town Most of the hotels in Trat Town are along or just off Sukhumvit Rd. The *Tang Nguan Seng 2* (tel 511028) at 66-71 Sukhumvit Rd has rooms from 80 to 150B. There's a cheaper *Tang Nguan Seng 1* (tel 511051) at No 44-77, where rooms are 70B a night, no air-con available. The *Thai Roong Roj* (*Rung Rot*) (tel 511141) at 196 Sukhumvit Rd (actually off Sukhumvit a bit) has rooms from 100B or from 180B with

air-con. Then at 234 Sukhumvit Rd is *Sukhumvit Inn* (tel 512151) with 100 to 200B rooms. Top end in town is the *Trat* (511091), off Sukhumvit Rd, which has standard fan rooms for 190B, air-con up to 450B.

Max and Tick, of Krabi fame, have moved their *Mad Max Guest House* to Trat. Rates are 30B for a dorm bed or 60/80B a single/double. Any songthaew driver will know the place and, since it's downtown, fares shouldn't be more than 10B. Max and Tick are a friendly young Thai couple who speak excellent English. Their tape collection is one of the best around.

Bo Rai If you need to stay overnight in this gem-market town, the *Honey Inn* near the market has rooms with bath for 100B, air-con for 200B. There's also the slightly more upscale *Paradise* near the post office, where doubles with fan and bath are 200B, 300B with air-con.

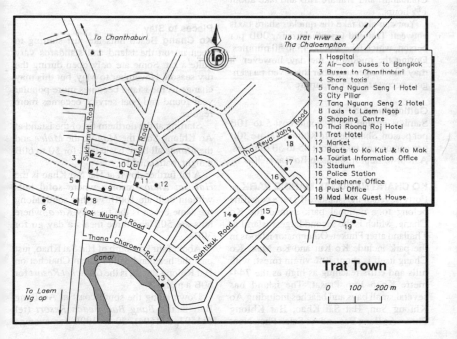

1 Hospital
2 Air-con buses to Bangkok
3 Buses to Chanthaburi
4 Share taxis
5 Tang Nguan Seng 1 Hotel
6 City Pillar
7 Tang Nguang Seng 2 Hotel
8 Taxis to Laem Ngop
9 Shopping Centre
10 Thai Roong Roj Hotel
11 Trat Hotel
12 Market
13 Boats to Ko Kut & Ko Mak
14 Tourist Information Office
15 Stadium
16 Police Station
17 Telephone Office
18 Post Office
19 Mad Max Guest House

Trat Town

0   100   200 m

Khlong Yai There are two hotels to choose from here: *Pawini* (*Pavinee*) near the share taxi stand for 60 to 100B without bath, 120B with; and *Suksamran*, 120 to 160B with fan, 200B with air-con.

Laem Ngop There's really no reason to stay here since most boats to the island leave in the afternoon and it's only 20 km from Trat. If you must, the *Sukjai, Paradise* and *Wang Mai Ngam* all have fan-cooled rooms for 150B.

Places to Eat

Next door to the Muang Trat is a good restaurant, the *Jiraporn*. On the Trat River in town is a decent night market.

Getting There & Away

Buses from Bangkok cost 112B air-con or 64B regular. The trip takes five to six hours one way by air-con bus or about eight hours by ordinary bus. Ordinary buses between Chantaburi and Trat are 18B and take about 1½ hours.

You can also take the quicker share taxis between Trat and Chanthaburi for 30B per person, which take around 45 to 50 minutes. During the middle of the day, however, it may take longer to gather the seven passengers necessary for a departure

Getting Around

Samlors around town should cost 5 to 10B per person. Share taxis to Khlong Yai are 30B per person and take about 45 to 50 minutes. A door-to-door minibus to Bo Rai is 30B.

KO CHANG NATIONAL MARINE PARK

Forty-seven of the islands off Trat's coastline belong to a national park named for Ko Chang, which is the second largest island in Thailand after Phuket. Other major islands in the park include Ko Kut and Ko Mak. Ko Chang itself is about 70% virgin forest, with hills and cliffs reaching as high as the 744-metre Khao Jom Prasat. The island has several small bays and beaches including Ao Khlong Son, Hat Sai Khao, Hat Khlong Phrao, Ao Bang Bao and Ao Salak Phet. Near each of these beaches are small villages, eg Ban Khlong Son, Ban Bang Bao and so on.

A series of three waterfalls along the stream of Khlong Mayom in the interior of the island, Than Mayom (or Thara Mayom) Falls, can be reached via Tha Than Mayom or Ban Dan Mai on the east coast. The waterfall closest to the shore can be climbed in about 45 minutes. The view from the top is quite good and there are two inscribed stones bearing the initials of Rama VI and Rama VII nearby. The second waterfall is about 500 metres further east along Khlong Mayom and the third is about three km from the first. At the third waterfall is another inscribed stone, this one with the initials of Rama V.

On Ko Kut you'll find beaches mostly along the west side, at Hat Taphao, Hat Khlong Chao and Hat Khlong Yai Kii. The main village on Ko Kut is Ban Khlong Hin Dam.

Ko Mak, the smallest of the three main islands, has a beach along the north-west bay and possibly others as yet undiscovered.

Places to Stay

Ko Chang Beach huts are just starting to open up on the island and standards vary quite a bit. Some are only open during the dry season, November to May, but this may change as the island becomes more popular year round and boat service becomes more regular.

Starting at the northern tip of the island at Ao Khlong Son, the *Manop*, the *Malee* and the *Manee* all have basic huts for 50 to 60B a night, bath outside.

A bit further down at Hat Sai Khao is the *Hat Sai Khao* 'resort', where solid huts without bath are 100B. Further south along the same beach is the friendly *Kaeo*, where huts are 50B and three meals a day go for 30B.

About four km south of Hat Sai Khao, just past the headland called Laem Chaichet on Hat Khlong Phrao, is the *Chaichet Resort* for 60B a night.

Down along the south coast at Ao Bang Bao is the *Bang Bao Beach Resort* (tel 511597, 511604), 50 to 100B for average bungalows. You may also be able to rent rooms cheaply in nearby Ban Bang Bao.

For now, there's no advertised accommodation at Ao Salak Phet, but as at Ao Bang Bao, you may be able to rent a room or house in Ban Salak Phet. Since Ko Chang is part of a national park, camping is allowed on any of the beaches.

Finally, at Than Mayom National Park on the east coast there are a few park bungalows at the usual national rates. A couple of private places, *Thanmayom* and *Maeo*, also rent huts for 60 to 100B a night.

As Ko Chang becomes more popular,

additional accommodation will undoubtedly spring up elsewhere around the island.

Ko Kut At Hat Taphao on the west coast, the aptly named *First* has basic huts for 50B, bath outside. If this one's closed when you arrive, try village homes in nearby Ban Hin Dam.

Ko Mak On the north-west bay is the rather exclusive *Ko Mak Resort* with rates starting at 800B including fan and bath.

Ko Kradat The *Ko Kradat* has air-con bun-

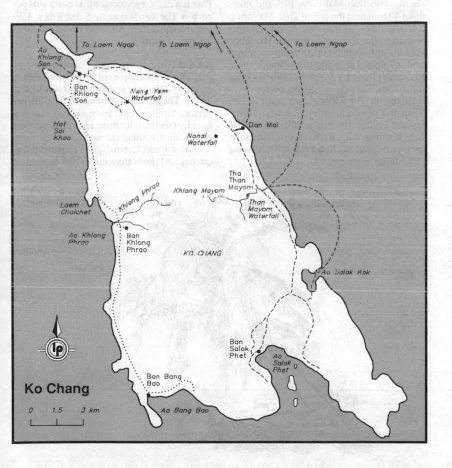

Ko Chang

0   1.5   3 km

galows for 600B. Mr. Chumpon in Bangkok (311-3668) can arrange accommodation at Ko Kradat and transport to the island in advance.

Getting There & Away

Ko Chang Take a songthaew (7B) from Trat to Laem Ngop on the coast, then a ferry to Ko Chang. You have a choice of several different ferries, depending on the day of the week and time of day. Two ferries leave daily for Ban Dan Mai and Tha Than Mayom on the north-east coast at 1 pm, returning to Laem Ngop at 7.30 am the following day. The ferry to Dan Mai costs 10B and takes about 40 minutes; the one to Than Mayom is 20B and takes 50 minutes. A faster, larger boat also plies the route between Tha Than Mayom and Laem Ngop, leaving the mainland at 9 am and arriving at Tha Than Mayom 40 minutes later; it returns the following day at 4.20 pm. The fare is 30B per person.

Ferries to Ao Khlong Son leave Laem Ngop at 1 pm on Monday, Tuesday, Thursday and Friday. The fare is 20B and the trip takes about an hour. In the reverse direction, ferries from Khlong Son leave at 4 am on the same days.

To get from one part of the island to another you have a choice of boat, foot or motorbike taxi. A motorcycle taxi from Ao Khlong Son all the way to Ban Bang Bao (about 15 km) costs 10 to 15B. You can also walk from Khlong Son to Hat Sai Khao in about half an hour; from Hat Sai Khao to Hat Khlong Phrao in about two hours; from Hat Khlong Phrao to Ao Bang Bao in about four hours.

There is a daily boat service between Than Mayom and Ao Salak Kok further south along the east coast of Ko Chang for 20B per person. Between Ao Salak Kok and Ao Salak Phet is a daily jeep service that costs 10B per person. The jeep leaves Ao Salak Kok at 4.30 pm, returning from Ao Salak Phet the following day at 6 am.

Ko Kut Two or three fishing boats a week go to Ko Kut from the pier of Tha Chaloemphon on the Trat River towards the east side of Trat Town. They'll take passengers for 50B per person. Similar boats leave slightly less frequently (six to eight times a month) from Ban Nam Chiaw, a village about halfway between Trat Town and Laem Ngop. Departure frequency and times from either pier depend on

the weather and the fishing season – it's best to enquire ahead of time. The boats take around six hours to reach Ko Kut.

Coconut boats go to Ko Kut once or twice a month from a pier next to the slaughterhouse in town – same fare and trip duration as the fishing boats.

If you want to charter a boat to Ko Kut, the best place to do so is from Ban Ta Neuk near Km 68 south-east of Trat, about six km before Khlong Yai off Highway 318. A long-tail boat, capable of carrying up to 10 people,

can be chartered here for 1000B. Travel time is about one hour. During the rainy season these boats may suspend service.

Ko Mak Coconut boats go to Ko Mak from the pier near the slaughterhouse in Trat Town once or twice a week. The trip takes five hours and costs 50B per person.

In future, as more travellers come to this area, regular ferry services to Ko Mak, Ko Kut and Ko Kradat may develop.

Northern Thailand

The first true Thai kingdoms (Sukhothai, Chiang Mai and Chiang Saen) arose in what is now northern Thailand, hence this region is dotted with great temple ruins. It is also the home of most of the Thai hill tribes, whose cultures are dissolving fast in the face of Thai modernisation and foreign tourism. Yet the scenic beauty of the north has been fairly well-preserved, and Chiang Mai is still probably Thailand's most livable city.

The northern Thai people are known for their relaxed, easy-going manner, which shows up in speech – the northern dialect has a rhythm which is slower than that of Thailand's other three main dialects.

The north also contains the infamous Golden Triangle, the region where Burma, Laos and Thailand meet and where most of the world's illicit opium is grown. Apart from the air of adventure and mystery surrounding the Golden Triangle, it is simply a beautiful area through which to travel.

The Northern Loop
While the straightforward way of travelling north is to head directly from Bangkok to Chiang Mai, there are many interesting alternatives.

The old Laotian Loop – from Bangkok to Vientiane, Luang Prabang and Ban Houei Sai, then back into Thailand to Chiang Rai and eventually Chiang Mai – has been cut short by the Lao Government. Still, you can make an interesting northern loop from Bangkok through Chiang Mai and the north-east and back to Bangkok.

Starting north, visit the ancient capitals of Ayuthaya, Lopburi and Sukhothai, or take a longer and less beaten route by heading west to Nakhon Pathom and Kanchanaburi and then travelling north-east by bus to Lopburi via Suphanburi (backtracking to Ayuthaya if desired).

From Lopburi, either head north to Chiang Mai, or stop at Phitsanulok for side trips to Sukhothai, Tak and Mae Sot. It is now pos-

sible to travel by road from Mae Sot to Mae Sarieng, then on to Mae Hong Son or Chiang Mai, though the last leg between Tha Song Yang and Mae Sarieng isn't paved yet and public transport is scarce.

Once you're in Chiang Mai, the usual route is to continue on to Fang for the Kok River boat ride to Chiang Rai, then on into the Golden Triangle towns of Mae Sai and Chiang Saen. Travellers with more time might add to this the Chiang Mai to Pai to Mae Hong Son to Mae Sariang to Chiang Mai circle. A very rough but traversable road between Tha Ton and Doi Mae Salong is an alternative to the Kok River trip once you get to the Fang area.

From the north, proceed to the north-east via Phitsanulok and Lom Sak, entering the north-east proper at either Loei or Khon Kaen. From there, Nong Khai, Udon Thani and Khon Kaen are all on the rail line back to Bangkok, but there are several other places in the area worth exploring before heading back to the capital.

Chiang Mai Province

CHIANG MAI TOWN เมือง เชียงใหม่
Over 700 km north-west of Bangkok, Chiang Mai (population 156,000) has more than 300 temples – almost as many as in Bangkok – making it visually striking. Doi Suthep Mount rises 1676 metres above and behind the city, providing a nice setting for this fast-developing centre.

Chiang Mai (new city) was built from scratch in 1296 under King Mengrai. Historically, Chiang Mai succeeded King Mengrai's Chiang Rai kingdom after he conquered the post-Dvaravati kingdom of Hariphunchai (modern Lamphun) in 1281. Mengrai had been a prince of Nan Chao, a Thai kingdom in south-west China.

Chiang Mai later became a part of the

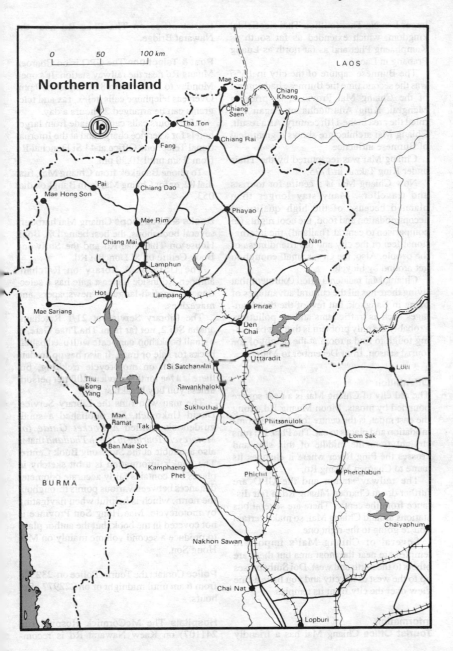

Northern Thailand

LAOS

Mae Sai

Chiang Khong

Chiang Saen

Tha Ton

Chiang Rai

Fang

Pai

Chiang Dao

Mae Hong Son

Phayao

Mae Rim

Nan

Chiang Mai

Lamphun

Lampang

Hot

Phrae

Mae Sariang

Den Chai

Uttaradit

Thung Song Yang

Si Satchanalai

Sawankhalok

Sukhothai

Loei

Mae Ramat

Tak

Phitsanulok

Lom Sak

Ban Mae Sot

Kamphaeng Phet

Phichit

Phetchabun

BURMA

Nakhon Sawan

Chaiyaphum

Chai Nat

Lopburi

0   50   100 km

larger Lan Na Thai (million Thai ricefields) kingdom, which extended as far south as Kamphaeng Phet and as far north as Luang Prabang in Laos.

The Burmese capture of the city in 1556 was the second time the Burmese had control of the Chiang Mai Province, as prior to Mengrai, King Anuruddha of Pagan had ruled the area in the 11th century. As a result, Chiang Mai architecture shows a great deal of Burmese influence.

Chiang Mai was recaptured by the Thais under King Taksin in 1775.

Now Chiang Mai is a centre for tourists and travellers. Many stay longer than planned because of the high quality of accommodation and food, the cool nights (in comparison to central Thailand), the international feel of the city and the friendliness of the people. Also, the city is small enough to get around by bicycle.

Chiang Mai residents often comment that living there has all the cultural advantages of being in Bangkok, but few of the disadvantages such as traffic jams and air pollution. Probably the only problem is that it's becoming tough to find a room at the height of the tourist season, from December to March.

Orientation

The old city of Chiang Mai is a neat square bounded by moats. Moon Muang Rd, along the east moat, is the centre for cheap accommodation and places to eat. Tha Phae Rd runs straight from the middle of this side and crosses the Ping River where it changes its name to Charoen Muang Rd.

The railway station and the GPO are further down Charoen Muang Rd, a fair distance from the centre. There are several bus stations around Chiang Mai, so make certain you're going to the right one.

Several of Chiang Mai's important temples are near the moat area but there are others to the north and west. Doi Suthep rises up to the west of the city and you have a fine view over the city from its temples.

Information

Tourist Office Chiang Mai has a friendly tourist office on Tha Phae Rd near the Nawarat Bridge.

Post & Telephone The GPO is on Charoen Muang Rd near the railway station. It's open Monday to Friday from 8.30 am to 4.30 pm. Overseas telephone calls, telex, fax and telegrams can be arranged 24 hours a day.

After-hours calls can be made from larger hotels for a service charge and at the International Telephone Office at 44 Si Donchai Rd from 9 am until 10.30 pm.

To phone Bangkok from Chiang Mai, first dial 02, or for Chiang Mai from Bangkok dial 053.

Books & Bookshops Chiang Mai harbours several bookshops, the best being DK Book House on Tha Phae Rd and the Suriwong Book Centre on Si Donchai Rd.

The USIS/AUA library on Ratchadamnoen Rd inside the east gate has a selection of English-language newspapers and magazines.

The Library Service at 21/1 Ratchamankha Soi 2, not far from Tha Phae Gate, is a small bookshop-cum-cafe with used paperbacks for sale or trade. It also has up-to-date information on motorcycle trekking, but there is a fee for this service (20B per person) unless you buy breakfast.

The man who runs the Library Service, David Unkovich, has published a small guidebook entitled *A Pocket Guide for Motorcycle Touring in North Thailand* that is also available at the Suriwong Book Centre. The book's information is a bit sketchy in places but contains fairly accurate odometer distances between various points throughout the north, which is helpful when navigating by motorcycle. Mae Hong Son Province is not covered in the book, but the author plans to produce a second volume mainly on Mae Hong Son.

Police Contact the Tourist Police on 232508 from 6 am until midnight or on 222977 after hours.

Hospitals The McCormick Hospital (tel 241107) on Kaew Nawarat Rd is recommended over the Suandok Hospital because 'they are more geared up to foreigners, speak better English and won't keep you waiting for so long'. A consultation and treatment for a simple ailment costs about 200B. Free *Fansidar* tablets are available at the Suandok Hospital's malaria centre.

Immigration The Immigration Office (tel 213510) is off Highway 1141 near the airport.

Maps Finding your way around Chiang Mai is fairly simple although a copy of Nancy Chandler's *Map of Chiang Mai* is a worthwhile investment for 60B. It shows all the main points of interest and innumerable oddities which you'd be most unlikely to stumble upon by yourself. Similar in scope are *DK's Chiang Mai Tourist Map* published by DK Book House (this has more emphasis on local transport information but very shaky transliteration) and TAT/Suriwong Book Centre's *Tourist Map of Chiang Mai*. TAT also puts out a sketchy city map that's free.

Wat Chiang Man
The oldest wat in the city, Wat Chiang Man was founded by King Mengrai in 1296 and features typical northern Thai architecture with massive teak columns inside the bot (main chapel). Two important Buddha images are kept in the smaller wiharn to the right of the bot. The monks once kept it locked, but now it's open daily from 9 am to 5 pm.

The Buddha Sila is a marble bas-relief standing 20 to 30 cm high. It's supposed to have come from Sri Lanka or India about 2500 years ago. The well-known Crystal Buddha, shuttled back and forth between Siam and Laos like the Emerald Buddha, is kept in the same glass cabinet. It's thought to have come from Lopburi 1800 years ago and stands just 10 cm high.

Wat Phra Singh
Started by King Pa Yo in 1345, the wiharn which houses the Phra Singh image was built between 1385 and 1400, and the bot was finished at about 1600. The Phra Singh

Buddha supposedly comes from Sri Lanka, but it is not particularly Sinhalese in style. As it is identical to two images in Nakhon Si Thammarat and Bangkok, and has quite a travel history (Sukhothai, Ayuthaya, Chiang Rai, Luang Prabang – the usual itinerary for a travelling Buddha image, involving much royal trickery), no one really knows which image is the real one or can document its provenance. It's kept in the smaller building behind and to the left of the bot.

Wat Chedi Luang
This has a very large and venerable chedi, which holds the image, dating from 1441. It's now in partial ruins, due to either a 16th century earthquake or the cannon fire of King Taksin in 1775. It's said that the Emerald Buddha was placed in the eastern niche here in 1475. The *lak muang* (guardian deity-post) for the city is within the wat compound in the small building to the left of the main entrance.

A few years ago, Thailand's Fine Arts Department had the financial support of the Japanese Government to restore the great chedi, but nothing seems to have come of these plans. Since no one knows for sure how the original spire looked, Thai artisans will have to design a new spire for the chedi if and when it is restored. It's still impressive the way it is, as long as it is kept from decaying further.

Wat Phan Tao
Adjacent to Wat Chedi Luang, this wat has a wooden wiharn and some old and interesting monk's quarters. Across Ratchadamnoen Rd from here, at the intersection with Phra Pokklao Rd, is an uninteresting monument marking the spot where King Mengrai was struck by lightning!

Wat Jet Yot
Out of town on the northern highway loop near the Chiang Mai Museum, this wat was built in the mid-15th century and based on the design of the Mahabodhi Temple in Bodhgaya, India. The seven spires represent the seven weeks Buddha spent in Bodhgaya after his enlightenment. The proportions for

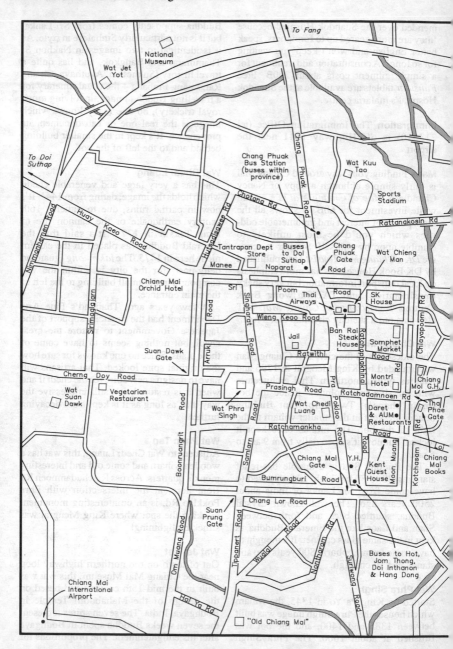

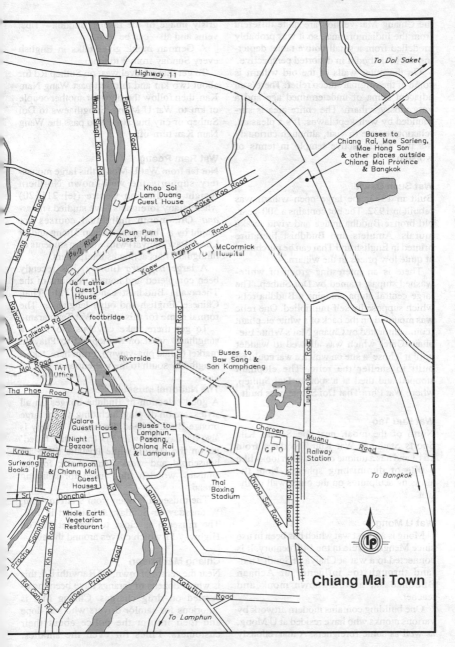

Chiang Mai Town

the Chiang Mai version are quite different from the Indian original, so it was probably modelled from a small votive tablet depicting the Mahabodhi in distorted perspective.

On the outer walls of the old wiharn is some of the original stucco relief. There's an adjacent stupa of undetermined age and a very glossy wiharn. The entire area is surrounded by well-kept lawns. It's a pleasant, relaxing temple to visit, although curiously it's not a very active temple in terms of worship.

Wat Suan Dawk

Built in 1383, the large open wiharn was rebuilt in 1932. The bot contains a 500-year-old bronze Buddha image and vivid Jataka murals. Amulets and Buddhist literature printed in English and Thai can be purchased at quite low prices in the wiharn.

There is an interesting group of whitewashed stupas, framed by Doi Suthep. The large central stupa contains a Buddha relic which supposedly self-multiplied. One relic was mounted on the back of a white elephant (commemorated by Chiang Mai's White Elephant Gate) which was allowed to wander until it 'chose' a site on which a wat could be built to shelter the relic. The elephant stopped and died at a spot on Doi Suthep, where Wat Phra That Doi Suthep was built.

Wat Kuu Tao

North of the moat, near the Sanam Kila Sports Stadium, Wat Kuu Tao dates from 1613 and has a unique chedi which looks like a pile of diminishing spheres. Note the amusing sculptures on the outer wall of the wat.

Wat U Mong

U Mong is a forest wat which has been in use since Mengrai's rule in the 14th century. It is connected to a wat at Chaiya in South Thailand through the influence of Achaan Buddhadasa, a well-known monk and teacher.

One building contains modern artwork by various monks who have resided at U Mong, as well as some foreigners. A marvellously grisly image of the fasting Buddha – ribs, veins and all – can be seen.

A German monk gives talks in English every Sunday from 3 to 6 pm.

To get there, travel west on Suthep Rd for about two km and turn left past Wang Nam Kan, then follow the signs for another couple of km to Wat U Mong. Songthaews to Doi Suthep or city bus No 1 also pass the Wang Nam Kan turn-off.

Wat Ram Poeng

Not far from Wat U Mong, this large monastery supports the well-known Northern Insight Meditation Centre (tel 211620) where many foreigners have studied *vipassana*. One-month individual courses are taught by a Thai monk (Ajaan Thong and/or Luang Paw Banyat) with western students or bilingual Thais acting as interpreters.

A large *tripitaka* (library) has recently been completed and houses versions of the Theravada Buddhist canon in Pali, Thai, Chinese, English and other languages. The formal name for this wat is Wat Tapotaram.

To get there, take city bus No 1 or a songthaew west on Suthep Rd to Phayom market (talaat pha-yawm). From here, take a songthaew south to the wat entrance (4B).

The National Museum

A good selection of Buddha images, in all styles, are on display, including a very large bronze Buddha head downstairs. Pottery is also displayed downstairs (note the 'failed' jar on the stairs), while upstairs there are household and work items. Look for the amusing wooden 'dog' used for spinning thread.

The museum is open from 9 am to 4 pm, Wednesday to Sunday. Admission is 10B. The museum is close to Wat Jet Yot on Highway 11 which curves around the city.

Chiang Mai Prison

Near the centre of town, off Ratwithi Rd, this is where dozens of farangs have been incarcerated on drug charges. Chiang Mai is notorious for samlor drivers who sell dope and then inform the police about their customers. Fines for even the smallest amounts of ganja are very high – 50,000B for a couple of grams is not unusual. Those who cannot afford to buy out of this dangerous game go to jail.

Night Market

An extensive night market sprawls over the area between Suriwong Rd and Tha Phae Rd, off Chang Klan Rd, just east of the Mae Kha canal, near the Chiang Inn. This market is made up of several different concession areas and dozens of street vendors displaying an incredible variety of Thai and northern Thai goods at very low prices – if you bargain well. Actually, many importers buy here because the prices are so good, especially when buying in quantity.

Good buys include Phrae-style *seua maw hawm* (blue denim farmers' shirts), northern and north-eastern handwoven fabrics, yams (shoulder bags), hill-tribe crafts (many tribespeople set up their own concessions here), opium scales, hats, silver jewellery, lacquerware and many other items. Cheap cassette tapes are plentiful too.

If you're in need of new travelling clothes, this is a good place to look. A light cotton dress, trousers or yams can be bought for between 45 and 60B, and work shirts cost between 45 and 50B, depending on size.

You must bargain patiently but mercilessly. There are so many different concessions selling the same type of items that competition effectively keeps prices low, if you haggle. Look over the whole bazaar before you begin buying. If you're not in the mood or don't have the money to buy, it's still worth a stroll, unless you don't like crowds – most nights it's elbow to elbow. Several restaurants and scores of food trolleys feed the hungry masses.

Other Attractions

The Old Chiang Mai Cultural Centre on Highway 108 south of town is a tourist centre where northern Thai and hill-tribe dances are performed nightly.

Laddaland has a dance performance every morning, but it's rather kitsch.

Out towards Doi Suthep, six km from the town centre, are the Chiang Mai Zoo and the nearby Chiang Mai Arboretum.

Near the night market is Kamphaeng Din Rd, the street of a thousand cut-rate prostitutes at night. It follows an old earthen rampart between Loi Kroa and Tha Phae Rds. This is strictly a Thai scene as well as most probably being dangerous.

The Chiang Mai University Campus is also an interesting place in the evenings, with a busy night bazaar of its own.

Festivals

The week-long Winter Fair in late December and early January is a great occasion, as is the April Songkran Water Festival which is celebrated with great enthusiasm.

Yet perhaps Chiang Mai's best celebrated festival is the Flower Festival, also called the Flower Carnival, which is held annually during the first week of February. Events occur over a three-day period and include displays of flower arrangement, a long parade of floats decorated with hundreds and thousands of flowers, folk music, cultural performances and the Queen of the Flower Festival Contest. Most activities are centred at Buak Hat Public Park in the south-west corner of the city moats. People from all over the province and the rest of the country turn out for this occasion, so book early if you want a room in town.

Places to Stay – bottom end

At any one time there are about 50 hotels and 100 guest houses in operation in Chiang Mai. Hotels range from 60B per room (*Thai Charoen*) to 1600B per room (*Chiang Mai Orchid*), with an average room costing from 100 to 300B per night. Guest houses range from 30B per person for a dorm bed to 300B for a room. A lot of cheap hotels have replaced the English word 'hotel' with the new buzzword 'guest house', although the Thai still reads *rohng raem* (hotel).

Hotels *Roong Ruang Hotel* (tel 236746), also spelt *Roong Raeng*, is well located at 398 Tha Phae Rd, near Tha Phae Gate, on the eastern side of the city moat. Its service is good and rooms are quiet and clean.

Singles/doubles with a fan and bath are 130/170B or 220/250B with air-con. A hot water shower is available. This is a good place to stay for the Flower Festival in early February as the Saturday parade passes right by the entrance. Another entrance is on Chang Moi Kao Rd.

YMCA International House (tel 221819 or 222366) is at 2/4 Mengrai-Rasmi Rd, above the north-west corner of the moat. Singles/doubles in the old wing with a fan and a shared bath are 95/155B, 160/220B with a fan and private bath or 230/280B with air-con. Dorm beds in the old wing are 60B. In the fully air-con new wing, singles/doubles with a fan and a private bath are 380/440B.

Sri Rajawong (tel 235864) at 103 Ratchawong Rd, between east moat and the Ping River, has singles with a fan and bath for 70B, or 50B without a bath.

Sri Santitham (tel 221585) at 15 Chotana Rd Soi 4, near Bus Station Number 1 (White Elephant station), has singles with a fan and bath from 60B, or for 150B with air-con.

Thai Charoen (tel 236640) at 165 Tha Phae Rd, towards the river and between the moat and the TAT office (the Seiko Tour office is out front), has singles with a fan and bath starting from 60B.

Muang Thong (tel 211438) at 5 Ratchamankha Rd, a good location inside the city moats, has singles with a fan and bath from 80B.

New Chiang Mai (tel 236561 or 236766) at 22 Chaiyaphum Rd, is pleasant, clean and well-located on the east moat. It has spacious rooms with a fan and bath for 130B. Air-con rooms start from 190B.

Miami, another reasonable hotel on Chaiyaphum Rd, has singles for 100B, and *Nakhorn Ping* (tel 236024) at 43 Taiwang Rd, offers similar but cheaper accommodation, from 80B per room.

Guest Houses Guest houses are clustered in several areas: along Charoen Rat Rd east of the Ping River, which is far from the centre of the city but near buses to Chiang Rai, Lamphun and the railway station; along Moon Muang Rd (the inside of the east moat) and on streets off Moon Muang; and along

Charoen Prathet Rd, parallel to Charoen Rat but west of the Ping River. Several others are scattered elsewhere around the west side of Chiang Mai.

Guest houses come and go with frequency in Chiang Mai. The best are owned and managed by local families. The worst are those opened by Bangkok Thais who fiddle with your stored belongings while you're off on a trek.

The cheaper guest houses make most money from food service and hill-tribe trekking rather than from room rates. Many of the guest houses can arrange bicycle and motorcycle rental. If you phone a guest house, most will collect you from the train or bus station for free if they have a room. You can assume that rooms under 80B will not have a private bath but will probably have a fan.

The following guest houses listed were checked by me and found to be adequate:

Chiang Mai Youth Hostel (tel 212863) at 31 Prapakklao Rd inside the moat has dorm beds for 40B and rooms from 60 to 100B. An ISIC card obtains a 10B discount. It's clean, secure and friendly and its treks get good reviews. A branch hostel (tel 236735) at 21/8 Chang Klan Rd has rooms from 100 to 180B.

Changmoi House (tel 251839) at 29 Chang Moi Kao, behind the New Chiang Mai Hotel, is an old favourite. Clean doubles are 50, 60 and 70B, depending on the size of the room. Changmoi House also has triples for 100B and may soon be adding a few new 80B rooms.

Nearby is the hotel-like *Happy House* at 11 Chiang Moi Kao Rd, towards Tha Phae Gate. Big rooms with a fan and bathroom range from 150 to 180B.

A bit further north on this soi is the fairly new *Eagle House* (tel 235387) which has clean, quiet rooms with a private bath for from 70 to 80B or 60B with a shared bath.

The long-standing *Gemini House* at 22 Ratchadamnoen Rd is an old teak house with a couple of dorms and several rooms. Dorm beds cost 30B per person while rooms with a shared bath cost 50B a single or 80B a double.

The Daret Restaurant on Moon Muang Rd owns another restaurant and a guest house

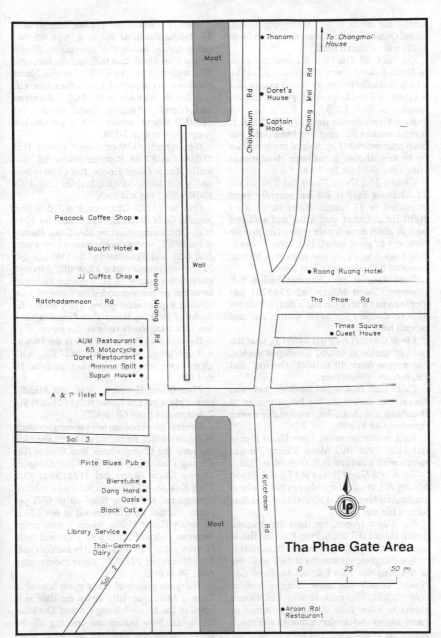

across the moat at 4/5 Chaiyaphum Rd, called *Daret's House*. Rates range from 60 to 100B with a shared bath.

On Soi 6 off Tha Phae Rd, near the gate, is *Times Square Guest House* (tel 232448), which is similar to Happy House except that it caters to French-speaking guests. Rooms range from 80 to 120B.

Kent Guest House (tel 217578), 5 Soi 1, Ratchamankha Rd, near Tha Phae Gate, has been recommended by several readers. Run by an Englishman, it has large clean rooms with a fan and bath for 100B.

Chiang Mai Guest House (tel 236501) at 91 Charoen Prathet Rd has recently been expanded to 27 rooms. Rates range from 100B for a double with a fan and a shared bath to 200B for a double with a fan, private bath and a 'good view'. Hot water is available from 6 to 10 am and from 6 to 10 pm. An extra bed costs only 30B more.

Next door at 89 Charoen Prathet Rd, *Chumpol Guest House* (tel 234526) has single rooms with a fan and a shared bath for 90B or doubles for 140B with a fan and private bath.

Linda Guest House (tel 246915), near the railway station at 454/67 Banditpattana Rd, has rooms from 40 to 60B. German and English are spoken here.

C&C Teak House (tel 246966), between the railway station and the Ping River at 39 Bamrungrat St, has quiet, comfortable rooms from only 40 to 60B.

Back inside the moat, *Peter Guest House* (tel 210617) at 46/3 Moon Muang Rd has rooms with a fan and bath from 60 to 80B.

Top North Guest House at 15 Soi 2, Moon Muang Rd, is an efficiently run place where singles/doubles cost 150/200B. All rooms have a fan and bath.

Nat Guest House, up from the original Youth Hostel at 7 Soi 6, Phra Pokklao Rd, is a comfortable place with rooms from 80B.

Another pleasant standby is the *Pao Come* at 9 Changmoi Kao Rd, not far from *Lek House*, outside the moat. Singles/doubles cost 50/70B. The once-famous Lek House seems to have gone downhill in terms of room quality and service, although its French restaurant is still supposed to be good.

Manit's Guest House is a one-man show at 44 Ratchaphakhinai Rd in a large off-the-street house inside the city moat. Single rooms with a bath cost 60B and doubles cost 80B without a bath or 130B with one. Manit handles every aspect of this business himself.

A few doors away at No 48/1 is the clean and friendly *Phathai Guest House* (tel 213013) where rooms with a private hot water shower cost 100B.

Chiangmai Garden Guest House (tel 210881) at 82-86 Ratchamankha Rd, formerly Racha Guest House, has clean rooms and good food. Singles/doubles cost 100/120B with a fan and bath.

Out at 282/3 Charoen Rat Rd is the popular *Gold Riverside* with rooms for 50 to 80B. On the same road are *Mee Guest House*, at No 193/1, where double rooms with a bath cost 60B and *Pun Pun* (tel 243362), at No 321, where rooms start at a low 40B. All three guest houses are a bit far from the centre of town but are recommended for those who are seeking a quiet atmosphere. They are on the banks of the Ping River. *Pun Pun* also has a few nice bungalows right on the river.

Beyond Pun Pun at No 365 is the Dutch-run *Hollanda Montri* (tel 242450), with clean rooms and hot water showers from 80 to 120B.

Tiwa Guest House, a clean and friendly newer place off Loi Khrao Rd at 101-106 Soi 2, has rooms from 60 to 80B.

Several guest houses have sprung up north of the city walls, far from the Tha Phae action but near the Chang Phuak Bus Station (for Chiang Dao, Fang and Tha Ton): *Camp of Troppo Guest House* (tel 213219) at 83/2 Ling Kok St, off Chotana Rd, has a relaxed atmosphere and costs from 40 to 60B per room. Further up Chotana Rd at No 129 is *Chawala Guest House* where rooms range between 100 and 220B with a fan and bath. Nearby at No 127 is a second branch of *C&C Teak House* (tel 232382), where rooms range from 30 to 60B.

There are plenty of other guest houses in Chiang Mai, especially down the little side lanes in the Moon Muang Rd and Tha Phae Rd areas. New places are opening all the time, due to the shortage of rooms from

December to February inclusive, and during festivals such as Songkhran and the Flower Festival.

Guest houses which belong to the Chiang Mai Guest House Association are probably more secure in terms of theft than those which are not. As members pay government taxes, they are generally more interested in long-term operation.

The TAT office on Tha Phae Rd can provide an up-to-date list of members.

Warning Lonely Planet has received many letters from travellers who have left their valuable belongings in a guest house safe while they were trekking. Unfortunately, upon their return, they discovered that their property had been removed from the safe and that items such as travellers' cheques, Swiss army pocket knives and sunglasses were missing. One Australian traveller discovered that A\$2500 had been spent on her Mastercard which had been left in a safe while she had been trekking. An Irish couple had £6000 worth of goods charged to their credit cards in Bangkok while they were on a three-day trek! If you leave your valuables in a safe, make sure you obtain a fully itemised receipt before departing on a trek.

Places to Stay – middle
Hotels The recently refurbished *Montri* (tel 211069 or 211070), on the corner of Moon Muang Rd and Ratchadamnoen Rd, has singles with a fan and bath from 200 to 250B, or 250 to 350B for a deluxe single with air-con.

A & P (tel 212309), also on Moon Muang Rd and next to the Daret Restaurant, has singles with a fan for 150B and air-con rooms for 250B. Both hotels are within the city moat area.

Guest Houses South of the city at 92 Wualai Rd Soi 2 is the *Srisupan Guest House* (tel 252811) which has fan-cooled and air-con rooms from 200B, including a private hot water shower.

Not far from the night bazaar is the *Galare Guest House* (tel 233885) at 7-7/1 Charoen

Prathet Rd Soi 2. It is fully air-con and has rooms from 240 to 340B.

Places to Stay – top end
Hotels Chiang Mai has plenty of more expensive hotels, several of which are along Huay Kaew Rd, towards Doi Suthep. These include the following, all of which have air-con and swimming pools:

Chiang Inn Hotel (tel 235655), 100 Chang Klan Rd, from 920B
Chiang Mai Hills (tel 210030), 18 Huay Kaew Rd, from 726B
Chiang Mai Orchid (tel 222099), 100 Huay Kaew Rd, from 1210B
Chiang Mai Plaza (tel 252050), 92 Si Donchai Rd, from 950B
Chiang Mai President (tel 253-2166), 226 Vitchayanon Rd, from 847B
Dusit Inn (tel 236835), formerly Chiang Mai Palace, 112 Chang Klan Rd, from 1000B
Poy Luang Hotel (tel 242633), 146 Super Highway, from 886B
Rincome Hotel (tel 221044), 301 Huay Kaew Rd, from 1331B
Suriwong Hotel (tel 236789), 110 Chang Klan Rd, from 1089B

Hotels one notch down, which have some rooms with air-con and some with a fan, include:

Anodard Hotel (tel 211055), 5 Ratchamankha Rd, from 280 to 480B
Bualuang Hotel (tel 221678), 16 Huay Kaew Rd, from 350B
Chang Phuak Hotel (tel 221755), 133 Chotana Rd, from 250 to 400B
Chiang Come Hotel (tel 222237), 7/35 Suthep Rd, from 300 to 500B
Chiang Mai Phucome Hotel (tel 211026), 21 Huay Kaew, from 550 to 880B
Diamond Hotel (tel 234155), 33/10 Charoen Prathet Rd, from 400 to 930B
Grand Apartment (tel 217291), 24/1 Ratchaphakhinai, from 300 to 550B
Iyara Hotel (tel 222723), 126 Chotana Rd, from 450 to 550B
Little Duck Hotel (tel 221750), 99/9 Huay Kaew Rd, from 400 to 500B
Muang Mai Hotel (tel 221392), 502 Huay Kaew Rd, from 420 to 480B
Nantana Pension (tel 232092), 72/76 Thiphanet Rd, from 250 to 350B
New Asia Hotel (tel 235288), 55 Ratchawong Rd, from 220 to 1200B

Northern Inn Hotel (tel 210002), 234/12 Maninoparat Rd, from 480 to 530B

Porn Ping (Phornphing) Hotel (tel 235099), 46 Charoen Prathet, from 650B

Prince Hotel (tel 236396), 3 Taiwang Rd, from 440 to 680B

River View Lodge (tel 251109), 25 Charoen Prathet Rd Soi 2, from 500 to 700B, with discounts May to August

Royal Park Hotel (tel 242755), 47 Charoen Muang Rd, from 300 to 750B

Sri Tokyo Hotel (tel 213899), 6 Boonruangrit Rd, from 220 to 680B

Sumit Hotel (tel 211033), 198 Ratchaphakhinai Rd, from 140 to 290B

Wiang Kaew Hotel (tel 221549), 7/9 Huay Kaew Rd, from 190 to 450B

Places to Eat

Chiang Mai has the best variety of restaurants of any city in Thailand, apart from Bangkok. Most travellers seem to have better luck here than in Bangkok though, simply because it's so much easier to get around and experiment.

Travellers' Food Three places where travellers like to hang out and eat western food and drink fruit smoothies are the *Daret Restaurant* near Tha Phae Gate on Moon Muang Rd, the *Thai-German Dairy Restaurant* at its old spot on the corner of Moon Muang Rd and Soi 2, and the *Ban Rai Steakhouse* in Wiang Kaew Rd next to Wat Chiang Man.

The Daret also serves some pretty fair Thai dishes. It has opened a second restaurant across the moat on Chaiyaphum Rd. Quite a few travellers have also raved about the Ban Rai's steak and potatoes.

Breakfast is good at the *Library Service*, around the corner from the Thai-German Dairy Restaurant on Soi 2. *Supun House* on Moon Muang Rd between the Daret and the Thai-German Dairy is also quite good for western breakfasts. For early risers (before 8 am), Supun House and the Daret are the only places open in this area.

The new *JJ Coffeeshop* under the Montri Hotel has a good menu of Thai, Chinese and western food at low prices, especially considering how clean the place is and that it's air-con. At the other end of the same building is the *Peacock Coffeeshop*, which specialises

in pizza but serves breakfasts too. Pizza at *Mr Chan's* at 2/5-6 Prachasamphan Rd is also supposed to be good.

The *Banana Split*, between Supun House and the Daret on Moon Muang Rd, are popular for ice cream and burgers.

Lek House at 22 Chaiyaphum Rd (a short way down a soi), still draws rave reviews from travellers. On New Year's Eve the place is packed and the owner/manager, Yves, sometimes gives away champagne.

The Pub, 88 Huay Kaew Rd, is one of the oldest restaurants in Chiang Mai serving continental food. It is not cheap, but *Newsweek* magazine did name it 'one of the world's best bars'.

Thai Food Two good Thai restaurants are the large, open-air *Aroon Rai*, across the moat on Kotchasan Rd, which specialises in northern dishes, and the smaller but better *Thanam Restaurant* on Chaiyaphum Rd near the New Chiang Mai Hotel and Tha Phae Gate.

Specialities at the super-clean Thanam include *phak nam phrik* (fresh vegetables in chili sauce), *plaa duk phat phet* (spicy fried catfish), *kaeng som* (hot and sour vegetable ragout with shrimp), as well as local dishes like *khao soi* (Burmese chicken curry soup with noodles) and *khanom jiin ngiaw* (Chinese noodles with spiced pureed fish and coconut milk). Thanam has a small English sign inside. It closes at about 8 pm, doesn't serve alcohol and won't serve people wearing beach clothes (tank tops, etc).

Out on Suthep Rd at No 1/10 is a small family-run restaurant serving some of the best southern Thai food in northern Thailand. Called the *Krua Phuket Laikhram* (Classical Phuket Kitchen), there's no English sign so far but it's worth hunting down for the delicious, cheap, yet large portions of authentic home-style Thai cooking. If there are no seats downstairs, try the upstairs dining room. Specialities include *yawt phrao phat phet kung* (spicy stir-fried shrimp with coconut shoots), *het huu nuu phat khai* (eggs stir-fried with mouse-ear mushrooms) and *yam phuket laikhram* (a delicious salad of cashew nuts and squid). It has daily specials, too. Ask for Khun Manop, who speaks English.

Lung Thaworn (Uncle Eternity), on Wiang Kaew Rd not far from Wat Chiang Man and the Ban Rai, serves good Thai and French food at very reasonable prices. Thaworn speaks French and was a cook at the French Embassy for 12 years.

Also good are the kai yang restaurants on Kotchasan Rd, south of the Loi Kroa Rd intersection. North-eastern food such as *somtam*, *laap* and sticky rice are their specialties, but other Thai foods are served also.

Another good place for north-eastern fare is *Phu Kradung*, a restaurant on the corner of Sam Larn Rd and Bamrungburi Rd, at Suan Prung Gate. Order the *nam phrik num* as a sauce to go with the kai yang. It's a northern Thai chilli sauce made from ground Thai eggplant, green chilli, salt and lime juice, and is similar to a savoury Mexican salsa.

Chinese Food A recommended Chinese restaurant is *Ruam Mit Phochana*, across from the public playground on Sithiwong Rd. The owner/cooks are from China's Yunnan Province, so the house specialities are naturally Yunnanese. The food is better than anything you'll find in Kunming, the main centre of the Yunnan Province.

The menu includes *pla thawt nam daeng* (red-sauce whole fried fish, cooked with large, semi-hot red peppers), *muu saam cham jim si-yu* (shredded white pork served with a chilli, garlic and soy sauce), *muu tom khem* (salty, boiled pork or Yunnanese ham) and *tao hu phat phrik daeng* (braised bean curd and red peppers). Apart from a rice accompaniment, you can order *mantou*, which are plain Chinese steamed buns, similar to the Thai *salabao* but without stuffing.

Another Yunnanese place is across from the police box on Loi Kroa Rd, near Wat Pan Tong.

Many of the Chinese living in Chiang Mai are Yunnanese immigrants or are direct descendants of Yunnanese immigrants who the Thais call *Jiin Haw* (galloping Chinese). This could be a reference to their migratory ways or to the fact that many brought pack horses from Yunnan.

Food Stalls Along Chaiyaphum Rd, north of Lek House, is a small but thriving night market where you can get everything from noodles and seafood to Yunnanese specialities at good prices.

The stalls across from the Montri Hotel on Ratchadamnoen Rd serve large rice plates for 10B and they have an English menu.

Another good hunting ground is the very large night market west of Chiang Mai Gate on Bamrungburi Rd. This is a great place to make an evening of eating and drinking.

Good *khao man kai* (chicken rice), *sate*, soups and dumplings are available along Intharawararot Rd, across from the south side of the old provincial office.

The Somphet market on Moon Muang Rd, north of the Ratwithi Rd intersection, sells cheap take-away curries, *yam*, *laap*, *thawt man*, sweets, seafood, etc.

Noodles Noodles in Chiang Mai are wonderful and the variety astounding. For boat noodles (rice noodles in a dark broth that contains that hunger-inducing herb *ganja*), try the *Kulian* on the corner of Moon Muang Rd and Ratchamankha Rd.

For *khao soi* – a Burmese concoction of chicken, spicy curried broth and flat, squiggly, wheat noodles which bears a slight resemblance to Malaysian *laksa* – your best bet is the *Khao Soi Lam Duang* on Charoen Rat Rd, not far from the Pun Pun Guest House on the same side of the road. The cook has prepared khao soi for no less a person than King Phumiphon (Bhumiphol). It only costs 8B per bowl. Also on the menu are *kao lao* (soup without noodles), *muu sate* (grilled spiced pork on bamboo skewers), khao soi with beef or pork instead of chicken, *khanom rang pheung* (beehive pastry, which is a coconut-flavoured waffle), Maekhong rice whiskey and beer.

Another khao soi place on the same road is *White House*, across from the Je T'aime Guest House. Other noodle places serving khao soi can be found around the city – just look for the distinctive noodle shape.

If you like khanom jiin, the thin white noodles served with spicy fish or chicken curry, don't miss the no-name khanom jiin stall off Moon Muang Rd on Soi 5, across from Wat Dawk Euang. It's on the left, about 50 metres from Moon Muang Rd, and serves possibly the best khanom jiin in town for 5B a plate.

For a variety of rice and wheat noodles, *Laggan* (The Noodle Shop) at 1/2 Soi 8, Moon Muang Rd, is a good place to try, especially if you're a noodle novice, as there is an English menu.

Great *kuaytiaw* (noodle soup) can be bought at the all-night food market (*aahaan toh rung*) in the night bazaar area. Especially recommended is *laat naa thaleh*, which is rice noodles heaped with squid, shrimp and other seafoods. Another good night market is the small one on Chaiyaphum Rd, north of the Chang Moi Rd intersection.

Vegetarian Food There are at least three vegetarian restaurants in Chiang Mai. One of the most popular is the *AUM Vegetarian Restaurant*, south of Daret's on Moon Muang Rd. The all-veggie menu features a varied list of traditional Thai and Chinese dishes (plus words of wisdom along the bottom of each page), including *kaeng khae*, a northern speciality and *laap tao-huu*, a north-eastern dish, prepared without meat or eggs. The muesli here is good, too. It's a bit more expensive than the veggie place near Wat Suan Dawk on Cherng Doy Rd, but it's still reasonable. There is also an upstairs eating area with cushions on the floor and low tables. AUM is open from 9 am to 2 pm and 5 to 9 pm.

West of town, on the left side of the Cherng Doy Rd and on the way to Wat Suan Dawk, is the *Vegetarian Restaurant* (*Raan Aahaan Mangsawirat*), Chiang Mai's oldest veggie eatery. Its Thai vegetarian fare uses lots of bean curd, mushrooms and coconut milk and is generally good. Prices are a low 7 to 8B per plate, with some large dishes costing 15B. The desserts are good too – try the *kluay buat chee* bananas in sweet coconut milk – and it has a good khao soi made with wheat gluten instead of meat. Years ago this place

was only open for lunch, but it now operates from 8 am to 7 pm daily. There are daily specials not listed on the standard bilingual menu, so ask about them.

Out along Si Donchai Rd, past the Chang Klan Rd intersection, is the *Whole Earth Vegetarian Restaurant* in a transcendental meditation centre. The food is Thai and Indian and the atmosphere is suitably mellow, although the food may be a bit over-priced.

Some Indian vegetarian dishes are served at the Indian, Pakistani and Middle Eastern *Al-Shiraz* restaurant at 123 Chang Klan Rd, across from the night bazaar. *The Cafeteria* at 27-29 Chang Klan also serves Arabic and Indian food in vegetarian variations.

Others If you like garden restaurants (*suan aahaans*), Chiang Mai has plenty. Several are along Highway 11 near Wat Jet Yot and the National Museum. The food can be very good, but it is the *banyaakaat* (atmosphere) that is most prized by Thais.

Finally, for a chuckle, check out the ostentatious *Nang Nual Seafood Restaurant* off the road to Lamphun, south of the city. This place, a branch of the Nang Nual in Pattaya, has large grounds with gardens, waterfalls, aviaries and attendants at every 10 paces along the path to the entrance who bow and *wai* as you approach. Inside, the pretentiousness doesn't stop, as more attendants in various costumes fuss over you and a bored Thai classical orchestra plays. If you can bring yourself to sit down and look at the menu, you'll see that the prices are not as high as the surroundings would lead you to expect. Still, it is probably the most expensive place in Chiang Mai and unbearably stuffy.

Entertainment
Anybody who's anybody makes the scene at the Riverside (*Rim Ping*), a restaurant-cafe on Charoen Rat Rd, on the Ping River. It has good food, fruitshakes, cocktails and live music nightly. It's usually packed with farangs on weekends, so arrive early to get a table on the outdoor verandah overlooking the river.

Another up-and-coming spot is *Six-Pole House,* a pub with 100-year-old teak floors, at 36-44 Charoen Rat Rd. This is a favourite spot for Thai musicians and hence the live music often involves impromptu jam sessions. Good regional Thai food is served, including a few vegetarian dishes and brown rice. It's open 11 am to 2 pm and 6 pm to midnight.

For dancing, the hot spot is the disco in the *Porn Ping Hotel* on Charoen Prathet Rd, where there is usually a good, live band. All the flash hotels like the *Chiangmai Orchid* and the *Dusit Inn* have discos with recorded music. Cover charges are usually between 50 and 90B.

Along Moon Muang Rd, between the Thai-German Dairy Restaurant and Soi 3, are a string of small bars with low-volume music that are good for a quiet drink. The *Pinte Blues Pub,* at 33/6 Moon Muang Rd, serves

espresso, beer and plays all pre-recorded blues. The *Bierstube* features German grub and beer, while the *Oasis* and *Black Cat Bar* are pretty featureless except that an inordinate number of Thai females seem to hang about.

For a traditional Thai massage, contact Rinkaew Povech (tel 234565 or 234567) at 183/4 Wualai Rd. If you telephone, they will provide free transportation to and from your hotel or guest house. Rates are 200B per hour in group or private rooms.

Things to Buy

There are numerous shops all over Chiang Mai selling hill-tribe crafts and other local work. Thai Tribal Crafts at 208 Bamrungrat Rd, near the McCormick Hospital, is run by two church groups on a non-profit basis and has the 'best selection, quality and prices'. The Hilltribe Products Foundation near the Vegetarian Restaurant is also reported to be good. You'll also find very competitive prices upcountry.

Although there are a lot of things to attract your money, Chiang Mai is basically a very commercial and touristy place and a lot of junk is churned out for the undiscerning. So bargain hard and buy carefully!

Cotton & Silk Very attractive lengths of material can be made into all sorts of things. Go to Pasang, south of Lamphun, for cotton. For Thai silk, with its lush colours and pleasantly rough texture, try San Kamphaeng. It's cheaper than in Bangkok.

Ceramics Thai Celadon, about six km north of Chiang Mai, turns out ceramic-ware modelled on the Sawankhalok pottery that used to be made hundreds of years ago at Sukhothai and exported all over the region. With their deep, cracked, glazed finish some pieces are very beautiful and prices are often lower than in Bangkok. The factory is closed on Sunday. Other ceramics can be seen close to the Old Chiang Mai centre.

Woodcarving Many types of carvings are available including countless elephants, but who wants a half-size wooden elephant anyway? Teak salad bowls are good and very cheap.

Antiques You'll see lots of these around, including opium weights – the little animal-shaped weights supposedly used to measure opium in the Golden Triangle. Check prices in Bangkok first, as Chiang Mai's shops are not always cheap. Also remember that world-wide there are a lot more instant antiques than authentic ones. The night bazaar area is probably the best place to look for fake antiques. For the real thing, visit the several stores along Tha Phae Rd.

Lacquerware Decorated plates, containers, utensils and other items are made by building up layers of lacquer over a wooden or woven bamboo base. Burmese lacquerware, smuggled into the north, can be seen, especially at Mae Sai.

Silverwork There are several silverwork shops close to the south moat gate. Hill-tribe jewellery, which is heavy, chunky stuff, is very nice.

Clothes All sorts of shirts, blouses and dresses, plain and embroidered, are available at very low prices, but check the quality carefully. The night bazaar and stores along Tha Phae Rd have good selections.

Umbrellas Go out to Baw Sang, the umbrella village, where beautiful paper umbrellas are handpainted. Framed, leaf paintings from there are also very attractive.

Getting There & Away

Air Thai International Airways has two offices in Chiang Mai. One is within the city moat area at 240 Phra Pokklao Rd (tel 211541), behind Wat Chiang Man, and the other (tel 233559) is outside the moat area at 183/3 Chang Klan Rd, close to the Si Donchai Rd intersection.

Thai Airways has several daily one-hour flights between Bangkok and Chiang Mai. The fare is 1275B or 1575B for business class.

Airfares between Chiang Mai and other Thai cities are:

Lampang	155B
Chiang Rai	300B
Mae Hong Son	310B
Nan	380B
Mae Sot	430B
Phitsanulok	505B
Khon Kaen	1780B
Udon	1945B
Ubon	2005B
Surat Thani	2260B
Phuket	2400B
Hat Yai	2580B

Bus From Bangkok's Northern Bus Terminal there are 14 ordinary buses daily to Chiang Mai, departing from 5.25 am to 10 pm. The nine-hour trip costs 133B via Nakhon Sawan and 140B via Ayuthaya. Four 1st-class air-con buses leave the adjacent air-con terminal between 9.10 and 10.30 am and eight buses leave from 8 to 9.45 pm. These buses take about eight hours and cost 242B one-way.

Ten or more private tour companies run air-con buses between Bangkok and Chiang Mai, departing from various points throughout both cities. Round-trip tickets are always somewhat cheaper than one-ways. The least expensive tour buses leave from the Khao San Rd area in Banglamphu, Bangkok. Fares range from 180 to 240B depending on the bus. VIP buses are the most expensive as these have fewer seats per coach to allow for reclining positions. Similar buses can be booked in the Ngam Duphli St area of Bangkok and near the Indra Hotel in Pratunam. Some bus tickets include a night's free stay at a guest house in Chiang Mai.

The public buses from the Northern Bus Terminal are generally more reliable and on schedule than the ones booked in Banglamphu, etc. The only advantage of the private buses is that they pick you up where you book the ticket. If you don't have a lot of baggage it's probably better to leave from the terminal, unless you score a ticket with free accommodation in Chiang Mai.

Public buses between Chiang Mai and

other towns in the north and north-east have frequent departures throughout the day (at least hourly), except for the Mae Sai, Khon Kaen, Udon and Khorat buses which have morning and evening departures only. Here are some fares and trip durations:

City	Fare	Duration
Chiang Rai	47B	4 hours
(air-con)	66B	3 hours
Fang*	32B	3 hours
Khon Kaen	153B	12 hours
(air-con, Route 12)	214B	12 hours
(air-con, R 11)	275B	11 hours
Lampang	25B	1½ hours
Lamphun*	6B	½ hour
(air-con)	50B	1 hour
Mae Hong Son		
(R 108)	97B	9 hours
Mae Hong Son		
(R 107/1095)	100B	9-10 hours
Mae Sai	59B	5 hours
(air-con)	83B	4 hours
Mae Sariang	50B	5 hours
Nan	71B	7 hours
(air-con)	100B	6 hours
Pai	50B	4-5 hours
Pasang*	10B	45 minutes
Phrae	49B	4 hours
(air-con)	68B	3½ hours
Phetchabun		
(air-con)	235B	8 hours
Phitsanulok	82B	5-6 hours
(air-con)	117B	5 hours
Thaton*	37B	4 hours

*Leaves from White Elephant (Chang Phuak) Bus Station, Chotana Rd. All other buses leave from the Chiang Mai Arcade Bus Station (New Station), off Kaew Nawarat Rd. For other buses leaving Chiang Mai, all buses to destinations within Chiang Mai Province use the Chang Phuak Station while all buses outside the province use the Chiang Mai Arcade Station.

Train The Chiang Mai Express leaves Bangkok's Hualamphong Station at 6 pm daily, arriving in Chiang Mai at 7.05 am. Its 1st and 2nd-class cars are air-con.

Rapid trains leave at 3 pm (air-con 2nd class) and 10 pm (no air-con), arriving at 4.50 and 11.45 am respectively. There is also a Special Express (no air-con) that leaves at 7.10 pm and gets into Chiang Mai at 7.55 am.

The basic 2nd-class fare is 255B, excluding either the Express (30B) or Rapid (20B) surcharges. Add 70B for an upper berth and 100B for a lower berth in a 2nd-class sleeping car (100 and 150B respectively on the Special Express). For air-con 2nd class, add 50B per ticket for chair cars and 100B for sleepers. For example, if you take a 2nd-class upper berth on a Rapid train, your total fare will be 345B (255+70+20B).

First-class berths are 250B per person in a double cabin, 350B in a single and are available on the Express only. Third class is 151B, which includes the Express surcharge. Subtract 10B for Rapid train fares. The Special Express is 2nd class only and not air-con.

Trains leave Lopburi for Chiang Mai at 9.07 am (Rapid), 5.27 pm (Rapid, air-con 2nd class), 8.20 pm (Express, air-con 2nd class) and 12.22 am (Rapid, no air-con), arriving at the times listed for the same trains from Bangkok. Fares are 245B 2nd class, 130B 3rd class Express and 10B less for the Rapid.

Berths on sleepers to Chiang Mai are increasingly hard to reserve without booking well in advance. Tour groups sometimes book entire cars. Chiang Mai to Bangkok doesn't seem to be as difficult as others, except at the Songkran (mid-April) and Chinese New Year (February) holiday periods.

The Chiang Mai Railway Station's cloak room has a left-luggage facility that is open from 6 am to 6 pm daily. The cost is 5B per piece for the first five days and 10B per piece thereafter.

Getting Around
Airport Transport You can get a taxi into the centre of Chiang Mai from the airport for less than 50B, although a songthaew would be less again. It's a neat little airport with a bank, post office, tourist information counter and two snack bars – one is out under the trees by the carpark and there is also a bar in an old

air force transport aircraft. The airport is only two or three km from the city centre.

Bus Large city buses cost 2B. The TAT office in Chiang Mai has a map with bus routes.

Songthaew These go anywhere on their route for 5B.

Samlor These three-wheel pedicabs cost between 5 and 10B for most trips.

Bicycle This is by far the best way to get around Chiang Mai. The city is small enough so that everywhere is accessible by bike, including Chiang Mai University, Wat U Mong, Wat Suan Dawk and the National Museum on the outskirts of town.

Bicycles can be rented for between 20 and 25B per day from several of the guest houses or from various places along the east moat.

Motorcycle These can be rented from 80B (Honda 80cc step-through) to 200B (Honda MTX 125 or Yamaha 175) per day, depending on the size of the motorcycle and the length of rental. Prices are very competitive in Chiang Mai because there's a real glut of motorcycles. For two people, it's cheaper to rent a small motorcycle for the day to visit Doi Suthep than to go up and back on a songthaew. One of the more reliable places to rent motorcycles for long-distance touring is 65 Motorcycle Rental Service (tel 213315) on Moon Muang Rd between the AUM and Daret restaurants, near Tha Phae Gate.

AROUND CHIANG MAI TOWN
Doi Suthep ดอยสุเทพ
Sixteen km north-west of Chiang Mai is Doi Suthep. Near its summit is Wat Phra That Doi Suthep, first established in 1383 under King Keu Na. A *naga* (dragon-headed serpent) staircase of 300 steps leads to the wat at the end of the winding road up the mountain. At the top, weather permitting, there are some fine aerial views of Chiang Mai. Inside the cloister is an intriguing copper-plated chedi topped by a five-tier gold umbrella.

About five km beyond Wat Phra That is Phra Tamnak Phu Phing, a winter palace for

the royal family, the gardens of which are open on weekends and holidays. The road that passes Phu Ping Palace splits off to the left, stopping at the peak of Doi Pui. From there a dirt road proceeds for two or three km to a nearby Meo hill-tribe village. If you won't have an opportunity to visit more remote villages, it's worth visiting this one, even though it is very well-touristed. Some Meo handiwork can be purchased and traditional homes and costumes can be seen, although it's mostly posed situations. 'Everyone knows some English,' wrote one visitor, such as 'you buy', 'money' and 'I'll have no profit'.

Getting There & Away Songthaews to Doi Suthep leave throughout the day from Chang Phuak Gate, along Manee Noparat Rd. The fare is 30B up and 20B down. A cable car to the peak from the foot of the hill costs 5B.

To Phu Phing Palace add 10B and to Doi Pui add 20B in each direction.

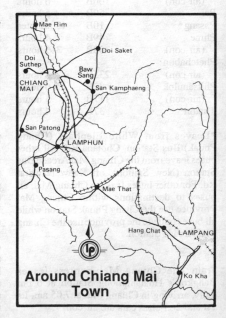

Around Chiang Mai Town

Tribal Research Institute

This research institute is on Chiang Mai University campus, five km west of the city. A No 1 bus goes by the university. The institute features a small hill-tribes museum, and literature on hill tribes is available. It's open Monday to Friday, from 8.30 am to 4.30 pm.

Baw Sang บ่อสร้าง

Baw Sang, nine km east of Chiang Mai on Highway 1006, is usually called the umbrella village because of its many umbrella manufacturers. Practically the entire village consists of craft shops selling painted umbrellas, fans, silverware, straw handiwork, bamboo and teak, statuary, china, celadon and lacquerware, along with the most tacky Chiang Mai and North Thailand souvenirs, as well as quality items. The larger shops can arrange overseas shipping at reasonable rates. As in Chiang Mai's night bazaar, discounts are offered for quantity purchases. Some of the places will pack and post parasols, apparently quite reliably.

San Kamphaeng สันกำแพง

Four or five km further down Highway 1006 is San Kamphaeng which flourishes on cotton and silk weaving. Stores offering finished products line the main street, although the actual weaving is done in small factories down side-streets. There are some deals to be had here, especially in silk. For cotton, you'd probably do better in Pasang, a lesser known village near Lamphun Town, although you may see shirt styles here not available in Pasang. A cotton shirt or blouse can cost between 60 and 250B.

Getting There & Away Buses to Baw Sang (sometimes spelled Bo Sang or Bor Sang) and San Kamphaeng leave Chiang Mai frequently during the day from the north side of Charoen Muang Rd, east of the Ping River. (This is towards the GPO and the railway station and across from San Pa Khoi Market. The fare is 4B to Baw Sang and 5B to San Kamphaeng.

Hang Dong หางดง

Thirteen km south of Chiang Mai on Route

108 is Hang Dong, which could be called the basket village. Catch a bus from the Chiang Mai Gate to Hang Dong (10B fare) where anything made of straw, bamboo or rattan can be found: hats, baskets, furniture, fish traps, rice winnowers, coconut strainers, mats, brooms, rice and fish steamers, fighting-cock cages, bird cages, etc. Most of the shops are actually about two km before Hang Dong.

Elephants

A daily 'elephants at work' show takes place near the 58 km marker on the Fang road. Arrive at about 9 am or earlier to see bath time in the river. It's really just a tourist trap but probably worth the admission price. Once the spectators have gone the logs are replaced for tomorrow's show!

It's a good idea to take a picture of an elephant to show the bus conductor or the word 'elephant' may get you to Fang, further north. Northern Thailand has an elephant meeting in November each year and hotel and food prices go up accordingly.

Another place to see elephants is at the Elephant Training School on the Lampang to Chiang Rai road. A big sign on the roadside in Thai and on the other side in English indicates the location. Walk a couple of km up and down hills to get to the well-hidden school – you might find an elephant to follow.

The place is geared for tourists with seats and even toilets, but nobody seems to know about it. When the trainer feels like it, some time between 8 am and 12 midday, the elephants are put through their paces. They appreciate a few pieces of fruit – 'feels like feeding a vacuum cleaner with a wet nozzle,' reported a visitor.

CHOM THONG จอมทอง

Chom Thong (pronounced 'jawm thawng') is another necessary stop between Chiang Mai and Doi Inthanon, Thailand's highest peak.

Wat Phra That Si Chom Thong

If you have time, walk down Chom Thong's main street to Wat Phra That Si Chom Thong.

The gilded Burmese chedi in the compound was built in 1451 and the Burmese-style bot, built in 1516, is one of the most beautiful in northern Thailand. Inside and out it is an integrated work of art that deserves admiration; it is well cared for by the local Thais. Fine wood carving can be seen along the eaves of the roof and inside on the ceiling, which is supported by massive teak columns. The impressive altar is designed like a small prasat and is said to contain a relic of the right side of the Buddha's skull. The abbot is a very serene old man, soft-spoken and radiant.

Behind the prasat-altar is a room containing religious antiques. More interesting is a glass case along one wall of the bot which contains ancient Thai weaponry – a little out of place in a wat maybe.

Wat Phra Nawn Yai

About halfway between Chiang Mai and Chom Thong you may see Wat Phra Nawn Yai off to the side of the highway (on the right heading towards Chom Thong) with its distinctive Disney-like Buddha figures standing, sitting and reclining, as well as sculptured scenes from selected Jatakas. The statuary is incredibly garish and cartoonish – good for a giggle.

Doi Inthanon ดอย อินทนนท์

Doi Inthanon, Thailand's highest peak (2595 metres), has three impressive waterfalls cascading down its slopes. Starting from the bottom, these are Mae Klang Falls, Wachiratan Falls and Siriphum Falls. The first two have picnic areas and food vendors nearby. Mae Klang is the largest waterfall and easiest to get to, as you must stop there to get a bus to the top of Doi Inthanon. Mae Klang Falls can be climbed on near the top, as there is a footbridge leading to massive rock formations over which the water falls. Wachiratan is also very nice and less crowded.

The views from Inthanon are best in the cool-dry season from November to February. You can expect the air to be quite chilly towards the top, so bring a jacket or sweater. For most of the year a mist, formed by the condensation of warm humid air below, hangs around the topmost peak. Along the 47 km road to the top are many terraced rice fields, tremendous valleys and a few small hill-tribe villages. The entire mountain is a national park, despite agriculture and human habitation.

Getting There & Away

Buses to Chom Thong leave regularly from just inside the Chiang Mai Gate at the south moat in Chiang Mai. Some buses go directly to Mae Klang Falls and some terminate in Hot, though the latter will let you off in Chom Thong. The fare to Chom Thong, 50 km away, is 11B.

From Chom Thong there are regular songthaews to Mae Klang, about eight km north, for 10B. Songthaews from Mae Klang to Doi Inthanon leave almost hourly until late afternoon and cost 25 to 30B per person. Most of the passengers are locals who get off at various points along the road up, thus allowing a few stationary views of the valleys below. If you're travelling by private vehicle, you'll have to pay a toll at the park entrance of 20B per car or 5B per motorcycle.

For another 10B you can go from Chom Thong to Hot, where you can get buses on to Mae Sariang or Mae Hong Son. However, if you've gone to Doi Inthanon and the waterfalls, you probably won't have time to make it all the way to Mae Sariang or Mae Hong Son in one day, so you may want to stay overnight in Chom Thong. Ask at the wat for a place to sleep. There's probably a hotel somewhere in town.

Lamphun Province

LAMPHUN TOWN เมือง ลำพูน

Best seen on a day trip from Chiang Mai, along with Pasang, Lamphun (population 14,000) was the centre of the small Hariphunchai principality ruled originally by the Mon princess Chama Thewi. Long after its progenitor, Dvaravati, was van-

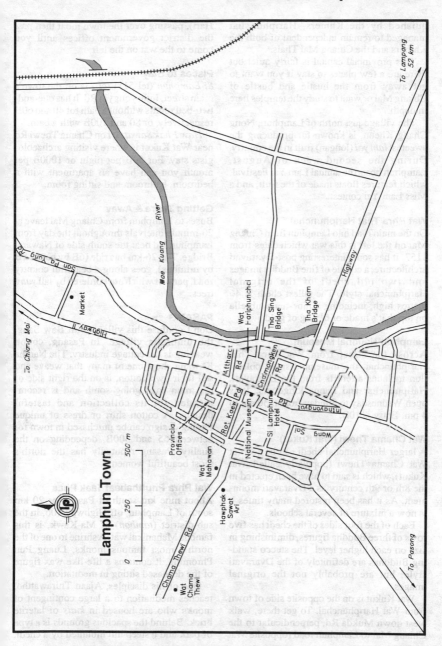

quished by the Khmers, Hariphunchai managed to remain independent of both the Khmers and the Chiang Mai Thais.

This provincial capital is fairly quiet but there are a few places to stay if you want to get away from the hustle and bustle of Chiang Mai or want to study the temples here in depth.

The village just north of Lamphun, Nong Chang Kheun, is known for producing the sweetest *lam yai* (longan) fruit in the country. During the second week of August, Lamphun hosts the annual Lam Yai Festival, which features floats made of the fruit, and a Miss Lam Yai contest.

Wat Phra That Hariphunchai

On the main road into Lamphun from Chiang Mai on the left is this wat which dates from 1157. It has some interesting post-Dvaravati architecture, a couple of fine Buddha images and two old chedi of the original Hariphunchai style. The tallest chedi is 46 metres high, including a nine-tier umbrella on top that's made of 6½ kg of gold.

Lamphun National Museum

Across the street from Wat Phra That Hariphunchai, the museum's small collection includes artefacts from the Dvaravati, Hariphunchai and Lanna kingdoms. It is open Wednesday to Sunday from 8.30 am to 4 pm. Entry is 10B.

Wat Chama Thewi (Wat Kukut)

A larger Hariphunchai chedi can be seen at Wat Chama Thewi (popularly called Wat Kukut), which is said to have been erected in the 8th or 9th century as a Dvaravati monument. As it has been restored many times it is now a mixture of several schools.

Each of the four sides of the chedi has five rows of three Buddha figures, diminishing in size on each higher level. The stucco standing Buddhas are definitely of the Dvaravati style, but are probably not the original images.

Wat Kukut is on the opposite side of town from Wat Hariphunchai. To get there, walk west down Mukda Rd, perpendicular to the Chiang Mai to Lamphun road (opposite Wat

Hari), passing over the town moat then past the district government offices until you come to the wat on the left.

Places to Stay

Si Lamphun (tel 5111760) is on the town's main street, Inthayongyot Rd. It has one-and-two-bed rooms without a bath for 40 and 60B respectively, or 80 and 100B with a bath.

Haw Phak Sawat Ari on Chama Thewi Rd near Wat Kukut is where visiting archaeologists stay. For 50B per night or 1000B per month you can have an apartment with a bedroom, bathroom and sitting room.

Getting There & Away

Buses to Lamphun from Chiang Mai leave at 20-minute intervals throughout the day from Lamphun Rd near the south side of Nawarat Bridge. The 26-km bus ride (6B by bus or 8B by minibus), goes along a beautiful country road, parts of which are bordered by tall *yang* trees.

PASANG ป่าซาง

Don't confuse this village with Baw Sang, the umbrella village. In Pasang, cotton weaving is the cottage industry. The Nantha Khwang shop, one of many that weave and sell their own cotton, is on the right side of the main road going south and is recommended for its collection and tasteful designs. A cotton shirt or dress of unique Pasang design can be purchased in town for between 65 and 300B, depending on the quality. Pasang reputedly has the north's most beautiful women.

Wat Phra Phutthabaat Taak Phaa

About nine km south of Pasang or 20 km south of Lamphun, off Highway 106, in the sub-district (*tambon*) of Ma-Kawk, is this famous Mahanikai wat. A shrine to one of the north's most famous monks, Luang Puu Phromma, it contains a life-like wax figure of the deceased sitting in meditation.

One of his disciples, Ajaan Thirawattho, teaches meditation to a large contingent of monks who are housed in *kutis* of laterite brick. Behind the spacious grounds is a type of park and a steep hill mounted by a chedi.

The wat is named for an unremarkable Buddha footprint (Phra Phutthabaat) shrine in the middle of the lower temple grounds where Buddha supposedly dried his robes (Taak Phaa) and left an imprint.

Getting There & Away

A songthaew will take you from Lamphun to Pasang for a few baht. From Chiang Mai it costs 10B by regular bus or 12B by minibus.

Hill-Tribe Treks

For years Chiang Mai has been a centre for treks into the mountainous northern areas inhabited by hill tribes. It used to be pretty exciting to knock about the dirt roads of rural Chiang Rai Province, do the boat trip between Fang and Chiang Rai and hike into the various villages of the Karen, Meo, Akha and Yao tribes and the Kuomintang settlements. You could spend the night in rustic surroundings and perhaps share some opium with the villagers.

Only a very few Thais living in Chiang Mai had the travel and linguistic knowledge necessary to lead adventurous foreigners through this area. Booking a trip usually meant waiting for optimum conditions and adequate numbers of participants which sometimes took quite a while.

The trips began to gain popularity in the early 1970s and now virtually every hotel and guest house in Chiang Mai books hill-tribe tours for countless tour organisations.

Soon the word was out that the area north of the Kok River in the Golden Triangle was being over-trekked, with treks criss-crossing the area in such a fashion that the hill-tribe villages were starting to become human zoos. When their only contact with the outside world was through a camera lens and a flow of sweets and cigarettes, it was no wonder that the villagers began to feel this way.

So the tours moved south of the Kok River, around Chiang Dao and Wieng Papao, then to Mae Hong Son where most of them

now operate. It's only a short time before this area suffers from the heavy traffic as well.

Meanwhile, hundreds of foreign travellers each year continue to take these treks. Most come away with a sense of adventure while a few are disillusioned. What makes a good trek is having primarily a good leader-organiser, followed by a good group of trekkers. Some travellers finish a tour complaining more about the other trekkers than about the itinerary, food or trek leader.

Before Trekking

Hill-tribe trekking isn't for everyone. Firstly, you must be physically fit to cope with the demands of sustained up and down walking, exposure to the elements and spotty food. Secondly, many people feel awkward walking through hill-tribe villages and playing the role of voyeur.

In cities and villages elsewhere in Thailand, Thais and other lowland groups are quite used to foreign faces and foreign ways (from television if nothing else), but in the hills of northern Thailand the tribes lead largely insular lives. Hence, hill-tribe tourism has pronounced effects, both positive and negative. On the positive side, travellers have a chance to see how traditional subsistence-oriented societies function. Also, since the Thai Government is sensitive about the image projected by their minority groups, tourism may actually have forced it to review and sometimes improve its policies toward hill tribes. On the negative side, trekkers introduce many cultural items and ideas from the outside world that may erode tribal customs to varying degrees.

If you have any qualms about interrupting the traditional patterns of life in hill-tribe areas, you probably should not go trekking. It is undeniable that trekking in northern Thailand is marketed like soap or any other commodity. Anyone who promises you an authentic experience is probably exaggerating at the very least, or at worst may be contributing to the decline of hill-tribe culture by leading foreigners into unhampered areas.

If you desire to make a trek keep these points in mind: choose your trek operator carefully, try to meet the others in the group (suggest a meeting) and find out exactly what the tour includes and does not include as usually there are additional expenses beyond the basic rate. If everything works out, even an organised tour can be worthwhile. A useful check list of questions to ask are:

1. How many people will there be in the group? Six is a good maximum, reported one traveller, although others have said that 10 is equally OK.

2. Can they guarantee that no other tourists will visit the same village on the same day, especially overnight?

3. Can the guide speak the language of each village to be visited?

4. Exactly when does the tour begin and end? Some three-day treks turn out to be less than 48 hours.

5. Do they provide transport before and after the trek or is it just by public bus – often with long waits?

Choosing a company TAT is making efforts to regulate trekking companies out of Chiang Mai and recommend that you trek only with members of the Professional Guide Association of Chiang Mai or the Jungle Tour Club of Northern Thailand. Still, with more than 100 companies operating out of Chiang Mai, it's very difficult to guarantee any kind of control.

These days there are plenty of places apart from Chiang Mai where you can arrange treks. Often these places have better and usually less expensive alternatives which originate closer to the more remote and untrekked areas. Also, they are generally smaller, friendlier operations and the trekkers are usually a more determined bunch since they're not looking for a quick in-and-out trek. The treks are often informally arranged, usually involving discussions of duration, destinations, cost, etc (it used to be like that in Chiang Mai).

You can easily arrange treks out of the following towns in the north: Chiang Rai, Mae Hong Son, Pai, Mae Sai and Tha Ton. With a little time to seek out the right people, you can also go on organised treks from Mae Sariang, Soppong (near Pai), Mae Sot, the

Akha Guest House on the road to Doi Tung and other out-of-the-way guest houses which are springing up all over northern Thailand.

The downside, of course, is that companies outside of Chiang Mai are generally subject to even less regulation than those in Chiang Mai, and there are fewer guarantees with regard to trekking terms and conditions.

Costs Organised treks out of Chiang Mai average from 800B for a four-day, three-night trek to 2500B for a deluxe seven-day, six-night trek which includes elephant riding and/or rafting. Rates vary, so it pays to shop around. You can count on an extra 1000B for elephants or other exotic additions to a basic trek. Elephant rides actually become quite boring and even uncomfortable after about an hour.

Don't choose a trek by price alone. It's better to talk to other travellers in town who have been on treks. Treks out of other towns in the north are usually between 100 and 150B per person per day.

The Professional Guide Association in Chiang Mai meets monthly to set trek prices

and to discuss problems, and issues regular, required reports to TAT about individual treks. All trekking guides and companies are supposed to be government licenced. As a result, a standard for trekking operators has emerged whereby you can expect the price you pay to include: transport to and from the starting/ending points of a trek (if outside Chiang Mai); food (three meals a day) and accommodation in all villages visited; basic first aid; pre-departure valuables storage; and sometimes the loan of specific equipment, such as sleeping bags in cool weather or water bottles.

Not included in the price are beverages other than drinking water or tea, the obligatory opium-smoking with the village headman (how many travellers have I heard say ' ... and then, oh wow, we actually smoked opium with the village headman!'), lunch on the first and last days and personal porters.

Seasons Probably the best time to trek is November to February when the weather is refreshing with little or no rain and poppies are in bloom everywhere. Between March and May the hills are dry and the weather is quite hot in most northern places. The second-best time to trek is early in the rainy season, between June and July, before the dirt roads become too saturated.

Safety Every year or so there's at least one trekking robbery in northern Thailand. Often the bandits are armed with guns which they will use without hesitation if they meet resistance. Once they collect a load of cameras, watches, money and jewellery, many bandit gangs hightail it across the border into Burma. In spite of this, police have had a good arrest record so far and have created hill-country patrols. Still, gangs can form at any time and anywhere. The problem is that most people living in the rural north believe that all foreigners are very rich (a fair assumption in relation to hill-tribe living standards). Most of these people have never been to Chiang Mai and, from what they have heard about Bangkok, they consider to be a virtual paradise of wealth and luxury. So

don't take anything with you trekking you can't afford to lose, and don't resist robbery attempts.

Conduct
Once trekking, there are several other guidelines to minimising the negative impact on the local people.

1. Always ask for permission before taking photos of tribal people and/or their dwellings. You can ask through your guide or by using sign language. Because of traditional belief systems, many individuals and even whole tribes may object strongly to being photographed.
2. Show respect for religious symbols and rituals. Don't touch totems at village entrances or other objects of obvious symbolic value without asking permission. Keep your distance from ceremonies being performed unless you're asked to participate.
3. Practise restraint in giving things to tribespeople or bartering with them. Food and medicine are not necessarily appropriate gifts if they result in altering traditional dietary and healing practices. The same goes for clothing. Tribespeople will abandon handwoven tunics for printed T-shirts if they are given a steady supply. If you want to give something to the people you encounter on a trek, the best thing is to make a donation to the village school or other community fund. Your guide can help arrange this.

Opium Smoking Some guides are very strict now about forbidding the smoking of opium on treks. This seems to be a good idea, since one of the problems trekking companies have had in the past is dealing with opium-addicted guides! Volunteers who work in tribal areas also say opium-smoking sets a bad example for young people in the villages.

Opium is traditionally a condoned vice of the elderly, yet an increasing number of young people in the villages are now taking opium and heroin. This is possibly due in part to the influence of young trekkers who may smoke once and a few weeks later be hundreds of km away while the villagers continue to face the temptation every day.

Independent trekking

You might consider striking out on your own in a small group of two to five people. Gather as much information as you can about the area you'd like to trek in from the Tribal Research Institute at Chiang Mai University. The institute has an informative pamphlet which is available at its library. Don't bother staff with questions about trekking as they are quite non-committal, either from fear of liability or fear of retribution from the Chiang Mai trekking companies.

Maps, mostly distributed by guest houses outside of Chiang Mai, pinpoint various hill-tribe areas in the north. DK Books in Chiang Mai sell two excellent maps on the Wawi area, south of the Kok River and the Kok River area itself. Both lie in Chiang Rai Province and are considered safe areas for do-it-yourself treks. DK Books plan to produce a series of trekking maps based on Tribal Research Institute research.

Be prepared for language difficulties. Few people you meet will know any English. Usually someone in a village will know some Thai, so a Thai phrasebook can be helpful (Lonely Planet publishes one).

As in Himalayan trekking in Nepal and India, many people now do short treks on their own at the lower elevations, staying in villages along the way. It is not necessary to bring a lot of food or equipment, just money for food which can be bought along the way in small Thai towns and occasionally in the hill-tribe settlements. However, TAT strongly discourages trekking on your own because of the safety risk. Check in with the police when you arrive in a new district so they can tell you if an area is considered safe or not. A lone trekker is an easy target (see the Safety section).

Trekking Companies

I won't make any specific recommendations for particular trekking companies in Chiang Mai. Many of the trekking guides are freelance and go from one company to the next, so there's no way to predict which companies are going to give the best service at any time.

The companies listed are recognised by TAT and the Professional Guide Association,

which means that they should be using licensed guides. Just about every guest house in Chiang Mai works through one of these companies. The list represents a mixture of companies which are directly affiliated with hotels/guest houses and those which are not. Ultimately, the best way to shop for a trek is to talk to travellers who have just returned from treks.

Bamboo Tour (tel 236501), Chiang Mai Guest House, 91 Charoen Prathet Rd
Camp of Troppo (tel 213219), 83/2 Chotana Rd
Changmoi Trekking (formerly Folkways) (tel 251839), Changmoi Guest House, 29 Chang Moi Kao Rd
Eagle Trekking (tel 235387), Eagle House, 16-18 Chang Moi Kao Rd, Soi 3
Enjoy Tour (tel 235791), 258 Tha Phae Rd
DNP Trekking, (tel 210447), Welcome Guest House, 37/1 Moon Muang Rd
Evergreen (tel 236710), 47 Moon Muang Rd
Family Tribal Trekking (tel 213939), Moon Muang Rd, 9 Soi 7
Inter Travel Agency (tel 252512), 17 Tha Phae Rd
Inthanon Tours (tel 232722), 100/19 Huay Kaew Rd
Lanna Travel & Tour Service (tel 251471), 94 Charoen Prathet Rd
Markes Travel (tel 236704), 2-4 Tha Phae Rd
Mau Tour (tel 211033), 106 Ratchapakhinai Rd
MEI Tour (tel 234358), 261 Tha Phae Rd
Northern Thailand Trekking (tel 214572), 59 Moon Muang Rd
New Wave Tour (tel 214040), 33/6 Moon Muang Rd
Pinan Tour (tel 236081), 235 Tha Phae Rd
PS Tours & Travel (tel 251721), New Chiang Mai Hotel, Chaiyaphum Rd
Sam Trekking & Service (tel 233885), Galare Guest House, 7 Charoen Prathet Rd
Seiko Tour (tel 236640), 164 Tha Phae Rd
Singha Travel (tel 233198), 277 Tha Phae Rd
Summit Tour & Trekking (tel 233351), 28-30 Tha Phae Rd
Top North Tours (tel 252050), Chiangmai Plaza Hotel, 92 Si Donchai Rd
Udom Tribal Trek (tel 232448), Times Square Guest House, 2/10 Tha Phae Rd
Unity Tour (tel 211033), 198 Ratchapakhinai Rd
Youth's Tour (tel 212863), Chiang Mai Youth Hostel, 31 Phra Pokklao Rd

Hill-Tribe Directory

The term hill tribe refers to ethnic minorities living in the mountainous regions of north and west Thailand. The Thais refer to them as *chao khao*, literally meaning mountain

Top: Wat Phra Singh, Chiang Mai (CT)
Left: Mosaic, Wat Chiang Man, Chiang Mai (JC)
Right: Wat Chedi Luang, Chiang Mai (CT)

Top: Wat Phra Singh, Chiang Mai (JC)
Left: Kamphaeng Phet Buddha (JC)
Right: Wat Chama Thevi (Wat Kukut), Lamphun (TW)

people. Each hill tribe has its own language, customs, mode of dress and spiritual beliefs.

Most are of semi-nomadic origins, having migrated to Thailand from Tibet, Burma, China and Laos during the past 200 years or so, although some groups may have been in Thailand much longer. They are fourth-world people in the sense that they belong neither to the main aligned powers nor to the third-world nations. Rather, they have crossed and continue to cross national borders without regard for recent nationhood. Language and culture constitute the borders of their world as some groups are caught between the 6th and 20th centuries while others are gradually being assimilated into modern Thai life.

The Tribal Research Institute in Chiang Mai recognises 10 different hill tribes but there may be up to 20 in Thailand. The institute's 1986 estimate of the total hill-tribe population was 550,000.

The following descriptions cover the largest tribes which are also the groups most likely to be encountered on treks. Linguistically, the tribes can be divided into three main groups: the Tibeto-Burman (Lisu, Lahu, Akha); the Karenic (Karen, Kayah); and the Austro-Thai (Hmong, Mien). Comments on ethnic dress refer mostly to the female members of each group as hill-tribe men tend to dress like rural Thais. Population figures are 1986 estimates.

The Shan (Thai Yai) are not included since they are not a hill-tribe group per se as they live in permanent locations, practice Theravada Buddhism and speak a language very similar to Thai. Thai scholars consider the Shan to have been the original inhabitants (Thai Yai means larger or majority Thais) of the area. Nevertheless, Shan villages are common stops on hill-tribe trekking itineraries.

Akha (Thai: *I-kaw*)
Population: 33,600
Origin: Tibet
Present locations: Thailand, Laos, Burma, Yunnan
Economy: rice, corn, opium
Belief system: animism, with an emphasis on ancestor worship.
Distinctive characteristics: head dresses of beads, feathers and dangling silver ornaments. Villages are along mountain ridges or on steep slopes from 1000 to 1400 metres in altitude. The Akha are amongst the poorest of Thailand's ethnic minorities and tend to resist assimilation into the Thai mainstream. Like the Lahu, they often cultivate opium for their own consumption.

Hmong (Thai: *Meo* or *Maew*)
Population: 80,000
Origin: south China
Present locations: south China, Thailand, Laos, Vietnam
Economy: rice, corn, opium
Belief system: animism
Distinctive characteristics: simple black jackets and indigo trousers with striped borders or indigo skirts, and silver jewellery. Most women wear their hair in a large bun. They usually live on mountain peaks or plateaus. Kinship is patrilineal and polygamy is permitted. They are Thailand's second largest hill-tribe group and are especially numerous in Chiang Mai Province.

Karen (Thai: *Yang* or *Kariang*)
Population: 265,600
Origin: Burma
Present locations: Thailand, Burma
Economy: rice, vegetables, livestock
Belief system: animism, Buddhism, Christianity, depending on the group.

Distinctive characteristics: thickly woven V-neck tunics of various colours (unmarried women wear white). Kinship is matrilineal and marriage is endogamous. They tend to live in lowland valleys and practice crop rotation rather than swidden (slash and burn) agriculture. There are four distinct Karen groups – the White Karen (Skaw Karen), Pwo Karen, Black Karen (Pa-o) and Kayah. These groups combined are the largest hill tribe in Thailand, numbering a quarter of a million people or about half of all hill-tribe people. Many Karen continue to migrate into Thailand from Burma, fleeing Burmese Government persecution.

Lahu (Thai: *Musoe*)
Population: 58,700
Origin: Tibet
Present locations: south China, Thailand, Burma
Economy: rice, corn, opium
Belief system: theistic animism (supreme deity is *Geusha*) and some groups are Christian.
Distinctive characteristics: black and red jackets with narrow skirts for women. They live in mountainous areas at about 1000 metres. Their intricately woven shoulder bags (*yaam*) are prized by collectors. There are four main groups – Red Lahu, Black Lahu, Yellow Lahu and Lahu Sheleh.

Lisu (Thai: *Lisaw*)
Population: 24,000
Origin: Tibet
Present locations: Thailand, Yunnan
Economy: rice, opium, corn, livestock
Belief system: animism with ancestor worship and spirit possession.
Distinctive characteristics: the women wear long multi-coloured tunics over trousers and sometimes black turbans with tassels. Men wear baggy green or blue pants pegged in at the ankles. They wear lots of bright colours. Premarital sex is said to be common, along with freedom in choosing marital partners. Patrilineal clans have pan-tribal jurisdiction, which makes the Lisu unique among hill-tribe groups (most tribes have power centred at the village level with either the shaman or a village headman). Their villages are usually in the mountains at about 1000 metres.

Mien (Thai: *Yao*)
Population: 35,500
Origin: central China
Present locations: Thailand, south China, Laos, Burma, Vietnam
Economy: rice, corn, opium
Belief system: animism with ancestor worship and Taoism.
Distinctive characteristics: women wear black jackets and trousers decorated with intricately embroidered patches and red fur-like collars, along with large dark blue or black turbans. They have been heavily influenced by Chinese traditions and use Chinese characters to write the Mien language. They tend to settle near mountain springs at between 1000 and 1200 metres. Kinship is patrilineal and marriage is polygamous.

Nakhon Sawan Province

NAKHON SAWAN TOWN นครสวรรค์
A fairly large town on the way north from Bangkok, Nakhon Sawan Town has an excellent view from the hilltop Wat Chom Khiri Nak Phrot. Thais and farangs agree that Nakhon Sawan is not known for its hospitality. The population (101,000) is largely Chinese and during Chinese New Year celebrations in February every hotel in town is booked.

Places to Stay
Si Phitak (tel 221076) at 109/5 Matuli Rd has rooms for between 80 and 100B. Also reasonably priced are the *Asia* (tel 213752) at 956 Phahonyothin Rd, where rooms range from 80 to 180B and the *New Thanchit* (tel 212027) at 110/1 Sawanwithi Rd, where the cost is from 90 to 120B. *Sala Thai* (tel 222938), 217-25 Matuli Rd, has air-con rooms for 200B and *Airawan* (*Irawan*) (tel 221889) at 1-5 Matuli Rd has all air-con rooms for between 200 and 450B.

A more expensive hotel is the *Phiman* (tel 222473), in front of the bus terminal at the Nakhon Sawan Shopping Centre, where air-con rooms range from 350 to 1500B.

Getting There & Away
The ordinary bus fare from Chiang Mai is 80B or 47B from Bangkok. Air-con buses from Bangkok cost 87B.

Kamphaeng Phet Province

KAMPHAENG PHET TOWN กำแพงเพชร
Kamphaeng Phet Town (population 23,000) was once an important front line of defence for the Sukhothai kingdom but is now mostly

known for producing the tastiest *kluay khai* (egg banana) in Thailand.

Old City

Only a couple of km off the Bangkok to Chiang Mai road are some ruins within the old city area of Kamphaeng Phet as well as some very fine remains of the long city wall.

A Kamphaeng Phet Historical Park has been established at the old city site and the area is now cared for by the Department of Fine Arts. There is a 20B entry fee to the ruins within the city wall. Here you'll find Wat Phra Kaew, which used to be adjacent to the

royal palace. The many weather-corroded Buddha statues here have assumed slender, porous forms which are reminiscent of Giaccobetti sculpture, as many visitors have commented. A little south-east of Wat Phra Kaew is Wat Phra That, distinguished by a large round-based chedi surrounded by laterite columns.

Kamphaeng Phet National Museum

Across the road from these temples is a national museum. The downstairs area contains the usual survey of Thai art periods while the upper floor has a collection of

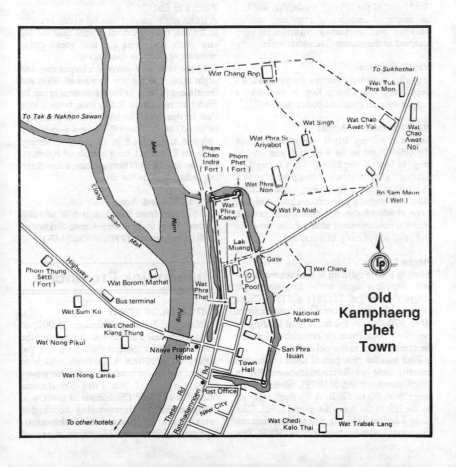

artefacts found in the Kamphaeng Phet area, including terracotta ornamentation from ruined temples and Buddha images in the Sukhothai and Ayuthaya styles. The museum is open Wednesday to Sunday from 8.30 am to 4 pm. Admission is 5B.

San Phra Isuan
Near the museum, San Phra Isuan is a shrine with a sandstone base, upon which is a Khmer-style bronze of Shiva (Isvara). This image is actually a replica, as the original is in the Kamphaeng Phet National Museum.

Wat Phra Si Ariyabot
North-east of the old city walls, this wat has the shattered remains of standing, sitting, walking and reclining Buddha images sculpted in the classic Sukhothai style.

Wat Chang Rop
Literally meaning 'temple surrounded by elephants', Wat Chang Rop is just that, a temple with an elephant-buttressed wall.

Wat Phra Borom Mathat
Across the Ping River are several more neglected ruins in an area that was settled long before Kamphaeng Phet's heyday, although visible remains are post-classical Sukhothai in design. Wat Phra Borom Mathat features a few small chedi and one large chedi of the late Sukhothai period, which is now crowned with a Burmese-style umbrella added early this century.

Places to Stay
It can be a little difficult to find accommodation since few signs are in English script. *Nitaya Prapha* (tel 711381) at 118/1 Thesa Rd is an old wooden hotel with rooms from 40 to 80B. It's on the main road leading to the river bridge (near the roundabout) and is the closest hotel to the old city.

Well into the new part of town on the left (north) side of Ratchadamnoen Rd is *Ratchadamnoen* (tel 711029), where rooms range from 80 to 120B. A bit further down on the left is the town's top-end hotel, *Cha Kang Rao* (tel 711315), where all rooms are air-con and rates run from 220 to 1500B. The *Phet Hotel* (tel 712810) near the municipal market at 99 Wijit Rd is also at the top end, with air-con rooms from 175B.

The next street over towards the river is Thesa Rd and down a couple of hundred metres on the right, set off the road, is the *Navarat (Nawarat)* (tel 711211), which has clean, comfortable rooms starting at 120B, and a coffee shop downstairs. In the centre of the new town not far from the municipal market is the bustling *Gor Choke Chai (Kaw Chok Chai)* (tel 711247). Rooms with a fan and bath cost between 100 and 200B and the staff is friendly.

Places to Eat
A small night market sets up every evening in front of the provincial offices near the old city walls and there are also some cheap restaurants near the roundabout.

In the centre of town is a larger day and night market at the intersection of Wijit and Banthoengjit Rds. Several restaurants can be found along Thesa Rd across from Sirijit Park by the river. The *Malai* (no English sign or menu) at 77 Thesa Rd serves good isaan (north-eastern) food in an outdoor setting. Also on Thesa Rd are a couple of bakeries, *Phayao* and *Tasty*. There are also a few floating restaurants on the river.

Getting There & Away
The bus fare from Bangkok is 69B or 126B air-con. Most visitors arrive from Sukhothai (20B), Phitsanulok (27B) or Tak (14B).

Phitsanulok Province

PHITSANULOK TOWN พิษณุโลก
Phitsanulok Town (population 75,000) is often abbreviated as Phi-lok. It straddles the Nan River about 390 km from Bangkok and makes an excellent base from which to explore the lower north. Besides the venerable temples of Wat Phra Sri Ratana Mahathat and Wat Chulamani in town, you can explore the surrounding accessible attractions of historical Sukhothai, Kamphaeng Phet and Si Satchanalai as well

as the national parks of Thung Salaeng Luang and Phu Hin Rong Kla, the former strategic headquarters of the Communist Party of Thailand. All of these places are within a 150 km radius of Phitsanulok Town.

Check out the markets by the Nan River for bargains on upcountry craft.

Information
The TAT office (tel 252742) at 209/7-8 Borom Trailokanat Rd has knowledgeable and helpful staff (some of TAT's best) whose members give out free maps of the town and a sheet that describes a suggested walking tour.

If you plan to do the trip from Phi-lok to Lom Sak, ask for their sketch map of Highway 12 which marks several waterfalls along the way.

Wat Phra Si
The full name of this temple is Wat Phra Si Ratana Wora Maha Wihan, but the locals call it Wat Phra Si or Wat Yai. The main wihan contains the Chinnarat Buddha (Phra Phuttha Chinnarat), one of Thailand's most revered and copied images. The wat is next to the bridge over the Nan River (on the right as you're heading out of Phi-lok towards Sukhothai). This famous bronze image is probably second in importance only to the Emerald Buddha in Bangkok's Wat Phra Kaew.

The image was cast in the late Sukhothai style, but what makes it strikingly unique is the flame-like halo around the head and torso that turns up at the bottom to become dragon-serpent heads on either side of the image. The head of this Buddha is a little wider than standard Sukhothai, giving the statue a very solid feel.

The story goes that construction of this wat was commissioned under the reign of King Li Thai in 1357. When it was completed, King Li Thai wanted it to contain three high-quality bronze images, so he sent for well-known sculptors, from Si Satchanalai, Chiang Saen and Hariphunchai (Lamphun), as well as five Brahmin priests. The first two castings worked well, but the third required three attempts before it was decreed the best of all. Legend has it that a white-robed sage appeared from nowhere to assist in the final casting, then disappeared. This last image was named the Chinnarat (Victorious King) Buddha and it became the centrepiece in the wihan. The other two images, Phra Chinnasi and Phra Si Satsada, were later moved to the royal temple of Wat Bowonniwet in Bangkok. Only the Chinnarat image has the flame-dragon halo.

The walls of the wihan are low to accommodate the low-swept roof, typical of northern temple architecture, so that the image takes on larger proportions than it might in a central or north-eastern wat. The doors of the building are inlaid with mother-of-pearl.

Dress appropriately when visiting this most sacred of temples – no shorts or revealing tops.

Near Wat Yai, on the same side of the river, are two other temples of the same period – Wat Ratburana and Wat Nang Phaya.

Wat Chulamani
Five km south of the city, a 2B bus trip on bus No 5 down Borom Trailokanat Rd, is Wat Chulamani, the ruins of which date from the Sukhothai period. The original buildings must have been impressive, judging from what remains of the ornate Khmer-style *prang* (tower). King Borom Trailokanat was ordained as a monk here and there is an old Thai inscription to that effect on the ruined wihan, dating from the reign of King Narai the Great.

The prang itself has little left of its original height, but Khmer-style door lintels remain, including a very nice one with a Sukhothai walking Buddha and a dhammachakka in the background.

Besides the prang and the wihan, the only original structures left are the remains of the monastery walls. Still, there is a peaceful, neglected atmosphere about the place.

Buddha-Casting Foundry
On Wisut Kasat Rd, not far from the Phitsanulok Youth Hostel, is a small factory where bronze Buddha images of all sizes are cast. Most are copies of the famous Phra Chinnarat Buddha at Wat Yai. Visitors are welcome to watch and there are even detailed

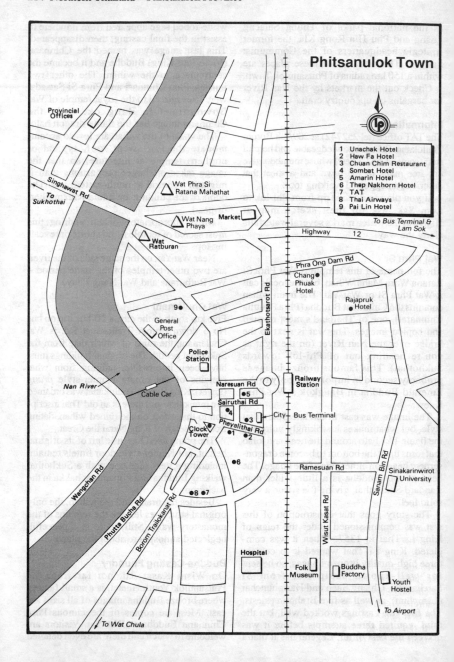

Phitsanulok Town

1 Unachak Hotel
2 Haw Fa Hotel
3 Chuan Chim Restaurant
4 Sombat Hotel
5 Amarin Hotel
6 Thep Nakhorn Hotel
7 TAT
8 Thai Airways
9 Pai Lin Hotel

Provincial Offices

Singhawat Rd

To Sukhothai

Wat Phra Si Ratana Mahathat

Wat Nang Phaya

Market

Wat Ratburan

To Bus Terminal & Lam Sok

Highway 12

Phra Ong Dam Rd

Chang Phuak Hotel

Rajapruk Hotel

9

General Post Office

Ekathotsarot Rd

Police Station

Nan River

Cable Car

Naresuan Rd

5

Sairuthai Rd

4

3

Phayalithai Rd

1

Clock Tower

2

6

Railway Station

City Bus Terminal

Ramesuan Rd

Sanam Bin Rd

Sinakarinwirot University

Wangchan Rd

8 7

Phutta Bucha Rd

Borom Trailokanat Rd

To Wat Chula

Wisut Kasat Rd

Hospital

Folk Museum

Buddha Factory

Youth Hostel

To Airport

photo exhibits describing step by step the 'lost wax' method of metal casting. Some of the larger images take a year or more to complete. The foundry is owned by Dr Thawi, an artisan and nationally renowned expert on northern Thai folklore.

There is a small gift shop at the foundry where you can purchase bronze images of various sizes.

Folk Museum

Across the street and north a short distance from the foundry is a folk museum established by Dr Thawi from his personal collection of traditional farm implements, cooking utensils, hunting equipment, musical instruments and other folkloric artefacts from throughout the northern region. It's the best collection of its kind in the country and many of the objects on display are virtually nonexistent in modern Thai life. If you're lucky, Dr Thawi may be around to offer you an impromptu demonstration of rustic devices used for calling birds and other animals, including elephants! Entrance to the museum is by donation.

Places to Stay – bottom end

Near the railway station are several inexpensive hotels and places to eat. If you turn left out of the station and then turn first right on to Sairuthat Rd you'll come to *Sombat Hotel* on the left side of the road. Rooms with a shower and a toilet down the hall are 70B, or 80B with a toilet. It's noisy and a bit of a brothel, however.

Further towards the river are the *Sukkit* and the *Chokprasit*, not quite as good but the rates are similar.

On the next street south, Phayalithai Rd, are two old standbys, the *Haw Fa* and the *Unachak*. Both have adequate rooms with a fan and bath for about 100B.

Better than any yet mentioned is the newly opened *Phitsanulok Youth Hostel* (tel 242060) at 38 Sanam Bin Rd. The hostel is in a 40-year-old house shaded by jasmine vines and is quite comfortable. Sapachai, the owner, worked as a systems analyst in Bangkok for 10 years before giving up the rat race to return to his boyhood home. Large

double rooms cost 100B and the dorm is 50B per person. Subtract 10B from these rates if you hold an IYH card. A third person can stay in a double for an added 40B. Breakfast costs 25B and includes two eggs, toast, milk and coffee or tea.

You can get here by samlor or by a No 4 city bus. From the railway station, catch the No 4 heading south on Ekathotsarot Rd. The bus will turn left on Ramesuan Rd and then right on Sanam Bin Rd. The hostel is about 100 metres down Sanam Bin Rd on the left. From the airport, the hostel is easy to reach – take a No 4 bus and it will be on the right. From the bus terminal, take a No 1 city bus going east on Highway 12. When the bus turns at Ramesuan Rd into the centre of town, get off and change to a No 4 bus or walk 100 metres or so to the hostel. Samlor rides should cost 5B per person from the airport, 5 to 10B from the railway station and 10 to 15B from the bus terminal.

Places to Stay – middle

Rajapruk Hotel (tel 258477) at 99/9 Phra Ong Dam Rd offers good value. Air-con rooms with hot water are available at 200B economy, 250B standard and 300B deluxe. Behind it is the *Guest House Hotel*, also owned by Rajapruk, where basic air-con rooms go for 160B.

Places to Stay – top end

More expensive hotels include the *Thepnakhon* at 43/1 Sithamtripidok Rd, which has air-con rooms from 400B, and the *Phailin* on Borom Trailokanat Rd, where air-con rooms start at 420B.

Places to Eat

Phitsanulok is a great town for eating. There must be more restaurants per capita here than just about any other town in Thailand.

Excellent, inexpensive Thai food can be had at the *Chuan Chim* (also called *Puun Sii*) across the street from the Haw Fa Hotel on Phayalithai Rd. There are plenty of other cheap Thai restaurants in this area too.

Floating restaurants light up the Nan River at night. The *River Pub & Restaurant* on the east side of the river near the centre of town has good food and live folk music. A corner of the dining area has traditional mawn khwan floor pillows and mats for eating at.

South of the main string of floating restaurants is a pier where you can board the *Yaat Fon* (Raindrop), a restaurant-boat that cruises the Nan River every night. You pay 10B to board the boat and then order from a menu as you please – no minimum charge.

Also along the river is a popular night market area with dozens of food vendors, a couple of whom specialise in *phak bung loi faa* (floating-in-the-sky morning glory vine), which usually translates simply as flying vegetable. This fad originated in Chonburi but has somehow taken root in Phi-lok. There are several of these places in town as well as on the river. The dish is basically morning glory vine stir-fried in soy bean sauce and garlic, but with a performance included. The cook fires up a batch in the wok and then flings it through the air to a waiting server who catches it on a plate. The eating places on the river are now so performance-oriented that the server climbs to the top of a van to catch the flying vegetable! Tour companies bring tour groups here and invite tourists to try the catch – it's as amusing watching the tourists drop phak bung all over the place as it is to watch the cook. During the day this area is a sundries market.

Close to the Phitsanulok Youth Hostel are several small noodle and rice shops. Across from the Sinakarinwirot University campus on Sanam Bin Rd is the very popular and very inexpensive *Sawng Anong* outdoor restaurant, open from 9 am to 3 pm daily. It's got a great selection of curries, noodles and Thai desserts, all priced at less than 10B. Try the *sao nam*, a mixture of pineapple, coconut, dried shrimp, ginger and garlic – delicious. Also good is the *kaeng yuak*, a curry made from the heart of a banana palm.

The cheapest meal in town has got to be *kuaytiaw phat thai* at the intersection of Phra Ong Dam Rd and Ekathotsarot Rd. The intersection is called Si-Yaek Baan Khaek (Indian village crossroads) and the vendor on the north-west corner has been serving up 3B dishes of phat thai for many years.

Getting There & Away

Air Thai Airways has two daily 45-minute flights to Phitsanulok from Bangkok, at 7.15 am and 3.50 pm. The one-way fare is 730B. There are direct flights between Phitsanulok and Loei (340B on Monday, Wednesday and Friday), Tak (215B on Tuesday, Thursday, Saturday and Sunday) and Phrae (290B on Tuesday and Thursday).

Phitsanulok's airport is just out of town. Songthaews leave every 20 minutes or so and go into town for 5B, otherwise catch the No 4 city bus for 2B. The big hotels in town run free buses from the airport.

Bus Transportation choices out of Phitsanulok are very good, as it's a junction for bus lines running both north and north-east. Bangkok is only five hours away by bus and Chiang Mai is five-and-a-half hours away. Ordinary buses leave for Phitsanulok from Bangkok's Northern Bus Terminal several times daily and cost 72B or 130B with aircon. Be sure to get the *sai mai* (new route) bus via Nakhon Sawan, as the old route via Tak Fa takes six hours and costs 6B more. Direct buses between Phitsanulok and Loei via Dan Sai cost 47B and takes four hours.

Buses between Phitsanulok and other provinces in the north and north-east leave several times a day, except for air-con buses which may depart only once or twice a day:

City	Fare	Duration
Chiang Mai		
(via Den Chai)	67B	5½ hours
(air-con)	120B	5½ hours
Chiang Mai		
(via Tak)	82B	6 hours
(air-con)	117B	6 hours
Chiang Rai		
(via Sukhothai)		7 hours
(air-con)	131B	7 hours
Chiang Rai		
(via Uttaradit)	81B	6 hours
(air-con)	110B	6 hours
Khon Kaen	76B	5 hours
(air-con)	106B	5 hours
Khorat		
(Nakhon Ratchasima)	81B	6 hours
(air-con)	146B	6 hours

Mae Sot	50B	5 hours
Phrae (new route)	37B	3 hours
Phrae (old route)	48B	5 hours
Udon Thani		7 hours
(air-con)	130B	7 hours

Buses to the following nearby points leave on the hour (*), every two hours (**) or every three hours (***) from early morning until 5 or 6 pm (except for Sukhothai buses, which leave every half hour):

City	Fare	Duration
Sukhothai	14B	1 hour
Kamphaeng Phet*	27B	3 hours
Uttaradit*	35B	3 hours
Phetchabun***	39B	3 hours
Lom Sak*	34B	2 hours
Dan Sai**	32B	3 hours
Tak*	30B	3 hours

Train The 6.40 am and 3 pm Rapid trains from Bangkok arrive in Phitsanulok at 12.56 and 9.17 pm. The basic fare is 143B 2nd class or 69B 3rd class, plus a 20B surcharge for the Rapid service. If you're going straight on to Sukhothai from Phitsanulok, the trishaw ride from the station to the bus station four km away is 15B. From there you can get a bus to Sukhothai or you can pick up a bus on Singhawat Rd on the west side of the river, which is a 5B ride from the railway station.

Getting Around

Samlor rides within the town centre should cost 5B per person. City buses are 2B and there are five lines making the rounds, so you should be able to get just about anywhere by bus. The terminal for city buses is near the railway station off Ekathotsarot Rd. You can cross the river by cable car, which costs 2B each way. The cable-car terminal on the east side of the river is near the police station.

PHU HIN RONG KLA NATIONAL PARK

อุทยานแห่งชาติ ภูหินร่องกล้า

From 1967 to 1982, Phu Hin Rong Kla was the strategic headquarters for the Communist Party of Thailand (CPT) and its tactical arm, the People's Liberation Army of Thailand (PLAT). The location was perfect for an insurgent army, as it was high in the mountains and there were very few roads into the CPT territory. Another benefit was that the headquarters were only 50 km from the Lao border, so lines of retreat were well-guarded after 1975 when Laos fell to the Pathet Lao. China's Yunnan Province was only 300 km away and it was in the provincial capital, Kunming, that CPT cadres received their training in revolutionary tactics.

The CPT camp at Phu Hin Rong Kla became especially active after the October 1976 student uprising in Bangkok in which hundreds of students were killed by the Thai military. Many students fled to the area to join the CPT and these students set up a hospital and a school of political and military tactics. For nearly 20 years the area around Phu Hin Rong Kla served as a battlefield for skirmishes between Thailand's 3rd Army Division, garrisoned in Phitsanulok, and the PLAT.

In 1972, the Thai Government launched the 1st, 2nd and 3rd Armies, plus the navy, air force, and national guard against PLAT in an attempt to rout them from Phu Hin Rong Kla, but the action was unsuccessful. In 1980 and 1981, they tried again and were able to recapture some parts of CPT territory. But the decisive blow to the CPT came in 1982 when the Government declared amnesty for all the students who had joined the communists after 1976. The departure of most of the students broke the spine of the movement, which had by this time become dependent on their membership. A final military push in 1982 effected the surrender of PLAT and Phu Hin Rong Kla was declared a national park.

Information

The park covers about 307 square km of rugged mountains and forest. The elevation at park headquarters is about 1000 metres, so the park is refreshingly cool even in the hot season. The main attractions are the remains of the CPT stronghold, including a rustic courthouse/meeting hall, the school of military tactics and politics and the CPT administration building. Across the road from the school is a waterwheel designed by exiled engineering students. In another area of the park is a trail that goes to Phaa Chu Thong (Flag Raising Cliff, sometimes called Red Flag Cliff), where the communists would raise the red flag to announce a military victory. Also in this area is an air-raid shelter, a viewing point and the remains of the main CPT headquarters – the most inaccessible point in the territory before a road was built by the Thai Government. The buildings are just bamboo and wood huts with no plumbing or electricity – a testament to how primitive the living conditions were for the insurgents.

At the park headquarters is a small

museum which displays relics from the CPT days such as medical instruments and weapons. At the end of the road into the park is a small Hmong village. When the CPT were here, the Hmong were their allies. Now they've switched allegiance to the Thai Government and are undergoing 'development'. One wonders what would have happened if the CPT had succeeded in its revolutionary goal. Maybe the 3rd Army headquarters in Phitsanulok would now be a museum instead.

If you're not interested in the history of Phu Hin Rong Kla, there are hiking trails,

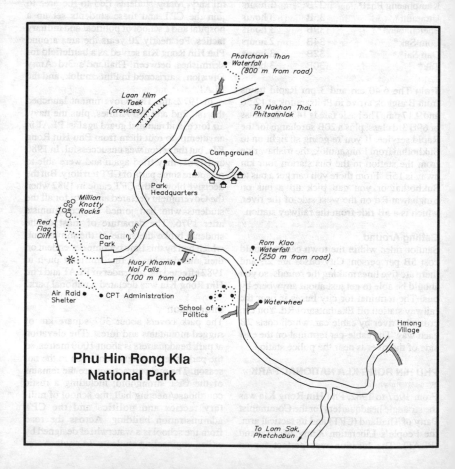

Phu Hin Rong Kla National Park

waterfalls and scenic views, plus some interesting rock formations – an area of jutting boulders called Laan Hin Pum (Million Knotty Rocks) and an area of deep rocky crevices where PLAT troops would hide during air raids, called Laan Hin Taek (Million Broken Rocks).

Places to Stay
The Forestry Department rents out two bungalows that sleep seven each for 400B, two bungalows that sleep 10 each for 600B and one bungalow which sleeps 15 people for 900B. You can pitch your own tent for 5B per person per night or sleep in park tents for 30B per person (no bedding provided). If you want to build a fire, you can buy chopped wood for 150B a night. Accommodation must be booked in advance through the Forestry Department's Bangkok office (tel 579-0529 or 579-4842). For some unknown reason, you can't book on the spot.

Places to Eat
Near the camping grounds and bungalows are a couple of food vendors. The best is *Duang Jai Cafeteria* – try its famous carrot somtam.

On the way to or from Phitsanulok, stop at *Kafae Sot* (also called *Queen Coffee*) at the 45 km spot on Highway 12. It has some of the best fresh coffee outside of Bangkok. It's near Ban Kaeng Sawng, close to Kaeng Sawng Waterfall. The beans are all locally grown but have names like Blue Mountain and Brazil. Freshly brewed coffee costs between 15 and 25B per cup, but it's worth it for 100% Arabica or Robusta beans. Ordinarily, Thai coffee is mixed with ground tamarind seed and other additives.

Getting There & Away
The park headquarters are about 125 km from Phitsanulok. To get there, take a Lom Sak bus east on Highway 12 as far as Ban Yaeng, then another bus 25 km north to Ban Nong Krathao (about four km south of Nakhon Thai). The road to the park is signposted at this point, so either hitch or grab a songthaew for the final 31 km to the park entrance. There are also occasional

direct buses to Nakhon Thai from Phi-lok, in which case you can go straight to Ban Nong Krathao first.

A small group could also charter a pick-up and driver in Nakhon Thai to visit all the spots for about 550B for the day. The Rang Thong Tour Co in Phitsanulok, near TAT, can do all-day tours for 800B that take up to eight people.

This is a delightful trip if you're on a motorcycle as there's not much traffic along the way.

Sukhothai Province

SUKHOTHAI TOWN เมือง สุโขทัย
As Thailand's first capital, Sukhothai flourished from the mid-13th century to the late-14th century. The new town of Sukhothai (population 23,000) is almost 450 km from Bangkok and is undistinguished except for its very good municipal market in the town centre.

The old city of Sukhothai (Dawn of Happiness) features quite an admirable spread of ruins covering 45 square km, making an overnight stay in new Sukhothai worthwhile, although you could make a day trip from Phitsanulok.

The Sukhothai kingdom is viewed as the Golden Age of Thai civilisation and the religious art and architecture of the Sukhothai era are considered to be the most classic of Thai styles.

The more remote ruins in the hills west of the old city walls, such as Saphan Hin, used to be considered a dangerous area, but since UNESCO and the Thai Government have joined in the development of the old city environs, all ruins are safe to visit with or without a guide. The Sukhothai ruins have been declared a historical park and are divided into five zones, each of which has a 20B admission fee.

Ramkhamhaeng National Museum
The museum provides a good starting point for an exploration of the ruins. Check the well-made miniature model of the old city

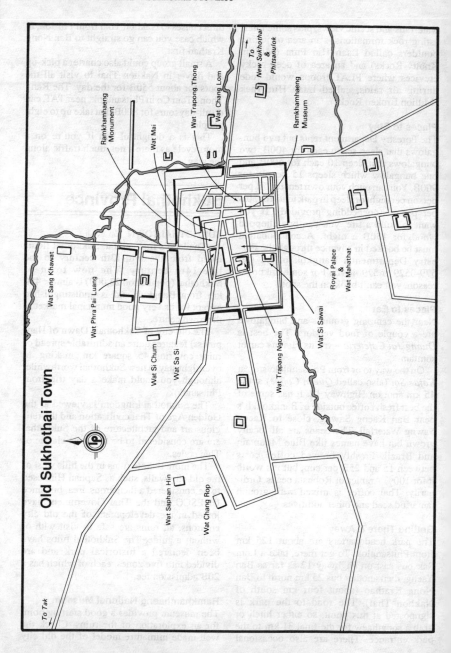

Old Sukhothai Town

and its environs for orientation and relative distances between sites. This will help in planning which sites to visit first and in what order. A replica of the famous Ramkhamhaeng inscription is kept here amongst a good collection of Sukhothai artefacts.

The museum is open daily from 9 am to 4 pm and admission is 20B.

Sukhothai Historical Park

All of the ruins listed are now part of the Sukhothai Historical Park. The official hours (when admission is collected) are from 6 am to 6 pm.

Wat Mahathat The largest in the city and built in the 13th century, this wat is surrounded by brick walls (206 by 200 metres) and a moat. The spires feature the famous lotus bud motif of Sukhothai architecture and some of the original stately Buddha figures still sit among the ruined columns of the old wihans. There are 198 chedi within the monastery walls – a lot to explore.

Wat Si Sawai Just south of Wat Mahathat stands this 12th-to-13th-century shrine, featuring three corn cob-like prangs and a picturesque moat. It was originally built by the Khmers as a Hindu temple.

Wat Sa Si This wat sits on an island west of the Ramkhamhaeng monument. It's a simple, classic Sukhothai-style wat with one large Buddha, one chedi and the columns of the ruined wihan.

Wat Trapang Thong Next to the museum, this small, still-inhabited wat is reached by a footbridge crossing the large lotus-filled pond which surrounds it. This reservoir, the original site of the Loy Krathong Festival in Thailand, supplies the Sukhothai community with most of its water.

Wat Phra Pai Luang Outside the city walls to the north, this somewhat isolated wat features three Khmer-style prangs, similar to those at Si Sawai but bigger, dating from the 12th century. This may have been the centre of Sukhothai when it was ruled by the Khmers of Angkor prior to the 13th century.

Wat Si Chum This wat is west of the old city and contains the impressive, much-photographed *mondop* (square building used by laypeople) with an 11-metre seated Buddha. A passage in the mondop wall leads to the top. Jataka inscriptions line the ceiling of the passageway, but these can only be seen by candle or torch.

Wat Chang Lom Off the main highway east of the old city, this wat is next to the Sukhothai Cultural Centre. A large chedi is supported by 36 elephants sculpted into its base.

Wat Saphan Hin Saphan Hin is a couple of km to the west of the old city walls, on the crest of a hill that rises about 200 metres above the plain. The name of the wat, which means stone bridge, is a reference to the slate path and staircase leading to the temple, which is still in place. The site affords a good view of the Sukhothai ruins to the south-east and the mountains to the north and south. All that remains of the original temple are a few chedi and the ruined wihan, consisting of two rows of laterite columns flanking a 12½-metre-high standing Buddha image on a brick terrace.

Wat Chang Rop On another hill west of the city, a bit south of Wat Saphan Hin, this wat features an elephant-base stupa, similar to that at Wat Chang Lom.

Places to Stay

Hotels There are several good hotels: *Chinnawat* (tel 611385), 1-3 Nikhon Kasem Rd, has clean and comfortable rooms, friendly and helpful staff and a good restaurant downstairs. Rooms with a fan and bath cost from 70 to 100B, depending on whether they are in the old or new wing – the old wing is cheaper and a bit quieter. There are air-con rooms for between 140 and 180B, plus a couple of large rooms with air-con, hot water and a bath for 400B. There is also an eight-bed dormitory that goes for 30B per person.

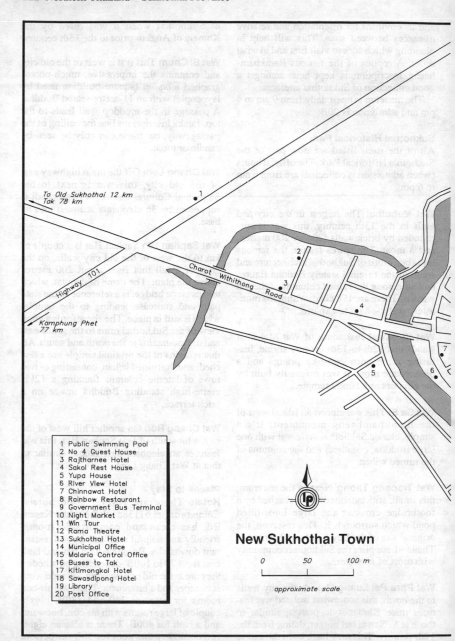

To Old Sukhothai 12 km
Tak 78 km

Kamphung Phet
77 km

Highway 101

Charot Withithong Road

1 Public Swimming Pool
2 No 4 Guest House
3 Rajtharnee Hotel
4 Sakol Rest House
5 Yupa House
6 River View Hotel
7 Chinnawat Hotel
8 Rainbow Restaurant
9 Government Bus Terminal
10 Night Market
11 Win Tour
12 Rama Theatre
13 Sukhothai Hotel
14 Municipal Office
15 Malaria Control Office
16 Buses to Tak
17 Kitimongkol Hotel
18 Sawasdipong Hotel
19 Library
20 Post Office

New Sukhothai Town

0   50   100 m

approximate scale

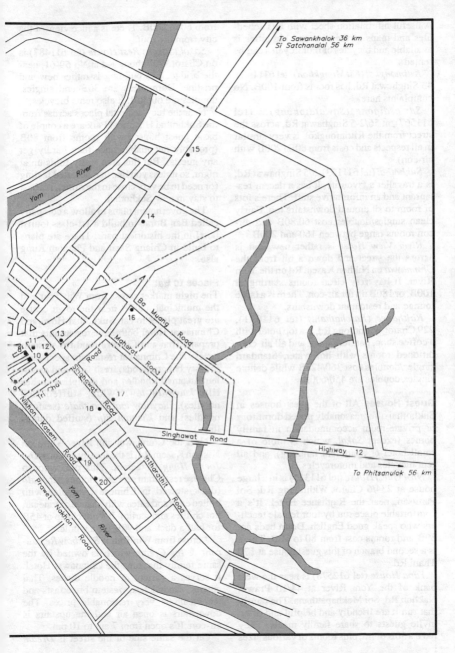

To Sawankhalok 36 km
Si Satchanalai 56 km

Yom River

To Phitsanulok 56 km

Singhawat Road   Highway 12

Ba Muang Road

Maharot Road

Nikhon Kasem Road

Singhawat Road

Prowet Nokhon Road

Si Intharathit Road

Tri Chot

Yom River

A useful information sheet with bus schedules and maps of the new and old cities is available and bicycles or motorcycles can be rented.

Kitimongkol (Kit Mongkhon) (tel 611193), 43 Singhawat Rd, has rooms from 100B. No complaints here.

Sawasdipong (Sawatdiphong) (tel 611567), at 56/2-5 Singhawat Rd, across the street from the Kittimongkol, is very similar in all respects and costs from 80B (200B with air-con).

Sukhothai (tel 611133), 5/5 Singhawat Rd, is a traveller's favourite. It has a decent restaurant and an informative staff. There's lots of room to sit around downstairs too. Fairly clean singles/doubles cost 60/80B and air-con rooms range between 160 and 200B.

River View Hotel is rather new and is across the street and down a bit from the *Chinnawat* on Nikhon Kasem Rd on the Yom River. It has very clean rooms starting at 100B, or 180B up for air-con. There is a large lounge and restaurant downstairs.

Rajthanee (Ratchathani) (tel 611031), 229 Charot Withithong Rd, is a top hotel with a coffee shop, bar, restaurant and all air-conditioned rooms with hot water. Standard singles/doubles cost 360/420B while deluxe singles/doubles are 450/600B.

Guest Houses All of the guest houses in Sukhothai offer reasonably priced dormitory or private-room accommodation in family homes (except *Sakol*, which is more of a small hotel or apartment building), and all rent bicycles and motorcycles.

No 4 Guest House (tel 611315) is in a large house at 234/6 Charot Withithong Rd, Soi Panitsan, near the Rajthanee Hotel. It's a comfortable place run by four female teachers who speak good English. Dorm beds are 30B and rooms cost from 80 to 90B. There is a second branch of this guest house at 170 Thani Rd.

Yupa House (tel 612578) is near the west bank of the Yom River at 44/10 Prawet Nakhon Rd, Soi Mekhapatthana. The family that run it are friendly and helpful and often invite guests to share family meals. They have a 30B dorm, plus rooms of various sizes

from 60 to 100B. There is a nice view of the city from the roof.

Sakol (Sakon) Rest House (tel 611487) is on Charot Withithong Rd at No 59-61, near the bridge. The building is rather new and pristine. Dorm beds are 30B and singles/doubles are 60/80B. It also rents bicycles.

Near the bicycle rental places across from the Sukhothai Historical Park are a couple of basic guest houses with rooms from 80B (probably negotiable since they hardly get any guests). But this area really folds up at night, so unless you like that deserted feeling (or need to be very close to the ruins), it's best to stay in new Sukhothai.

The government plans to allow a company called Ban Boran to build a 1st-class tourist hotel in the historical park. There are plans to build in Chiang Saen and Phanom Rung also.

Places to Eat

The night market across from Win Tour and the municipal market near the town centre are great places to eat. Sukhothai Hotel and Chinnawat Hotel both have restaurants that prepare Thai and Chinese food for western tastes. The Chinnawat restaurant specialises in tasty bakery goods, fresh fruit and excellent steamed noodles and dumpling dishes like *kuaytiaw lawt* (wide, stuffed rice noodles), *kuaytiaw laat naa thale* (seafood noodles) and *khanom jiip* (stuffed dumplings).

Near the Chinnawat and River View, on Nikhon Kasem Rd, is the locally famous *Kho Joeng Hong* restaurant. This old, wooden Chinese restaurant serves delicious *pet phalo* (duck stewed in Chinese five-spice with boiled eggs and eaten with a sauce of vinegar, hot chillies and garlic). It's not cheap at 45B for half a duck and 90B for a whole.

Across from Win Tour is *Rainbow Restaurant & Ice Cream* which is owned by the same family that runs the Chinnawat Hotel. It serves a variety of noodle dishes, Thai curries, sandwiches, western breakfasts and ice cream at very reasonable prices. The downstairs is open air and the upstairs is air-con. It's open from 7 am to 10 pm.

On the same side of the street is *Dream*

Cafe, an air-con cafe that serves espresso and other 100% coffee drinks, plus Thai herbal liquors and beer. The food is a bit more expensive than at the Rainbow, but the place has character.

The No 4 Guest Houses have information about free dinners put on by the Volunteer English School at Udom Daruni High School. In exchange for helping with one English lesson, travellers are served a large free meal 'to accommodate all tastes including vegetarian'.

Getting There & Away

Bus Sukhothai can be reached by road from Phitsanulok, Tak or Kamphaeng Phet. If you've just arrived in Phitsanulok by rail or air, take a city bus No 1 (2B) to the centre or Baw Kaw Saw Terminal, for buses out of town. The bus to Sukhothai costs 14B, takes about an hour and leaves regularly throughout the day. You could also catch this bus on the road to Sukhothai out near the bridge over the Nan River, near Wat Mahathat.

From Tak, get a Sukhothai bus at the Baw Kaw Saw Terminal just outside of town. The fare is 19B and the trip takes about an hour. Buses from Kamphaeng Phet are 20B and take from one to 1½ hours.

Buses to/from Chiang Mai cost 72B via Tak or 100B via Lampang and take from 4½ to five hours. Buses between Bangkok and Sukhothai are 87B or 153B air-con and take seven hours. Buses to Chiang Rai cost 80 or 120B air-con and take six hours. Buses to Khon Kaen cost 100 or 155B air-con and take from six to seven hours.

Phitsanulok Yan Yon Tour has a daily VIP bus (with reclining seats) to Bangkok for 205B that leaves at 10.45 pm. Ordinary buses to destinations outside the Sukhothai Province leave from the Baw Kaw Saw government terminal and tour buses leave from Win Tour or Phitsanulok Yan Yon Tour near the night market area. Buses to Tak leave from Ban Muang Rd, two streets east from Singhawat Rd.

Buses to Sawankhalok and Si Satchanalai (18B, one hour) leave hourly from the intersection across from the Sukhothai Hotel, between about 6 am and 6 pm.

Getting Around

Songthaew A songthaew to the old city (muang kao) from Sukhothai costs 5B and takes between 20 and 30 minutes. A tuk-tuk and driver can be hired for between 40 and 50B an hour (depending on whether you hire them in town or at the old city), which can save you a lot of time and sore feet in touring the ruins. In addition, guides of varying ages and knowledge hang around hotels and markets in Sukhothai as well as around the ruins. If you have lots of time and stamina you can walk from site to site, though it might take two days to see it all.

Bicycles & Motorcycles These can be rented across from the national museum in the old city for between 20 and 80B a day. This is probably the best way to tour the ruins.

Tours The Chinnawat Hotel runs van tours to old Sukhothai and Si Satchanalai. The Sukhothai tour is from 8.45 am to 12.10 pm and costs 80B per person for three or more. The Si Satchanalai tour is in the afternoon and costs 150B per person for three or more. This is a fairly economical way to see the ruins considering what groups of three or more might pay for tuk-tuks or motorcycles. Admission fees to the museum and ruins are not included in the tour price.

AROUND SUKHOTHAI TOWN

Si Satchanalai ศรีสัชนาลัย

The Sukhothai period ruins in Si Satchanalai and Chaliang are in the same basic stylistic range as those in old Sukhothai, but with some slightly larger sites. The Si Satchanalai ruins have recently been declared a national historical park. After getting off the bus at old Si Satchanalai you'll have to follow the sign (in Thai and English) down a side road to the Yom River and cross by ferry near Keng Luang (Royal Rapids). The ruins are set among hills and are very attractive in the sense that they're not as developed a tourist attraction as are the Sukhothai ruins. The Si Satchanalai Historical Park has an admission fee of 20B.

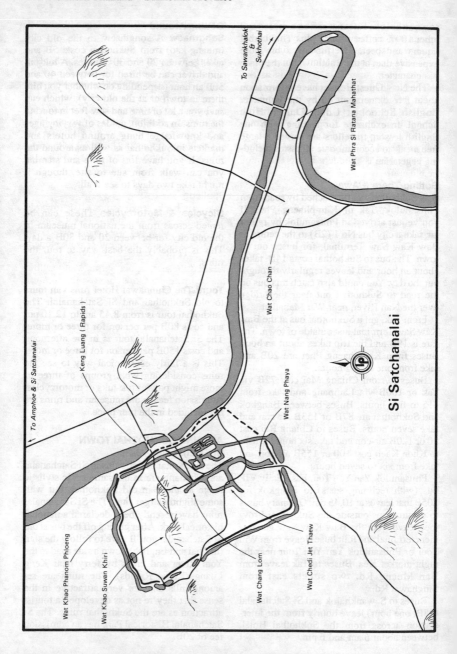

Si Satchanalai

To Sawankhalok & Sukhothai

Wat Phra Si Ratana Mahathat

Wat Chao Chan

Wat Nang Phaya

To Amphoe & Si Satchanalai

Keng Luang (Rapids)

Wat Khao Phanom Phloeng

Wat Khao Suwan Khiri

Wat Chang Lom

Wat Chedi Jet Thaew

Sawankhalok Pottery Sukhothai was famous for its beautiful pottery, much of which was exported. Particularly fine specimens can be seen in the national museums of Jakarta and Pontianak in Indonesia as the Indonesians of the time were keen collectors. A lot of the pottery was made in Si Satchanalai and rejects, buried in the fields, are still being found. Shops have misfired, broken, warped and fused pieces at Sukhothai and Si Satchanalai. Thai Celadon in Chiang Mai is a modern interpretation of the old craft.

Wat Chang Lom This is the first temple you'll come to after crossing the Yom River. It has the same name and style as the one in Sukhothai – elephants surrounding a stupa – but is somewhat better preserved.

Wat Khao Phanom Phloeng On the hill overlooking Wat Chang Lom to the right are the remains of Wat Khao Phanom Phloeng – a large seated Buddha, a chedi and stone columns which once supported the roof of the wihan. From this hill you can make out the general design of the once great city. The slightly higher hill west of Phanom Phloeng is capped by a large Sukhothai chedi, all that remains of Wat Khao Suwan Khiri.

Wat Chedi Jet Thaew Next to Wat Chang Lom, these ruins contain seven rows of lotus-bud chedi, the largest of which is a copy of one at Wat Mahathat in old Sukhothai. There is also an interesting brick and plaster wihan designed to look like a wooden structure (an ancient Indian technique used all over South-East Asia). A prasat and chedi are stacked on the roof.

Wat Nang Phaya South of Wat Chang Lom and Wat Chedi Jet Thaew, this stupa is Sinhalese in style and was built in the 15th or 16th century, a bit later than other monuments at Si Satchanalai.

Places to Stay In nearby Sawankhalok, the *Muang In* (tel 642622) at 21 Kasemrat Rd has rooms from 150B. Just outside Si Satchanalai is the *59 Bungalow* with similar rates.

Getting There & Away The Si Satchanalai ruins are off the road between new Si Satchanalai and Sawankhalok. You can either take the Si Satchanalai bus from Sukhothai or Sawankhalok all the way into the new city, then hire a taxi or minibus back to the ruins, or ask to be let off the bus at the old city (muang kao), 12 km short of the new city. A bus from Sukhothai to Si Satchanalai costs 18B.

Chaliang
Two km back down Route 101 towards Sawankhalok are the ruins of Wat Phra Si Ratana Mahathat and Wat Chao Chan. From the Si Satchanalai ruins, either walk along a path following the left bank of the Yom River or cross the river again by ferry and follow the highway until you come to the turn-off

Wat Phra Si Ratana Mahathat

on the right which crosses over a bridge to Chaliang. It's worth the walk. Any wat called the Temple of the Great and Sacred Jewel Relic usually is.

Wat Phra Si Ratana Mahathat These ruins consist of a large Sukhothai-style chedi between two wihans, one of which contains a large seated Sukhothai Buddha image, a smaller standing image and a bas-relief of the famous walking Buddha, so exemplary of the flowing, boneless Sukhothai style. The other wihan contains less distinguished images.

Wat Chao Chan These wat ruins are about 500 metres west of Wat Phra Si Ratana Mahathat. The central attraction is a large Khmer-style prang similar to later prangs in Lopburi and probably built during the Ayuthaya period. The prang has been restored and is in fairly good shape. The roofless wihan on the right contains a large, ruined, standing Buddha.

Tak Province

Tak, like Loei, Nan, Phetchabun, Krabi and certain other provinces, has traditionally been considered a remote province, that is, one which the central Bangkok Government has had little control over. In the 1970s, the mountains of west Tak were a hotbed of communist guerrilla activity. Now the former leader of the local CPT movement is involved in resort hotel development and Tak is open to outsiders, but the area still has an untamed feeling about it.

Western Tak has always presented a distinct contrast with other parts of Thailand because of heavy Karen and Burmese cultural influences. The Thai-Burmese border districts of Mae Ramat, Tha Song Yang and Mae Sot are dotted with Karen refugee camps, a result of recent fighting between the Karen National Union (KNU) and the Burmese Government which is driving Karen civilians across the border.

The main source of income for people living on both sides of the border is legal and illegal international trade. Black market dealings are estimated to account for at least 100 million baht per year in local income. The main smuggling gateways on the Thai side are Tha Song Yang, Mae Sarit, Mae Tan, Wangkha, Mae Sot and Waley. On the Burmese side, all of these gateways except Mae Sot are controlled by the KNU. Only Myawaddy, across the Moei River from Mae Sot, is under full Burmese Government control.

One important contraband product is teak, brought into Thailand from Burma on big tractor trailers at night. More than 125,000B in bribes per truckload is distributed among the local Thai authorities responsible for looking the other way.

Most of the province is forested and mountainous and is excellent for trekking. Organised trekking occurs, some from out of Chiang Mai further north. There are Hmong (Meo), Musoe (Lahu), Lisu and White and Red Karen settlements throughout the west and north. Many Thais come to Tak to hunt, as the province is known for its abundance of wild animals, especially in the northern part of Tak Province towards Mae Hong Son Province. Much of the hunting is illegal, such as tiger and elephant hunts in national wildlife preserves.

TAK TOWN เมือง ตาก
Tak Town (population 21,000) is not very interesting, except as a point from which to visit Lang Sang National Park to the west or Phumiphon Yanhi Dam to the north.

Places to Stay & Eat
Most of Tak's hotels are lined up on Mahat Thai Bamrung Rd in the town centre. The biggest hotel, *Wiang Tak* (tel 511910), at 25/3 Mahat Tahi Bamrung Rd, has air-con rooms from 410B.

Nearby on the same road, but less expensive, are the *Tak* (tel 511234), which has rooms with a fan and bath from 90B, and the *Mae Ping* (tel 511807), with similar accommodation for 80B.

On the next street over is the *Sa-nguan Thai* (tel 511265) at 619 Taksin Rd. Rooms

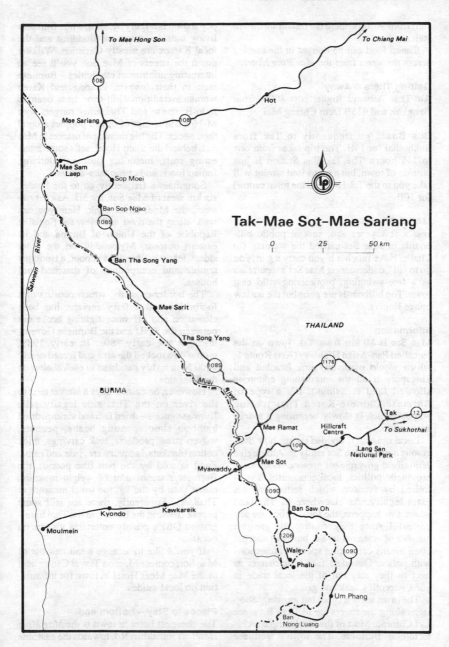

Tak-Mae Sot-Mae Sariang

0   25   50 km

THAILAND

BURMA

start from 90B and there is a restaurant downstairs.

Cheap food can be bought in the market across the street from the *Mae Ping Hotel*.

Getting There & Away
Air Thai Airways flights cost 800B from Bangkok and 415B from Chiang Mai.

Bus Buses go frequently to Tak from Sukhothai for 19B. The trip takes from one to 1½ hours. The Tak Bus Station is just outside of town, but a motorised samlor will take you to the Tak Hotel (at the town centre) for 10B.

MAE SOT แม่สอด
Just a few years ago, several public billboards in Mae Sot carried the warning (in Thai): 'Have fun, but if you carry a gun, you go to jail', underscoring Mae Sot's reputation as a free-swinging, profiteering wild east town. The billboards are gone but the outlaw image lingers.

Information
Mae Sot is 80 km from Tak Town on the so-called Pan-Asian Highway (Asia Route 1, which would ostensibly link Istanbul and Singapore if all the intervening countries allowed land crossings). It's a type of Burmese-Chinese-Karen-Thai trading outpost which is slowly becoming a tourist destination.

Local opinion is divided on just how dangerous a place Mae Sot really is. Although a centralised government presence dominates provincial politics, local economics is controlled by factions which settle conflicts extra-legally. As elsewhere in Thailand where this happens, the local police are all-powerful since they control the greatest number of armaments. So, business success often means cultivating special connections with police. Outsiders face little danger as long as they stay out of the local trade in guns, narcotics, teak and gems.

The town itself is small but growing. Shop signs along the streets are in Thai, Burmese and Chinese. Most of the local temple architecture is Burmese. The town's Burmese population is largely Muslim, while Burmese living outside town are Buddhist and the local Karens are mostly Christian. Walking down the streets of Mae Sot, you'll see an interesting mixture of ethnicities – Burmese men in their *longyis*, Hmong and Karen women in traditional hill-tribe dress, bearded Indo-Burmese and Thai army rangers with M-16's and strings of opium poppies around their necks. The big municipal market in Mae Sot, behind the Siam Hotel, sells some interesting stuff, including Burmese clothing, Indian foods and cheap take-aways.

Songthaews frequently go to the border, six km west of Mae Sot, for 5B. Ask for *rim moei*, the Moei River bank. Here you can walk along the river and view the Socialist Republic of the Union of Burma and its eastern outpost, Myawaddy, on the other side. Clearly visible are a school, a Buddhist temple and compounds of thatched-roof houses.

The border crossing, which consists of a footbridge and a ferry service, has been closed on and off since fighting broke out between the KNU and the Burmese Government in the early '80s. In early 1989, mortar-fire rocked the area and forced nearly 1000 Myawaddy residents to seek shelter on the Thai side.

However, on calmer days a market next to the river on the Thai side legally sells Burmese goods – dried fish and shrimp, dried bamboo shoots, mung beans, peanuts, woven-straw products, teak carvings, thick cotton blankets, lacquerware, jade and gems. Food is sold by the *pan* (the pound), the Burmese/Karenni unit of weight measure, rather than by the kg, the usual measure in Thailand. Apparently, there are still some people crossing the border, as the Thai Immigration Office plainly entertains visitors on occasion.

If you'd like to arrange a hill trek out of Mae Sot, contact Maesod Travel Centre next to the Mae Moei Hotel in town for information on local guides.

Places to Stay – bottom end
The cheapest hotel in town is the *Mae Moei Hotel* on Inthakhiri Rd, towards the east side

of town near the post office. The quite adequate rooms in this old wooden hotel cost 40B without a bath and 50B with one. A bit nicer is the *Suwannavit (Suwan Wit) Hotel* (tel 531162) around the corner on Soi Wat Luang. Rooms cost 60B in the old wing and 70B in the new building, both with bath.

You can get adequate rooms with a bath at the *Siam Hotel* (tel 531376) on Prasat Withi Rd, Mae Sot's other main street, starting from 100B. The Siam also has some more expensive air-con rooms.

Places to Stay – middle
Near the Siam is the newer *Porn Thep Hotel* (tel 532590) at 25/4 Soi Si Wieng, off Prasat Withi Rd near the day market. Air-con singles/doubles with hot water cost 260/280B, while rooms with a fan and bath are 200D.

The top digs in town used to be at the *First Hotel*, on Inthakhiri Rd across from the Mae Sot Bus Station and behind the police station. It seems pretty ordinary now, with faded but comfortable rooms starting at 140B with a fan and bath or up to 300B with air-con.

Places to Stay – top end
The top end is now the *Mae Sot Hills Hotel* (tel 532601/8, Bangkok reservations tel 224-7916/8) on the highway to Tak, just outside of town. The 120-room hotel has a swimming pool, tennis courts, a good restaurant that's open until 3 am, a discotheque and a Thai cocktail lounge (very dark). All rooms come with air-con, hot water, a fridge, TV/video and telephone. Rates are reasonable considering the relative luxury. Singles/doubles cost 450/500B and it's 900B for a suite.

Places to Eat
Near the Siam Hotel are several good places to eat including the *Kan Eng* for its Chinese/Thai food. Next door on Prasat Withi Rd is a small food centre with several different vendors serving noodles and curry.

Down the road a bit from the Mae Moei Hotel is a nice garden restaurant called *Neung Nut Restaurant*. The atmosphere is very pleasant, the service and food are of a high standard and the prices are quite reasonable.

The best Chinese restaurant in town is the unassuming *Kwangtung Restaurant*, which specialises in Cantonese cooking. It's next to the big market which is on a back road behind the Siam Hotel.

A favourite among Burmese Muslims is the fried chicken prepared and sold in the market.

Getting There & Away
Air Thai Airways flies between Phitsanulok and Mae Sot via Tak on Tuesday, Thursday, Saturday and Sunday at 8.50 am (9.40 am from Tak), arriving at 10.05 am. In the reverse direction, flights leave Mae Sot at 3.05 pm, arriving in Phitsanulok at 4.20 pm. The fare is 370B.

Bus Buses to Mae Sot leave hourly from the Tak Bus Station, from 6 am until 6 pm. An air-con minibus (rot tuu) costs 25B or you might share a taxi for 50B. The trip takes 1½ hours on a beautiful winding road through forested mountains and passes several hill-tribe villages.

From Bangkok's Northern AC Terminal there is one air-con bus per day to Mae Sot, which leaves at 10.15 pm and costs 179B.

Getting Around
Most of Mae Sot town can be visited on foot. A motorcycle dealer on Prasat Withi Rd rents motorcycles for from 100B (100cc) to 130B (125cc) a day.

AROUND MAE SOT
Ban Mae Tao แม่เต๊า
Wat Wattanaram (Phattanaram) is a Burmese temple at Ban Mae Tao, three km west of Mae Sot on the road to the border. A large alabaster, sitting Buddha is in a shrine with glass-tile walls, very Burmese in style. In the main wihan on the 2nd floor is a collection of Burmese musical instruments, including tuned drums and gongs.

Wat Phra That Doi Din Kiu (JI)
This is a forest temple 11 km north-west of the Mae Sot town on a 300-metre hill over-

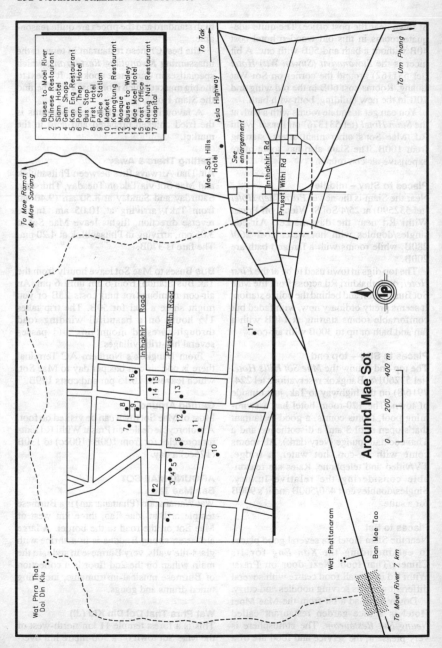

Around Mae Sot

1 Buses to Moei River
2 Chinese Restaurant
3 Siam Hotel
4 Gem Shops
5 Kan Eng Restaurant
6 Porn Thep Hotel
7 Bus Stop
8 First Hotel
9 Police Station
10 Market
11 Kwongtung Restaurant
12 Mosque
13 Buses to Waley
14 Mae Moei Hotel
15 Post Office
16 Neung Nut Restaurant
17 Hospital

To Tak

To Um Phang

Asia Highway

Mae Sot Hills Hotel

See enlargement

Inthakhiri Rd

Prusat Withi Rd

To Mae Ramat & Mae Sariang

Wat Phra That Doi Din Kiu

Inthakhiri Road

Prusat Withi Road

Wat Phattanaram

Ban Mae Tao

To Moei River 7 km

0   200   400 m

looking the Moei River and Burma. A small chedi mounted on what looks like a boulder that is balanced on the edge of a cliff is one of the attractions and is reminiscent of the Kyaiktiyo Pagoda in Burma.

The trail that winds up the hill provides good views of thick teak forests across the river in Burma. On the Thai side a scattering of smaller trees is visible. There are a couple of small limestone caves in the side of the hill on the way to the peak. The dirt road that leads to the wat from Mae Tao passes through a couple of Karen villages.

Mae Kit Saam Thaa แม่กิตสามท่า
Only 13 km north of Mae Sot is this lovely Thai village of peaceful corn growers. The temple abbot here is well known for his *metta* (loving-kindness) and the village seems to project a rural nirvana as you walk down its dirt roads. The Ban Ramat bus from Mae Sot stops here.

Waley วาเลย์
Twenty-six km from Mae Sot, Route 1206 splits south-west off Highway 1090 at Ban Saw Oh and terminates 15 km south at the border town of Waley, an important smuggling point. On the Burmese side is Phalu, one of the two main gateways to Kawthoolei, the Karen nation, still under Karen control since the Burmese began putting military pressure on the KNU. The other gateway is Three Pagodas Pass, further south in Kanchanaburi Province, though both the Burmese Government forces and the Mon insurgent army are vying for control there. Opium is cultivated extensively in this area, much to the chagrin of Thai authorities who send rangers in every year to cut down the production.

There are several daily songthaews to Waley from Mae Sot. Your passport may be checked at a police outpost before Waley.

Places to Stay
Outside of Mae Sot towards Tak is *Thawichailand*, a development of resort bungalows in castle-style architecture set off the highway and decorated with rather tasteless Thai and Chinese sculptures. The owner,

Thawichai, is a well-known right-winger and devotee of local-born Field Marshall Sarit (see History section in Facts for the Visitor), a dictator who ruled Thailand on and off from 1951 to 1963. The centrepiece of the garden area is a statue of the deceased Sarit (he died of cirrhosis). Bungalows start at 300B, but there doesn't seem to be a lot of business.

Still further afield is *Ban Ramat Village*, a jungle resort north of Mae Sot between the towns of Mae Ramat and Mae Sarit. Bungalows start at a reasonable 100B per night and staff arrange wildlife sightings for guests as this area is a natural habitat for wild deer, boar, tigers and other forest animals. Contact the *Mae Sot Hills Hotel* (tel 532601/8) for more information.

Getting There & Away
Songthaews to Waley depart Mae Sot frequently from near the mosque for 30B per person.

Buses to the Moei River (the border) leave from Prasat Withi Rd in Mae Sot, a block west of the Siam Hotel, every half-hour or so. The fare is 5B.

Highway 1085 runs north out of Mae Sot and all the way to Mae Hong Son Province. However, the section of the road north of Tha Song Yang is not yet sealed and the final 75 km was still very rough in 1989. The Government has plans to complete the sealing of the highway in the next two years or so, which will make it fairly easy to travel along the Burmese border from Mae Sot to Mae Sariang, passing through Mae Ramat, Mae Sarit, Tha Song Yang and Ban Sop Ngao.

To date, it has only been possible to get public transport out of Mae Sot as far as Tha Song Yang. The first leg is by songthaew to Mae Sarit (100B), then to Mae Ta-Waw (near Ban Tha Song Yang) there are occasional songthaews for 40B. At this point the traffic really thins out and about the only way you'll make it to Mae Sariang is to hitch (which could be a day's wait or more) or charter a pick-up from Mae Ta-Waw for 700B. You'd then have to hold on tight for the crunchy three to four-hour ride to Mae Sariang along a very bad road. Along the way you'll pass through thick forest, including a few stands of teak, Karen villages, the occasional work elephant and a Thai ranger post called the Black Warrior Kingdom.

UM PHANG กุ้มผาง

Highway 1090 goes south from Mae Sot to Um Phang, 150 km away. This road used to be called Death Highway because of the guerrilla activity in the area which hindered highway development. Those days are past, but lives are still lost because of brake failure or treacherous turns on this steep, winding road which passes through incredible mountain scenery.

In Um Phang district, you can hire rafts down the Mae Klong River for 300B plus 100B for the navigator (enquire at Um Phang Huts). The scenery along the river is stunning, especially just after the rainy season (November and December) when the cliffs are streaming with water and Thi Lachu Waterfall is at its best.

Near the Burmese border in Um Phang district is the culturally singular village of Leh Tawng Khu (Letongkhu). The villagers are for the most part Karen in language and dress, but their spiritual beliefs are unique to this area. They will eat only the meat of wild animals and hence do not raise chickens, ducks, pigs or beef cattle. They do, however, keep buffalo, oxen and elephants as work animals. Some of the men wear their hair in long topknots. The village priests, whom the Thais call *reu-sii* (rishi or sage) have long hair and beards and dress in brown robes. The priests live apart from the village in a temple and practise traditional medicine based on knowledge of herbs and ritual magic. Nobody seems to know where their religion comes from, although there are indications that it may be Hindu-related.

Places to Stay

Your choice is between *Um Phang Huts* (tel 513316) at 200B or accommodation provided by the *kamnoen* (precinct mayor) at a negotiable price.

Getting There & Away

Buses to Um Phang cost 70B and there's only one trip each day which usually leaves at about 8 am.

Lampang Province

LAMPANG TOWN เมือง ลำปาง

One hundred km from Chiang Mai is Lampang Town (population 47,000), which was inhabited as far back as the 7th century in the Dvaravati period and played an important part in the history of Hariphunchai. Many rich Thais have retired here so the wats of Lampang are well endowed. Two typical, well-cared for northern-style temples, Wat Phra Saeng and Wat Phra Kaew Don Tao (which for 32 years housed the Emerald Buddha), can be seen on opposite sides of the Wang River in the northern end of town.

Places to Stay

There are several economical choices along Boonyawat Rd, which runs through the centre of town. *Si Sa-Nga* (tel 217070) at No 213-215 has rooms with a fan and bath from 80B and air-con rooms from 200B. *Arunsak* (tel 217344) at No 90/9 is similar but starts at 100B. *Suandok* at No 168 has slightly better rooms from 150B with a fan and bath. Cheaper hotels are *Lucky* and *Thap Thim Thong*, both on Kao Mithuna Rd, with basic rooms from 60B with a fan and bath.

More upmarket is the refurbished *Asia Lampang* (tel 217844) at 229 Boonyawat Rd. It's now all air-con and costs from 300B. At the top end, *Thip Chang Garnet Lampang* (tel 218450 or 218337) at 54/22 Thakraw Noi Rd has air-con rooms from 300 to 800B.

Places to Eat

There are several good food stalls near the railway station. The *Jamthewi* restaurant, across from the slaughterhouse, has northern specialities such as laap and naem as well as fresh pig and calf brains, if you like that sort of thing.

Getting There & Away

The 7 am bus to Lampang from Phitsan-ulok's main bus station costs 63B and takes four hours. From Chiang Mai, buses for Lampang leave from the Chiang Mai Arcade Station and also from next to the Nawarat Bridge in the direction of Lamphun. The fare is 25B and the trip takes 1½ hours.

The bus station in Lampang is some way out of town – 5 to 10B by samlor if you arrive late at night.

To book an air-con bus from Lampang to Bangkok or Chiang Mai there is no need to go out to the bus station as the tour bus companies have offices in town.

AROUND LAMPANG PROVINCE
Wat Phra That Lampang Luang

Out of Lampang Town, this is a fantastic walled temple originally constructed during the Hariphunchai period (10th to 11th century) but restored in the 16th century. It is unique in overall design, inside and out, as it once served as both temple and fort against invading Burmese.

To get to the wat, you must catch a songthaew along Lampang's Praisani Rd to the small town of Ko Kha, about 20 km south-west of Lampang city. The fare should be about 10B. The wat is about three km from Ko Kha – either walk or catch a songthaew (3B) or motorcycle taxi (10B).

Young Elephant Training Centre

Fifty-four km north-east of Lampang Town, outside Ban Pang La, is a camp for the training of young elephants. Training takes place daily between 7 and 11 am except on public holidays and during the elephants' summer vacation from March to May. Elephants begin training when they're between three and five years old and the training continues for five years. Tasks they learn under the direction of their mahouts include pushing, carrying and piling logs, as well as bathing and walking in procession. Now that logging has been banned in Thailand, one wonders if there is going to be less demand for trained elephants.

Working elephants have a career of about 50 years, hence when young they are given two mahouts, one older and one younger (sometimes a father and son team) who can see the animal through its lifetime. Thai law

requires that elephants be retired and released into the wild at age 61. They often live 80 years or more.

Elephant mothers carry their calves for 22 months. An adult can run at speeds of up to 23 km per hour and put less weight on the ground per centimetre than a deer. Estimates put the number of wild elephants in Thailand at between 3000 and 4000. In 1952 there were 13,397 domestic elephants in Thailand and at the turn of the century it is estimated that there were at least 100,000 elephants working in Thailand. Until 1917, a white elephant appeared on the Thai national flag.

To get to the camp, take a bus from Lampang to Ban Pang La (18B) and follow the signs west off the highway for 1½ km.

Mae Hong Son Province

Mae Hong Son Province is 368 km from Chiang Mai by the southern road through Mae Sariang on Route 108, or 270 km by the northern road through Pai on Route 1095. Thailand's most north-western province is a crossroads for hill tribes (mostly Karen, with some Hmong, Lisu and Lahu), Burmese immigrants and opium traders living in and around the forested Pai River Valley.

As the province is so far from the influence of seawinds and is thickly forested and mountainous, the temperature seldom rises above 40°C, while in January the temperature can drop to 2°C. The air is often misty with ground fog in the winter and smoke from slash-and-burn agriculture in the hot season.

MAE HONG SON TOWN เมือง แม่ฮ่องสอน

The provincial capital (population 6600) is peaceful (boring to some), despite the intrusion of daily flights from Chiang Mai. Climb the hill west of town, Doi Kong Mu (1500 metres), to the Burmese-built Wat Phra That Doi Kong Mufor, from where there is a nice view of the valley. A lot of Burma-watching journalists and hill-tribe linguists/anthropologists hang out in Mae Hong Son – look for the khaki safari jackets. It is also becoming

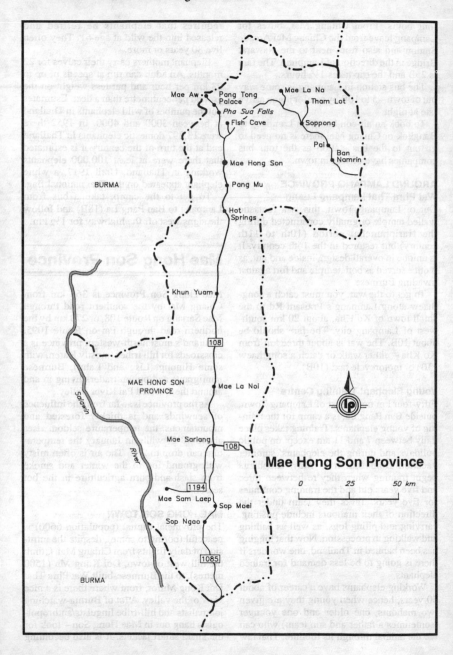

something of a traveller scene – there being more than 20 guest houses at last count.

Mae Hong Son is best visited between November and March when its beauty is at its peak. During the rainy season from June to October travel in the province can be difficult because there are few paved roads. During the hot season the Pai Valley fills with smoke from swidden agriculture. The only problem with going in the cool season is that the nights are downright cold – you'll need at least one thick sweater and a good pair of socks for mornings and evenings and a sleeping bag or several blankets for sleeping. If you're caught short, you might consider buying a blanket at the market (the made-in-China acrylic blankets are cheap) and cutting a hole in the middle for use as a poncho.

Wat Jong Kham & Jong Klang

Next to a large pond in the southern part of town are a couple of semi-interesting Burmese-style wats – Wat Jong Kham and Wat Jong Klang. Jong Kham was built nearly 200 years ago by Thai Yai or Shan people, who make up about 50% of the population of Mae Hong Son Province. Jong Klang houses 100-year-old glass paintings and wood carvings from Burma which depict the various lives of the Buddha, but you must ask to see them as they are kept locked away.

These wats are the focal point of the Poi Sang Long Festival in March when young Shan boys are ordained as novice monks (*buat luuk kaew*) during the school holidays. Like elsewhere in Thailand, the ordinants are carried on the shoulders of friends or relatives and paraded around the wat under festive parasols, but in the Shan custom the boys are dressed in ornate costumes (rather than simple white robes) and wear flower headdresses and facial make-up. Sometimes they ride on ponies.

Places to Stay

Most of the hotels in Mae Hong Son are along the main north-south road, Khunlum Praphat. *Siam Hotel* (tel 611148), next to the bus station, has decent rooms from 120B. Down the street the *Methi (Mae Tee)* (tel 611121) at No 55 is similar. Both have air-con rooms for 250B.

Sa-nguan Sin Hotel on Singhanat Bamrung Rd, which runs east-west, is an old wooden hotel with fairly clean rooms for 50B with a shared bath, or 70B with a private bath. Every room has two beds, which seems to be a tradition among old wooden hotels in the north.

Three years ago there were only two guest houses in town, but now Mae Hong Son has become so popular that I lost count at 20. Not far from the bus station, the original *Mae Hong Son Guest House* is still going strong on Khunlum Praphat Rd, Soi 2, but may be moving to a more secluded spot at the south end of the road beyond the Baiyoke Chalet Hotel. The guest house is a good source of information and inexpensive meals. Rates are still 30B per person in shared rooms.

North of there on Panglo Nikhom Rd is the *Galare Guest House* with bamboo-walled rooms for 40B. The Galare gets a few traveller complaints because it's near a slaughterhouse – pigs start squealing at about 3 am in the morning when the killing begins.

Also at this end of town (but far from the slaughterhouse) is the larger *Guysorn Guest House* (Sumpow's Place) at 6 Pracha Uthit Rd, with rates at 30B per person. In the hills beyond Guysorn are the secluded *Sang Tong Huts* which have panoramic views. The setting is pretty but it's not cheap at 50B for a dorm bed and up to 250B for a hut. Nearer to town and off the same road is *SR House*, a bit motel-like but singles/doubles are only 40/60B.

Back on Khunlum Praphat Rd, south of the bus terminal on the right and set back off the road a bit, is *Garden House*, where rustic singles/doubles are 50/80B.

Just a bit further down is *Khun Tu Guest House* (Khun Tu Trading) where one-bed rooms are 80B and two-bed rooms are 160B with a shared bath. The one four-bed air-con room with a hot bath costs 300B. Khun Tu also sells air tickets and rents motorcycles and bicycles. It has another guest house north of town called *Khun Tu Tarzan's House Resort*, with similar rates.

Down near the end of Khunlum Praphat

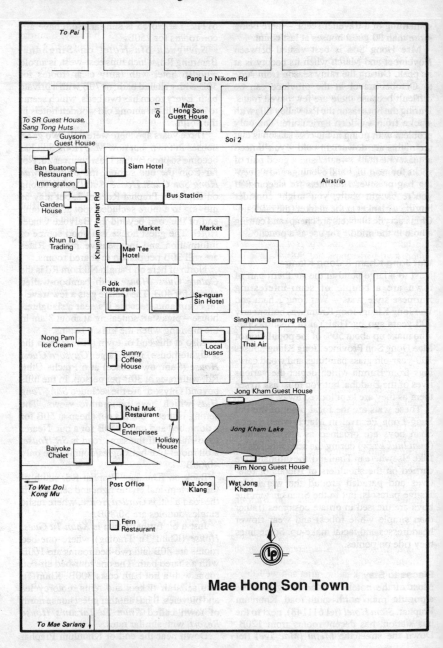

Mae Hong Son Town

To Pai

Pang Lo Nikom Rd

Soi 1

Mae
Hong Son
Guest House

Soi 2

To SR Guest House,
Sang Tong Huts

Guysorn
Guest House

Ban Buatong
Restaurant

Immigration

Garden
House

Khun Tu
Trading

Siam Hotel

Bus Station

Market

Market

Mae Tee
Hotel

Jok
Restaurant

Sa-nguan
Sin Hotel

Airstrip

Singhanat Bamrung Rd

Nong Pam
Ice Cream

Sunny
Coffee
House

Local
buses

Thai Air

Khai Muk
Restaurant

Don
Enterprises

Holiday
House

Baiyoke
Chalet

Jong Kham
Guest House

Jong Kham Lake

Rim Nong Guest House

To Wat Doi
Kong Mu

Post Office

Wat Jong
Klang

Wat Jong
Kham

Fern
Restaurant

To Mae Sariang

Rd next to the Khai Muk Restaurant and behind Don Enterprises is *Don Guest House*, where very basic singles cost 30B and doubles are from 40 to 50B.

Fern House (tel 611374), 87 Khunlum Praphat Rd, has been recommended and costs 60B for a double with a shared bath.

The top-end hotel in Mae Hong Son is *Baiyoke Chalet Hotel* (tel 611486), formerly the Mitniyom, at 90 Khunlum Praphat. It's got all the typical amenities for 650B standard and 1000B superior.

In the area of Jong Kham Lake are three very pleasant guest houses. *Jong Kham Guest House* overlooks the lake from the north and has very clean singles/doubles for 50/100B. A shared hot shower is available and towels are provided. On the west side of the lake and also good is *Holiday House*, where two-bed rooms are 80B, with a hot shower available. On the south side of the lake is *Rim Nong Guest House*, a friendly place with a little restaurant on the water's edge. Rates are a low 25B per person in the house on the lake, or 30B per person in the larger house back across the road.

Places to Eat

Mae Hong Son isn't known for its food, but there are a few decent places to eat besides the guest houses. *Khai Muk* is one of the better Thai-Chinese restaurants on Khunlum Praphat Rd. There is also a *jok* (broken-rice soup) place near the Mae Tee Hotel that sells American breakfasts for 20 to 25B. The morning market behind the Mae Tee Hotel is a good place to buy food for trekking. Get there before 8 am.

Across from the Siam Hotel on Khunlum Praphat Rd is the pleasant *Ban Buatong* cafe/restaurant, which has good Thai food and western breakfasts. Down the road on the left, across from Nong Pam Ice Cream, is the air-con *Sunny Coffee House*, a big night hangout for young Thais. A better place for an evening drink is the quiet and well-decorated *Lai Phat* at 52/11 Khunlum Praphat Rd, near the Mae Tee Hotel.

Getting There & Away

Air Thai Airways flies to Mae Hong Son from Chiang Mai twice a day at 11.25 am and 4.15 pm. On Tuesday, Thursday, Saturday and Sunday there's a third flight at 12.15 pm. The fare is 310B and the flight takes 35 minutes. From Bangkok it's 1420B and requires a change of plane in Chiang Mai.

Bus From Chiang Mai the bus trip is rather gruelling over the northern route through Pai – only go this way if you plan to stop in Pai and/or Soppong. The southern route through Mae Sariang is much more manageable, not only because it's over sealed roads but because the bus stops every two hours for a 10 to 15-minute break. Either way the trip takes eight to nine hours and costs 100B (97B via Mae Sariang). The old Pai road, built by the Japanese in WW II, will probably be completely sealed and restructured within the next few years.

The bus to Mae Hong Son via Mae Sariang leaves Chiang Mai (Arcade Bus Station) every two hours between 6.30 am and 9 pm. The fare is 97B. There is also one daily air-con minibus to Mae Hong Son via Mae Sariang at 9 pm for 175B, which takes eight hours. The Pai bus leaves the same station four times a day at 7, 8.30 and 11 am and 2 pm. The fare is 50B (you must change buses in Pai to continue on to Mae Hong Son). Departure times may change as the Government paves more of the Chiang Mai to Pai to Mae Hong Son road.

Getting Around

Most of the Mae Hong Son town is walkable. To points outside of town, songthaews leave from Singhanat Bamrung Rd. Several guest houses rent bicycles and motorcycles, including Khun Tu on Khunlum Praphat Rd.

AROUND MAE HONG SON TOWN
Trekking & Rafting

Trekking out of Mae Hong Son can be arranged at Mae Hong Son Guest House or at Don Enterprises, 77/1 Khunlum Praphat Rd. Other trekking agencies are along Khunlum Praphat Rd and Singhanat Bamrung Rd. There is a nearby Karen village which can be visited without a guide by walking one or two hours outside of town.

Raft trips on the Pai River to Pai and beyond are gaining in popularity, as are boat trips into the Karen state (or nation, depending on your political alliances) of Burma. The Pai River raft trips can be good if the raft holds up (it's not uncommon for them to fall apart and/or sink), but the Burma trip, which attracts travellers who want to see the Padaung or long-necked people, is a bit of a rip-off, costing about 700B for a four-hour trip through unspectacular scenery to see maybe four Padaung people who are practically captives of the Karen operators involved.

Mae Aw แม่แอ่

One of the best day trips you can do out of the provincial capital is to Mae Aw, north of Mae Hong Son on a mountain peak at the Burmese border. A songthaew there costs 100B return per person during the dry season or 200B in the rainy season and leaves from Singhanat Bamrung Rd near the telephone office – get there at about 8 am. The trip takes two hours and passes Shan, Karen and Meo villages, the Pang Tong Summer Palace and waterfalls.

Mae Aw is a settlement of Hmong (Meo) and KMT peoples, one of the last true KMT outposts in Thailand. Occasionally there is fighting along the border between the KMT and the Shan United Army, led by the infamous opium warlord Khun Sa. When this happens, public transport to these areas is usually suspended and you are advised against going without a guide.

You can also walk from Mae Hong Son to Chiang Mai if you're up to it. A very high, steep mountain path begins in the mountains on the south-east side of town. The trip is said to take seven days and is supposed to be safe. There are only a few villages along the route, but the scenery is incredible. Food must be carried part of the way (this is a trek for the hardy and experienced). Ask at the Mae Hong Son Guest House for details.

Mae La-Na แม่ลานา

Between Mae Hong Son and Pai is an area of forests, mountains, streams and limestone caves dotted with Shan and hill-tribe villages. Some of Mae Hong Son's most beautiful scenery is within a day's walk of the Shan villages of Mae La-Na and Soppong, both of which have accommodation.

The Mae La-Na junction is 55 km from Mae Hong Son Town or 56 km from Pai. The village of Mae La-Na is six km north of the junction and from here you can trek to several Red and Black Lahu villages and a couple of large caves.

Soppong สบป่อง

Soppong is a small but relatively prosperous market village a couple of hours north-west of Pai and about 70 km from Mae Hong Son.

Close to Soppong are several Lisu, Karen and Lahu hill-tribe villages that can easily be visited on foot. Enquire at the Jungle Guest House or Cave Lodge for reliable information. It's important to ask about the current situation as the Burma border area is somewhat sensitive due to the opium trade.

Tham Lot About eight km north of Soppong is Tham Lot, a large limestone cave with a wide stream running through it. It is possible to hike all the way through the cave (approximately 400 metres) by following the stream, though it requires some wading back and forth. Besides the main chamber there are three side chambers that can be reached by ladders – it takes two or three hours to see the whole thing. The national park caretakers at the entrance to the park will rent you a gas lantern for 50B to take into the caverns. A guide will cost another 50B.

Tham Lot is one of two local caves which happen to be the longest, known caves in mainland South-East Asia, though some as yet unexplored caves in southern Thailand may be even longer. The other is Tham Nam Lang.

Tham Nam Lang Near Ban Nam Khong, 30 km north-west of Soppong, this cave is nine km long and is said to be one of the largest caves in the world in terms of volume. There are many other caves in the area, some of which contain 2000-year-old wooden coffins.

Top: Abbot, Wat Si Nong Song, Chiang Khan (JC)
Bottom: Akha house, Doi Tung (JC)

Top: Monk, Wat Phra Phutthabaat, Pasang (JC)
Left: Avalokitesvara, Muang Singh (DS)
Right: Rice farmers near Ayuthaya (TM)

Places to Stay

There is a sprinkling of accommodation in the area, mostly concentrated around Soppong. The *Soppong Guest House* has several simple A-frame huts for 50B. Behind the Muslim Restaurant next door are a few rooms called the *Central Guest House*. Better accommodation is at the friendly *Jungle Guest House*, one km west on the road to Mae Hong Son, where well-designed huts are 30B per person and there is also a good restaurant.

Lisu Lodge, a few km east of Soppong off Highway 1095 in Ban Namrin, is run by a very friendly and helpful Lisu family. A bed is 30B per night and large meals are 20B.

The popular *Cave Lodge*, run by a former trekking guide from Chiang Mai and her Australian husband, is near Tham Lot. Word has it the atmosphere at the Cave Lodge is quite business-like these days, however. A sign in the lodge expresses regret that other guest houses in the area are getting a piece 'of the cake we baked'! Beds are 30B in a large commonroom and meals are from 20 to 30B.

Nearer to the cave, on Huay Nam Lang (the stream that flows into the cave), is *Tum Lod (Tham Lot)*, which has 30B huts on the water and on a hill overlooking the stream. Follow signs in Soppong to get to either of these guest houses – it's about a 1½-hour walk to Ban Tham, the village closest to Tham Lot cave. The village headman rents rooms to travellers and the Forestry Department has a few bungalows near the cave for 20B per person.

At Ban Nam Khong is the *Wilderness Lodge*, run by the same family that owns the Cave Lodge. Huts are 30B per person.

Just outside Mae La-Na village is the *Mae Lana Guest House* which has four large doubles with mosquito nets for 50B per night and a four-bed dorm for 20B per person. Isabelle and Niwet cook French and Thai food for travellers, and plan to expand the facilities so that they can accommodate a maximum of 16 guests.

About 12 km north of Mae La-Na in the Black Lahu village of Ban Huay Hea (very close to the Burmese border) is the *Lahu Guest House*, run by a village teacher who speaks English. Simple accommodation is 20B per person and the money goes into a community fund.

Other less convenient guest houses can be found around Mae Hong Son – the touts will find you at the bus terminal. On the road to Mae Aw, 54 km away and six km before the KMT village, is the *Hill Guest House* where a dorm bed is 20B and singles/doubles are 30/50B.

Places to Eat

In Soppong, try eating at a noodle stand where the bus stops and/or across the road at a Muslim restaurant which serves khao soi and other dishes. Aside from these, you're at the mercy of the guest-house kitchens.

Getting There & Away

Pai to Mae Hong Son buses stop in Soppong and there are two or three each day in either direction. From Mae Hong Son, it's about 2½ hours by bus and costs 30B. The trip between Pai and Soppong costs 20B and takes from 1½ to two hours.

MAE SARIANG แม่สะเรียง

Many of the hill-tribe settlements in Mae Hong Son Province are concentrated in the districts/towns of Khun Yuam, Mae La Noi and Mae Sariang (population 7400), which are good departure points for treks. Of these three small towns, Mae Sariang is the largest and offers the most facilities for use as a base. Near Mae Sam Laep, west on the Burmese border, can be reached by songthaew or motorcycle, and from there you can hire boats for trips down the scenic Salawin River.

Although there is little to see in Mae Sariang, it's a pleasant enough town and the travel scene is slowly expanding. Two Burmese/Shan temples, Wat Jong Sung (Uthayarom) and Wat Si Bunruang, just off Mae Sariang's main street not far from the bus station, are worth a visit if you have time.

Salawin Jungle Tours at the Riverside View Guest House can arrange day and overnight boat trips on the Salawin River that

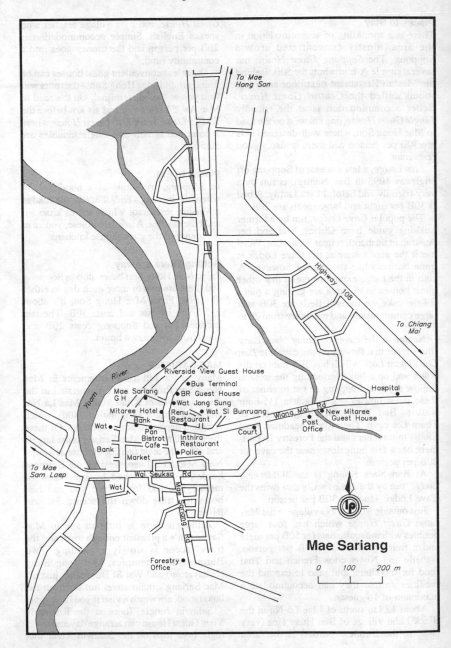

To Mae
Hong Son

Highway 108

To Chiang
Mai

River

Yuam

Riverside View Guest House

Bus Terminal

Mae Sariang
G H

BR Guest House

Wat Jong Sung

Mitaree Hotel

Renu
Restaurant

Wat Si Bunruang

Bank

Wiang Mai Rd

Hospital

New Mitaree
Guest House

Wat

Bank

Pan
Bistrot
Cafe

Inthira
Restaurant

Court

Post
Office

Market

Police

To Mae
Sam Laep

Wat

Wai Seuksa Rd

Mae Sariang Rd

Forestry
Office

Mae Sariang

0   100   200 m

include stops in Karen villages and Mae Sam Laep.

About 36 km south-east of Mae Sariang at Ban Mae Waen is Pan House, where a guide named T Weerapan (Mr Pan) leads local treks. To get to Ban Mae Waen, take a Chiang Mai-bound bus east on Route 108 and get out at the 68 km marker. Mae Waen is a five-km walk south up a mountain.

Next to the service station across from the bus terminal is a small motorcycle rental place.

Places to Stay

Mae Sariang's one hotel, *Mitaree Hotel*, near the bus station on Mae Sariang Rd, has doubles for 100B in the old wooden wing (which they call Mitaree Guest House) or for 150B in the new wing. Air-con rooms in the new wing cost 300B.

On Wiang Mai Rd near the post office is *New Mitaree Guest House* run by the same people. It has large but rather cheerless concrete doubles for 100B. A better place is *BR Guest House* next to the bus terminal, where a clean two-bed room is 80B.

If you turn left out of the bus terminal and then make the first right you'll come to the popular *Mae Sariang Guest House* on Mongkhonchai Rd, opposite the entrance to Wat Uthayarom. Rooms are 50B without a bath or 100B with one. Around the corner on Laeng Phanit Rd on the Yuam River is the newer *Riverside View Guest House* where rooms are 50B per person.

Out of town, the village headman in Mae Sam Laep lets rooms for 50B per person. In the nearby village of Mae Khong Kha, the *Salween Guest House* also has rooms for 50B per person. There's no public transport to Mae Khong Kha. You can either be dropped off there on a trek or rent a motorcycle.

In Khun Yuam, *Mit Khun Yuam Hotel* has rooms from 60B.

Places to Eat

The *Riverside View Guest House* on Laeng Phanit Rd has a pleasant restaurant area downstairs.

The *Inthira Restaurant*, on the left side of Wiang Mai Rd as you enter town from

Chiang Mai (not far from the Mae Sariang Rd intersection), serves what is considered some of Thailand's best *kai phat bai kaphrao* (chicken fried in holy basil and chillies). The Inthira is also well known for its batter-fried frogs, though you won't see them on the English menu.

Across the street is the similar but less popular *Renu Restaurant*. Both places have English menus. Around the corner on the lane leading to Wat Si Bunruang is *Reuan Phrae Restaurant*, which serves Chinese, Thai, Muslim and vegetarian food. Prices on the bilingual menu are moderate and it's a clean, quiet place.

The *Pan Bistrot Cafe* at 158 Wiang Mai Rd, between Mae Sariang Rd and the river, serves medium-priced western and Thai food. The food stall next to the BR Guest House on Mae Sariang Rd serves excellent khao soi and khanom jiin for less than 10B.

Getting There & Away

Bus Buses to Mae Sariang leave Chiang Mai's Arcade Station about every two hours between 6.30 and 9 pm. The trip takes about four hours and costs 50B. From Mae Sariang to Khun Yuam it's another 30B or 47B to Mae Hong Son. There's one daily bus between Tak and Mae Sariang for 77B which takes six hours.

A bus for Bangkok leaves Mae Sariang daily at 5 pm, arriving in Bangkok at 6 am. The fare is 152B.

Songthaew Local songthaews go from Mae Sariang to the following Karen villages: Sop Han (20B); Mae Han (40B); and Huay Khong (35B).

Songthaews also ply Route 1085, the road south to Mae Sot, as far as Mae Ngao (Sop Ngao), the closest you can get to Tha Song Yang or Mae Sarit by public transport from Mae Sariang. To Pha Pha it's 50B, to Huay Pho it's 70B, to Mae Kha-Tuan it's 100B and to Mae Ngao it's 200B. (See Mae Sot's Getting There & Away section)

One songthaew goes to Mae Sam Laep on the Salawin River every morning. The fare for men is 50B and for women it's 100B –

the men have to get out and push the truck on bad sections of the road.

PAI ปาย

It first appears that there's not a lot to see in Pai, a peaceful crossroads town about halfway between Chiang Mai and Mae Hong Son on Route 1095. But if you stick around a few days and talk to some of the locals, you may discover some beautiful out-of-town spots in the surrounding hills. Any of the guest houses in town can provide information on local trekking (there are Shan, Lahu, KMT and Lisu villages nearby) and some do guided treks for about 100B per day. Rafting from Pai to Mae Hong Son is also possible – it takes five days when conditions are favourable.

Wat Phra That Mae Yen

Simply known as Wat Mae Yen, this is a newish temple built on a hill with a good view overlooking the valley. Walk one km east from the main intersection in town, across a stream and through a village, to get to the stairs (353 steps) which lead to the top. The monks are vegetarian, uncommon in Thai Buddhist temples. Six k... further down the same road is a waterfall.

Places to Stay

Across from the bus terminal is the friendly *Duang Guest House*, where clean rooms are 30B per person. A big plus is their hot-water shower. Further east on this road in an old wooden house is the *Family Guest House*, which charges 20B per person, but fighting cocks are raised out the back so it's not too quiet. At the far west end of this road, past the hospital, is *Kim Guest House*, which is a bit isolated but quiet. Rooms without a bath are 30B per person or 40B with a bath.

Out on the main road through town is the *Pai Guest House*, the town's first. It's back towards Chiang Mai, where the bus from Chiang Mai stops on the main street. Rates are 30B per person. You might run into the infamous Buffalo Bill, who helped to start an informal chain of guest houses throughout the north, recognisable by the water buffalo skull hanging out the front. These places are not actually owned by any one group, but they all know each other and share a staff of young Thais. These days Bill divides his time between Pai, Chiang Rai and trekking in the hills.

Across the street behind the Pai in the Sky Cafe is the *Pai in the Sky Guest House* with none-too-special rooms for 30B per person.

A little further down the street in the same direction, the *Wiang Pai Hotel* is a traditional wooden hotel with 15 spacious rooms. Two can sleep in one bed for 50B, otherwise the charge is 40B for one person alone. A two-bed room is 80B. Behind the old hotel is a new wing where a double with a bath is 100B. Hot water is available on request.

On the southern edge of town, off the road a bit, is the *Shan Guest House* run by Boonyang, a Shan who has worked in Bangkok and Saudi Arabia. The atmosphere and food are good and Boonyang tries hard to please. Shan-style bungalows are single/double 40/50B with a bath. If these are full, singles/doubles in the main building are 30/50B with a shared bath. A hot shower is available.

Further still, on the other side of the road, is the *New Pai in the Sky Guest House* with clean rooms for 60B without a bath or 80B with one.

Along the Pai River east of town are three bungalow operations. Just off the road to Wat Mae Yen and next to the bridge is the *Riverside Guest House*, which has places to sit along the river and huts for 40B single or 60B double. Further down the river, the *Pai River Lodge* has nice huts arranged in a large circle with a dining/lounge area on stilts in the middle. Rates are only 25B per person. North along the river not far from the bus terminal is the slightly up-market (for Pai) *Pai Resort*. Its clean, quiet, A-frames with two beds, a bath, electricity and mosquito net go for 50B per person. All three places have hot-water showers.

Places to Eat

Most of the places to eat in Pai are along the main north-south and east-west roads. The *Homesick Restaurant* and *Pai in the Sky Cafe* get most of the traveller business. Both serve

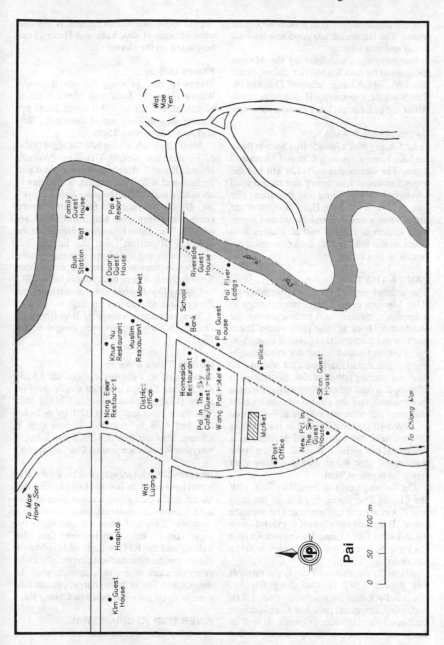

western and modified Thai food at moderate prices. The Homesick has good wholewheat bread and mat seating.

For authentic local food try the *Muslim Restaurant* for noodles and rice dishes, or the *Khun Nu*, which has a variety of Thai dishes. The *Nong Beer* restaurant is also quite good. All of the guest houses in Pai serve food too.

Getting There & Away
From Chiang Mai's Arcade Bus Station there are four buses a day at 7, 8.30 and 11 am and 2 pm. The distance is only 134 km but the trip takes about four hours due to the road conditions in Mae Hong Son Province. The fare is 50B. From Mae Hong Son there are three buses a day at 7 and 11 am and 2 pm. This stretch is 111 km and also takes four hours as the road is also under re-construction. The fare is 50B.

FANG & THA TON ฝาง ท่าตอน
The present city of Fang was founded by King Mengrai in the 13th century, though as a human settlement and trading centre the locale dates back at least 1000 years. There are Yao and Karen villages nearby which you can visit on your own, but for most people Fang is just a road marker on the way to Tha Ton, the starting point for Kok River trips to Chiang Rai (and other points along the river in between), and for guided or solo treks to the many hill-tribe settlements in the region.

About 10 km west of Fang at Ban Muang Chom, near the agricultural station, is a system of hot springs. Just ask for the 'baw nam rawn' (hot water springs), 'baw nam hawn' in northern Thai.

On the way north to Fang/Tha Ton, visit the Chiang Dao caves, five km off the road and 72 km north of Chiang Mai. The entrance fee is 5B and the cave is said to extend some 10 to 14 km into Chiang Dao mountain (but the lighting system only runs in about half a km or so).

About 20 km short of Fang is the turn-off for Route 1249 to Doi Ang Khang, Thailand's Little Switzerland. This 1300-metre (approximate) peak has a cool climate year-round and produces flowers, as well as fruits and vegetables that are usually found only in more temperate climates. A few hill-tribe villages (Lahu, Lisu and Hmong) can be visited on the slopes.

Places to Stay
Places to stay in Fang include the older *Wiang Fang*, *Si Sukit* and *Metta Wattana* hotels, all for about 70B a room. More up-market digs in Fang are at the *Chok Thani* and *Roza*, both from 150B.

Most travellers who spend the night prefer to be near the pier in Tha Ton. *Phanga's House* (Karen Coffeehouse) is the old stand-by here and is 30B per person, but it's nearly an hour's walk from the pier. *Thip's Travellers House* has received favourable reports from travellers and singles/doubles are 40/50B. The *Siam Kok Guest House*, in the opposite direction from the bridge, has similar rates and a pleasant cafe downstairs. Further on this road nearest the pier is *Chan Kasem Guest House* with rooms from 40B.

Chiang Dao has one old wooden hotel, the *Pieng Dao*, with rooms for 80B.

The Yunnanese village of Ban Khum on Doi Ang Khang also has some bungalows for rent.

Getting There & Away
Bus Buses to Fang leave from the Chang Phuak Bus Station north of the White Elephant (Chang Phuak) Gate in Chiang Mai. The three-hour trip costs 32B by ordinary bus and 40B by minibus. If you stop at Chiang Dao the fare is 18B. From Fang, a songthaew will take you to Tha Ton for 6B.

Motorcycle Motorcycle trekkers can also travel between Tha Ton and Doi Mae Salong, 48 km north-east along a sometimes treacherous, unpaved mountain road. There are a couple of Lisu and Akha villages along the way. The 27 km or so between Doi Mae Salong and the KMT village of Hua Muang Ngam are the most difficult, especially in the rainy season when this stretch may be impassable. For an extra charge, you can take a motorcycle on some boats to Chiang Rai.

RIVER TRIP TO CHIANG RAI
From Tha Ton you can make a five-hour boat

trip to Chiang Rai down the Kok River. The boat leaves at about 12 noon and costs about 160B per person, depending on the boat. You can also charter a boat, which between eight or 10 people works out at much the same cost per person but gives you more room. The trip is a bit of a tourist trap these days as the villages along the way sell coke and there are lots of TV aerials – but it's still fun. To catch a boat on the same day from Chiang Mai you'd have to leave by 7 or 7.30 am at the latest and make no stops on the way. The 6 am bus is the best bet.

The travel time downriver depends to some extent on the river height, but usually takes from three or four hours. Sometimes you get an armed guard on the boat but he seems to spend most of the time asleep with his machine gun in a plastic sack. You could actually make this trip in a day from Chiang Mai, catching a bus back from Chiang Rai as soon as you arrive, but it's far better to stay in Fang or Tha Ton, then Chiang Rai or Chiang Saen and travelling on. You may sometimes have to get off and walk and it's also possible to make the trip (much more slowly) upriver, despite the rapids.

These days some travellers take the boat to Chiang Rai in two stages, stopping first in Mae Salak, a large Lahu village which is about a third of the distance. The boat fare to Mae Salak is 40B. From here you can trek in the vicinity of the river to other Shan, Thai and hill-tribe villages, or do longer treks south to Wawi, a large multi-ethnic community of Jiin Haw (Chinese refugees), Lahu, Lisu, Akha, Shan, Karen, Yao and Thai peoples. The Wawi area has dozens of hill-tribe villages of various ethnicities, including the largest Akha community in Thailand (Saen Charoen) and the oldest Lisu settlement (Doi Chang). If this kind of trip appeals to you, pick up the Wawi or Kok River trekking maps at DK Books in Chiang Mai. The maps mark trails and village locations.

Another alternative is to trek south from Mae Salak all the way to the town of Mae Suai, where you can catch a bus on to Chiang Rai or back to Chiang Mai.

Several of the guest houses in Tha Ton now organise raft trips down the river – you pay for a raft to be built and then pole yourself with or without a guide. This can easily take days, especially when the raft falls apart and has to be rebuilt. A better way is to pull together a small group of travellers and charter one of the house rafts with a guide and cook for a two or three-day journey down the river, stopping off in villages along the way. A house raft generally goes for 2400B and takes up to six people.

Warning In February 1988 a couple of boats going down the Kok were ambushed by Akha bandits who shot and killed two passengers (one Briton and one Thai) and wounded two others. The bandits, armed with assault rifles, fired from the shore and forced the boats to turn into the bank. The boats were part of an organised tour, so ostensibly the regularly scheduled boats are less of a target. The rafts, on the other hand, make an especially easy target. Chiang Rai police have tightened security on the river and now have regular river patrols and identity checks. Nevertheless, don't travel on your own down the river with any valuables you can't afford to lose. If you go on a tour boat, insist on an armed guard.

Chiang Rai Province

CHIANG RAI TOWN เมือง เชียงราย

A little more than 100 km from Chiang Mai, Chiang Rai Town (population 41,000) is known as the gateway to the Golden Triangle. The main reasons to come here are to do a hill-tribe trek out of Chiang Rai or to travel by boat up the Kok River. Otherwise, the town is simply a main bus junction for proceeding on to Mae Chan, Chiang Saen and Mae Sai in the Golden Triangle proper.

Chiang Rai was founded by King Mengrai in 1262 as part of the Lanna kingdom. It became a Thai territory in 1786. Its most historic monument, Wat Phra Kaew, once hosted the Emerald Buddha during its circuitous travels (the image eventually ended up at the wat of the same name in Bangkok). It now houses a replica of Chiang Mai's Wat

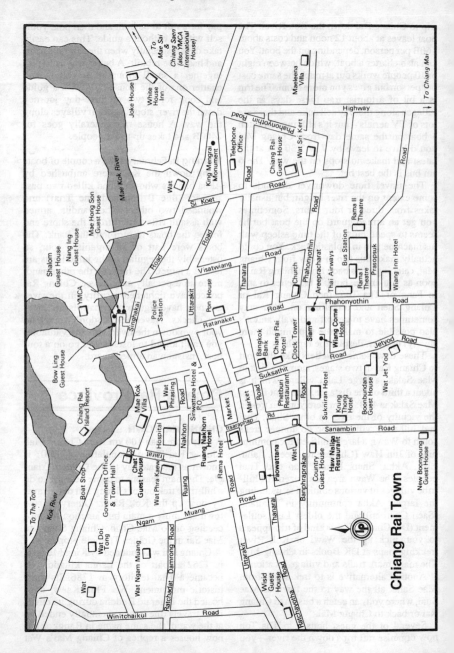

To Mae Sai &
Chiang Saen
(also YMCA
International
House)

To Chiang Mai

Joke House

White
House
Inn

Maeleena
Villa

Highway

Telephone
Office

King Mengrai
Monument

Phahonyothin Road

Chiang Rai
Guest House

Wat Sri Kert

Wat

Road

Si Koet

Road

Rama II
Theatre

Mae Hong Son
Guest House

Nang Ing
Guest House

Thanarai

Road

Bus Station

Prasopsuk

Wiang Inn Hotel

Shalom
Guest House

Visatwiang

Road

Church

Rama I
Theatre

YMCA

Uttarakit

Road

Phahonyothin

Thai Airways

Areepracharat

Singhakai

Pon House

Ratanaket

Road

Phahonyothin

Road

Road

Police Station

Siam

Wiang Come
Hotel

Bow Ling
Guest House

Bangkok
Bank

Chiang Rai
Hotel

Clock Tower

Road

Jetyod

Road

Wat Jet Yod

Chiang Rai
Island Resort

Mae Kok
Villa

Wat
Phrasing

Sirwattana Hotel &
P.O.

Suksathit

Road

Phetburi
Restaurant

Sukniran Hotel

Krung
Thong
Hotel

Boonbundan
Guest House

Boat Stop

Hospital

Market

Market

Road

Itsaraphap

Nakhon

Ruang Nakhorn
Hotel

Rama Hotel

Sanambin

Road

To Tha Ton

Thararat

Rd

Chat
Guest House

Wat Phra Kaew

Ruang

Road

Paowattana

Wat

Haw Naliga
Restaurant

Country
Guest House

New Boonyoung
Guest House

Kok River

Government Office
& Town Hall

Wat Doi
Tong

Ngam

Muang

Thanarai

Road

Banphraprakan

Road

Wat Ngam Muang

Ratchadan

Damrong

Road

Road

Uttarakit

Road

Wisid
Guest House

Wat

Winitchaikul

Road

Ratchayotha

Road

Chiang Rai Town

Phra Singh Buddha image. Other temples of mild interest in Chiang Rai are Wat Jet Yot and Wat Klang Muang.

From the Kok River pier, boats can take you upriver as far as Fang. An hour's boat ride from Chiang Rai is Ban Ruammit, a fair-sized Karen village. From here you can trek to Lahu, Yao, Akha and Lisu villages – all within a day. Inexpensive room and board (20B per person, meals 10B) are available in many villages in the river area. Another popular area for do-it-yourself trekkers is Wawi, south of the river town of Mae Salak near the end of the river route. (See River Trip to Chiang Rai.)

Places to Stay

Guest Houses Near the Kok River boat pier for boats from Tha Ton is *Mae Kok Villa*, 445 Singhakai Rd, which has dorm accommodation for 30B, bungalows with a fan and hot bath for 120B and large singles/doubles with a fan and hot bath for 140/160B. IYH cardholders get a 10% discount on these rates. Another nice place near the Kok River pier is *Chat House*, at 1 Trairat Rd. It's an old Thai house with singles/doubles with a shared bath for 30/50B, or 60/70B with a private bath. Bicycles are for rent and it offers several treks.

A bit east of here in a network of sois off Singakai Rd are several small family guest houses which are fairly new on the scene. First is the clean and friendly *Bow Ling House* (tel 712704) which has singles/doubles with a shared bath for 40/60B and rooms with a private bath for 80B. A hot-water shower is available. Next is *Shalom Guest House*, which so far is two brick bungalows, each with two beds and a private bath for 100B a night. Down the soi from Shalom is the *Nang Ing Guest House* where dorm beds are 30B and private rooms without a bath are from 60 to 100B. The rooms at Nang Ing are a bit overpriced for what you get. Next is the very pleasant *Mae Hong Son Guest House of Chiang Rai*, run by the same family as the original guest house in Mae Hong Son. Rooms are 40B with a shared bath or 80B with a private bath. This one has a very nice garden cafe and a

hot-water shower. It also rents motorcycles and organises treks.

Down in the centre of town are several larger guest houses. *Chiang Rai Guest House* at 717/2 Srikerd (Si Koet) Rd is the typical (in this case, the original) northern guest house with a water buffalo skull out front, although it's a bit run down. Rooms are 50B or 30B per person. It's near the bus station but a bit away from everything else in Chiang Rai.

Pon House, at 503 Ratanaket Rd, is better located and better value with clean rooms for 50B per person. The food is good and it now has a hot-water shower too.

Out on Ratchayotha Rd, west of the clock tower, is *Wisid (Wisit) Guest House* (tel 713279) at No 21/4. Rooms in this old teak and bamboo house are 60B with a shared hot bath. It lends motorcycles for in-town trips at no charge and organises treks. A bit closer in at 389 Banphaprakan Rd is *Country Guest House* (tel 712994), another old Thai house. Singles/doubles are 40/60B with a shared bath and motorcycles are for rent. The atmosphere seems rather cold and business-like.

In the southern part of town are *Boonbundan Guest House* (tel 712914) and *New Boonyoung Guest House* (tel 712893), both in walled compounds. The Boonbundan is at 1005/13 Jetyod Rd and offers a choice of accommodation – in small rooms off the garden, in huts or in the new air-con building overlooking the garden – something to suit all budgets. Small rooms without a bath are 40B, slightly larger singles/doubles with a hot bath are 50/80B. Hut singles/doubles with a fan and a bath are 100/150B and large singles/doubles with a fan in the new building are 150/200B or 300/350B with air-con. The Boonbundan loans bicycles, rents out motorcycles and runs treks. *New Boonyoung* at 1054/5 Sanambin Rd has a similar arrangement minus the new building. Singles/doubles without a bath are 40/60B and 80/100B with a hot bath.

The north-eastern part of town near the highway to Mae Sai has a couple of guest houses. *White House Inn* is just off the highway and has large singles/doubles for

40/60B and a few motorcycles for rent. A bit further north down Rong Kasat Rd is *Joke House* (tel 712945), another Buffalo Bill project. Dorm beds are 30B, huts are 70B and singles/doubles in a long concrete building are 40/80B with a fan and a hot shower. Joke House runs treks and rents out motorcycles and cars.

Finally, there's *Maleena Villa*, 863 Wat Phra Non Rd, with rath dull bungalows from 160B.

Also out of town, on the highway to Mae Sai past the touristy handicraft centre, is the YMCA's *Golden Triangle International House* (tel 713785). This is a very modern establishment with dorm beds for 50B, singles/doubles with a fan and private bath for 140/180B, or 225/300B air-con. All rooms come with hot water and a telephone. *Lanna Guest House* (tel 713924) is also off the highway about 1½ km past the river bridge. Singles/doubles in the wooden bungalows are 30/50B and dorm beds are 20B. Phone from town or contact its office at Discovery Tours opposite the Wiang Come Hotel and free transport will be provided to the guest house. You can get to either of these two by hopping on any bus (about 5B) heading up Highway 110 (Phahonyothin Rd).

Hotels *Rama Hotel* (tel 311344) is at 331/4 Trairat Rd in the town centre, a couple of blocks from the clock tower and next to Wat Moon Muang. It has clean rooms from 180B or from 275B with air-con. Restaurants, night clubs and theatres are nearby.

On Suksathit Rd near the clock tower and district government building is *Chiang Rai Hotel* (tel 311266) where rooms with a fan cost from 80B. Also centrally located is the *Sukniran* (tel 311055) at 424/1 Banphraprakan Rd, between the clock tower and Wat Ming Muang, and around the corner from the Chiang Rai Hotel. Rooms start at 140B.

Similar to the Sukniran but cheaper is the *Siam* at 531/6-8 Banphraprakan, where rates start at 100B with a fan and bath.

Ruang Nakhorn, 25 Ruang Nakhon Rd, near the hospital, allows four people to share

a room with a bath for 200B. Bungalows are 140B and doubles are 180B or 220B air-con.

If you favour the old Thai-Chinese type of hotel, check out the *Areepracharat* at 541 Phahonyothin, where rooms start at 60B, or the *Paowattana* at 150 Thanarai Rd, which has rooms for 80B. Another cheap hotel is the *Siriwattana* at 485 Uttarakit Rd next to the post office, where singles/doubles are 50/70B and a couple of bungalows are 40 to 50B.

Near the bus station is the clean and efficient *Krung Thong Hotel* (tel 711033) at 412 Sanambin Rd. Large rooms with a fan and a bath start at 120B, while air-con rooms cost 250B.

Near the top of the price scale is the *Wiang Inn* (tel 711543) at 893 Phahonyothin Rd, with rooms, all air-con, from 450B. It has a swimming pool and other luxuries too.

Chiang Rai's newest hotel, *Wiang Come* (tel 711800), at 869/90 Premawiphat Rd in the Chiang Rai Trade Centre, is of international class with air-con rooms from 500 to 800B, complete with a TV and refrigerator. The hotel has a discotheque.

Places to Eat
There are plenty of restaurants in Chiang Rai, especially along Banphraprakan and Thanarai Rds. Near the bus station are the usual food stalls, but these are cheap and tasty.

Haw Naliga (the clock tower restaurant) has good Thai-Chinese food at reasonable prices. The locals say you haven't been to Chiang Rai if you haven't eaten at this place (near the clock tower on Banphraprakan Rd).

Especially good are the baked and steamed dishes *plaa neua awn pae sa* (moist and tender whole butterfish steamed in a spicy-sour broth with mushrooms), *tao hu maw din* (bean curd stew, baked in a clay pot) and *plaa nin thawt krathiam phrik Thai* (Blue Nile fish fried in garlic and black pepper). An outdoor garden section has been opened recently.

Just east of here on the same side of the street are the *Phetburi* and *Ratburi* restaurants. The Phetburi has a particularly good selection of curries and other Thai dishes.

One speciality is *cha-om thawt*, a type of fried quiche of cha-om greens cut in squares and served with a delicious chili sauce.

The ice-cream parlour next to the New Boonyoung Guest House has good noodle and rice dishes. The two large open-air restaurants on either side of Phahonyothin Rd, near the Areepracharat Hotel, also make especially good rice dishes for 10B – one is open during the day, the other at night. The night market next to the bus terminal and Rama I cinema is also good.

Bierstube on Phahonyothin Rd south of the Wiang Inn has been recommended for German food, and there are several other western-style pubs along here and on the street in front of the Wiang Come Hotel.

Next to the mosque on Itsaraphap Rd is a Thai Muslim restaurant with *khao mok kai*, a Thai version of chicken briyani.

Getting There & Away

Air Thai Airways has daily flights to Chiang Rai from Chiang Mai International Airport at 9.10 and 11.25 am and 1.45 pm. The flight takes 50 minutes and costs 300B.

Bus There are two bus routes (old and new) to Chiang Rai from Chiang Mai. The old route (*sai kao*) heads south from Chiang Mai to Lampang before heading north through Ngao, Phayao, Mae Chai and finally to Chiang Rai. If you want to stop at any of these cities, this is the bus to catch, but the trip will take up to seven hours. This bus leaves from Chiang Mai-Lamphun Rd near the Nawarat Bridge.

The new route (*sai mai*) heads north-east along Route 1019 to Chiang Rai, stopping in Doi Saket and Wiang Papao, and takes about four hours. The fare is 47B ordinary or 66B air-con. New-route buses and air-con buses leave from the Arcade Bus Station. Chiang Mai to Chiang Rai buses are sometimes stopped for drug searches by police.

Boat One of the most popular ways of getting to Chiang Rai is the river trip from Tha Ton (see River Trip to Chiang Rai).

For boats upriver on the Mae Kok, go to the pier in the north-western corner of town.

Regular longboats from Chiang Rai stop at the following villages along the Kok (times are approximate for ideal river conditions):

Destination	Fare	Duration
Ban Ruammit	20B	1 hour
Pong Nam Rawn	25B	1 hour, 20 min
Phaa Muup	30B	1 hour, 45 min
Hat Yao	50B	2 hours, 15 min
Phaa Khwang	60B	2½ hours
Kok Noi	80B	3 hours
Phaa Tai	100B	3½ hours
Mae Salak	120B	4 hours
Tha Ton	160B	4½ to 5 hours

Getting Around

Most of the guest houses in town rent or lend bicycles, which are a good way to get around town. Motorcycles are also easily rented through guest houses. A reliable motorcycle rental and repair shop is Soon, on the east side of Trairat Rd, between Banphraprakan and Thanarai Rds. Another place that rents motorcycles is next to the Sukniran Hotel.

A city bus system circulates along the main city streets. The fare is 2B.

MAE SALONG (SANTIKHIRI) แม่สลอง สันติคีรี

The village of Mae Salong was originally settled by the renegade Kuomintang 93rd Regiment, which fled to Burma from China after the 1949 Chinese revolution. The renegades were again forced to flee in 1961 when the Burmese Government decided they wouldn't allow the KMT to remain legally in northern Burma (some still hide out in the hills).

Ever since the Thai Government granted these renegades refugee status in the '60s, the Thais have been trying to incorporate the Yunnanese KMT and their families into the Thai nation. Before now they weren't having much success, as the KMT persisted in involving themselves in the Golden Triangle opium trade, along with opium warlord Khun Sa and the Shan United Army (SUA).

This area is very mountainous and there are few paved roads, so the outside world has always been somewhat cut off from the goings-on in Mae Salong. Hence, for years the KMT were able to ignore attempts by

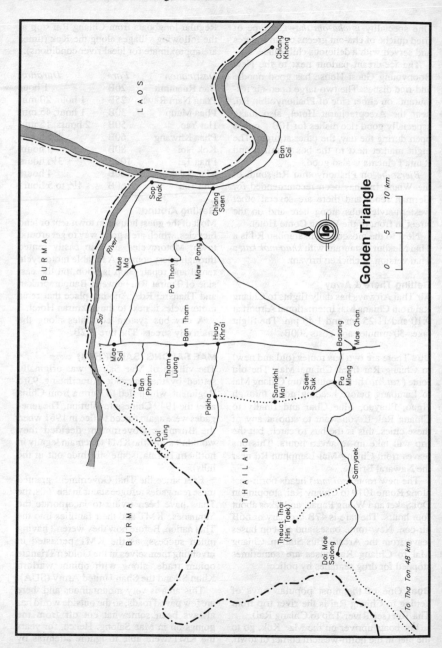

Thai authorities to suppress opium activity and tame the region. Khun Sa, in fact, made his home in nearby Ban Hin Taek (now Ban Thoet Thai) until the early '80s when he was finally routed by the Thai military. Khun Sa's retreat to Burma seemed to signal a change in local attitudes and the Thai Government finally began making progress in its pacification of Mae Salong and the surrounding area. (See Opium & the Golden Triangle in Facts about the Country).

The Thai Government officially changed the name of the village from Mae Salong to Santikhiri, which means Hill of Peace.

The 36-km road from Basang, near Mae Chan, to Santikhiri, has been paved (beforehand, pack horses were used to move goods up the mountain to Mae Salong) and a Thai language elementary school has been established. There are also evening adult classes in the Thai language.

Most people in the area speak Yunnanese, except of course for members of the local hill tribes, who are mainly Akha and speak hill-tribe dialects. Like other villages throughout rural Thailand undergoing similar pacification programmes, Mae Salong is wired with a loudspeaker system that broadcasts official programming in the streets, starting at 6 am. The locals are reluctant to speak of their KMT past and deny that there are any KMT regulars left in the area. To the Thais, they are simply the Jiin Haw (galloping Chinese), a reference either to their use of horses or their migratory status.

One of the most important government programmes is the crop substitution plan to encourage hill tribes to cultivate tea, coffee, corn and fruit trees. This seems to be somewhat successful, as there are plenty of these products for sale in the town markets and tea and corn are abundant in the surrounding fields. There is a tea factory in town where you can taste the fragrant Mae Salong teas (originally from Taiwan), and there are many fruit wines and liquors for sale at the markets. The local illicit corn whisky is much in demand – perhaps an all too obvious substitution for the poppy.

Another local speciality is Chinese herbs, particularly the kind that are mixed with liquor, called *yaa dong* in Thai. Thai and Chinese tourists who come to Mae Salong always take back a bag or two of assorted Chinese herbs.

Mae Salong is unlike any other town in Thailand. The combination of pack horses, hill tribes (Akha, Lisu, Mien, Yao) and southern Chinese-style houses conjures up the picture of a small town or village in Yunnan Province in China.

It is possible to walk south from Mae Salong to Chiang Rai in three or four days, following trails which pass through hill-tribe villages. Ask about political conditions before heading off in the opposite direction (toward Burma), however. In February 1989 Khun Sa sent SUA troops to Ban Mae Chan Luang, an Akha village on Doi Mae Salong. The troops sealed off the village and abducted several villagers including the headman. The conflict had to do with opium-smuggling routes in the area. SUA and Wa National Army forces are competing for control over this section of the Thai-Burmese border and often clash in the area.

Places to Stay

The *Mae Salong Guest House* is at the high end of town and the couple who run it are very friendly. Clean one-bed rooms without a bath are 50B, or 70B for the same with two beds and 100B for a room with a bath, single or double. Good Yunnanese food is served and they also sell several varieties of local fruit spirits, Mae Salong tea and Chinese herbal medicines. The owners can arrange treks on horseback for 100B per person per day or advise you on making treks on your own.

Shin Sane (Sin Sae) Guest House, Mae Salong's original hotel, is a wooden Chinese affair around the corner from the Mae Salong Guest House. Singles/doubles are 50/70B. It has information on trekking and a nice little cafe. Further along this road is the *Rainbow Guest House* which is nothing special at 50B per person, but the family that run it are friendly.

At the top of the price range is the *Sakura Resort* above the town where rooms are from 200 to 300B. A new hotel is going up just below the town centre and looks to be in the 100 to 300B range, perhaps more.

Three km from Basang on the road to Mae Salong is a turn-off to *Winnipa Lodge* on a hillside overlooking the road. From here you can see Doi Tung in the distance.

If you're hiking to Chiang Rai from Doi Mae Salong, you could stop off in Ban Hin Fon and stay at *Laan Tong Lodge*, which is about 13 km west of Mae Chan and has huts for 30B per person. Otherwise you can reach it by taking a songthaew from Mae Chan to the village (20B) and then hiking the three km to the lodge. One of the activities here is tubing along the Mae Chan River. Laan Tong can also arrange treks.

Places to Eat
Don't miss the many street noodle vendors who sell *khanom jiin nam ngiaw*, a delicious Yunnanese rice-noodle concoction topped with spicy chicken curry – Mae Salong's most famous local dish and a gourmet bargain at 5B per bowl.

On the road to the Rainbow Guest House are two good noodle restaurants with *khanom jiin* and khao soi. One of them also sells fluffy *mantou* (plain steamed Chinese buns) and *salabao* (pork-stuffed Chinese buns) with delicious pickled vegetables. Many of the Chinese in Santikhiri are Muslims, so you'll find several Muslim restaurants.

Getting There & Away
To get to Mae Salong by public transport, take a bus from Mae Sai or Chiang Rai to Ban Basang, which is about two km north of Mae Chan. From Ban Basang, there are songthaews up the mountain to Mae Salong for 40B per person (down again costs 30B). The trip takes about an hour. The bus fare from Chiang Rai to Ban Basang is 10B.

MAE SAI แม่สาย
The northernmost point in Thailand, Mae Sai is a good place from which to explore the Golden Triangle, Doi Tung and Mae Salong. It's also the spot to observe border life, as Mae Sai is the only official land crossing open between Burma and Thailand. Only Burmese and Thai nationals are allowed to cross the bridge which spans the Sai River border, although there is talk of allowing foreigners to cross the border for the day in the future.

Burmese lacquerware, gems, jade and other goods from Laos and Burma are sold in shops along the main street in Mae Sai, although the trade is mainly a tourist scene now.

Many Burmese come over during the day from Thakhilek to work or do business, hurrying back by sunset.

Take the steps up the hill near the border to Wat Phra That Doi Wao, west of the main street, for superb views over Burma and Mae Sai. There are also some interesting trails in the cliffs and hills overlooking the Mae Sai Guest House and the river.

Motorcycle trekking in the area is quite good due to plenty of challenging back roads and trails. Chad Guest House in Mae Sai has good information on motorcycle treks and its own excellent well-researched maps.

Tham Luang (Great Cave) ถ้ำหลวง
About six km south of Mae Sai off Highway 110 is a large cave that extends into the hills for at least a couple of km, possibly more. The first cavern is huge and a narrow passage at the back leads to a series of other chambers and side tunnels of varying sizes. The first km is fairly easy going but after that you do some climbing over piles of rocks to get further in. For 15B you can borrow a gas lantern from the caretakers in front of the cave or you can take someone along as a guide (for which there's no fixed fee; just give him whatever you want). The roof formations in places are fantastic and tiny crystals make them change colour according to the angle of the light.

Tham Pum/Tham Pla ถ้ำพุ่ม/ถ้ำพลา
Only 13 km south of Mae Sai, just off Highway 110 at Ban Tham, are a couple of caves with freshwater lakes inside. Bring a torch to explore the caves as there are no lights. The real attraction here, though, is the very unique Khmer-style chedi in front of the

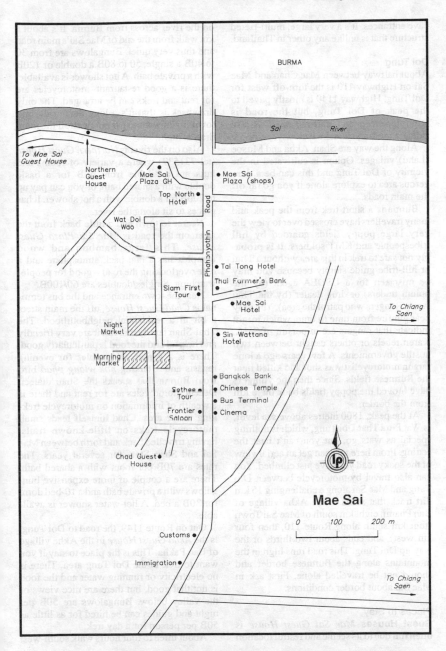

cave entrances. It's a very large, multi-tiered structure that is unlike any other in Thailand.

Doi Tung ดอยตุง

About halfway between Mae Chan and Mae Sai on Highway 110 is the turn-off west for Doi Tung. Highway 1149 is mostly paved to the peak of Doi Tung, but the road is winding, steep and narrow, so if you're riding a motorcycle, take it slowly.

Along the way are Shan, Akha and Musoe (Lahu) villages. Opium is cultivated in the vicinity of Doi Tung and this can be a dangerous area to explore alone if you go far off the main roads.

Burma is a short trek from the peak and many travellers have crossed over to view the very large poppy fields guarded by hill tribespeople and KMT soldiers. It is probably not safe to trek in this area without a Thai or hill-tribe guide simply because you may be mistaken for a USDEA agent (by the opium traders) or drug dealer (by the Thai Army Rangers who patrol the area). You may hear gunfire from time to time, which might indicate that rangers are in pursuit of SUA, Karen rebels or others caught between two hostile governments. A few years ago a lone farang motorcyclist was shot and killed near the Burmese fields. Since then the villagers have moved the poppy fields back three km from the border.

At the peak, 1800 metres above sea level, is Wat Phra That Doi Tung, which is nothing special as wats go, but you can't beat the setting. From here you can get an aerial view of the snaky road you have just climbed. You can also travel by motorcycle between Doi Tung and Mae Sai along a challenging 15 km dirt track that starts in the Akha village of Ban Phami, eight km south of Mae Sai Town (four km south along Route 110, then four km west), and ends about two-thirds of the way up Doi Tung. This road runs high in the mountains along the Burmese border and should not be travelled alone. First ask in Mae Sai about border conditions.

Places to Stay

Guest Houses Mae Sai Guest House is often full due to its scenic and restful location on the river across from Burma. It's about a km walk from the end of Mae Sai's main road and thus very quiet. Bungalows are from 30 to 40B a single, 50 to 80B a double or 120B with a private bath. A hot shower is available, there is a good restaurant, motorcycles are for rent and treks can be arranged. The only drawback is that it's a long dark walk into town if you want to eat out or stroll the main drag at night.

Also on the river is *Northern Guest House* (tel 731537) where a variety of rooms and huts are available from 60B for a basic double with a shared bath, or you can pay up to 200B for a double with a hot shower. It has places to sit along the river.

Nearer to town and a little back from the river on the road is *Mae Sai Plaza Guest House*. This large bamboo and wood complex has a laid-back atmosphere and a cafe overlooking the road – good for people-watching. Singles/doubles are 60/100B.

Near the town entrance and the bus terminal is *Chad Guest House*, off the main street a bit in a residential neighbourhood. The Thai-Shan family that run it are very friendly and helpful and the food is particularly good. There is a garden with tables for evening repasts and a talking *nok wiang phao* bird from Burma that speaks the Shan dialect. Decent motorcycles are for rent and there is a wealth of information on motorcycle trekking in the area. Chad himself leads small motorcycle treks on little-known trails, having travelled back and forth between Mae Sai and Shan State for several years. The rates are 70B per room with a shared bath. There are a couple of more expensive bungalows with a private bath and a 10-bed dorm for 30B a bed. A hot-water shower is available.

Out on Route 1149, the road to Doi Tung, is the *Akha Guest House* in the Akha village of Ban Pakha. This is the place to stay if you want to trek in the Doi Tung area. There is no electricity or running water and the food is not that good, but there are nice views of the valley below. Bungalows are 50B per night and guides can be hired for as little as 50B per person for a day trek.

About three to four hours walk south-west

of Ban Pakha is *Chiang Rai Mountain Guest House* on the Mae Kham River near Samakhee Mai village, from where you can trek to Mae Salong.

Hotels *Top North Hotel* (tel 731955) on Phahonyothin Rd (the main road) has singles/doubles for 140/170B, or for 340B with air-con and hot water.

Mae Sai Hotel (tel 721462), off Phahonyothin Rd on the other side, has been refurbished and is good value. Singles/doubles with a fan and private bath are 100/150B, while air-con rooms with a hot bath are 280B.

Sin Wattana (tel 731950) is on Phahonyothin Rd across from the market and costs from 120B for fairly well-kept rooms.

At the top end is the new *Tai Tong (Thai Thong) Hotel* (tel 731975) at 6 Phahonyothin Rd, where standard rooms are 400B and somewhat larger rooms are 450B. Considering the rooms, these rates are perhaps a tad high. All come with air-con and hot water.

Places to Eat
The night market is rather small but the Chinese vendors do excellent *kuaytiaw phat si-yu* and other noodle dishes. You can also get fresh *pa-thong ko* (Chinese doughnuts) and hot *nam tao-hu* (soy milk).

Jojo's on Phahonyothin Rd serves ice cream and western snacks. Down near the bridge on the river is a floating restaurant that's OK. The 'in' night spot is the *Frontier Saloon*, down near the Chad Guest House, where they serve draft beer and Maekhong whisky in an old west setting.

Getting There & Away
Bus Buses to Mae Sai frequently leave from Chiang Rai and cost 15B for the 1½-hour trip. From Chiang Saen it costs 14B. Sethee Tour and Siam First Tour each have VIP 'sleeper' buses from Mae Sai to Bangkok that leave at about 5.30 or 6 pm daily.

Buses to the turn-off for Doi Tung are 7B from either Mae Chan or Mae Sai.

Motorcycle By motorcycle from Mae Sai to Chiang Saen there's a choice of two half-

paved roads (one from the centre of town and one near the town entrance) or a fully paved road via Highway 110 to Mae Chan and then Highway 1016 to Chiang Saen.

The roads out of Mae Sai are considerably more direct but there are several forks where you have to make educated guesses on which way to go (there are occasional signs). The two roads join near the village of Mae Ma where you have a choice of going east through Sop Ruak or south through Pa Thon. The eastern route is more scenic.

Songthaew From Ban Huai Khrai, at the Doi Tung turn-off, a songthaew to the Akha Guest House at Ban Pakha is 10B or 30B all the way to Doi Tung, 18 km away. The road to Doi Tung has seriously deteriorated above Pakha in the last few years and this section is becoming more of a challenge to climb, whether you're in a truck, jeep or motorcycle. Meanwhile, the Highway Department is busy building a new road parallel to, but several km away from, the present one.

CHIANG SAEN เชียงแสน
A little more than 30 km from Chiang Rai, Chiang Saen is a small but lively crossroads town on the banks of the Maekhong (often spelt Mekong) River. Scattered throughout the town are the ruins of the Chiang Saen Kingdom, founded in 1325, including chedi, images of the Buddha and earthen city ramparts. A few of the old monuments still standing pre-date Chiang Saen by a couple of hundred years.

National Museum
Near the town entrance, a small national museum displays artefacts from the Chiang Saen and Lanna periods as well as prehistoric stone tools from the area and hill-tribe crafts, dress and musical instruments. It's open daily from 9 am to 4 pm and admission is 5B. The archaeological station behind the museum has a large detailed wall map of Chiang Saen and the surrounding area.

Wat Chedi Luang
Behind the museum to the east, this wat has

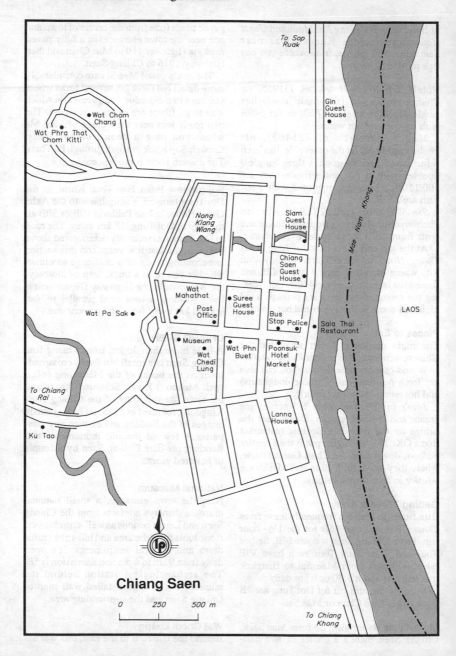

To Sop Ruak

Gin Guest House

Wat Chom Chang

Wat Phra That Chom Kitti

Nong Klang Wiang

Siam Guest House

Chiang Saen Guest House

Wat Mahathat

Post Office

Wat Pa Sak

Suree Guest House

Bus Stop

Police

Sala Thai Restaurant

Mae Nam Khong

LAOS

Museum

Wat Chedi Lung

Wat Phn Buet

Poonsuk Hotel

Market

To Chiang Rai

Ku Tao

Lanna House

Chiang Saen

0   250   500 m

To Chiang Khong

a remarkable eight-sided chedi. It's 58 metres tall and was built in the 12th century.

Wat Pa Sak

About 200 metres from the Chiang Saen gate are the remains of Wat Pa Sak, which is undergoing restoration by the Fine Arts Department. The ruins of seven monuments are visible. The main mid-14th century stupa combines elements of the Hariphunchai and Sukhothai styles with a possible Pagan Burmese influence. Since these ruins are a historical park, there is a 20B admission fee into the wat's grounds.

Wat Phra That Chom Kitti

Between two and three km north of Wat Pa Sak are the remains of Wat Phra That Chom Kitti and Wat Chom Chang on top of a hill. The round chedi of Wat Phra That is thought to have been constructed before the founding of the kingdom. The smaller chedi a bit below this belonged to Wat Chom Chang. These chedi aren't really much to see but there's a good view of Chiang Saen and the river from the top of the hill.

The Lao side of the mighty Maekhong looks deserted, but Lao boats flying Pathet Lao flags do occasionally float by. Hill-tribe crafts can be bought in a few shops along the river. Some of the townspeople, Lao immigrants, speak French.

Places to Stay

Most budget travellers stay in Chiang Saen these days. The *Chiang Saen Guest House* is under new management and is said to have improved. Small singles/doubles are 30/50B while larger ones with a private bath are 80/100B. It's on the road to Sop Ruak, opposite the river. Bicycles and motorcycles can be rented at the Chiang Saen and interesting bike trips can be made in the vicinity.

A bit further along this road on the same side is the newer *Siam Guest House*. It has singles/doubles in its huts for 40/60B without a bath, or 70B with one. It also has a pleasant cafe, and rents out bicycles and motorcycles.

Further north on the edge of town overlooking the river is the cosy and quiet *Gin Guest House* (formerly *Kim's*). Singles/doubles in the big house are 30/50B or a hut costs 80B.

In the opposite direction on the same road, towards Chiang Khong, is the very popular *Lanna House*. Lanna has two kinds of bungalows – those for 80B or a slightly nicer one for 100B. It rents out bicycles, motorcycles and jeeps and dispenses information about local trekking.

Inside the town is the *Suree Guest House*, about 100 metres off the main road near Wat Mung Muang and the post office. A big house run by friendly folk, the cost is 50B per double or 75B for a three-bed room.

If all these places are full, the only other choice is the *Poonsuk Hotel*, a bright blue ramshackle building near the end of Chiang Saen's main street, towards the river. Double rooms are from 40 to 70B, and mosquito nets are provided.

Places to Eat

The long-standing *Sala Thai Restaurant* overlooks the Maekhong River and serves fair chow (though they don't really have everything listed on the menu) and cheap eats are available in and near the market on the river road.

A good garden restaurant, *Yonok*, is outside of town, five km towards Mae Chan and one km off the highway next to Chiang Saen Lake. It specialises in freshwater seafood – try the *plaa nin thawt* (fresh fried Nile fish). It has no English menu, so bring your eating guide if your Thai isn't up to it. It also rents out a few 500B bungalows which have a refrigerator and a hot shower.

Getting There & Away

There are frequent buses from Chiang Rai to Chiang Saen for 15B. The trip takes between 40 minutes and 1½ hours.

Returning from Chiang Saen, don't take a Chiang Mai bus (out of Chiang Saen directly) unless you want to travel along the old road, which means passing through Pham, Payao, Ngao, Lampang and Lamphun before arriving in Chiang Mai – a seven-to-nine-hour trip. First go to Chiang Rai (on a Chiang Rai bus of course) then change to a

Chiang Mai bus which goes along the new road (sai mai), a trip of about 4½ hours.

AROUND CHIANG SAEN

Sop Ruak สบรวก

Further north, 14 km from Chiang Saen up the road which runs alongside the river, is Sop Ruak, the official centre of the Golden Triangle. This is where the borders of Burma, Thailand and Laos meet, at the confluence of the Sop Ruak and Maekhong rivers. Sop Ruak has become something of a tourist trap, with souvenir stalls, restaurants and busloads of package tour visitors during the day.

Chiang Khong เชียงของ

Across the river from Ban Houei Sai in Laos, this was the place where you began or finished the old Laotian Loop. There's no real reason to go to Chiang Khong now but there are several cheap hotels along the main street. If boat travel along the Maekhong River is allowed, there will probably be boat trips between Chiang Saen and Chiang Khong.

Places to Stay

There used to be several places to stay for travellers who wanted to be at the centre of the Golden Triangle, but the budget places at Sop Ruak are slowly giving way to souvenir stalls and larger tourist hotels. *Golden Triangle Guest House* still has your typical tropical bungalows overlooking the Maekhong for 60B with a private bath, which is a good price. The place is clean and well-run, has electricity, and there's swimming below.

The other choice is *Poppy Guest House*, which has a good restaurant, but only three huts for 80B with a private bath.

The 150-room *Golden Triangle Resort Hotel* is being built on a hillside overlooking the river and will be a 1st-class place with rooms from 500B. It is supposed to be completed by the end of 1989. Others will no doubt follow.

Getting There & Away

From Chiang Saen to Sop Ruak, a share-taxi costs 10B and these leave several times a day. You can also hitch hike from the front of the

Sala Thai Restaurant in Chiang Saen or hire a long-tail boat.

A good way to see the Golden Triangle is by motorcycle and these can be rented either in Chiang Saen or in Mae Sai. There's usually a better choice of machines in Mae Sai, but either town could serve as a base for covering the territory.

Phrae Province

Phrae Province is probably most famous for the distinctive seua maw hawm, the indigo-dyed cotton farmer's shirt seen all over Thailand. 'Made in Phrae' has always been a sign of distinction for these staples of rural Thai life and since the student-worker-farmer political solidarity of the 1970s, even Thai university professors like to wear them. The cloth is made in Ban Thung Hong outside of town.

The provinces of Phrae and Nan have been neglected by tourists and travellers alike because of their remoteness from Chiang Mai, but from Den Chai they're easily reached by bus along Highway 101.

PHRAE TOWN เมืองแพร่

This provincial capital (population 20,000) is only 23 km from the Den Chai Railway Station on the Chiang Mai line.

Temples

Temple architecture in Phrae is a bit unusual since you'll find both Burmese and Lao styles. In town, visit Wat Chom Sawan, a Burmese-style temple built by local Shans early this century. There's a large copper-crowned chedi on the grounds and the wihan is a fine example of northern temple architecture.

Wat Phra Non and Wat Phong Sunan have Lao-style wihans with carved-wood pediments.

On a hill about nine km south-east of town off Route 1022 is Wat Phra That Cho Hae, famous for its 33-metre-high gilded chedi. Cho Hae is the name of the cloth that worshippers wrap around the chedi – it's a type of satin said to be woven in Xishuangbanna (Northern Thai: Sip-Song Ban Na, meaning 12,000 fields). The Phra Jao Than Jai Buddha image here is reputed to impart fertility to women who make offerings to it.

Dan Prathup Jai บ้านประทับใจ

You can see lots of good wood carving in Phrae. In town is the Ban Prathup Jai, also called Ban Soi Roi Tan, a large northern-style teak house which was built using more than 130 teak logs. The interior is ornately carved. Phrae is a centre for teak craft and in Sung Men district just south of Phrae is the Hua Dong Market, a trading place for teakwood carving.

Muang Phi เมืองผี

Also called Ghost-Land, this is a strange geological phenomenon about 18 km north of Phrae off Highway 101. Erosion has created bizarre pillars of soil and rock that look like giant fungi.

Mrabri Hill Tribe

Along the border of Phrae and Nan provinces live the remaining members of the Mrabri hill tribe, whom the Thais call *phii thong leuang* (spirits of the yellow leaves). The most nomadic of all the tribes in Thailand, the Mrabri customarily move on when the leaves of their temporary huts turn yellow, hence their Thai name. Now, however, their numbers have been greatly reduced (to possibly as few as 150) and experts suspect that few of the Mrabri still migrate in the traditional way.

Traditionally they are strict hunter-gatherers but many now work as field labourers for Thais or other hill-tribe groups such as the Hmong, in exchange for pigs and cloth. It is said that the Mrabri believe they are not entitled to cultivate the land for themselves. When one of their members dies, the body is put in a treetop to be eaten by birds.

Places to Stay

Several cheap hotels can be found along Charoen Muang Rd, including *Kanchana*, *Siriwattana* and *Thep Wiman*, all of which have rooms starting at between 60 and 70B.

Paradorn (Pharadon) (tel 511177), 177 Yantara Kit-koson, has moderately priced singles/doubles with a fan and bath for 130/150B or air-con rooms from 220B. It also has information on local attractions. On the same road are *Thung Si Phibun* at No 84 and *Sawat-dikan* at No 76-8, with rooms from 70B.

Just a cut above the *Paradorn* in price and amenities is the *Nakhon Phrae Hotel* (tel 511969) at 29 Ratchadamnoen Rd, which has singles/doubles with a fan for 135/200B, or with air-con for 350/400B. It has tourist information, and outside the front of the hotel you may meet a diligent samlor driver named Suksom who is so proud of Phrae that he wrote a letter to us complaining that Phrae was missing from this guidebook (until now)!

Getting There & Away

Bus A bus from Bangkok's Northern Bus Terminal is 120B for ordinary buses departing hourly between 5 and 9.30 pm. Air-con buses are 213B and leave at 8.30 and 8.50 pm.

From Chiang Mai's Arcade Bus Station, ordinary buses leave at 8 and 11 am, and 3 and 5 pm. The fare is 49B and the trip takes four hours. An air-con bus leaves from the same station at 10 am and 10 pm and costs 68B.

Train Trains to Den Chai Railway Station from Bangkok are 188B 2nd class or 90B 3rd class, plus supplementary charges as these apply. The only trains that arrive at a decent hour are the No 59 Rapid (departs Bangkok at 6.40 am and arrives in Den Chai at 3.33 pm) and the No 35 Rapid (leaves at 10 pm and arrives at 7.15 am). On the No 35 you can get a 2nd-class sleeper for 70B upper berth or 100B lower berth.

Buses and songthaews leave Den Chai frequently for Phrae and cost about 20B.

UTTARADIT TOWN เมือง อุตรดิตถ์

Continue north by rail from Si Satchanalai and Sawankhalok to Uttaradit Town (population 33,000). Uttaradit Province is noted for its fruit and for the largest earth-filled dam in Thailand, the Sirikit Dam, which is 55 km from the town.

Buses from Bangkok cost 102B or 186B air-con.

Places to Stay

P. Vanich (Phaw Wanit) 2 (tel 411499 or 411749) is by the river at 1 Sri Uttara Rd, within walking distance of the railway station. Rooms start from 90B, or from 200B with air-con. The *Uttaradit* at 24-28 Rasanarn Rd and the *Anothai* at 149-153 Kasemrat are similarly priced.

Nan Province

One of Thailand's remote provinces (an official Thai Government designation), Nan was formerly so choked with bandits and PLAT insurgents that travellers were discouraged from visiting. The Thai Government couldn't get any roads built in the province because guerrillas would periodically destroy highway building equipment at night.

With the successes of the Thai army and a more stable political machine in Bangkok during the last few years, Nan is opening up and more roads are being built. The roads that link the provincial capital with the nearby provinces of Chiang Rai, Phrae, Uttaradit, etc pass through exquisite scenery of rich river valleys and rice fields. Like Loei Province in the north-east, this is a province to be explored for its natural beauty and its likable people – living close to traditional rural rhythms.

NAN TOWN เมืองน่าน

A little more than 340 km from Chiang Mai and 295 km from Sukhothai, the main attraction of Nan Town (population 23,000) is getting there.

There are a couple of historic temples to see in Nan Town.

Wat Phumin

Near the municipal buildings off Suriyaphong Rd, the bot, like many northern

temples, was built on a cruciform plan with carved doors and ceilings. The altar in the centre has four sides with Sukhothai-style sitting Buddhas in *marawichai* (victory over Mara, one hand touching the ground) pose facing each direction. The temple was first built in 1496 but has been restored over the centuries.

Wat Phra That Chae Haeng

Two km past the bridge which spans the Nan River, heading west out of town, this very old temple dating from 1355 is the most sacred wat in Nan Province. It is set on a hill with a view of Nan and the valley. The bot features a five-level roof with carved wooden eaves. A gilded Lao-style chedi sits on a large square base. Each side is 22½ metres long and the entire chedi is 55½ metres high.

Boat Races

During *thawt kathin*, mid-October to mid-November, the city of Nan holds boat races (khaeng reua) on the river. The all-wooden 30-metre-long boats display sculpted naga heads and tails and hold up to 50 rowers.

Places to Stay

If you want to stay in Nan (you'll probably have to if you've come this far) you could try the basic *Amorn Si* at 97 Mahayot Rd where rooms start at 80B. *Nan Fah* (tel 710284) at 438-440 Sumonthewarat and *Sukkasem* (tel 710141) at 29/31 Ananworaritdet Rd are more expensive with rooms from 100B or 160B with air-con.

The all air-con *Dhevaraj (Thewarat) Hotel* (tel 710094) at 466 Sumonthewarat Rd has rooms with a private bath from 200B.

Getting There & Away

Air You can fly to Nan from Chiang Mai (380B), Phitsanulok (480B) or Phrae (190B).

Bus Buses run from Chiang Mai, Chiang Rai and Phrae to Nan. The fare from Chiang Mai's Arcade Bus Station is 71B (99B air-con) and the trip takes from seven to eight hours along the old route through Lampang and Phrae. (See Phrae's Getting There &

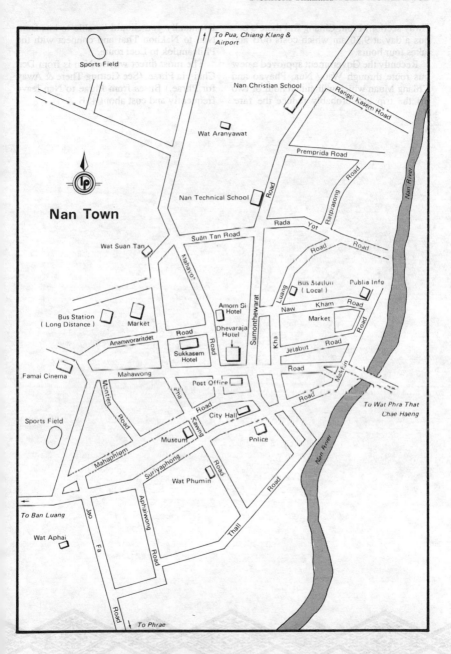

Away section) From Chiang Rai there's one bus a day at 9.30 am which costs 60B and takes four hours.

Recently the Government approved a new bus route through Wang Nua, Phayao and Chiang Muan which will cut an hour or two off the trip and probably reduce the fare.

Eventually you should be able to bus from Nan to Nakhon Thai and connect with the Phitsanulok to Loei route.

The most direct way to Nan is from Den Chai via Phrae. (See Getting There & Away for Phrae.) Buses from Phrae to Nan leave frequently and cost about 45B.

North-East Thailand

In many ways, the north-eastern region of Thailand is the kingdom's heartland. The older Thai customs remain more intact here than elsewhere in the country, and so, partly due to the area's general non-development, the north-east has hosted less tourism.

Sites of historical and archaeological significance abound in the north-east, several of which have been restored or excavated so that visitors are finally beginning to discover north-eastern travel. The pace is slower, the people friendlier and inflation is less effective in its provinces, known collectively as *isaan*, than in Thailand's other main regions.

The term isaan is also used to classify the local people (*khon isaan*) and the local food (*aahaan isaan*). It comes from the Sanskrit name for the Mon Khmer kingdom Isana which flourished in (what is now) north-eastern Thailand and pre-Angkor Cambodia. A mixture of Lao and Khmer influence is a mark of isaan culture and language. The Khmers have left behind several Angkor Wat-like monuments near Surin, Khorat, Buriram and other north-eastern towns. Near the Maekhong River/Lao border in the town of That Phanom is the famous Lao-style temple, Wat That Phanom. Many of the people living in this area speak Lao or a Thai dialect which is very close to Lao.

Isaan food is famous for its pungency and choice of ingredients. Well-known dishes include kai yang (roast spiced chicken) and somtam (spicy salad made with grated unripe papaya, lime juice, garlic, fish sauce and fresh hot pepper). North-easterners eat glutinous rice with their meals, rolling the almost translucent grains into balls with their hands.

The music of the north-east is also highly distinctive in its folk tradition, using instruments such as the *khaen*, a reed instrument with two long rows of bamboo pipes strung together, the *pong lang*, a xylophone-like instrument made of short wooden logs and the *pin*, a type of small three-stringed lute played with a large plectrum. The most popular song forms are of the *luuk thung* (children of the fields) type, a very rhythmic style in comparison to the classical music of central Thailand.

The best silk in Thailand is said to come from the north-east, around Khorat (Nakhon Ratchasima) and Roi Et. A visit to north-eastern silk-weaving towns can produce bargains as well as an education in Thai weaving techniques.

For real antiquity, Udon Province offers prehistoric cave drawings at Ban Pheu, north of Udon Thani, and a look at the ancient ceramic and bronze culture at Ban Chiang to the east. This latter site, excavated by the late Chester Gorman and his team of University-of-Pennsylvania anthropologists, may prove to be the remains of the world's oldest agricultural society and first bronze metallurgy, predating by centuries developments in the Tigris-Euphrates Valley and in China.

Travellers who want to know more about north-eastern Thailand should read the works of Pira Sudham, a Thai author born in Buriram. His autobiographical *People of Esarn (Isaan)* is especially recommended.

Main transportation lines (train and bus) in the north-east are along the routes between Bangkok and Nong Khai and between Bangkok and Ubon Ratchathani. The north east can also be reached from northern Thailand by bus or plane from Phitsanulok, with Khon Kaen as the gateway, as travel agents put it.

Isaan officially consists of 17 provinces: Buriram, Chaiyaphum, Kalasin, Khon Kaen, Loei, Mahasarakham, Mukdahan, Nakhon Ratchasima (Khorat), Nakhon Phanom, Nong Khai, Roi Et, Sakhon Nakhon, Si Saket, Surin, Ubon Ratchathani, Udon Thani and Yasothon.

If you proceed to the north-east from Bangkok, the first principal stop is Khorat.

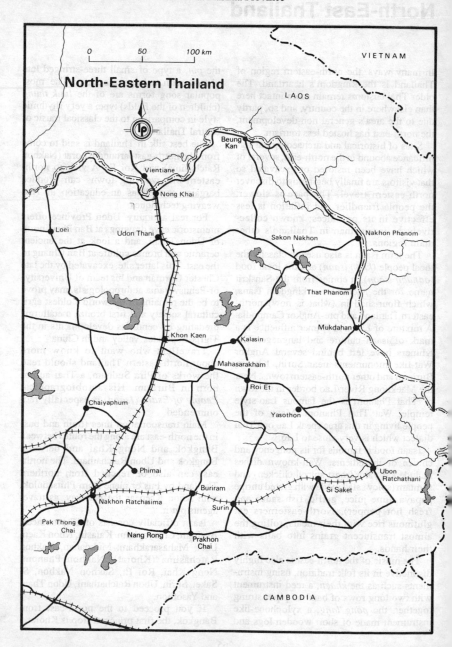

Nakhon Ratchasima Province

Nakhon Ratchasima (also known as Khorat) Province is well known for silk weaving. Some of Thailand's best woven silk is made in the village of Pak Thong Chai, 30 km south-west of Khorat Town on Highway 24. Many of the Bangkok silk houses have their cloth made there, so don't expect to get any special bargains just because you went all that way. There are also a couple of silk shops in Khorat Town (Ratri Thai Silk on Ratchadamnoen Rd near the Thao Surinari shrine and Thusnee (Thatsani) Thai Silk on Buarong Rd), which are just as good for their selection and price. Still, Pak Thong Chai is worth a trip if you're interested in observing Thai silk-weaving methods.

Travellers interested in Thai ceramics can watch beautiful pottery being made at the village of Dan Kwian, 15 km south-east of Khorat.

NAKHON RATCHASIMA TOWN นครราชสีมา

Exactly 250 km from Bangkok, Nakhon Ratchasima Town (population 205,000) is also known as Khorat. It is often cited as only a train or bus stop from the nearby Phimai ruins, but is a fairly interesting stop in itself. Up until the mid-Ayuthaya period it was actually two towns, Sema and Khorakpura, which were merged under the reign of King Narai. To this day, Khorat has a split personality of sorts, with the older less commercial half to the west, and the newer downtown half inside the city moats to the east, although neither town was originally here.

One of the seven air bases in Thailand used by USA armed forces to launch air strikes on Laos and Vietnam in the '60s and '70s was here. A few retired GIs still live in the area with their Thai families and the Veterans of Foreign Wars Cafeteria is still open on Phoklang Rd. But the heavy American influence that was obvious in the late '70s after the base was closed has all but faded away. Yes, the big massage parlours are still here but the clientele is almost exclusively Thai.

Information

The TAT office on Mittaphap Rd (west edge of town) is worth a visit since it has plenty of information on the north-east. To get there, walk straight across from the entrance to the Nakhon Ratchasima Railway Station to Mukkhamontri Rd, turn left and walk (or catch a No 2 bus) west until you reach the highway to Bangkok – Mitthaphap Rd. TAT is just across the road, on the north-west corner.

Mahawirong National Museum

In the grounds of Wat Sutchinda, directly across from the government buildings off Ratchadamnoen Rd and just outside the city moat, this museum has a good collection of Khmer art objects, especially door lintels, as well as objects from other periods. It's open from 9 am to 12 noon and 1 to 4 pm, Wednesday to Sunday. Admission is 5B.

Thao Suranari Shrine

At the Chumphon Gate to downtown Khorat, on the west side, is this much-worshipped shrine to Khun Ying Mo, a courageous Thai woman who led the local citizens in a battle against Lao invaders from Vientiane during the rule of Rama III. There is a curious miniature model of a bus at the shrine, donated by local bus drivers perhaps in the hope that they will be protected from danger by Khun Ying Mo's spirit.

Next to the shrine in the evenings you can see performances of *phlaeng khorat*, the traditional Khorat folk song. It's usually performed by couples who are hired by people whose supplications to Thao Surinari have been honoured. To show gratitude to the spirit, they pay for the performance.

Wat Sala Loi

This distinctive modern Temple of the Floating Pavilion is 400 metres east of the north-eastern corner of the city moat and has a bot shaped like a Chinese junk.

Silver Lake Water Park

Near the Amphawan intersection toward Mittaphap Rd, Silver Lake is a water recreation park with a large swimming pool and water slides. In the pool, female attendants float by in boats hawking snacks. The restaurant is open at night and there are free performances of north-eastern folk dancing (including Khmer and Lao forms) and *luuk thung*, north-eastern country music. During the day, admission to Silver Lake is 20B.

Places to Stay – bottom end

Hotels Visit the TAT office for a map and complete list of hotels, as well as names of night clubs, restaurants, theatres and Turkish baths. *Fah Sang*, 68-70 Mukkhamontri Rd, not far from the Nakhorn Ratchasima Railway Station, has clean rooms and friendly staff. Singles are from 75 to 100B

and doubles are from 120 to 150B, with a fan and bath. Air-con singles/doubles with hot water cost 180/240B.

Pho Thong, 658 Phoklang Rd, has rooms from 80 to 120B with a fan and bath. Noisy but livable, it's on the corner of Ratchadamnoen Rd at the west city gate, right in the centre of things.

Siri Hotel, 167-8 Phoklang Rd, is well located a couple of blocks west of the city moats. Quiet and friendly, singles start at 70B with a fan or 150B air-con. The VFW Cafeteria is next door.

Thai Phokaphan, 104-6 Atsadang Rd, is inside the city moats, across the street from the expensive *Khorat Hotel* and CP Turkish

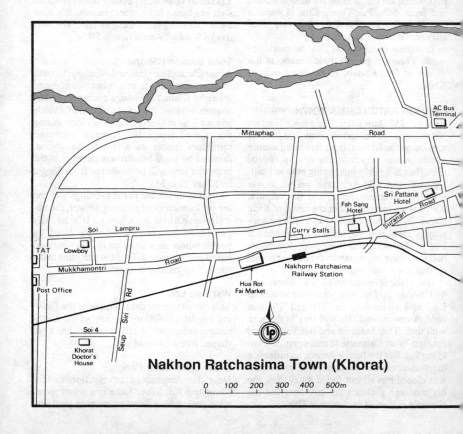

Nakhon Ratchasima Town (Khorat)

0   100   200   300   400   500m

Bath, near the Charoen Rat Theatre and the post office. Good singles/doubles are 90/150B or 180/220B air-con.

Cathay, 3692/5-6 Ratchadamnoen Rd, has reasonable rates (90 to 120B), but is a bit out of the way.

Khorat Hotel (tel 242260), 191 Atsadang Rd, has singles/doubles for 160/220B, or from 250B air-con.

Guest Houses Khorat's first guest house, *Khorat Doctor's House* (tel 255846), opened recently. It's at 78 Suep Siri Rd Soi 4, near Silver Lake Park. The house is quiet and comfortable and has four large singles/doubles for 50/80B, or 100B air-con. Khun

Surit is opening another branch nearer the town centre, close to the Hua Rot Fai Market and the Nakhorn Ratchasima Railway Station. All rooms at this second location will be 50B. If you phone from the bus or train station, transport will be provided to the guest house.

Next door to the *Tokyo Hotel* on Suranari Rd is the *Tokyo Guest House*, actually an extension of the hotel, where large rooms with a bath cost 70B.

Places to Stay – top end
Sri Pattana (tel 242944) on Suranari Rd has air-con rooms from 300B and a swimming pool. *Chom Surang* (tel 242940) has rooms

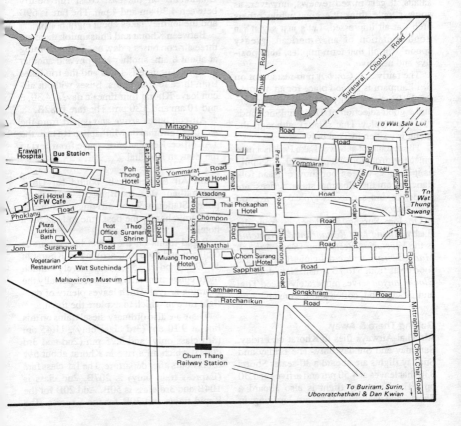

from 500B, again with a pool and all air-con. The newer *Muangmai Chao Phraya* (tel 244906) has rates from 400 to 650B.

Places to Eat
Khorat has many excellent Thai and Chinese restaurants, especially along the western gates to downtown Khorat, near the Thao Surinari Shrine. The curry stalls across from the Nakhorn Ratchasima Railway Station are also very good and cheap, but they're only open from about 10 am until 3 pm. The nearby Hua Rot Fai Market on Mukkhamontri Rd is a great place to eat at night.

VFW Cafeteria next to the Siri Hotel on Phoklang Rd has American breakfasts from 14B, as well as steaks, ice cream, pizza and salads. It gets mixed reviews, however, as some people think it's great while others aren't at all impressed. Let's just say it's a good imitation of an American 'greasy spoon', for all that term implies, both positive and negative.

The fairly new *Cowboy* pub-restaurant on Soi Lamparu is a good place for an evening drink. It's got a funky old west atmosphere and a good selection of Thai drinking foods like yam (spicy Thai salads), although the menu is written in Thai only.

The restaurant at Silver Lake Park is a nice place for an outdoor evening meal, especially as it includes a free floor show of isaan folk dancing on the floating stage. Prices are moderate and service is typical of a good *suan aahaan*.

On Jom Surangyat Rd across from the flashy *Muang Mai Restaurant & Nightclub* is the *Vegetarian Restaurant* (*Raan Aahaan Mangsawirat*), where delicious Thai veggie food costs from 5 to 7B a dish. Next door the *Black Canyon* serves moderately priced Thai and farang food, coffee and ice cream.

Getting There & Away
Air Thai Airways flies to Khorat on Friday, Saturday and Sunday only. The Friday and Sunday flights are aboard a 30-seater Shorts 330 that leaves at 4.50 pm and arrives at 5.30 pm. The Thursday flight is also aboard a Shorts and leaves at 9.45 am, arriving in Khorat at 10.25 am. The fare is 480B one-way.

The privately owned Bangkok Airways once had frequent flights to Khorat, but these were suspended a couple of years ago along with all its other routes. Now that Bangkok Airways is flying to southern Thailand again, there's a possibility it'll re-establish the north-eastern flights.

Bus Ordinary buses leave the Northern Bus Terminal in Bangkok every 15 or 20 minutes from 5 am to 9.30 pm. The fare is 51B and the trip takes four hours. Air-con buses cost 92B.

Buses between Khorat and Khon Kaen cost 39B. Direct buses between Khorat and Chantaburi on the east coast run hourly between 4.30 am and 4 pm. The fare is 69B and the journey takes about eight hours.

Between Khorat and Phitsanulok there are three air-con buses a day, one in the morning at about 8 am, another at 5 pm and another at 8 pm. The fare is 146B and the trip takes from three to four hours. Buses without air-con leave Khorat four times a day, at 4.30, 6 and 10 am and 3.30 pm. The fare is 82B.

Air-con buses arrive and depart from the AC Bus Terminal on Mitthaphap Rd near the TAT office. Regular buses leave from next to the Erawan Hospital.

Train An Express train bound for Ubon Ratchathani departs Bangkok's Hualamphong Station at 9 pm, arriving in Khorat at 1.44 am – hardly the best time to look for a hotel.

Rapid trains on the Ubon line depart at 6.50 am and 6.45 pm, arriving in Khorat at 11.42 am and 11.35 pm respectively – much more convenient arrival times, especially the morning arrival which leaves plenty of daylight time in which to explore the town.

There are also ordinary diesel trains on this line at 9.10 am (3rd class only), 11.45 am (3rd class only) and 3.25 pm (2nd and 3rd class), which all arrive in Khorat about 5½ to six hours after departure. The 1st-class fare (Express train only) is 207B, 2nd class is 104B and 3rd class is 50B. Add 20B for the Rapid trains and 30B for the Express. The train passes through some great scenery on the Khorat Plateau, including a view of the enormous white Buddha figure at Wat Theppitak on a thickly forested hillside.

AROUND NAKON RATCHASIMA TOWN
Pak Thong Chai

Thirty km south of Nakhon Ratchasima Town, on Route 24, is Pak Thong Chai, Thailand's most famous silk-weaving village. Several varieties and prices of silk are available and most weavers sell directly to the public. However, prices are not necessarily lower than in Khorat or Bangkok.

A bus to Pak Thong Chai leaves the bus station in Khorat every 30 minutes, the last at 4 pm. The fare is 10B.

Places to Stay *Achaan Pan* and *Pak Thong Chai* hotels are both on the main road through town and have rooms from 60B.

Phimai พิมาย

The small town of Phimai is nothing much, but staying the night here seems pleasant anyway. Outside the town entrance, a couple of km down Route 206, is Thailand's largest banyan tree, spread over an island in a state irrigation reservoir. The locals call it *sai ngam*, meaning beautiful banyan

Prasat Hin Phimai This Angkor-period Khmer shrine, 60 km north-east of Khorat, makes Phimai worth a visit. Originally started by Khmer King Jayavarman VII in the late 10th century and finished by King Suriyavarman I in the early 11th century, this Mahayana Buddhist temple projects a majesty that transcends its size. The main shrine, of cruciform design, is made of white sandstone, while the adjunct shrines are of pink sandstone and laterite. The lintel sculpture over the doorways to the main shrine are particularly impressive. The Phimai temple,

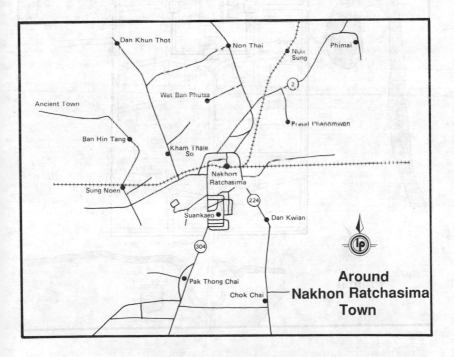

Around Nakhon Ratchasima Town

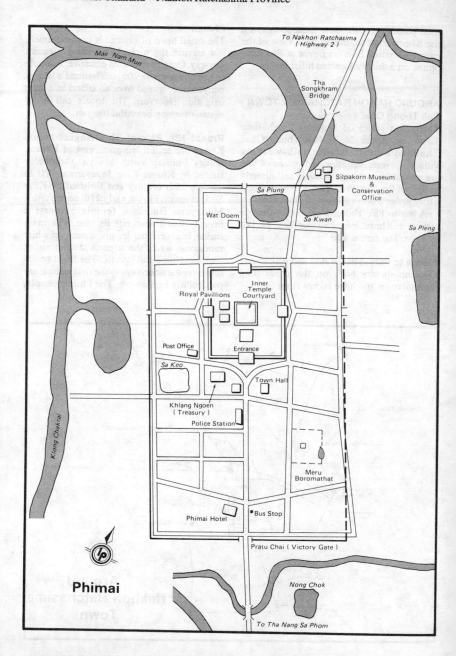

To Nakhon Ratchasima
(Highway 2)

Mae Nam Mun

Tha
Songkhram
Bridge

Silpakorn Museum
& Conservation
Office

Sa Plung

Sa Kwan

Sa Pleng

Wat Doem

Inner
Temple
Courtyard

Royal Pavillions

Post Office

Entrance

Sa Keo

Khlong Chakai

Town Hall

Khlang Ngoen
(Treasury)

Police Station

Meru
Boromathat

Phimai Hotel

Bus Stop

Pratu Chai (Victory Gate)

Nong Chok

To Tha Nang Sa Phom

Phimai

as well as other Khmer monuments in this part of Thailand, pre-dates the famous Angkor Wat complex in Cambodia. When the Angkor Empire was at its peak and encompassed parts of Thailand, Phimai was directly connected to the Angkor capital by road.

Reconstruction work by the Fine Arts Department has been completed. The fact that all the pieces do not quite fit together as they must have originally only seems to add to the monument's somewhat eerie quality. Admission to the complex is 20B. Between the main entrance and the main street of the small town is a ruined palace and, further on, an open-air museum features Khmer sculpture.

Places to Stay The town's one hotel, *Phimai Hotel*, is around the corner from the bus terminal and has very clean and comfortable rooms from 80 to 130B without a bath, 120 to 170B with a bath or from 200 to 260B with air-con. A recent letter, however, indicated that standards may have taken a plunge – 'maybe they need some competition,' the writer concluded.

Places to Eat The *Baiteiy (Bai Toey)* restaurant down the street from the hotel has been recommended as a good place to eat.

Getting There & Away Buses to Phimai from Khorat leave every half-hour during the day from the main bus station behind the Erawan Hospital on Suranari Rd. Take the No 2 city bus (2B) east on Mukkhamontri Rd (from the railway station) and get off at the hospital, then walk through a side-street to the bus station.

The trip to Phimai takes about one to 1½ hours, depending on the number of passengers that are picked up along the way. The terminal in Phimai is around the corner from the Phimai Hotel and down the street from Prasat Hin Phimai. The fare is 14B.

Prasat Phanomwan ปราสาทพนมวัน
Although not as large as Prasat Hin Phimai, Phanomwan is equally impressive. It's off Highway 2 about halfway between Phimai

and Khorat – ask to be let off the Khorat-Phimai bus at Ban Long Thong (4B), then hop a local songthaew, hitchhike or walk the six km through Ban Long Thong and Ban Makha, both knife-making places, to get to Prasat Phanomwan. Though basically unrestored, Phanomwan is an in-worship temple with resident monks.

Buriram Province

Buriram (population 29,000) is a large province (number 18 out of 74) with a small capital and a long history. During the Angkor period this area was an important part of the Khmer Empire.

Visit the restored temple of Prasat Hin Khao Phanom Rung, the most impressive of all Angkor monuments in Thailand, as well as the lesser-known ruins of Prasat Hin Muang Tham, Ku Rasi, Prasat Ban Khok Ngiu, Prasat Nong Hong, Prasat Ban Thai Charoen, Prasat Nong Kong, Prang Ku Samathom, Prang Ku Khao Plaibat, Prang Ku Suwan Taeng, Prang Ku Khao Kadong and many others.

Generally speaking, prasat (from the Sanskrit architectural term *prasada*) refers to large temple sanctuaries with a cruciform floor plan while ku and prang ku are smaller Khmer-style chedi or stupas. However, many Thais use these terms interchangeably. Prasat is sometimes translated in Thai tourist literature as castle or palace, but these Khmer monuments were never used as royal residences.

Most of the ruins in Buriram are little more than piles of bricks by the side of a road or in a field somewhere. As the Fine Arts Department and/or the local community accomplish more restoration in the province, more of the mentioned Khmer monuments may become worth seeing.

PRASAT HIN KHAO PHANOM RUNG HISTORICAL PARK
อุทยานประวัติศาสตร์ ปราสาทหิน เขาพนมรุ้ง
Phanom Rung is Khmer for Big Hill, but the Thais have added their own word for hill

(khao) to the name as well as the word for stone (hin) to describe the prasat.

Prasat Phanom Rung is on an extinct volcanic cone, 383 metres above sea level, that dominates the flat countryside for some distance in all directions. To the south-east you can clearly see Cambodia's Dongrek Mountain Range and it's in this direction that the capital of the Angkor Empire once lay. The prasat's temple complex is the largest and best restored of all the Khmer monuments in Thailand (it took 17 years to complete the restoration) and although it's not the easiest place to reach, it's well worth the effort.

The temple was constructed between the 10th and 13th centuries with the bulk of the work done during the reign of King Suriyavarman II (1113 to 1150 AD), which by all accounts was the apex of Angkor architecture. The complex faces east, toward the original Angkor capital. Of the three other great Khmer monuments of South-East Asia, Angkor Wat faces west, Prasat Khao Viharn faces north and Prasat Hin Phimai faces south-east. Nobody knows for sure whether these orientations have any special significance, especially as most smaller Khmer monuments in Thailand face east (toward the dawn – typical of Hindu temple orientation).

One of the most remarkable design aspects of Phanom Rung is the promenade leading to the main gate. This is the best surviving example in Thailand. It begins on a slope 400 metres east of the main tower with three earthen terraces. Next comes a cruciform base for what may have been a wooden pavilion. To the right of this is a stone hall known locally as the White Elephant Hall. On the north side of this hall are two pools that were probably once used for ritual ablutions before entering the temple complex. Flower garlands to be used as offerings in the temple may also have been handed out here. After you step down from the pavilion area, you'll come to a 160-metre avenue paved with laterite and sandstone blocks and flanked by sandstone pillars with lotus-bud tops, said to be early Angkor style (1100 to 1180 AD). The avenue ends at the first and largest of three naga bridges at Phanom Rung.

The naga bridges are the only three which have survived in Thailand. The first is flanked by 16 five-headed nagas (cobra deities) in the classic Angkor style. After passing this bridge and climbing the stairway you come to the magnificent east gallery leading into the main sanctuary. The central prasat has a gallery on each of four sides and the entrance to each gallery is itself a smaller version of the main tower. The galleries have curvilinear roofs and false balustraded windows. Once inside the temple walls, look at each of the galleries and the gopura entranceways, paying particular attention to the lintels over the porticos. The craftsmanship at Phanom Rung represents the pinnacle of Khmer artistic achievement, on a par with the reliefs at Angkor Wat in Cambodia.

The Phanom Rung complex was originally built as a Hindu monument and exhibits iconography related to the worship of Vishnu and Shiva. Excellent sculptures of both Vaishnava and Shaiva deities can be seen in the lintels or pediments over the doorways to the central monuments and in various other key points on the sanctuary exterior.

On the east portico of the mondop (antechamber to the prasat or main sanctuary) is a Nataraja, or Dancing Shiva, in the late Baphuan or early Angkor style, while on the south entrance are the remains of Shiva and Uma riding their bull mount, Nandi. The central cell of the prasat contains a Shivalingam or phallus image.

Several sculptured images of Vishnu and his incarnations Rama and Krishna can be found on various other lintels and cornices. Probably the most beautiful is the relief of Lord Narayana, a reclining Vishnu in the midst of the Hindu creation myth. Growing from his navel is a lotus that branches into several blossoms, on one of which sits the creator god Brahma. On either side of Vishnu are heads of Kala, the god of Time and Death. He is asleep on the milky sea of eternity, here represented by a naga snake. This lintel sits above the eastern gate (the main entrance) beneath the Shiva Nataraja relief.

An interesting story goes with the Phra Narai (Thai for Lord Narayana) lintel. In the '60s it was noticed that the lintel was missing from the sanctuary and an investigation

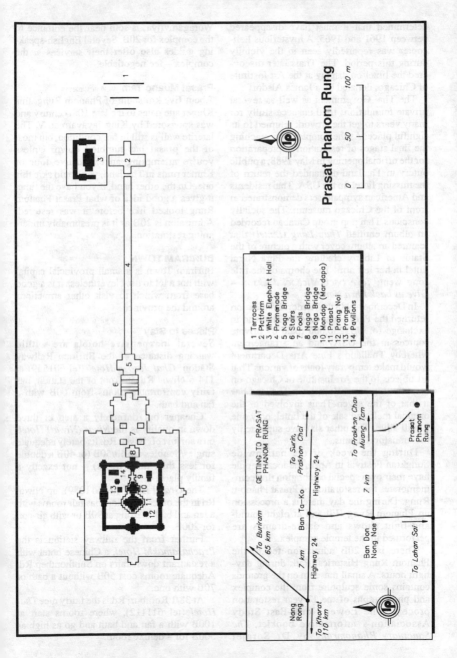

determined that it must have disappeared between 1961 and 1965. A mysterious helicopter was reportedly seen in the vicinity during this period. The Thais later discovered the lintel on display at the Art Institute of Chicago, donated by a James Alsdorf.

The Thai Government as well as several private foundations tried unsuccessfully for many years to get the artwork returned to its rightful place. As the complex was reaching the final stages of restoration in preparation for the official opening in May 1988, a public outcry in Thailand demanded the return of the missing lintel. In the USA, Thai residents and American sympathisers demonstrated in front of the Chicago museum. The socially conscious Thai pop group Carabao recorded an album entitled *Thap Lang* (*Lintel*) that featured an album cover with a picture of the Statue of Liberty cradling the Phra Narai lintel in her left arm! The chorus of the title song went: *Take back Michael Jackson – Give us back Phra Narai.*

In December 1988 the Alsdorf Foundation returned the Phra Narai lintel to Thailand in exchange for US$250,000 (paid by private sources in the USA) and an arrangement whereby Thailand's Fine Arts Department would make temporary loans of various Thai art objects to the Art Institute of Chicago on a continuing basis. Rumour in Thailand has it that of the seven Thais involved in the original theft and sale of the lintel, only one is still alive. The other six have supposedly met unnatural deaths.

During the week of the nationwide Songkran Festival in April, the local people have their own special celebration that commemorates the restoration of Prasat Phanom Rung. During the day there is a procession up Phanom Rung Hill and at night sound-and-light shows and dance-dramas are performed in the temple complex.

There is a 20B admission fee to the Phanom Rung Historical Park during daylight hours. A small museum on the grounds contains some sculpture from the complex and photographs of the 17-year restoration process. The Lower North-East Study Association's informative booklet, *The Sanctuary Phanomrung* by Dr Sorajet

Woragamvijya, is sold near the entrance to the complex for 20B. Several English-speaking guides also offer their services at the complex – fee negotiable.

Prasat Muang Tam ปราสาท เมืองธรรม
About five km south of Phanom Rung, this Khmer site dates to the late 10th century and was sponsored by King Jayavarman V. The laterite wall is still in fair condition, but most of the prasat has tumbled down. Unless you're attempting an exhaustive tour of Khmer ruins in Thailand, you could skip this one. On the other hand, if you have the time, it gives a good idea of what Prasat Phanom Rung looked like before it was restored. Admission is 20B as it is presumably undergoing restoration.

BURIRAM TOWN
Buriram Town is a small provincial capital with not a lot to do. Nevertheless it is a good base from which to visit other attractions around the province

Places to Stay
Several inexpensive hotels are within walking distance of the Buriram Railway Station. *Chai Jaroen Hotel* (tel 601559) at 114-6 Niwat Rd, in front of the station, has fairly comfortable rooms from 60B with a fan and bath.

Cheaper but definitely a step or three down in quality is the *Nivas (Niwat) Hotel*, on a soi just off Niwat Rd. Its barely adequate singles/doubles are 40/50B (or 40B a double for less than three hours) – not exactly a family place.

The *Grand Hotel* (tel 611089), up Niwat Rd in the other direction, has fair rooms with a fan and bath starting at 90B or with air-con for 200B.

Further from the railway station is the *Prachasamakhi Hotel*, a Chinese hotel with a restaurant downstairs on Sunthonthep Rd. Adequate rooms cost 50B without a bath or 70B with one.

At 38/1 Romburi Rd is the fairly nice *Thai Hotel* (tel 611112), where rooms start at 100B with a fan and bath and go as high as 500B for a deluxe room.

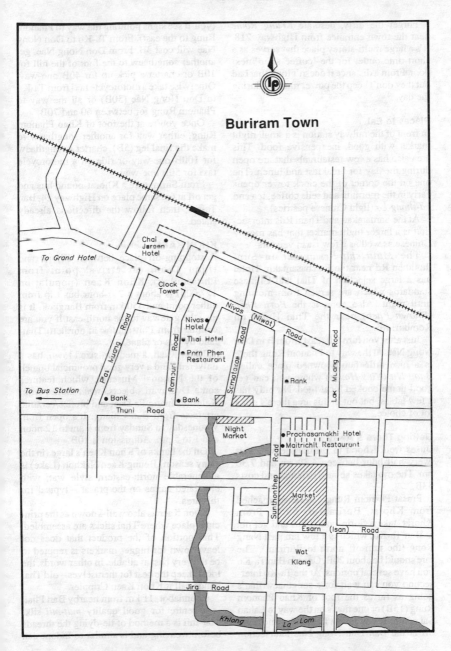

Buriram Town

Forget the dirty, desolate *Krung Rome* near the town entrance from Highway 218. It's a large multi-storey place that serves as a short-time outlet for the 'coffee shop' next door. From a distance it doesn't look that bad but they don't keep the power running during the day.

Places to Eat

In front of the railway station is a small night market with good, inexpensive food. This area also has a few restaurants that are open during the day for breakfast and lunch. The one on the corner of the clock tower opens early in the morning and sells coffee, tea and *pa-thong-ko* (light Chinese pastries).

At the Samatakan and Thani Rds intersection is a larger night market that has mostly Chinese as well as a few isaan vendors.

The *Maitrichit Restaurant* on Sunthonthep Rd near the Prachasamakhi Hotel has a large selection of Thai and Chinese standards which are served from morning until night. Also good is the *Porn Phen* (*Phawn Phen*) near the Thai Hotel on Romburi Rd.

Just after you turn left (east) from Ban Don Nong Nae on the way to Phanom Rung there is a nice little family-owned place called *Baan Nit* (*Nit's House*) where you can get good home-cooked local food. Nit only has a few tables, but out in this area there's not a lot of choice.

Getting There & Away

Buses from Khorat to Buriram leave about every half-hour between 4.30 am and 7.30 pm. The trip takes about 2½ hours and costs 33B.

Prasat Phanom Rung can be approached from Khorat, Buriram or Surin. From Khorat, take a Surin-bound bus and get out at Ban Ta-Ko, which is a few km past Nang Rong (the turn-off north to Buriram). The fare should be about 20B. Once in Ban Ta-Ko you have several options. At the Ta-Ko intersection you can wait for a songthaew that's going as far as the foot of Khao Phanom Rung (15B) or one that's on the way to Lahan Sai south. If you take a Lahan Sai truck, get off at the Ban Don Nong Nae intersection

(you'll see signs pointing the way to Phanom Rung to the east). From Ta-Ko to Don Nong Nae will cost 3B. From Don Nong Nae, get another songthaew to the foot of the hill for 10B or charter a pick-up for 40B one-way. Otherwise take a motorcycle taxi from Ta-Ko to Don Nong Nae (30B) or all the way to Phanom Rung for between 60 and 70B.

Once you're at the foot of Khao Phanom Rung, either wait for another songthaew to make the final leg (5B), charter a songthaew for 100B one-way or ride on a motorcycle taxi for 50B one-way.

From Surin, take a Khorat-bound bus and get off at the same place on Highway 24, Ban Ta-Ko, then follow the directions already stated.

KHON KAEN เมือง ขอนแก่น

A stopping-off place between Khorat and Udon Thani (or arrival point from Phitsanulok), Khon Kaen (population 127,000) is about a 2½-hour bus trip from either point and 450 km from Bangkok. It is also the gateway to the north-east if you are coming from Phitsanulok in northern Thailand by bus or plane.

Khon Kaen, a medium-sized town, has a university and a very good provincial branch of the National Museum, which features some Dvaravati objects, *sema* stones from Kalasin/Muang Fa Daet and bronze/ceramic artefacts from Ban Chiang. It's open from Wednesday to Sunday from 9 am to 12 noon and 1 to 5 pm. Admission is 10B.

On the banks of Khon Kaen's large (in the rainy season) Beung Kaen Nakhon (Lake) is a venerable north-eastern style wat, with elongated spires on the prasat – typical for this area.

Khon Kaen is also well-known as the principal place where Thai sticks are assembled. That portion of the product that does not leave town for bigger markets is reputed to be the very best available. In other words, the locals keep the best for themselves – old Thai hands call it Khon Kaen Crippler.

Chonnabot, 11 km from nearby Ban Phai, is a centre for good quality *mat-mii* silk. Mat-mii is a method of tie-dying the threads before weaving and is similar to Indonesian

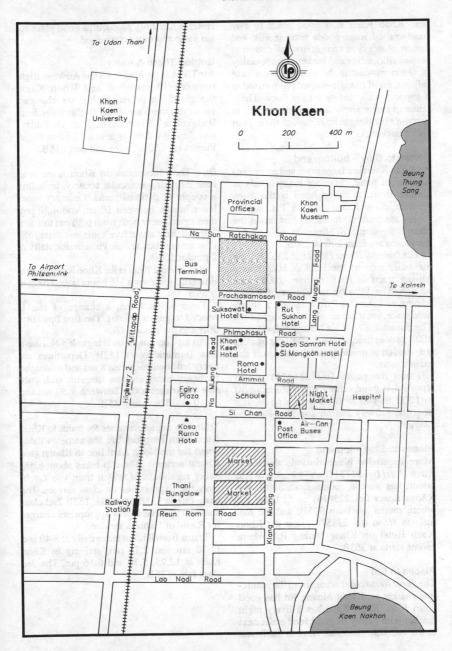

Khon Kaen

0   200   400 m

To Udon Thani

Khon
Kaen
University

To Airport
Phitsanulok

Beung
Thung
Sang

Provincial
Offices

Khon
Kaen
Museum

Na Sun Ratchakan   Road

Bus
Terminal

To Kalasin

Prachasamoson   Road

Suksawat
Hotel

Rot
Sukhon
Hotel

Phimphasut   Road

Saen Samran Hotel
Si Mongkôn Hotel

Khon
Kaen
Hotel

Roma
Hotel

Ammat   Road

Fairy
Plaza

School

Night
Market

Hospital

Si Chan   Road

Kosa
Ruma
Hotel

Post
Office

Air–Con
Buses

Market

Thani
Bungalow

Market

Railway
Station

Reun Rom   Road

Lao Nadi Road

Beung
Kaen Nakhon

ikat. Khon Kaen is a good place to buy hand-crafted isaan goods such as silk and cotton fabrics (you can get mat-mii cotton as well as silk), silver and basketry. A speciality of the north-east is the *mawn khwan* (axe pillow), a stiff triangle-shaped pillow used as a support while sitting on the floor. These come in many sizes, from small enough to carry in a handbag to large enough to fill your entire backpack.

Places to Stay – bottom end
As Khon Kaen is a large town and an important transit point, there are many hotels to choose from. A cheap hotel is the *Saen Samran*, 55-9 Klang Muang Rd, where rooms are from 60 to 100B. Just down the street is the similar *Si Mongkon* at No 61-67, but rooms are from 100 to 150B.

The friendly *Roma Hotel* (tel 236276), on the other side of the road at 50/2 Klang Muang starts at 100B or from 200B with air-con. The *Villa* on the corner of Klang Muang and Ammat Rds is mostly a short-time place, but it has air-con rooms for 220B. The *Sawatdi*, 177-9 Na Muang Rd, starts at 100B as does the *Suksawat*, off Klang Muang Rd, which is quieter since it's a bit off the main streets.

Thani Bungalow (tel 221470), Reun Rom Rd, is good value with rooms from 80 to 120B or 140 to 200B with air-con. It's near the railway station and Hua Rot Fai Market.

Places to Stay – top end
More expensive places include the *Khon Kaen Hotel* (tel 237711) on Phimphasut Rd, which has air-con rooms from 300B, the *Khosa Rama* (tel 225014) on Si Chan Rd where rooms are from 375B, and the *Rot Sukhon Hotel* (tel 238576), near the Khon Kaen Hotel on Klang Muang Rd, where rooms starts at 363B.

Places to Eat
The *Jerat Restaurant* across from the municipal market on Klang Muang Rd has good isaan food. Khon Kaen has a lively night market with plenty of good food stalls next to the AC Bus Terminal. Next to the Roma Hotel is *Kai Yang Thiparot*, a good place for kai yang and other isaan food.

Getting There & Away
Air There is no longer a Thai Airways flight between Phitsanulok and Khon Kaen, though check to see if this has changed. However, there are direct flights daily from Bangkok at 7.30 am and 6.35 pm. On Fridays and Sundays there is also a 12 noon flight. Flights take 50 minutes and cost 815B.

Bus The Phitsanulok to Khon Kaen road runs through spectacular scenery, including a couple of national parks. Ordinary buses leave hourly between 10 am and 4.30 pm, then again every hour from 6.30 pm to 1 am. The trip takes about five hours and costs 76B. One air-con bus leaves Phitsanulok daily at 2 pm for 106B.

Buses leave Khorat for Khon Kaen several times daily, arriving 2½ hours later. The cost is 39B.

From Khon Kaen, a change of bus is needed to get to Phimai. The first bus costs 30B and the second 4B.

An air-con bus from Bangkok's Northern Bus Terminal costs 153B. Departures are every half hour between 8 am and midnight. Ordinary buses are less frequent with only five departures a day between 9.30 am and 11.10 pm. The fare is 85B.

Train The departure times for trains to Khon Kaen from Bangkok are the same as those noted for the Nong Khai line to Khorat (see Khorat section). The trip takes about eight hours regardless of which train you catch. Only the Express has 1st-class service. The basic fare is 333B 1st class, 162B 2nd class and 77B 3rd class, plus appropriate charges for Rapid or Express service.

Trains from Khorat leave daily at 8.40 and 11.20 am and 2.55 pm, arriving in Khon Kaen at 12.25, 5.30 and 6.16 pm. The 3rd class fare is 35B.

Roi Et Province

Roi Et Province is known for the crafting of the quintessential isaan musical instrument, the khaen, a kind of pan pipe made of the *mai kuu* reed and wood. The best khaens are reputedly made in the village of Si Kaew, 15 km north-west of Roi Et Town. It generally takes about three days to make one khaen, depending on its size. The straight, sturdy reeds, which resemble bamboo, are cut and bound together in pairs of six, eight or nine. The sound box that fits in the middle is made of *ton pratu*, a hardwood that's resistant to moisture.

ROI ET TOWN

Roi Et Town (population 34,000) is a fairly small but growing capital of a province that three centuries ago was an important city state which probably served as a buffer between Thai and Lao political conflict.

Old Roi Et had 11 city gates and was surrounded by its 11 vassal colonies. The name of the province means One Hundred and One and may be an exaggeration of the number 11.

The capital is now on an entirely new site with the large Beung Phlan Chai artificial lake in the centre. Silk and cotton fabrics from Roi Et are high in quality and generally cheaper than in Khorat and Khon Kaen.

Wat Neua

This wat in the northern quarter of town is worth seeing for its 1200-year-old chedi from the Dvaravati period called Phra Satuup Jedi. This chedi exhibits an unusual four-cornered bell-shaped form that is rare in Thailand. Around the bot are a few old Dvaravati sema stones and to one side of the wat is an inscribed pillar erected by the Khmers when they controlled this area during the 11th and 12th centuries.

Wat Burapha

The tall, standing Buddha that towers above Roi Et's minimal skyline is the Phra Phuttha-ratana-mongkon-mahamuni (Phra Sung Yai for short) at Wat Burapha. Despite being of little artistic significance, it's hard to ignore. From the ground to the tip of the *usnisa* (flame-top), it's 67.8 metres high, including the base. You can climb a staircase through a building which supports the figure to about as high as the Buddha's knees and get a view of the town.

Places to Stay

Ban Chong (Banjong) (tel 511235) at 99-101 Suriyadet Bamrung Rd has adequate rooms with a fan and bath from 90 to 150B. On the same street at No 133 is the *Saithip* where rooms start at 150B with a fan or 170B with air-con. There are cheaper hotels along Rattakit Khlaikhla Rd including the *Thian Di* at No 52-62, where basic rooms start at 50B.

Places to Eat

Around the edge of Beung Phalan Chai are several medium-priced garden restaurants. The *Khao Laeng* is on the north-eastern side and has a pleasant atmosphere, an English menu and good food. You'll also find a string of cheaper restaurants along Ratsadan Uthit Rd, which runs east off the lake from the north-eastern corner.

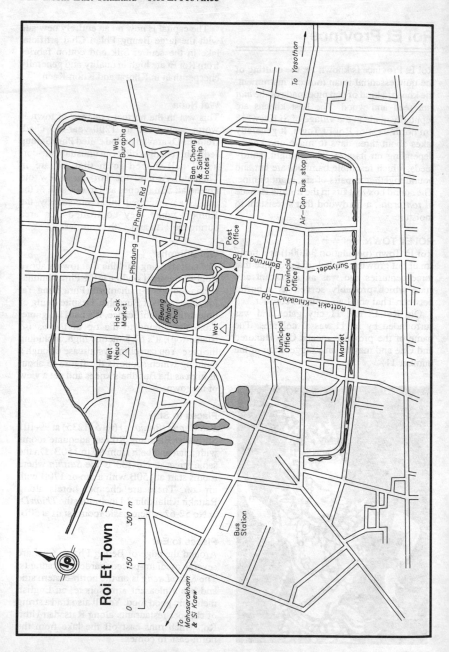

Roi Et Town

0   150   300 m

To Yasothon

To Mahasarakham
& Si Kaew

Wat Burapha

Ban Chong & Saithip Hotels

Air-Con Bus stop

Post Office

Phanit – Rd

Phadung

Bamrung Rd

Suriyadet

Provincial Office

Rattakit Khlaikhid Rd

Hai Sok Market

Beung Phlan Chai

Wat Neua

Wat

Municipal Office

Market

Bus Station

The night market area is a couple of streets east of the Banjong and Saithip hotels.

Things to Buy

If you want to buy local handicrafts, the best place to go is the shopping area along Phadung Phanit Rd where you'll find mawn khwan (triangular floor pillows), phaa mat-mii (tie-dyed silk and cotton fabric), sticky rice baskets, khaens and Buddhist paraphernalia. *Phaw Kaan Khaa* at 377-9 Phadung Phanit has a particularly good selection of fabrics, but as always you must bargain well to get good prices.

Udon Thani Province

UDON THANI TOWN   เมืองอุดรธานี

Just over 560 km from Bangkok, Udon (often spelt Udorn) is one of three north-eastern cities (including Ubon and Khorat) that boomed virtually overnight when an American military base was established in each during the Vietnam War (there were seven USA bases in Thailand during that period, but since 1976 there have been none).

Except for nearby Dan Chiang and Dan Pheu, Udon (population 83,000) has nothing much to offer unless you've spent a long time already in the north-east and seek western amenities like air-con coffee houses, flashy ice cream and massage parlours or farang food. However, Udon does have possibly the best kai yang in the north-east, outside of Si Saket.

Places to Stay – bottom end

The following hotels are recommended.

Queen Hotel, 6-8 Udon-dutsadi Rd, which has rooms with a fan and bath from 80B. It's a 5B samlor ride from the railway station.

Tokyo Hotel, 147 Prachak Rd, in the centre of town, has 100B rooms with a fan and bath or air-con rooms for 280B.

Si Sawat, at 123 Prachak Rd, near the Tokyo Hotel, costs 60B for a room with a fan and a shared bath in the old building or 80B for a room with a fan and private bath in the

new building. It's a bit noisy, according to one report.

Paradise Hotel, 44/29 Pho Si Rd, near the bus station and the fancy *Charoen Hotel*, charges from 150 to 200B for air-con rooms with a bath and hot water, while *Suk Somjai*, 226 Pho Si Rd, charges from 60 to 120B for a room with a fan and bath.

Thailand, 4/5 Surakon Rd, near the bus station, charges from 100B for not-so-clean rooms with a fan and bath.

Saiwong at 39 Adunyadet (Adulyadet) Rd, off Prachak Rd near the Chinese temple, is a small wooden Chinese hotel with rooms for 50B with a fan and shared bath.

There are several other small, inexpensive hotels along Prachak Rd, including the *Mit Sahai* and the *Malasi Saengden*, which both have rooms for 60B.

Places to Stay – top end

The *Charoen* (tel 221331) at 549 Pho Si Rd has air-con rooms from 380B. The *Chaiyaporn* (tel 221913 or 222144) at 209-211 Mak Khaeng Rd has rooms from 100B or from 250B with air-con, and *Charoensi Palace* (tel 222601), 60 Pho Si Rd, has air-con rooms from 250 to 500B.

Places to Eat

There is plenty of good food in Udon, especially isaan fare. The best kai yang shops are along Prachak Rd, west of the clock tower and just before Prachak Rd crosses Mak kaeng Rd. Try Khun Phaen beer, a brand mostly available in Thailand's east and north-east. It's very similar in taste to Singha, but is 5 to 10B cheaper.

Rung Thong sells excellent Thai curries at the west side of the clock tower traffic circle and is also cheap.

There's also *Rama Pastry*, an air-con pastry and coffee shop with good pastries, on Prachak Rd between Adunyadet and Mak kaeng Rds, a few blocks towards the clock tower from the kai yang shops.

Six km north of Udon on the road to Nong Khai is a very good (and inexpensive) seafood-isaan restaurant park called *Suan Kaset Rang San*. On an island among several small lakes, it serves great food in a rustic

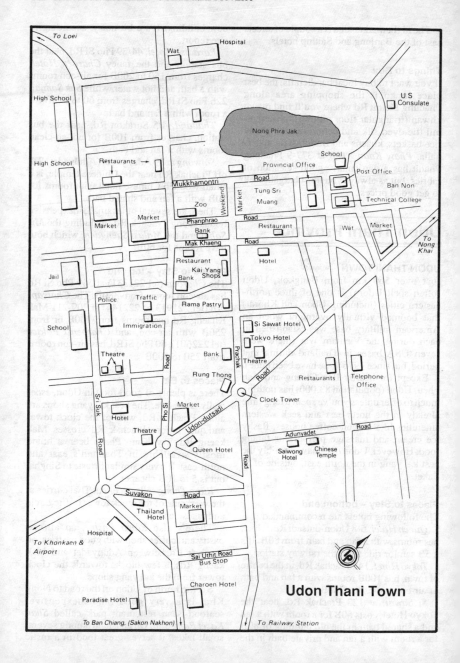

Udon Thani Town

atmosphere. Many of the types of fish served are caught in the lakes, which are owned by the restaurant. These include pla nin (Nile fish or Tilapia), *plaa taphian* (carp), *plaa nai* (wheel fish), *plaa yisok* (Probarbus carp) and *plaa jiin* (freshwater catfish). Recommended dishes include: *plaan nin phao* (grilled Nile fish), *tom yam plaa* (seafood soup seasoned with lemon grass, mushrooms and a few chillies) and *plaa nai jian puay* (a fantastic dish of steamed whole pla nai smothered in coriander, ginger and *puay*, a salty and sour Chinese plum).

It also has good isaan food and an English menu is available. Fishing in the lakes during the day is allowed. You are charged a flat rate of 10B per day to fish, plus 20B per kg of fish caught. However, you are welcome to enjoy the surroundings, without a fishing rod, for free.

Entertainment

For somewhere to go at night, the *Charoen Hotel* has a very dark cafe with live music – quite a scene. The other big night spot in Udon is the *Tibet* club.

Getting There & Away

Air Thai Airways flies to Udon from Bangkok daily by way of Khon Kaen (see Khon Kaen for departure times). The flight takes 1½ hours and costs 870B by Boeing 737 (flying upcountry) or 750B by Shorts 330 (flying back to Bangkok).

Bus Buses for Udon leave Bangkok's Northern Bus Terminal throughout the day from 9 am to 11.30 pm. The trip takes 11 to 12 hours and the fare is 106B or 191B air-con.

From Khorat, buses leave the main bus station for Udon every half-hour during the day and arrive five hours later. The cost is 60B (110B air-con).

Train The 9 pm Nong Khai Express from Bangkok arrives in Udon at 6.50 am the next day. The 1st-class fare is 413B, 2nd class is 198B and 3rd class is 95B, plus applicable charges for sleeper and Express service. A special, all-inclusive 3rd-class fare (110B) applies on Rapid trains to Udon.

Rapid trains leave Bangkok on the Nong Khai line at 6.10 am and 6.30 pm, arriving in Udon at 4.17 pm and 4.55 am. The Express to Bangkok leaves Udon at 8.02 pm and arrives at Hualamphong at 5.58 am. Rapid trains also leave Udon at 7.32 am and 7.01 pm, arriving in Bangkok at 5.45 pm and 5.32 am.

AROUND UDON THANI PROVINCE

Ban Chiang บ้านเชียง

Ban Chiang, 50 km east of Udon Thani Town, now plays host to a steady trickle of tourists from all over Thailand and a few from beyond. As well as the original excavation at Wat Pho Si Nai at the village edge (open to the public), there is a recently constructed museum with extensive Ban Chiang exhibits. This is worth a trip if you're at all interested in the historic Ban Chiang culture, which goes back at least 5000 years and quite possibly 7000. The museum is closed Mondays and Tuesdays.

This agricultural society, which once thrived in north-eastern Thailand, is known for its early bronze metallurgy and clay pottery, especially pots and vases with distinctive burnt-ochre swirl designs, most of which were associated with burial sites. The locals attempt to sell Ban Chiang artefacts, real and fake, but neither type will be allowed out of the country, so don't buy them. Some of the local handicrafts, such as thick handwoven cotton fabric, are good buys.

Getting There & Away

There is a regular bus between Udon and Ban Chiang for 20B. Buses leave in either direction several times a day, but the last leaves Ban Chiang in the late afternoon.

Ban Pheu บ้านผือ

Ban Pheu district is about 42 km north-west of Udon Thani Town and has a strange mix of prehistoric cave paintings and bizarre geological formations, the bulk of which are at Phra Phutthabat Bua Bok, 12 km outside of Ban Pheu on Phra Bat hill.

The formations are a 'madhouse of balanced rocks, spires and whale-sized boulders' said one traveller. Several shrines and three wats are built in and around the formations.

At the entrance to the area is the largest temple, Wat Phra That Phra Phutthabat Bua Bok. Prehistoric paintings are in several caves and feature wild animals, humans and cryptic symbols. To the south-east of the main wat are the caves of Tham Lai Meu and Tham Non Sao Eh and to the west are Tham Khon and Tham Wua Daeng. For isaan residents, this is an important place of pilgrimage.

Getting There & Away Ban Pheu has one hotel if you want to spend some time here. Otherwise, it can be visited as a day trip from either Udon or Nong Khai. From Udon it's a 14B songthaew ride to Ban Pheu or 20B from Nong Khai. From Ban Pheu, take a songthaew for 4B to the village nearest the site, Ban Tiu, then walk or hitch the three km to Wat Phra Phutthabat. You could also charter a motorcycle in the Ban Pheu market to take you all the way to Phra Phutthabat.

Nong Khai Province

Nong Khai Province is long and narrow, with 300 km of its length along the Maekhong River. Yet at its widest point, the province is only 50 km across. Even if you can't cross into Laos, Nong Khai is a fascinating province to explore. It has long, open views of the Maekhong River and Laos on the other side. There are touches of Lao-French influence on local culture which has made for good food and interesting wats.

The Thai name for the river is Mae Nam Khong. Mae Nam means river (literally 'mother water') and Khong is its name, hence the term 'Maekhong River' is a bit redundant. Westerners have called it the 'Mekong River' for decades and the Thais themselves sometimes call it 'Maekhong' for short, so I'm compromising and calling it the 'Maekhong River'.

NONG KHAI TOWN   เมืองหนองคาย
More than 620 km from Bangkok and 55 km

from Udon Thani Town, Nong Khai is where Route 2, the Friendship Highway, ends at the Maekhong River. Across the river is Laos.

Nong Khai (population 25,000) is one of four crossings open along the Thai-Lao border (the other three are Nakhon Phanom, That Phanom and Mukdahan) and citizens of the two countries are allowed to cross at will for day trips. Thais can fairly easily get visas for longer trips.

Check with the Lao Embassy in Bangkok for the possibility of farangs getting visas to visit Vientiane (Wieng Chan), 20 km north-west of Nong Khai. Also try the Immigration Office in Nong Khai in case they've decided to let foreigners across for day trips too (probably not yet).

If your visit is approved, take a ferry across to Tha Deua in Laos and catch a bus or taxi to Wieng Chan. The Thai and Lao Governments plan to build a bridge over the river from Ban Chommani (near the Nong Khai railhead) to Tha Na Laeng on the Lao side. The Australian-financed bridge is expected to be completed by 1992. Nong Khai is fast becoming a bona fide scene as travellers gather in anticipation of the expected opening of Laos.

Nong Khai Town has a row of old buildings of French-Chinese architecture along the east stretch of Meechai Rd, parallel to the river. Unfortunately, on my last visit I noticed that local developers are razing some of the most historic buildings in Nong Khai and replacing them with the ugly egg-carton architecture common all over urban Asia. Let's hope Nong Khai residents make a plea for historical preservation or they'll soon be no historic buildings left in Nong Khai.

The restaurant next to the Immigration Office and pier is a good place to sit and watch the small ferry boats flying Pathet Lao flags cross back and forth between Thailand and the Lao People's Democratic Republic. Obviously a great deal of travel is allowed between shores, as the boats always have passengers.

In the river is Phra That Nong Khai, a Lao chedi which can be seen in the dry season when the Maekhong lowers about 30 metres. The chedi slipped into the river in 1847 and is continuing to slide – it's near the middle now.

In the second week of March the Nong Kai Show is held with lots of festivities.

Wat Phra Thal Bang Phuan
วัดพระธาตุ บางเผือน

Twelve km south of Nong Khai Town, on Route 2 and then west on Route 211, Wat Bang Phuan is one of the most sacred sites in the north-east because of the old Indian-style stupa originally found here. It's similar to the original chedi beneath the Phra Pathom Chedi in Nakhon Pathom, but no-one knows when either chedi was built. Speculation has it that it must have been in the early centuries AD or possibly even earlier.

In 1559 King Jayachettha of Chantaburi (not the present Chantaburi in Thailand, but Wieng Chan known as Vientiane – in Laos) extended his capital across the Maekhong and built a newer, taller, Lao-style chedi over the original as a demonstration of faith (just as King Mongkut did in Nakhon Pathom). Vientiane is the French spelling of the Lao name Wieng Chan which, like the Thai Chantaburi, means City of the Moon. Rain caused the chedi to lean precariously and in 1970 it fell over. The Fine Arts Department restored it in 1978 with the Sangharaja, Thailand's Supreme Buddhist Patriarch, presiding over the rededication.

Actually, it is the remaining 16th-century Lao chedi in the compound (two contain semi-intact Buddha images in their niches) that give the wat its charm. There is also a roofless wihan with a large Buddha image and a massive round brick base that must have supported another large chedi at one time.

Getting There & Away To get to Wat Phra That Bang Phuan, get a Si Chiangmai or Sangkhom songthaew or bus in Nong Khai and ask for Ban Bang Phuan (12B). Otherwise get any bus south on Route 2 and get off in Ban Nong Hong Song, the junction for Route 211. From there you can grab the next bus from either Udon or Nong Khai that's going to Si Chiangmai and get off near the wat. The fare should be about 10B to the road leading off Route 211, an easy walk to the wat from that point.

Wat Hin Maak Peng วัดหินหมากเป้ง
Sixty km north-west of Nong Khai between Si Chiangmai and Sangkhom, Wat Hin is worth a trip just for the scenery along Route 211 from Nong Khai Town. This monastery is locally known for its *thutong* (Pali: *dhutanga*) monks – men who have taken ascetic vows in addition to the standard 227 precepts. These vows include eating only once a day, wearing only forest robes made from discarded cloth and having a strong emphasis on meditation. There are also several *mae chii* (Buddhist nuns, not actually ordained *bhikkhunis*) living here.

The place is very quiet and peaceful, set in a cool forest with lots of bamboo groves overlooking the Maekhong. The monastic kutis are built among giant boulders that form a cliff high above the river. Below the cliff is a sandy beach and more rock formations. Directly across the river a Lao forest temple can be seen. Fishermen occasionally drift by on house rafts. It's very atmospheric.

Getting There & Away To get there take a songthaew from Nong Khai to Si Chiangmai (13B) and ask for a songthaew directly to Wat Hin (there are a few) or to Sangkhom, which is just past the entrance to Wat Hin – the other passengers will let you know when the truck passes it. The second songthaew is 10B. On the way to Wat Hin you might notice a large topiary at Ban Phran Phrao on the right side of the highway.

Phutthamamakasamakhom พุทธมามกสมาคม
Also called Wat Khaek (a lot easier to pronounce) by locals, this strange Hindu-Buddhist temple, established in 1978, is a tribute to the wild imagination of Luang Pu Bunleua Surirat. Luang Pu (Venerable Grandfather) is a Brahminic yogi-priest-shaman who merges Hindu and Buddhist philosophy, mythology and iconography into a cryptic whole. He has developed a very large following in north-eastern Thailand and Laos, where he lived for many years before moving to Nong Khai (he still main-

tains a temple in Laos). He is supposed to have studied under a Hindu *rishi* in Vietnam.

The focus of the temple are many bizarre cement statues of Shiva, Vishnu, Buddha and every other Hindu or Buddhist deity imaginable, as well as numerous secular figures, all supposedly cast by unskilled artists under Luang Pu's direction. The style of the figures is remarkably uniform, with faces which look like benign African masks. In the shrine building there are two large rooms, upstairs and down, full of framed pictures of Hindu or Buddhist deities, temple donors, Luang Pu at various ages plus smaller bronze and

wooden figures of every description and provenance, guaranteed to throw an art historian into a state of disorientation.

In Nong Khai, it is said that any person who drinks water offered by Luang Pu will turn all his possessions over to the temple, so bring your canteen.

Getting There & Away Board a songthaew heading east towards Beung Kan and ask to get off at Wat Khaek, the Indian temple, which is four or five km outside of town, near St Paul Nong Khai School. The fare should be about 8B.

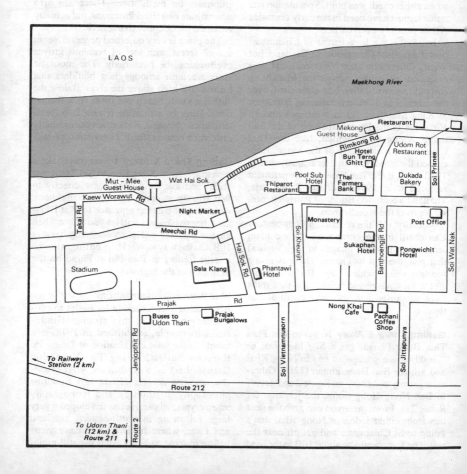

Festivals
Like many other cities in the north-east, Nong Khai has a large rocket festival (*ngaan bun bong fai*) during the full moon of May and a candle festival (*ngaan hae thian*) at the beginning of *phansaa*, or the Buddhist rains retreat, in late July.

Places to Stay
Hotels *Prajak Bungalows* (tel 411116), 1178 Prajak Rd, has good air-con rooms for 170B and rooms with a fan from 80 to 100B.

The *Phunsap Hotel* (its English sign reads Pool Sub), on Meechai Rd parallel to the river, costs 70B for OK rooms with a fan and bath.

The *Sukhaphan Hotel* on Banthoengjit Rd, across the street from the *Phongwichit Hotel*, is an old wooden Chinese hotel that has recently been nicely renovated. Rooms have screened windows and singles/doubles cost 60/70B with a fan and shared bath. This hotel has information on travel in Laos and even sells Lao postcards. Two other cheapies on Banthoengjit Rd, but which are not nearly as good as the Sukhaphan, are the *Banthoengjit* and the *Kheng Houng (Huang)*, both with rooms for 60B.

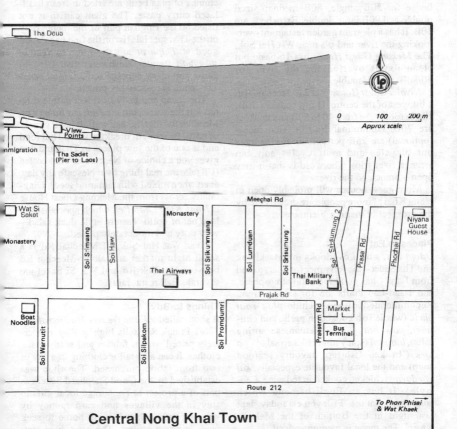

Central Nong Khai Town

Pongvichet (Phongwichit) at 723 Banth-oengjit Rd, across the street from the Sukhaphan, is fairly clean and businesslike and costs 80B for a room with a fan and bath.

At the top end in Nong Khai is the *Phantawi* (tel 411568), 1241 Hai Sok Rd, where very tidy rooms with a fan and bath start at 100B and go to 300B with air-con. Across the street are the *Phantawi Bungalows* under the same management and at the same rates. A decent coffee shop is downstairs.

Guest Houses *Mutmee (Mat-mii) Guest House* is on the river and has rooms in an old house for 50B single, 80B medium-sized double and 90B large double. Extra beds are 30B. It has a pleasant garden restaurant overlooking the river and it's near Wat Hai Sok. The *Mekong Guest House* has 16 basic but clean rooms overlooking the river for 50/80B, single/double.

Niyana Guest House is at 239 Meechai Rd, a bit west of the centre. Dorm beds are 30B, single rooms are from 40 to 50B and doubles are 70B. Communal Lao or Thai meals (optional) are 25B per person. It also rents out bicycles and motorcycles and can arrange river trips. The word is that it may open a branch on the river.

More guest houses will probably open in Nong Khai as more people are drawn here by the prospect of visiting Vientiane.

Places to Eat
Udom Rot, which overlooks the Maekhong and Tha Sadet – the ferry pier for boats to and from Laos – has good food and atmosphere, and isaan-Lao crafts are for sale in front. Recommended dishes include *plaa raat phrik* (whole fish cooked in garlic and chillies), *paw pia yuan* (Vietnamese spring rolls), *laap kai* (spicy mint chicken salad), *po taek* ('broken fishtrap' savoury seafood soup) and the local favourite especially, *kai lao daeng* (chicken cooked in red wine, Lao-style). It has an English menu which announces that the 'Fish you eat today slept last night in the Bottom of the Mekong River'. The menu is medium-priced.

On the other side of the pier is the more expensive *Tha Dan* (Customs Pier) restaurant, also with a souvenir shop in front.

Thiparot, next to the Pool Sub Hotel on Meechai Rd, serves excellent Chinese, Thai and Lao food. The speciality of the house is *plaa beuk*, the giant Maekhong catfish (*Pangasianodon gigas*) – the largest fish in the Maekhong River, sometimes reaching 400 kg. Locals say this fish must swim all the way from Qinghai Province in China where the Maekhong originates. The texture is very meaty but it has a delicate flavour, similar to tuna or swordfish, only whiter in colour. It's best prepared as *plaa beuk phat phet* in which chunks of plaa beuk are fried in fresh basil-laced curry paste. The giant catfish is not listed on the English part of the menu, only on the Thai specials list on the first page. Also good at *Thiparot* are the *plaa sa-nguang sa-nguan* (tender freshwater fish fried in garlic and black pepper) and *kai lao daeng*. The menu is reasonably priced.

The cheap and tasty Loet Rot coffee shop has left the scene, but the *Dukada Bakery* on Meechai Rd fills the gap well. It has a variety of pastries, western breakfasts and Thai food and is one of the few places in Thailand that gives you a choice of Nescafe or Thai coffee (I'll take the real thing over Nescafe any day, even when mixed with tamarind seed). Diagonally across from the Mekong Guest House is *Nong Khai Laap Pet*, which specialises in laap pet of north- eastern style duck salad – very tasty and moderately priced.

Near Wat Hai Sok off Meechai Rd is a small night market and along Meechai Rd between Hai Sok Rd and Wat Si Saket are several small restaurants.

Things to Buy
A shop called *Village Weaver Handicrafts* at 786/1 Prajak Rd, sells high quality, moderately priced woven fabrics and ready-made clothes. It can also tailor clothing in a day or two from fabric purchased. The shop was established by the Good Shepherd Sisters as part of a project to encourage local girls to stay in the villages and earn money by weaving rather than leaving home to seek work in urban centres. The hand-dyed mat-mii cotton is particularly good here, and

visitors are welcome to observe the methods in the weavery behind the shop. It's down Prajak Rd past the ordinary bus terminal – five to 10B by samlor from the centre of town. The Thai name of the project is *Hattakam Sing Thaw*.

Getting There & Away
Bus Buses to Nong Khai leave Udon approximately every 30 minutes throughout the day from the Udon Bus Station. The trip takes a little more than 1¼ hours and costs 20B.

Buses to Nong Khai from Bangkok's Northern Bus Terminal leave during the early morning from 5 to 8.30 am and in the evening at 8.10 and 8.54 pm. The trip is a long nine to 10 hours and costs 120B for an ordinary (no air-con) bus. Air-con buses are 209B and leave three times a day at 9 am, 9 and 9.30 pm. Most people take the train.

Buses from Khorat start running in the afternoon and continue into the early evening. The fare is 75B and the trip takes six to seven hours.

If you're coming from Loei Province you can get buses from Chiang Khan or Pak Chom, without having to double back to Udon. It's 65B from Chiang Khan and 50B from Pak Chom.

Train From Bangkok, the Nong Khai Express leaves Hualamphong daily at 8.30 pm, arriving in Nong Khai at 7.05 am. Two Rapid trains leave daily at 6.30 am and 7 pm, arriving at 5.10 pm and 6.05 am. Basic one-way fares are 450B 1st class, 215B 2nd class and 103B 3rd class, not including surcharges for Express or Rapid service (30B and 20B) or sleeping berths. The State Railway runs a 3rd-class special on Rapid trains for 115B inclusive, a saving of 8B.

AROUND NONG KHAI PROVINCE
Si Chiangmai ศรีเชียงใหม่
Along the Maekhong River and Route 211 between Nong Khai Town and the Loei Province line are several smaller towns and villages where life revolves around farming and minimal trade between Laos and Thailand.

Travelling west, one of the first is Si Chiangmai, just across the river from Vien-

tiane. Si Chiangmai has a large number of Vietnamese, who make their living from the manufacture of spring-roll wrappers made of rice flour. You can see the translucent disks drying in the sun on bamboo racks all over town. Si Chiangmai is one of the leading exporters of spring-roll wrappers in the world! Many of the Vietnamese and Lao residents are Roman Catholic and there is a small cathedral in town. A local bakery bakes fresh French rolls every morning.

The Australian-financed bridge between Thailand and Laos may be sited at Si Chiangmai, whenever they get around to building it.

Places to Stay There is only one guest house in town but more will surely start up. *Tim Guest House* is run by a friendly young Swiss French man (who speaks English, French, German and Thai) and his Thai wife. Rooms run from 40B for a small single to 100B for a large double. The couple serve food in a dining area downstairs. They also arrange boat trips and rent out bicycles and motorcycles. The guest house is on Rim Khong Rd near the river in the centre of town – walk west from the bus terminal and turn right at Soi 17, then turn left at the end of the road and you'll come to *Tim Guest House* on the left.

Getting There & Away Probably because of its importance as a spring-roll wrapper capital, Si Chiangmai has an abundance of public transport in and out. Bus fares to/from Si Chiangmai are:

Nong Khai	13B
Sangkhom	10B
Udon Thani	20B
Khon Kaen	41B
(air-con)	80B
Khorat	75B
(air-con)	120B
Bangkok	
(air-con)	160B

Sangkhom แสงขอม
The tiny town of Sangkhom could be used as a rest stop on a slow journey along the Maekhong River between Loei and Nong

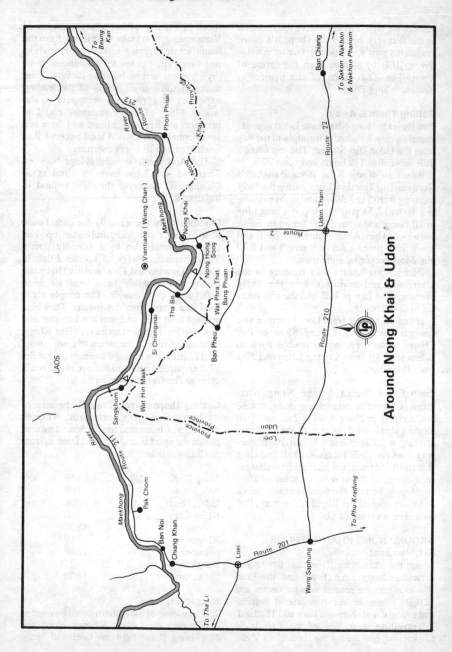

Khai. Wat Hin Maak Peng is nearby (see Nong Khai section) and there are some good hikes in the area to caves and waterfalls. The guest houses hand out maps of the area.

Places to Stay The town's three guest houses are off the main road through town near the river. *TXK Guest House* had two locations, one near the market and bus station and one further west, but it may have closed the former. Its original location is right on the river in the centre of town. Singles/doubles are 40/70B. TXK serves food, has good information and also rents out bicycles and motorcycles.

The second branch near the market has a nice sitting area that overlooks the river and a basic Thai restaurant next door that is also the town's night spot. It also serves good tom yam soup. If this place (*TXK 2*) is closed, it's still worth coming to the little restaurant.

Further along toward Loei is the *Bouy Guest House*, a pleasant place with huts on the river. Singles/doubles next to the river are 50/70B or 40/60B nearer the road. Next door is the similar *DD Guest House* with similar rates.

Getting There & Away Buses from Nong Khai are 25B and the trip takes about two hours. From Loei it's 45B and three or four hours. Pak Chom is 1½ hours away and the fare is 20B. From nearby Si Chiangmai, it's 10B.

Loei Province

Nearly 520 km from Bangkok, 150 km from Udo, 269 km from Phitsanulok via Lom Sak and 200 km via Nakhon Thai, Loei is one of Thailand's most beautiful and unspoiled provinces. The geography is mountainous and the temperature goes from one extreme to the other, the weather being hotter here than elsewhere in Thailand during the hot season and colder during the cold season. This is the only province in Thailand where temperatures occasionally drop to 0°C.

The culture is an unusual mix of northern and north-eastern influences which have pro-

duced many local dialects. The rural life of Loei outside of the provincial capital has retained more of a traditional village flavour than elsewhere in Thailand, with the possible exceptions of Nan and Phetchabun, also once classified as remote or closed provinces.

LOEI TOWN เมืองเลย

In the provincial capital of Loei (population 20,000) there is little to see or do. Cotton is one of Loei's big crops, so it's a pretty good place to buy cotton goods, especially the heavy cotton quilts (quite necessary in the cool months) made in Chiang Khan district – they're priced by the kg. During the first week of February, Loei holds a Cotton Blossom Festival which culminates in a parade of cotton-decorated floats and naturally a Cotton Blossom Queen beauty contest.

Within the province, Phu Kradung National Park, Phu Luang National Park and the districts of Tha Li and Chiang Khan are good places to explore for natural attractions.

About three km north of Loei Town is a water recreation park with a large swimming pool called Loei Land. The admission is a reasonable 30B per day.

Places to Stay

Guest Houses *Pin Can Saw Guest House* at 35/10 Soi Saeng Sawang has small but tidy singles/doubles for 50/70B. The young Thais that run it are friendly and helpful. Ask to try their *lao ya dong* (herbal whisky). To get there from the bus terminal, walk east along Ruamjai Rd (left out of the terminal), then turn first right. Pin Can Saw is about 50 metres down on the left.

If you go up one more street from Soi Saeng Sawang and make a left, you'll come to the *Muang Loei Guest House* on the right. Rates are the same as at Pin Can Saw and the English-speaking management distributes travel information. Downstairs is a small, reasonably priced restaurant.

Hotels *Sarai Thong Hotel,* on Ruamjit Rd, has 56 rooms in three buildings, costing from 50 to 120B. All rooms have a fan and bath.

It's off the street but not very clean. However, it is undergoing renovation.

Phu Luang Hotel (tel 811532 or 811570) at 55 Charoen Rat Rd near the market costs from 120B for rooms with a fan and bath, or from 250B for air-con. It has a restaurant and night club.

At 122/1 Charoen Rat Rd, across from the Bangkok Bank, is the *Thai Udom Hotel* (tel 811763), where rooms with a fan and bath cost 100B and rooms with air-con are from 180 to 220B – good value.

Srisawat (Si Sawat) on Ruamjit Rd near Sarai Thong, has singles/doubles for 60/100B and similar facilities to Sarai Thong.

The *Di Phakdi* (tel 811294) on Ua Ari Rd, around the corner from the Thai Udom and across from the cinema, has fair rooms from 60B with a fan and bath.

Over on Chumsai Rd near the Green Garden and Thip night clubs is the *King* (tel 811701), where rooms cost from 150B with a fan and bath or 500B with air-con and hot water.

Places to Eat

The market at the intersection of Ruamjai

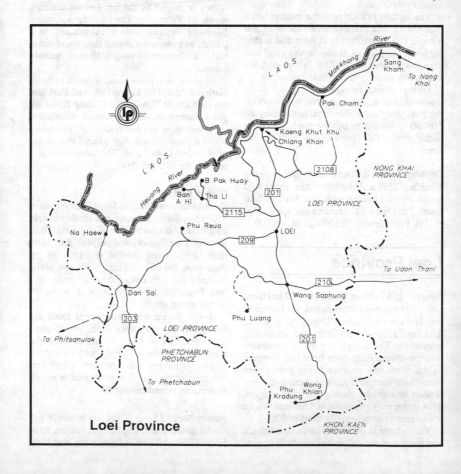

Loei Province

and Charoen Rat Rds has cheap eats and other items of local provenance. Look for the local speciality, *kai ping* (eggs-in-the-shell toasted on skewers).

Chuan Lee and *Sawita Bakery* are two pastry/coffee shops on the same side of Charoen Rat Rd, not far from the Thai Udom Hotel and Bangkok Bank. Chuan Lee is the older of the two and is more of a traditional Chinese coffee shop – very good. At lunch and dinner it also serves a few curries. Sawita is newer, has air-con and a long menu of Thai and farang dishes, including fruit salads, spaghetti, ice cream and cookies. Its prices are very reasonable.

Nawng Neung Restaurant, on the west side of Ruamjai Rd around the corner from the bus station, has great *khao man kai* (sliced chicken over marinated rice) and *kuaytiaw pet* (duck noodles). *Nam cha yen* is served in engraved aluminium cups and the soup in Chinese porcelain, yet most dishes are 12B or less. It closes at 4 pm.

Along Nok Kaew Rd between Soi Saeng Sawang and the traffic circle are two moderately priced Thai restaurants. The *Isaan* specialises in north-eastern food and *Saw Ahaan Thai* serves all kinds of Thai dishes. A simpler place on Nok Kaew Rd near Soi Saeng Sawang does just kai yang and somtam.

Entertainment
Further up Nok Kaew Rd from the Isaan restaurant and across from the King Hotel are two Thai night clubs with live music, the *Thip* and the *Green Garden*. Younger Thais go dancing at clubs near the Phu Luang Hotel and the night market, such as the *Rim Nam* and the *Tharn Thong*.

About a km out of town on the highway to Khon Kaen is a good garden restaurant called *Khrua Thong*.

Getting There & Away
Buses to Loei leave Udon regularly until late

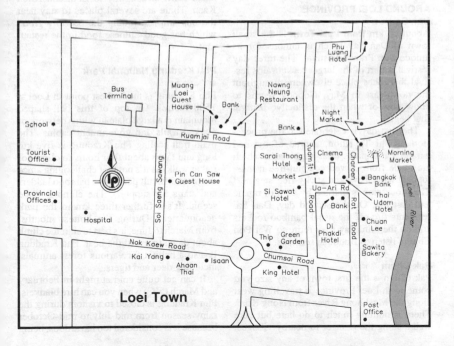

Loei Town

afternoon for 31B. The 150-km trip takes about four hours. From Nong Khai the fare is 65B and the trip takes five or six hours.

Loei can also be approached from Phitsanulok by bus via Lom Sak or Nakhon Thai. The Phitsanulok to Lom Sak leg takes 2½ hours and costs 34B. Lom Sak to Loei costs 45B and takes 3½ hours. The road from Nakhon Thai to Dan Sai is open, so there are direct buses from Phitsanulok to Loei via Dan Sai. The cost is 60B and the trip takes four hours. Buses between Loei and Dan Sai cost about 25B.

Air-con buses from Bangkok's Northern Terminal cost 191B and leave at 9 am and 8, 9, 9.30 and 10 pm, arriving in Loei about 10 hours later. Ordinary buses are 106B and leave at 4.30 and 5.30 am and 2, 8.30 and 9.30 pm.

If you want to see one of Loei's model villages, catch a songthaew east on Route 211 to Ban Noi (very near Kaeng Khut Ku).

AROUND LOEI PROVINCE

Dan Sai ด่านซ้าย

About 60 km from Loei Town is the small town of Dan Sai which is famous for its unique Bun Prawet Festival. The three-day festival is part of the larger rocket/rains festival that takes place elsewhere throughout the north-east in May. Nobody seems to know how or when the distinctive festival first began.

The first day is celebrated in the procession of Phi Ta Khon, a type of masked parade. Participants wear huge masks which are made from carved coconut-tree trunks, topped with a wicker sticky-rice steamer! The procession is marked by a lot of music and dancing. On the second day, Dan Sai residents fire off the usual bamboo rockets and on the third day they retire to Wat Pon Chai to listen to Buddhist sermons.

Pak Chom ปากชม

Pak Chom is the first town of any size you come to in Loei Province if travelling west along the Maekhong River from Nong Khai. There is nothing much to do here but take walks along the river or to nearby villages.

Ban Winai, a large Lao and Hmong refugee camp, is nearby but is not open to casual visitors.

After Pak Chom, travelling west, you come to Chiang Khan.

Places to Stay *Mae Khong Bungalows*, on the west edge of town next to the river, has singles/doubles for 40/70B. *Chumpee (Jampi) Guest House*, which is more or less in the centre, but also on the river, charges the same rates.

Getting There & Away From Chiang Khan, buses to Pak Chom are 14B. Buses from Sangkhom or Loei cost 25B. Songthaews between Pak Chom and Ban Winai (11 km) are 5B and leave Pak Chom about every half-hour in the morning and less frequently in the afternoon.

Lom Sak หล่มสัก

It's a scenic trip from Phitsanulok to this small town on the way to Loei and Khon Kaen. There are several places to stay near the bus stop, including the *Sawang Hotel* which has good Chinese food in the restaurant.

Phu Kradung National Park
อุทยานแห่งชาติภูกระดึง

Phu Kradung is the highest point in Loei at 1500 metres. On top of this bell-shaped mountain is a large plateau with a network of marked trails and government cabins. The main trail scaling Phu Kradung is five km long and takes about four hours to climb (or rather walk, as it's not that challenging since the most difficult parts have bamboo ladders and stairs for support). The climb is quite scenic. It's a further three km to the park headquarters. During the hottest months, from March to June, it's best to start the climb about dawn to avoid the heat. Phu Kradung is also a habitat for various forest animals, including deer and tigers.

It can get quite cold at night in February and March (5°C) when you can hire blankets. Phu Kradung is closed to visitors during the rainy season from mid-July to mid-October because it is considered too hazardous, being very slippery and subject to mud slides. The park can get crowded during school holidays.

Buses to Phu Kradung leave the Loei Bus Station in the morning for the 75-km trip.

Places to Stay Lots of young Thais, mainly friendly college students, camp here. Tents already set up cost 40B a night and boards for the bottom of the tents are available. Blankets and pillows cost extra. Set up your own tent for 5B per person. Cabins cost from 400 to 1200B depending on size, but will sleep five or more people. The cabins have water and electricity, but food must be brought with you from the villages below. The park gates open at 8 am. There are several small restaurants at the top of the park.

THA LI ท่าลี่
Perhaps the most beautiful part of Loei is the area which borders Laos from Dan Sai district in the west to Pak Chom in the east, including the districts of Tha Li and Chiang Khan.

Tha Li is 50 km from amphoe muang Loei Town, on Route 2115, and the village is only about eight km from the Lao border, formed here by the Heuang River, a tributary of the Maekhong (which joins the border east of here towards Chiang Khan).

Much of Tha Li district is the Thai half of a valley surrounded by the Khao Noi, Khao Laem and Khao Ngu mountains on the Thai side, and Phu Lane, Phu Hat Sone and Phu Nam Kieng on the Lao side.

When relations between Laos and Thailand were normal there was undoubtedly a lot of local commerce back and forth across the Mae Heuang. Now Ban A Hi and Ban Nong Pheu, perched on the border, thrive on black market trade. Handmade products such as cotton fabrics and straw mats, as well as contraband goods such as ganja and lao khao (white liquor), come across from Laos in exchange for finished goods from Thailand such as medicine and machine parts. These are Wild West villages where travellers go at their own risk. The local border police have been known to go fishing in the Heuang

River using hand grenades. The village brothels hire young Lao refugees.

The village men are prodigious drinkers but rarely touch beer or Maekhong whisky. Instead they drink lao khao, a clear, colourless, fiery liquid with a very high alcohol content, distilled from glutinous rice. In a pun referring to Thailand's famous Maekhong whisky, they call it 'Mae Heuang' after the local tributary. Inside nearly every bottle (20B per litre) is inserted a thick black medicinal root called *ya dong*, which is said to dissolve away the aches and pains of the day's work and prevent hangovers. It does seem to mellow the flavour of the lao khao, which has a taste somewhere in between high-proof rum and tequila.

In vivid contrast to these villages are several model villages (*muu baan tua yang*) organised by government officials as showcases for counter-insurgency in Loei Province. You'll know if you've stumbled upon one of these by the fenced-in houses with name tags on the doors. They also seem to be mostly empty of people – all hard at work in the fields, say officials. Some model villages even have model families (only one per village) which you are invited to visit. Walk right in and see Model Dad and Model Mum.

Near Ban Pak Huay is one of the best places for swimming in the Heuang River between January and May when the water is clear. None of these villages, including Tha Li, has a hotel or guest house, but you can usually spend the night at a village temple for a small donation.

Getting There & Away
See the Chiang Khan section for details of transport from Loei. Songthaews between Tha Li and Ban A Hi or Ban Pak Huay cost 7B.

CHIANG KHAN เชียงกาญจน์
Chiang Khan is also about 50 km from Loei Town, on the Maekhong River. Like Tha Li, the town is in a large valley surrounded by mountains, but unlike Tha Li, Chiang Khan has a couple of hotels and a few restaurants.

The place has a bit of the frontier atmosphere and some nice Maekhong-River views.

Visas can be extended at the Immigration Office, next to the post office, in Chiang Khan.

WATS

The town's wats feature a style of architecture rarely seen in Thailand – wihans with colonnaded fronts and painted shutters that seem to indicate a French (via Laos) influence. A good example in the centre of town is Wat Pa Klang (Wat Machatimaram), which is about 100 years old. Wat Santi and Wat Thakhok have similar characteristics. The walls of the temple buildings are stained red from all the red dust and mud that builds up in the dry and rainy seasons.

Wat Tha Khaek

Wat Tha Khaek is a 600-to-700-year-old temple, two km outside of Chiang Khan, on the way to Ban Noi and Kaeng Khut Khu.

The seated Buddha image in the bot is very sacred and it is said that holy water prepared in front of the image has the power to cure any ailing person who drinks or bathes in it.

Other well-known wats in the area include Wat Phu Pha Baen, 10 km east of Chiang Khan, where monks meditate in caves and on tree platforms, and Wat Si Song Nong, west of Kaeng Khut Ku (within easy walking distance) on the river. This is a small forest wat where the highly respected Achaan Maha Bun Nak resides.

Kaeng Khut Khu

About four km downstream from Chiang Khan Town is the Kaeng Khut Khu, a stretch of rapids (best in the dry/hot season) with a park on the Thai side and a village on the Laos side. You can hire a boat to reach the rapids. The park has a viewing tower and roofed picnic areas. Vendors sell delicious isaan food – kai yang, somtam and *khao niaw* – as well as *kung ten* 'dancing shrimp' (fresh,

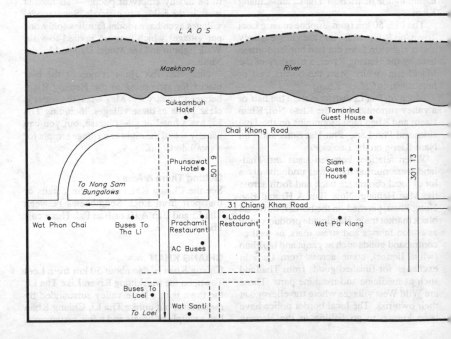

river prawns served live in a light sauce of lime juice and chillies), and *kung thawt* (the same fried whole in batter) and drinks. This is a nice place to spend a few hours.

Festivals

Chiang Khan comes alive at the end of the Buddhist rains retreat (*awk phansaa*) in October. At that time there's a week-long festival which features displays of large carved wax prasat at each of the temples in town as well as boat races on the river. At night there are performances of maw lam (isaan musical comedy), in the field facing the post office.

Places to Stay

The Amnatsiri Hotel has changed its name to *Chiang Khan Guest House* to cash in on the many travellers doing the Maekhong route these days. Fair rooms are 60B, or 70B with two beds and a shared bath. The dining area overlooks the river and good, inexpensive

food is served. At night it's a bit of a Thai hang-out. It's between Soi 19 and 20 on Chai Khong Rd, which runs along the Maekhong.

Down near Soi 17 is the easy-going *Nong Sam Guest House* which is run by an Englishman and his Thai wife. Large, comfortable, screened singles/doubles in this old wooden house on the river are 50/70B with a fan and shared bath. The couple are building some bungalows on the river on one edge of town and may possibly move all operations there. Nong Sam serves no alcohol, which tends to make it one of the quieter places in town to stay.

Further west on Chai Khong Rd, between Soi 12 and 13, is the *Tamarind Guest House*. It's OK, but rooms are rather small with singles/doubles at 50/70B. Turn away from the river altogether on Soi 12 and you'll find *Siam Guest House*, which is not recommended.

For a hotel, there's the *Souksomboon (Suksambun)* on Chai Khong Rd just past

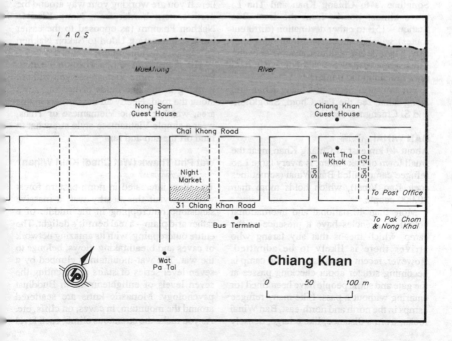

Chiang Khan

0   50   100 m

Soi 9 – look for the entranceway sign that says 'In–Out Hotel'. Rooms are 60B with a fan and shared bath or 80B with a private bath. Around the corner of Soi 9 is the *Phoonsawad (Phunsawat)*, which has similar facilities and rates.

Places to Eat

Most of the better eating places in Chiang Khan are clustered on Soi 9 and around the intersection of Soi 9 and Si Chiang Khan Rd. On the south-east corner, *Ladda* has decent khao kaeng (rice with curry) for 7B a plate. Across the street the *Prachamit* specialises in noodles. The most popular dish in town seems to be phat thai, thin rice noodles fried with bean sprouts, soy curd, peanuts and dried shrimp. Practically every restaurant in town lists this dish first on its menu! A few places serve khanom jiin (thin white wheat noodles with chilli sauce), which the locals call *khao pun*.

Getting There & Away

Songthaews to Chiang Khan and Tha Li leave almost hourly from the Loei Bus Station – 15B to either destination (different routes), which is about a two-hour ride either way. There is no regular transport between Tha Li and Chiang Khan, although a dirt road does run along the border.

For transport between Chiang Khan and Nong Khai, see the Pak Chom, Sangkhom and Si Chiangmai sections.

BAN WINAI บ้านวินัย

About 40 km east of Chiang Khan, near the small town of Pak Chom, is a very large Lao refugee camp called Ban Winai (sometimes spelt Ban Vinai), which holds more than 30,000 people.

More than 40 national and international volunteer agencies have a presence at the camp, which means that any farang who arrives there is likely to be admitted. However, recent reports say that the camp is becoming stricter about checking passes at the gate and some people have been fined for entering without a pass. Like many refugee camps in the north and north-east, Ban Winai looks, from a distance, like a large, densely populated but prosperous hill-tribe village, with thatched roofs and dirt roads. As you get closer, tank trucks and basketball courts tell the tale. Most of the refugees are Lao hill-tribe people, especially Hmong (also called 'Meo'), but there are also some lowland Lao, Khmer and Vietnamese.

You may get an entry pass to Ban Winai through the provincial offices in Loei, that's if you can give a good reason for your visit.

Getting There & Away

There are songthaews to Ban Winai from Chiang Khan and Pak Chom. The latter are easier to get, as there are regular songthaews stationed along the route. A songthaew from Chiang Khan to Pak Chom is 15B, and from Pak Chom songthaews leave in the morning for Ban Winai (5B).

BEUNG KAN บึงกาฬ

This is a small dusty town on the Maekhong River, 185 km from Nong Khai by Route 212. You may want to break your journey here if you are working your way around the north-eastern border from Nong Khai to Nakhon Phanom (as opposed to the easier but less interesting Udon to Sakon Nakhon to Nakhon Phanom route).

The closer you get to Nakhon Phanom Province, the more Vietnamese you will see working in the rice fields or herding cows along the road. Nearly all the farmers in this area, whether ethnic Vietnamese or Thais, wear a simple Vietnamese-style straw hat to fend off the sun and rain.

Wat Phu Thawk (Wat Chedi Khiri Wihan)
วัดภูทอก (วัดเจดีย์คีรีวิหาร)

Travellers interested in north-eastern forest wats can visit this nearby wat, a massive sandstone outcropping in the middle of a rather arid plain – a real hermit's delight. The entire outcropping, with its amazing network of caves and breathtaking views, belongs to the wat. The wat-mountain is climbed by a seven-level series of stairs representing the seven levels of enlightenment in Buddhist psychology. Monastic kutis are scattered around the mountain, in caves, on cliffs, etc. As you make the strenuous climb, each level is cooler than the one before. It is the cool and quiet isolation of this wat that entices monks and mae chiis from all over the north-east to come and meditate here.

This wat used to be the domain of the famous meditation master Achaan Juan – a disciple of the fierce Achaan Man who disappeared many years ago. Achaan Juan died in a plane crash a few years ago, along with several other monks who were flying to Bangkok for Queen Sirikhit's birthday celebration. The plane went down just outside Don Muang Airport. Many north-easterners have taken this incident as proof that the present queen is a source of misfortune.

To get to Wat Phu Thawk, you'll have to take an early morning songthaew south on Route 222 to Ban Siwilai (25 km, 7B), then another songthaew east (left) on a dirt road, 20 km to the wat (10B). This songthaew carries meritmakers. Hitching might be possible if you miss the truck. A reader reported getting a type of local tuk-tuk to the wat in the afternoon from Siwilai for 10B.

Places to Stay

Hotels in Beung Kan are all in the 40 to 80B price range (forget air-con). The *Samanmit, Neramit* and *Santisuk* are on Prasatchai Rd while the *Chuntha* is on Chansin Rd.

Getting There & Away

The bus from Nong Khai to Beung Kan is 40B. Nakhon Phanom to Beung Kan buses are 45B.

Nakhon Phanom Province

Nakhon Phanom Province has a large Lao and Vietnamese presence, although the capital is in the hands of ethnic Chinese. If you've come to this province to visit That Phanom, you'll probably have to stop here first to change buses, unless you go directly to That Phanom from Sakon Nakhon via Route 223.

NAKHON PHANOM TOWN นครพนม

Nakhon Phanom Town (population 33,000) is 242 km from Udon and 296 km from Nong Kai. It's a dull town which just happens to have a really panoramic view of the Maekhong River and the craggy mountains of Laos beyond.

Wat Si Thep, in town on the street of the same name, has a display of murals which one traveller reported to be as good as those in the Sistine Chapel!

Places to Stay

The top end in town is the *Nakhon Phanom Hotel* at 403 Aphiban Bancha Rd (tel 511455), where rooms with a fan and bath cost 120B and air-con rooms are from 220B.

The *Pong Hotel*, on the corner of Pon Keo and Bamrung Muang Rds, is 60B per room with a fan and bath, but it is run down and not very clean. The *Charoensuk Hotel*, at 692/45 Bamrung Muang Rd, is adequate for 80B with a fan and bath.

The *Si Thep Hotel* (tel 511036), 708/11 Si Thep Rd, costs 60B for a bungalow, 120B for a room with a fan and bath and 180B with air-con.

A good bet is the *First Hotel*, 370 Si Thep Rd, which has clean rooms with a fan and bath for 90B and air-con rooms for 200B. It's recommended.

Also good is the *Windsor Hotel*, 692/19 Bamrung Muang Rd, which has very nice rooms for 90B with a fan and bath and air-con rooms for 200B. It's not as quiet as the *First Hotel*.

Behind the Windsor, on the corner of Si Thep and Ruamjit Rds, is the *Grand Hotel* which has similar rooms for 70B or 200B air-con.

Another good place is the *River Inn* on the Maekhong River, where rooms with a fan and bath cost from 100B, with some air-con rooms available. The terrace restaurant that overlooks the river has a good atmosphere.

Places to Eat

Most of the town's better Thai and Chinese restaurants are along the river on Sunthon Wichit Rd and include *99 Phochana*, *VIP* and *Pla Beuk Thong*.

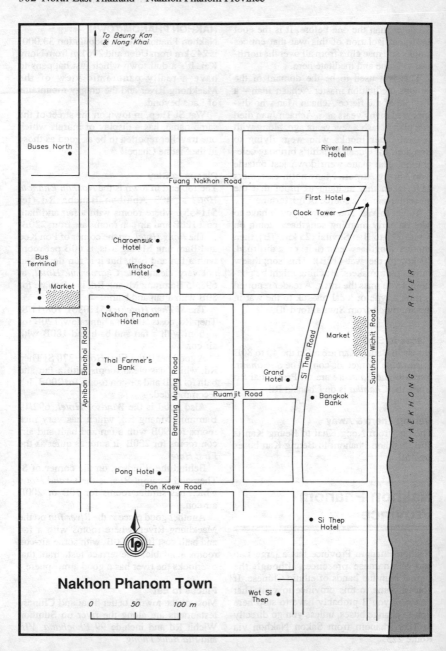

Nakhon Phanom Town

0   50   100 m

Several good, inexpensive restaurants serving noodles, curry and rice, etc, are along Bamrung Muang Rd near the Windsor Hotel. For local food, try *Rot Det* or *Nakhon Pho-chana*, across from the Charoensuk Hotel on Bamrung Muang Rd.

Entertainment

The hottest night spot in town is the *Tatiya Club* on the corner of Fuang Nakhon and Bamrung Muang Rds. It has a real variety show with glittery Thai pop singers.

Getting There & Away

Regular buses run from Nong Khai to Nakhon Phanom via Sakon Nakhon for 50B. There is a direct bus at 9.30 am (leaves Udon at about 8 am), which costs 70B and takes 7½ hours. If you want to go through Beung Kan, you can get a bus to Beung Kan first (40B), then change to a Nakhon Phanom bus (45B). Air-con buses run between Khorat and Nakhon Phanom thrice daily for 160B.

AROUND NAKHON PHANOM PROVINCE

Renu Nakhon   เรณูนคร

The village of Renu Nakhon is known for the weaving of cotton and silk fabrics, especially mat-mii designs. On Wednesdays there's a big handicraft market near Wat Phra That Renu Nakhon. On other days you can buy from a smaller number of vendors near the temple.

The turn-off to Renu Nakhon is south of Nakhon Phanom at the 44 km marker on Highway 212. Since it's only 10 km further to That Phanom, you could visit Renu on the way, or if you are staying a while in That Phanom, visit here as a day trip. From Highway 212 it's seven km west of Nakhon Phanom Town on Route 2031 (5B by songthaew from the junction).

Tha Khaek   ท่าแขก

This Lao town is across the river from Nakhon Phanom. Some travel is allowed across the river for residents of Thailand and Laos, but not for farangs (at least not yet, although this may soon change as the two governments get closer).

THAT PHANOM   ธาตุพนม

Fifty-three km from Nakhon Phanom Town and 107 km from Sakon Nakhon, the centre of activity in this small town is Wat That Phanom.

The short road between Wat That Phanom and the old town on the Maekhong River passes under a large Lao arch of victory which is almost identical to the arch at the end of Lane Xang Rd in Wieng Chan (which also leads to Wieng Chan's Wat That). This section of That Phanom is interesting, with French-Chinese architecture reminiscent of old Vientiane or Saigon.

In mid-February, the annual Phra That Phanom fair attracts quite a crowd to the town.

If you need to change money, go to the Thai Military Bank which is on the road to Nakhon Phanom.

Hundreds of Lao merchants cross the river for the market on Mondays and Thursdays.

That Phanom has hotels and restaurants, so it is not necessary to backtrack to Nakhon Phanom for these.

Wat That Phanom

This is a Lao-style wat that is very similar to Wat That Luang in Wieng Chan (Vientiane), Laos. The impressive chedi, which caved in during heavy rains in 1975 and was restored in 1978, is a talismanic symbol of isaan and is highly revered by Buddhists all over Thailand. The dating of the wat is disputed but some archaeologists set its age at about 1500 years. The chedi is 57 (or 52, depending on whom you believe) metres high and the spire is decorated with 10 kg of gold. Surrounding the famous chedi is a cloister filled with Buddha images and behind the wat is a shady park.

Places to Stay

The old town has three hotels. To reach *Saeng Thong Hotel*, turn right on to Phanom Phanarak Rd as you pass under the arch and it's on the left side of the street 30 metres down. An adequate room with a fan and shared bath costs 60B. It's a funky place with an inner courtyard and lots of character, and looks about 100 years old.

Chai Von (Wan) Hotel, on the opposite side of Phanom Phanarak Rd to the north of the arch (turn left as you pass under the arch), is similar to Sang Thong and costs 50B.

Lim-Charoen Hotel, on Chayangkun Rd near the bus terminal, has rooms for 80B, but one reader says you're better off at the cheaper hotels.

Places to Eat

There are plenty of noodle shops along Kuson Ratchadamnoen Rd, which leads from Phra That Phanom to the river. A good place to go for an early breakfast is near the pier where there are French-speaking coffee vendors and girls on bicycles selling warm, freshly baked French bread.

Getting There & Away

Bus The air-con Khorat to Nakhon Phanom

bus stops at That Phanom. The fare (160B) is the same as all the way to Nakhon Phanom.

Songthaew Songthaews to That Phanom leave regularly from the intersection near the Nakhon Phanom Hotel in Nakhon Phanom and cost 12B. Stay on it until you see the chedi on the right. The trip takes about 1½ hours.

Sakon Nakhon Province

Sakon Nakhon Province is well-known among Thais as the one-time home of two of the most famous Buddhist monks in Thai history, Achaan Man and Achaan Fan. Both were ascetic *thutong* monks who were thought to have attained high levels of profi-

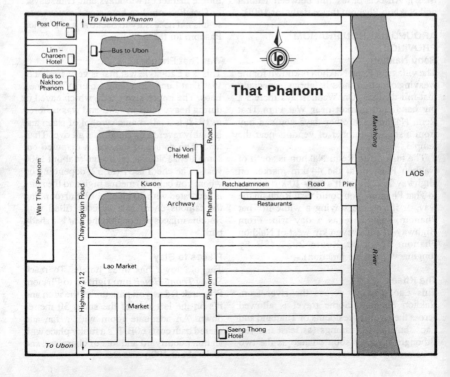

Top: Prasat Hin Phimai (JC)
Left: Wat That Phanom, That Phanom (JC)
Right: Chedi at Ban Tham, near Mae Sai (JC)

Top: 'Papa Taraporn', Ko Tao (MH)
Left: Khaen-maker, Roi Et (JC)
Right: Spirit house, Prachinburi (TM)

ciency in vipassana meditation. Though born in Ubon, Achaan Man spent most of his later years at Wat Pa Sutthawat in Sakon Nakhon Town. Some say he died here, while others say he wandered off into the jungle in 1949 and disappeared. Whatever the story, the wat now has an Achaan Man museum with an amazingly life-like wax figure of the monk as well as a display of some of his monkly possessions.

Achaan Fan Ajaro, a student of Achaan Man, established a cave hermitage for the study of meditation at Tham Kham on the mountain of Khao Phu Phaan. He was also affiliated with Wat Pa Udom Somphon in his home district of Phanna Nikhom, 37 km from Sakon Nakhon towards Udon Thani on Highway 22. A museum commemorating the life of Achaan Fan is there. Achaan Fan died in 1963.

The end of the Buddhist rains retreat in November is fervently celebrated in Sakon with the carving and display of wax prasats as well as parades.

SAKON NAKHON TOWN สกลนคร

The name for this town (and the province of course) can be translated as either Universal City (as intended) or Part City (more appropriate). Actually it's a very nice place, famous for its strong north-eastern brand of Thai Buddhism.

Wat Phra That Choeng Chum

Next to the Nong Han Lake in town, this wat features a 25-metre high Lao-style chedi which was erected during the Ayuthaya period over a smaller 10th-century Khmer chedi.

Wat Phra That Narai Jeng Weng

A 10th-to-11th-century Khmer prang in the Bapuan style can be seen at this wat, about five km outside of town at Ban That. The wat is called Phra That Naweng for short.

Phu Phaan National Park
อุทยานแห่งชาติภูพาน

This 645-square-km nature preserve is in the Phu Phaan Mountains near the Sakon Nakhon-Kalasin border. Deer, monkeys and other smaller forest animals are common to the park and wild elephants and tigers are occasionally seen as well.

The mountain forests are thick and the area is fairly undeveloped. It has been used as a hiding spot by two guerrilla forces – the Thai resistance against the Japanese in WW II and later the PLAT guerrillas in the '70s.

The park has few hiking trails but there are good views along Highway 213 between Sakon Nakhon and Kalasin. Three waterfalls – Tat Ton, Hew Sin Chai and Kham Hom – can be visited fairly easily.

The Tham Seri Thai cave was used by the Thai Seri during WW II as an arsenal and mess hall.

Places to Stay

The *Araya* on Prem Prida Rd has rooms with a fan for 100B and air-con rooms for 200B. At 645/2 Charoen Muang Rd is the less expensive *Krong Thong* (tel 711097), where rooms start at 60B. Also along Charoen Muang Rd are several hotels in the 60 to 80B price range, including the *Kusuma*, *Charoensuk* and *Sakon*. The *Imperial*, at 1892 Sukkasem Rd, has rooms for 160B with a fan and bath or 230B with air-con.

Getting There & Away

Direct buses to Sakon are available in Ubon (55B), Nakhon Phanom (20B), Kalasin (35B), That Phanom (17B) and Udon (45B).

Buses from Sakon to Bangkok are 119B (three departures a day) or 215B air-con (there is one evening departure a day). Buses between Khorat and Sakon (air-con only) are 138B and leave six times daily.

Yasathon & Mukdahan Provinces

YASATHON TOWN เมือง ยโสธร

Yasathon Town (population 20,000) is difficult to get to, but if you happen to be in the area (say, in Ubon, which is about 100 km away) during May, it might be worth a two-hour bus trip (from Ubon) to catch the annual rocket festival which takes place from 8 May to 10 May. The rocket festival, prevalent throughout the north-east as a rain and fertility rite, is celebrated most fervently in Yasothon where it involves a fantastic fireworks display. The name of the town, which has the largest Muslim population in the north-east, comes from the sanskrit *Yasodhara* which means preserver or maintainer of glory, and is also the name of one of Krishna's sons by Rukmini in the Mahabharata.

Places to Stay

Udomporn (Udomphon) at 80/1-2 Uthairamrit Rd costs from 70 to 80B for rooms with a fan and bath, while the *Surawet Wattana*, 128/1 Changsanit Rd, costs from 80 to 100B. If you can't get into either of these try the *Yothnakhon* (tel 711122), 141-143/1-3 Uthairamrit Rd, where rooms are from 100B or from 150B with air-con.

Getting There & Away

A bus to Yasothon from Ubon costs 23B and from Khorat it's 56B ordinary or 114B air-con.

MUKDAHAN TOWN เมือง มุกดาหาร

Exactly 55 km south of That Phanom and 170 km north of Ubon Ratchathani, Mukdahan Town (population 23,000) was formerly part of Nakhon Phanom and Ubon provinces, but since September 1982 Mukdahan has been Thailand's newest province.

Mukdahan Town is known for its beautiful Maekhong scenery and as a Thai-Lao trade centre. It's directly opposite the city of Suwannakhet in Laos.

Mukdahan might make a nice stopover between Nakhon Phanom or That Phanom and Ubon. For a view of the town, climb the 353-metre Phu Muu (Pig Hill, named for the wild pigs that used to live there).

Phu Pha Thoep National Park
อุทยานแห่งชาติ ภูผาเทพ

South of Mukdahan Town is a hilly area of caves and unusual mushroom-shaped rock formations. This is 16 km south of

Mukdahan on Route 2034 and there's a natural forest reserve in the centre of this area. Besides the rock formations, it has a habitat for barking deer, wild boar, monkeys and civets.

Places to Stay

The *Hua Nam Hotel* (tel 611137) at 20 Samut Sakdarak has rooms from 70B with a fan and bath or from 180B with air-con. On the same road is the cheaper *Banthom Kasem Hotel*, but it's a real dive. There is also the *Hong Kong Hotel* at 161/1-2 Phitak Santirat Rd where rooms are 80B with a fan and bath, and the *Si Siam Hotel* on Wiwit Surakan Rd which has rooms for 100B with a fan and bath or 200B air-con.

Places to Eat

A good place to eat and relax on the river is *Suan Malakaw* (Papaya Garden), which sells fruit and north-eastern food. The restaurant opposite the Banthom Kasem is open all night.

Getting There & Away

There are regular buses from either direction – 40B from Nakhon Phanom (and half that from That Phanom) or 50B from Ubon.

Ubon Ratchathani Province

Ubon (also known as Ubol) is 557 km from Bangkok, 271 km from Nakhon Phanom and 311 km from Khorat. It's the north-east's largest province and the provincial capital is its largest town. Despite this, there is not a lot to see here, outside of the annual candle festival and a few wats.

UBON RATCHATHANI TOWN เมือง อุบล

Ubon Town (population 100,000) has some good accommodation and restaurants as it was another main American base in the Vietnam days. Getting around the town on city buses is relatively easy. Ubon also has a very helpful TAT office next to the town shrine.

Wat Thung Si Muang

Off Luang Rd, near the centre of town, this wat was originally built during the reign of Rama III (1824 to 1851) and has a *haw trai* (Tripitaka library) in good shape. It rests on high-angled stilts in the middle of a small pond. Nearby is an old mondop with a Buddha footprint symbol.

Wat Phra That Nong Bua

This wat is on the road to Nakhon Phanom on the outskirts of town (catch a white city bus for 2B) and is based almost exactly on the Mahabodhi stupa in Bodhgaya, India. It is much better than Wat Jet Yot in Chiang Mai, which is purported to be a Mahabodhi reproduction, but was designed by people who never saw the real thing. The jataka reliefs on the outside of the chedi are very good. There are two groups of four niches on each side of the four-sided chedi which contain Buddhas in different standing postures. The stances look like stylised Gupta or Dvaravati closed-robe poses.

Wat Nong Pa Phong

South of Ubon in Warin Chamrap district, about 10 km past the railway station, is Wat Nong Pa Phong. This very famous forest wat is in the care of Achaan Chaa, who has many other branch temples in the Ubon Province and one in Sussex, England. All of these temples are known for their quiet discipline and daily routine of work and meditation.

Dozens of westerners have studied here during the past 20 years and many live here or at branch temples as ordained monks.

Achaan Chaa, a former disciple of the most famous north-eastern teacher of them all, Achaan Man (who disappeared from sight some years ago), is known for his simple and direct teaching method which seems to cross all international barriers.

To get to the wat from Ubon, take a pink city bus No 3 to the *baw khaw saw* terminal, then catch a songthaew going to the wat.

Wat Pa Nanachat Beung Wai

Nearby to Wat Nong Pa Phong, Wat Pa Nanachat Beung Wai's abbot is Canadian, the vice-abbot is Japanese and most of the monks are European. As Achaan Chaa is quite old and has been very ill, Wat Pa Nanachat is where you should go if you are interested in more than sightseeing. The wat is very clean, cool and quiet. Both men and women are welcome, but men are required to shave their heads if they want to stay beyond three days.

Getting There & Away From Ubon, take a white, city bus No 1 south down Uparat Rd, cross the bridge over the Mun River and get off as the bus turns right in Warin Chamrap for the railway station. From there, catch any songthaew heading south (though heading west eventually, towards Si Saket) and ask to be let off at Wat Nanachat – everybody knows it.

You can also get there by catching a Si Saket bus from Ubon for 3B to Beung Wai, the village across the road from Wat Nanachat. There is a sign in English at the edge of the road – the wat is in the forest behind the rice fields.

You can also hire a tuk-tuk direct to the wat from town for about 50B.

Ko Hat Wat Tai เกาะหาดวัดใต้

This is a small island in the Mun River on the southern edge of town. During the hot and dry months, from March to May, it is a favourite picnic spot and there are 'beaches' on the island where you can swim. You can get there by boat or by walking across a wooden bridge that connects the island to the north bank.

Festivals

The candle festival is most grandly celebrated in Ubon, with music, parades, floats, beauty contests and enormous carved candles of all shapes – human, animal, divine and abstract. The evening processions are impressive. The festival begins around khao phansaa, the first day of the Buddhist rains retreat in late July, and lasts five days. Spirits

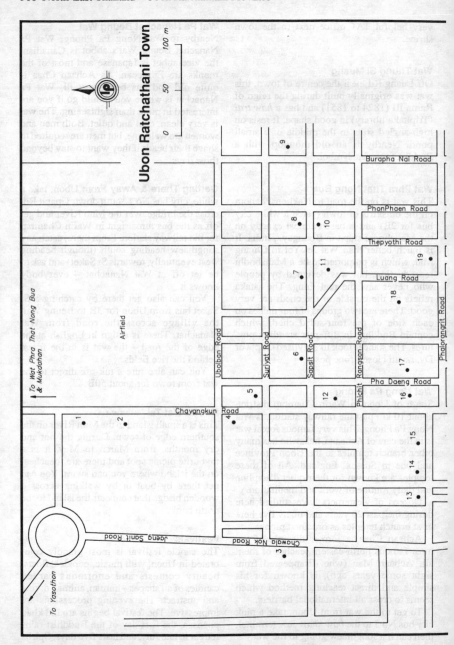

Ubon Ratchathani Town

100 m

50

0

Burapha Nai Road

PhonPhaen Road

Thepyothi Road

Luang Road

Pha Daeng Road

Chayangkun Road

Chawala Nok Road

Jaeng Sanit Road

Ubolban Road

Suriyat Road

Sapsit Road

Phichit Road

Rangsan Road

Phalorangrit Road

To Wat Phra That Nong Bua

Airfield

To Wat Phra That Nong Bua & Mukdahan

To Yasothon

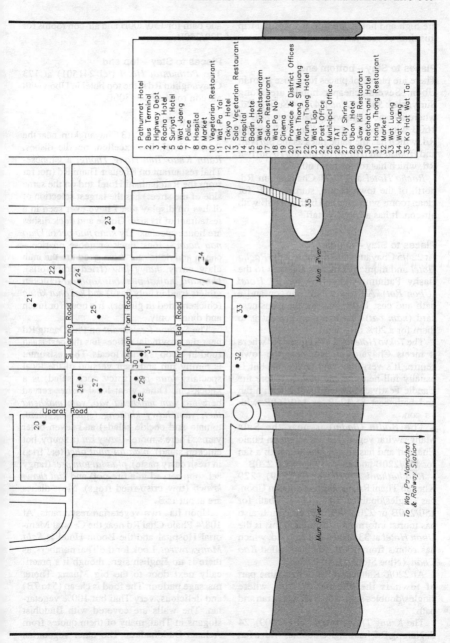

1 Pathumrat Hotel
2 Bus Terminal
3 Highway Dept
4 Racha Hotel
5 Suriyat Hotel
6 Wat Jaeng
7 Police
8 Hospital
9 Market
10 Vegetarian Restaurant
11 Wat Pa Yai
12 Tokyo Hotel
13 Sala Vegetarian Restaurant
14 Hospital
15 Bodin Hote
16 Wat Suthatsanaram
17 Sakon Restaurant
18 Wat Pa No
19 Cinema
20 Province & District Offices
21 Wat Thong Si Muang
22 Krung Tnong Hotel
23 Wat Liap
24 Post Office
25 Municipcl Office
26 TAT
27 City Shrine
28 Ubon Hotel
29 Jiaw Kii Restaurant
30 Ratchathani Hotel
31 Hong Thong Restaurant
32 Market
33 Wat Luang
34 Wat Klang
35 Ko Hat Wat Tai

Si Narong Road

Kheuan Thani Road

Phrom Bat Road

Uparat Road

Mun River

Mun River

To Wat Pa Namechot
& Railway Station

are high and hotels are full. It's worth a trip this time of year just to see the festival.

Places to Stay – bottom end

There are plenty of places to choose from in Ubon. Several cheaper hotels are along Suriyat Rd: *Suriyat Hotel*, 47/1-4 Suriyat Rd, where a basic room with a fan costs 80B or 160B with air-con; the *Dollar*, 39/5 Suriyat Rd, which has the same rates as the *Suriyat*; and *Homsa-ad (Hawm Sa-at)*, 80/10 Suriyat Rd, which has rooms from 60 to 80B.

Racha Hotel at 149/21 Chayangkun Rd, north of the town centre, starts at 90B for clean rooms with a fan and bath or 180B with air-con. It has a friendly staff.

Places to Stay – middle

At 224/5 Chayangkun Rd, north of the *Racha Hotel* and municipal market and next to the flashy Pathumrat Hotel, is the *99 Hotel (Ubon Rat)*. All rooms have air-con and a bath and cost 160B. Ask for their business card (*nam bat*) first and then present it to them for a 20% discount.

The *Tokyo Hotel* is at 178 Uparat Rd where it meets Chayangkun Rd, near the town centre. It's very nice and well-kept, but is usually full near the end of July before the Candle Festival. Singles/doubles with a fan and bath cost 85/120B or 140/160B with air-con.

The *Bodin (Badin)* is near the Sala Mangsawirat vegetarian restaurant on Phalo Chai Rd and has singles/doubles with a fan for 150/220B and air-con rooms for 220B.

Ratchathani Hotel (tel 254599), 229 Kheuan Thani Rd, the biggest hotel in Ubon, has singles/doubles with a fan and bath for 150/200B or 220/280B with air-con. It also has tourist information. Similar to this is the *Ubon Hotel* at 333 Kheuan Thani Rd, which has rooms from 150B. It's also called *Kao Chan* (Nine Storeys).

At 220/6 Ratchabut Rd in this same part of town is the cheaper *Si Isan*, where singles/doubles start at 60/80B with a fan and bath.

The *Krung Thong Hotel* (tel 241609), 24 Si Narong Rd, has singles/doubles with a fan and bath for 150/200B and air-con rooms for 220/250B.

Places to Stay – top end

The *Pathumrat Hotel* (tel 241501) at 173 Chayangkun Rd is the top hotel in Ubon with air-con rooms from 300B.

Places to Eat

The *Loet Rot* at 147/13 Chayangkun, near the Racha Hotel, has excellent noodle dishes. *Raan Khao Tom Hong Thong*, a Chinese-Thai restaurant on Kheuan Thani Rd (not far from the Ratchathani Hotel and on the same side of the street) has the largest selection of dishes on display that I have ever seen in a restaurant of its size. Goose and duck dishes are house specials. Try *khao naa pet* or *khao naa haan* – roast duck or goose on rice – cheap and delicious. Also good are the crab claw curry, *hawy jaw* (fried crab rolls), *khreuang naikai phat bai kaphrao* (chicken giblets fried in holy basil) and *kai phat khing* (chicken fried in ginger). It's open for lunch and dinner only.

The *Sakhon Restaurant* on Pha Daeng Rd near the provincial offices has the best isaan food in Ubon, say the locals. The restaurant is family run and their version of the local specialty *laap pet* (spicy duck salad) is a knock-out. Other great local dishes served here are *yam makheua yao, yam makheua thet, yam hawy khraeng* (spicy eggplant, tomato and cockle salads) and seven other yams. There's more – *kawy kai* (a soupy, hot chicken salad), *plaa lai phat phet* (eel fried in fresh curry paste), *plaa lai tom pret* (tangy eel soup served in a fire-pot) and *kiat thawt krawp* (tiny crisp-fried frogs). Most dishes are about 15B.

Ubon has two vegetarian restaurants. At 108/4 Phalo Chai Rd near the Central Memorial Hospital and the Bodin Hotel is *Sala Mangsawirat*. Look for the Thai numbers, as there is no English sign, though it's practically next door to the big Muang Thong massage parlour. The food is cheap (5 to 7B) and delicious, very Thai but 100% vegetarian. The walls are covered with Buddhist slogans in Thai, many of them quotes from Achaan Buddhadasa. The other vegetarian place is across from Sapsit Prasong Hospital on Sapsit Rd and has similar Thai vegetarian cuisine at about the same prices.

The Fern Bakery near the teacher's college (Thai: *withayalai khruu*) sells good cakes and other baked items. Take a city bus north and get off near the clock tower.

Ubon has two night markets which are open from dusk to dawn, one at the talaat yai by the river near the bridge and the other near the bus terminal on Chayangkun Rd – convenient to hotels on Chayangkun and Suriyat Rds.

For breakfast, *Chiokee (Jiaw Kii)* on Kheuan Thani Rd is very popular among local office workers. Prices are good and it has everything from *khao tom* to ham and eggs. One of their specialities is jok (broken-rice soup).

Getting There & Away

Air Thai Airways flies daily from Bangkok to Ubon at 7.10 am, except on Friday and Sunday when flights leave at 2.55 pm. On Tuesday, Wednesday, Thursday and Saturday, a second flight departs Bangkok at 10.25 am. The fare is 1080B and the flight takes an hour.

Bus Two tour buses a day go to Ubon from Nakhon Phanom at 7 am and 2 pm, leaving from the intersection of Bamrung Muang and Ratsadorn Uthit Rds near the Windsor Hotel. The fare is 96B. Ordinary buses from the Baw Kaw Saw Station leave regularly from morning until late afternoon for 60B. The trip takes 5½ hours on the tour bus and six to seven hours on the rot thammada (ordinary bus).

Buses for Ubon leave the Northern Bus Terminal in Bangkok up to 15 times a day from 4.30 am through to nearly midnight. These cost 126B or 227B with air-con, but the air-con buses only run between 7.30 and 9.30 pm. Other fares to/from Ubon are:

Khong Jiam	30B
Yasothon	23B
Si Saket	14B
Mukdahan	34B
Sakon Nakhon	55B
(air-con)	100B
Udon Thani	80B
(air-con)	140B
Khon Kaen	56B
(air-con)	101B
Mahasarakham	42B
(air-con)	78B
Roi Et	36B
(air-con)	65B
Khorat	80B
(air-con)	146B
That Phanom	35B
(air-con)	80B

Train The Ubon Ratchathani Express leaves Bangkok daily at 9 pm, arriving in Ubon at 6.30 am the next morning. The basic 1st-class fare is 416B, 2nd class is 200B and 3rd class is 95B, not including surcharges for Express service or a sleeping berth. Rapid trains leave at 6.50 am, 6.45 and 10.40 pm, arriving in Ubon about 11 hours later. There is no 1st class on Rapid trains.

Rapid trains from Khorat leave at 11.47 am and 11.40 pm, arriving in Ubon at 5 pm and 4.45 am. The basic fares are 121B 2nd class and 58B 3rd class.

The Express back to Bangkok leaves Ubon at 7.35 pm, arriving at Hualamphong Station at 5.15 am. There are Rapid trains at 6.35 am, 5.25 and 6.20 pm, arriving in Bangkok at 4.30 pm, 4.05 and 4.40 am respectively. Ordinary trains only take an hour longer and depart at 7 am, 3.20 and 11.20 pm.

AROUND UBON

Si Saket ศรีสะเกษ

Si Saket, 63 km west of Ubon, is famous for its kai yang. Vendors line the road outside of town and people in Bangkok ask friends from Ubon to bring Si Saket kai yang with them when they visit.

Pha Taem ผาแต้ม

In Khong Chiam district, 65 km east of Ubon Town, near the confluence of the Mun and Maekhong rivers, is a stone cliff called Pha Taem. Pha Taem is about 200 metres long and features prehistoric colour paintings that are 4000 or more years old. Nearby is Sao

Chaliang, an area of unusual stone formations similar to Phu Thoep in Mukdahan.

It's difficult to reach Pha Taem by public transport. By car or motorcycle, go east on Route 217 to Phibun Mangsahan, then turn left (north-east) on Route 222 and follow this road to Khong Chiam. From Khong Chiam, take Route 2134 north-west to Ban Huay Phai and then go north-east again to the village of Nong Pheu. From Nong Pheu you can walk to the river and see the cliff paintings.

The tourist office in Ubon runs van tours to Pha Taem, Sao Chaliang and several other remote places east of Ubon including the rapids of Kaeng Tana and Kaeng Sapheu, Wat Phu Khao Kaew, Hehw Sinchai Falls and Two-Colour River (the junction of the Mun and Maekhong rivers) on Saturdays and Sundays. The tours leave at 8 am from the town shrine in Ubon (San Chao Phaw Lak Muang) next to the tourist office. The cost is reasonable at 50B per person.

Surin Province

SURIN TOWN เมือง สุรินทร์

Surin (population 40,000), 452 km from Bangkok, is a forgettable town except during the Elephant Round-Up in late November. At that time a carnival atmosphere reigns with elephants providing the entertainment. If ever you wanted to see a lot of elephants in one place (there are more elephants now in Thailand than in India), this is your chance.

Places to Stay

Hotel rates may increase during the Elephant Round-Up and hotels may fill up, but otherwise, *Krung Si* (tel 511037), 15/11-4 Krung Si Nai Rd, charges from 90 to 100B, and *New Hotel* (tel 511341, 511322), 22 Thanasan Rd, charges from 100 to 150B and has some air-con rooms from 180B. Also on Thanasan Rd at No 155-61 is *Saeng Thong*, which has rooms from 100 to 200B.

The *Amarin* (tel 511407), Tesaban 1 Rd, costs from 85 to 150B or from 160B with air-con. Not far from it is a similar place, the *Thanachai*.

The top digs is the *Phetkasem Hotel* (tel 511274) at 104 Jit Bamrung Rd. All rooms are air-con, with rates from 300 to 650B.

Getting There & Away

Bus Surin buses leave several times a day from Bangkok's Northern Bus Terminal between 6 am and 10.15 pm for 86B one-way. During the Elephant Round-Up, there are many special air-con buses to Surin, organised by major hotels and tour companies. The regular government-run air-con bus costs 155B and leaves the AC Northern Terminal daily at 11 am, 9.30, 10 and 10.10 pm.

Buses from Khorat are 40B and take about four hours.

Train Most people travel to Surin by Rapid train No 31, which leaves Bangkok at 6.50 am, arriving in Surin at 2.29 pm. The fares are 173B 2nd class and 93B 3rd class, including the Rapid surcharge. Book your seats at least two weeks in advance for travel during November. A faster train is the air-con diesel No 931 to Surin at 10.55 am, arriving at 5.15 pm for 20B less (no Rapid surcharge).

Southern Thailand

Although under Thai political domination for several centuries, the south has always remained culturally apart from the other regions of Thailand. Historically the peninsula has been linked to cultures in ancient Indonesia, particularly the Srivijaya Empire, which ruled a string of principalities in what is today Malaysia, southern Thailand and Indonesia. The Srivijaya Dynasty was based in Sumatra and lasted nearly 500 years (8th to 13th centuries). The influence of Malay-Indonesian culture is still apparent in the ethnicity, religion, art and language of the *Thai pak tai*, the southern Thais.

The Thai pak tai dress differently, build their houses differently and eat differently from Thais in the north. Many are followers of Islam, so there are quite a few mosques in southern cities; men often cover their heads and the long sarong is favoured over the shorter phaakamaa worn in the northern, central and north-eastern regions. There are also a good many Chinese living in the south – the influence of whom can be seen in the old architecture and in the baggy Chinese pants worn by non-Muslims. All speak a dialect common among southern Thais that confounds even visitors from other Thai regions – diction is short and fast: *pai nai* (Where are you going?) becomes *p' nai; tham arai* (What are you doing?) becomes *tham' rai*, and the clipped tones fly into the outer regions of intelligibility, giving the aural impression of a tape played at the wrong speed. In the provinces nearest Malaysia – Yala, Pattani, Narathiwat and Satun – many Thai Muslims speak Yawi, an old Malay dialect with some similarities to modern Bahasa Malaysia and Bahasa Indonesia.

Southern Thais are stereotypically regarded as rebellious folk, considering themselves reluctant subjects of Bangkok rule and Thai (central Thai) custom. Indeed, Thai Muslims (ethnically Malay) living in the provinces bordering on Malaysia complain of persecution by Thai government troops who police the area for insurgent activity. There has even been some talk of these provinces seceding from Thailand, an event that is unlikely to occur in the near future.

Bounded by water on two sides, the people of south Thailand are by and large a seafaring lot. One consequence of this natural affinity with the ocean is the abundance of delectable seafood, prepared southern-style. Brightly painted fishing boats, hanging nets and neat thatched huts add to the pak tai setting; travellers who do a stint in south Thailand are likely to come face to face with more than a few visions of 'tropical paradise', whatever their expectations might be.

Three of Thailand's most important exports – rubber, tin and coconut – are produced in the south so that the standard of living is a bit higher here than in other provincial regions. However, southern Thais claim that most of the wealth is in the hands of ethnic Chinese. In any of the truly southern Thai provinces (from Chumphon south), it is obvious that the Chinese are concentrated in the urban provincial capitals while the poorer Muslims live in the rural areas. Actually, the urban concentration of Chinese is a fact of life throughout South-East Asia which becomes more noticeable in south Thailand and the Islamic state of Malaysia because of religious-cultural differences.

In official government terms, southern Thailand is made up of 14 provinces: Chumphon, Krabi, Nakhon Si Thammarat, Narathiwat, Pattani, Phang-Nga, Phattalung, Phuket, Ranong, Satun, Songkhla, Surat Thani, Trang and Yala. For the purposes of this guide, we've included all provinces on the southern peninsula, taking Ratburi, Phetburi, and Prachuap Khiri Khan from central Thailand and putting them alongside the others on the official list.

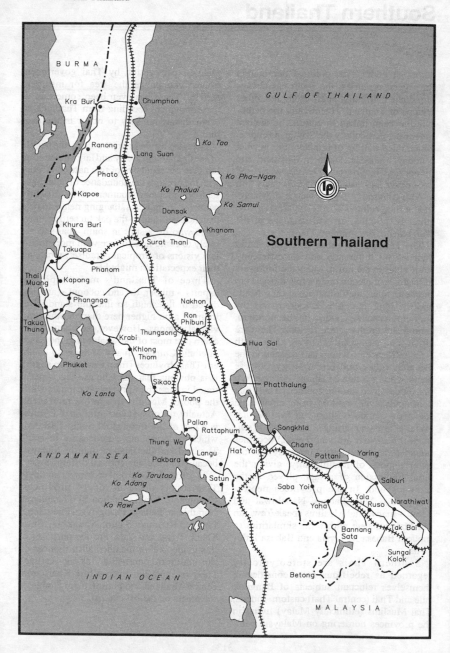

Southern Thailand

RATCHABURI เมืองราชบุรี

While Ratchaburi (population 43,000) is actually the provincial capital of the province of the same name, it is the first major town you reach on the way south from Nakhon Pathom, well before you get to the coast and Hua Hin. North-east of Ratchaburi, about 20 km towards Bangkok, are the famous floating markets of Damnoen Saduak. For details, see the Bangkok Floating Market section.

Places to Stay

The *Zin Zin Hotel* on Railway Rd is cheap. Other hotels include the *Araya* (tel 337781/2) on Kraiphet Rd, with rooms from 100B, or from 175B with air-con.

Phetburi Province

PHETBURI TOWN เมืองเพชรบุรี

Situated 160 km south of Bangkok, Phetburi (or Phetchaburi) (population 35,000) is worth a stopover for its many old temples spanning several centuries. Six or seven temples can be seen while taking a circular walk of two or three hours through the city. Also noteworthy is Khao Wang, just west of the city, which has the remains of a King Mongkut palace and several wats, plus a good aerial view of the city. The underground Buddhist shrine at the Khao Luang Caves is also worth seeing.

Information & Orientation

If you arrive at the railway station, follow the road south-east of the tracks until you come to Ratchadamnoen Rd, then turn right. Follow Ratchadamnoen Rd south to the second major intersection and turn left towards downtown Phetburi to begin the walk. Or take a samlor from the railway station to Chomrut Bridge (Saphan Chomrut) over the Phetburi River, for 8B. If you've come by bus, you'll be getting off very near the Chomrut Bridge. This is the centre of Phetburi, more or less – from here you can check out hotels if you're spending

the night, or, if you're not, stow your gear at the Anglican Church next to the bus station.

Samlor drivers in Phet are very hard to negotiate with, even for Thais. All in all, it's better to walk or ride on the *rot leng*, small minivans that run all over town for 3B per person.

Wats

Cross the bridge to begin a long walk that passes Wat Yai Suwannaram, Wat Trailok, Wat Kamphaeng Laeng, Wat Phra Suang, Wat Ko Kaew Sutharam and Wat Mahathat. These temples have made very few concessions to the 20th century and thus provide a glimpse of the traditional Siamese urban wat.

Wat Yai Suwannaram

After you've crossed the Phetburi River by Chomrut Bridge (the second northernmost bridge in Phetburi) and passed the Nam Chai Hotel on the left, walk a little further until you see a big temple on the right. This is Wat Yai, dating from the reign of King Chulalongkorn (1851 to 1868). The main bot is surrounded by a cloister filled with sober Buddha images. The murals inside the bot are in good condition. Next to the bot is a beautifully designed old *haw trai*, a Tripitaka (Buddhist scripture) library.

Wat Borom & Wat Trailok

These two wats are next to one another on the opposite side of the road from Wat Yai, a little east. They are distinctive for their monastic halls and long, graceful wooden 'dormitories' on stilts.

Turn right onto the road heading south from Wat Trai Lok and follow this road down past a bamboo fence on the right to the entrance for Wat Kamphaeng Laeng.

Wat Kamphaeng Laeng

This is a very old (13th century) Khmer site with five Khmer prangs and part of the original wall still standing. The prang in front contains a Buddha footprint. Of the other four, two contain images dedicated to famous Luang Po (venerable elderly monks), one was in ruins (but is being restored) and the fifth has recently been uncovered from a mound of dirt. The Khmers built these as Hindu monuments, so the Buddhist symbols are late additions.

Wat Phra Suang & Wat Lat

Follow the road next to Wat Kamphaeng Laeng, heading west back towards the river until you pass Wat Phra Suang on the left, undistinguished except for one very nice Ayuthaya-style prasat. Turn left immediately after this wat, heading south again until you come to the clock tower at the south edge of town. You'll have passed Wat Lat on the left side of the street along the way, but it's not worth breaking your momentum for; this is a long walk.

Wat Ko Kaew Sutharam

Turn right at the clock tower and look for signs leading to Wat Ko. Two different sois on the left lead to the wat, which is behind the shops along the curving street. The bot features early 18th-century murals. There is also a large wooden monastic hall on stilts similar to the one at Wat Borom-Wat Trailok, but in much better condition.

Wat Mahathat

Follow the street in front of Wat Ko north (back towards downtown Phetburi), and walk over the first bridge you come to on the left, which leads to Wat Mahathat. Alternatively, you can cross the river at Wat Ko, near the clock tower and take the street on the other side of the river around to Wat Mahathat. The large white prang of Wat Mahathat can be seen from a distance – a typical late Ayuthaya-early Rattanakosin adaptation of the Khmer prangs of Lopburi, Phimai, etc. This is obviously an important temple in Phetburi, judging from all the activity here.

Khao Wang & Phra Nakhon Khiri Historical Park

เขาวังอุทยานแห่งประวัติศาสตร์พระนครคีรี

Just west of the city, a 5B samlor ride from the bus station, is Khao Wang. Cobblestone paths lead up and around the hill, which is studded with wats and various components of King Mongkut's Phra Nakhon Khiri palace (Holy City Hill). The views are great, especially at sunset. The walk up looks easy but is fairly strenuous. Fat monkeys loll about in the trees and on the walls along the main paths. In 1988, Phra Nakhon Khiri was declared a national historical park so there is now an entry fee of 20B. A tram has been installed so that you can reach the peak without walking for 5B per person each way.

Khao Luang Caves ถ้ำเขาหลวง

Five km north of Phet Town is the cave sanctuary of Khao Luang (Great Hill). Concrete steps lead into the main cavern, which is filled with old Buddha images, many of them put in place by King Mongkut (Rama IV). Sunlight from two holes in the chamber ceiling spray light on the images, a favourite subject for photographers. On the right of the entrance is Wat Bunthawi, with a sala designed by the abbot himself.

Places to Stay

Of the variety of places to stay here, the following are recommended. On the east side of Chomrut Bridge, on the right bank of Phetburi River, is the *Chom Klao Hotel*, an ordinary semi-clean Chinese hotel with friendly staff. It costs 60B for rooms with fan and shared bath, or 80B with private bath.

The *Nam Chai Hotel* is a block further east from Chomrut Bridge and the Chom Klao Hotel, and has rooms for 70 to 120B, but is not such good value as the Chom Klao.

Then there's the *Phetburi Hotel*, on the next street north of Chomrut, behind the Chom Klao, with rooms for 80B with fan and bath.

The *Khao Wang Hotel* (tel 425167), opposite Khao Wang (the Hill Palace) used to be my favourite in Phet, but reports indicate the rooms may have gone downhill recently. A fairly clean room with fan and bath cost 90/130B for a single/double. Air-con rooms are 150/200B.

A reader has recommended the *Phetkasem Hotel*, 86/1 Phetkasem Rd, which is on the highway north to Bangkok on the edge of town. Rooms are 100 to 150B.

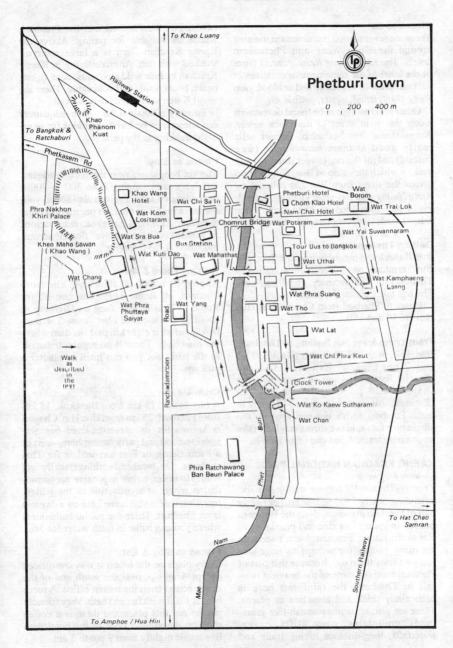

Phetburi Town

0   200   400 m

To Khao Luang

To Bangkok & Ratchaburi

Phetkasem Rd

Railway Station

Khao Phanom Kuat

Phra Nakhon Khiri Palace

Khao Maha Sawan (Khao Wang)

Wat Chang

Wat Phra Phuttaya Saiyat

Khao Wang Hotel

Wat Kom Lositaram

Wat Sra Bua

Wat Kuti Dao

Wat Chi Sa In

Bus Station

Wat Mahathat

Wat Yang

Ratchadamnoen Road

Phetburi Hotel

Chom Klao Hotel

Nam Chai Hotel

Chomrut Bridge

Wat Potaram

Wat Uthai

Wat Phra Suang

Wat Tho

Wat Borom

Wat Trai Lok

Wat Yai Suwannaram

Tour Bus to Bangkok

Wat Kamphaeng Laeng

Wat Lat

Wat Chi Phra Keut

Clock Tower

Wat Ko Kaew Sutharam

Wat Chan

Phra Ratchawang Ban Beun Palace

Walk as described in the text

Phet Buri

Mae Nam

To Amphoe / Hua Hin

To Hat Chao Samran

Southern Railway

Places to Eat

There are several good restaurants in the area around the Khao Wang and Phetkasem hotels. The *Khao Wang Restaurant* in front of the hotel of the same name specialises in various kinds of vegetable and seafood yam – egg plant, squid, oyster, catfish, etc.

Other good eating can be found downtown along the main street to the clock tower. Across from Wat Mahathat, *Lamiet* sells really good *khanom maw kaeng* (egg custard) and *foi thawng* (sweet shredded egg yolk) – which they ship to Bangkok. A shop across the street from Wat Lat called *Saw Rung Huang* also has great khanom, including a delicious kind of khao kriap (rice crisps) made with coconut and sesame.

Getting There & Away

Bus Buses leave regularly from the Southern Bus Terminals on Charan Sanitwong Rd in Thonburi for 35B ordinary, or 54B air-con. The bus takes about 2½ hours.

Buses to Phetburi from Cha-am and Hua Hin are 10 and 15B.

Train Trains leave Noi Station, in Thonburi, Bangkok, at 9 am, 12.30 pm (Rapid), 1.40 and 2 pm (Special Express), 3.15 pm (Special Express), 4 pm (Rapid), 5.30 pm (Rapid), 6.30 pm (Rapid) and 7.20 pm (Express). All trains take about 3½ hours to reach Phetburi so it's not really worth the surcharges for rapid or express service – take an ordinary train. A 3rd-class fare is 34B.

KAENG KRACHAN NATIONAL PARK

อุทยานแห่งชาติ แก่งกระจาน

This is Thailand's largest national park, extending nearly 3000 square km, or nearly half of Phetburi Province, along the Burmese border. In spite of its size and proximity to Bangkok, Kaeng Krachan doesn't seem to get many visitors (or perhaps its huge size just swallows them up). Because this part of Phetburi receives some of the heaviest rainfall in Thailand, the rainforest here is particularly thick and abundant in places. There are also areas of savannah-like grasslands, mountains, steep cliffs, caves, waterfalls, long-distance hiking trails and two rivers, the Phetburi and the Pranburi, which are suitable for rafting. Above the Kaeng Krachan Dam is a large reservoir stocked with fish. Animals living in Kaeng Krachan include wild elephants, deer, tigers, bears, boars, gaurs and wild cattle. There are small Karen settlements here as well.

Forestry officials at the park headquarters can sometimes be hired as guides for overnight trekking in the park.

Places to Stay

The six bungalows near the park headquarters have rates ranging from 300 to 700B, depending on size. You can also set up your own tent for 5B per person per night. *Kaeng Krachan Resorts* (Bangkok reservations 513-3238) offers expensive 'floatel' accommodation at the reservoir.

Getting There & Away

Kaeng Krachan is about 60 km from Phetburi, off Route 3175. The turn-off for Route 3175 is at Tha Yang on Highway 4, about 18 km south of Phet Town. The park headquarters is eight km past the dam where the road ends. There is no regular transport to the park, but you can hitch or charter a pick-up.

CHA-AM ชะอำ

A tiny town 178 km from Bangkok, 18 km from Phetburi, 25 km from Hua Hin, Cha-am is known for its casuarina-lined beaches, good seafood and party atmosphere – sort of a Palm Beach or Fort Lauderdale for Thai students. On weekends, things really get wild. However, rather expensive accommodation makes it unattractive to the budget traveller, unless you come here on a day trip from Phetburi. There are public bathhouses where you can bathe in fresh water for 5B.

Places to Stay & Eat

Every place on the beach is way overpriced except *Arunthip*, near the south end of the beach across from the tourist office. A room here is 120B with fan and bath. Very friendly people run this place and there is a coffee shop on the ground floor of the hotel with live music nightly from 9 pm to 3 am.

The next cheapest places are *Jitravee Bungalow* and *Cha-am Villa* (tel 471010, 471241), which will let you have rooms for 200B mid-week (300B on weekends). Next up in price are *Saeng Thong Resort* (tel 471440) and *Cha-Am Inn* (tel 471154), which have rooms for 250B mid week. Also reasonable are *Santisuk Bungalows* and *Kaen Chan Bungalow* at 300B. The rest of the places are 500B and over.

Out of town a bit is the *Regent Cha-am* for 1400B up. One traveller said he stayed in a dormitory here for 50B.

Vendors on the beach sell fair chow. Opposite the beach are several good seafood restaurants which, unlike the bungalows, are reasonably priced.

Getting There & Away

Bus Buses from Phetburi are 10B, buses from Hua Hin are 5B (from Hua Hin, take a Phetburi-bound bus). Ask to be let off at Hat Cha-am (Cha-am Beach).

Buses from Bangkok to Cha-am cost 38B for ordinary or 55B for air-con. Buses leave from the Southern Bus Terminals.

Prachuap Khiri Khan Province

HUA HIN เมืองหัวหิน

A favourite beach resort for Thais, Hua Hin (population 31,000) is 230 km from Bangkok, in Prachuap Khiri Khan Province. The Thais seem to want to keep this one for themselves, since it is seldom mentioned in the TAT literature. I don't blame them: Hua Hin is a nice, quiet, and fairly economical place to get away from it all, and yet is a convenient distance from Bangkok. The private sector in Hua Hin, however, have begun promoting Hua Hin tourism, so it's beginning to see more and more farangs and will probably be changing rapidly in the years to come.

Rama VII had a summer residence built here, right on the beach, which is still used by the royal family. Just north of the palace are Hua Hin's rickety piers, bustling with activity in the early morning when the fishing boats go out and in the evening when they return. A few of the piers are used exclusively for drying squid – thousands of them – and this part of town exudes a powerful aroma.

The main swimming beach, not Thailand's best, has thatched umbrellas and long chairs. Vendors from the nearby food stalls will bring loungers steamed crab, mussels, beer, etc, and there are pony rides for the kids.

Eight or nine km south of Hua Hin are the slightly more secluded beaches of Khao Takiap, Suan Son and Khao Tao. Pranburi is a small town 24 km south of Hua Hin that's trying to become a mini-Hua Hin.

Places to Stay – bottom end & middle

Prices are moving up quickly for places near the beach. Hotels in town are still reasonable and it's only a five or 10-minute walk to the beach from most of them.

Hua Hin Ralug (Raluk) Hotel (tel 511940), 16 Damnoen Kasem, has rooms with fan for 100B, with fan and bath for 150B, and is only a couple of hundred metres from the beach. They also have some large bungalows for 350B with fan, 450B with air-con. Across the street from the Raluk is the newer *Jed Pee Nong* (tel 512381), where very modern, clean rooms are 300B with fan, 400B with air-con; not exactly bottom-end prices, but not bad value for the money. Next door the *Gee Cuisine* restaurant has a few basic rooms at the back for 80 to 130B. Back across the street again next to the more top-end Sirin Hotel is the *Thai Tae (Thae) Guest House* with basic rooms for 150B, larger rooms for 200B. Rooms come with fan and bath.

If you turn left at Thai Tae Guest House coming from the railway station, you'll enter Naretdamri Rd, which has become a hot spot for small hotels and guest houses almost overnight. On the left a few doors down from the corner is *Dang's House*, where there are small rooms for 60B and larger rooms for 120B and 150B. The proprietors jack up the price further on weekends and holidays. A bit

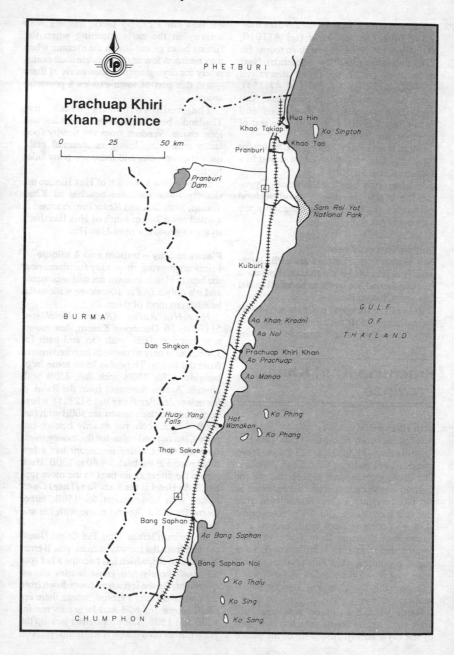

Prachuap Khiri Khan Province

0   25   50 km

PHETBURI

Hua Hin
Ko Singtoh
Khao Takiap
Khao Tao
Pranburi
Pranburi Dam
Sam Roi Yot National Park

Kuiburi

GULF
OF
THAILAND

BURMA

Ao Khan Kradni
Ao Noi
Dan Singkon
Prachuap Khiri Khan
Ao Prachuap
Ao Manao

Ko Phing

Huay Yang Falls
Hat Wanakon
Ko Phang

Thap Sakae

Bang Saphan

Ao Bang Saphan

Bang Saphan Noi

Ko Thalu

Ko Sing

CHUMPHON

Ko Sang

beyond Dang's are a couple of places with 'Rooms for Rent' signs out front, including the *Kak Guest House*. Both have basic rooms for 100B. There are probably other places on this part of Naretdamri Rd that let rooms. Further down Naretdamri near the pier, the *Mee Karuna Restaurant & Guest House* has four air-con rooms for 300 to 500B.

The next street up away from the beach is Poonsuk Rd. It's mostly a restaurant street at the moment, but one new hotel has been built here so far. The *Ban Boosarin* (tel 512076) calls itself a 'mini-deluxe hotel' and although it's 550B a night, all rooms come with air-con, hot water, telephone, colour TV, fridge and private terrace. It's super-clean and they claim they charge the same rates on weekends as weekdays. They give a 10% discount for stays of a week or more.

Running east from Chomsin Rd (the road leading to the main pier) is Naep Khehat Rd. At 73/5-7 is the *Phananchai Hotel* (tel 511707) with fan/bath rooms for 250B and air-con for 350B. It's fairly clean but a bit of a walk from the swimming beaches.

To find hotels under 200B, you'll have to go up to Phetkasem Rd, the main north-south road through town. *Chaat Chai* at 59/1 Phetkasem Rd has rooms with fan and bath for 90 to 180B. Just off Phetkasem, behind the bank, is *Subhamitra (Suphamit)* (tel 511208, 511487) with very clean rooms with fan and bath for 170B. Suphamit also has a few more expensive air-con rooms. Just past the market at 46 Phetkasem is *Damrong* (tel 511574), 120B for rooms with fan and bath, more for air-con.

Behind the Chatchai market area on Sasong Rd is the *Siripetchkasem (Siri Phetkasem)* (tel 511394), similar to the hotels along Phetkasem Rd. Fan rooms are 150B and air-con rooms are 300B.

Finally, a bit further north, at 11 Damrong Rat Rd, is the *Tananchai* (tel 511755), a middle-range place for 200B with fan and bath, more for air-con. The Tanachai accepts credit cards.

Places to Stay – top end

The air-con *Sirin Hotel* (tel 511150) is on Damnoen Kasem Rd down from the Raluk toward the beach. The rooms here are well kept and come with hot water and fridge. The semi-outdoor restaurant area is pleasant. Double rooms are 590B during the week and 990B on weekends and holidays.

The only other top-end hotel in town is the former Railway Hotel, but there are a few top-end places on beaches just north and south of town:

Royal Garden Resort (tel 511881, Bangkok reservations 251-8659) 107/1 Phetkasem Rd, 1500B up plus 300B peak season supplement November to April.
Royal Garden Village (tel 512412/5, Bangkok reservations 251 8659) 45 Phetkasem Rd, 1200B up plus 300B peak season supplement November to April.
Sailom Hotel (tel 511890/1, Bangkok reservations 258-0652), 750B up Sunday to Thursday, add 700B on weekends.
Hua Hin Highland Resort (tel 211-2579), 460 to 680B. On a hill north of town, this one is a favourite of golfers who frequent the nearby Royal Hua Hin Golf Course.
Hotel Sofitel Central Hua Hin (Hua Hin Railway Hotel) (tel 512021/40, Bangkok reservations 233-0974, 233-0980), 1600B up. From December 20 to February 20 there's a 400B peak season supplement on all room charges.

Hua Hin Railway Hotel

In 1922 the State Railway of Thailand (then the Royal Thai Railway) extended the national rail network to Hua Hin to allow easier access to the Hua Hin summer palace. The area proved to be a popular vacation spot among non-royals too, so in the following year they built the Hua Hin Railway Hotel, a graceful colonial-style inn on the sea, with sweeping teak stairways and high-ceiling rooms. When I researched the first edition of this guide in 1981, a double room was still only 90B and the service was just as unhurried as it had been when I first stayed here in 1977. It probably hadn't changed much since 1923, except for the addition of electric lighting and screened doors and windows. Big-bladed ceiling fans stirred the humid sea air and in the dining room one ate using State Railway silverware and thick china from the '20s. Unfortunately, when Bangkok's Central Department Store took over the management of the hotel they floundered in their attempt to upgrade the facilities, failing to take advantage of the hotel's original ambience.

In 1986 the French hotel chain of Sofitel became part of a joint venture with Central and together they restored the hotel to most of its former glory. It now bears the awkward name *Hotel Sofitel Central Hua Hin*, but if you've been looking for a historical South-East Asian hotel to spend some money on, this might be it. All of the wood panelling and brass fixtures

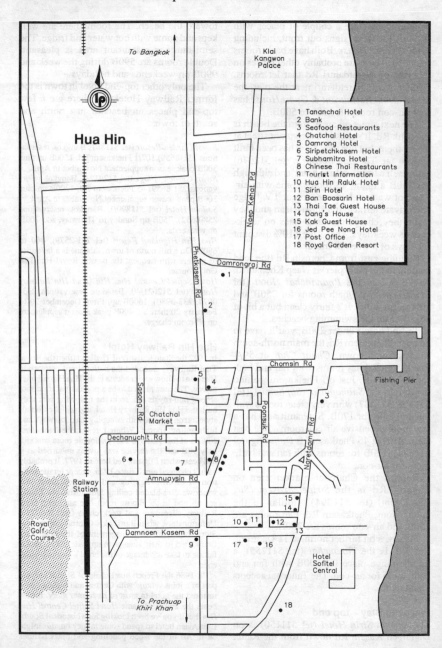

To Bangkok

Klai Kangwon Palace

Hua Hin

1 Tananchai Hotel
2 Bank
3 Seafood Restaurants
4 Chatchai Hotel
5 Damrong Hotel
6 Siripetchkasem Hotel
7 Subhamitra Hotel
8 Chinese Thai Restaurants
9 Tourist Information
10 Hua Hin Raluk Hotel
11 Sirin Hotel
12 Ban Boosarin Hotel
13 Thai Tae Guest House
14 Dang's House
15 Kak Guest House
16 Jed Pee Nong Hotel
17 Post Office
18 Royal Garden Resort

Naep Kehat Rd

Damrongraj Rd

Phetkasem Rd

Chomsin Rd

Fishing Pier

Sasong Rd

Chatchai Market

Poonsuk Rd

Naretdamri Rd

Dechanuchit Rd

Amnuaysin Rd

Railway Station

Royal Golf Course

Damnoen Kasem Rd

Hotel Sofitel Central

To Prachuap Khiri Khan

throughout the rooms and open hallways have been restored. While the old railway silverware and china have been resigned to antique cabinet displays, the spacious, lazy ambience of a previous age remains. Even if you don't want to spend the money to stay here, it's worth a stroll through the grounds and open sitting areas for a little history. It's more interesting in terms of atmosphere than either the Raffles in Singapore or the Oriental in Bangkok (neither of which have eight-hectare grounds), and somewhere in between in terms of luxury.

All rooms and bungalows are air-con and come with TV, fridge, etc. In the new wing that's been built off the original colonial wing, rooms range in price from 1600B for a 'standard' room to 2200B for a 'superior'. Rooms in the old wing are 1900B. Across Damnoen Kasem Rd is the Villa Wing, a collection of large beach bungalows that are part of the original Railway Hotel as well. One-bedroom/two-bedroom villas are 1600/2500B.

Incidentally, in 1983 this hotel was used as Hotel Le Phnom for the filming of *Killing Fields*. And the State Railway Hotel still owns the hotel; Sofitel/Central are just leasing it.

Places to Stay – out of town
Hat Takiap The *Charoensuk Guest House* (tel 512339) has 12 rooms ranging in price from 600B upwards. The *Fongkhlun Guest House* (tel 512402) has six rooms from 400 to 500B. The *Khao Takiap Resort* (tel 512405) has six rooms from 300 to 800B. The *Rung Arun Guest House* (tel 512554) has two rooms from 150 to 700B, and the *Vegas Guest House* (tel 512290) has 32 rooms priced from 390B.

Hat Khao Tao The *Nanthasuda Guest House (Nanthasuda Restaurant)* has rooms priced from 300B.

Hat Suan Son The *Suan Son Padiphat* (tel 511239) has 37 rooms priced from 150B.

Pranburi The *Pranburi Beach Resort* (tel Bangkok reservations 233-3871) has rooms priced from 1400B, and the *Pransiri Hotel* (tel 621061), 283 Phetkasem Rd has rooms from 140B.

Places to Eat
The best seafood in Hua Hin is concentrated in three main areas. Firstly, along Damnoen Kasem Rd near the Jed Pee Nong and Raluk

hotels, and off Damnoen Kasem, on Poonsuk Rd and Naretdamri Rd, there are some medium-priced restaurants. Secondly, there's excellent and inexpensive food in the Chatchai night market, off Phetkasem on Dechanit Rd, and in nearby Chinese-Thai restaurants. The third area is next to Tha Thiap Reua Pramong, the big fishing pier at the end of Chonsin Rd. The fish here, of course, is fresh off the boats but not necessarily the cheapest in town. One of the places near the pier, *Saeng Thai*, is the oldest seafood restaurant in Hua Hin and quite reliable if you know how to order. The best value for money can be found in the smaller eating places on and off Chonsin Rd and in the Chatchai night market. There is also a night market on Chonsin Rd.

The best seafood to order in Hua Hin is plaa samlee (cotton fish or kingfish), plaa kapong (perch), plaa meuk (squid), hawy maleng phu (mussels), and pu (crab) in any of several forms: phat (sliced, filleted and fried), yang (roast, squid only), phao (grilled), neung (steamed), tom yam (in a hot and tangy broth), raat phrik (smothered in garlic and chillies), thawt (fried whole) and dip (raw).

The central market is excellent for Thai breakfast – they sell very good jok and khao tom (rice soups) Fresh-fried pathong-ko, Hua Hin-style (small and crispy, not oily), are 1B for four. A few vendors also serve hot soy milk in bowls (4B) – break a few pathong-ko into the soy milk and drink free nam cha – a very tasty and filling breakfast for 7B if you can eat 12 pathong-ko.

Poonsuk and Naretdamri Rd is becoming a centre for farang-oriented eateries. The *Tan Thong* does good seafood and also has a bar. The *Beergarden* is just what it sounds like – an outdoor pub with western food. The *Headrock Cafe* (not a mis-spelling but a pun on the name Hua Hin – 'head rock') is more of a drinking place, but also has Thai and western food. On the next street up, Poonsuk Rd, is the Italian *La Villa* with pizza, spaghetti, lasagne and so on.

Getting There & Away
Bus Buses from Bangkok's Southern Bus

Terminal are 74B air-con, 41B ordinary. The trip takes about four hours.

Buses for Hua Hin leave Phetburi regularly for 15B. The same bus can be picked up in Cha-am for 10B. From Nakhon Pathom an ordinary bus is 32B.

Train The same trains south apply here as those described under Phetburi – Getting There & Away. The train trip takes 4½ hours; 1st-class fare is 182B (Express only), 2nd class 92B (Rapid and Express only), 3rd class is 44B.

You can also come by train from any other station on the southern rail line, including Phetburi (3rd class, 13B), Nakhon Pathom (2nd/3rd class 52/33B), Prachuap (3rd class, 19B), Surat Thani (2nd/3rd class, 116/74B) and Hat Yai (2nd/3rd class, 183/116B).

Getting Around
Samlor fares in Hua Hin have been set by the municipal authorities so there shouldn't be any haggling. Here are some sample fares: the railway station to the beach, 10B; the bus terminal to Sofitel Central, 15B; Chatchai market to the fishing pier, 5B.

For local buses to the beaches of Khao Takiap, Khao Tam and Suan Son, go to the ordinary bus terminal on Sasong Rd. Fares are: Khao Takiap 5B, Khao Tao 4B and Suan Son 4B. These buses run from around 6 am until 5 pm. Buses to Pranburi are 7B.

Motorcycles and bicycles can be rented from a place on Damnoen Kasem Rd near the Jed Pee Nong Hotel. They ask 200B per day for a motorbike (could be negotiated down for longer term rentals) and 20 to 40B for bicycles.

At the fishing pier in Hua Hin you can hire boats out to Singtoh Island for 600B a day. On Hat Takiap you can get boats for 500B.

KHAO SAM ROI YOT NATIONAL PARK
อุทยานแห่งชาติ เขาสามร้อยยอด
This 98-square-km park has magnificent views of the Prachuap coastline if you can stand a little climbing. Khao Daeng is only about half an hour's walk from the park headquarters, and from here you can see the ocean as well as some freshwater lagoons. If

you have the time and energy, climb the 605-metre Khao Krachom for even better views. If you're lucky, you may come across the rare serow, or Asian mountain goat, while hiking. The lagoons are great places for bird-watching.

The other big attraction at Sam Roi Yot (Three Hundred Peaks) are the three caves of Tham Kaew, Tham Sai and Tham Phraya Nakhon. Tham Phraya Nakhon is the most interesting and can be reached by boat or on foot. The boat trip only takes about half an hour there and back, while it's half an hour each way on foot along a steep trail. There are actually two large caverns, both with sinkholes that allow light in. In one cave is a royal sala, or resting pavilion, built for King Chulalongkorn, who would stop off here when travelling back and forth between Bangkok and Nakhon Si Thammarat.

English-speaking guides can be hired at the park office for 50B per hike.

Places to Stay
The Forestry Department hires out two-person tents for 30B per night and large bungalows for 500 to 1000B per night that sleep 10 to 20 people. You can also pitch your own tent for 5B per person on Laem Sala or Hat Sam Phraya, which are just beyond the visitors' centre. There is a restaurant on Hat Laem Sala. Bring repellent along as the park is rife with mosquitoes.

Getting There & Away
Catch a bus to Pranburi (7B from Hua Hin) and then another to the park for 10B. Sometimes it's necessary to change buses in Bang Phu. If you're coming by car or motorcyle from Hua Hin, it's about 25 km to the park turn-off, then another 38 km to park headquarters.

PRACHUAP KHIRI KHAN TOWN
เมือง ประจวบคีรีขันธ์
Roughly 80 km south of Hua Hin, Prachuap Khiri Khan Town (population 14,000) is the provincial capital, though it is somewhat smaller than Hua Hin. There are no real swimming beaches in town, though the eight-km-long bay of Ao Prachuap is pretty

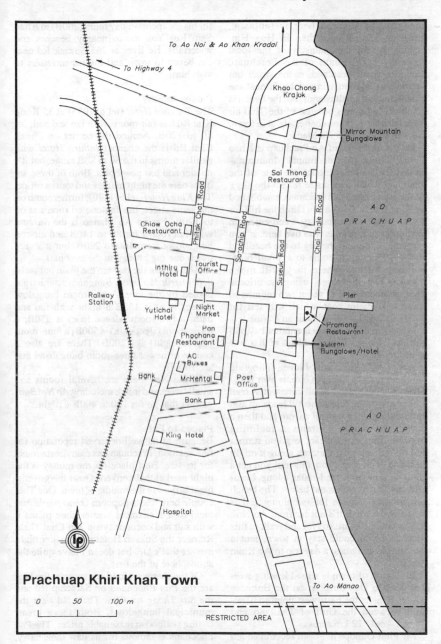

To Ao Noi & Ao Khan Kradai

To Highway 4

Khao Chong Krajok

Mirror Mountain Bungalows

Sai Thong Restaurant

AO PRACHUAP

Chiow Ocha Restaurant

Phitak Chat Road

Sarachip Road

Suseuk Road

Chai Thale Road

Inthira Hotel

Tourist Office

Pier

Railway Station

Yutichai Hotel

Night Market

Pramong Restaurant

Pan Phochana Restaurant

Sukson Bungalows/Hotel

AC Buses

McRental

Bank

Post Office

Bank

AO PRACHUAP

King Hotel

Hospital

To Ao Manao

Prachuap Khiri Khan Town

0   50   100 m

RESTRICTED AREA

enough. The seafood here is fantastic, however, and cheaper than in Hua Hin. Fishing is still the mainstay of the local economy here. South of Ao Prachuap, around a small headland, is the small but scenic Ao Manao, ringed by limestone mountains and small islands, but the beach is off limits to farangs because of the Thai air force base there. If you charter a boat in town, you can sail through Ao Manao.

On the north end of Ao Prachuap is Khao Chong Krajok (Mirror Tunnel Mountain – named for the hole through the side of the mountain which appears to reflect the sky). At the top is Wat Thammikaram, established by King Rama VI. You can climb the hill for a view of the town and bay – and entertain the hordes of monkeys who live here. If you continue on around the bay to the headland at the north, you'll come to a small boat-building village where they still make wooden fishing vessels using traditional Thai methods. It takes about two months to finish a 12-metre boat, which will sell for 300,000 to 400,000B without an engine.

A few km north of here is another bay, Ao Noi, and a small fishing village with a few rooms to let.

About eight km north of town, following the same road beyond Ao Noi, is Wat Khao Tham Khan Kradai, a small cave wat. A trail at the base of the limestone hill leads up and around the side to a small cavern and then a larger one which contains a reclining Buddha. The cave appears to go on further and if you've brought a torch along it might be worth exploring. From this trail you get a good view of Ao Khan Kradai, a long, beautiful bay that stretches out below. The beach here is very suitable for swimming and is virtually deserted. It's not far from Ao Noi, so you could stay in Ao Noi and walk to this beach. Or you could stay in town, rent a motorcycle and make a day trip to Ao Khan Kradai.

Just south of town is a road leading west that goes to Dan Singkon on the Burmese border. This is the narrowest point in Thailand between the Gulf of Thailand and Burma – only 12 km across.

Mr Pinit Ounope has been recommended

for his inexpensive day tours (200B) to Khao Sam Roi Yot and to nearby beaches and waterfalls. He lives at 265 Susuak Rd near the beach in town and invites travellers to visit him.

Places to Stay

The *Yutichai Hotel* (tel 611055) at 35 Kong Kiat Rd has fair rooms with fan and bath for 80 to 120B. Around the corner on Phitak Chat Rd is the cheaper *Inthira Hotel* with similar rooms in the 60 to 80B range, but it's noisier and has peepholes. Both of these are quite near the night market and tourist office. The *King Hotel* (tel 611170), further south on the same street, has fan-cooled rooms at 60 to 120B. Facing Ao Manao is the *Suksan*, with fan rooms for 80 to 140B and air-con bungalows from 160 to 220B, but it's very much one big brothel in the evenings.

Also facing the bay are the plain but well-kept *Mirror Mountain Bungalows*, which are owned by the city. A one-room bungalow (sleeps two) is 150B a night with fan and bath; a two-room (sleeps four) is 350B; a three-room (sleeps six) is 500B; a four- room (sleeps eight) is 1200B. There are also a couple of newer three-room bungalows that are 1000B.

In Ao Noi there are several rooms and small 'weekend inns', including *Ao Noi Bungalows* that go for 100 to 400B a night.

Places to Eat

Because of its well-deserved reputation for fine seafood, Prachuap has many restaurants for its size. Best place for the money is the night market that convenes near the government offices in the middle of town. One Thai couple here roasts popcorn (*khao phoht hua taek*) over a charcoal brazier, then mixes it with salt and coconut syrup. On Chai Thale Rd near the Suksan Hotel is a smaller night market that's OK but doesn't have quite the atmosphere of the first.

Of the many seafood restaurants, the best are the *Pan Phochana* on Sarachip Rd and the *Sai Thong* on Chai Thale Rd near the municipal bungalows. Both serve great-tasting seafood at reasonable prices. The Pan Phochana is famous for its haw mok hawy, ground fish curry steamed in mussels on the half-shell. Other good restaurants include the *Chiow Ocha* (a bit higher-priced – this is where the Thai tour buses stop), the *Pramong* and the *Chao Reua*. One of the seafood specialities of Prachuap that you shouldn't miss is *plaa samlii taet diaw*, whole cottonfish that's sliced lengthways and left to dry in the sun half a day, than fried quickly in a wok. It's often served with mango salad on the side. It may sound awful, but the taste is sublime.

Across from the Inthira Hotel is a small morning market with tea stalls that serve cheap curries and noodles.

Getting There & Away

Bus From Bangkok, ordinary buses are 63B and they leave the Southern Bus Terminal frequently between 4.30 and 5.20 pm. For air-con, it's 105B from the Southern AC Terminal. From Hua Hin buses are 21B and they leave from the bus station on Sasong Rd every 20 minutes from 7 am to 3 pm.

Train For departure details from Bangkok, see Phetburi – Getting There & Away: the same services apply. Fares from Bangkok are 122B for 2nd class and 58B for 3rd class. Trains between Hua Hin and Prachuap are 19B; the 11.57 am ordinary train arrives in Prachuap at 1.20 pm. Rapid trains leave Hua Hin at 4.16 pm and 7.58 pm, arriving in Prachuap at 5.29 pm and 9.27 pm respectively.

Getting Around

Prachuap Town is small enough to get around on foot. You can hire a tuk-tuk to Ao Noi for 20B. The motorcycle dealer on Sarachip Rd rents motorcycles.

THAP SAKAE & BANG SAPHAN

ทับสะแก   บางสะพาน

These two districts lie south of Prachuap Khiri Khan and together they offer a string of fairly good beaches that hardly get any tourists.

The town of Thap Sakae is set back from the coast and isn't much, but along the seashore there are a few places to stay (see below). The beach opposite Thap Sakae isn't anything special either but north and south of town are the beaches of Hat Wanakon and Hat Laem Kum. There is no private accommodation at these beaches at the moment, but you could ask permission to camp at Wat Laem Kum, which is on a prime spot right in the middle of Hat Laem Kum. Laem Kum is only 3½ km from Thap Sakae and at the north end is the fishing village of Ban Don Sai, where you can buy food.

Bang Saphan is no great shakes as a town either, but the long beaches here are beginning to attract some speculative development. Between Bang Saphan and Bang Saphan Noi you'll find the beaches of Hat Sai Kaew, Hat Ban Krut, Hat Ban Nong Mongkon, Hat (Ao) Baw Thawng Lang, Hat Pha Daeng and Hat Bang Boet, all of which are worth looking up. Getting around can be a problem since there isn't much public transport between these beaches. The manager at the Talay Inn in Thap Sakae has a truck that he lets guests use sometimes to go to the nearby beaches.

Places to Stay & Eat

Thap Sakae In Thap Sakae Town, there are three hotels to choose from: the *Chawalit*, right off the highway with rooms for 100 to 200B with fan and bath; the *Sukkasem*, near the centre of town with rooms for 100 to 180B; and the *Thiparot*, with rooms for 100 to 200B. On the coast opposite Thap Sakae are a couple of concrete block-style bungalows for 150 to 300B, eg *Chan Reua*. Much more congenial and economical is the *Talay Inn* (tel 671417), a cluster of nine bamboo huts on a lake fed by the Huay Yang Waterfall, but back from the beach a bit in the fishing village. Accommodation is 50B per person. The owner-manager, Khun Yo, was a nurse in England for 12 years and he takes good care of his guests. His place is about one km east of the Thap Sakae Railway Station, which is about 1½ km from Thap Sakae Town. Talay Inn is within easy walking distance of the sea and there is fishing and swimming in the lake.

Bang Saphan Along the bay of Ao Bang Saphan are several beach hotels and bungalows. The *Hat Somboon Sea View* is 250B per room with private bath. For 150B a night you could stay at any of the following: *Sarika Villa, Sung Haeng Hotel, Hat Sai Kaew Resort* or *Wanwina Bungalows*. The *Krua Klang Ao* restaurant is a good place for seafood, right near the centre of Ao Bang Saphan.

Hat Kaew Between Thap Sakae and Bang Saphan on the beach of Hat Kaew (Km 372, Highway 4) is Haad Kaeo Beach Resort (tel 611035). It's actually just 200 metres from the Ban Koktahom Railway Station, which can only be reached by ordinary train from the Hua Hin, Prachuap, Thap Sakae, Bang Saphan or Chumphon terminals. Pretty white bungalows with green roofs are 200B per day.

Getting There & Away

Buses from Prachuap to Thap Sakae are 6B and from Thap Sakae to Bang Saphan 8B. If you're coming from further south, buses from Chumphon to Bang Saphan are 25B.

You can also get 3rd-class trains between Hua Hin, Prachuap, Thap Sakae, Ban Koktahom and Bang Saphan for a few baht on each leg, as all of them have railway stations (the Rapid and Express lines do not stop in Thap Sakae or Bang Saphan).

Chumphon Province

CHUMPHON TOWN เมืองชุมพร

Nearly 500 km south of Bangkok, Chumphon Town (population 15,000) is the junction town (the name is derived from *chumnumphon*, which means 'meeting place') where you turn west to Ranong and Phuket or continue south on the newer road to Surat Thani, Nakhon Si Thammarat and Songkhla. The provincial capital is a busy place but of no particular interest except that this is where south Thailand really begins in terms of ethnic markers like dialect and religion. The port of Chumphon is 10 km from Chumphon Town, and in this area there are a few beaches and a handful of islands with good reefs for diving.

The nearest islands are Ko Samet, Ko Mattara, Ko Rang Kachiu and Ko Raet. Landing on Ko Rang Kachiu is restricted as this is where the precious swallow's nest is collected for the gourmet market. If you want to visit, you can request permission from the Laem Thong Bird Nest Company in Chumphon. The other islands are uninhabited. The reefs around Ko Raet and Ko Mattara are the most colourful. There are many other islands a bit further out that are also suitable for diving – get information from the diving centre at Chumphon Cabana Resort on Thung Wua Laen beach. You can hire boats and diving equipment here as well during the diving season, June to October. Fishing is also popular around the islands.

Places to Stay

The cheaper hotels in Chumphon are along Sala Daeng Rd in the centre of town. The *Si Taifa Hotel* on Sala Daeng Rd is a clean, old Chinese hotel built over a restaurant with rooms for 70B with shared bath, 90B with basin and shower, or 100B with shower and Thai-style toilet. Each floor has a terrace where you can watch the sun set over the city. There's also the *Thai Prasert*, 202-204 Sala Daeng Rd, with rooms from 60 to 80B, and the *Suriya*, 125/24-26 Sala Daeng Rd, which has the same rates – neither of them are particularly good.

Further north on Sala Daeng Rd are the nearly identical *Si Chumphon Hotel* (tel 511280) and *Chumphon Suriwong Hotel*, both clean and efficient Chinese hotels with rooms for 100B up with fan and bath, 250B for air-con. The fairly new *Tha Taphao Hotel* (511479) is on Tha Taphao Rd near the bus terminal. Rooms here are 145/190B for comfortable singles/doubles with fan and bath or 180/210B with air-con.

More expensive is the *Paradorn Inn* (tel 511598) at 180/12 Paradorn Rd where standard air-con rooms cost 350B, or 400B with TV and fridge. They also have a few rooms with fan for 220B.

Places to Eat

Around the corner from the Si Chumphon Hotel on Kommaluang Chumphon Rd is a

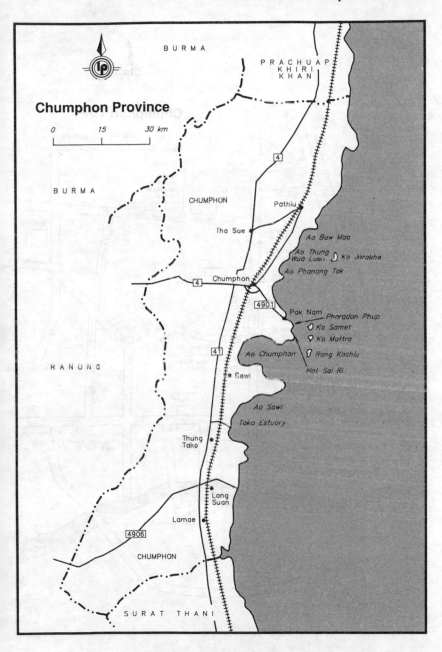

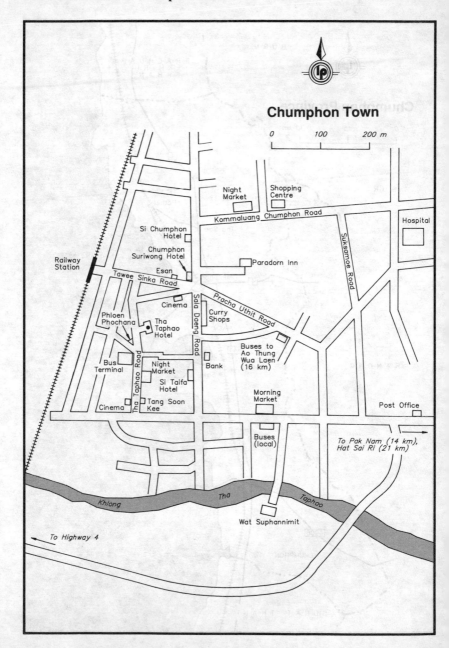

Chumphon Town

big night market with all kinds of vendors, including one place that serves espresso and other coffee drinks as well as ice cream (try the brandy coffee ice).

The several curry shops along Sala Daeng Rd are proof that you are now in southern Thailand. Over on Tha Taphao Rd is a smaller night market and a very popular Chinese place called *Tang Soon Kee*. Further north on this street just past the bus terminal on the left is another Chinese place, *Phloen Phochana*, which opens early in the morning with 1B pathong-ko, soy milk and coffee or tea. Up on Tawee Sinka Rd near the Chumphon Suriwong Hotel is the *Esan* with good north-eastern food in the evenings.

Getting There & Away
Bus From Bangkok's Southern Bus Terminals ordinary buses are 89B and depart at 4 am and 6.05 am only. Air-con buses are 160B and leave every 10 minutes from 9.30 am to 10 pm.

Buses run regularly between Surat Thani and Chumphon for 45B or to/from Ranong for 27B. Bang Saphan to Chumphon is 25B.

Train Rapid and Express trains from Bangkok (Bangkok Noi station in Thonburi) take about 7½ hours to reach Chumphon and cost 82B 3rd class, 172B 2nd class, or 356B 1st class (Express only). See Phetburi – Getting There & Away for departure times.

Getting Around
Songthaews to the Chumphon Estuary (Pak Nam Chumphon) are 5B per person. To Hat Sai Ri they're 8B and to Thung Wua Laen 15B. Buses to Tako Estuary (for Hat Arunothai) are 13B. A motorcycle taxi out to Thung Wua Laen should be no more than 50B.

AROUND CHUMPHON PROVINCE
The best beaches in Chumphon Province are north of Chumphon Town at Ao Phanang Tak, Ao Thung Wua Laen and Ao Baw Mao. Nearer town, in the vicinity of the Chumphon Estuary, are the lesser beaches of Hat Pharadon Phap and Hat Sai Rii. Then about 40 km south of Chumphon Town, past the town

of Sawi, is the Tako Estuary and the fair beach of Hat Arunothai. Most of these beaches have at least one set of resort bungalows.

On Tha Taphao Rd in town near the bus terminal is a private tourist information centre whose primary purpose seems to be to steer you toward the Chumphon Cabana Resort.

Places to Stay
The air-con *Porn Sawan Home Beach Resort* (tel 521031) is at the Chumphon Estuary on Pharadon Phap beach and has rooms starting at 550B.

The *Chumphon Cabana Resort* (tel 501990, Bangkok reservations 224-1994) on Hat Thung Wua Laen (12 km north of Chumphon) has 22 well-appointed bungalows and 20 sets of diving equipment. The nightly tariff ranges from 300 to 1000B.

Chumphon Sunny Beach (Bangkok reservations 511-3746) is at the Tako Estuary on Hat Arunothai, about 50 km south of Chumphon. Bungalows are 300 to 450B with fan or 550B for air-con.

Ranong Province

This is Thailand's least populous province, 67% of it is mountains, over 80% forests. Like much of southern Thailand, it undergoes two monsoons, but its mountains tend to hold the rains over the area longer, so it gets the highest average annual rainfall in the country. Hence it's incredibly green overall, with lots of waterfalls, but is swampy near the coastline, so there isn't much in the way of beaches. The provincial economy is supported mainly by mineral extraction and fishing, and rubber, coconut and cashew nut production. In Ranong they call cashews *ka-yuu* (in other southern provinces the word is *ka-yii* and in the rest of Thailand it's *met ma-muang*).

RANONG TOWN เมืองระนอง
The small capital and port of Ranong Town (population 17,000) is only separated from

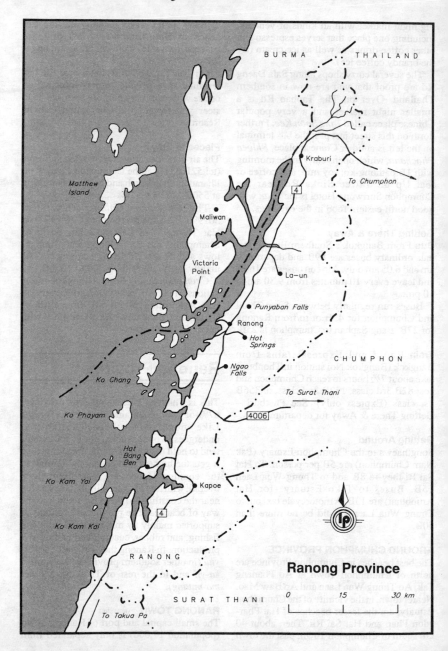

BURMA   THAILAND

Matthew Island

● Kraburi

4

To Chumphon

● Maliwan

Victoria Point

● La-un

● *Punyaban Falls*

● Ranong

● *Hot Springs*

● *Ngao Falls*

CHUMPHON

Ko Chang

To Surat Thani

Ko Phayam

4006

Hat Bang Ben

● Kapoe

Ko Kam Yai

4

Ko Kam Kai

RANONG

Ranong Province

0   15   30 km

SURAT THANI

To Takua Pa

Burma by the Chan River. Burmese from nearby Victoria Point (called Kaw/Ko Sawng by the Thais, meaning 'second island', or Kaw Thaung in the Burmese pronunciation) hop across to trade in Thailand or work on fishing boats. Although there is nothing of great cultural interest in the town, the buildings are architecturally interesting since this area was originally settled by Hokkien Chinese.

During the reign of King Rama V, a Hokkien named Koh Su Chiang was made governor of Ranong (gaining the new name Phraya Damrong Na Ranong) and his former residence, Nai Khai Ranong has become a combination clan house and shrine. It's on the northern edge of town and is worth a visit if you're looking for something to do in Ranong. Of the three original buildings, one still stands and is filled with mementos of the Koh family glory-days. The main gate and part of the original wall remain as well. Koh Su Chiang's great-grandson Koh Sim Kong is the caretaker and he speaks a little English. Several of the shop houses on Ruangrat Rd preserve the old Hokkien style, too. Koh Su Chiang's mausoleum is set into the side of a hill a bit further north on the road to Hat Chandamri.

About one km east of the Jansom Thara Hotel is the Ranong Mineral Hot Springs at Wat Tapotaram. Water temperature hovers around 65°C, hot enough to boil eggs. The Jansom Thara pipes water from the springs into the hotel where you can take a 42°C mineral bath in their large public jacuzzi for 50B. If you continue on the same road past the hot springs for about seven km, you'll come to the village of Hat Som Paen, a former tin-mining community. At Wat Hat Som Paen, visitors feed fruit to the huge black carp (plaa phluang) in the temple stream. The faithful believe these carp are actually thewada, a type of angel, and it's forbidden to catch and eat them. Legend has it that those who do will contract leprosy. Another three km down a bumpy dirt road is Marakot Thara, an emerald-green reservoir that fills an old tin quarry. Although tin production in Ranong has slackened off due to the depressed global market, the mining of

calcium compounds, used to make porcelain, is still profitable.

Hat Chandamri is touted as the nearest beach to Ranong Town but it's really more of a mud flat. From the dining terrace of the Jansom Thara Resort overlooking the bay, you can eat seafood and watch the sun set over Victoria Point. It's 10 km north-west of town, about 15B by motorcycle taxi or 4 to 5B by songthaew. Jansom Thara does boat trips to nearby islands, including Ko Phayam, which is said to have a fairly good beach for swimming. The average cost for a day trip is 300B per person, including lunch. Their boat, the JS Queen, can also be chartered for trips to further islands like the Ko Surin group. It holds up to 40 people.

The provincial fishing port, Tha Thiap Reua Pramong, is eight km south-west of town. It's called Saphaan Plaa (Fish Bridge) for short and is always bustling with activity as fishing boats are loaded and unloaded with great cargoes of flapping fish. About half the boats are Burmese, as the fish traders buy from anyone who lands fish here. Boats can be chartered here for day trips to nearby islands. Unless you want to see heaps of fish or charter a fishing boat, though, there's really no reason to go out to the port.

About 60 km north of Ranong Town, in Kraburi district, is the Isthmus of Kra, the narrowest point in Thailand. Barely 22 km separates the Gulf of Thailand from the Indian Ocean at this point. Just off Highway 4 is a monument commemorating this geographical wonder. At one time the Thai government had plans to construct the so-called Kra Canal here, but the latest word is that the canal will run east from Satun Province through Songkhla, about 500 km further south.

Of the several well-known waterfalls in Ranong Province, Ngao Falls and Punyaban Falls are within walking distance of Highway 4. Ngao is 13 km south of Ranong Town while Punyaban is 15 km north. Just ride a songthaew in either direction and ask to be let off at the nam tok (waterfall).

Information

Ranong is about 600 km south of Bangkok,

300 km north of Phuket. Most of Ranong's banks are on Tha Muang Rd, the road to the fishing pier. There is a post office on Ruangrat Rd in the old town district.

Places to Stay & Eat

The *Asia Hotel* (tel 811113) at 39/9 Ruangrat Rd near the day market has clean rooms with fan and bath for 150B and air-con rooms for 250B. Across from the market is the *Sin Ranong Hotel* with adequate rooms for 100B. North a bit, at No 81/1 Ruangrat Rd, is the *Sin Tavee (Thawi) Hotel* (811213) with

similar rooms for 120B, plus air-con rooms for 240B.

Further up Ruangrat Rd and cheaper are the *Rattanasin Hotel* on the right and the *Suriyanon Hotel* on the left across from the post office. The Rattanasin is the better of the two and has fair rooms from 70B with fan and bath. The Suriyonon is dark and decaying, but the staff are friendly and claim they don't allow any hookers in the hotel. A basic room with just a bed is 40B, with a fan it's 50B and with a fan and bath it's 60B.

Across Phetkasem Highway on the road to the hot springs is *Jansom Thara Hotel*, which

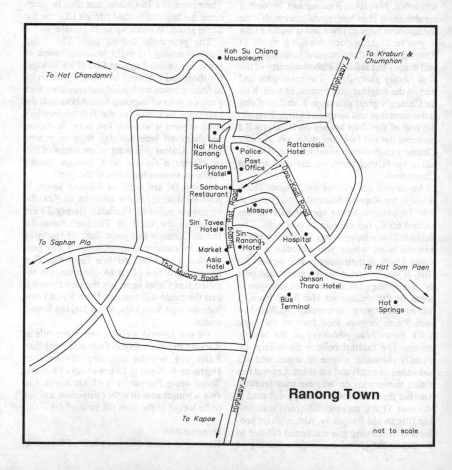

Ranong Town

not to scale

has just about everything you could possibly want in a hotel. Standard rooms come with air-con, colour TV with in-house video, hot water bath with jacuzzi (piped in from the hot springs), and a refrigerator stocked with booze. There are also two restaurants, one of which specialises in Chinese dim sum and noodles, two large mineral jacuzzis, a fitness centre, a disco, coffee house/cocktail lounge, a swimming pool and a travel agency. Rates start at 1000B. At their sister hotel, the *Jansom Thara Resort* at Hat Chandamri, similarly equipped bungalows (but no jacuzzis) cost 1200B.

For inexpensive Thai and Burmese breakfasts, try the morning market on Ruangrat Rd. Also along Ruangrat Rd are several traditional Hokkien coffee shops with marble-topped tables and enamelled metal teapots. One of the best restaurants in town is the *Sombun Restaurant*, across from the Rattanasin Hotel, with great seafood and standard Thai-Chinese dishes.

Getting There & Away

You can get to Ranong via Chumphon, Surat Thani or Takua Pa/Phuket. Buses from Chumphon are 27B, or from Surat 45B. Buses from Takua Pa are 32B, from Phuket 60B. The bus terminal in Ranong is out of town near the Jansom Thara Hotel, but buses stop in town on Ruangrat Rd before proceeding on to the terminal.

Air-con minivans run between Phuket (opposite the Imperial Hotel) and the Jansom Thara Hotel in Ranong for 180B. The van leaves Ranong at 8 am and arrives in Phuket at 12.30 am; in the opposite direction it leaves Phuket at 2 pm and arrives in Ranong at 6.30 pm. In either direction the van stops in Takua Pa for a meal (not included in the fare). They also have a minivan that runs between Surat (Muang Tai Hotel) and Ranong for 150B. Departure from Ranong is at 8 am, arriving in Surat at 11.30 am. From Surat the van leaves at 12.10 pm and arrives in Ranong at 3.40 pm.

Getting Around

Songthaews ply the roads around Ranong Town and out to the hot springs and Hat Som Paen (No 2), Hat Chandamri (No 3) and Saphan Pla (No 2). The fare is 4 to 5B to any of these places. Motorcycle taxis (look for the orange vests) will take you anywhere in town for 5B, or for 10 to 15B to the other places.

LAEM SON NATIONAL PARK
อุทยานแห่งชาติแหลมสน

The Laem Son (Pine Cape) Wildlife and Forest Preserve, stretches 315 square km over the Kapoe district of Ranong and Khuraburi district, Phang-Nga. This area includes about 100 km of Andaman Sea coastline as well as over 20 islands. Much of the coast here is covered with mangrove swamps, home to various species of birds, fish, deer and monkeys, including the crab-eating macaques which are easily seen while driving along the road to the park headquarters. The best-known and most accessible beach is Hat Bang Ben, where the main park offices, restaurant and bungalows are. This is a long, sandy beach backed by shady casuarina trees and it is said to be safe for swimming year-round. From here you can see several islands, including the nearby Ko Kam Yai, Ko Kam Nui, Mu Ko Yipun, Ko Kang Kao and, to the north, Ko Phayam. The park staff can arrange boat trips out to any of these islands.

Ko Phayam is inhabited by around 100 Thais, who mostly make their living by fishing or growing cashews. There is a good swimming beach on Phayam and on the west side of some of the Kam islands, as well as some live coral. The beach on Ko Kam Nui has particularly clear water for swimming and snorkelling plus the added bonus of fresh water year-round and plenty of grassy areas for camping. One island on the other side of Ko Kam Yai which can't be seen from the beach is Ko Kam Tok (also called Ko Ao Khao Khwai). It's only about 200 metres from Ko Kam Yai, and, like Ko Kam Nui, has a good beach, coral, fresh water and a camping area. Ko Kam Yai is 14 km southwest of Hat Bang Ben. During low tide you can walk to a nearby island just a couple of hundred metres away from Hat Bang Ben.

About three km north of Hat Bang Ben,

across the canal, is another beach, Hat Laem Son, which is almost always deserted and is 'undeveloped' according to park authorities (which means they won't guarantee your safety). The only way to get there is to hike from Bang Ben. In the opposite direction, about 50 km south of Hat Bang Ben, is Hat Praphat, very similar to Bang Ben with casuarina trees and a long beach. A second park office is located here and this one can be reached by road via the Phetkasem Highway.

In the canals you ford coming into the park, you may notice large wooden racks which are used for raising oysters.

Places to Stay & Eat
According to park authorities at Laem Son, the cost for accommodation in any of the park bungalows is 'by donation', which means you should be able to stay there for about 100B per person. Camping is allowed anywhere amongst the casuarina trees for 5B per person. Just outside the park entrance is the private *Komain Villa* where small bungalows are 100B per night. The food at the park cafe is rather pricey, but considering it has to be brought over 10 km of rough road, the prices are understandable. Slightly cheaper places can be found near Komain Villa.

Getting There & Away
The turn-off for Laem Son is about 58 km down the Phetkasem Highway (No 4) from Ranong Town, between Km 657 and 658. Any bus heading south from Ranong can drop you off here or you could hitch fairly easily as there is plenty of traffic along Highway 4. Once you're off Highway 4, however, you'll have to wait a bit to flag down pick-up trucks going to the village near Laem Son. If you can't get a ride all the way, it's a two-km walk from the village to the park. If you have your own vehicle, don't attempt this road when it's wet unless you have 4WD or a good dirt-bike.

SURIN ISLANDS NATIONAL PARK
อุทยานแห่งชาติ หมู่เกาะสุรินทร์

A national park since 1981, the Surin Islands are famous for excellent diving and sport-fishing. The two main islands (there are five in all) of Ko Surin Nua and Ko Surin Tai (North Surin Island and South Surin Island) are about 60 km from Khuraburi. The park office and visitors' centre is on the southwest side of the north island at Ao Mae Yai where boats anchor. Admission to the park is 5B.

On the southern island is a village of sea gypsies (*chao le* or *chao nam*) and this is also where the official camp ground is located. The best diving is said to be in the channel between these two islands. The chao nam hold a large ceremony, involving ancestral worship, on Ko Surin Tai during the full moon in March. The island may be off limits during that time, so ask at the park office.

Places to Stay
Accommodation at the park bungalows is 100B per person. At the campground two-person tents are 60B a night or you can use you own (or camp without a tent) for 5B per night per person.

Getting There & Away
The mainland office of Surin Islands National Park is in Khuraburi, about 70 km south of Ranong. You can charter a boat out to the Surin Islands from Khuraburi either through the park officers (who will merely serve as brokers/interpreters) or from the Phae Pla Chumphon Pier at Ban Hin Lat. The road to Ban Hin Lat runs off Highway 4 at Km 110, just north of the Khuraburi turn-off. A 15-metre boat that takes up to eight persons can be chartered for around 2000B for a round trip – it takes four to five hours each way. Ordinarily boat travel is only considered safe between December and early May, between the two monsoons.

You can also get boats to the Surin Islands from Hat Patong or Hat Rawai in Phuket. A regular charter boat from Phuket takes 10 hours or you can get a Songserm express boat during the diving season (December to April) that takes only three hours 15 minutes. However, the fare for the express boat is 1500B per person – if you have more than a couple of people it's cheaper to go from

Top: School children at Wat Kuhasawan, Phattalung (MH)
Bottom: Pattani market (JC)

Top: Palm trees, Ko Pha–Ngan (MH)
Bottom: Ko Phi Phi (Don Sai Beach) (JC)

Khuraburi. Group tours sometimes go from Khuraburi for 500B per person.

SIMILAN ISLANDS NATIONAL PARK
อุทยานแห่งชาติหมู่เกาะสิมิลัน

The Similan Islands are world-renowned among diving enthusiasts for incredible underwater sightseeing at depths ranging from two to 30 metres. As elsewhere in the Andaman Sea, the best diving months are December to May when the weather is good and the sea is at its clearest (and boat trips are much safer). The Similans are also sometimes called Ko Kao, or Nine Islands, because there are nine of them – each has a number as well as a name. The word 'Similan' in fact comes from the Malay word 'sembilan' for 'nine'. Counting in order from the north, they are Ko Bon, Ko Ba Ngu, Ko Similan, Ko Payu and Ko Miang (two islands close together), Ko Payan, Ko Payang and Ko Hu Yong. Sometimes you see these listed in the reverse order. They're relatively small islands and uninhabited except for park offi-

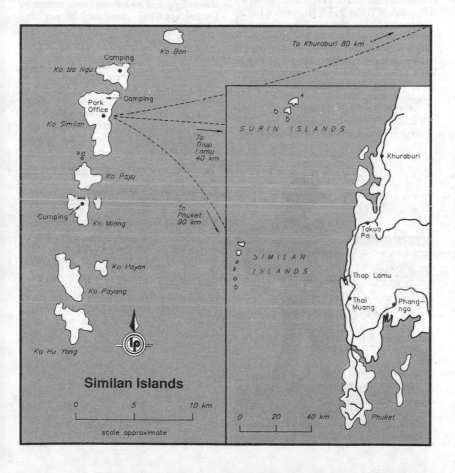

Similan Islands

cials and occasional tourist groups from Phuket. The park office is on the largest island, Ko Similan. Admission to the park is 5B.

Places to Stay
Bungalows and camping cost the same in the Similans as in the Surin Islands. There are camping areas on Ko Ba Ngu, Ko Similan and Ko Miang.

Getting There & Away
The Similans can be reached from either Khuraburi (same pier as for the Surin Islands) or the pier at Thap Lamu, about 40 km south of Takua Pa off Highway 4 (or 20 km north of Thai Muang). From Khuraburi the Similans are about 80 km away, about five hours by boat, and from Thap Lamu it's only 40 km, about three hours by boat. Figure on roughly 2500B to charter a boat for eight people from Khuraburi, less from Thap Lamu.

As with the Surin Islands, boats to the Similans leave most frequently from Hat Patong in Phuket, at least for the time being.

As demand for boats from Khuraburi and Takua Pa increases, a regularly scheduled boat service from these points is bound to start. Overnight diving excursions from Patong are fairly reasonable in cost – about 1500B a day including food, accommodation and underwater guides. Equipment is extra. Non-divers can join these trips for around half the cost – snorkellers are welcome. Songserm Travel does a deal where they pick you up at your Phuket hotel at 6.30 am and drive to Thap Lamu for the boat to the islands. The Songserm boat goes to two islands, Ko Similan and Ko Miang, for snorkelling and swimming, then returns to Phuket via Thap Lamu at 7.30 pm. The 1500B price includes a seafood lunch, light dinner, snacks, beverages and snorkelling equipment.

Seatran Travel, 65 Phuket Rd, Phuket Town, runs their excursion boat *Seatran Queen* between November and March. An overnight trip is 1370B – you sleep on board in a four-berth cabin. On Phuket's Hat Rawai you're supposed to be able to charter your own boat for about 5000B – one that will take up to 30 people.

Phuket Province

Exactly 885 km from Bangkok, the 'Pearl of the South', as the tourist industry has dubbed it, Phuket is Thailand's largest island (810 square km) and a province in itself. While tourism and tin are Phuket's major moneymakers the island is still big enough to accommodate escapists of nearly all budget levels. Formerly called Ko Thalang ('Phuket' and 'Thalang' are both Malay names), Phuket has a culture all of its own, combining Chinese and Portuguese influences, like Songkhla, with that of the indigenous ocean-going people. In the Andaman Sea off south Thailand's west coast, the island's terrain is incredibly varied, with rocky beaches, long, broad, sandy beaches, limestone cliffs, forested hills and tropical vegetation of all kinds. Great seafood is available all over the island and

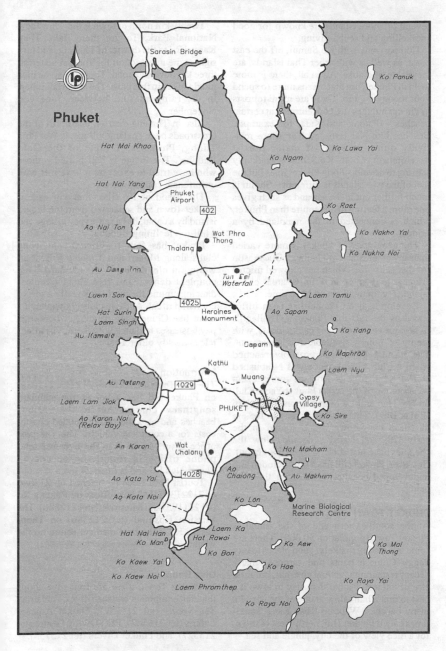

Phuket

Sarasin Bridge

Ko Panuk

Hat Mai Khao

Ko Lawa Yai

Ko Ngam

Hat Nai Yang

Phuket
Airport

402

Ko Raet

Ao Nai Ton

Wat Phra
Thong

Ko Nakha Yai

Thalang

Ko Nakha Noi

Ao Bang Tao

Ton Sai
Waterfall

Luem Son

Laem Yamu

4025

Hat Surin

Heroines
Monument

Laem Singh

Ao Sapam

Au Kamala

Ko Rang

Capam

Ko Maphrao

Kathu

Laem Ngu

Au Patong

Muang

4029

Gypsy
Village

Laem Lam Jiok

PHUKET

Ko Sire

Ao Karon Noi
(Relax Bay)

Wat
Chalong

An Karon

Hat Makham

4028

Ao
Chalong

Ao Makham

Ao Kata Yai

Ao Kata Noi

Ko Lon

Marine Biological
Research Centre

Laem Ka

Hat Nai Han

Hat Rawai

Ko Man

Ko Aew

Ko Mai
Thong

Ko Kaew Yai

Ko Bon

Ko Kaew Noi

Ko Hae

Laem Phromthep

Ko Raya Yai

Ko Raya Noi

several offshore islands are known for good snorkelling and scuba-diving.

Comparisons with Ko Samui, off the east coast, as well as with other Thai islands, are inevitable of course. All in all, there is more to do in Phuket, but that means more to spend your money on, too. There are more tourists in Phuket but they are concentrated at certain beaches – Patong and Kata, for example. Beaches like Nai Han and Karon are relatively quiet, in spite of major tourist development at both. Ko Samui is gradually starting to develop along Phuket lines but the feel of the two islands is different – Samui is much further out in the sea and as such gives one more a feeling of adventure than Phuket, which is connected to the mainland by a bridge.

The geography of Phuket is more varied than any other island in Thailand. One reason for this is its size, which has allowed microclimates to develop in different areas of the island. Try them all if you have time.

Development on Phuket has been influenced by the fact that Phuket is Thailand's richest province (on a per capita basis), with plenty of money available for investment. The turning point was probably reached when a Club Méditerranée was established at Hat Kata, followed by the more recent construction of the lavish Phuket Yacht Club on Nai Han and Le Meridien on Karon Noi (Relax Bay). This marked an end to the era of cheap bungalows which started in the early '70s and lasted a decade. Now the cheapies have just about all been bought out. However, Phuket still has a few secluded and undeveloped beaches, at least for the time being.

PHUKET TOWN เมืองภูเก็ต

At the south-eastern end of the island is Phuket Town (population 50,000). There are some interesting markets (good places to buy baggy Chinese pants and sarongs) many decent restaurants, several cinemas, but little else of interest. Rather than stay in town it's best to rent a bungalow at one of the island's many beaches. Walk up Khao Rang, sometimes called Phuket Hill, north-west of town, for a nice view of the city, jungle and sea.

Twenty km north of town is the Phra Taew National Park. To get there, take Thep Kasatri Rd to the district of Thalang, and turn right at the intersection for Ton Sai waterfall three km down the road. There are some nice jungle hikes in this park. The waterfall is best in the rainy season, between June and November.

Also in Thalang district, just north of the crossroads near Thalang village, is Wat Phra Thong, Phuket's 'Temple of the Gold Buddha'. The image is half buried – those who have tried to excavate it have met with unfortunate consequences.

The island of Ko Sire, four km east of Phuket Town and separated from the bigger island by a canal, has a sea-gypsy village and a hill-top reclining Buddha.

Phuket has four traditional *ram wong* clubs along Montri and Thalang Rds. Ram wong (circle dance) is a standard Thai couples' dance, and like most couples' dancing around the world, it's really a sort of courtship ritual. At these clubs, however, it's more like Chinese tea-dancing, where men pay hostesses to dance with them. The clientele is mostly older Thais.

Information
The TAT Tourist Office (tel 212213, 211036) on Phuket Rd has a list of the standard songthaew charges out to the various beaches and also the recommended charter costs for a complete vehicle. The The post office is on Montri Rd. The overseas telephone office is round the corner on Phang-Nga Rd and is open 24 hrs.

Tourist Police can be reached on 212046 or 212213. THAI has offices on Ranong Rd (tel 211195) and Montri Rd (tel 212880). The Mission Hospital (tel 212386) on Thepkasatri Rd is the best medical centre on the island.

Dive Shops
In Phuket Town, there are four dive shops that rent equipment and lead dives: Andaman Sea Sports (tel 211752); Phuket Aquatic Safaris (tel 216562); PFC Diving Centre (tel 215527); and Phuket Divers (tel 215738).

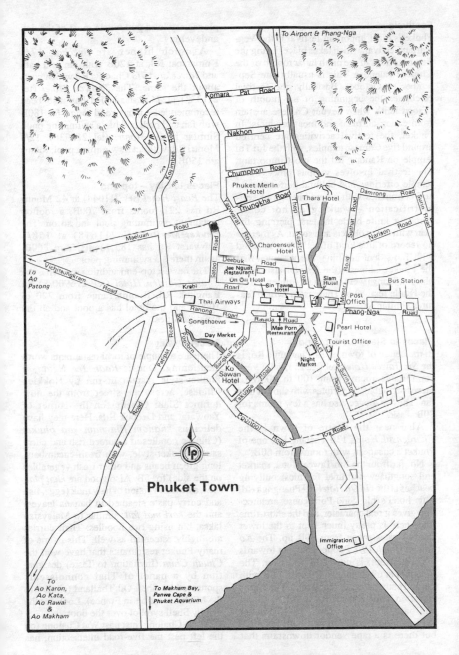

To Airport & Phang-Nga

Komara Pat Road

Nakhon Road

Chumphon Road

Phuket Merlin Hotel

Damrong Road

Thara Hotel

Thungkha Road

Maeluan Road

Charoensuk Hotel

Narison Road

Deebuk Road

Jee Nguat Restaurant

On On Hotel

Krabi Road

Sin Tawee Hotel

Siam Hotel

Bus Station

Post Office

Thai Airways

Ranong Road

Phang-Nga Road

Songthaews

Rasada Road

Pearl Hotel

Day Market

Mae Porn Restaurant

Tourist Office

Night Market

Ko Sawan Hotel

To Ao Patong

Vichitsongkram Road

Kosumbee Road

Yaowarat Road

Sattoi Road

Soi Rom Manee

Phuket Road

Phang-Nga Road

Montri Road

Suthat Road

Surin Road

Thep Kasatri Road

Satun Road

Takua Pa Road

Phoonphol Road

Tilok Uthit Road

Kra Road

Phuket Town

Chao Fa Road

Patpat Road

Soi Rom

Bangkok Road

To
Ao Karon,
Ao Kata,
Ao Rawai
&
Ao Makham

To Makham Bay,
Panwa Cape &
Phuket Aquarium

Immigration Office

Festivals

Phuket's most important festival is the Vegetarian Festival, which takes place during the first nine days of the ninth lunar month of the Chinese calendar. This is usually late September or October. Basically, the festival celebrates the beginning of the month of 'Taoist lent', when devout Chinese abstain from eating all meat and meat products. In Phuket, the festival activities are centred around five Chinese temples, with the Jui Tui temple on Ranong Rd the most important. The festival involves various processions, temple offerings and cultural performances and culminates with incredible acts of self-mortification – walking on hot coals, climbing knife-blade ladders, piercing the skin with sharp objects and so on. As there is no record of this kind of activity associated with Taoist lent in China, it is assumed that the Phuket Chinese (the festival also takes place in Trang) were somehow influenced by the Hindu festival of Thaipusam, which features similar acts.

Places to Stay – bottom end

In the centre of town, at 81 Phangnga Rd, is the *Sin Tawee Hotel* (tel 212153) with very comfortable rooms from 100 to 200B or more for doubles and triples with shower and fan. The Sin Tawee also has a few rooms for 80B – ask.

Also near the centre of town is the *Charoensuk Hotel*, 136 Thalang Rd, one of Phuket's cheapest, with rooms from 60B.

Not far from the Sin Tawee Hotel, market and songthaew terminal for most outlying beaches is the *On On Hotel*, 19 Phangnga Rd. This hotel's old Sino-Portuguese architecture gives it real character, and the short-time trade here is pretty much kept to the lower floors - rates range from 80B up. The *Ko Sawan Hotel*, 19/8 Poonpol Rd, out towards the waterfront, is now 80B and over. The *Pengmin* at 69 Phangnga Rd costs 60B with fan and bath, but is not too special. The *Thara Hotel* on Thep Kasatri Rd is 70B with fan and bath. The *Siam Hotel*, 13-15 Phuket Rd has rooms with fan and bath for 80B, but there is a tape vendor downstairs that

plays very loud pop music most of the day and evening.

A notch higher are *Sukchai*, 17/1 Komarapat Rd, at 120B with fan and bath and *Taweekit* at 7/3 Chao Fa Rd which costs about the same. The *Thawon Hotel* (tel 211333) at 74 Ratsada Rd has also been recommended – it has good rooms for 180B with fan and bath and has a swimming pool. Similar is the *Montri* (tel 212936), 12/6 Montri Rd, without a swimming pool; rooms are 150B.

Places to Stay – top end

The *Pearl Hotel* (tel 211044) at 42 Montri Rd has 221 rooms from 700B, a rooftop restaurant, swimming pool and so on. The *Phuket Merlin* (tel 211618) at 158/1 Yaowarat Rd has 185 rooms from 860B, again there's a swimming pool.

The newest top-end addition in town is the *Phuket Garden Hotel* (tel 216900/8) on Bangkok Rd. Rooms range from 720 to 1000B and the hotel has a pool and all the usual facilities.

Places to Eat

There are a couple of local restaurants worth mentioning. One is *Raan Jee Nguat*, a Phuket-style restaurant run by Hokkien Chinese, across the street from the now defunct Siam Cinema on the corner of Yaowarat and Deebuk Rds. Here they have delicious *khanom jiin nam yaa phuket* (Chinese noodles in a pureed fish and curry sauce, Phuket-style, with fresh cucumbers, long green beans and other fresh vegetables on the side) for 5B. Also good are *khai plaa mok*, a Phuket version of haw mok (eggs, fish and curry paste steamed in banana leaves) and the *kari mai fan*, similar to Malaysian laksa, but using rice noodles. Their curries are highly esteemed as well. This is one of many Phuket restaurants that have won the *Chuan Chim* (Invitation to Taste) designation by a panel of Thai connoisseurs sponsored by Shell Oil Thailand (similar to the Michelin rating in France). Look for the yellow Shell symbol over the doorway.

At Ao Chalong, just past Wat Chalong (on the left past the five-road intersection, haa yaek Wat Chalong) is *Kan Aeng*, a good fresh seafood place. You order by weight, choosing from squid, oysters, cockles, crab, mussels and several kinds of fish, and then specify the method of cooking, whether grilled (phao), steamed (neung), fried (thawt), parboiled (luak – for squid), or in soup (tom yam). Large grilled crabs are about 40 to 50B apiece. It used to be out on a pier over the bay itself, but is now housed in a new enclosed restaurant, not as cheap as the old location.

Thungka Kafae is an outdoor restaurant at the top of Khao Rang, which has a nice atmosphere and good food. Try *tom kha kai* (chicken coconut soup) or *khai jiaw hawy nang rom* (oyster omelette). They're open from 11 am to 11 pm daily. Very popular with Thais and farangs alike and deservedly so, is the *Mae Porn*, a restaurant with everything, at the corner of Phangnga and Soi Pradit Rds, close to the On On and Sin Tawee Hotels. There's an air-con room and an open-air room and they sell curries, seafood, fruit shakes, you name it and Mae Porn has it.

Another popular spot in town is *Kanda Bakery* on Ratsada Rd. They're open early in the morning with fresh-baked

whole wheat bread, baguettes, croissants and real brewed coffee.

Finally, there's the ever dependable and ever tasty night market on Phuket Rd near the Ratsada Rd intersection, which is fast and cheap. If there's one thing the town of Phuket has, it's good food.

Getting There & Away

Bus From Bangkok, one air-con bus leaves the Southern Bus Terminal at 8 am, and then nine buses leave at 15-minute intervals between 6.30 and 8.30 pm. The trip takes 13 to 14 hours and the one-way fare is 299B. Ordinary buses leave seven times a day from 7.30 am until 10.30 pm for 166B. Advance bookings are not possible.

Several private tour buses run to Phuket regularly with fares of 299B one way or 540B round trip. Most have one bus a day which leaves at 6 pm or 7 pm. Try *Thai Transport* on Ratchadamnoen Klang near the Benz showroom. The ride along the west coast between Ranong and Phuket can be hair-raising if you are awake, so it is fortunate that this part of the trip takes place during the wee hours of the morning.

From Phuket, most tour buses to Bangkok

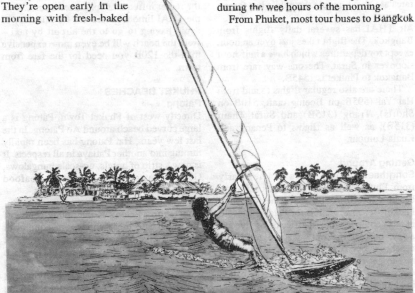

leave at 3 pm. Several agencies have their offices on Ratsada and Phangnga Rds downtown.

Fares and trip durations for local bus trips to and from Phuket include:

destination	fare	hours
Surat Thani	61B	6
Trang	62B	6
Hat Yai	91B	8
(air-con)	154B	8
Nakhon Si Thammarat	75B	8
Krabi	38B	3½
Phang-Nga	22B	1¾

Taxis & Minivans There are also share taxis between Phuket and other provincial capitals in the south; taxi fares are generally about double the fare of an ordinary bus. The taxi stand for Nakhorn Si Thammarat, Surat Thani, Krabi, Trang and Hat Yai is on Phangnga Rd, near the Pearl Cinema.

Some companies run minivans with through tickets to Ko Samui from Phuket – part of a minivan circuit that goes Phuket, Surat, Krabi and Ranong. As in share taxis, fares are about double the public bus fares.

Air THAI has several daily flights from Bangkok. The flight takes just over an hour, except for departures which have a half-hour stopover in Surat. The one-way fare from Bangkok to Phuket is 1545B.

There are also regular flights to and from Hat Yai (595B on Boeing craft, 510B on Shorts), Trang (315B) and Surat Thani (315B), as well as flights to Penang and Kuala Lumpur.

Getting Around
Songthaews Songthaews run regularly from Phuket Town to the various Phuket beaches for 10 to 20B – see the following Phuket Beaches section for details. Beware of tales about the tourist office being five km away, or that the only way to reach the beaches is by taxi, or even that you'll need a taxi to get from the bus station to the town centre. Bus station rip-offs are a way of life in Phuket!

Songthaews or tuk-tuks around town cost a standard 5B. Songthaews to the beaches depart from close to the town centre and the tourist office. Officially the songthaews all stop running at 5 pm so after that time the 'official' fares are likely to increase. You can charter your own songthaew for about 100B to most of the beaches.

Motorcycles You can hire motorcycles (usually 80 to 125cc Japanese bikes) from various places at the beaches or in Phuket Town. Costs are in the 150 to 250B per day range. Take care when riding a bike – if you have an accident you're unlikely to find that medical attention is as good as you get back home. People who ride around in shorts and T-shirt and a pair of thongs are asking for trouble. A minor spill whilst wearing reasonable clothes would leave you bruised and shaken, but, for somebody clad in shorts, it could result in enough skin loss to end their travels right there. It's also said that riding after dark in Phuket is not safe due to robberies.

Airport To get from the airport (11 km from town) to Phuket Town, you can take one of the rather infrequent songthaews for 15B or the THAI limousine service for 50B. Try to avoid having to go to the airport by taxi – from the beach will be even more expensive than the 120B you need for the fare from town.

PHUKET BEACHES
Patong ป่าตอง
Directly west of Phuket Town, Patong is a large curved beach around Ao Patong. In the last few years, Hat Patong has been rapidly turning into another Pattaya in all respects. It is now a strip of hotels, up-scale bungalows, German restaurants, expensive seafood places, night clubs and coffee houses.

Dive Shops Patong is the diving centre of the island and these shops rent equipment and lead dive tours: Andaman Divers (tel 321155); Diving Tours (tel 321141); Ocean Divers at the Patong Beach Hotel (tel 321166); Santana International Diving (tel 321360); and Phuket International Diving Centre, Coral Beach Hotel (tel 321166).

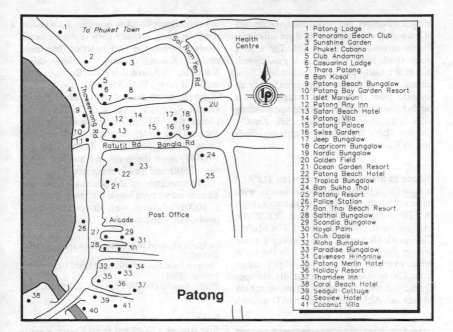

```
 1 Patong Lodge
 2 Panorama Beach Club
 3 Sunshine Garden
 4 Phuket Cabana
 5 Club Andaman
 6 Casuarina Lodge
 7 Thara Patong
 8 Ban Kosol
 9 Patong Beach Bungalow
10 Patong Bay Garden Resort
11 Islet Mansion
12 Patong Bay Inn
13 Safari Beach Hotel
14 Patong Villa
15 Patong Palace
16 Swiss Garden
17 Jeep Bungalow
18 Capricorn Bungalow
19 Nordic Bungalow
20 Golden Field
21 Ocean Garden Resort
22 Patong Beach Hotel
23 Tropica Bungalow
24 Ban Sukho Thai
25 Patong Resort
26 Police Station
27 Ban Thai Beach Resort
28 Salthai Bungalow
29 Scandia Bungalow
30 Royal Palm
31 Club Oasis
32 Aloha Bungalow
33 Paradise Bungalow
34 Cavaneea Bungalow
35 Patong Merlin Hotel
36 Holiday Resort
37 Thamdee Inn
38 Coral Beach Hotel
39 Seagull Cottage
40 Seaview Hotel
41 Coconut Villa
```

Boat Trips Several different companies on Patong do one-day cruises to nearby islands. For excursions to the Similan and Surin Islands off the Andaman coast of Phang-Nga Province, see the sections on these islands in the Ranong Province section.

Places to Stay Rates on Patong really vary according to season. In the high season (December to March, and August) you'll be doing very well to find something under 300B a night. During off-months some of the 300B places will drop as low as 150B or even 100B but that's about it. The cheapest bungalows are the *Bangla*, 100 to 200B and the *Seven Seas* at 150B. In the 200 to 300B range are *Happy Heart, Paradise, Royal Palm, Sunshine Garden* and *Sala Thai* bungalows. These five will discount their bungalows around 30% to 40% in the low season, from May to October.

At the other end of the price range the *Patong Beach Hotel* (tel 321301) has rooms

from 680B. *Patong Bay Garden Resort* (tel 321297/9) has rooms from 720B, *Club Andaman* (tel 211451) has bungalows from 580B and the *Phuket Cabana* (tel 321135) starts at 1200B and goes up to 2400B. At the very pinnacle of expense, perched on a cliff over Hat Patong, is the *Coral Beach Hotel* (tel 321106) with rooms from 1460 to 4040B.

Getting There & Away Songthaews to Patong leave from Ranong Rd, near the day market and Fountain Circle; the fare is 10B.

Karon กะรน
Karon is a long, gently curving beach with small sand dunes and a few evergreen trees. Some insist on calling this two beaches: Karon Yai and Karon Noi. Karon Noi, also known as Relax Bay, can only be reached from Hat Patong. It's completely monopolised by the relatively new Le Meridien Hotel. Karon used to be quite a spot for

budget travellers, but now there are nine sets of bungalows, of which only three offer any rooms or huts for under 150B. There isn't much shade here, so a suntan is guaranteed. It is still a fairly peaceful beach where fishermen cast nets, and where you can buy fresh seafood from their boats, though the rice fields between the beach and the surrounding hills have been abandoned. See Kata – Getting There & Away for details on transport to Karon.

Places to Stay *Marina Cottage* (tel 212901) is now the cheapest digs on the beach, with basic rooms starting at 40B and going as high as 1200B for a nice bungalow. It's at the extreme south end of the beach. The Marina Cottage also has a dive shop. Next up in price are the *Kata Villa* (tel 211014), in the same area, where rooms and bungalows range from 150 to 600B, and the slightly cheaper *Tropicana*, a bit to the north, on the other side of the road. Although the Kata and Tropicana

are sometimes listed as being on Kata beach, south of here, actually they're on the headlands between the two beaches (but more towards Karon), an area sometimes called Kata-Karon. Also at this end is the *Shangrila*, which is now 150 to 350B.

At the north end of the beach is *Phuket Ocean Resort*, a hotel with 26 fan-cooled rooms for 300/350B a single/double. The *Ruam Thep Hotel* is at the south end and costs around 500B. The *Karon Villa* (tel 216547) is on the north end and has rooms from 850B and a swimming pool.

The remainder of the places on Karon are all new resort-type hotels with rooms starting at 1000B or above, with air-con, swimming pools, etc. The top end is:

Le Meridien Hotel (tel 321480), 464 rooms, 1900 to 2300B
Thavorn Palm Beach Hotel (tel 215557), 250 rooms, 1600 to 2800B
Phuket Arcadia Hotel (tel 214841), 225 rooms, 1750 to 2500B

Kata กะตะ

Just around a headland from Karon, Kata is more interesting as a beach than Karon, and is divided into two – Ao Kata Yai (Big Kata Bay) and Ao Kata Noi (Little Kata Bay). The small island of Ko Pu is within swimming distance of the shore and on the way are some pretty nice coral reefs. The water here is very clear and snorkelling gear can be rented from

Kata & Karon

1	Karon on Sea
2	Kampong Karon
3	Phuket Golden Sand Inn
4	Phuket Ocean Resort
5	Karon Villa
6	Karon Sea View
7	Karon Inn
8	Kata Inn'85
9	Shangrila
10	Ruamthep Inn
11	Kata Villa
12	Marina Cottage
13	Kata Guest House
14	Club Med
15	Kakata Inn
16	Chao Kuan Bungalow
17	Kata Thani

several of the bungalow groups. With 11 sets of bungalows and a Club Med it can get a bit crowded, and the video bars are starting to take over. The centre for this kind of development seems to be the Kata-Karon area, the hills at the north end that lead to either Karon or Kata Yai.

There has been a bit of friction between Club Med and local residents, firstly because Club Med tried to make the beach area private, and, secondly, because they tried to bar people from using the road to that end of Kata. Club Med is now trying to win local approval by offering discount memberships to local residents and by building a computer lab at the local public school.

Places to Stay Bungalow rates have really gone up in Kata in recent years; 10 years ago there was only one bungalow village, with bungalows for 10B. Now the crowd ranges from 50B at the *Mabuhay* and *Western Inn* at Kata Noi (certain huts only, others with toilet and shower are more expensive) to 2900B at the *Club Méditerranée* on Kata Yai. The *Kata Guest House*, almost on Karon, is now 130B up.

The *Friendship* at the headland between Kata Yai and Kata Noi is 100B. A sprinkling of others in the 150 to 300B range include *Kata Noi Resort* at Kata Noi and *Chao Khuan* at Kata Yai. All of the bungalows except for Club Med will give discounts during the low season, from May to October.

The *Kata Thani* (tel 216632) on Kata Noi beach has upscale rooms and bungalows for 1200 to 1600B. The *Kakata Inn* (tel 214824/7) right on Hat Kata Yai has 95 large air-con bungalows for 1000 to 1400B.

Getting There & Away Songthaews to both Kata and Karon leave frequently from the Ranong Rd market in Phuket Town for 10B per person.

Nai Han ไนหาน

A few km south of Kata, in a small bay, this beach is similar to Kata and Karon. It used to be less frequented, as there was not much room for bungalow development until they started cutting away the forests on the hillsides overlooking the beach. Now every inch of space is developed and Nai Han bay somehow looks twice as big as it did a decade ago. The opening of the Phuket Yacht Club in early 1986 has changed the atmosphere of this beach considerably – this used to be the bottom-end place to hang out. The TAT says Nai Han beach is a dangerous place to swim during the monsoon season (May to October) but it really varies according to daily or weekly weather changes.

Growth at Nai Han is far from reaching its peak – I'd predict rapid changes here over the next two or three years, along the lines of Karon beach perhaps.

Places to Stay For the moment, there are still some budget-priced bungalow operations here for around 50B per night: *Ao Sane (Saen)* is off the beach, but has huts from 50 to 150B; *Coconut* is the lowest with some 50B huts; the *Sunset* and *Grandpa's* rent places for 40 to 150B. The Sunset is nicely situated on a hillside along the south end of the beach, opposite the Phuket Yacht Club, which occupies the north end.

The *Phuket Yacht Club* is in a class by itself, built at a cost of 145 million baht. It sits on the northern end of Nai Han, with 120 'state rooms' and suites catering to the world yachting community. There is a mobile pier that swings back and forth in front of the Club to transport yachties from boat to landing. Nightly rates start at 1950B for a double room and reach 7000B for the better suites.

At the end of the cape, to Nai Han's north is *Jungle Beach Resort* with rooms and bungalows from 400B.

Getting There & Away Nai Han is 18 km from town and a songthaew (leaving from the intersection of Bangkok Rd and Fountain Circle) costs 20B per person.

Rawai ราไวย์

Rawai was one of the first coastal areas on Phuket to be developed, simply because it was near Phuket Town and there was already a rather large fishing community there. Once other nicer beach areas like Patong and Karon were 'discovered', Rawai began to gradually lose popularity and today it is a rather spiritless place. The big 88-room Rawai Resort Hotel, as well as other Rawai hotel and bungalow operations, are in danger of going out of business. The beach is not so great, but there is a lot happening in or near Rawai – a local sea gypsy village: Hat Laem Ka (better than Rawai) to the north; boats to the nearby islands of Ko Lon, Ko Hae, Ko Hew, Ko Phi Phi and others; and good snorkelling off Laem Phromthep at the southern tip of the island, easy to approach from Rawai. In fact, most of the visitors who stay at Rawai these days are divers who want to be near Phromthep and/or boat facilities for off-island diving trips.

The diving around the offshore islands is not bad, especially at Kaew Yai/Kaew Noi, off Phromthep and at Ko Hae. Shop around for boat trips to these islands for the least expensive passage – the larger the group, the cheaper the cost per person.

Places to Stay *Pornmae Bungalows*, 58/1 Wiset Rd, has bungalows for 100 to 200B and at the *Salaloi Bungalows* rates range from 100 to 250B.

Moving upscale, the *Rawai Resort Hotel* (tel 212943) has rooms from 380 to 650B. The *Rawai Garden Resort* has eight rooms for 200 to 300B. Round at Laem Ka the big *Phuket Island Resort* (tel 212676, 212910) has rooms from 850B, all air-con, swimming pool and all mod-cons. The *Promthep Palace Bungalows* (tel 211599) at Laem Phromthep go for 300 to 450B.

Getting There & Away Rawai is about 16 km from town and getting there costs 10B by songthaew from the circle at Bangkok Rd.

Surin สุรินทร์
North of Ao Patong, 24 km from Phuket Town, Surin has a long beach and sometimes fairly heavy surf. Surin used to be a popular

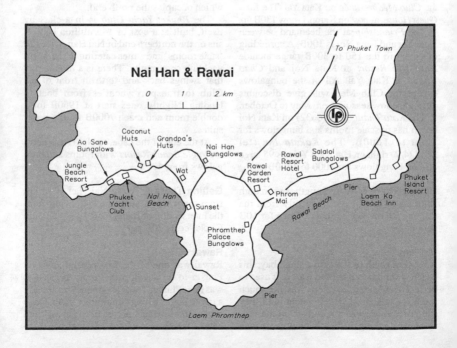

Nai Han & Rawai

place for local Thais to come and nibble at seafood snacks and *mieng kham* sold by vendors along the beach before *Amanpuri* built their ultra-exclusive resort here.

The Amanpuri plays host to Thailand's celebrity traffic, each of whom gets a 133-square-metre pavilion and a personal attendant; the staff to guest ratio is in fact 3.5 to one. It's owned by Indonesian Adrian Zecah and designed by the architect who designed the former Shah of Iran's winter palace. You can expect to pay US$250 to US$350 a day for a room here.

There is a golf course nearby and an older resort hotel on the north end, the *Pansea* (tel 212901), with rooms from 1410B including breakfast and dinner.

Laem Singh & Hat Kamala
แหลมสิงห์   กมลา

Just south of Surin is Laem Singh (Cape Singh), a beautiful little rock-dominated beach. You could camp here and eat on Surin beach or in Ban Kamala, a village further south.

Hat Kamala is a lovely stretch of sand and sea south of Surin and Laem Singh. Down a road, at the north end, there is *Kratomthip Cottages*, a set of very well-designed, screened bungalows that go for 200B, including maid service. There is also a restaurant/bar at the south end, next to Ban Kamala village. The Sheraton Hotel chain is constructing a large hotel here.

If you're renting a motorbike, this is a nice little trip down Route 402 and then over dirt roads from Surin to Kamala. Just before Surin, in Ban Thao village number two, is one of south Thailand's most beautiful mosques, a large whitewashed, immaculate structure with lacquered wooden doors.

Bang Tao บางเต่า

North of Surin around a cape is Ao Bang Tao, a long sandy beach with two up-market places to stay, *Bang Tao Huts* and the recently built *Dusit Laguna Resort*. Rooms at the well-managed Dusit are 2350 to 2600B and suites are 5450B, including tax. From 20 December to 20 February there is a 400B peak season surcharge.

Getting There & Away A songthaew from Ranong Rd to Surin or Bang Tao costs 10B, to Kamala 15B.

Nai Yang & Mai Khao
ในยาง   ไม้ขาว

Both of these beaches are near the Phuket airport, about 30 km from town. Nai Yang, a fairly secluded beach favoured by Thais, is actually a national park, with one set of government-run bungalows. It's about five km further north along Route 402 (Thep Kasatri Rd) to Phuket's longest beach, Hat Mai Khao, where sea turtles lay their eggs between November and February each year. About a km off Nai Yang is a decent reef at a depth of 10 to 20 metres.

Camping is allowed on both Nai Yang and Mai Khao beaches. The park bungalows on Nai Yang are 500B and sleep up to 12 people. Two-person tents can be rented for 60B a night.

Although this is a national park, somehow the fancy *Pearl Village Beach Hotel* (311338) managed to slip in on 20 acres of the south end of the beach. Air-con rooms and cottages start at 1500B.

Getting There & Away A songthaew to Nai Yang costs 15B.

Surat Thani Province

CHAIYA ไชยา

About 640 km from Bangkok, just north of Surat, Chaiya is best visited as a day trip from Surat Thani. Chaiya is one of the oldest cities in Thailand, dating back to the Srivijaya Empire. In fact, the name may be a contraction of Siwichaiya, the Thai pronunciation of the city that was a regional capital between the 8th and 10th centuries. Previous to this time the area was on the Indian trade route in South-East Asia. Many Srivijaya artefacts at the National Museum in Bangkok were found in Chaiya, including the Avalokitesvara Bodhisattva bronze, considered to be a masterpiece of Buddhist art.

The restored Borom That Chaiya stupa at

Wat Phra Mahathat, just outside of town, is a fine example of Srivijaya architecture and strongly resembles the *candis* of central Java. A ruined stupa at nearby Wat Kaew, also from the Srivijaya period, again shows central Javanese influence (or perhaps vice versa) as well as Cham (9th-century South Vietnam) characteristics.

Wat Suan Mokkaphalaram

Another attraction for visitors to Chaiya is Wat Suanmok, west of Wat Kaew, a modern forest wat founded by Buddhadasa Bhikkhu (Thai: *Phutthathat*), Thailand's most famous monk. Buddhadasa, a rotund octogenarian, ordained as a monk when he was 21 years old, spent many years studying the Pali scriptures and then retired to the forest for six years of solitary meditation. Returning to ecclesiastical society, he was made abbot of Wat Phra Mahathat, a high distinction, but conceived of Suanmok (short for Suan Mokkhaphalaram, 'garden of liberation') as an alternative to orthodox Thai temples.

The philosophy that has guided Buddhadasa is ecumenical in nature, comprising Zen, Taoist and Christian elements, as well as the traditional Theravada schemata. Today the hermitage is spread over 60 hectares of wooded hillside and features huts for 40 monks, a museum-library, and a 'spiritual theatre'. This latter building has bas-reliefs on the outer walls which are facsimiles of sculpture at Sanchi, Bharhut and Amaravati in India. The interior walls feature modern Buddhist painting, eclectic to say the least, executed by the resident monks. Resident farang monks here hold meditation retreats the first 10 days of every month. Anyone is welcome to participate; a 40B donation per day is requested to cover food costs. A book that contains the gist of Buddhadasa's perspective is *Emptiness & Nibbana* (Wayfarer Books, PO Box 5927, Concord, California 94524, USA), an English translation of two of his classic lectures.

Places to Stay

Stay in Surat for visits to Chaiya or request permission to stay in the guest quarters at Wat Suanmok. There is also a 'nice, old Chinese hotel' in Chaiya for 60B, reported one traveller, just ask the locals where it is.

Getting There & Away

If you're going to Surat by train, you can get off at the small Chaiya Railway Station, then later catch another train to Surat. From Surat you can either hire a taxi or get a train going north from Surat's railway station at Phun Phin. Taxis are best hired from Phun Phin, too. The trains between Surat and Chaiya may be full but you can always stand or squat in a 3rd-class car for the short trip.

The ordinary train costs 7B 3rd class from Phun Phin to Chaiya and takes about an hour to get there. Until late afternoon there are songthaews from the Chaiya Railway Station to Wat Suanmok for 5B per passenger. There are also buses (bound for Surat) from the front of the movie theatre on Chaiya's main street. Turn right on the road in front of the railway station. The fare to Wat Suanmok is 3B. Suanmok is about seven km outside of town on the highway to Surat and Chumphon. If buses aren't running you can hire a motorcycle (and driver) for 10 to 15B anywhere along Chaiya's main street.

Coming from Surat Thani it isn't necessary to go to Chaiya at all if you're heading for Wat Suanmok. Buses run there frequently and directly from Surat Thani Bus Station. The trip takes about 45 minutes and costs 10B.

SURAT THANI TOWN/BAN DON
เมืองสุราษฎร์ธานี บ้านดอน

There is little of particular historical interest at Surat (population 41,000), a busy commercial centre and port dealing in rubber and coconut, but the town has character nonetheless. It's 651 km from Bangkok and the first point in a southbound journey towards Malaysia that really feels and looks like south Thailand. For most people Surat is only a stop on the way to Ko Samui or Ko Pha-Ngan, luscious islands 32 km off the coast, so that the Ban Don Bus Station and the ferry piers to the east become the centre of attention.

Your boat to Ko Samui could leave from

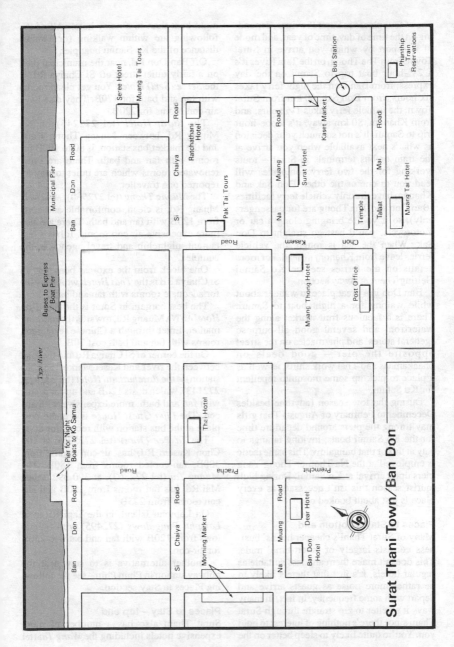

Surat Thani Town/Ban Don

one of four places in Surat Province, depending on the time of day, time of year, and mode of transport by which you arrive in Surat Town: from Tha Thong, on the Tapi River it's a 2½-hour boat trip to Samui on the day express; from Ban Don the night ferry takes six hours; from Don Sak, 60 km from Surat Town, the vehicle ferry takes 1½ hours; and from Khanom, 80 km away, it's a one-hour trip to Samui. It's not so much your decision as what's next available when you arrive at the train or bus terminals in Surat – touts working for the two ferry companies will lead you to one or the other. Don Sak and Khanom have the only vehicle ferry facilities (Ban Don and Tha Thong are for passengers only), so if you're bringing along a car or motorcycle, you'd best go straight to Don Sak. When the sea is rough, the vehicle ferries leave from Khanom instead. For more details on the ferries see the Ko Samui Getting There & Away section.

Ban Don is a great place to wander about while waiting for a night boat to Samui. There is a fabulous fruit market along the waterfront and several good all-purpose 'general stores' and pharmacies on the street opposite the pier – good deals on phaakamaas and Thai work shirts, as well as a place to pick up some mosquito repellent for Ko Samui.

During the low season (anytime besides December to February or August) Thai girls may throng the piers around departure time for the Ko Samui boats, inviting farangs to stay at this or that bungalow. This same tactic is employed at the Na Thon or Thong Yang piers upon arrival at Ko Samui. During high tourist season this isn't necessary as every place is just about booked out.

Places to Stay – bottom end
Many of Surat Thani's cheaper hotels' business consists largely of 'short-time' trade. This doesn't make them any less suitable as regular hotels, it's just that there's likely to be rather more noise as guests arrive and depart with some frequency. In fact, in many ways it's better to zip straight through Surat Thani since there's nothing of interest to hold you. You're quite likely to sleep better on the

night boat than in a noisy hotel. All of the following are within walking (or samlor) distance of the Ko Samui boat pier.

Off Ban Don Rd, near the municipal pier, on a fairly quiet street off Si Chaiya Rd, is the Seree (Seri) Hotel. You get clean rooms with fan and bath for 120B. They also have air-con rooms for 220B.

The Surat Hotel (tel 272243) on Na Muang Rd, between Muang Thong Hotel and the market/bus station, is 80 to 100B for rooms with fan and bath. There are some renovated rooms which are quiet to stay in, reported one traveller.

The Muang Thong (tel 272560), at 428 Na Muang Rd, is clean, comfortable and costs from 120B with fan and bath. There are also more expensive air-con rooms. It has a restaurant, nightclub and travel agency in the complex.

One block from the express boat pier on Si Chaiya Rd is the Thai Hotel, which is 80B for adequate rooms with fan and bath.

The best bargain in Surat is the Ban Don Hotel on Na Muang Rd, towards the morning market. Enter through a Chinese restaurant, rooms with fan and bath cost 70B.

On the corner of Si Chaiya Rd and the road between the river and Kaset Market (and bus station) is the Ratchathani Hotel (tel 272972, 272143), which costs 120B and up for rooms with fan and bath, more expensive with air-con. The Lipa Guest House is a brand new place at the bus station with rooms for 80B.

The Ta Pee (Tapi) (tel 272575), at 100 Chon Kasem Rd, has air-con rooms from 300B, fan-cooled rooms from 180B. The Muang Tai (tel 272367), at 390-392 Talaat Mai Rd, has fan rooms from 150B and air-con rooms from 225B.

On Lamphu Island, in the Tapi River, is Lamphu Bungalows (272495) with bungalows from 120B with fan and bath, to 250B for air-con.

Another alternative is to stay near the railway station in Phun Phin – see the following Places to Stay section.

Places to Stay – top end
Surat Thani also has a number of more expensive hotels including the Wang Tai (tel

273410/1) at 1 Talaat Mai Rd. It's a big hotel with nearly 300 rooms, a swimming pool and prices from 450B. The *Siam Thani* (tel 391-0280) at 180 Surat Thani-Phun Phin Rd costs 480B but during the low season they offer 50% discount. They have a good restaurant reported one traveller The *Siam Thara*, on Don Nok Rd near the Talaat Mai Rd intersection, has air-con rooms for 480 to 560B.

Places to Stay – Phun Phin

You may find yourself needing accommodation in Phun Phin, either because you've become stranded there due to booked-out trains or because you've come in from Samui in the evening and plan to get an early morning train out of Surat before the Surat to Phun Phin bus service starts. If so, there are several good places to stay. Right across from the railway station are several cheap but adequate hotels. The best is probably the *Tai Fah*. The family that runs it is very helpful to travellers and they allow people to sleep on the floor of the restaurant downstairs if they're full, no charge. Rooms are 70B without a bath. Another satisfactory place in the same location is the *Sri Thani*, with rooms for 60B.

Around the corner on the road to Surat, also quite close to the railway station, are the *Kaew Fah* for 70B and the nicer *Queen* for 100B.

Across from the Queen and Kaew Fah is a good night market with cheap eats. The Tai Fah does Thai, Chinese and farang food at reasonable prices.

Places to Eat

The Kaset Market area next to the bus terminal and the morning market between Na Muang and Si Chaiya are good food-hunting places. Many stalls near the bus station specialise in *khao kai op*, a marinated baked chicken on rice which is very tasty. During mango season, a lot of street vendors in Surat sell incredible khao niaw ma-muang, coconut-sweetened sticky rice with sliced ripe mango.

Getting There & Away

Bus Air-con buses leave the Southern AC Bus Terminal in Thonburi daily at 8 pm and 8.30 pm, arriving in Surat 11 hours later; the fare is 225B. Ordinary buses leave the ordinary Southern Bus Terminal at 8 am, 8 and 9.30 pm for 125B. Special 'VIP' buses for overnight trips to Ban Don from Bangkok with only 30 seats (more reclining room) cost 320B.

Several private tour companies run buses to Surat from Bangkok for 200 to 300B.

Buses to Surat from Phuket are 61B and the trip takes six to seven hours.

In Surat, a good place to get tour bus tickets to Bangkok, Phuket or Hat Yai is Muang Tai Tour, next door to the Seree Hotel. But there are several tour bus companies along Tallat Mai and Na Muang Rds.

From Nakhon Si Thammarat you can take an air-con bus to Surat for 60B which includes a substantial Thai meal – check Muang Tai Tours at 1487/9 Jamroenwithi Rd in Nakhon Si Thammarat. Ordinary buses from the Baw Kaw Saw Station are about half that fare.

Train Trains for Surat, which don't really stop in Surat Town but in Phun Phin, 14 km west of town, leave Bangkok's Hualamphong Terminal at 12.30 pm (Rapid), 2 pm (Special Express), 3.15 pm (Special Express), 4 pm (Rapid), 5.30 pm (Rapid), 6.30 pm (Rapid), and 7.20 pm (Express), arriving 10½ to 11 hours later. The 6.30 pm train (Rapid No 41) is the most convenient, arriving at 6.03 am, giving you plenty of time to catch a boat to Samui, if that's your destination. Fares are 470B in 1st class (available only on the 2 and 3.15 pm Special Express), 224B in 2nd class, 107B in 3rd class, not including Rapid/Express/Special Express surcharges or berths.

It can be difficult to book a train out of Surat (Phun Phin) – it's better to book a bus, especially if proceeding south. The trains are very often full and it's a drag to take the bus 14 km from town to the Phun Phin Railway Station and be turned away. Although the railway will sell you 'standing room only' 3rd-class tickets, this is a reasonable alternative if you can tolerate standing for an hour or two until someone vacates a seat down the line.

Advance train reservations can be made without going all the way out to Phun Phin station, at Phanthip travel agency on Talaat Mai Rd in Ban Don, near the market/bus station. You might try making a reservation *before* boarding a boat for Samui. The Songserm Travel Service on Samui also does reservations.

Train, Bus & Boat Combinations These days many travellers are buying tickets from the State Railway that go straight through to Ko Samui or Ko Pha-Ngan from Bangkok on a train, bus & boat combination. For example, a 2nd-class seat that includes bus to boat transfers through to Samui costs 284B. See the Getting There & Away sections under each island for details.

Getting Around
Phun Phin to Tha Thong Buses to Ban Don from Phun Phin Railway Station leave every 10 minutes or so from 6 am to 8 pm for 5B per person. Some buses drive straight to the pier (if they have enough tourists on the bus), while others will terminate at the Ban Don Bus Station, from where you must get another bus to Tha Thong (or to Ban Don if you're taking the night ferry). If you arrive in Phun Phin on one of the night trains, you can get a free bus from the railway station to the pier, courtesy of the boat service, for the morning boat departures. If your train arrives in Phun Phin when the buses aren't running (which includes all trains except No 41 trains), you're out of luck and will have to hire a taxi to Ban Don, for about 60 to 70B, or hang out in one of the Phun Phin street cafes until buses start running.

Buses from Ban Don Bus Station to Phun Phin Railway Station run every five minutes from 5 am to 7.30 pm. Empty buses also wait at the Tha Thong Pier for passengers arriving from Ko Samui on the express boat, ready to drive them directly to the railway station or destinations further afield.

KHAO SOK NATIONAL PARK
อุทยานแห่งชาติ เขาสก

This 646-square-km park is in the western part of Surat Thani Province, off Route 401 about a third of the way between Takua Pa and Surat Thani Town. The park features thick rainforest, waterfalls, limestone cliffs, numerous streams and a lake formed by the Chiaw Lan Dam.

Places to Stay
Khao Sok has a camping area and a few bungalows, rates negotiable. A small restaurant near the entrance serves inexpensive meals.

Accommodation is also available just outside the park at *Tree Tops Guest House* (Bangkok reservations 233-0196, 236-7919). A tree house costs 300B a day and a hut is 200B, both with attached bath. Tents can be rented for 50B per person. The staff also does jungle tours and/or rafting trips for 150B per day. Meals are available for 30 to 50B. The entrance to Tree Tops is at Km 108 – look for the signs.

KO SAMUI เกาะสมุย
Ko Samui (population 32,000) long ago attained a somewhat legendary status among Asian travellers, yet until recently it never really escalated to the touristic proportions of other similar getaways found between Goa and Bali. With the advent of the Don Sak auto/bus ferry a few years ago and the airport opening, things are now changing fast. During the high seasons, January to February and July to August, it can be difficult to find a place to stay, even though most beaches are crowded with bungalows. The port town teems with farangs getting on and off the ferry boats, booking tickets onward, collecting mail at the post office. Now that Bangkok Airways has daily flights to Samui, the island is rushing headlong into top-end development.

Airport or no airport, Samui is still an enjoyable place to spend some time. It still has some of the best accommodation values in Thailand and a laid-back atmosphere that makes it quite relaxing. If Samui survives its current identity crisis, it may yet escape the fate of Pattaya and Phuket. Even with an airport, it still has the advantage of being off the mainland and far away from Bangkok. Coconuts are still the mainstay of the local economy and in fact, two million are shipped to Bangkok each month. But there's no going back to 1971, when the first two tourists arrived on a coconut boat from Bangkok.

Samui is different from other islands in south Thailand and its inhabitants refer to themselves as *chao samui* – 'Samui folk' – rather than Thais. They are even friendlier than the average upcountry Thai, in my opinion, and have a great sense of humour, although those who are in constant contact with tourists may be a bit jaded. The island also has a distinctive cuisine, influenced by the omnipresent coconut, the main source of income for chao samui. Coconut palms blanket the island, from the hillocks right up

to the beaches. The durian, rambutan and langsat fruits are also cultivated on Samui.

Ko Samui is part of an island group that used to be called Mu Ko Samui, though you rarely hear that term these days. It's Thailand's third largest island, at 247 square km, and is surrounded by 80 smaller islands. Six of these, Pha-Ngan, Ta Loy, Tao, Taen, Ma Ko and Ta Pao, are inhabited as well.

The population of Ko Samui is for the most part concentrated in the port town of Na Thon, on the west side of the island facing the mainland and in 10 or 11 small villages scattered around the island. One road encircles the island with several side roads poking into the interior; this main road is now paved all the way around.

Information

The best time to visit the Samui group of

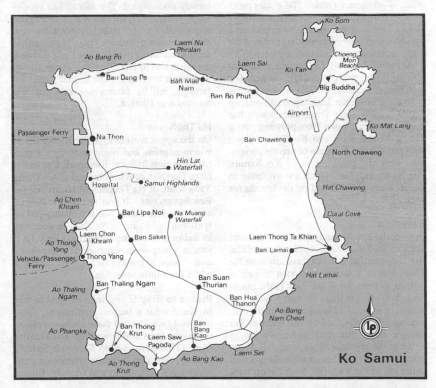

Ko Samui

islands is during the hot and dry season, February to late June. From July to October it can be raining on and off, and from October to January there are sometimes heavy winds. However, many travellers have reported fine weather (and fewer crowds) in September and October. November tends to get some of the rain which also affects the east coast of Malaysia at this time. Prices tend to soar from December to July, whatever the weather.

Travellers have been able to extend their tourist visas at the Ko Samui Immigration Office in Na Thon for 500B. Several travellers have written to say take care with local agents for train and bus bookings. Bookings sometimes don't get made at all, the bus turns out to be far inferior to what was expected or other hassles develop.

Great 45-minute massages for 40B are often available at the sala opposite the post office – masseurs (male). Take care with local boat trips to nearby islands reported one visitor. His boat was nearly swamped on a windy day and he eventually had to spend the night stranded on an uninhabited island.

At the north end of Na Thon there's a Thai boxing ring with regularly scheduled matches. Admission is 100B to most fights.

In Surat or on Ko Samui, you can pick up TAT's helpful Surat Thani map, which has maps of Surat Town, the province, Ang Thong Marine Park and Ko Samui, along with travel info. A couple of private companies now do good maps of Ko Samui, Pha-Ngan and Tao, which are available in tourist areas of Surat and on the islands for 35B.

Waterfalls

Besides the beaches and rustic, thatched roof bungalows, Samui has a couple of waterfalls. Hin Lat waterfall is about three km from Na Thon and is a worthwhile visit if you're waiting in town for a boat back to the mainland. You can get there on foot – walk 100 metres or so south of town on the main road, turning left at the road by the hospital. Go straight along this road about two km to arrive at the entrance to the waterfall. From here, it's about a half-hour walk along a trail to the top of the waterfall. Near the car park

at the entrance is another trail left to Suan Dharmapala, a meditation temple. Na Muang waterfall, in the centre of the island 10 km from Na Thon, is more scenic and less frequented. A songthaew from Na Thon to these latter waterfalls should be about 20B. Songthaews can also be hired at Chaweng and Lamai beaches.

Temples

For temple enthusiasts, at the southern end of the island, near the village of Bang Kao, there is Wat Laem Saw with an interesting old chedi. At the northern end, on a small rocky island joined to Samui by a causeway, is the so-called Temple of the Big Buddha. The modern image, about 12 metres in height, makes a nice silhouette against the tropical sky and sea behind it. The image is surrounded by kutis, or meditation huts, mostly unoccupied. The monks like receiving visitors there, though a sign in English requests that proper attire (no shorts) be worn on the temple premises. There is also an old semi-abandoned temple (Wat Pang Ba) near the north end of Hat Chaweng where 10-day vipassana courses are occasionally held for farangs, led by farang monks from Wat Suanmok in Chaiya.

Na Thon นาธร

On the upper west side of the island, this is where express and night passenger ferries from the piers in Surat disembark. Car ferries from Don Sak or Khanom land at Ao Thong Yang south of Na Thon about 10 km (see the Beaches section). If you're not travelling on a combination ticket you'll probably end up spending some time in Na Thon on your way in and/or out, waiting for the next ferry. Or if you're a long-term beachcomber, it makes a nice change to come into Na Thon once in a while for a little town life.

Places to Stay If you want or need to stay in Ko Samui's largest settlement, (pronounced Naa Thawn) there are seven places to choose from at this writing. The *Seaview Hotel* (Thai name is *Santi Kasem*) is Samui's oldest, a wooden building overlooking the water - it's safe, clean and friendly. Rooms

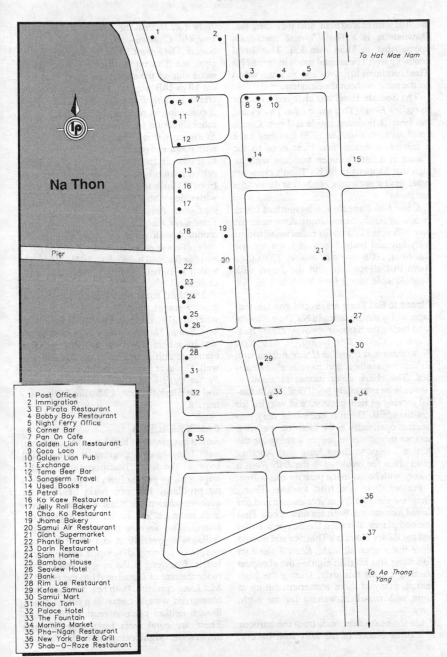

Na Thon

To Hat Mae Nam

Pier

To Ao Thong Yang

1 Post Office
2 Immigration
3 El Pirata Restaurant
4 Bobby Boy Restaurant
5 Night Ferry Office
6 Corner Bar
7 Pan On Cafe
8 Golden Lion Restaurant
9 Coco Loco
10 Golden Lion Pub
11 Exchange
12 Teme Beer Bar
13 Songserm Travel
14 Used Books
15 Petrol
16 Ko Kaew Restaurant
17 Jelly Roll Bakery
18 Chao Ko Restaurant
19 Jhome Bakery
20 Samui Air Restaurant
21 Giant Supermarket
22 Phantip Travel
23 Darin Restaurant
24 Siam Home
25 Bamboo House
26 Seaview Hotel
27 Bank
28 Rim Lae Restaurant
29 Kafae Samui
30 Samui Mart
31 Khao Tom
32 Palace Hotel
33 The Fountain
34 Morning Market
35 Pha-Ngan Restaurant
36 New York Bar & Grill
37 Shab-O-Roze Restaurant

are 70B with shared bath, 80B including fan. Downstairs is a Thai-Chinese restaurant specialising in khao man kai. This hotel probably won't be around much longer as Na Thon continues to grow – and Na Thon won't be the same without the Seaview.

The Seaside Hotel has changed its name to *Palace Hotel* (Thai name *Chai Thale*) and has been remodelled inside and out. Clean, spacious rooms start at 120B and they have a restaurant downstairs. Next door to the Palace is a dark wooden building with no sign that happens to be Na Thon's cheapest hotel (and a notorious brothel) at 40 to 45B per room.

Chao Koh Bungalow, a bit north of town, is 300 to 600B. *Samui Bungalow*, near the post office, is 120B up for rather small rooms with fan and bath. South of town are the *Chokana*, 200B single or double, 250B for a room that sleeps four and the *Jinta*, with single/double rooms for 100/150B.

Places to Eat There are several good restaurants and watering holes in Na Thon. On the road facing the harbour are *Siam Home Restaurant*, *Darin Restaurant*, *Chao Koh Restaurant* and *Bamboo House Restaurant*, all serving seafood and travellers' specialities. The shark steak dinner at Bamboo House is an especially good deal, a substantial serving of fish, potatoes and veggies for less than 50B. Darin is one of the only restaurants open early in the morning (before 8 am), so this is where people waiting for the 7.30 am ferry to Surat hang out. Another good place for breakfast is the *Jelly Roll*, a bakery with home-made pastries and coffee.

Further down the road towards Thong Yang are the *Pha-Ngan Restaurant* and *Sri Samui Restaurant*. Both are quite good Thai seafood places. Between the Seaview Hotel and the Palace Hotel is a Thai rice and noodle place that's open all night, *Raan Khao Tom Toh Rung* (no English sign) – the cheapest place to eat on this strip. During the high season, many of these restaurants fill up at night with travellers waiting for the night ferry.

On the next street back from the harbour is another branch of the Jelly Roll bakery,

Jelly Roll II, then the *J Home Bakery* and a few old Chinese coffee shops like *Kafae Samui*. The *Samui Air* restaurant (no English sign, but it's near the Jhome Bakery on the same side of the street) has good Thai food for 10 to 18B per dish. Further south on this street is *The Fountain*, an Italian place specialising in pasta and pizza. Back in the other direction (north) on an intersection is *El Pirata*, a small Spanish garden restaurant with pizza and paella. Across the street from El Pirata is the *Golden Lion*, a medium-priced seafood place. Down the street a bit from El Pirata is *Bobby Boy*, a restaurant-bar with video. Other bars in the vicinity include the *Corner Bar*, the *Golden Lion Pub* and the *Teme Beer Bar*, all open only at night from around 6 pm to midnight. After midnight the only places open are the *Khao Tom Toh Rung* and the flashy Thai nightclub *Pan On Cafe*, which is rather expensive, dark and well-chilled.

The third street back from the harbour is mostly travel agencies, photo shops and other small businesses. Two small supermarkets, *Samui Mart* and *Giant Supermarket* are also back here. The Charoen Laap morning market is still in operation on this street as well. Down at the south end is the *New York Bar & Grill* with American-style deli food and the *Shab-O-Roze*, a Muslim Indian restaurant.

SAMUI BEACHES

Samui has plenty of beaches to choose from, with bungalows appearing at more small bays all the time. Transportation has also improved, so getting from beach to beach is no problem. The two main beaches for accommodation are Chaweng and Lamai, both more or less on the east side of the island. The former has more bungalow 'villages' – over 40 at last count – plus a couple of recently developed flashy tourist hotels. Chaweng is the longest beach, over twice the size of Lamai, and has the island of Mat Lang opposite. Both beaches have clear blue-green waters. Lamai is a little quieter, though neither place is particularly lively. There are coral reefs for snorkelling and underwater sightseeing at both. Perhaps there's a bit more to do in Hat Lamai because of its proximity to two villages – Ban Lamai and Ban Hua Thanon. At the wat in Ban Lamai is the Ban Lamai Cultural Hall, a sort of folk museum displaying local ceramics, household utensils, hunting weapons and musical instruments. Chaweng is definitely the target of current upscale development because of its long beach.

For more peace and quiet, try the beaches along the north, south and west coasts. Mae Nam, Bo Phut and Big Buddha along the north end; Bo Phut and Big Buddha are part of a bay that holds Ko Fan (the island with the 'big Buddha'), separated by a small headland. The water here is not quite as clear as at Chaweng or Lamai, but the feeling of seclusion is greater, although it is becoming a little more touristed these days. Hat Thong Yang is on the west side of the island and is even more secluded (only a few sets of bun-

Typical bungalow, Ko Samui

galows there), but the beach isn't that great by Samui standards. There is also Hat Ang Thong, just north of Na Thon, very rocky but with more local colour (eg fishing boats) than the others. The south end of the island now has many bungalows as well, set in little out-of-the-way coves – worth seeking out. And then there's everywhere in between – every bay, cove or cape with a strip of sand gets a bungalow nowadays, right around the island.

Prices vary considerably according to the time of year and occupancy rates. Some of the bungalow operators on Samui have a nasty habit of tripling room rates when rooms are scarce, so that a hut that's 30B in June could be 100B in August. Rates given in this section can only serve as a guideline – they could go lower if you bargain or higher if space is tight.

Places to Stay & Eat

Everyone has his or her own idea of what the perfect beach bungalow is. At Ko Samui, the search could take a month or two, with over 130 operations to choose from. Most offer roughly the same services and accommodation for 50 to 150B, though some are quite a bit more. The best thing to do is to go to the beach you think you want to stay at and pick one you like – look inside the huts, check out the restaurant, the menu, the guests. You can always move if you're not satisfied. I prefer the smaller, four to eight-bungalow sites, some of which are only 40 to 50B per night. They don't have the Singha-bottle porch banisters and stained wooden frames of the larger sites, but can be just as comfortable. Generally anything that costs less than 100B a night will mean a shared bath, which may be preferable when you remember that mosquitoes breed in standing water. For a pretty basic bungalow with private bath, 100B is the minimum on Ko Samui.

Food is touch and go at all the beaches – one meal can be great, the next at the very same place not so great. Fresh seafood is usually what they do best and the cheapest way to eat it is to catch it yourself and have the bungalow cooks prepare it for you, or buy it in one of the many fishing villages around the island, direct from the fishermen themselves, or in the village markets. Good places to buy are in the relatively large Muslim fishing villages of Mae Nam, Bo Phut and Hua Thanon.

The island has changed so much in the years between editions of this book (not to mention the way it has changed since 1971, when the first tourists arrived), that I hesitate to name favourites. Cooks come and go, bungalows flourish and go bankrupt, owners die (my favourite, Niyom, in 1981) – you never can tell from season to season. Prices have remained fairly stable in recent years, unlike at Phuket, but they are creeping up. It's easy to get from one beach to another, so you can always change bungalows. The jet set seem to be discovering Samui but, thank goodness, Club Med and Amanpuri decided to build on Phuket rather than here. Finally, if Samui isn't to your liking, move islands! Think about Ko Pha-Ngan or Ko Tao.

What follows are some general comments on staying at Samui's various beaches, moving clockwise around the island from Na Thon.

Ao Bang Po & Hat Mae Nam
อ่าวบางโพธิ์   หาดแม่น้ำ

Ao Bang Po and Hat Mae Nam are 14 km from Na Thon and expanding rapidly in terms of bungalow development. At the headland (Laem Na Phra Laan) where Ao Bang Po ends and Mae Nam begins is the *Plant Inn*, also spelled *Phalarn*, with bungalows from 70 to 200B. A second branch, the *Phalarn Inn II*, has recently opened with the same rates. In Ao Bang Po itself is *Sunbeam*, a set of bungalows in a very nice setting. Huts are 250 to 300B, all with private bath. It has a good setting with fair snorkelling and swimming. *Thong Thip Villa* is also building some middle-range bungalows at Ao Bang Po.

Down on Hat Mae Nam proper is *Friendly*, which has clean, well-kept huts for 40B per person, and good food too. Also good are *LaPaz Villa* (50 to 80B), *Silent* (70 to 150B) and, in Mae Nam, the *Holiday*, *Golden Hut* and *Shangri-La*, the last three being still new enough for the staff to try hard to please, yet experienced enough to know what they're doing.

There are at least 10 or 15 other bungalow operations between Laem Na Phra Laan and Laem Sai, where Ao Mae Nam ends. The *Ubon Villa* (30 to 40B) has been recommended by a few readers.

Hat Bo Phut   หาดบ่อผุด
This beach has a reputation for peace and quiet; there are about 15 places to stay here in total. Before you arrive at Bo Phut village is a string of 30 to 100B places, including *Sunny*, *Bophut Guest House* and *Sala Thai*. Also here is the long-running *Peace*, with huts ranging from 40 to 200B. Food at the Peace is good but also expensive. *Calm* bungalows are nice and go for 50 to 60B. *World* has moved up-market with new bungalows from 60 to 400B.

Proceeding east, a road off the main round-island road runs to the left and along the bay towards the village. Here you'll find the original *Boon Bungalows*, a small operation with 30 to 50B huts, as well as the *New Boon Privacy*, owned by the same family. At New Boon large, comfortable bungalows with two beds, fan and fridge go for 400 to 500B. The restaurants at both Boons are good. West of Boon's is *Ziggy Stardust*, a clean place with huts for 150 to 250B. Next to Ziggy's is the new *Siam Sea Lodge*, a small hotel with rooms for 300B with fan, hot water and fridge, or 400B with ocean view. You'll find several more cheapies along this strip, including *Smile House*, *Miami* and *Oasis*, all with huts in the 30 to 100B range.

If you continue through the village along the water, you'll find *Blue Sky*, a place off by itself with huts for 40B. This area is sometimes called Hat Bang Rak.

The village has a couple of cheap local-style restaurants as well as a couple of farang places with French names.

Big Buddha Beach (Hat Phra Yai)
หาดพระใหญ่

This now has nearly a dozen bungalow operations, including the moderately expensive air-con *Nara Bungalows* (tel 421364) with rooms for 380 to 600B and a swimming pool. *Family Village* gets good reviews and costs 50 to 150B. *Big Buddha Bungalows* (50 to

150B) is still OK. *Ocean View* is about the cheapest place here now, 50 to 80B for simple huts. The rest are in the 100 to 200B range.

Hat Choeng Mon หาดช่องมน

The big headland between Big Buddha and Chaweng is actually a series of four capes and coves, but the largest is Choeng Mon. Between Laem Thongson and Laem Thong Po, on the northern end, are three places; *Golden Pine* and *Ban Thongson* in the 200B range, as well as the cheaper *Thongson Bay* at 80 to 100B.

The next cove over is where beautiful Hat Choeng Mon starts, but just before that is a smaller cove with only one development, *Tongsai Bay Hotel and Cottages*, a resort with a private beach, swimming pool and tennis courts. Rates are 1800B up. Another km on is Choeng Mon with *PS Villa* (40 to 150B), *Su's Place* (300B), *Choeng Mon* (50 to 200B), *Chat Kaew* (100 to 200B), and *Island View* (40 to 60B). Across from the beach is Ko Fan Yai, an island that can be reached on foot in low tide.

Next is the smaller bay called Ao Yai Noi, just before north Chaweng. This little bay is quite picturesque, with large boulders framing the beach. The *IKK* bungalows are 200B and the *Coral Bay Resort* has larger bungalows that range from 450B with fan to 800B with air-con.

Hat Chaweng หาดเฉวง

Hat Chaweng, Samui's longest beach, also has the island's highest concentration of bungalows and is even getting a few tourist hotels. Prices are moving up-market fast; accommodation is now maybe 50B at the lowest in the off months, and up to 2600B at the *The Imperial Samui*. There is now a little commercial 'strip' behind the central beach with restaurants, souvenir shops and discos. If there are a lot of vacant huts (there usually are during the low season) you can sometimes talk prices down to 40B for a basic hut. The beach is beautiful here, and local developers are finally cleaning up some of the trashy areas behind the bungalows that were becoming a problem in the early '80s.

Chaweng has km after km of beach and bungalows – perhaps 50 or more in all – so have a look around before deciding on a place. There are basically three sections: North Chaweng, Hat Chaweng proper and Chaweng Noi.

North Chaweng places are mostly in the 80 to 200B range, with simple bungalows with private bath at the northernmost end. These include the *Matlang Resort, Blue Lagoon, Samui Island Resort, Marine, Moon, Family, Poppy Inn* and *K John Resort*. Poppy Inn has the best lay-out of this group. Then at the end nearest to central Chaweng are a group of 300 to 500B places: *Chaweng Palace Resort, Samui Cabana, Samui Country Resort* and *Samui Palace*. These places are all nice enough, if somewhat lacking in character.

The central area, Hat Chaweng proper, is the longest and has the most bungalows and hotels. This is also where the strip behind the hotels and huts is centred, with restaurants, bars, discos, video parlours, tourist police and even a mobile currency exchange. The *Manohra* restaurant here features classical southern Thai dancing performances with dinner. Water sports are big here, too, so you can rent wind-surfing equipment, go scuba diving, sail a catamaran, charter a junk and so on. This area also has the highest average prices on the island, not only because accommodation is more up-market but simply because this is/was the prettiest beach on the island. In general, the places get more expensive as you move from north to south. Rather than list all the places on Chaweng Central, I'll just give examples across the spectrum, starting at the north:

Chaweng Villa, 80 to 200B
Lucky Mother, 50 to 120B
Coconut Grove, 60 to 200B
Chaweng Garden, 150 to 200B
Malibu Resort, 150 to 350B
Long Beach, 50 to 200B
Thai House, 80 to 200B
The Village, 450 to 800B
Samui Pansea, 950 to 2000B
Joy Resort, 350 to 800B
Munchies, 400 to 700B

If you're getting the idea that this isn't the beach for backpackers, you're right. To save money, it's better to stay at the cheaper places at North Chaweng or Chaweng Noi and make use of all three beach areas, or go to another beach entirely.

Chaweng Noi is off by itself around a headland· at the south end of central Hat Chaweng. Samui's top property at the moment, the *Imperial Samui*, is built on a slope here and costs 1600 to 2600B for air-con accommodation with telephone and colour TV. The Imperial's 56 cottages and 24-room hotel are built in a pseudo-Mediterranean style with a 700-square-metre swimming pool (saltwater) and a terrace restaurant with a view. Not very far from the Imperial is one of Chaweng's less expensive digs, the *Sunshine*, where huts are 50 to 150B. The *Maew* is a pre-Imperial hold-out where huts are still 40 to 80B – if it hasn't disappeared yet. The *Thawee* is another oldie for 50 to 100B and the *Sak* is similarly priced. Finally there's the *Tropicana Beach Resort* with all air-con rooms at 1200 to 1500B.

Coral Cove

Another series of capes and coves starts at the end of Chaweng Noi, beginning with scenic Coral Cove. Somehow the Thais have managed to squeeze three places around the cove, plus one across the road. The only one with immediate beach access is *Coral Cove*, where basic huts are 70 to 200B. The *Hi Coral Cove* above is 100 to 200B. The *Hillside Hut* on the hill opposite the road and the *Coral Cove Resort* are in the same price range.

Ao Thong Ta Khian   อ่าวท้องตาเคียน

This is another small, steep-sided cove, similar to Coral Cove and banked by huge boulders. At this writing there is one small set of bungalows here, *Thong Ta Khian Kata Garden*. The huts overlook the bay and cost 50B. There are a couple of good seafood restaurants down on the bay, and this is a good place for fishing.

Hat Lamai   หาดละไม

After Chaweng, this is Samui's most popular

beach for farangs. Hat Lamai rates are just a bit lower than at Chaweng overall, without the larger places like the Pansea or Imperial (yet) and fewer of the 500B-plus places. It also has more of a relaxed, village feel to it. As at Chaweng, the bay has developed in sections, with a long central beach flanked by hilly areas.

Cheaper huts at the north-east end are at *Comfort* (50 to 150B), *No Name* (40B), *Suan Thong Kaid* (50 to 80B), *Blue Lagoon* (40 to 150B), *Silver Cliff* (60 to 80B) and, back from the beach, *My Friend* (50B). More expensive are the newer places, including *Island Resort* (200 to 500B), *Rose Garden* (50 to 200B) and *Spanish Eyes* (100 to 150B). There are a sprinkling of others here that seem to come and go with the seasons.

Down into the main section of Lamai begins a string of places for 100 to 400B including *Mui*, *Fantasy Villa*, *Magic*, *Coconut Villa* and the *Weekender*. The Weekender has a wide variety of bungalows and activities to choose from, including a bit of a nightlife. Moving into the centre of Ao Lamai, you'll come across *Coconut Beach* (40 to 80B), *Animal House* (skip this one, it's received several complaints), *Lamai Inn* (80 to 150B) and the *Best Resort* (250 to 500B). This is the part of the bay closest to Ban Lamai village and the beginning of the Lamai 'scene'. The *Flamingo Party House* is a big market/restaurant/bar/disco on the road to Na Thon.

Next comes a string of slightly up-market 100 to 350B places: *Marina Villa*, *Sawatdi*, *Mira Mare*, *Sea Breeze*, *Aloha* and *Vineyard Haven*. All of these have fairly elaborate dining areas; the *Aloha* (tel 421418) is said to have a good Italian restaurant and the Vineyard Haven is known for its happy hours.

Finishing up central Hat Lamai is a mixture of 50 to 80B and 100 to 200B places. The *White Sand* is one of the Lamai originals and huts are still 40B. A farang flea market is held here on Sundays – many travellers sell hand-made jewellery. The long-standing *Palm* is still here as well, but they've upgraded the bungalows to the 100 to 200B price-range. The *Nice Resort* has huts for

80B up but they're really too close together. Finally, there's the *Sun Rise* with acceptable 40 to 80B huts.

At this point a headland interrupts Ao Lamai and the bay beyond is known as Ao Bang Nam Cheut, named for the freshwater stream that runs into the bay here. During the dry months the sea is too shallow for swimming here, but in the late rainy season when the surf is too high elsewhere on the island's beaches, south Lamai is one of the best for swimming. Way out on the rocky point is *Rock* with simple huts interspersed between boulders for 30 to 60B. Down farther is *Anika, Noi* and *Best Wishes*, all with huts for 30 to 50B. The *Swiss Chalet* has large bungalows overlooking the sea for 150 to 200B and the restaurant does Swiss as well as Thai food. Then comes the old-timer *Rocky* with the same rates.

South End

Bungalow development is under way in some of the smaller bays and coves on Samui's south end. If the development along Chaweng and Lamai is too much for you, this area might be just the ticket.

Ao Na Khai & Laem Set Just beyond the village of Ban Hua Thanon at the south end of Ao Na Khai is an area sometimes called Hat Na Thian. As at Lamai, the places along the south end of the island are pretty rocky, which means good snorkelling (there's a long reef here), but perhaps not such good swimming. Prices in this area seem fairly reasonable – 100B here gets you what 200B might in Chaweng. The hard part is finding these places, since they're off the round-island road, down dirt tracks, and most don't have phones. You might try exploring this area on a motorcycle first. The *Cozy Resort* has huts for 80 to 200B and at the end of the same road is the slightly less expensive *Honey*. Down a different road in the same area is the *Samui Orchid Resort* (tel 421079), which, with huts and a swimming pool for 450 to 750B, is slightly up-market. Turn right here, follow the coast and you'll come to the basic *Sonny View* (50B) and the nicely designed *Na Thian* (70 to 100B). At the end

of the road is the well-run and secluded *Laem Set Inn* (tel 077 273130). It's supposedly a members-only place, but the proprietor, an Englishman, will occasionally take on new guests if there is room. Rates vary from 100 to 350B.

Ao Bang Kao This bay is at the very south end of the island between Laem Set and Laem So (Saw). Again, you have to go off the round-island road a couple of km to find these places: *Diamond Villa* (50 to 80B), *Samui Coral Beach* (100 to 300B), *Sea Hill* (50 to 150B) and *Laem So Beach* (50 to 250B).

Ao Thong Krut Next to the village of Ban Thong Krut on Ao Thong Krut is, what else, *Thong Krut*, where huts with private bath are only 80B.

West Coast

Several bays along Samui's west side have places to stay, including Thong Yang, where the Don Sak ferry docks. The beaches here turn to mud flats during low tide, however, so they're more or less for people seeking to get away from the east coast scene, not for beach fanatics.

Ao Phangka Around Laem Hin Khom on the bottom of Samui's west side is this little bay, sometimes called Emerald Cove. The secluded *Emerald Cove* and *Sea Gull* have huts with rates from 40 to 80B – it's a nice setting and perfectly quiet.

Ao Thong Yang The car ferry jetty is here in Ao Thong Yang. Near the pier are *Sunflower* (30 to 150B), *Coco Cabana Beach Club* (150 to 300B) and the motel-like *Samui Ferry Inn* (400 to 600B). The Coco Cabana is the best of the lot.

Ao Chon Khram On the way to Na Thon is sweeping Ao Chon Khram with the *Lipa Lodge* and *International*. The Lipa Lodge is especially nice, with a good site on the bay. Rates start at 40B, most huts are about 80B, with a few as high as 350B. There is a good restaurant and bar here, not bad for the money. On the other hand, the International is nothing special at 150 to 400B.

Getting There & Away

Air Bangkok Airways (tel 253-4014), 144 Sukhumvit Rd, Bangkok, now flies daily to Ko Samui. The fare is 1650B one way – no discount for a return ticket. The flight duration is one hour and 10 minutes, with flights departing Bangkok at 7.30 and 10.40 am, 1.50 and 5 pm. Return flights from Samui to Bangkok depart at 9 am, 12.10, 3.20 and 6.30 pm.

Ferry To sort out the ferry situation you have to first understand that there are two ferry companies and three ferry piers (actually four but only three are in use at one time) on the Surat Thani coast and two on Ko Samui. Neither ferry company is going to tell you about the other. Songserm Travel runs the express ferry boats from the Tha Thong Pier, six km from downtown Surat, and the slow night boats from the Ban Don Pier in town. These take passengers only. The express boats used to leave from the same pier in Ban Don as the night ferry – when the river is unusually high they may use this pier again.

Samui Ferry Co runs the vehicle ferries from Don Sak (or Khanom when the sea is high). This is the company that gets most of the bus/boat and some of the train, bus & boat combination business.

Express Boats from Tha Thong

From November to May three express boats go to Samui (Na Thon) daily from Tha Thong and each takes two to 2½ hours to reach the island. From November to May the departure times are usually 7.30 am, 12 noon and 2.30 pm, though these change from time to time. From June to October there are only two express boats a day at 7.30 am and 12.30 pm – the seas usually are too high in the late afternoon for a third sailing in this direction during the rainy season. Passage is 80B one way, 150B round trip. The express ferry boats have two decks, one with seats below and an upper deck that is really just a big luggage rack – good for sunbathing.

From Na Thon back to Surat, there are departures at 7.15 am, noon and 3 pm from November to May, or 7.30 am and 3 pm June to October. The 7.15 or 7.30 am boat includes a bus ride to the train station in Phun Phin; the afternoon boats include a bus to the railway station and to the bus station.

Night Ferry There is also a slow boat for Samui that leaves the Ban Don Pier each night at 11 pm, reaching Na Thon around 5 am. This one costs 60B for the upper deck (includes pillows and mattresses), or 30B down below (straw mats only). This trip is not particularly recommended unless you arrive in Surat Thani too late for the fast boat and don't want to stay in Ban Don. Some travellers have reported, however, that a night on the boat is preferable to a night in a noisy Surat Thani short-time hotel. And it does give you more sun time on Samui, after all. The night ferry back to Samui leaves Na Thon at 9 pm, arriving at 3 am.

Vehicle Ferry Tour buses run directly from Bangkok to Ko Samui, via the car ferry from Don Sak in Surat Thani Province, for around 230B. Check with the big tour bus companies or any travel agency. From Talaat Mai Rd in Surat Thani you can also get bus/ferry combination tickets straight through to Na Thon, Samui. These cost 50B on an ordinary bus, 80B for an air-con bus. Pedestrians or people in private vehicles can also take the ferry directly from Don Sak, which leaves at 9 am, 2 and 5.30 pm, and takes one hour to reach the Thong Yang pier on Samui. The fare for pedestrians is 40B, for a motorcycle and driver 70B, and for a car and driver 180B. Passengers on private vehicles pay the pedestrian fare. Don Sak is about 60 km from Surat Thani. A bus from the Surat Thani Bus Station is 10B and takes 45 minutes to an hour to arrive at the Don Sak Ferry. If you're coming north from Nakhon Si Thammarat, this might be the ferry to take, though from Surat Thani the Tha Thong ferry is definitely more convenient.

From Ko Samui, air-con buses to Bangkok leave from near the pier in Na Thon at 1.30 and 3.30 pm daily, both arriving at 5 am due to the stopover in Surat. Through buses to

Hat Yai from Samui cost 230B and leave Na Thon at 7.30 am, 3 and 9 pm, arriving six hours later. Check with the several travel agencies in Na Thon for the latest routes.

Train The State Railway also does rail/bus/ferry tickets straight through to Samui from Bangkok. The fares are 399B for a 2nd-class upper berth, 429B for a 2nd-class lower berth, 284B for a 2nd-class seat and 210B for a 3rd-class seat. This includes Rapid service and berth charges; add 100B for air-con. This only comes out cheaper (less 10B) than doing the connections yourself if you buy the 2nd-class seat. For all other tickets it's 30 to 50B more expensive.

Getting Around

It's quite possible to hitch around the island, despite the fact that anyone on the island with a car is likely to want to boost their income by charging for rides. The official songthaew fares are 10B from Na Thon to Lamai, Mae Nam or Bo Phut, 15B to Big Buddha or Chaweng, 20B to Choeng Mon. From the car ferry landing in Thong Yang, rates are 15B for Lamai, Mae Nam and Bo Phut/Big Buddha, 20B for Chaweng, 25B for Choeng Mon. These minibuses run regularly during daylight hours only. A bus between Thong Yang and Na Thon is 5B. Note that if you're arriving in Thong Yang on a bus (via the vehicle ferry), your bus/boat fare includes a ride into Na Thon.

Several places rent motorcycles in Na Thon and at various bungalows around the island. The going rate is 150B per day, but on longer periods you can get the price down (say 280B for two days, 400B for three days, etc). Rates are generally lower in Na Thon and it makes more sense to rent them there if you're going back that way. Take it easy on the bikes; several farangs die or are seriously injured in motorcycle accidents every year on Samui, and, besides, the locals really don't like seeing their roads become race tracks.

KO PHA-NGAN เกาะพะงัน

Ko Pha-Ngan, about a half-hour boat ride north of Ko Samui, has become the island of choice for those who find Samui too well touristed. It started out as sort of a 'back-door escape' from Samui but is pretty well established now, with a regular boat service and 50 or 60 places to stay around the 190-square-km island. It's definitely worth a visit for its remaining deserted beaches (they haven't all been built upon) and, if you like snorkelling, for its live-coral formations. In the interior of this somewhat smaller island are the Than Sadet and Phaeng Waterfalls.

Wat Khao Tham is a cave temple beautifully situated on top of a hill near the little village of Ban Khai. An American monk lived here for over a decade and his ashes are interred on a cliff overlooking a field of palms below the wat. Several times a year 10-day meditation retreats are held at this wat.

Although hordes of backpackers have discovered Ko Pha-Ngan, a lack of roads has so far spared it from tourist hotel and package tour development. Compared to Samui, Pha-Ngan has a lower concentration of bungalows, less crowded beaches and coves, and an overall less 'spoiled' atmosphere. Pha-Ngan aficionados say the seafood is fresher and cheaper than on Samui's beaches, but it really varies from place to place. As Samui becomes more expensive for both travellers and investors, more and more people will be drawn to Pha-Ngan. But for the time being, overall living costs are about half what you'd pay on Samui.

Thong Sala ทองศาลา

Ko Pha-Ngan has a total population of roughly 7500 and about half of them live in and around the small port town of Thong Sala. This is where the Songserm Co ferry boats from Surat and Samui (Na Thon) dock although there are also smaller boats from Mae Nam and Bo Phut on Samui.

Thong Sala is the only place on the island where you can change money at regular bank rates and post or receive mail. You can also rent motorcycles here for 150 to 250B per day.

Although it is possible to rent rooms in Thong Sala, most people of course choose to stay at one of Pha-Ngan's beaches.

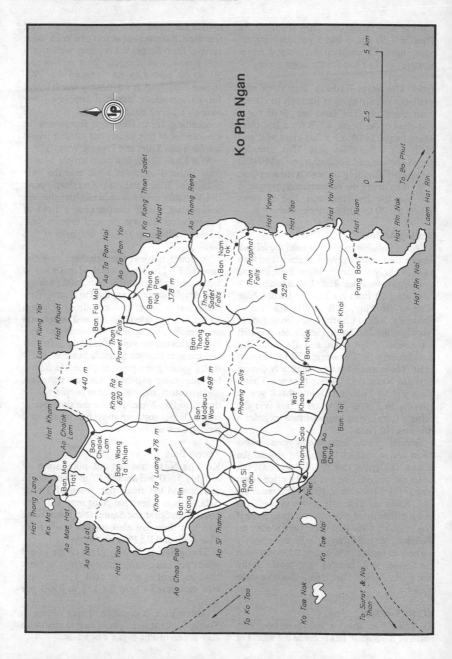

Ko Pha Ngan

5 km

2.5

0

To Bo Phut

Laem Hat Rin

Hat Rin Nok

Hat Rin Nai

Hat Yuan

Hat Yai Nam

Hat Yao

Hat Yang

Ko Kong Than Sadet

Ao Thong Reng

Hat Kruat

Ao Ta Pan Noi

Ao Ta Pan Yai

Laem Kung Yai

Hat Khuat

Ban Fai Mai

Than Prawet Falls

Ban Thong Nai Pan

378 m

Than Sadet Falls

Ban Nam Tok

Than Praphat Falls

525 m

Ban Thong Nang

Pang Bon

440 m

Khao Ra 620 m

Ban Madeua Wan 498 m

Phaeng Falls

Ban Nok

Ban Khai

Hat Khom

Ao Chalok Lam

Ban Chalok Lam

Ban Wong Ta Khian

Khao Ta Luang 476 m

Wat Khao Tham

Ban Tham

Hat Thong Lang

Ko Ma

Ban Mae Hat

Ao Mae Hat

Ao Not Lat

Hat Yao

Ban Hin Kong

Ban Si Thanu

Thong Sala

Bang Ao Charu

Ban Tai

Ao Chao Pao

Ao Si Thanu

Pier

Ko Tae Nai

Ko Tae Nok

To Ko Tao

To Surat & Na Thon

A few foreigners have stayed at Wat Khao Tham – there's plenty of room there if you don't mind very basic accommodation. You'll have to walk down the steep hill every day for food. Ten-day meditation retreats are held here from time to time.

Beaches

A few years ago the only beaches with accommodation were just north and south of Thong Sala and on the southern end of the island at Hat Rin. The bungalow operations are still mostly concentrated in these areas, but now there are many other places to stay around the island as well. Because there are almost no paved roads on Pha-Ngan, transport can be a bit of a problem, though the situation is constantly improving as enterprising Thais set up taxi and boat services between the various beaches.

Many of the huts on Pha Ngan have been established by entrepreneurs from Ko Samui with several years experience in the bungalow business. Huts go for 30 to 50B a night on average; many do not have electricity or running water. Some have generators which are only on for limited hours in the evening – the lights dim when they make a fruit shake. For many people, of course, this adds to Pha-Ngan's appeal. Other places are moving into the 80-to-150B range, which almost always includes a private bath. As travel to Pha-Ngan seems particularly seasonal, you should be able to talk bungalow rates down when occupancy is low. During the peak months, December to February and July and August, there can be an acute shortage of rooms at the most popular beaches. Even the boats coming here then can be dangerously overcrowded.

Since many of the cheaper bungalows make the bulk of their profits from their restaurants rather than from renting huts, bungalow owners have been known to eject guests who don't take meals where they're staying after a few days. The only way to avoid this, besides foregoing your own choice of restaurants, is to get a clear agreement beforehand on how many days you can stay. This only seems to be a problem at the cheaper 30 to 50B places.

There are a number of beaches with accommodation on Pha-Ngan; the following are listed moving in a counter-clockwise direction away from Thong Sala.

Bang Ao Charu The beach here is not one of the island's best, but it's close to town so people waiting for an early boat back to Surat or on to Ko Tao may choose to stay here (or north of Thong Sala on Nai Wok Ao) since transport times from other parts of the island can be unpredictable.

Sea Surf, Phangan Villa, Moonlight, Sun Dance, Half Moon, Coco Club and *Chokkhana Beach* are all in the 40-to-100B range. Further south-east towards Ban Tai are a few other places strung along the coast including the *Windward, Boon* and *P Park*, all for 30 to 40B.

Ban Tai & Ban Khai Between the villages of Ban Tai and Ban Khai is a series of sandy beaches with well-spaced bungalow operations, all in the 30 to 40B range. Here you can find *Pink, Liberty, Jup, No Name, Windy Huts, Green Peace, Laem Thong, Thong Yang, Booms Cafe* and *Silvery Moon*.

In Ban Khai the locals also rent rooms to travellers, especially from December to February when just about everything is filled up. You can get a hut for a month at very low rates here.

Laem Hat Rin This long cape juts south-east and has beaches along both its westward and eastward sides. The eastward side has the best beach, Hat Rin Nok, a long sandy strip lined with coconut palms. The snorkelling here is pretty good, but between October and March the surf can be a little hairy.

Along the west side, sometimes called Hat Rin Nai (Inner Rin Beach) you'll find longrunners *Palm Beach* and *Sunset*, both for 30 to 50B. Newer places that offer similarly priced accommodation are *Rainbow, Coral, Chok Chai* and, down near the tip of the cape, *Lighthouse*. The *Rin Beach Resort* has a few larger huts with private bath for 150B as well as the 30B cheapies.

Across the ridge on the east side is Hat Rin Nok (Outer Rin Beach), with the *Seaview,*

Tommy, Sunrise, Hat Rin and *Paradise.*
These are all in the 40-to-80B range. The
Palita Lodge has huts with private bath for
100B, plus cheaper 50B huts. The Paradise
and the Hat Rin are very popular eating
places and the Palita is well known for its
cheese buns.

On both sides of Hat Rin, hammers and
saws are busy putting together new huts, so
there may be quite a few more places by now.

East Coast Beaches Above Hat Rin Nok
there is no accommodation (except one place
in Ao Thong Reng), at this writing, until you
reach Ao Ta Pan Yai, about 17 km north. But
a dirt track (traversable on foot but only
partially by motorcycle) does run along the
coast from Hat Rin about half that distance
before heading inland to Ban Nam Tok and
Than Sadet Falls. Between Hat Rin and the
village of Ban Nam Tok are several little
coves with the white-sand beaches of Hat
Yuan (2½ km north of Hat Rin), Hat Yai Nam
(3½ km), Hat Yao (five km) and Hat Yang
(six km), all virtually deserted. Then 2½ km
north of Ban Nam Tok by dirt track is the
pretty, double bay of Ao Thong Reng, where
No Name bungalows are 30B.

Ao Thong Nai Pan This bay is really made
up of two bays, Ao Ta Pan Yai and Ao Ta Pan
Noi. On the beach at Ta Pan Yai, near Ban
Thong Nai Pan village, are the *White Sand*
and the *Nice Beach*, both with 10 or 11 huts
for 30 to 40B each. Up on Thong Ta Pan Noi
are the very nicely situated *Panviman Resort*
and the *Thong Nai Pan Resort*. The Panviman overlooks the bay and is run by a retired
Thai boxer. Huts are 60B up, all with private
bath. The more basic Thong Nai Pan Resort
costs 30 to 50B.

Chalok Lam & Hat Khuat These are two
pretty bays with beaches on the north end of
Pha-Ngan, still largely undeveloped because
of the distances involved from major transport points to Samui and the mainland. Hat
Khuat (Bottle Beach) is the smaller of the
two and currently has only one set of bungalows. Huts at the *Bottle Beach* are 40B. West
of Hat Khuat, 2½ km, across Laem Kung

Yai, is Hat Khom, where the *Coral Bay* goes
for 30 to 40B.

It's a further two km to the village of Ban
Chalok Lam. The long Chalok Lam beach
has two places to stay, *Thai Life*, with the
usual 30-to-40B huts, and *Wattana*, with
slightly nicer huts for 60 to 150B.

Ao Mae Hat As you move west on Pha-Ngan,
as on Samui, the sand gets browner and
coarser. The beach at Ao Mae is no great
shakes, but there is a bit of coral offshore.
The *Mae Hat Bay Resort* is only 30B while
the *Island View Cabana* has huts up to 150B
with private bath. The Island View also has
a good restaurant. The village of Ban Mae
Hat is nearby.

Hat Yao This beach is nothing special but if
you want to stay over the *Hat Yao* has basic
30B huts.

Ao Chao Pao In this area you begin to see
the occasional mangrove along the coast.
The beach in Ao Chao Pao is sometimes
called Si Thanu, though strictly speaking Ao
Si Thanu is the next bay south after Laem Si
Thanu. There are four places to stay along
the beach here, perhaps too many for the
attractions this part of the island holds. The
30B *Laem Son* is at the south end of the bay,
right on the cape. The *Sea Flower, Si Thanu,*
and *Gornviga Resort and Laem Niat* all have
bungalows with private bath for 80 to 150B.

Ao Wok Tum & Ao Nai Wok These two
nondescript bays are just a few km north of
Thong Sala. At the southern end of Wok Tum
are the basic 30B *Tuk, Kiat, OK* and *Darin.*
A little further down around the cape of Hin
Nok are *Porn Sawan, Cookies* and *Beach*, all
with simple 30 to 40B huts.

Just north of Thong Sala are the 30B *F-
One, Chan* and *Vantana* and the more
expensive *Siripun* and *Phangan*, both with
private bath huts from 80B.

Ko Tae Nai This little island is right across
the bay from the Thon Sala Pier and the *Koh
Tae Nai* rents huts for 100 to 200B with

shared bath. The island is not really worth the short trip.

Getting There & Away
Express Boats Songserm express boats to Ko Pha-Ngan leave from the Na Thon Pier on Ko Samui every day at 10 am and 3 pm from November to May or 10 am and 4 pm from June to October. The trip takes 40 minutes and costs 55B one way. Boats back to Samui leave Pha-Ngan's Thong Sala Pier at 6.20 and 11 am daily from November to May, or 6.30 am and 1 pm from June to October. The express-boat routes to Pha-Ngan are extensions of the Surat to Ko Samui routes, so you can go straight to Pha-Ngan from Surat with a short stopover in Na Thon (see Ko Samui, Getting There & Away, for express boat times from Surat).

Night Ferry You can also take the slow night ferry direct to Pha-Ngan from the Ban Don Pier in Surat. It leaves nightly at 11 pm, takes six hours to arrive at Thong Sala, and costs 60B on the upper deck, 30B on the lower.

Getting Around
Road A couple of roads branch out from Thong Sala, primarily to the north and the south. One road goes north-west from Thong Sala a few km along the shoreline to the villages of Ban Hin Kong and Ban Si Thanu. From Ban Si Thanu the road travels north-east across the island to Ban Chalok Lam. Another road goes straight north from Thong Sala to Chalok Lam. The road south to Ban Khai passes an intersection where another road goes north to Ban Thong Nang and Ban Thong Nai Pan. Songthaews and motorcycle taxis handle all the public transport along island roads. Some places can only be reached by motorcycle; some places only by boat or foot.

From Thong Sala, a songthaew to Ban Hin Kong (for Ao Si Thanu and Hat Yao) is 20B per person, a motorcycle taxi 25B. To Wat Khao Tham, Ban Tai or Ban Khai, it's 15B by songthaew, 20B by motorcycle.

A songthaew from Thong Sala to Chalok Lam is 25B, a motorcycle 30B.

To get to Hat Rin from Thong Sala, you have to take a taxi to Ban Khai and then walk three km. You can also get there by boat; see the following Boat section.

Thong Nai Pan can be reached by motorcycle from Thong Sala (130B) or Ban Tai (120B). See the following Boat section for water transport to Thong Nai Pan.

You can also rent motorcycles in Thong Sala for 150 to 250B a day.

Boat Hat Khuat (Bottle Beach) can be reached on foot from Ban Fai Mai (two km) or Ban Chalok Lam (four km). There are also daily boats from Ao Chalok Lam in the late afternoon for 20B. The boats leave Hat Khuat around 9 am.

Thong Nai Pan can be reached by boat from Hat Rin on south Pha-Ngan at 7 am for 40B, but these boats generally run only between April and September. When the express boat arrives at the Thong Sala Pier from Surat/Samui, there are usually boats waiting to take passengers on to Hat Rin for 30B – it takes about 45 minutes. Passengers already on Pha-Ngan can take these boats, too – they go in each direction two or three times daily.

Bo Phut & Hat Rin A small boat goes direct from Samui's Bo Phut village to Hat Rin on Ko Pha-Ngan for 50B. The boat leaves just about every day at 9.30 am, depending on the weather and number of prospective passengers, and takes 40 to 45 minutes to reach the bay at Hat Rin. Sometimes there is also an afternoon boat at 3.30 pm. As more and more people choose this route to Ko Pha-Ngan, service will probably get more regular. In the reverse direction it usually leaves at 9 am and 2.30 pm.

Mae Nam & Thong Nai Pan From April to September there is also one boat a day between Hat Mae Nam on Samui and Ao Thong Nai Pan on Pha-Ngan. The fare is 60B and the boat usually leaves around 9 am.

Ko Pha-Ngan & Ko Tao During the high travel season, January to March, there are about five boats a week between Thong Sala and Ko Tao, 47 km north. The trip takes three hours and costs 80B one way. From April to December the boats to/from Ko Tao only leave two or three times a week, depending on the weather.

Train, Bus & Ferry Combinations At Bangkok's Hualamphong Railway Station you can purchase train tickets that include a bus from the Surat Thani Railway Station to the Ban Don Pier and then a ferry to Ko Pha-Ngan. A 2nd-class seat costs 309B inclusive, while a 3rd-class seat is 235B. Second-class sleeper combinations cost 424B for an upper berth, 459B for a lower. Add 100B for an air-con coach.

KO TAO เกาะเต่า
Ko Tao translates as 'Turtle Island', named for its shape. It's only about 21 square km in area and the population of 750 are mostly involved in fishing and growing coconuts. If you want to enjoy palm-studded Samui-style geography without the crowds, this might be the place. Since it takes at least five hours to get there from the mainland (from Surat via Ko Pha-Ngan), Ko Tao doesn't get people coming over for day trips or for quick overnighters.

Ban Mae Hat is on the west side of the island and is where inter-island boats land. The only other villages on the island are Ban Hat Sai Ri in the centre of the northern part and Ban Chalok Ban Kao to the south. Just a km off the north-west shore of the island is Ko Nang Yuan, which is really three islands joined by a sand bar.

The granite promontory of Laem Tato at the southern tip of Ko Tao makes a nice hike from Ban Chalok Ban Kao.

Places to Stay
Huts are very simple and inexpensive on Ko Tao as they have only used local materials up to now. On Ao Mae beach just north of Ban Mae Hat are *Nuan Nang*, with basic huts for 30 to 50B and huts with bath for 60 to 80B, then *Dam* for 30 to 40B. A bit further north on this beach at Laem Cho Po Ro (Jaw Paw Raw) is *Khao* for 50B.

Around this headland, to the north, is the long Hat Sai Ri with only one bungalow

operation at this writing, the *O-Chai* for 30 to 40B. Nearby is Ban Hat Sai Ri, about 2½ km from Ban Mae Hat. A couple of km south of Ban Mae Hat at Laem Hin Sam Kon is the nicely situated *Neptune* for 30 to 40B. Below this promontory is Hat Sai Nuan, where you can find the *Sai Thong* and the *Cha*, both from 50B. The only way to get there is to walk along the dirt track from Mae Hat.

About two km east of Sai Nuan there are two small beaches on Ao Chalok Ban Kao. On the first is *Taraporn* (30 to 40B) and on the second *Laem Khlong* (50B). The village of Chalok Ban Kao is quite close and there's a road between here and Ban Mae Hat.

On the other side of the impressive Laem Tato to the east is pretty Ao Thian Ok with *Hope* and *Niyom*, both 30 to 50B. Another km or so east is Hat Sai Daeng where *Kiat* offers simple huts for 50B.

North-east of Ban Chalok Ban Kao on the lower east coast of the island at tiny Ao Leuk beach is the 30B *Chamnan*. Two km to the north is another beach at Ao Tanot, but so far no accommodation.

At Ao Hin Wong two km east of Ban Hat Sai Ri are a handful of huts called *Sahat*, for 30B.

Finally, on Ko Nang Yuan are the *Nang Yuan* bungalows for 70 to 80B. One problem in staying on Ko Nang Yuan might be putting up with diving groups that occasionally take over the island. Regular twice-daily boats to Nang Yuan from the Ban Mae Hat Pier are 15B per person. You can charter a ride there for 50B.

Getting There & Away
Depending on weather conditions, anywhere from two to five boats a week go between the Thong Sala pier on Ko Pha-Ngan and Ban Mae Hat on Ko Tao. The trip takes three hours and costs 80B per person.

From Chumphon on the mainland there are occasional scheduled boats to Ko Tao. From January to March they leave two or three times a week, but the rest of the year there are only two or three boats a month. These scheduled boats are 95B per person and take six to seven hours to reach Ko Tao. You can charter a boat to Ko Tao from Chumphon for maybe 2500B. Try the pier at Pak Nam, the Chumphon estuary.

ANG THONG NATIONAL MARINE PARK

อุทยานทางทะเลแห่งชาติจังหวัดอ่างทอง

From Ko Samui, a couple of tour operators run day trips out to the Ang Thong archipelago, 31 km north-west. A typical tour costs 150 to 180B per person, leaves Na Thon at 8.30 am and returns at 5 pm. Lunch is included, along with snorkelling in a sort of lagoon formed by one of the islands, from which Ang Thong gets its name (Golden Jar), and a climb to the top of a 240-metre hill to view the whole island group. Departures are usually only twice a week. At least once a month there's also an overnight tour, as there are bungalows on Ko Wua Ta Lap. These cost 250B per person and include three meals and accommodation at the bungalows. You may be able to book a passage alone to the Ang Thong islands; enquire at Songserm Travel Service or Ko Samui Travel Centre in Na Thon.

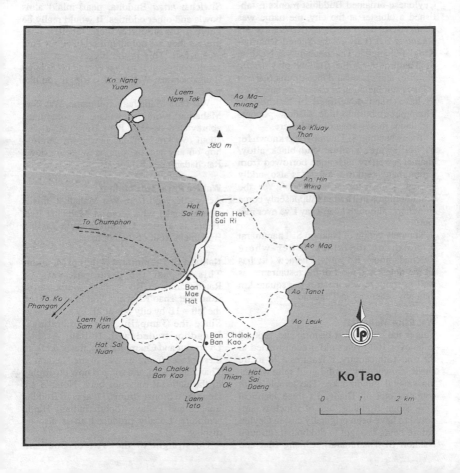

Nakhon Si Thammarat Province

NAKHON SI THAMMARAT TOWN

เมือง นครศรีธรรมราช

Nakhon Si Thammarat Town (population 72,000) is 780 km from Bangkok. Centuries before the 8th-century Srivijaya Empire subjugated the peninsula, there was a city-state here called Ligor or Lagor, capital of the Tambralinga Kingdom, which was well known throughout Oceania. Later, when Ceylonese-ordained Buddhist monks established a cloister at the city, the name was changed to the Pali-Sanskrit *Nagara Sri Dhammaraja* (City of the Sacred Dharma-King), rendered in Thai phonetics as Nakhon Si Thammarat. Thai shadow play (*nang thalung*) and classical dance-drama (*lakhon* – Thai pronunciation of Lagor) are supposed to have been developed in Nakhon Si Thammarat; buffalo-hide shadow puppets and dance masks are still made here.

Today Nakhon Si Thammarat is known for its neilloware, a silver and black alloy/enamel jewellery technique borrowed from China many centuries ago. It is also, oddly enough, known for its 'gangsters'. Yes, the best hoodlums in Thailand supposedly come from here, although I can't say I've ever met one.

The new centre of Nakhon Si Thammarat is north of the clock tower where Ratchadamnoen Rd splits. The new city has all the hotels and most of the restaurants, as well as more movie theatres per square km than any other city in Thailand.

Wat Phra Mahathat

This is the city's most historic site, reputed to be over 1000 years old. Reconstructed in the mid-13th century, it features a 78-metre chedi, crowned by a solid gold spire weighing several hundred kg. The temple's bot contains one of Thailand's three identical Phra Singh Buddhas, one of which is supposed to have been originally cast in Ceylon before being brought to Sukhothai (through Nakhon Si Thammarat), Chiang Mai and later, Ayuthaya. The other images are at Wat Phra Singh in Chiang Mai and the National Museum in Bangkok – each is claimed to be the original.

Besides the distinctive bot and chedi there are many intricately designed wihans surrounding the chedi, several of which contain crowned Nakhon Si Thammarat/Ayuthaya-style Buddhas in glass cabinets. One wihan houses a funky museum (5B admission) with carved wooden kruts (garudas, Vishnu's mythical bird-mount), old Siwichai votive tablets, Buddha figures of every description including a standing Dvaravati figure and a Siwichai *naga* Buddha, pearl-inlaid alms bowls and other oddities. It would really be good if the artefacts were labelled – at present they are not identified in either Thai or English. This is the biggest wat in the south, comparable to Wat Po and other large Bangkok wats. Well worth a trip, if you like wats.

Wat Phra Mahathat's full name, Wat Phra Mahathat Woramahawihan, is sometimes abbreviated as Wat Phra Boromathat. It's about two km from the new town centre – hop on any bus or songthaew going down Ratchadamnoen Rd for 2B.

Wat Na Phra Boromathat

Across the road from Wat Mahathat, this is where monks who serve at Mahathat live. There is a nice Gandhara-style fasting Buddha in front of the bot here.

Nakhon Si Thammarat National Museum

This is past the principal wats on Ratchadamnoen Rd heading south, across from Wat Thao Khot and Wat Phet Jarik, on the left – 1B by city bus or 2B by songthaew. Since the Tampaling (or Tambralinga) Kingdom traded with Indian, Arabic, Dvaravati and Champa states, much art from these places found its way to the Nakhon Si Thammarat area, and some is now on display in the national museum here. Notable are Dong-Son bronze drums, Dvaravati Buddha images and Pallava (South Indian) Hindu sculpture. Locally produced art is also on display.

Go straight to the 'Art of Southern

Thailand' exhibit in a room on the left of the foyer, if you've already had your fill of the usual Thai art history surveys from Ban Chiang to Ayuthaya. This room has many fine images of Nakhon Si Thammarat provenance, including Phutthasihing, U Thong and late Ayuthaya styles. The Nakhon Si Thammarat-produced Ayuthaya style seems to be the most common, with distinctive, almost comical, crowned faces. The so-called Phutthasihing-style Buddha looks a little like the Palla-influenced Chiang Saen Buddha, but is shorter and more 'pneumatic'.

Admission to the museum is 10B and hours are Wednesday to Sunday, from 9 am to 4 pm.

Hindu Temples

There are also three Hindu temples in Nakhon Si Thammarat, along Ratchadamnoen, inside the city walls. Brahmin priests from these temples take part each year in the royal ploughing ceremony in Bangkok. One temple houses a locally famous Shivalingam (phallic shrine) which is worshipped, among others, by women hoping to bear children.

Other

Every year in mid-October there is a southern Thai festival called Chaak Phra Pak Tai held in Songkhla, Surat Thani and Nakhon Si Thammarat. In Nakhon Si Thammarat the festival is centred around Wat Mahathat and includes performances of nang thalung, lakhon, etc.

Places to Stay – bottom end

Most of Nakhon Si Thammarat's hotels are near the train and bus stations.

On Yammaraj (Yomarat) Rd, across from the railway station, is the *Si Thong Hotel*, with adequate rooms for 80B with fan and bath. Also on Yomarat Rd are the *Nakhon Hotel* and *Yaowarat*, with the same rates and facilities as Si Thong.

On Chamnemvithee (Jamroenwithi) Rd (walk straight down Neramit Rd opposite the railway station two blocks and make a right on Jamroenwithi Rd) is the *Siam Hotel*, a large hotel with rooms with fan and bath for

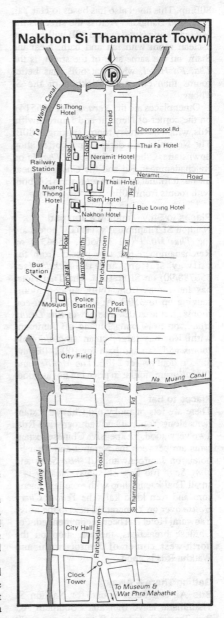

80B up. This hotel also has buses to Hat Yai, Surat and Bangkok. Across the street is the *Muang Thong Hotel*, where 80B will get you a clean room with fan and bath. Near the Siam, on the same side of the street, is the *Thai Fa Hotel*, which, at 60B, has better rooms than either the Nakhon or the Si Thong.

Other places are the *Neramit* (tel 356514), on the corner of Neramit and Jamroenwithi Rds, which has dreary rooms starting at 80B. The Neramit has a dark, sleazy coffee shop downstairs. Others are the newer *Thai Li* on Ratchadamnoen Rd and the *Chokchai* near the bus terminal on Phosadet Karom Rd, both with rooms from 80B.

Places to Stay – middle & top end
Nakhon Si Thammarat's flashiest hotels are the *Thai Hotel* (tel 356505, 356451) on Ratchadamnoen Rd, two blocks from the railway station, and the *Taksin* (tel 356788/90) on Si Prat Rd. The Thai Hotel has fan rooms from 160B, air-con rooms ranging up to 350B. At the Taksin air-con rooms start at 200B. The newer *Bue Loung Hotel*, on Soi Loung Muang off Jamroenwithi Rd, has large, clean single/double rooms with fan and bath for 100/140B and air-con doubles for 240B. The *Montien* and *Petpailin* are similar in price but not as good.

Places to Eat
There are lots of funky old Chinese restaurants along Yomarat and Jamroenwithi Rds. Two very good, inexpensive Chinese restaurants are between the Neramit and Thai Fa hotels on Jamroenwithi Rd – *Bo Seng* and *Yong Seng* (no English signs). Nearby is a small Thai kaeng shop with excellent kaeng som and tom khaa kai. The *Yellow Curry House* over on Yomarat Rd next to the noisy Yaowaraj Hotel has been recommended. For Chinese breakfasts, the jok shop on the north-west corner of Jamroenwithi and Watkhit Rds is good.

Getting There & Away
Bus Air-con buses bound for Nakhon Si Thammarat leave Bangkok's Southern AC Bus Terminal daily at 9 am and every 20 minutes from 6.30 to 7.50 pm, arriving 12 hours later, fare 270B. Air-con buses in the reverse direction leave at about the same hours. Ordinary buses leave Bangkok at 6.50, 8 am, 5 and 9.30 pm for 150B.

From Surat Thani there are daily buses to Nakhon. Check with the tour bus companies on Na Muang Rd. A tour bus from Surat to Nakhon should cost 60 to 65B one way. Buses run from Songkhla to Hat Yai to Nakhon. From Songkhla to Nakhon, you cross the river by ferry – there can be long delays here. Check with the Choke Dee Hotel in Songkhla or at one of the tour bus companies on Niphat Uthit 2 Rd in Hat Yai. Muang Tai Tours, on Jamroenwithi Rd in Nakhon Si Thammarat, does a 60B trip to Surat that includes a good meal and a video movie.

Hourly buses to Nakhon Si Thammarat leave Krabi's Talaat Kao for 50B per person and take about four hours.

Train Most southbound trains stop at the junction of Khao Chum Thong, about 30 km west of Nakhon Si Thammarat, from where you must take a bus or taxi to the coast. However, two trains actually go all the way to Nakhon Si Thammarat (there is a branch line from Khao Chum Thong to Nakhon Si Thammarat): the Rapid No 47, which leaves Bangkok's Hualamphong Station at 5.30 pm, arriving in Nakhon Si Thammarat at 8.35 am, and the Express No 15, which leaves Bangkok at 7.20 pm and arrives in Nakhon Si Thammarat at 10 am. Most travellers will not be booking a train directly to Nakhon Si Thammarat, but if you want to, a 1st-class fare is 590B, 2nd class 279B, 3rd class 133B, not including surcharges for Rapid/Express service or sleeping berths.

AROUND NAKHON SI THAMMARAT PROVINCE
Laem Talumpuk
This is a small scenic cape not far from Nakhon Si Thammarat Town. Take a bus from Neramit Rd going east to Pak Nakhon for 8B, then cross the inlet by ferry to Laem Talumpuk.

Hat Sa Bua หาดสระบัว

Sixteen km north of Nakhon Si Thammarat in the Tha Sala district, about 9B by songthaew, off Route 401 to Surat, are some semideserted white sand beaches – no tourists. There are some very reasonably priced restaurants here, and there are also vendors selling prawn-cakes, reported one traveller.

Hat Sichon & Hin Ngam
หาดสิชล   หินงาม

Hat Sichon and Hat Hin Ngam are stunning beaches 37 km north of Nakhon Si Thammarat in Sichon district. Get the bus for Hat Hin Ngam or Sichon from the bus station for 15B. Hat Sichon comes first; Hin Ngam is another 1½ km. *Prasansuk Villa* has 30 bungalows for rent at 200 to 300B.

Ao Khanom อ่าวขนอม

About 25 km from Sichon, 70 km from Surat or 80 km from Nakhon Si Thammarat. Not far from the vehicle ferry landing for Ko Samui in Khanom is a string of three white-sand beaches, Hat Nai Praet, Hat Nai Phlao and Hat Pak Nam. *Khanom Beach Resort* has 10 bungalows for 200 to 300B. *Fern Bay Resort* and *Nai Phlao Bay Resort* are similar.

Phattalung Province

Over 840 km from Bangkok and 95 km from Hat Yai, Phattalung is one of the south's only rice-growing provinces and it has prospered as a result.

PHATTALUNG TOWN เมืองพัทลุง

The provincial capital (population 33,000) is fairly small (you can walk around the perimeter of downtown Phattalung in an hour, even stopping for rice), but it is unique among southern Thai towns. Judging from the number of *hang thong* – gold dealers – on Poh Saat Rd, there must be a large Chinese population.

Phattalung is also famous for the original nang thalung, Thai shadow play named most likely for Phattalung – nang means hide (untanned leather), and thalung is taken from Phattalung. The Thai shadow-play tradition remains only in Nakhon Si Thammarat and Phattalung, though the best performances are seen in the latter. A typical performance begins at midnight and lasts four to five hours. Usually they take place during *ngaan wat* or temple fairs.

The town is situated between two pictur-esque, foliage-trimmed limestone peaks, Khao Ok Thalu (punctured-chest mountain) and Khao Hua Taek (broken-head mountain). Local myth has it that these two mountains were the wife and mistress of a third mountain to the north, Khao Muang, who fought a fierce battle over the adulterous husband, leaving them with their 'wounds'. The names refer to their geographic peculiarities – Ok Thalu has a tunnel through its upper peak, while Hua Taek is sort of split at the top.

Like most Thai towns, Phattalung's street plan is laid out in a grid pattern. Most of the local sights are nearby. To change money it's best to go to the Thai Farmer's Bank on Ramet Rd.

Wat Wang

Over 100 years old, this is the oldest wat in Phattalung. Originally the palace of a Thai prince was located just east of the wat (*wang* means palace), but only the wall remains. The original chedi is in front of the wat. A closed bot has a decaying set of murals with Buddhist and Ramayana themes. You have to open the doors and windows to see them. Wat Wang is four to five km east of Phattalung Town on the road to Lam Bam. Take a songthaew next to the post office for the 3B ride to Wat Wang.

Wat Kuhasawan

On the west side of town – from the railway station Kuhasawan Rd leads right to it – Wat Kuhasawan comprises one large cave with rather ugly statues, but the cave is high and cool. A tall passageway leads deeper into the cave – lights can be switched on by the monks. Steps lead around the cave to the top of the mountain for a nice view of rice fields and mountains further west.

To the right of the main cave is an old

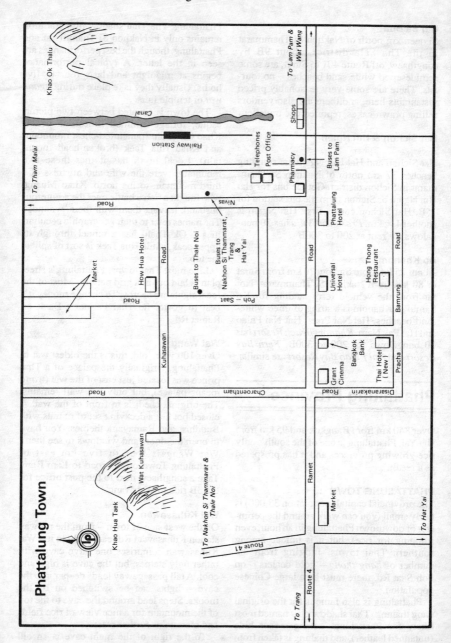

Phattalung Town

hermit's cave – the monk died in 1973 and his form is commemorated by a statue at the second level of stairs. Good views of Khao Ok Thalu and most of Phattalung City can be had from certain points around this cave.

Lam Pam ถ้ำป่า

If you follow Phattalung's main street, Ramet Rd, east over the railway tracks past Wat Wang, you'll come to Lam Pam on the banks of the Thale Luang, the upper part of the south's inland sea. For 5B you can ride a songthaew from next to the post office out to Lam Pam in 15 minutes, or hire a motorcycle for 10B.

Under shady trees next to the sea (which is freshwater), are beach chairs and tables where you can relax, enjoy the breeze and order food – crab, mussels, other shellfish, squid, plus beer, soda, etc. Although the inland sea itself is not at all spectacular, this is a nice spot to while away a few hours drinking beer and eating the fabulous *plaa meuk kluay yaang* ('banana' squid – egg-carrying squid, roasted over charcoal), along with *mieng kham*, that unique do-it-yourself concoction of dried shrimp, peanuts, lime, garlic, ginger, chilli, toasted coconut and salty-sweet sauce wrapped in wild tea leaves – cheap, too.

Thale Noi Waterbird Sanctuary

สวนนกน้ำเป็ด ทะเลน้อย

Thale Noi is a small inland sea or lake, 32 km north-east of Phattalung Town, which is a waterbird sanctuary protected by the Forestry Department. Among the 182 species of waterbird here, the most prominent is the *nok i kong*, with its long funny feet which quiver like malfunctioning landing gear as the bird takes flight, and the *nok pet daeng*, a small, red-headed 'duck bird', related to the whistling teal, that skitters along the water.

The sea itself is sort of a large swamp similar to the Everglades in the southern USA. The major forms of vegetation are water vines and *don kok*, a reed which the nok i kong uses to build large 'platforms' over the water for nesting purposes. The local Thais use these same reeds, after drying them in the sun, to make floor mats which are

sold throughout Phattalung. The village near the park entrance to Thale Noi is a good place to observe the reed-weaving methods.

To get there, take a Thale Noi bus from the local bus stop on Poh Saat Rd in Phattalung. The bus stops at the sanctuary after about an hour's journey and costs 8B. Long boats can be hired at the pier to take passengers out and around the Thale Noi for two hours for 150B.

Tham Malai ถ้ำมาลัย

Three km north of Phattalung near the railway is a hill with a large cave, Tham Malai, at its base. On the top of the hill are some Chinese shrines, though a Thai Theravada monk resides there. There are excellent views of Phattalung and surrounding mountains from the top.

The cave itself is more interesting than the shrines. Bring a torch (flashlight) and you can explore the various rooms within the cavern. The cave is more or less in its natural state, with its stalagmites and stalactites still intact. Even without a light, it's worth exploring a bit – when the cave reaches its darkest point, you'll come upon an opening leading back around to daylight.

If the canal running parallel to the railway has enough water, you can get a boat for 5B as far as Tham Malai – easiest in December and January. If the water is too low, walk along the tracks until you come to a footbridge which will take you over the canal onto a path leading to the cave.

Places to Stay

Ramet Rd is the main drag where you will find two of Phattalung's four principal hotels.

At 43 Ramet Rd, the *Phattalung Hotel* is dingy and costs 70B with fan and shared bath. The *Sakon* (the English sign reads 'Universal Hotel') is a short distance west of the Phattalung Hotel on Ramet Rd, at the intersection with Poh-Saat Rd. It's clean and has adequate rooms with fan and bath for 70B.

The *Thai Hotel* is a new, large hotel on Disara-Nakarin Rd, off Ramet near the Rama Cafe and Bangkok Bank. Rooms start at 120B with fan and bath, up to 250B with air-con.

The *How Hua Hotel* (Haw Far?), on the corner of Poh-Saat and Kuhasawan Rds, has rooms with fan and bath for 100B, air-con rooms for 200B. It's also very clean.

Out at Thale Noi, the Forestry Department has a few bungalows for rent for 300B.

Places to Eat

The best restaurant in town is the well-known *Hong Thong Restaurant* on Pracha Bamrung Rd – turn left off Disara-Nakarin Rd just past the new Thai Hotel. This is a family-run Chinese place and the seafood is excellent since Phattalung is only a few km from the inland sea. *Hawy jaw*, crab sausage served with sliced pineapple on the side, is very nice. Also excellent are *plaa kao neung puay* (whole fish steamed in a broth of onions, peppers, Chinese mushrooms and tangy plums), *plaa tuk phat phet* (catfish fried in chilli and fresh holy basil), *yam ma-muang* (spicy mango salad), *kai manao raat nam krewi* (chicken in lime sauce), *plaa kapong khao thawt* (fresh-water perch fried whole) and *kung nam jeut phao* (grilled freshwater shrimp). Prices are not high.

Most cheap restaurants in Phattalung are on the grubby side. The market off Poh-Saat Rd is a good place for cheap take-aways. For breakfast, try the local speciality *khao yam*, dry rice mixed with coconut, peanuts, lime leaves and shrimp – delicious. About three km west of town where Route 4 meets Route 41 is a Muslim market. Several food stalls here sell Muslim food like *khao mok kai* (chicken biryani) and the southern Thai version of *kai yang*.

Getting There & Away

Bus Buses from the Baw Kaw Saw station in Nakhon Si Thammarat take two hours and cost 30B. Buses from Hat Yai and Songkhla are 22 and 30B respectively and take about the same time.

Buses from Trang are 15B and take 1½ hours. Phattalung to Phuket buses are 75B and take seven hours.

Train Special Express trains from Bangkok leave Hualamphong Station at 2 and 3.15 pm, arriving in Phattalung at 5.47 and 7.04

am. The cheaper Rapid No 43 leaves Bangkok at 4 pm and arrives in Phattalung at 8.50 am. Basic fares are 611B 1st class (Express only), 288B 2nd class, 137B 3rd class, plus appropriate surcharges.

Songkhla Province

SONGKHLA TOWN เมืองสงขลา

Songkhla Town (population 84,000), 950 km from Bangkok, is another former Srivijaya satellite on the east coast. Not much is known about the pre-8th century history of Songkhla, called Singora by the Malays. The town, small in area and population, is on a peninsula between the Thale Sap Songkhla (an inland sea) and the South China Sea (or Gulf of Thailand, depending on how you look at it). The inhabitants are a colourful mixture of Thais, Chinese and Muslims (ethnic Malays), and the local architecture and cuisine reflect the combination. The seafood served along the white Hat Samila is excellent, though the beach itself is not that great for swimming, especially if you've just come from Ko Samui. However, beaches are not Songkhla's main attraction, even if the TAT so promotes them – the town has plenty of other curiosities to offer, and the evergreen trees along Hat Samila give it a rather nice visual effect.

Information

The Malaysian Consulate is next to Khao Noi near Hat Samila. There is also an American Consulate next to the governor's residence on Sadao Rd.

The Waterfront

The waterfront on the inland sea is buzzing with activity most of the time. Ice is loaded onto fishing boats on their way out to sea, baskets and baskets of fish are unloaded onto the pier from boats just arrived, fish markets are setting up and disassembling, long boats doing taxi business between islands and mainland are tooling about. The fish smell along the piers is pretty powerful – be warned.

Around Town

For interesting Songkhla architecture, walk along the back streets parallel to the inland sea waterfront – Nakhon Nai and Nakhon Nawk Rds. Some of the buildings here are very old and show Chinese, Portuguese and Malay influence, but they're disappearing fast. South of Hat Samila a few km is a quaint Muslim fishing village – this is where the tourist photos of gaily painted fishing vessels are taken.

National Museum

This is in a 100-year-old building of southern Sino-Portuguese architecture, between Rong Muang Rd and Jana Rd (off Vichianchom Rd), next to Songkhla's bus station. Admission is free and there are exhibits from all national art-style periods, especially Srivijaya. Hours are the usual 9 am to 4 pm, Wednesday to Sunday, and admission is 10D.

Wat Matchimawat

On Saiburi Rd towards Hat Yai, this wat has an old marble Buddha image and a small museum. There is also an old Sinhalese-style chedi and royal pavilion at the top of Khao Tang Kuan, a hill rising up at the north end of the peninsula.

Other

Songkhla is south Thailand's educational centre; there is one university, several colleges, technical schools and research institutes, a nursing college and a military training camp, all in or near the town. The Institute of Southern Thai Studies is headquartered at Si Nakharinwirot University, four km from Songkhla on the road to Hat Yai. The folklore museum at the Institute is open from 8.30 am to 4.30 pm, Monday to Friday.

Suan Tun, a topiary park across from the Samila Hotel, has yew hedges trimmed into animal shapes.

Places to Stay – bottom end

The best deal in Songkhla is the *Narai Hotel* (tel 311078), 14 Chai Khao Rd, at the foot of Khao Tang Kuan. It's an older wooden hotel with clean quiet singles/doubles for 80/90B, with fan and shared bath. A huge double with bath is 150B.

The *Songkhla Hotel*, on Vichianchom Rd, across from the Fishing Station, has 100B rooms that are OK, but the standards are going downhill. The *Choke Dee Hotel*, just down the road from the Songkhla, is a depressing place that costs 120B.

The *Suk Somboon II* on Saiburi Rd, near the museum, is not bad for 100B a double, although they're just wooden rooms, off a large central area, and you have to ask for that price – posted rates start at 130B. There's also a more expensive *Suk Somboon I* on the same road a block south, with rooms from 140B up. The *Wiang Sawan*, in the middle of the block between Saiburi and Ramwithi Rds not far from Wat Matchimawat, has rooms from 140B, a bit overpriced for what you get.

The *Saen Sabai* (tel 311090) at 1 Phetkhiri Rd is well located and has clean, if small, rooms from 150B with fan or 220B with air-con.

Places to Stay – top end

The *Samila Hotel* (tel 311310/4) on the beachfront has air-con rooms starting from 700B; it has a swimming pool and other luxuries. Other expensive hotels include the *Queen* (tel 311138) at 20 Saiburi Rd, next door to the Suksomboon 2, with good air-con rooms from 280B. The similarly priced *Charn (Chan)* (tel 311903) is on the same road but on the outskirts of the downtown area on the way to Hat Yai. The new *Royal Crown* on Chai Nam Rd has air-con rooms from 450B with colour TV and fridge.

Also new is the *Lake Inn*, a place with great views right on the Thale Sap. Very nice air-con rooms start at 280B.

Places to Eat

There are lots of good restaurants in Songkhla but a few tend to overcharge foreign tourists. The Chinese restaurant on the corner opposite the Choke Dee Hotel is a rip-off; it looks good, but walk on by, unless you think 35B for fried rice is reasonable. The *Khao Noi* (no English sign), next door to the Chinese place at 12/22 Vichianchom Rd, is better. The best seafood place, accord-

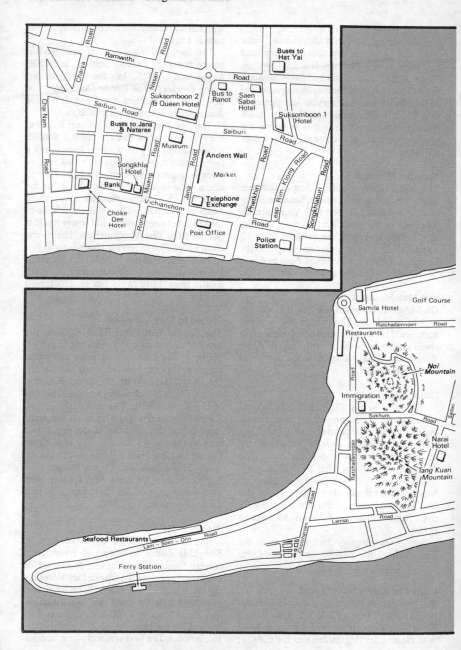

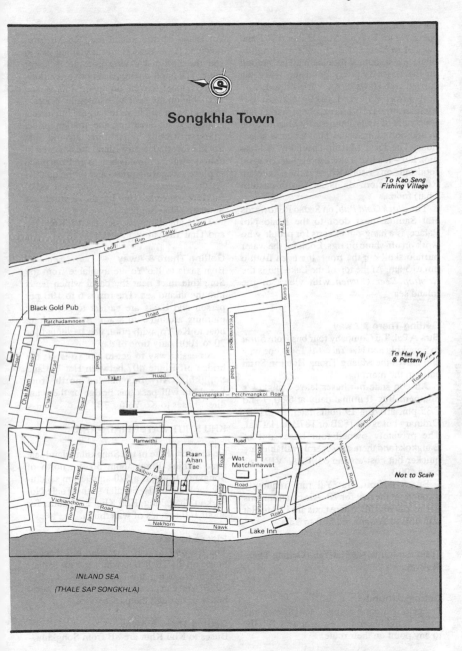

Songkhla Town

To Kao Seng
Fishing Village

Black Gold Pub

To Hat Yai
& Pattani

Chaimangkal – Petchmangkol Road

Not to Scale

Raan
Ahan
Tae

Wat
Matchimawat

Lake Inn

INLAND SEA
(THALE SAP SONGKHLA)

ing to locals, is the *Raan Aahaan Tae* on Nang Ngam Rd (off Songkhlaburi Rd and parallel to Saiburi Rd). Look for a brightly lit place just south of the cinema. The seafood on the beach is pretty good too – try the curried crab claws or spicy fried squid.

A great day and night market off Vichianchom Rd offers excellent market fare – a couple of stalls feature tasty Muslim food in addition to the usual Thai-Chinese selections. The local Muslim speciality is khao mok kai – it's like a chicken biryani. Several foodstalls on Srisuda Rd, near the Chai Nam Rd intersection, do isaan (north-eastern Thai) food.

The *Black Gold Pub*, on Sadao Rd towards Hat Samila, next door to the Khao Noi Palace, is a hang-out of sorts for people who work on off-shore oil rigs. Look for the water buffalo skull out the front. It's open from 6 pm to 3 am. At the top of the Lake Inn is the *Rooftop Beer Garden* with views of the inland sea.

Getting There & Away
Bus A Pak Tai Company tour bus from Surat to Songkhla and Hat Yai costs 130B one way and leaves the Muang Thong Hotel in Surat early in the morning.

Air-con state-run buses leave Bangkok's Southern Bus Terminal daily at 6.30, 7 and 7.35 pm, arriving 19 hours later, for 319B. Ordinary buses are 182B or 187B to Hat Yai. The privately owned tour buses out of Bangkok (and there are several available) are quicker but cost around 350B. A 'VIP' bus costs 400B.

Buses to/from Hat Yai run frequently throughout the day for 7B. Air-con minivans to Hat Yai are 10B. Share taxis are 12B to Hat Yai, 40B to Pattani and 50B to Yala.

Train For trains, see Hat Yai – Getting There & Away.

Getting Around
For getting around in town, songthaews circulate Songkhla and take passengers, for 3B, to any point on their route.

KO YO เกาะยอ
An island on the inland sea, Ko Yo (pronounced Kaw Yaw) is worth visiting just to see the cotton-weaving cottage industry there. The good-quality, distinctive phaa kaw yaw is hand-woven on rustic looms and available on the spot at 'wholesale' prices – meaning you still have to bargain but have a chance of undercutting the market price. Many different households around this thickly forested, sultry island are engaged in cotton-weaving, so it is best to go from place to place comparing prices and fabric quality. At the north end of the island is a small folklore museum run by the Institute of Southern Thai Studies.

There are also a couple of wats, Khao Bo and Thai Yaw, to visit.

Getting There & Away
Boat taxis to Ko Yo are available from the Songkhla inlet near the canal which feeds into the inland sea. The trip is 6 to 10B per person and boats are easiest to get in the morning around 7 to 8 am. An entire long boat to Ko Yo, with pilot, can be rented for 70 to 100B, any time of day.

An easier way to get to Ko Yo is via the bridge off Route 407 between Hat Yai and Songkhla. Any bus headed north from Songkhla will pass this bridge or there are direct buses to Ko Yo for 7B.

KHU KHUT WATERBIRD PARK
นวฐุทยานนกน้ำ ขุขุต
On the east shore of the Songkhla inland sea, near Sathing Phra, about 50 km north of Songkhla Town, is a 520-square-km sanctuary for waterbirds. Similar to the Thale Noi Park in Phattalung, Khu Khut is a habitat for about 140 species of waterbirds.

Places to Stay
The *Kukon Guest House* is an old wooden house on the Thale Sap with a terrace restaurant overlooking the lake. A room here is 100B. You can arrange boat trips at the guest house or through the park service.

Getting There & Away
Buses to Khu Khut are 8B from Songkhla –

take a Ranot-bound bus. In Khu Khut you can walk the three km to the park or get a motorcycle taxi for 5B.

HAT YAI หาดใหญ่

Hat Yai (population 130,000), 933 km from Bangkok, is south Thailand's commercial centre and one of the kingdom's largest cities, though it is only a district of Songkhla Province. A steady stream of customers from Malaysia keep Hat Yai's downtown business district booming. Everything from dried fruit to stereos are sold in the shops along Niphat Uthit Rds Nos 1, 2 and 3, not far from the railway station. Many travellers stay in Hat Yai, taking side trips to Songkhla.

Information & Orientation

The TAT Tourist Office (tel 243747) is at 1/1 Soi 2 Niphat Uthit 3 Rd. The Tourist Police can also be found here. THAI (tel 243711) has offices on Niphat Uthit 2 Rd in the centre of town and on Niphat Songkhrao 1 Rd near the traffic circle. Malaysian Airlines System (tel 243729, 245443) is on Thamnoonvithi Rd near the Nora Hotel.

The GPO is just north of the railway station before you get to the U Taphao Bridge leading out of town to the airport.

The Immigration office is near the same bridge on Nasathanee Rd. The nearest Malaysian Consulate is in Songkhla.

Wat Hat Yai Nai

West of town a few km, off Phetkasem Rd towards the airport, is Wat Hat Yai Nai. A very large (35 metres) reclining Buddha on the premises (Phra Phut Mahatamongkon) is currently being restored along with the wihan to house it. Inside the image's gigantic base is a curious little museum/souvenir shop/mausoleum. The old abbot likes receiving visitors. To get there, hop on a songthaew near the intersection of Niphat Uthit 1 Rd and Phetkasem Rds, get off after crossing the U Taphao Bridge.

Bullfights

Bullfighting, involving two bulls in opposition rather than man and bull, takes place as a spectator sport twice monthly in Hat Yai.

On the first Sunday of each month it's at an arena next to the Nora Hotel off Thamnoonvithi Rd (the same road which leads to the railway station, pronounced Thammanun Withi), and on the second Sunday it is at the Hat Yai Arena on Route 4, near the airport. Matches take place continuously all day from 10.30 am until 6 pm and admission is 30B – although many hundred times that amount changes hands during the non-stop betting by Thai spectators.

Places to Stay – bottom end

Hat Yai has dozens of hotels within walking distance of the railway station.

Cheaper places nearby include the *Cathay Guest House*, on the corner of Thamnoonvithi and Niphat Uthit 2, three blocks from the station, with rooms ranging from 80 to 150B; there is also a 50B dorm. The Cathay has become a travellers' centre in Hat Yai because of its good location, helpful staff and plentiful travel info for trips onward, including tips on travel in Malaysia. They serve food (and also don't mind if you bring takeways in and eat in the lounge). There is a bus ticket agency downstairs. The *Angel Guest House*, 127 Thamnoonvithi Rd, has basically the same rates as the Cathay except that for 50B you can get a closet-like room instead of a dorm bed.

The *Saeng Fa Hotel*, off Niphat Uthit 3 Rd at No 98-100, has clean 120B rooms with fan and bath or 240B for air-con. Also on Niphat Uthit 3 Rd is the *Tong Nam Hotel*, a rather basic Chinese hotel with 80/100B rooms, shared bath/private bath. *Kim Hua*, further south on the same road, is 100 to 150B for fan and bath.

The *Savoy Hotel*, 3½ blocks from the station on Niphat Uthit 2 Rd, has fair 80B rooms, although doubles are often 120B or more. The name's been changed to New Savoy, but it's as rundown as ever.

On Niphat Uthit 1 Rd is the *Mandarin Hotel*, with rather overpriced rooms for 120B with fan and bath. *Seiko Hotel*, five blocks from the station on the corner of Thamnoonvithi and Sanchanusorn Rds, is just liveable, with 100B rooms with fan and bath. The *Grand Hotel*, at 257-9 Thamnoonvithi Rd, is

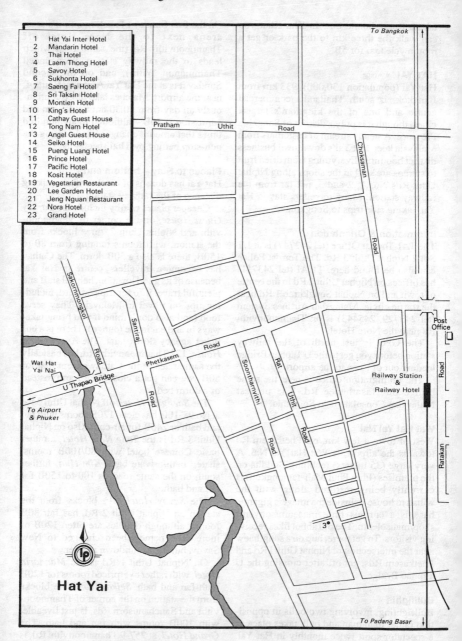

1	Hat Yai Inter Hotel
2	Mandarin Hotel
3	Thai Hotel
4	Laem Thong Hotel
5	Savoy Hotel
6	Sukhonta Hotel
7	Saeng Fa Hotel
8	Sri Taksin Hotel
9	Montien Hotel
10	King's Hotel
11	Cathay Guest House
12	Tong Nam Hotel
13	Angel Guest House
14	Seiko Hotel
15	Pueng Luang Hotel
16	Prince Hotel
17	Pacific Hotel
18	Kosit Hotel
19	Vegetarian Restaurant
20	Lee Garden Hotel
21	Jeng Nguan Restaurant
22	Nora Hotel
23	Grand Hotel

To Bangkok

Pratham   Uthit   Road

Choksaman   Road

Post Office

Road

Ratakan   Road

Sakornmongkol   Road

Santiraj

Road

Phetkasem   Road

Soontharnvithi   Road

Rat   Uthit   Road

Wat Hat Yai Nai

U Thapao Bridge

To Airport & Phuket

Railway Station & Railway Hotel

3°

Hat Yai

To Padang Basar

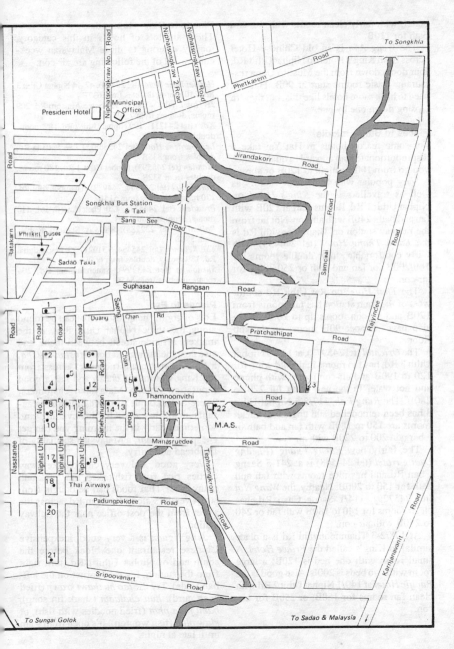

better, with fairly clean rooms with fan and bath for 110B.

The *Weng Aun* is an old Chinese Hotel across from King's Hotel on Niphat Uthit Rd, four doors down from the Muslim Ocha restaurant. Basic rooms start at 90B. Hat Yai used to have more hotels like this, but they're closing down one by one.

Places to Stay – middle

For some reason hotels in Hat Yai take a disproportionate leap upward in quality once you go from 100B a night to 120B or above.

Very popular with Malaysian visitors as well as travellers is the *King's Hotel* on Niphat Uthit 1 Rd. Rooms start at 120B with fan and bath, 240B with air-con. Not far from the railway station on Thamnoonvithi Rd is the *Laem Thong Hotel* (tel 244433) with fairly comfortable single/double rooms for 160/200B for fan and bath or 250/280B for air-con.

The *Thai Hotel* on Rat Uthit Rd southwest of the train station has fan rooms from 120B and air-con rooms up to 260B. They also have cheaper 90B rooms on the top floor.

The *Oriental* (tel 245977), at 137-9 Niphat Uthit 3 Rd, has fan rooms in the old wing for 120 to 190B and air-con rooms with phone and hot water in the new wing for 220 to 280B. The *Rung Fah*, 117/5-6 Niphat Uthit 3 has been remodelled and upgraded. Clean rooms are 150 to 180B with fan and bath or a bargain 200 to 220B with air-con.

The fairly new *Pueng Luang* (*Pheung Luang Hotel* (tel 244548) is at 241-5 Saeng Chan Rd and has nice rooms with fan and bath for 150 to 200B. Nearby, the *Wang Noi* (tel 245729), 114/1 Saeng Chan Rd, has clean rooms for 140 to 180B with fan or 240 to 250B with air-con.

At 138/2-3 Thamnoonvithi Rd is a place similar to King's called the *Prince Hotel*. A small room with one bed is 120B; a large room with two beds is 200B. Also good is the *Pacific Hotel* at 149/1 Niphat Uthit 2 Rd with clean fan rooms for 150B, or 250B for air-con.

Places to Stay – top end

There are lots of hotels in this category, mainly catering to those Malaysian weekenders. All of the following are air-con:

Hat Yai Inter Hotel (tel 24474), 42-44 Niphat Uthit 3 Rd, 210 rooms, doubles from 637B

JB Hotel (tel 234300/8), 99 Jootee Aunsorn Rd, 209 rooms, doubles from 750B

Kosit (tel 244711), 199 Niphat Uthit 2 Rd, 182 rooms, doubles from 506B

Lee Gardens Hotel (tel 245888), 1 Lee Pattana Rd, doubles from 835B

Montien (tel 245593), Niphat Uthit 1 Rd, 180 rooms, doubles from 532B

Nora Hotel (tel 244944, 244982), Thamoonvithi Rd, 170 rooms, doubles from 515B

President (tel 244477), 420 Phetchkasem Rd, 110 rooms, doubles from 620B

Rajthanee (tel 232288), Railway Station, doubles from 580B

The Regency (tel 245454, 231021) 23 Prachatiphat Rd, 189 rooms, doubles from 660B

Sukhontha (tel 243999), Sanehanusom Rd, 204 rooms, doubles from 545B

Places to Eat

Lots of good, cheap restaurants can be found along the three Niphat Uthit Rds, in the markets off side streets between them, and also near the railway station. *Muslim-O-Cha*, a Muslim restaurant (no pork) across from the King's Hotel, is cheap and has a good reputation among Malaysian customers. There are a couple of other Muslim restaurants near this one. In the evening and sometimes early in the morning you can get cheap *roti chanai*, a Malaysian speciality of flat bread and curry.

Very good and very cheap take-away curries, rice, fried fish cakes, haw mok and many other Thai foods can be bought from street vendors along Ratakan Rd, across the street from the post office near the railway station.

Jeng Nguan is a very good, inexpensive Chinese restaurant one block before the south end of Niphat Uthit 1 Rd (turn right from the station, it's on a corner on the left-hand side). Try the *tao hu thawt krawp* (fried bean curd), *huu chalaam* (shark fin soup), *bami plaa phat* (fried noodles with fish), or *kiaw plaa* (fish wonton). It's open from 9 am until late at night.

At this same end of Niphat Uthit 1, near the Dianna Club, are two or three places specialising in isaan food.

Another good restaurant in Hat Yai is *Niyom Rot* (the English sign says 'Niyom Rosh') in front of the expensive Nora Hotel on Thamnoonvithi Rd. The *plua krabawk thawt*, whole sea mullet fried with eggs intact, is particularly good.

On Thamnoonvithi Rd between Niphat Uthit Rds 1 and 2 are the *Thanad Sri Number 1* and *Thanad Sri Number 2* noodle shops, which serve very tasty and inexpensive noodle and rice dishes. They close at about 6 pm.

There's a hole-in-the-wall Thai vegetarian restaurant down Niphat Uthit 3 Rd. Rice plates with two choices of curry or whatever are 10B. Unfortunately, it's only open between 10.30 am and 2 pm.

Hat Yai restaurants have some intriguing names. Look for the *Plain Restaurant* and *Beatles Seafood*.

Nightlife

Most of the many clubs and coffee shops in town cater almost exclusively to Malaysian clientele. The bigger hotels like *The Regent* and *Sukhontha* have discos. The *Post Laserdisc* on Thamnoonvithi Rd, near the Indra Hotel, is a music video/laserdisc bar with an excellent sound system and well-placed monitors. It has mostly western movies, and programmes change nightly – the fairly up-to-date music videos are a filler between the films. The daily schedule starts at 10 am and goes until 1 am – mostly Thais and farangs come here.

Near the Post Laserdisc are *Sugar Rock* and *One of the Few*, trendy coffee houses popular with young Thais.

Four of Hat Yai's six cinemas have sound rooms where the original English soundtrack of English-language films can be heard while watching films that have been dubbed in Thai for the rest of the theatre: *Siam* (Phetkasem Rd), *Coliseum* (Pratchathipat Rd), *Chalerm Thai* (Suphasan Rangsan Rd) and the *Hat Yai Rama* (Phetkasem Rd).

Getting There & Away

Hat Yai is a very important travel junction – almost any Thailand-Malaysia trip involves a stop here.

Bus From Songkhla, big green buses leave every 15 minutes from Rong Muang Rd, across from the Songkhla National Museum, around the corner from the Songkhla Hotel, or they can be flagged down anywhere along Vichianchom Rd or Saiburi Rd, towards Hat Yai. The fare for these buses is 7B.

To Songkhla from Hat Yai, the green buses start from the Municipal Market. Share taxis also start from the market and from the corner of Supphasan Rangsan Rd. For buses from Bangkok to Hat Yai, see the Songkhla – Getting There & Away section.

Tour buses from Bangkok are 339B and they leave the Southern AC Bus Terminal every 15 minutes from 5.30 to 8.15 pm. The trip takes 13 hours. Ordinary buses cost 187B and they leave Bangkok at 9.45 and 10.50 pm.

From Padang Besar at the Malaysian border, buses are 13B and take an hour to reach Hat Yai. Bus services operate between 6 am and 4 pm.

There are also buses running between Phuket and Hat Yai; ordinary buses are 91B and air-con is 154B. The trip takes six hours.

Magic Tour, a travel agency downstairs from the Cathay Guest House, does express air-con buses and minivans to Penang, Kuala Lumpur, Singapore, Phuket, Krabi, Ko Samui and Bangkok. The Angel Guest House on Thamnoonvithi has a similar service.

Other bus information out of Hat Yai:

destination	fare	hours
Kuala Lumpur*	250B	12
Narathiwat	50B	3
(air-con)	60B	3
Pattani	30B	2½
Phattalung	22B	2
Satun	22B	2
(air-con)	30B	2
Singapore*	330B	15
SuratThani	67B	5
SuratThani*	150B	4½
Trang	35B	3
Yala	35B	2½

*Private tour bus companies:

Magic Tour (tel 234535), bottom floor Cathay Guest House

Hat Yai Swanthai Tours (tel 246706), 108 Thamnoonvithi Rd

Sunny Tour (tel 244156), Niphat Uthit 2 Rd

Pan Siam (tel 237440), 99 Niphat Uthit 2 Rd

Share Taxi Share taxis are an important way of getting from one province to another quickly in the south. There are five share taxi stands in Hat Yai, each specialising in certain destinations. Taxis to Songkhla, Phattalung, Trang, Narathiwat, Sungei Kolok and Nakhon Si Thammarat leave from Suphasan Rangsan Rd near Wat Cheu Chang.

Taxis to Phuket, Surat Thani, Padang Besar and Krabi leave from behind the Hat Yai Inter Hotel on Duang Chan Rd.

To Narathiwat and Penang, taxis leave from Niphat Uthit 1 Rd near the old An An Hotel.

To Sadao, Khu Khut and Ranot, taxis leave from near the President Hotel on Phetkasem Rd.

Finally, taxis to Yala leave from in front of the Cathay Guest House.

In general, share taxi fares cost about the same as an air-con bus, but they're about 30% faster. Share taxis also offer door-to-door drop-offs at the destination. A share taxi to Songkhla is 12B. A share taxi to/from Padang Besar is 25B. To Penang, they're 200B.

Train Trains from Bangkok to Hat Yai leave Hualamphong Station daily at 2 pm (Special Express No 19), 3.15 pm (Express 11) and 4 pm (Rapid No 43), arriving in Hat Yai at 5.47 am, 7.04 am and 8.50 am. The basic fare is 664B 1st class (Express only), 313B 2nd class or 149B 3rd class.

Surat Thani to Hat Yai costs 55B, 3rd class.

Air THAI flies to Hat Yai from Bangkok daily at 7.45 am, except Thursday when it leaves at 4.30 pm; on Wednesdays and Saturdays there is also a 10.45 am flight. Flights take an hour and 15 minutes. The fare is 1760B one way.

There are also flights to Hat Yai from

Phuket for 510B (Shorts) and 595B (Boeing) and from Hat Yai to Penang for 820B. Both THAI and MAS fly to Penang.

Getting Around

The innumerable songthaews around Hat Yai cost 4B per person. Watch out when you cross the street or they'll mow you down.

Phang-Nga Province

AO PHANG-NGA อ่าวพังงา

Over 94 km from Phuket Town, the area around Ao Phang-Nga is quite scenic – lots of limestone cliffs, odd rock formations, islands that rise out of the sea like inverted mountains, not to mention caves and quaint fishing villages. Phang-Nga would make a good motorcycle trip from Phuket, or, if you have time, you could spend a few days there.

On the way to Phang-Nga Town (population 9000), turn left off Route 4 just five km past the small town of Takua Thung, to get to Tham Suwan Kuha, a cave temple full of Buddha images. Between Takua Thung and Phang-Nga Town is the road to Tha Don, where you can find the Phang-Nga Customs Pier. It is at this pier that boats can be hired to tour Ao Phang-Nga, visiting a Muslim fishing village on stilts, half-submerged caves, strangely shaped islands (yes, including those filmed in the 007 flick, *Man with the Golden Gun*) and other local oddities. Worthwhile if you have the bread – say 400B for five hours for a whole boat.

Tours from Phuket cost around 300B per person, but one traveller related how he bargained a seat down to 50B by explaining that he didn't really care about air-con buses or seafood lunches! A postman from Ko Panyi named Sayan has been doing overnight tours of Ao Phang-Nga from Tha Don for several years now. They continue to receive good reviews from travellers. The tour is 200B per person and includes a boat tour of Tham Lot, a large water cave, Ko Phing Kan (Leaning Island), Ko Khao Tapu (Nail Mountain Island) and Ko Panyi, plus dinner, breakfast and accommodation in a Muslim fishing village on Ko Panyi. Look for him at Tha Don or in front of the market on the main street of Phang-Nga Town – he has his own bus and is usually there every morning around 8.30 or 9 am. He can be contacted through the Thawisuk Hotel as well. You can also take a ferry to Ko Panyi on your own for 20B.

Whatever you do, try to avoid touring the bay in the middle of the day (10 am to 4 pm) when hundreds of package tourists crowd the islands. On Ko Panyi always ask the price before eating as the restaurants often overcharge.

Phang-Nga's best beach areas are on the west coast facing the Andaman Sea. Between Thai Muang in the south and Takua Pa in the north are the beaches of Hat Thai Muang and Hat Bang Sak see the Khuraburi, Takua Pa & Thai Muang section for more detail.

Places to Stay & Eat

There are several small hotels in Phang-Nga Town. The *Thawisuk* is right in the middle of town, a bright blue building with the English sign 'Hotel'. Fairly clean, quiet rooms upstairs go for 80B, with fan, bath, towel, soap and boiled water – the best value in Phang-Nga. On the rooftop of Thawisuk you can sit and have a beer while watching the sun set over Phang-Nga's rooftops and the limestone cliffs surrounding the town.

The *Lak Muang* (tel 411125, 411288), on Phetkasem Rd, just outside town, towards Krabi, has rooms from 100B and a restaurant. The *Rak Phang-nga*, across the street from Thawisuk toward Phuket, is 80B but somewhat dirty and noisy. Further down the road towards Phuket is the *Muang Thong*, with adequate rooms for 100/150B a single/double. Outside town even further towards Phuket is *Lak Muang II* with all air-con rooms from 230B.

Several food stalls on the main street of Phang-Nga Town sell cheap and delicious khanom jiin with chicken curry, nam yaa, or nam phrik. There are also the usual Chinese khao man kai places.

The *Phang-Nga Bay Resort Hotel* (tel 411067/70) near the customs pier out of town is beyond the means of most budget travel-

lers (726 to 847B) but has a swimming pool and a decent restaurant. All rooms come with TV, telephone and fridge.

Getting There & Away

Buses for Phang-Nga leave from the Phuket Bus Terminal on Phang-Nga Rd, near the Thep Kasatri Rd intersection, hourly between 6.20 am and 6 pm. The trip to Phang-Nga Town takes 1¾ hours and the one-way fare is 22B. Alternatively you can rent a motorcycle from Phuket.

From Krabi a bus is 25B and takes 1½ hours. Songthaews between Phang-Nga Town and Tha Don (the Phang-Nga Customs Pier) are 7B.

HAT BANG SAK & HAT KHAO LAK
หาดบางลึก   หาดเขาหลัก

South of Takua Pa Town, 13 and 25 km respectively, are the beaches of Bang Sak and Khao Lak. The beach at Khao Lak is pretty, but somewhat stoney. Accommodation is available at *Khao Lak Bungalows* from 60B. Bang Sak is a long sandy beach backed by casuarina trees. Thais claim the roasted fish sold by vendors in Bang Sak is the best in Thailand. Both beaches are just a km or two off Highway 4.

KHURABURI, TAKUA PA & THAI MUANG
คุระบุรี   ตะกั่วป่า   เมืองไทย

These districts of Phang-nga Province are of little interest in themselves but are departure points for other destinations. From Khuraburi you can reach the remote Surin and Similan Islands or from Takua Pa you can head east to Khao Sok National Park and Surat Thani.

Takua Pa is also about halfway between Ranong and Phuket so buses often make rest stops here. Just off the highway is the *Extra Hotel* with rooms from 120B if you want to stop for the night.

In the district of Thai Muang is Thai Muang Beach National Park, where sea turtles come to lay eggs between November and February.

Krabi Province

Krabi Province has scenic karst formations near the coast, similar to those in Phang-Nga Province, even in the middle of the Krabi River. Krabi Town itself sits on the banks of the river right before it empties into the Andaman. Near town you can see Bird, Cat and Mouse Islands, named for their shapes. There is some excellent snorkelling offshore and among the 130 islands in the province. Hundreds of years ago, Krabi's waters were a favourite hide-out for Asian pirates because of all the islands and water caves. The interior, noted for its tropical forests and the Phanom Bencha mountain range, has barely been explored.

Krabi has a nearly new but, hardly used deep-sea port financed by local speculators in tin, rubber and palm oil, Krabi's most important sources of income. The occasional ship from Singapore (sometimes even a Singapore or Penang junk) anchors here and if you know the right people you can buy tax-free cigarettes and other luxury items while one of these boats is in port.

KRABI TOWN เมืองกระบี่

Nearly 1000 km from Bangkok and 180 km from Phuket Town, the fast-developing provincial capital, Krabi Town (population 16,000), has good beaches nearby, friendly townspeople and good food. Beach accommodation is reasonably priced (though not as cheap as Ko Pha-Ngan) and there are regular boats to Ko Phi Phi, 42 km west. Boats to Ko Phi Phi do not sail though during the monsoon season which begins in late May and ends in late September. The beaches of Krabi are nearly deserted in the rainy season, however, so this is still a good time to go. From December to March, the hotels and bungalows along Krabi's beaches can fill up. This part of Krabi has been 'discovered' by world travellers and beach bungalows are expanding operations to accommodate them.

Information

The post and telephone office is on Utarakit Rd past the turn-off for the Jao Fa pier. Visas can easily be extended at the Immigration Office, which is a bit further along the same road.

Krabi has dozens of fly-by-night travel agencies that book accommodation at beaches and islands as well as tour bus and boat tickets. Two good places for general travel info on Krabi as well as boat and bus bookings are Chan Phen on Utarakit Rd and Tip House on Prachacheun Rd.

Bangkok Guide has just begun issuing a *Guide Map of Krabi*, for 35B, that contains several mini-maps of areas of interest throughout the province. If it's kept up to date it should prove to be very useful for travel in the area.

A joint venture between THAI and the Thailand Cultural Centre is currently planning to renovate the Krabi Customs House on Jao Fa Rd and transform the building into a southern Thai cultural museum. When the project is completed, the museum will contain a collection of 30,000 year-old artefacts of local provenance, a seashell collection, and various folk items from southern Thai culture, such as chao nam (sea gypsies) folkcraft and costumes from *likhe ba* (jungle theatre) to other local performing arts.

Hat Nopparat Thara หาดนพรัตน์ธารา

Eighteen km north-west of Krabi Town, this beach used to be called Hat Khlong Haeng (Dry Canal Beach) because the canal that flows into the Andaman Sea here is dry except during and just after the monsoon season. Field Marshal Sarit gave the beach its current Pali-Sanskrit name, which means 'Beach of the Nine-Gemmed Stream', as a tribute to its beauty. The two-km-long beach is part of Hat Nopparat Thara, Phi Phi Islands National Marine Park, and is a favourite spot for Thai picnickers. It is a good place for shell-hunting. There are some government bungalows for rent and a visitors' centre of sorts, with wall maps of the marine park.

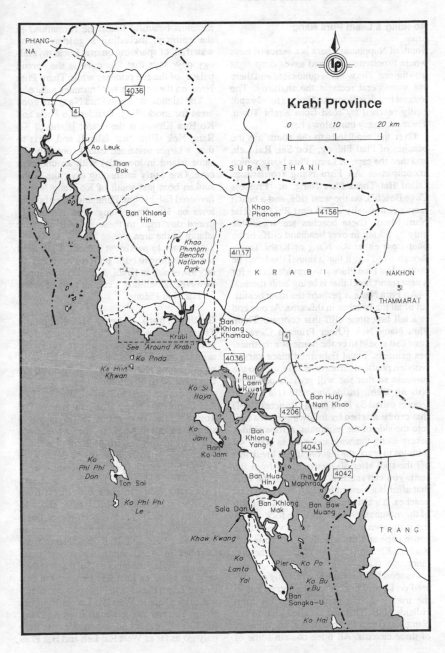

Krabi Province

0   10   20 km

PHANG-
NA

SURAT THANI

4036

4

Ao Leuk

Than
Bok

Ban Khlong
Hin

Khao
Phanom

4156

Khao
Phanom
Bencha
National
Park

4037

K R A B I

NAKHON
THAMMARAT

Ban
Khlong
Khamao

4036

Krabi

See 'Around Krabi'

Ko Pnda

Ko Hin
Khwan

Bun
Laem
Kruat

4

Ban Huay
Nam Khao

4206

Ko Si
Hoya

Ban
Khlong
Yang

Ko
Jam

4043

Ban
Ko Jam

Ko
Phi Phi
Don

Ton Sai

Ban Huay
Hin

Thai
Maphrao

4042

Ban Baw
Muang

Ko Phi Phi
Le

Ban Khlong
Mak

T R A N G

Sala Dan

Khaw Kwang

Ko
Lanta
Yai

Pier   Ko Po

Ko Bu
Bu

Ban
Sangka-U

Ko Hai

Ao Nang & Laem Phra Nang

ยาวนาง   แหลมพระนาง

South of Noppharat Thara is a series of bays where limestone cliffs and caves drop right into the sea. The water is quite clear and there are some coral reefs in the shallows. The longest beach is along Ao Nang, a lovely spot easily reached by road from Krabi Town. There are many bungalows here.

Over the headlands to the south are the beaches of Phai Phlong, Ton Sai, Rai Leh, and then the cape of Laem Phra Nang which encompasses Ao Phra Nang (sometimes called Hat Tham Phra Nang, or 'Princess Cave Beach'), on the west side, and a beach facing east usually called East Rai Leh (Hat Nam Mao). These beaches are accessible only by hiking in over headland cliffs or by boat from either Ao Nang or Krabi Town, though word has it that a tunnel road will be built to Hat Phai Phlong to provide access for a new resort hotel that is being built there.

Ao Phra Nang is perhaps the most beautiful of all the beaches in this area. At one end is a tall limestone cliff that contains Tham Phra Nang Nok (Outer Princess Cave), a cave that is said to be the home of a mythical sea princess. Local fishermen place carved wooden phalli in the cave as offerings to the princess so that she will provide plenty of fish for them. Inside the cliff is a hidden lagoon called Sa Phra Nang (Princess Pool) that can be reached by following a cave trail into the side of the mountain. A rope guides hikers along the way and it takes about 40 minutes to reach the lagoon. If you break left off the trail after 50 metres or so from the start, you can reach a 'window' in the cliff that affords a view of Rai Leh West and East beaches. It's also possible to climb to the top of the mountain from here (some rock climbing is involved) and get an aerial view of the entire cape and the islands of Ko Poda and Ko Hua Khwan (Chicken Island) in the distance.

A second, larger cave was recently discovered on Laem Phra Nang. The entrance is in the middle of the peninsula not far from Hillside Huts. This one is called Tham Phra Nang Nai (Inner Princess Cave) and consists of three caverns. All three contain some of the most beautiful limestone formations in the country, including a golden 'stone waterfall' of sparkling quartz. Local mythology now says that this cave is the 'grand palace' of the sea princess while Tham Phra Nang on the beach is her 'summer palace'.

The islands off Laem Phra Nang are good areas for snorkelling. Besides Ko Poda and Ko Hua Khwan is the nearer island of Ko Rang Nok (Bird Nest Island) and, next to that, a larger unnamed island (possibly the same island in low tide) with an undersea cave. One fairly interesting dive site is the sunken boat just south of Ko Rang Nok, a favoured fish habitat. Phranang Place bungalows on Hat Phra Nang does reasonably priced day trips to these as well as other islands in the area.

Contrary to persistent rumour, Club Med is *not* planning to build on Hat Phra Nang, or anywhere else in Krabi. A Phuket developer, however, is building a similar type of resort on Hat Phai Phlong.

Getting There & Away Hat Noppharat Thara and Ao Nang can be reached by songthaews that leave about every 15 minutes from 7 am to 5 pm from Utarakit Rd near the New Hotel. The fare is 15B and the trip takes 30 to 40 minutes.

You can get boats to Ton Sai, West Rai Leh and Laem Phra Nang at several places. For Ton Sai, the best thing to do is get a songthaew out to Ao Nang, then a boat from Ao Nang to Ton Sai. It's 15B per person for two people or more, 30B if you don't want to wait for a second passenger to show up.

For West Rai Leh or anywhere on Laem Phra Nang, you can get a boat direct from Krabi's Jao Fa Pier for 30B. It takes about 45 minutes to reach Phra Nang. However, boats will only go all the way round the cape to West Rai Leh and Hat Phra Nang from October to April when the sea is tame enough. During the other half of the year they only go as far as East Rai Leh, on the east side of Laem Phra Nang – but you can easily walk from here to West Rai Leh or Hat Phra Nang. You can also get boats from Ao Nang for 20B all year round, but in this case they only go as far as West Rai Leh and Hat Phra

Nang (again, you can walk to East Rai Leh from here).

Another alternative is to take a songthaew as far as Ao Nam Mao, a small fishing bay near the Shell Cemetery for 15B, and then a boat to Laem Phra Nang for 20B (three people or more required).

Some of the beach bungalows have agents in town who can help arrange boats – but there's still a charge.

Su-Saan Hawy (Shell Cemetery)
สุสานหอย

Nineteen km west of town, on Laem Pho, is the so-called Shell Fossil Cemetery, a shell 'graveyard', where 75-million-year-old shell fossils have formed giant slabs jutting into the sea. To get there, take a songthaew from the Krabi waterfront for 15B – ask for 'Su-Saan hawy'.

Wat Tham Seua   วัดถ้ำเสือ

In the other direction, about six km north and then eight km east of town, is Wat Tham Seua (Tiger Cave Temple), one of south Thailand's most famous forest wats. The main bot is built into a long, shallow limestone cave, on either side of which are dozens of kutis, or monastic cells, built into various cliffs and caves. The abbot is Achaan Jamnien, a Thai monk in his forties who has allowed a rather obvious personality cult to develop around him. The usual pictures of split cadavers and decaying corpses on the walls (useful meditation objects for countering lust) are interspersed with large portraits of Achaan Jamnien, who is well known as a teacher of vipassana (insight meditation) and metta (loving-kindness). It is said that he was apprenticed at an early age to a blind lay priest and astrologer who practised folk medicine and that he has been a celibate his entire life. Many young women come here to practise as eight-precept nuns.

The best part of the temple grounds can be found in a little valley behind the ridge where the bot is located. Follow the path past the main wat buildings, through a little village with nuns quarters, until you come to some steep stairways on the left. The first leads to an arduous climb to the top of a karst hill with a good view of the area. The second stairway leads over a gap in the ridge and into a valley of tall trees and limestone caves. Enter the caves on your left and look for light switches on the walls - the network of caves is wired so that you can light your way chamber by chamber through the labyrinth until you rejoin the path on the other side. There are several kutis in and around the caves, and it's interesting to see the differences in interior decorating – some are very spartan and others are outfitted like oriental bachelor pads. A path winds through a grove of trees surrounded by tall limestone cliffs covered with a patchwork of foliage. If you continue to follow the path you'll eventually end up where you started, at the bottom of the staircase.

Getting There & Away To get to Wat Tham Seua, take a songthaew from Utarakit Rd to the Talaat Kao junction for 3B, then change to any bus or songthaew going up Highway 4 towards Trang and Hat Yai and get off at the road on the left just after Km 108 – if you tell the bus operators 'Wat Tham Seua' they'll let you off in the right place. It's a two-km walk straight up this road to the wat.

In the mornings there are a few songthaews from Phattana Rd in town that pass the turn-off for Wat Tham Seua (10B) on their way to Ban Hua Hin. Also in the morning there is usually a songthaew or two going direct to Wat Tham Seua from Talaat Kao for around 5B.

Than Bokkharani Botanical Gardens
สวนพฤกษชาติ ธารโบกขรณี

Just after the rainy season, this place looks like a Disney fantasy, but it's real and entirely natural. Emerald green waters flow out of a cave cleft in a tall cliff and into a large lotus pool, which overflows steadily into a wide stream, itself dividing into many smaller streams in several stages. At each stage there's a pool and a little waterfall. Tall trees spread over 40 rai (6.4 square km) provide plenty of cool shade. Thais from Ao Leuk come to bathe here on weekends and then it's full of laughing people playing in the streams and pools. During the week there are only a

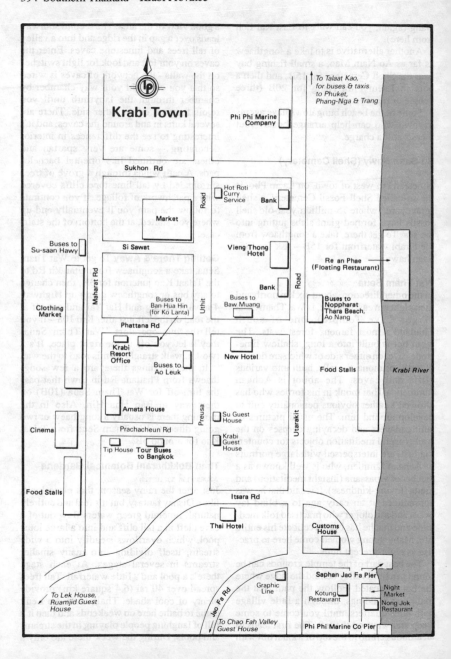

Krabi Town

Sukhon Rd

Market

Si Sawat

Buses to
Su-saan Hawy

Clothing
Market

Phattana Rd

Krabi
Resort
Office

Buses to
Ao Leuk

Amata House

Cinema

Prachacheun Rd

Tip House

Food Stalls

Maharat Rd

Buses to
Ban Hua Hin
(for Ko Lanta)

Tour Buses
to Bangkok

Road

Phi Phi Marine
Company

Hot Roti
Curry Service

Bank

Vieng Thong
Hotel

Bank

Buses to
Baw Muang

New Hotel

Preusa

Su Guest
House

Krabi
Guest
House

Itsara Rd

Thai Hotel

Uthit

Utarakit

Road

To Talaat Kao,
for buses & taxis
to Phuket,
Phang-Nga & Trang

Re an Phae
(Floating Restaurant)

Buses to
Noppharat
Thara Beach,
Ao Nang

Food Stalls

Krabi River

Customs
House

Saphan Jao Fa Pier

Graphic
Line

To Lek House,
Ruamjid Guest
House

Jao Fa Rd

Kotung
Restaurant

To Chao Fah Valley
Guest House

Phi Phi Marine Co Pier

Night
Market

Nong Jok
Restaurant

few people about, mostly kids doing a little fishing. Vendors sell noodles, roast chicken, delicious batter-fried squid and som-tam under the trees.

Getting There & Away Than-Bok, as the locals call it, is off Highway 4 between Krabi and Phang-Nga Towns, near the town of Ao Leuk, one km south-west toward Laem Sak. To get there, take a songthaew from the intersection of Phattana and Preusa Uthit Rds in Krabi Town to Ao Leuk for 10B; get off just before town and it's an easy walk to the park entrance on the left. The park looks its best in December, just after the monsoons – when it's been dry a long time, the water levels go down and in the midst of the rains it can be a bit murky.

Khao Phanom Bencha National Park
อุทยานแห่งชาติ เขาพนมเบญจา
This 50-square-km park is in the middle of virgin rainforest along the Phanom Bencha mountain range. The main scenic attractions are the three-level Huay To Falls, Khao Pheung Cave and Huay Sadeh Falls, all within three km of the park office. Other less well-known streams and waterfalls can be discovered here as well. Clouded leopards, black panthers, Asiatic black bears, deer, leaf monkeys, gibbons and various tropical birds make their home here. The park has a camp ground where you are welcome to pitch your own tent for 5B per person per night.

Getting There & Away Public transport direct to Khao Phanom Bencha National Park from Krabi Town or Talaat Kao are rare. Two roads run to the park off Highway 4. One is only about half a km from Talaat Kao – you could walk to this junction and hitch, or hire a truck in Talaat Kao all the way for a 100B or so. The other road is about 10 km north of Krabi off Highway 4. You could get to this junction via a songthaew or a bus heading north to Ao Leuk. It would be cheaper to rent a motorcycle in Krabi for a day trip to Phanom Bencha than to charter a pick-up.

Places to Stay – Town
Guest Houses The cheapest places in Krabi Town are the many guest houses which seem to be springing up everywhere. Some only stay around a season or two, others seem fairly stable. The ones in the business district feature closet-like rooms above modern shop buildings – OK for one night before heading to a nearby beach or island but not very suitable for long-term stays. Downtown you'll find the *Su Guest House* on Preusa Uthit Rd, with 60 to 70B rooms with shared bath. Similar to Su Guest House is the *Pee Pee Guest House* across the street. On Prachacheun Rd, *Fairly Tour* has clean rooms upstairs for 70 to 80B, or 40B for a dorm bed. There are others – *Krabi Guest House* on Preusa Uthit, *Jungle Book Guest House* – across from the floating restaurant on Utarakit Rd, each with 60B rooms without bath or 80 to 100B with.

Quieter and more comfortable are the guest houses just south-west of town near the courthouse. Out on Jao Fa Rd is the rather plain *Fawlty Tower Guest House* for 30B per person. Beyond, on the opposite side of the road, is the slightly up-market *Chao Fa Valley Guest House & Resort*, which has clean fan-cooled rooms for 80 to 300B, or air-con rooms for 350 to 500B, as well as a restaurant out front.

On Soi Ruam Jit, which is more or less parallel to Jao Fa Rd, are the *Ruamjid* and *Lek* guest houses, both with fair rooms for 70 to 80B. Between Soi Ruam Jit and Jao Fa Rd, accessed by an alley off Jao Fa, is *Sabai Guest House* for 60B a room. One more block west from Soi Ruam Jit on Itsara Rd is *Lek House* with large doubles for 60B or dorm for 30B.

Hotels Hotels in Krabi Town have always been lacking and the situation has not improved. The *New Hotel* (tel 611318) on Phattana Rd has adequate rooms for 120B with fan and bath, from 140B for air-con. The old wing of the *Thai Hotel* on Itsara Rd has disappeared, leaving only the new building with overpriced rooms. This used to be good value, but they seem to have raised the rates and lowered the standards. Rooms with fan start at 250B, air-con from 360B.

Better is the recently refurbished *Vieng (Wiang) Thong* (tel 611188, 611288) at 155 Utarakit Rd. Large doubles with fan and bath are 250B, with air-con 350B. Travellers seeking mid-range comfort would do better to lodge at the *Chao Valley Resort* or one of the other guest houses.

Outside town near the Talaat Kao Bus Terminal are the sleazy *Kittisuk*, on Si Phang-Nga Rd, and *Naowarat* on Utarakit Rd. The Kittisuk has a few 80B rooms, while the Naowarat starts at 180B.

Places to Eat

What Krabi Town lacks in hotels it more than makes up for in good eating places. Forget the expensive and not-so-tasty *Reuan Phae*, a floating restaurant on the river in front of town (though this might be a nice place to have a beer or rice whisky and watch the river rise and fall with the tide); next to it is a row of food stalls with cheap rice plates and noodles, including Muslim food like khao mok kai. Further south down Utarakit Rd is a night market next to the big pier (called Saphan Jao Fa) with great seafood at low prices and a host of Thai dessert vendors.

The fabulous *Tamarind Tree* is a small, family-run, open-air restaurant on the right side of Jao Fa Rd, just past the Chao Fa Valley Resort. Delicious southern Thai-style curries are only 10B per plate with rice, or you can get *khanom jiin nam yaa*, thin white wheat noodles with ground fish curry, for 5B. In the mornings they also serve khao yam, the southern Thai breakfast of rice mixed with dried shrimp, toasted coconut, ginger and lime – sort of the Thai equivalent of Swiss muesli – for 8B.

The *Thammachat* restaurant, at 15 Phattana Rd, has decent seafood and vegetarian dishes at reasonable prices. There are also food stalls next to the movie theatre on Maharat Rd and across the street from the theatre. Among these latter places is the *Amata House*, a thatched-roof cafe/bar favoured by young Thais and travellers. Amata House is open from 8 am until after midnight and is a good place to meet people.

They serve beer, coffee, tea, fruit shakes, western breakfasts and a few snacks and baked goods. Similar, and in the same vicinity, is *Tip House* at 49 Prachacheun Rd.

One of the best restaurants in town for standard Thai dishes and local cuisine is the *Kotung* near Saphan Jao Fa Pier. The tom yam kung is especially good, as is anything else made with fresh seafood. One of the specialities of the house is *hawy lawt*, a tube-like shellfish that looks something like 'squid-in-a-shell', quickly steamed/stir-fried in a sauce of basil and garlic – delectable. Two people can order three dishes, rice and a large Singha for about 100B, a bargain when you remember the beer costs half that. Also excellent for seafood, and very popular among locals, is the *Nong Jok* across the street next to the night market.

For cheap Thai breakfasts, the morning market off Si Sawat Rd in the middle of town is good. Not far from the morning market on Preusa Uthit Rd is a Muslim place that serves roti chanai, the Malaysian-style breakfast of flat bread and curry. Look for a sign that says 'Hot Roti Curry Service'.

Places to Stay – Beaches

Ao Nang The *Krabi Resort* (tel 611300, 611198) is at the north end of Ao Nang and has overpriced bungalows that cost 1100B up on the water, 880B off. They also have a dorm for 50B per person but reports say it's dirty and has rats. Most of the guests are with package tours or conferences. There are the usual resort amenities, including a swimming pool, bar and restaurant. Bookings can be made at the Krabi Resort office in town on Phattana Rd and they'll provide free transport out to the resort for guests.

Also along Ao Nang are several budget bungalow operations, though rates are gradually increasing with demand. Near the turn-off for the Krabi Resort but not on the beach are *Ao Nang Ban Leh* with 70B huts, shared bath, and the *Ao Nang Hill* for 40 to 60B. On the water is *PS Cottage* with huts for 150B with private bath. Going south along the beach you'll come to *Ao Nang Beach*, 50B for simple huts or 150B for larger huts with bath. Next is the *Coconut*

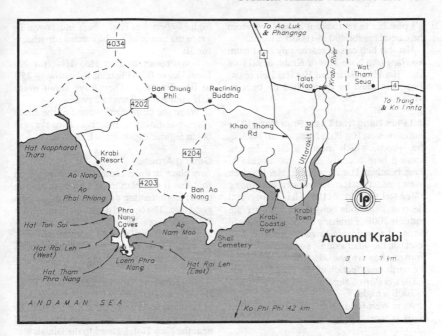

Around Krabi

Garden bungalows for 60B without bath, 150B with.

The beach road intersects with Route 4203 to Krabi Town just before you arrive at *Phra-Nang Inn* (tel 612173, 612174), a tastefully designed 'tropical hotel' with sweeping views of the bay. Roomy bungalows with fan and bath are 150 to 250B while large air-con rooms are 666 to 1000B a night. They also have a good restaurant.

Next door is the *Ao Nang Villa*, also a good place, with a few bungalows without bath for 60B, or 150 to 300B with.

Up Route 4023, a hundred or so metres from the beach, is the *Princess Garden*, which has 45B huts with shared bath or 120B with private bath. Further up the road are the *Apex*, 150B with bath, and the *Krabi Seaview Resort*, which costs 80B for simple huts, and up to 450B for larger huts with air-con and bath.

Hat Phai Phlong The *Phai Phlong Bungalows* was forced to close when the land-owners sold this beach to a Bangkok hotel conglomerate. At the moment there is no accommodation here, but if they haven't started building the planned resort yet, it might be worth boating over for the day – nice beach.

Ao Ton Sai This beach can only be reached by boat from Ao Nang, Ao Nam Mao or Krabi. Until very recently, *Andaman Bungalows* provided highly praised accommodation, but a new owner has moved in and at this writing there's no word on prospective development, though it will probably be something up-market.

Hat Rai Leh (West) There are three places to choose from here. *Railay Village* has 150B huts with bath, and *Railae Beach* has the same plus 50B huts without bath. *Sunset* has larger bungalows, all with private bath, for 200 to 300B for three to four people. All have dining areas. At the north end of the beach is a private beach condominium development.

It's possible to rent vacant bungalows from the caretakers for 400 to 1000B a night.

Hat Rai Leh can be reached by boat from Ao Nang, Ao Nam Mao or Krabi, or on foot from Hat Phra Nang and Hat Rai Leh (east) (but these must be approached by boat as well).

Hat Phra Nang (Hat Tham Phra Nang)
The bungalows on Hat Phra Nang are all back in the woods, which means a clean beach. Staying here actually gives you access to three beaches: Hat Phra Nang, Hat Rai Leh (west) and Hat Rai Leh (east). *Phranang Place* (tel 611944, 611955) has nearly 100 clean and spacious bungalows with private bath for 200B. Phranang Place spreads right across the peninsula towards Hat Rai Leh (east) on the other side – you can easily walk from one beach to the other. Next door, along the north-west section of Hat Phra Nang, are the newer *Phra Nang Bay* bungalows for 150 to 200B a night.

As at West Rai Leh and Hat Ton Sai, Phra Nang is accessible by boat only.

Hat Rai Leh (East)
Besides Phranang Place, there are three other smaller bungalow operations here. *Queen* has standard bungalows for 150B, while *Ya-Ya* has tree houses for 50 to 100B. At the north end of the beach is *Hill Side Huts* for 70B with shared bath, 150B with private bath. This beach tends toward mud flats during low tide.

Getting There & Away
Catch buses to Krabi from Phuket's bus terminal on Phang-Nga Rd at 12.50 pm or 2.30 pm. The price is 38B. More expensive minivans can be arranged at various travel agencies as well.

Buses for Krabi leave Phang-Nga Town several times a day for 20B. Direct Krabi to Surat buses take 4½ hours for 50B. From Hat Yai it's 60B and four hours; from Trang, 30B, 2½ hours. There are also share taxis to/from Trang, Hat Yai and Satun. The share taxi fare is roughly twice ordinary bus fare.

Out-of-province buses to/from Krabi arrive at and depart from Talaat Kao, a junction about four km north of Krabi on the highway between Phang-Nga and Trang. To get to the centre of Krabi, catch a songthaew for 3B.

Songthaews to Ban Hua Hin (for Ko Lanta) leave from Phattana Rd in town – 25B to Ban Hua Hin. They leave about every half-hour from 10 am to 2 pm.

When the current renovation of the Krabi Airport is finished, Bangkok Airways will begin regular flights from Bangkok.

Getting Around
Any place in town can easily be reached on foot, but if you plan to do a lot of exploring out of town, renting a motorcycle might be a good idea. The Suzuki dealer on Preusa Uthit Rd rents bikes for 150 to 200B a day. A couple of other places do motorcycle rental as well, including the Graphic Line travel agency on the corner of Jao Fa and Utarakit Rds.

Songthaews to Ao Leuk (for Than Bokkharani Park) leave from the intersection of Phattana and Preusa Uthit Rds for 10B. To Ao Nang (15B) they leave from Utarakit Rd near the New Hotel. Boats to the islands and beaches mostly leave from Jao Fa Pier. See the Ao Nang & Laem Phra Nang section for boat details.

KO PHI PHI เกาะ พี พี
Ko Phi Phi actually consists of two islands about 40 km from Krabi Town, Phi Phi Le and Phi Phi Don.

Phi Phi Don พีพี ดอน
Phi Phi Don is the larger of the two islands, sort of a dumb-bell shaped island with scenic hills, awesome cliffs, long beaches, emerald waters and remarkable bird and sea life. The 'handle' in the middle has long white-sand beaches on either side, only a few hundred metres apart. The beach on the south side curves around Ao Ton Sai, where boats from Phuket and Krabi dock. There is also a Thai Muslim village here. On the north side of the handle is Ao Lo Dalam. The uninhabited (except for beach huts) western section of the island is called Ko Nawk (outer island), and the eastern section, which is much larger, is Ko Nai (inner island). At the north of the east

end is Laem Tong, where the island's chao nam (sea gypsies) population lives. The number of chao nam here varies from time to time, as they are still a somewhat nomadic people, sailing from island to island, stopping off to repair their boats or fishing nets, but there are generally about 100. Like Pacific islanders of perhaps 100 years ago, they tend to be very warm and friendly horizon-gazers.

Hat Yao (Long Beach) faces south and has some of Phi Phi Don's best coral reefs. Ton Sai, Lo Dalam and Hat Yao all have beach bungalows. Over a ridge, north-west from

Hat Yao, is another very beautiful beach, Hat Lanti, with good surf, but the locals won't allow any bungalows here out of respect for the large village mosque situated in a coconut grove above the beach. Further north is the sizeable bay of Lo Bakao, where there is a small resort, and near the tip of Laem Tong is yet another resort.

Phi Phi Le พีพีเล

Phi Phi Le is almost all sheer cliffs, with a few caves and a sea lake formed by a cleft between two cliffs that allows water to enter into a bowl-shaped canyon. The so-called

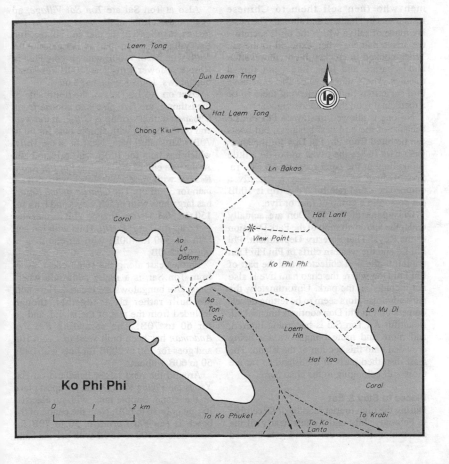

Ko Phi Phi

Viking Cave contains prehistoric paintings of ships (Asian junks) and is also a collection point for sea swallow nests. The swallows like to build their nests high up in the caves in rocky hollows which can be very difficult to reach. Agile collectors build bamboo scaffolding to get at the nests but are occasionally injured or killed in falls. People who want to collect sea swallow nests must bid for a licence in competition with other collectors which gives them a franchise to harvest the nests for four years. In one year there are only three harvests, as the birds build seasonally, and the first harvest fetches the highest prices. The collectors sell the nests to middlemen who then sell them to Chinese restaurants in Thailand and abroad. The nests are made of saliva which the birds secrete – the saliva hardens when exposed to the air. When cooked in chicken broth, they soften and separate and look like bean thread noodles. The Chinese value the expensive bird secretions highly, believing them to be a medicinal food that imparts vigour.

No-one is allowed to stay on Phi Phi Le because of the bird nest business, but boats can be hired from Phi Phi Don for the short jaunt over to see the caves and to do a little snorkelling at the coral reefs in Ao Ma-Ya. Spear-fishing here is so easy it's nearly a crime. The usual rate for a day trip is 100B per person in a group of four or five.

Only parts of Phi Phi Don are actually under the administration of the Park Division of the Royal Thai Forestry Department. Phi Phi Le and the western cliffs of Phi Phi Don are left to the nest collectors and the part of Phi Phi Don where the chao nam live is also not included in the park. Unfortunately, the park administrators seem to be letting development on Phi Phi Don continue unchecked. Beautiful Ao Ton Sai is becoming littered, and more and more bungalows are being crowded onto this section of the island. The least disturbed parts of the island so far are those still belonging to the chao nam.

Places to Stay & Eat

During the high tourist months of December to February, July and August nearly all the accommodation on the island gets booked out. As elsewhere during these months, it's best to arrive early in the morning to stake out a room or bungalow.

At Ao Ton Sai, there are three places to stay. The *Pee Pee Islands Cabana* has the greatest capacity and variety of accommodation, with quite nice one-bed bungalows for 100B, two-bed bungalows with bath for 500B and a nine-person bungalow for 630B. Dorm accommodation is also available for 70B per person and there are tents for 50B. The restaurant, *Ma-Yah Kitchen*, is a bit on the expensive side. To book in advance, contact the Phi Phi Marine Travel Co in Krabi.

Also at Ton Sai are *Ton Sai Village*, up against the cliffs to the west and *Phi Phi Resort*, to the east of the pier and village. Ton Sai Village has up-market bungalows for 750B with fan or 1100B with air-con. Phi Phi Resort is lower priced at 100B for small bungalows, 150B for the large ones.

Over on Ao Lo Dalam, the north side of the isthmus, are five places to choose from. Cheapest at this writing is *Gift 2*, at the west end of the beach, with simple huts for 50 to 70B with shared bath. Next in is the *Vally*, which has huts for 100B with private bath. At the east end of the beach is *Phi Phi Krabi Resort*, with nice bungalows with private bath for 300B up. The *Charlie Beach Resort* has large huts with beach views and bath for 150 to 350B. On the hillside a bit further east is the up-market *P P Hill*. Huts with fan and bath are 300 to 400B; with air-con they're 600 to 1200B.

Further east along the south coast, away from Ton Sai, is a rocky peninsula where *Laem Hin* bungalows are located. Here huts are built rather close together, though secluded from the rest of the island, and go for 60 to 70B. The sprawling *Phi Phi Andaman* has been built west of Laem Hin and goes for 150 to 200B for huts with bath, 50 to 60B without.

Around the next larger headland on Hat Yao is the *Viking Village*, the cheapest place on the island. Simple huts, with no electricity, are only 30 to 60B. Near the centre of the beach is *Phi Phi Paradise*, 50 to 70B for basic huts or 100 to 150B with private bath.

Finally, near the end of the beach, is the long-running *Long Beach*. Since they've added a generator, bungalow rates have gone up to 80B without bath, 150B with. Nearby snorkelling is good. The best way to get to Hat Yao is to walk along the trail through the centre of the island over the hills to the beach, where the bungalows are located, although it is possible to walk along the shoreline all the way, if you don't mind picking your way across rocky points.

The two resorts on the north end of the island are *Pee Pee Island Village*, at Lo Bakao, and *P P International Resort* near Chong Kiu village on Laem Tong. Pee Pee Island has some 60 air-con bungalows on stilts for 950B up. They also offer water sports like wind-surfing and diving. P P International is similar and starts at 1200B.

Food on Ko Phi Phi is touch and go, varying according to how recently a boat delivery of food has been made. Seafood is always abundant, but vegetables scarce. Most bungalows' kitchens are rather so-so, except for more expensive places like the Pee Pee Cabana, which have their own boats.

Getting There & Away

Ko Phi Phi is equidistant from Phuket and Krabi Town, but Krabi Town is your most economical point of departure. From either place, boats only travel during the dry season, from late October to May, as the seas are too rough during the monsoons. Sometimes when there's a lull in the weather, they'll risk sending boats out during the monsoons.

From Krabi Town's Jao Fa Pier, there are usually three boats a day (during the season) leaving at 9 am, 1 and 3 pm. Passage is 100 to 125B per person, depending on the boat, and the trip takes about 1 hour 45 minutes on the faster boats, or 2½ hours on the slower ones. You can also get boats from Ao Nang on the Krabi Province coast for 100B from October to April; the fare is 100B per person and there's only one departure a day at around 2 pm.

From Phuket, boats leave Hat Patong at 9 am, 1, 2, 3 and 4 pm for 150 to 200B per person. This trip takes 1½ hours on the fast

boat, and up to three hours on the slow boat. During the rainy season, there is occasionally a 1 pm boat to Ko Phi Phi.

Various tour companies in Phuket offer day trips to Phi Phi, for 350 to 450B per person, that include round-trip transport, lunch and a tour. If you want to stay overnight and catch another tour boat back, you have to pay another 100B. Of course it's cheaper to book a one-way passage on the regular ferry service.

Pee Pee Islands Cabana also does package deals from Krabi or Phuket that include accommodation and a tour of Phi Phi Le.

As Ko Lanta is becoming more touristed, there are now fairly regular boats between that island and Ko Phi Phi from October to April. Boats generally leave from the pier on Lanta Yai around 10.30 pm, arriving at Phi Phi Don around 12.30 pm. In the reverse direction the departure is usually at 2.30 pm. Passage is 100B per person. It's also possible to get boats to/from Ko Jam; the same approximate departure time, fare and trip duration applies.

See the Krabi Town Getting There & Away section for transport to Krabi.

KO JAM (KO PU) & KO SI BOYA
เกาะ พยาม   เกาะสีบอยหน้า

These large islands are inhabited by a small number of fishing families. At this writing there is one set of bungalows on the west side of Ko Si Boya called *Islander Hut* for 70B per night, and another on Ko Jam's southern end called *Jum Island Resort*. The latter costs from 50B up, but will soon be replaced by a 40-house, 120-room hotel development called *Starry Nights Over the Andaman*. Ko Jam is also called Ko Pu.

Getting There & Away

Boats to both islands leave two or three times a day from Ban Laem Kruat, a village about 30 km from Krabi Town, at the end of Route 4036, off Highway 4. Passage is 15B to Si Boya, 20B to Ban Ko Jam.

You can also get direct boats from Krabi's Jao Fa Pier for 50B. At this point, there is only one daily boat which leaves around 2 pm, but service from Krabi is liable to increase after the new hotel is built.

KO LANTA เกาะลันตา

Ko Lanta (population 18,000) is an island district of Krabi Province south of the provincial capital that consists of 52 islands. Twelve of those islands are inhabited and, of these, three are large enough to be worth exploring, Ko Klang, Ko Lanta Noi and Ko Lanta Yai. At present you have to get there by ferry from either Ban Hua Hin, on the mainland across from Ko Lanta Noi, or from Baw Muang, further south. Ko Lanta Yai is the largest of the three islands – this is also where the district offices are. The west sides of all the islands have beaches. The best are along the south-west end of Lanta Yai, but practically the whole west coast of Lanta Yai is one long beach interrupted by the occasional stream or shell bed. Coral reefs are located along parts of the west side of Lanta Yai and along the Khaw Kwang (Deer Neck) cape at its north-western tip. A hill on the cape gives a good aerial view of the island.

The people in this district are a mixture of Muslim Thais and chao nam who settled here long ago. There are now several inexpensive bungalow operations on Lanta Yai and you can camp on any of the islands – all have sources of fresh water. The village of Ban Sangka-U on Lanta Yai's southern tip is a traditional Muslim fishing village and the people are friendly. Ban Sala Dan at the northern end is the largest village on the island and even has a few TVs.

The little island between Ko Lanta Noi and Ko Klang has a nice beach called Hat Thung Thale – hire a boat from Ko Klang. Also worth exploring is Ko Hai – see the Trang Province section for more details as Ko Hai is more accessible from that province.

Places to Stay

None of the beach places on Ko Lanta have electricity so far – quiet, lamplit nights are the rule. At the northern end of Lanta Yai near Ban Sala Dan is the *Khaw Kwang Beach Bungalows*. It's actually on the south-east side of the small peninsula of the same name

that juts west from the island. Nicely separated huts on a long curving beach are 50B per person, or you can rent tents for 50B per night.

About three km south of Ban Sala Dan along the west side of the island are two more places, *Lanta Villa* and *Lanta Sea House*. Both have basic huts for 50B or 80 to 100B with private bath.

Another 11 km or so down the beach is *Lanta Marina Hut*, a nicely designed place on shady grounds, with large bungalows for 80B, with toilet inside and shower outside. They also have a few huts without toilet for 50 to 70B. Four or five km further, near the end of the district road, is the *Lanta Palace*, which is similar to the Lanta Marina Hut in price and facilities.

After this the road ends, but a dirt track continues to Ban Sangka-U. At the last beach on the south-western tip of the island should be the *Amata* bungalows, a project planned by the same Krabi Town residents who used to manage the now-defunct Phai Plong Bungalows near Ao Nang.

If you get tired of bungalow food there are a couple of basic places to eat in Sala Dan village at the northern end of Lanta Yai. One place near the pier has great khao yam and pa-thong-ko in the mornings.

Getting There & Away

The usual way to get to Ko Lanta is to get a songthaew, for 25B, from the Talaat Kao junction outside Krabi Town all the way to Ban Hua Hin, and then a boat across the narrow channel, for 10B, to Ban Khlong Mak on Ko Lanta Noi. From there, you get a motorcycle taxi, for 20B, across to another pier on the other side, and get another boat, for 5B, to Ban Sala Dan on Ko Lanta Yai. Ban Hua Hin is 26 km, down Route 4206, from Ban Huay Nam Khao, which is about 44 km from Krabi Town along Highway 4. If you're travelling by private car or motorcycle, the turn-off for Route 4023 is near Km 63 on Highway 4. Songthaews from Krabi Town (Talaat Kao junction) to Ban Hua Hin run regularly until about 2 pm. It takes about two hours because most of 4023 is unpaved (though locals say it should be paved within the next two years).

From Ban Sala Dan on Lanta Yai you can get a motorcycle taxi to Hat Khaw Kwang for 10B, or pay 30 to 40B to other beaches. You can also hike to Khaw Kwang from Sala Dan, as it's only two km

If you're travelling by car, you'll have to park near the pier in Ban Hua Hin. If you have a motorcycle, you can take it on both ferries all the way to Ko Lanta Yai.

The other way to get to Ko Lanta from the mainland is to get a boat from Ban Baw Muang, which is about 35 km from Ban

Huay Nam Khao at the end of Route 4042 (about 80 km in total from Krabi Town). The turn-off for Route 4042 is at Km 46 near the village of Sai Khao. It's 13 km from Ban Sai Khao to Ban Baw Muang on this dirt road. The boats from Ban Baw Muang are fairly large, holding up to 80 people, and they sail for an hour before reaching Lanta Yai. The fare is 30B.

During the dry season, October to April, there are fairly regular boats from Ko Phi Phi for 100B per person. They take about 1½ hours to reach Ban Sala Dan. There are also occasional boats to Lanta from the Saphan

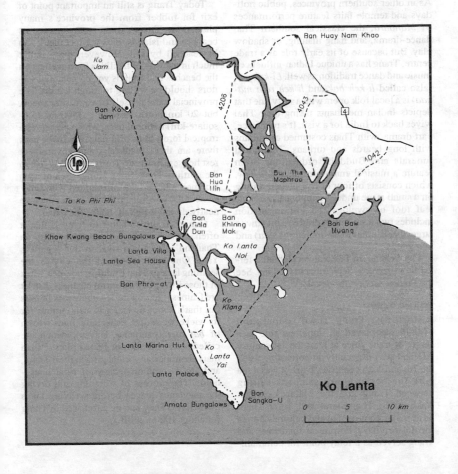

Ko Lanta

0   5   10 km

Jao Fa pier in Krabi – ask at Phi Phi Marine Transport, on Utarakit Rd, or at any of the guest houses in town – and from the pier on Ko Jam.

Trang Province

The province of Trang has a geography similar to that of Krabi and Phang-Nga, but is much less frequented by tourists.

Music and Dance

As in other southern provinces, public holidays and temple fairs feature performances of *Manohra*, the classical southern Thai dance-drama, and nang thalung, or shadow play. But because of its early role as a trade centre, Trang has a unique Indian-influenced music and dance tradition as well. *Li-keh paa* (also called *li-keh bok* and *li-keh ram manaa*) is a local folk opera with a story line that depicts Indian merchants taking their Thai wives back to India for a visit. It's part farce, part drama, with Thais costumed as Indians with long beards and turbans. Traditional funerals and Buddhist ordinations often feature a musical ensemble called *kaa-law*, which consists of four or five players sitting on a small stage under a temporary coconut-leaf roof or awning. The instrumentation includes two long Indian drums, a *pii haw* (a large oboe similar to the Indian *shahnai*) and two gongs.

The Vegetarian Festival is celebrated fervently in Trang in September or October. See the Phuket section for details.

TRANG TOWN เมืองตรัง

Historically, Trang Town (population 47,000) has played an important role as a centre of trade since at least the 1st century AD and was especially important between the 7th and 12th centuries, when it was a sea port for ocean-going sampans sailing between Trang and the Malacca Straits. Nakhorn Si Thammarat and Surat Thani were major commercial and cultural centres for the Srivijaya Empire at this time, and Trang served as a relay point for communi-

cations between the east coast of the Thai peninsula and Palembang, Sumatra. Trang was then known as Krung Thani and later as Trangkhapura (City of Waves) until the name was shortened during the early years of the Rattanakosin period. During the Ayuthaya period, Trang was a common port of entry for seafaring western visitors, who continued by land to Nakhorn Si Thammarat or Ayuthaya. The town was then located right at the mouth of the Trang River, but later King Mongkut gave orders to move the city to its present location inland because of frequent flooding.

Today Trang is still an important point of exit for rubber from the province's many plantations. Trang's main attractions are its beaches and islands, plus the fact that it can be reached by rail. However, there is not much in the way of facilities for travellers on the beaches and islands yet, so potential visitors should be willing to rough it a bit. The provincial capital itself doesn't offer much, but 20 km north there is a 3500-rai (5.6-square-km) national park, which preserves a tropical forest in its original state. In the park there are three waterfalls and government rest houses. Between Trang and Huay Yot to the north is Thale Song Hong (Sea of Two Rooms), a large lake surrounded with limestone hills. The hills in the middle of the lake nearly divide it in half, hence the name.

One of Trang's claims to fame is that it often wins awards for 'Cleanest City in Thailand' – its main rival in this regard is Yala. One odd aspect of the city is the seeming lack of Thai Buddhist temples. Most of those living in the central business district are Chinese, so you do see a few joss houses but that's about it. Trang is also famous for its wickerwork and, especially, mats woven of *bai toei* (pandanus leaves), which are called *seua paa-nan*, or Panan mats. Panan mats are important bridal gifts in rural Trang, and are a common feature of rural households. The process of softening and drying the pandanus leaves before weaving takes many days. They can be purchased in Trang for about 100 to 200B.

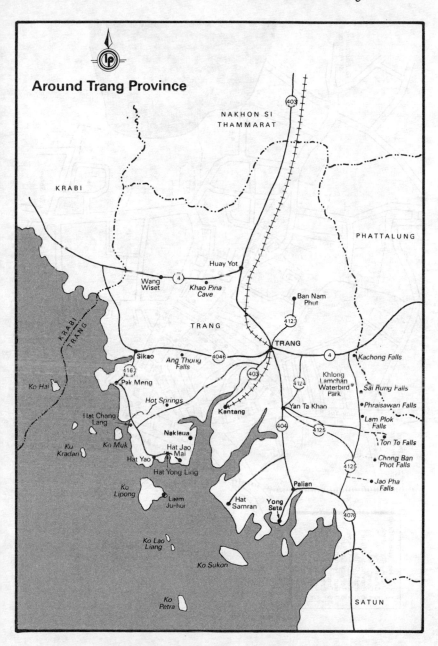

Around Trang Province

NAKHON SI THAMMARAT

KRABI

PHATTALUNG

Huay Yot

Wang Wiset

④

Khao Pina Cave

Ban Nam Phut

403

TRANG

4123

K R A B I   T R A N G

Sikao

Ang Thong Falls

4046

TRANG

④

Kachong Falls

Ko Hai

4162

Pak Meng

403

4124

Khlong Lamchan Waterbird Park

Sai Rung Falls

Hot Springs

Kantang

Yan Ta Khan

Phraisawan Falls

Hat Chang Lang

Nakleua

404

4125

Lam Plok Falls

Ko Kradan

Ko Muk

Hat Jao Mai

Ton Te Falls

Hat Yao

Hat Yong Ling

Chong Ban Phot Falls

4125

Ko Lipong

Laem Ju-hoi

Palian

Jao Pha Falls

Hat Samran

Yong Sata

4078

Ko Lao Liang

Ko Sukon

SATUN

Ko Petra

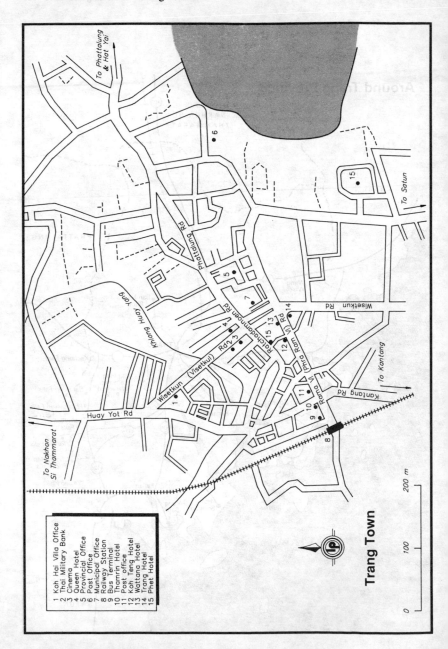

1 Koh Hai Villa Office
2 Thai Military Bank
3 Cinema
4 Queen Hotel
5 Provincial Office
6 Post Office
7 Municipal Office
8 Railway Station
9 Bus Terminal
10 Thamrin Hotel
11 Post Office
12 Koh Teng Hotel
13 Wattana Hotel
14 Trang Hotel
15 Phet Hotel

Trang Town

To Phattalung & Hat Yai
To Satun
To Kantang
To Nakhon Si Thammarat

Phattalung Rd
Phattalung Rd
Wisetkun Rd
Khlong Yong
Wisetkun (Visetkul) Rd
Ratchadamnoen Rd
Rama VI (Phra Ram VI) Rd
Kantang Rd
Huay Yot Rd

0   100   200 m

Places to Stay & Eat

There are a number of places on the main streets, Phra Ram VI Rd, Visetkul (Wisetkun) Rd and Ratchadamnoen Rd, which run from the clock tower. The *Ko Teng* (tel 218622) on Phra Ram VI Rd has clean single/double rooms for 110/150B and a good restaurant downstairs. They also have an information board of sorts with details on Trang attractions. The *Wattana Hotel* (tel 218184) is on the same stretch, and a little more expensive, but not good at all.

Over on Ratchadamnoen Rd is the inexpensive *Petch (Phet) Hotel* (tel 218002), with fair rooms with fan and bath for 70B. They also have a restaurant downstairs.

On Visetkul Rd are the *Queen Hotel* (tel 218522), with large clean rooms for 140B, or 220 B with air-con, and the *Trang Hotel* (tel 218944), near the clock tower, with fan rooms from 160B, air-con for 240B. Queen is the better value of the two.

Top end is the *Thamrin* (tel 218507) on Kantang Rd near the train and bus stations. Air-con rooms are 420 to 700B.

Plenty of good restaurants can be found in the vicinity of these hotels. Next door to the Queen Hotel is the *Phloen Restaurant*, which has a very broad selection of rice and noodle dishes. The menu (Thai only) has several vegetarian dishes including *wun-sen phat jeh sai phong kari*, bean-thread noodles stir-fried with curry powder, *kwetiaw phat haeng tao-huu*, rice noodles fried with tofu, and *khao naa ka-phrao tao-hu*, tofu stir-fried with holy basil over rice. Or make it simple and get *khao phat jeh*, vegetarian fried rice. Another house speciality is *kafae phloen*, a spiced coffee made with local Khao Chong coffee.

Another good place for the local coffee is the *Kafae Khao Chong* food stall on Phattalung Rd, open from 7 am until 10 pm. The *Sinjew* on Kantang Rd also has Khao Chong coffee and is open all night.

Trang Town is justly famous for *khanom jiin* (Chinese pasta). One of the best places to try it is at the tables set up at the corner of Visetkul and Phra Ram VI Rds. You have a choice of dousing your noodles in *nam yaa* (a spicy ground fish curry), *nam phrik* (a sweet and slightly spicy peanut sauce), or

kaeng tai plaa (a very spicy mixture of green beans, fish, bamboo shoots and potato). To this you can add your choice of fresh grated papaya, pickled veggies, cucumber and bean sprouts – all for 5B per bowl. Across the street from this vendor is a small night market in front of the municipal offices.

Getting There & Away

Bus & Share Taxi A bus from Satun, Hat Yai or Krabi to Trang is 35B. A share taxi from the same cities is around 50B. From Phattalung it's 15B by bus, 20B by share taxi.

From Ban Huay Nam Khao, the junction for Highway 4 and the road to Ko Lanta, a bus to Trang is 20B.

Air-con buses to/from Bangkok are 288B (160B for an ordinary bus). The air-con buses take about 12 hours to do the route.

Train Only one train goes all the way from Bangkok to Trang, the Rapid No 41, which leaves Hualamphong Station at 6.30 pm, arriving in Trang at 10.10 am the next day. You can also catch a train in Thung Song, a rail junction town in Nakhorn Si Thammarat Province. From here, there are two trains daily to Trang, leaving at 9.25 am and 3.35 pm, arriving an hour and 45 minutes later.

If you want to continue on to Kantang on the coast, there is one daily train out of Trang at 5.18 pm which arrives in Kantang at 6 pm. The Bangkok to Trang fare is 301B 2nd class, 155B 3rd class, including the Rapid surcharge. Trang-Kantang is 4B in 3rd class.

Air THAI has one daily flight to Trang from Phuket at 4.25 pm, arriving 30 minutes later. The closest Bangkok-Phuket flight to that departure time is the 11.15 am flight which arrives in Phuket at 12.30 pm. The Phuket to Trang fare is 315B; from Bangkok the through fare is 1660B, a savings of 200B over separate tickets.

BEACHES

Trang Province has several sandy beaches and coves along the coast, especially in the Sikao and Kantang districts. From Route 403 between Trang Town and Kantang is a turn-off west onto an unpaved road that leads down to the coast. At the end, it splits north and south. The road south leads to Hat Yao, Hat Yong Ling and Hat Jao Mai. The road north leads to Hat Chang Lang and Hat Pak Meng.

Hat Jao Mai & Ko Lipong
หาด เจ้าไหม́   เกาะลิ้พอง

Both Hat Jao Mai and Ko Lipong can be found in Kantang district, about 35 km from Trang. The wide white-sand beach is five km long and gets some of Thailand's biggest surf (probably the source of the Trang's original unshortened name, City of Waves). Hat Jao Mai is backed by pine trees and limestone hills with caves, some of which contain pre-historic human skeletal remains. Tham Jao Mai is the most interesting of the caves, a large cavern with lots of stalactites and stalagmites. This beach is part of Hat Jao Mai National Park, which includes Hat Chang Lang further north and the islands of Ko Muk, Ko Kradan, Ko Jao Mai, Ko Waen, Ko Cheuak, Ko Pling and Ko Meng. Camping is permitted on Jao Mai and there are a few bungalows for rent as well.

Off the coast here is Ko Lipong, Trang's largest island. There are three fishing villages on the island, so boats from Kantang port are easy to get for the one-hour trip. The Botanical Department maintains free shelters on Laem Ju-Hoi, a cape on the western tip of Ko Lipong. On the south-western side of the island is a beach where camping is permitted.

Hat Yong Ling & Hat Yao
หาดยองลิ่ง   หาดยาว

North of Hat Jao Mai a few km are these two white-sand beaches separated by limestone cliffs. There is no accommodation here as yet.

Hat Chang Lang, Ko Muk & Ko Kradan
หาดฉางลาง   เกาะมุกข์   เกาะกระดาน

Hat Chang Lang is part of the Hat Jao Mai National Park, and this is where the park office is located. The beach is about two km long and very flat and shallow. At the north end is Khlong Chang Lang, a stream that empties into the sea.

Ko Muk is nearly opposite and can be

reached by boat from Kantang or Pak Meng. The coral around Ko Muk is lively, and there are several small beaches on the island suitable for camping and swimming. Near the north end is Tham Morakot (Emerald Cave), a beautiful limestone tunnel that can be entered by boat during low tide. At the south end of the island is pretty Phangka Cove and the fishing village of Hua Laem.

Ko Kradan is the largest of the islands that belong to Hat Jao Mai National Park. Actually, only five of six precincts on the island belong to the park; one is devoted to coconut and rubber plantation. There are fewer white-sand beaches on Ko Kradan than on Ko Muk, but the reef on the side facing Ko Muk is said to be good for diving. Private accommodation is available on Ko Kradan.

Hat Pak Meng
หาดแพกเม้ง

Thirty-nine km from Trang in Sikao district, north of Hat Jao Mai, Yao and Yong Ling, is another long, fine sand beach near the village of Ban Pak Meng. A couple of hundred metres offshore are several limestone rock formations, including a very large one with caves. To get there, take a bus to Sikao from Trang, and then a songthaew to Ban Pak Meng. Total fare should be about 20B. A road now connects Pak Meng with the other beaches south, so if you have your own wheels there's no need to backtrack through Sikao.

Around the beginning of November, locals flock to Hat Pak Meng to collect *hawy taphao*, a delicious type of clam. The tide reaches its lowest this time of year, so it's relatively easy to pick up the shells.

About halfway between Pak Meng and Trang, off Route 4046, is the 20-metre-high Ang Thong Falls.

Hat Samran & Ko Sukon
หาดสำราญ   เกาะสุรินทร์

Hat Samran is a beautiful and shady white-sand beach in Palian district, about 40 km south-west of Trang city. From the customs pier at nearby Yong Sata you should be able to get a boat to Ko Sukon (also called Ko Muu), an island populated by Thai Muslims, where there are more beaches.

Ko Hai เกาะ ไห

This island is actually part of Krabi Province to the north, but is most accessible from Trang. It's a fairly small island, covering about 3000 rai (4.8 square km), but the beaches are fine white sand and the water is clear.

Places to Stay Along the east shore of Ko Hai are three places to stay. Near the north end is *Koh Hai Village* (tel 218674) with air-con bungalows for 980B (extra bed 120B) or tents for 150B a day. Further south, towards the middle of the island, is *Koh Hai Villa* (218923), with less expensive fan-cooled bungalows for 300B a day and tents for 150B. At the south end is *Hai Island Resort* (tel 210317) where rooms are 490/630B for singles/doubles or 840B for a seven-bed room. Two-person tents are 150B a night, while larger four-person tents are 300B.

You can book any of these through the Koh Hai Villa Travel Agency in Trang, 8/19 Visetkul (Wisetkun) Rd. Each has its own office in the city, but this one is the most conveniently located if you're staying in the central business district.

Getting There & Away Two boats a day leave the pier at Pak Meng for Ko Hai at 10 am and 2 pm. The fare is 50B and the trip takes about 40 minutes. You can also charter a boat at the pier for 300B. A taxi from Trang to Pak Meng is 25B per person.

WATERFALLS

Trang Province recently paved a road that runs south from Highway 4 near the Trang-Phattalung border past a number of scenic waterfalls. The waterfalls are created by the meeting of the Trang and Palian Rivers (and/or their tributaries) and the Khao Banthat Mountains. Ton Te Falls is probably the most striking. It's 46 km from Trang Town. Ton Te is best seen during, or just after the rainy season, say from September to November, when the 320-metre waterfall is at its fullest.

Chao Pha Falls in the Palian district near Laem Som has about 25 levels of five to 10 metres each, with pools at every level. The semi-nomadic Sakai tribe are sometimes seen in this area.

KHLONG LAMCHAN WATERBIRD PARK
นวอุทยานนกน้ำ คลองลำชาน

This is a large swampy area similar to Thale Noi or Ku Khut on the east coast of Songkhla, where many waterbird species congregate. Accommodation is available.

Satun Province

Satun (sometimes spelled Satul) is Thailand's southernmost province, on the west coast, bordering Malaysia.

SATUN TOWN เมือง สตูล

Satun Town itself is not that interesting, but you may enter or leave Thailand here by boat via Kuala Perlis in Malaysia. Sixty km north of Satun is the small port of Pak Bara, the departure point for boats to Ko Tarutao National Park, Satun's big attraction.

Eighty percent of Satun's population is Muslim; in fact, throughout the entire province there are only 11 or 12 Buddhist temples, in contrast to 117 mosques. As in Thailand's other three predominantly Muslim provinces, (Yala, Pattani and Narathiwat) the Thai government has installed a loudspeaker system in the streets which broadcasts government programmes at 6 am and 6 pm (beginning with a wake-up call to work and ending with the Thai national anthem, for which everyone must stop and stand in the streets), either to instil a sense of nationalism in the typically rebellious southern Thais, or perhaps to try and drown out the prayer calls and amplified sermons from local mosques. As in Pattani and Narathiwat, one hears a lot of Yawi spoken in the streets.

If you are going to Kuala Perlis in Malaysia, remember that banks in Malaysia are not open on Thursday afternoons or Friday, due to the observance of Islam.

Places to Stay & Eat

Satun The *Rian Thong Hotel* (English sign says 'Rain Tong') is at the end of Samanta

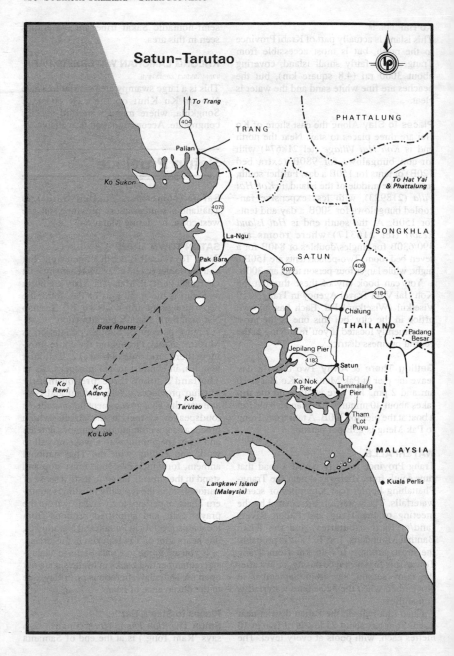

Satun-Tarutao

To Trang

PHATTALUNG

TRANG

Palian

Ko Sukon

To Hat Yai
& Phattalung

La-Ngu

Pak Bara

SATUN

SONGKHLA

Boat Routes

Chalung

THAILAND

Padang
Besar

Ko Rawi

Ko Adang

Jepilang Pier

Ko Tarutao

Satun

Ko Nok
Pier

Ko Lipe

Tammalang
Pier

Tham Lot
Puyu

Langkawi Island
(Malaysia)

MALAYSIA

Kuala Perlis

Prasit Rd, next to the Rian Thong Pier, an embarkation point for boats to and from Malaysia. Large, clean rooms are 100B. The *Satun Thani Hotel*, near the centre of town is OK, with 100B rooms, air-con for 220B. Also in the centre of town is the not-so-clean *Thai Niyom Hotel*, with rooms from 60B.

Near the municipal offices on Hatthakam Seuksa Rd is the clean and friendly *Udomsuk Hotel* (tel 711006), where rooms start at 80B.

South of town a bit, on Wiset Mayura Rd, is the *Slinda (Salinda) Hotel*, which caters mostly to Malaysian tourists. Rooms start at 100B, but are not very well kept.

Top end in Satun is the newish *Satun Wang Mai Hotel* (tel 711607/8), near the north end of town on Satun Thani Rd. All rooms have air-con and start at 270B.

Near the gold-domed Bambang Mosque in the centre of town are several cheap Muslim food shops. The roti shop across from the Shell service station on Satun Thani Rd serves great *roti kaeng*, roti with curry, all day and into the night. It's 3B per roti or 5B with egg – the curry dip is free. Two *roti khai* (egg roti) make a filling breakfast.

The *Ajjara (Atjara)* garden restaurant near the municipal office and the Udomsuk Hotel has good isaan food and is not too expensive.

For Chinese food, wander about the little Chinese district near the Rian Thong Hotel. There's nothing fancy, just a few noodle shops and small seafood places.

La-Ngu & Pak Bara La-Ngu has a couple of cheap hotels. The *G Guest House*, in Pak Bara, is about 200 metres before the pier. Clean rooms are 50B and can sleep two to three people. There are several food stalls near the Pak Bara pier that do fruit shakes and seafood.

Getting There & Away
Bus & Share Taxi A share taxi to Satun from Hat Yai is 35B. The taxi stand in Hat Yai is opposite the post office near the railway station. A bus is about half that. Buses from Trang are 35B, share taxis 50B.

An air-con bus from Bangkok's Southern AC Bus Terminal leaves once a day at 6.30 pm, and costs 355B. But this is really too long a bus trip – if you want to get to Satun from Bangkok, it would be better to take a train to Padang Besar on the Malaysian border and then a bus or taxi to Satun. Padang Besar is 60 km from Satun. See the following Train section.

Boat From Kuala Perlis, in Malaysia, boats are M$4. Depending on the time of year and the tides, boats from Malaysia will either dock at Tammalang Pier, in the estuary south of Satun Town, or right in Satun, on Khlong Bambang, near the Rian Thong Hotel. From Satun, the boats cost 40B from the river pier in Satun or 20B from Tammalang.

Train The only train that goes all the way to Padang Besar is the Special Express No 11, which leaves Hualamphong Station at 3.15 pm and arrives in Padang Besar around 8 am the next day. The basic fare is 744B for 1st class, 376B for 2nd class, including the Special Express surcharge.

Getting Around
A songthaew to Tammalang Pier (for boats to Malaysia) costs 6B from Satun. A motorcycle taxi costs 15 to 20B.

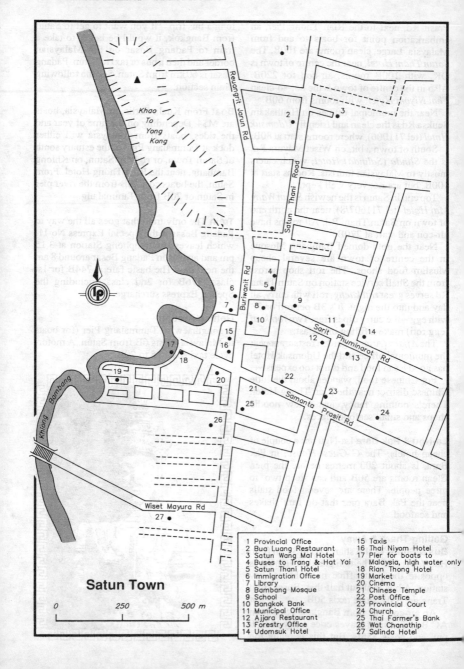

Satun Town

0   250   500 m

1 Provincial Office
2 Bua Luang Restaurant
3 Satun Wang Mai Hotel
4 Buses to Trang & Hat Yai
5 Satun Thani Hotel
6 Immigration Office
7 Library
8 Bambang Mosque
9 School
10 Bangkok Bank
11 Municipal Office
12 Ajjara Restaurant
13 Forestry Office
14 Udomsuk Hotel

15 Taxis
16 Thai Niyom Hotel
17 Pier for boats to
   Malaysia, high water only
18 Rian Thong Hotel
19 Market
20 Cinema
21 Chinese Temple
22 Post Office
23 Provincial Court
24 Church
25 Thai Farmer's Bank
26 Wat Chanathip
27 Salinda Hotel

Khao To Yong Kong

Reuangrit Jarun Rd

Satun Thani Road

Buriwanit Rd

Sarit Phuminarot Rd

Samanta Prasit Rd

Wiset Mayura Rd

Khlong Bambang

KO TARUTAO MARINE PARK

อุทยานฉัตว์น้ำ เกาะตะรุเตา

This park is actually a large archipelago of 51 islands, approximately 30 km from Pak Bara in La-Ngu district, which is 40 km from Satun Town. Ko Tarutao, the biggest of the group, is only five km from Langkawi Island in Malaysia. Only five of the islands have any kind of regular boat service to them, Tarutao, Adang, Rawi, Lipe and Klang, and, of these, only the first three are generally visited by tourists.

Ko Tarutao is about 151 square km in size, and features waterfalls, inland streams, beaches, caves and protected wildlife that includes dolphins, sea turtles and lobster. Nobody lives on this island except for employees of the Royal Forest Department. The island was a place of exile for political prisoners between 1939 and 1947, and remains of the prisons can be seen near Ao Talo Udang, on the southern tip of the island, and at Ao Talo Wao, on the middle of the east coast. There is also a graveyard, charcoal furnaces and fermentation tanks for making fish sauce. Tarutao's largest stream, Khlong Phante Malaka, enters the sea at the north-west tip of the island at Ao Phante; the brackish waters flow out of Tham Jara-Khe (Crocodile Cave - the stream was once inhabited by ferocious crocodiles, which seem to have disappeared). The cave extends for at least a km under a limestone mountain — no-one has yet followed the stream to the cave's end. The mangrove-lined watercourse should not be navigated at high tide, when the mouth of the cave fills.

The park pier, headquarters and bungalows are also here at Ao Phante Malaka. The best camping is at the beaches of Ao Jak and Ao San, two bays south of park headquarters. For a view of the bays, climb Topu Hill, 500 metres north of the park office. There is also camping at Ao Makham (Tamarind Bay), at the south-west end of the island, about 2½ km from another park office at Ao Talo Udang. There is a road between Ao Phante, in the north, and Ao Talo Udang, in the south, of which 11 km were constructed by political prisoners in the '40s, and 12 km were more recently constructed by the park division.

The road is, for the most part, overgrown, but park personnel have kept a path open to make it easier to get from north to south without having to climb over rocky headlands along the shore. Ko Rang Nok (Bird Nest Island), in Ao Talo Udang, is another collection place for the expensive swallow nests craved by Chinese throughout the world. Good coral reefs are at the north-west part of the island at Pha Papinyong (Papillon Cliffs), at Ao San and in the channel between Ko Tarutao and Ko Takiang (Ko Lela) off the north-west shore.

Ko Adang is 43 km west of Tarutao, and about 80 km from Pak Bara. Ko Adang's 30 square km are covered with forests and fresh-water streams, which fortunately supply water year-round. There is a park office here, as well as a few bungalows. Camping is allowed. Ko Rawi is just east of Ko Adang, and a bit smaller. Off the west coast of Ko Adang, and the south-east coast of Ko Rawi, are coral reefs with many live species of coral and tropical fish. Ko Lipe is immediately south of Ko Adang, and is inhabited by about 500 'sea gypsies', known by the Thais as chao leh or chao nam, and by the Malays as *orang rawot* or *orang laut*. They subsist on fishing and some cultivation of vegetables and rice on the flatter parts of the island. They are said to have originated from the Lanta islands in Krabi Province. One can camp here, or rent a hut from the chao nam. There is a coral reef along the south side of the small island and several small beachy coves.

Between Ko Tarutao and Ko Adang-Rawi, there is a small cluster of three islands, called Mu Ko Klang (Middle Island Group), where there is good snorkelling. One of the islands, Ko Khai, also has a good white-sand beach. Boats from Ko Tarutao take about 40 minutes to reach Ko Khai.

Places to Stay

Park accommodation on Ko Tarutao is 800B for a large 'deluxe' bungalow, or 200B for the smaller 'standard'. A longhouse has four-bed rooms for 50B per person. The park also rents tents for 60B, or you may pitch your own for 5B per person. Bungalows may be booked in advance at the park office in Pak

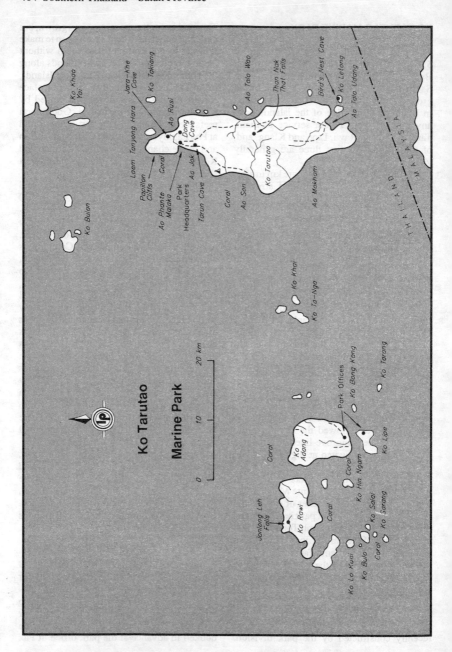

Ko Tarutao

Marine Park

Bara. Bungalows on Ko Adang are only 50B per person. For Ko Tarutao and/or Ko Adang, bring as much of your own food as you can from Satun or Pak Bara – the park restaurant is horrendous and expensive. On Ko Lipe you have a choice of places to stay and eat among the chao nam – a plus.

The Forestry Department is considering requests from private firms to build hotels and bungalows in Tarutao National Park. This is a very unfortunate event if it means Ko Tarutao is going to become like Ko Phi Phi or Ko Samet, both of which are national parks that have permitted private development, with disastrous results.

Getting There & Away

Boats to Tarutao leave regularly between November and April from the pier in Pak Bara, 65 km north of Satun Town and 22 km from Ko Tarutao. The rest of the year there is no boat service and the park is supposedly closed. Satun Province officials are planning to construct a new pier in Tan Yong Po district nearer Satun Town, that will serve tourist boats to Tarutao and other islands, possibly on a year-round basis.

For now, the park service has given the boat concession over to a private company in Pak Bara, Nong Darin. Their boats leave Pak Bara for Tarutao daily at 10.30 am and 2 pm. The fare is 120B, round trip, and it takes one to two hours, depending on the boat. Food and beverages are available on the boat.

From Tarutao there are three boat departures a week to Ko Adang and Ko Lipe. These are at 12 noon on Tuesday, Thursday and Saturday. The boats return to Tarutao from Ko Adang on Wednesday, Friday and Sunday at 8 am. Tickets for the Tarutao-Adang boat are 250B, round trip, if you stay one night only, 350B if you stay more than one night. This trip takes 2½ hours each way. As more people travel to Ko Tarutao, ticket prices will probably come down. Boats back to Pak Bara from Tarutao leave daily at 9 am and 2 pm.

There are also occasional tour boats out to Tarutao, but these are usually several hundred baht per person, as they include a guided tour, meals, etc. Your final alternative is to charter a boat with a group of people.

The cheapest are the hang yao (long-tail boats), which can take eight to 10 people out from Pak Bara's commercial pier for 500B. On holidays, boats may travel back and forth to Tarutao every hour or so to accommodate the increased traffic.

To get to Pak Bara from Satun, you must take a share taxi or bus to La-Ngu, then a songthaew on to Pak Bara. Taxis to La-Ngu leave from in front of the Thai Niyom hotel when there are enough people to fill a taxi for 20B per person. Frequent buses leave from the same place for 10B. From La-Ngu, songthaew rides to Pak Bara are 6 to 8B and terminate right at the harbour.

You can also travel to La-ngu from Trang by songthaew for 20B. From Hat Yai you would take a bus to the junction town of Chalung (19B, 1½ hours), which is about 15 km short of Satun, then get a songthaew north on Route 4078 for the 10B, 45 minute trip to La-ngu. Once a day, at 7.45 am, there is a direct bus to Pak Bara from Hat Yai for 29B. In the reverse direction, it leaves Pak Bara for Hat Yai at 4.30 pm.

It is also possible to hire boats to Ko Tarutao from three different piers (*thuu reua*) on the coast near Satun Town. The nearest is the Ko Nok Pier, three km south of Satun (40 km from Tarutao). Then there is the Tammalang Pier, nine km from Satun, on the opposite side of the estuary from Ko Nok Pier. Tammalang is 35 km from Tarutao. Finally there's the Jepilang pier 13 km east of Satun (30 km from Tarutao).

Yala Province

Yala is the most prosperous of the four predominantly Muslim provinces in south Thailand, mainly due to income from rubber production, but also because it is the number one business and education centre for the region.

YALA TOWN เมืองยะลา

The fast-developing capital (population 65,000) is known as 'the cleanest city in Thailand' and has won awards to that effect

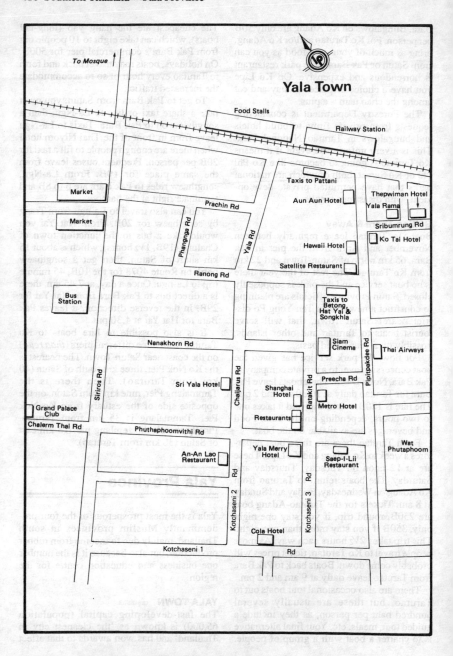

Yala Town

To Mosque

Food Stalls

Railway Station

Market

Market

Prachin Rd

Taxis to Pattani

Aun Aun Hotel

Thepwiman Hotel

Yala Rama

Sribumrung Rd

Ko Tai Hotel

Phangnga Rd

Yala Rd

Hawaii Hotel

Satellite Restaurant

Ranong Rd

Bus Station

Taxis to Betong, Hat Yai & Songkhla

Siam Cinema

Thai Airways

Pipitpakdee Rd

Nanakhorn Rd

Preecha Rd

Metro Hotel

Thai Rd

Siriros Rd

Sri Yala Hotel

Chaijarus Rd

Shanghai Hotel

Ratakit Rd

Restaurants

Grand Palace Club

Chalerm Thai Rd

Phuthaphoomvithi Rd

Wat Phuthaphoom

An-An Lao Restaurant

Yala Merry Hotel

Saep-I-Lii Restaurant

Kotchaseni 2 Rd

Kotchaseni 3 Rd

Cola Hotel

Kotchaseni 1

Rd

three times in the last 25 years (its main competitor is Trang). It's a city of parks, wide boulevards and orderly traffic. During the dry season there are nightly musical performances in Chang Phuak Park, in the south-east part of the city just before the big Lak Muang traffic circle, off Pipitpakdee Rd. The new Phrupakoi Park, just west of the *lak muang* (city pillar), has a big man-made lake where people can fish, go boating and eat in floating restaurants. Yala residents seem obsessed with water recreation, possibly as a consequence of living in the only landlocked province in the entire south. There is a public swimming pool in town at the Grand Palace restaurant and disco.

One of the biggest regional festivals in Thailand is held in Yala Town each year, during the last six days of June, to pay respect to the city guardian spirit, Jao Paw Lak Muang. Chinese New Year is also celebrated here with some zest, as there are many Chinese living in the capital. The Muslim population is settled in the rural areas of the province, for the most part, though there is a sizeable Muslim quarter near the railway station in town – you'll know it by the sheep and goats wandering in the streets and by the modern mosque – Yala's tallest building and the largest mosque in Thailand.

Wat Naa Tham

Outside of town, about eight km east off the Yala to Hat Yai highway, is Wat Khuhaphimuk (also called Wat Naa Tham the cavefront temple), a Srivijaya-period cave temple established around 750 AD. Inside the cave is Phra Phutthasaiyat, a long reclining Buddha image sculpted in the Srivijaya style. For Thais, this is one of the three most venerated Buddhist pilgrimage points in southern Thailand (the other two are Wat Boromthat in Nakhon Si Thammarat and Wat Phra That Chaiya in Surat Thani). There is a small museum in front of the cave, with artefacts of local provenance.

Two km past Wat Naa Tham is Tham Silpa, a cave with murals from the Srivijaya era. A monk from Wat Naa Tham may be able to guide you there. There are several other caves in the vicinity worth exploring for their impressive stalactite and stalagmite formations.

Getting There & Away Take a songthaew going east towards the town of Yaha or Hat Yai and ask to get off at the road to Wat Naa Tham – fare is 2B. It's about a one-km walk to the wat from the highway.

Places to Stay

Yala has quite a few hotels at all price levels. Starting from the bottom, the *Shanghai Hotel*, *Metro Hotel* and the *Saen Suk* are all nearly identical Chinese hotels with Chinese restaurants on the ground floor. All are on the same block on Ratakit Rd, in the business district, not far from the railway station. All three have somewhat dreary rooms from 60B; the Saen Suk is a bit cleaner than the other two, and its restaurant is also better, specialising in generous plates of chicken rice (khao man kai) for 15B.

At the next level is the *Sri Yala Hotel* (tel 212815) at 16-22 Chai Jarat Rd (the street sign says Chaijarus), with clean rooms for 120B, a restaurant and a popular coffee shop. The *Hawaii* and *Aun Aun* hotels, on Pipitpakdee Rd, are the first hotels you see as you walk into town from the railway station. The Hawaii is over-priced for what you get at 120B, but the Aun Aun is OK at 60B without bath, 80 to 90B with. The *Thepwiman Hotel*, a left turn from the station on Sribumrung (Si Bamrung) Rd, across from the Yala Rama, with rooms from 100B, aircon for 200B, is better.

Moving up a bit more, the *Yala Merry* (tel 212693), on Phutthaphumwithi and Kotchaseni 3 Rds, is a clean and quiet place at 120B for a very nice room with fan and bath (150B for two beds), or 170B for air-con. At the south end of this block, around the corner on Kotchaseni 1 Rd, is the *Cola Hotel* with 100B rooms similar to the Thepwiman.

Top end is the *Yala Rama* on Sribumrung Rd near the station. Here, a room with fan and bath is 170B, while air-con rooms are 250 to 299B. All rooms have two beds. The coffee shop and the night club here are quite popular.

Places to Eat

There are plenty of inexpensive places to eat in downtown Yala, near all the hotels, especially Chinese restaurants along Ratakit and Ranong Rds. The *Saen Suk* hotel restaurant has good khao man kai, and the food stall next door, *Mae Prapai*, has good curry and rice plates for 8B – both Malaysian and Thai curries.

The *Suay Suay* indoor/outdoor restaurant, on Sri Bumrung Rd near the Rama Hotel, and the big *Satellite* restaurant on the corner of Pipitpakdee and Ranong Rds specialise in steamed cockles. On Phuthaphumwithi Rd between the Yala Merry Hotel and Wat Phuthaphoom are *Laila*, a Muslim garden restaurant and, directly across the street, the *Saep-I-Lii Restaurant*, a small, cheap, north-eastern Thai restaurant.

On Kotchaseni 2 Rd, a couple of blocks down the street from Sri Yala Hotel, is the *An An Lao Restaurant*, a large garden restaurant specialising in kai betong, quite good and reasonably priced. The *Grand Palace Club*, at the end of Phuthaphumwithi Rd, in the opposite direction from Wat Phuthaphum, serves fancy Thai and Chinese food at fancy prices.

The day market on Siroros (Sirorot) Rd has a good selection of fresh fruit. The Muslim foodstalls nearby serve roti kaeng in the early morning – a cheap and filling breakfast.

Getting There & Away

From Hat Yai, ordinary trains are 23B 3rd class, and take three hours. By share taxi the trip is 50B and takes about one hour.

From Sungai Kolok, at the Malaysian border, trains are 22B for a 2½-hour trip, or 60B by share taxi. Buses to/from Pattani are 9B for the one-hour trip. Buses south to Sungai Kolok or Pattani leave from Siroros Rd near the Ranong Rd intersection. Buses north (to Hat Yai, etc) leave from Siroros Rd, north of the railway tracks.

Air-con buses between Bangkok and Yala are 384B. A 2nd-class seat on the train is 366B, including Rapid surcharge. The Rapid No 45 leaves Bangkok daily at 12.30 pm and arrives in Yala at 6.34 am the next day. The Special Express leaves at 1.40 pm and arrives at 9.45 am – add 100B for mandatory air-con and Special Express surcharges to the above fare.

BAN SAKAI   บ้านซาไก

The well-known village of Ban Sakai is in Tharato district, about 80 km south of Yala on the way to Betong. Ban Sakai is the home of some of Thailand's last remaining Sakai tribes, called 'Ngaw' by Thais because their frizzy heads and dark complexions remind Thais of the outer skin of the rambutan fruit (*ngaw* in Thai). Anthropologists speculate that the Sakai are the direct descendants of a Proto-Malay race that once inhabited the entire Thai-Malay peninsula and beyond (also called Negritos, 'an aboriginal jungle race allied to negroid pygmies found in the Philippines, New Guinea and parts of Africa', according to George McFarland). It is maintained that they were subjugated by technologically more advanced Austro-Thai cultures from the north. At any rate, the peaceful, short-statured Sakai still lead a traditional village life of hunting and gathering, practice very little agriculture and express themselves through their own unique language, music and dance. Recently a development project has got the Sakai involved in tending rubber plantations.

Also in Tharato district is Tharato Falls, which is now a national park.

BETONG   เบตง

Betong is 140 km south-west of Yala Town on the Malaysian border, and is Thailand's southern-most point. The area surrounding Betong is mountainous and jungle-foliated and morning fog is not uncommon in the district. Both Thai and Malaysian authorities believe that the Communist Party of Malaysia has its hidden headquarters somewhere in the vicinity. Occasionally, there are joint Thai-Malaysian military operations here in search of so-called 'Target 1', so this is a bit of a hot spot – a large contingent of Thai troops are in fact stationed at Camp Sirinthon, an Army base near Yala Town. The Pattani United Liberation Organization (PULO), Thai Muslim separatists who want

Yala and other Muslim provinces to secede from Thailand, also have forces in this area. The occasional truck is hijacked by one or the other of the insurgent groups. Farangs don't seem to be a target, but travel at night in this area is not recommended.

Malaysians are allowed to cross the border at Betong, so the little town is often crowded on weekends as they come across to shop for cheaper Thai merchandise, including, for the Malay men, Thai women. The town of Betong is famous for *kai betong*, the delicious local chicken, and also roast or fried mountain frogs, which are said to be even more delicious than the mountain frogs of Mae Hong Son. Many townspeople speak English as well as Thai and Malay.

Places to Stay
Most hotels in Betong are in the 120-to-200B range for basic rooms – Malaysian price levels – eg the *Cathay, Fortuna, Khong Kha, Thai, King's, Venus* and *My House*. The *Betong Hotel*, 13/6 Sarit Det Rd, has rooms for 70 to 140B, and the *Si Betong 2*, 14/4 Chaiya Chaowalit Rd, is 80 to 120B. Betong has more Muslim and Chinese restaurants than Thai.

Getting There & Away
A share taxi to Betong from Yala is 50B; bus is 25B.

RAMAN รามัน
Twenty-five km south-east of Yala Town by road or train, Raman is well known as a centre for the Malay-Indonesian martial art of *silat*. Two very famous teachers of silat reside here, Hajisa Haji Sama-ae and Je Wae. If you're interested in pure Thai Muslim culture, this is the place.

Pattani Province

PATTANI TOWN เมืองปัตตานี
The provincial capital of Pattani (population 38,000) provides a heavy contrast with Yala Town. In spite of its basic function as a trading post operated by the Chinese for the

benefit (or exploitation, depending on your perspective) of the surrounding Muslim villages, the town has a more Muslim character than Yala Town. In the streets, you are more likely to hear Yawi, the traditional language of Java, Sumatra and the Malay peninsula (which when written uses the classic Arabic script plus five more letters), than any Thai dialect. The markets are visually quite similar to markets in Kota Baru in Malaysia. The town as a whole is as dirty as Yala Town is clean.

The centre of this concrete town is at the intersection of Naklua/Yarang Rd, the north-south road between Yala and Pattani harbour, and Ramkomud Rd, which runs east-west between Songkhla and Narathiwat. Inter-city buses and taxis stop at this intersection. Ramkomud Rd becomes Rudee Rd after crossing Naklua Rd and it is along Rudee Rd that you can see what is left of old Pattani architecture – the Sino-Portuguese style that was once so prevalent in south Thailand. Pattani, in fact, was until rather recent history, the centre of an independent principality that included Yala and Narathiwat.

Mosques
Thailand's second largest mosque is the Matsayit Klang, in Pattani Town, a large traditional structure of green hue, probably still the south's most important mosque. It was built in the early '60s and is on Yarang Rd, about 200 metres south of Pipit Rd intersection.

The oldest mosque in Pattani is the Matsayit Kreu-Se, built in 1578 by an immigrant Chinese named Lim To Khieng who had married a Pattani woman and converted to Islam. Actually, neither To Khieng, nor anyone else, ever completed the construction of the mosque. The story goes that his sister, Lim Ko Niaw, sailed from China on a sampan to try and persuade her brother to abandon Islam and return to his homeland. To demonstrate the strength of his faith, he began building the Matsayit Kreu-Se. His sister then put a Chinese curse on the mosque, saying it would never be completed. Then, in a final attempt to dissuade To Khieng, she hanged herself from a nearby cashew-nut tree. In his grief, Khieng was unable to complete the mosque, and to this day it remains unfinished – supposedly every time someone tries to work on it, lightning strikes. The brick, Arab-style building has been left in its original semi-completed, semi-ruined form, but the faithful keep up the surrounding grounds. The mosque is in Ban Kreu-Se, about seven km east of Pattani Town, off Highway 42.

The tree that Ko Niaw hanged herself from has been enshrined at the San Jao Leng Ju Kieng (or San Jao Lim Ko Niaw), the site of an important Chinese Muslim festival in late February or early March. The shrine is in the north end of town towards the harbour.

Batik

Thai Muslims in southern Thailand have their own traditional batik methods that are similar but not identical to the batik of north-east Malaysia. The best place to shop for local batik is at the Palat Market (talaat nat Palat), which is off Highway 42 between Pattani and Saiburi in Ban Palat. The market is held all day Wednesdays and Sundays only. If you can't make it to this market, the shops of Muslim Phanit and Nadi Brothers on Rudee Rd sell local and Malaysian batik as well at perhaps slightly higher prices.

Beaches

The only beach near town is at Laem Tachi, a cape that juts out over the north end of Ao Pattani. You must take a boat taxi to get there, either from the Pattani Pier or from Yari district at the mouth of the Pattani River. This white-sand beach is about 11 km long, but is sometimes marred by refuse from Ao Pattani, depending on the time of year and the tides. Hat Ratchadaphisek (or Hat Sai Maw) is about 15 km west of Pattani. It's a relaxing spot, with lots of sea pines for shade, but the water is a bit on the murky side. Then there's Hat Talo Kapo, 14 km east of Pattani Town, near Yaring district, a pretty beach that's also

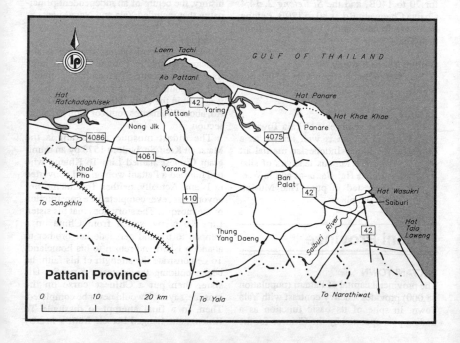

a harbour for *kaw-lae*, the traditional fishing boats of south Thailand. Better beaches can be found south of Pattani, on the way to Narathiwat, especially in the Panare and Saiburi districts where there are kilometres of virtually deserted beach. Hat Chala Lai is a broad white-sand beach 43 km south-east of Pattani Town, near Panare. Eight km further, toward Narathiwat, is Hat Khae Khae, a pretty beach studded with boulders. Three km north of Panare Town is Hat Panare, which is another colourful kaw-lae harbour.

Near Saiburi is Hat Wasukri, also called Chaihat Ban Patatimaw, a beautiful white-sand beach with shade. It's 53 km from Pattani Town. Some private bungalows here rent for 200B, but this may be negotiable when occupancy is low. Further south still, a few km before you reach the Narathiwat provincial border, is Hat Talo Laweng, possibly Pattani Province's prettiest beach.

A good place to watch the building of kaw-lae is in the village of Pase Yawo (Ya-Waw), near the mouth of the Saiburi River. It's a tradition that is slowly dying out as the kaw-lae is replaced by long-tail boats with auto engines.

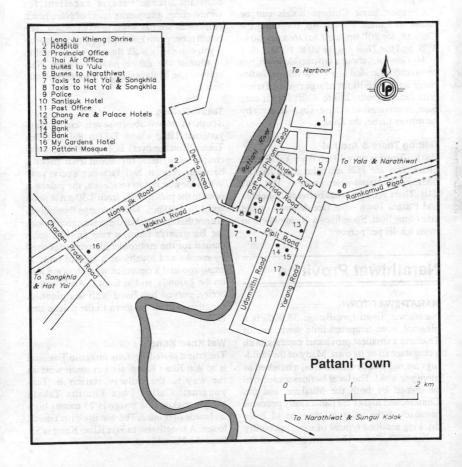

1 Leng Ju Khieng Shrine
2 Hospital
3 Provincial Office
4 Thai Air Office
5 Buses to Yulu
6 Buses to Narathiwat
7 Taxis to Hat Yai & Songkhla
8 Taxis to Hat Yai & Songkhla
9 Police
10 Santisuk Hotel
11 Post Office
12 Chong Are & Palace Hotels
13 Bank
14 Bank
15 Bank
16 My Gardens Hotel
17 Pattani Mosque

Pattani Town

Places to Stay

The *Chong Are (Jong Ah) Hotel* is a Chinese place on Thanon Prida with rooms for 70B without a bath, 100B with. Attached to the Chong Are, with an entrance around the corner, is the *Palace*, a decent place whose rooms are 110B with fan and bath, 160B with two beds, or 180B for air-con.

The *Santisuk*, at 1/16 Pipit Rd, has OK rooms for 80B without a bath, 100 to 140B with. As in Yala, Narathiwat, Satun and Trang, all street signs are in tortured English transliterations of Thai (better than no transliterations at all, for those who can't read Thai).

Cheaper, basic Chinese hotels can be found on Pattani Phirom Rd, including the *Chin Ah*, for 80B up, the *Thai Hua*, for 60 to 80B, and the *Thai An*, for 60 to 100B.

My Gardens, about a km outside town, has been recommended as a good-value middle-range hotel – 180B for a large two-bed room with fan and bath, 280 to 330B for air-con. Samlor or songthaew drivers may know it by its former name, the Dina.

Getting There & Around

Pattani Town is only 40 km from Yala Town. Share taxis are 18B and take about half an hour. From Narathiwat, a taxi is 35B, bus 24B. There are also boats between Songkhla and Pattani Town – the fare depends on the size of the boat. Songthaews go anywhere in town for 4B per person.

Narathiwat Province

NARATHIWAT TOWN   เมืองนราธิวาส

Narathiwat Town (population 38,000) is a pleasant, even-tempered little town, one of Thailand's smallest provincial capitals, with a character all of its own. Many of the buildings are old wooden structures, a hundred or more years old. The local businesses seem to be owned by both the Muslims and the Chinese, and nights are particularly peaceful because of the relative absence of male drinking sessions typical of most upcountry towns in Thailand. The town is right on the sea, and some of the prettiest beaches on south Thailand's east coast are just outside town.

Hat Narathat   หาดนราธาวาส

Just north of town is a small Thai Muslim fishing village at the mouth of the Bang Nara River, lined with the large painted fishing boats called *reua kaw-lae* which are peculiar to Narathiwat and Pattani. Near the fishing village is Hat Narathat, a sandy beach, four to five km long, which serves as a kind of public park for locals, with outdoor seafood restaurants, tables and umbrellas, etc. The constant breeze here is excellent for windsurfing, a favourite sport of Narathiwat citizens as well as visiting Malaysians. The beach is only two km north of the town centre – you can easily walk there or take a samlor.

Almost the entire coast between Narathiwat and Malaysia, 40 km south, is sandy beach.

Taksin Palace

South of town about seven km is Tanyongmat Hill, where Taksin Palace (Phra Taksin Ratchaniwet) is located. The royal couple stay here for about two months between August and October every year. When they're not in residence, the palace is open to the public daily from 8.30 am to noon and 1 to 4.30 pm. The buildings themselves are not that special, but there are gardens with the Bangsuriya palm, a rare fan-like palm named for the embroidered sunshades used by monks and royalty as a sign of rank. A small zoo and a ceramics workshop are also on the grounds, and in front is Ao Manao, a pretty, curved bay lined with sea pines. A songthaew from the town to the palace area is 7B.

Wat Khao Kong

The tallest seated-Buddha image in Thailand is at Wat Khao Kong, six km south-west on the way to the railway station in Tanyongmat. Called Phra Phuttha Taksin Mingmongkon, the image is 25 metres high and made of bronze. The wat itself isn't much to see. A songthaew to Wat Khao Kong is 5B from the Narathiwat.

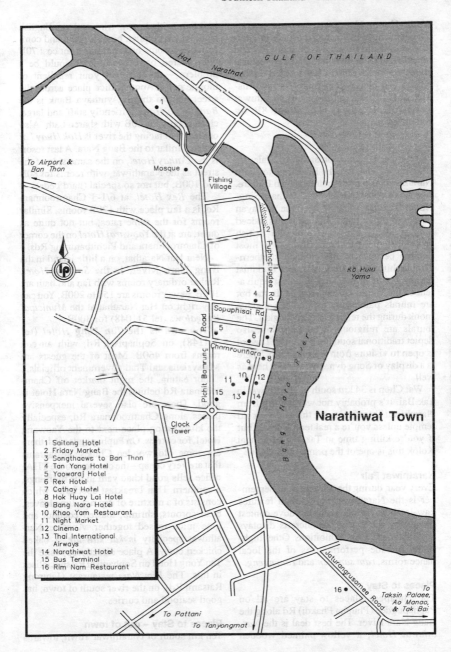

GULF OF THAILAND

Hat Narathat

To Airport &
Ban Thon

Mosque

Fishing
Village

Ko Puilu
Yama

Pupharabgdee Rd

Sopuphisai Rd

Chamrounnara

Pichit Bamrung Road

Clock
Tower

Bang Nara River

Narathiwat Town

1 Saitong Hotel
2 Friday Market
3 Songthaews to Ban Thon
4 Tan Yong Hotel
5 Yaowaraj Hotel
6 Rex Hotel
7 Cathay Hotel
8 Hok Huay Lai Hotel
9 Bang Nara Hotel
10 Khao Yam Restaurant
11 Night Market
12 Cinema
13 Thai International
   Airways
14 Narathiwat Hotel
15 Bus Terminal
16 Rim Nam Restaurant

Jaturangrusomee Road

To Pattani

To Tanyongmat

To Taksin Palaee,
Ao Manao,
& Tak Bai

Wadin Husen Mosque

One of the most interesting mosques in Thailand, the Wadin Husen was built in 1769 and mixes Thai, Chinese and Malay architectural styles to good effect. It's located in the village of Lubosawo in Bajo (Ba-Jaw) district, about 15 km north-west of Narathiwat Town off Highway 42, about 8B by songthaew.

Wat Chonthara Sing-He

During the British colonisation of Malaysia (then called Malaya), the Brits tried to claim Narathiwat as part of their Malayan Empire. The Thais constructed Wat Chonthara Sing-He in Tak Bai district near the Malayan border to prove that Narathiwat was indeed part of Siam, and as a result the British relinquished their claim. Today it's most notable because of the genuine southern-Thai architecture, rarely seen in a Buddhist temple – sort of the Thai-Buddhist equivalent of the Wadin Husen Mosque. In the bot are murals painted by a famous Songkhla monk during the reign of King Mongkut. The murals are religious in message but also depict traditional southern Thai life. The bot is open to visitors from 8 am to 5 pm. There is a display of Song dynasty ceramics here as well.

Wat Chon is 34 km south of Narathiwat in Tak Bai. It's probably not worth a trip from Narathiwat Town just to see this 100-year old temple unless you're a real temple freak, but if you're killing time in Tak Bai or Sungai Kolok this is one of the prime local sights.

Narathiwat Fair

Every year, during the third week of September is the Narathiwat Fair, which features kaw-lae boat racing, a singing dove contest judged by the Queen, handicrafts displays and silat martial arts exhibitions. Other highlights include performances of the local dance forms, ram sam pen and ram ngeng.

Places to Stay

The cheapest places to stay are all on Puphapugdee (Phupha Phakdi) Rd along the Bang Nara River. The best deal is the Narathiwat Hotel, a yellow-painted wooden building with brown trim and no English sign, which is quiet, breezy, clean and comfortable. Rooms on the water front cost 70B with shared bath. Mosquitoes could be a problem – don't forget your repellent or mossie coils. Another nice place across the street next to the Si Ayuthaya Bank is the Bang Nara Hotel – friendly staff and large, clean rooms for 60B with shared bath. Also on this road facing the river is Hok Huay Lai Hotel, similar to the Bang Nara. A last resort is the Cathay Hotel, on the same side of the street as the Narathiwat, with rooms for 80B and 100B, but not so special (hard beds).

The Rex Hotel, at 6/1-3 Chamroonnara Rd, is a fair place with 120B rooms. Similar rooms for the same rates, but not quite as quiet, are at the Yaowaraj Hotel on the corner of Chamroonnara and Pichitbamrung Rds.

Near Hat Narathat, on a little island in the Bang Nara River, is the Saitong Hotel. Rather ordinary rooms with fan and bath are 100B, newer rooms are 150 to 200B. You can stay right on Hat Narathat at the Municipal Bungalows (tel 511048) for 300B.

Top end is the Tan Yong Hotel (tel 511148), on Sophapisai Rd, with air-con rooms from 460B. Most of the guests are Malaysians and Thai government officials.

For eating, the night market off Chamroonnara Rd behind the Bang Nara Hotel is good. There are also several inexpensive places along Chamroonnara Rd, especially the khao kaeng place next to the Yaowaraj Hotel, for curries. On Puphapugdee Rd, there are some old wooden Chinese restaurants that are very cheap – the one next to the THAI office sells good khao yam in the mornings, a southern Thai breakfast speciality which consists of a mixture of dry rice, lime leaves, bean sprouts, shrimp, toasted coconut and lime juice tossed together. Another Narathiwat specialty is kai kaw-lae, a baked chicken curry. A place directly opposite the Tan Yong Hotel on Sophapisai Rd specialises in this. The Rim Nam restaurant (Jaturong Ratsami Rd), on the river south of town, has good seafood and curries.

Places to Stay – out of town

Ten km south of Narathiwat Town, towards

Tak Bai, is *Thanon Resort*, a quiet beach place with bungalows for 170B with fan and bath. The staff will provide free transport to and from town.

Getting There & Away

Share taxis between Yala Town and Narathiwat Town are 50B. The bus is 30B. The train is 13B for 3rd-class seats to Tanyongmat, 20 km west of Narathiwat, then it's either a 15B taxi to Narathiwat, or 8B by songthaew. From Sungai Kolok, buses are 15B, share taxis 30B. To/from Tak Bai, the other border crossing, is 10B by songthaew.

It's best not to travel around Narathiwat Province at night, because that's when the Muslim separatist guerrillas go around shooting up trucks and buses. In early 1989 a truck was hit by automatic weapons fire on Highway 42 between the capital and Bajo, wounding four people. A splinter group of the PULO took credit.

SUNGAI KOLOK & BAN TABA

These small towns in the south-east of Narathiwat Province are departure points for the east coast of Malaysia. The river forms the border here, and Rantau Panjang is the Malaysian border town on the south bank of the river. There is a fair batik ('Thai: *pa-te*') cottage industry in this district.

Sungai Kolok สุไหง-โกลก

The Thai government once planned to move the border crossing from Sungai Kolok to Ban Taba in Tak Bai district, which is on the coast 32 km east. The Taba crossing is now open and is a shorter and quicker route to Kota Baru, the first Malaysian town of any size. But it looks like Sungai Kolok will remain open as well for a long time. They're even building new hotels in Sungai Kolok and establishing a TAT office next to the immigration post.

The border is open from 5 am to 5 pm (6 am to 6 pm Malaysian time). On slow days they may close the border as early as 4.30 pm.

Ban Taba บ้าน ตะบะ

Ban Taba, five km south of bustling Tak Bai,

is just a blip of a town with only one bank and a couple of hotels. A ferry across the river into Malaysia is 5B. The border crossing here is open the same hours as in Sungai Kolok.

Places to Stay – Sungai Kolok

The Tourist Business Association brochure says there are 59 hotels in Sungai Kolok, but we only found 38. The main reason Sungai Kolok has so many hotels is to accommodate the weekend trips of Malaysian males. Of these cheaper hotels, only a handful are under 100B and they're mainly for those only crossing for a couple of hours. So if you have to spend the night here it's best to pay a little more and get away from the short-time trade.

The most reasonably priced places are along Charoenkhet Rd. Here you can find the fairly clean *Thailiang Hotel* for 80B, the *Savoy Hotel* for 100B, and the *Asia Hotel* for 150B, or 200 to 250B with air-con. The *Pimarn Hotel* is also quite good at 140B with fan and bath, 230B with air-con.

Over on the corner of Arifmankha and Waman Amnoey Rds is the pleasant *Valentine Hotel*, 170B with fan, 260B with air-con. There's a coffee shop downstairs; free fruit and coffee are provided to guests.

Other fairly decent hotels in the 100-to-150B range include the *Star Hotel*, at 20 Saritwong Rd, the *An An Hotel*, at 183/1-2 Prachawiwat Rd, the *Taksin 2*, at 4 Prachasamran Rd, the *Sansabai 2*, at 38 Chuenmankha Rd, the *Sansabai 1*, at 32/34 Bussayapan Rd, and the *Chonun*, at Soi Phuthon, Charoenkhet Rd.

Top end hotels in Sungai Kolok include:

Genting, Asia 18 Rd, from 462B
Grand Garden (tel 611389), 104 Arifmankha Rd, from 435B
Inter Hotel, Prachawiwat Rd, from 396B
Merlin Hotel (tel 611003), 40 Charoenkhet Rd, from 190B
Plaza Htel, Bussayapan Rd, from 360B
Tara Regent Hotel (tel 611401), Soi Phuthon, Charoenkhet Rd, from 230B

The town has plenty of food stalls selling Thai, Chinese and Malaysian food. The *Siam*

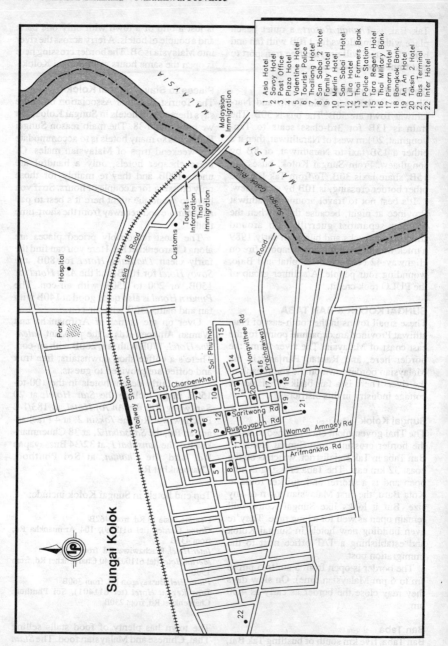

MALAYSIA

Malaysian Immigration

Tourist Information
Thai Immigration

Customs

Asia 18 Road

Hospital

Park

Railway Station

Sungai Kolok River

Sungai Kolok

Soi Phuthon

Charoenkhet

Saritwong Rd

Bussayapoch Rd

Waman Amnoey Rd

Arifmankha Rd

Vongavithee Rd

Prachawiwat

1 Asia Hotel
2 Savoy Hotel
3 Post Office
4 Plaza Hotel
5 Valentine Hotel
6 Tourist Police
7 Thailiang Hotel
8 San Sabai 2 Hotel
9 Family Hotel
10 Merlin Hotel
11 San Sabai 1 Hotel
12 Lilla Hotel
13 Thai Farmers Bank
14 Police Station
15 Tara Regent Hotel
16 Thai Military Bank
17 Pimarn Hotel
18 Bangkok Bank
19 An An Hotel
20 Taksin 2 Hotel
21 Bus Terminal
22 Inter Hotel

restaurant next to the Merlin is good for Thai food, and the *Bak Mui* near the Tara Regent for Chinese. For an economical and delicious breakfast very early in the morning try coffee and doughnuts at the station buffet. Some of the Malay shops also do roti kaeng (Malay; roti chanai), flat bread with curry dip, in the mornings.

Most places in Sungai Kolok will take Malaysian ringgit as well as Thai baht for food or accommodation.

Places to Stay – Ban Taba

Masya has good rooms for 230B with fan and bath, 270B with air-con. It's set back off the road leading from the Malaysian border. Another, newer hotel is being constructed nearby. Further from the border is a no-name motel for 150B – look for *Ta Wan Seafood*.

Getting There & Around

Bus & Share Taxi A share taxi from Yala to Sungai Kolok is 60B. A taxi between Narathiwat Town and Sungai Kolok is 30B, the bus is 16B (21B for an air-con bus).

Air-con buses to Hat Yai are 77B, and leave from the Valentine Hotel at 7, 12.30 am, 1 and 3 pm. From Hat Yai, departure times are the same. The trip takes about four hours.

The border is about a km from the centre of Sungai Kolok or the railway station. Transport around town is by motorcycle taxi – it's 10B for a ride to the border.

From Rantau Panjang (Malaysian side), a share taxi to Kota Baru costs M$3.50 per person (M$14 to charter the whole car) and takes about an hour.

Train You can get trains to Sungai Kolok from Yala Town and Tanyongmat (Narathiwat), but buses are really faster and more convenient along these routes. From Sungai Kolok to points further north (via Yala Town), however, the train is a reasonable alternative. A train to Hat Yai takes about 4½ hours and costs 31B for a 3rd-class seat, 65B 2nd class. Train Nos 124 and 132 leave Sungai Kolok at 6 and 8.40 am, arriving in Hat Yai at 10.33 am and 1.12 pm.

FURTHER SOUTH
Air
Phuket to Penang Wednesday and Saturday Thai International flies to Penang at 11.40 am. Arrival time in Penang is 1.30 pm. The fare is 1318B.

Bus & Share Taxi
Share taxis are a popular way of travelling between Hat Yai and Penang. They're big old Thai-registered Chevys or Mercedes which depart from Hat Yai around 9 am every morning. You'll find them at the railway station or along Niphat Uthit 2. In Penang you can find them around the cheap travellers' hotels in Georgetown. The cost is about 220B, or M$22 – this is probably the fastest way of travelling between the two countries, and you cross the border with a minimum of fuss. Cheaper and more comfortable, though less fast, are tour buses between Hat Yai and Penang. Magic Tour, downstairs from the Cathay Guest House in Hat Yai, has buses for 200B which leave twice daily and arrive in Penang in five hours.

You can cross the west coast border by taking a bus to one side and another from the other, but don't take the most obvious direct route between Hat Yai and Alor Setar. This is the route used by taxis and buses but there's a long stretch of no-man's-land between the Thai border control at Sadao and the Malaysian one at Changlun. Finding transport across this empty stretch is difficult. It's much easier to go to Padang Besar, where the railway line crosses the border. Here you can get a bus right up to the border, walk across and take another bus or taxi on the other side. On either side you'll most likely be mobbed by taxi and motorcycle drivers wanting to take you to immigration. It's better to walk over the railway by bridge into Thailand, and then ignore the touts asking $M until you get to 'official' Thai taxis who will transport you to all the way to Hat Yai, with a stop at the immigration office (2½ km from the border), for 25B.

There's a daily bus running between Alor Setar, Hat Yai and Kota Bahru and reverse. There's also a road crossing at Keroh (Thai side – Betong), right in the middle between the east and west coasts. This may be used more now that the Penang to Kota Baru road is open. For more info on Betong, see the Yala Province section.

See the Sungai Kolok & Ban Taba section (or Bangkok to Sungai Kolok section) for crossing the border on the east coast.

Train

Bangkok to Butterworth/Penang The daily Special Express No 11 leaves Bangkok's Hualamphong Station at 3.15 pm, arriving in Hat Yai at 7.04 am the next day, and in Butterworth, Malaysia, at 12.25 pm (Malaysian time, one hour ahead of Thai time). The fare to Butterworth is 927B for 1st class, 431B for 2nd, plus a 50B Special Express charge. There is no 3rd-class seating on this train.

For a sleeping berth in 2nd class add 100B for an upper berth, 150B for a lower. In 1st class it's 250B a bed in a double cabin, 350B for a single.

Bangkok to Kuala Lumpur For Kuala Lumpur take the Butterworth/Penang train, changing to the Malaysian Day Express No 3 in Butterworth, departing there for Kuala Lumpur at 2.15 pm, arriving in Kuala Lumpur at 8.15 pm the same day. The fare from Bangkok is 1432B 1st class, 659B 2nd class.

Bangkok to Singapore For Singapore, the final leg leaves Kuala Lumpur aboard Night Express No 61 at 10 pm, arriving in Singapore at 6.55 am the next day. The entire two-day journey costs 1965B 1st class, 899B 2nd class, not including Express surcharge or berth charges if you get a sleeper. If you're going straight through, when you get to Butterworth get off quickly and re-book a sleeping berth to Kuala Lumpur (M$2 to M$3). In Kuala Lumpur you have to get a 2nd-class seat allocation – insist on 2nd or you may be fobbed off with 3rd class on a slower Biasa train.

Bangkok to Sungai Kolok If you prefer the east coast passage to Malaysia (by train it's cheaper), take the daily Special Express No 19 to Sungai Kolok at 2 pm, which arrives in Sungai Kolok at 9.45 am the next day. This train has 1st (808B), 2nd (378B) and 3rd-class (180B) fares, not including the Special Express surcharge of 50B (and sleeping berths for 1st or 2nd class if you so choose).

It's about a km from Sungai Kolok Town or railway station to the Malaysian border. You can walk or take a motorcycle taxi for 10B. Coming from Malaysia, just follow the old railway tracks to your right, or, for the town, turn left at the first junction and head for the high-rises.

Be prepared for culture shock coming from Malaysia, warned one traveller. Not only are most signs in Thai script, but fewer people speak English in Thailand. The 3rd-class rail fare to Hat Yai is 65B.

Boat

Coast Route There are several ways of travelling between Malaysia and the south of Thailand by sea. Simplest is to take a long-tail boat between Satun Town, right down in the south-west corner of Thailand and Kuala Perlis. The cost is about M$4, or 40B, and boats cross over fairly regularly. Kuala Perlis is the departure point for the ferries across to the Malaysian island of Langkawi. There are immigration posts at both ports so you can make the crossing quite officially, but they're a bit slack at Satun Town (since they don't get many foreigners arriving this way) so make sure they stamp your passport. The immigration office in Satun is in the centre of town near the Bambang Mosque.

There are two piers in Satun where boats to/from Malaysia arrive and depart – Tammalang at the mouth of the Bambang River and the pier in town on the river near the Rian Thong Hotel. The pier they use is determined by water level and time of year.

From Satun Town you can take a bus to Hat Yai and then arrange transport to other points in the south or further north. It's possible to bypass Hat Yai altogether, by heading directly for Phuket or Krabi via Trang. Hat Yai is nothing special after all.

You can also take a ferry to Ban Taba on the east coast of Thailand from near Kota

Baru as well – see the section on Sungai Kolok & Ban Taba.

Ocean Route An alternative sea route is to travel by yacht between Phuket and Penang. The *Szygie* sails from Phuket to Penang periodically between 1 December and 30 April. Contact the operators at Restaurant Number Four, Hat Patong, Phuket or J Travel, Chulia St, Georgetown, Penang. They sail Phuket, Ko Phi Phi, Langkawi and Penang.

You can also find yachts going further afield, particularly to Sri Lanka. December and early January is the best month to look for them. The crossing takes about 10 to 15 days.

Glossary

achaan – respectful title for teacher, from the Sanskrit term *acharya*
aahaan – food
aahaan baa – forest food
ao – bay or gulf
amphoe – district; next subdivision down from province, sometimes spelled *amphur*
amphoe muang – provincial capital

ban – house or village; often spelt *ban*
bai toey – pandanus leaf
baw nam rawn – hot springs
bhikku – Buddhist monk; Thai pronunciation *phik-ku*
bot – central sanctuary or chapel in a Thai temple; from Pali *uposatha*

cha – tea
chaihaat – beach; often spelt *chaihat*
chao le/chao nam – sea gypsies
chedi – stupa; monument erected to house a Buddha relic; called *pagoda* in Burma, *dagoba* in Sri Lanka, *cetiya* in India

dhammachakha – Buddhist wheel of law
doi – peak, as in mountain

farang – foreigner of European descent

hang yao – long-tailed boat
hat – beach; short for *chaihaat*; also *hat*
haw trai – a Tripitaka (Buddhist scripture) library
hin – stone

iihen – palm civet (a cat/racoon/monkey-type creature)
isaan – general term for north-east Thailand, from the Sanskrit name for the mediaeval kingdom *Isana*, which encompassed parts of Cambodia and north-east Thailand

jangwat – province
Jataka – life-stories of the Buddha
Jiin – Chinese

kaew – also spelled *keo*; crystal, jewel, glass, or gem
kap klaem – drinking food
ka-toey – Thai transvestite
kaw lae – traditional fishing boats of southern Thailand
khaen – reed instrument common in north-east Thailand
khao man kai – chicken rice
khlong – canal
ko – island; also spelt *koh*; pronounced *kaw*

khao – hill or mountain
khon – masked dance-drama based on stories from the Ramakien
khon isaan – the people of north-east Thailand
klawng – Thai drums
kuay haeng – Chinese-style work shirt
kuti – meditation hut

laap – spicy mint salad with mint leaves
laem – cape (in the geographical sense)
lakhon – classical Thai dance-drama
lak muang – city pillar/phallus
lao khao – white liquor
lao theuan – jungle liquor
li-khe – Thai folk dance-drama
longyi – Burmese sarong

mae chii – Buddhist nuns
mae nam – river; literally 'mother water'
Maha That – literally 'great element', from the Sanskrit-Pali *mahadhatu*; common name for temples which contain Buddha relics
mai kuu – pan pipe
mat-mii – tie-dye silk method
maw hawm – Thai work shirt
mawn khwan – triangular shaped pillow popular in the north and north-east
metta – Buddhist practice of loving kindness
mondop – small square building in a *wat* complex generally used by lay people, as opposed to monks; from the Sanskrit *mandapa*
muang – city; pronounced *meu-ang*
muay Thai – Thai boxing

naem – raw sausage, popular in the north and north-east
naga – dragon-headed serpent
nakhon – city; from Sanskrit-Pali *nagara*; also spelt *nakhorn*
nam – water
nam phrik – chili sauce
nam plaa – fish sauce
nam tok – waterfall
nang – Thai shadow play
ngaan wat – temple fair
noeng khao – hill
ngop – traditional Khmer rice farmer's hat

pak nam – estuary
pak tai – southern Thai
pa-te – batik
phaa-khamaa – piece of cotton cloth worn as a wraparound by men

430

phaasin – same as above for women

phi pat – classical Thai orchestra

phra – monk or Buddha image; an honorific term from the Pali *vara*, ' excellent'

phra phum – earth spirits

phuu khao – mountain in central Thai

pong lang – north-east Thai marimba made of short logs

prang – Khmer-style tower on temples

prasat – small ornate building with a cruciform ground plan and needle-like spire, used for religious/royal purposes, located on *wat* grounds. From the Sanskrit term *prasada*

rai – one *rai* is equal to 1600 square metres

ram muay – boxing dance

reua duan – river express boat

reua hang yao – long-tail taxi boat

reua kam fak – cross-river ferry

reuan thaew – long-houses

reu-sii – a Hindu *rishi* , 'sage'

rot thammada – ordinary bus (non air-conditioned) or ordinary train (not rapid or express)

rot thua – tour bus; any air-con bus. Also called rot ae, 'air vehicle'

roti – round flatbread, common street food; also found in Muslim restaurants

sala – an open-sided, covered meeting hall or resting place

sala klang – provincial offices and/or city hall

samlor – literally 'three wheels'; three-wheeled pedicab used predominantly in provincial Thailand; prounounced as *sam-law*

sema – boundary stones used to consecrate ground

used for monastic ordinations; from the Sanskrit-Pali *sima*

serow – Asian mountain goat

seua maw hawm – blue cotton farmer's shirt

soi – lane

songkran – Thai new year

somtam – green papaya salad

soon – centre; from the Pali *sunya*; also *sun*

songthaew – literally 'two rows'; common name for small pick-up trucks with two benches in the back, used as buses/taxis

susaan – cemetery

talaat nam – floating market

tambon – also spelled *tambol*; next subdivision below *amphoe*; 'precinct'

thale sap – inland sea or large lake

thep – angel or divine being; from Sanskrit *deva*

thewada – a kind of angel

thutong – monks who have taken ascetic vows

tripitaka – Theravada Buddhist scriptures

tuk-tuk – motorised *samlor*

vipassana – Buddhist insight meditation

wang – palace

wai – palms-together Thai greeting

wat – temple-monastery; from Pali *avasa*, monk's dwelling

wiharn – counterpart to *bot* in Thai temple, containing Buddha images but not circumscribed by *sema* stones. Also spelt *wihan* or *viharn*; from Sanskrit *vihara*

yaa dong – herbal liquor; also the herbs inserted in *lao khao*

yam – Thai style salad; usually made with meat or seafood

Index

Maps

436 Map Index

Temperature

To convert °C to °F multiply by 1.8 and add 32

To convert °F to °C subtract 32 and multiply by ·55

Length, Distance & Area

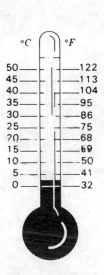

	multiply by
inches to centimetres	2.54
centimetres to inches	0.39
feet to metres	0.30
metres to feet	3.28
yards to metres	0.91
metres to yards	1.09
miles to kilometres	1.61
kilometres to miles	0.62
acres to hectares	0.40
hectares to acres	2.47

Weight

	multiply by
ounces to grams	28.35
grams to ounces	0.035
pounds to kilograms	0.45
kilograms to pounds	2.21
British tons to kilograms	1016
US tons to kilograms	907

A British ton is 2240 lbs, a US ton is 2000 lbs

Volume

	multiply by
Imperial gallons to litres	4.55
litres to imperial gallons	0.22
US gallons to litres	3.79
litres to US gallons	0.26

5 imperial gallons equals 6 US gallons
a litre is slightly more than a US quart, slightly less
than a British one

Temperature

To convert °C to °F, multiply by 1.8 and add 32

To convert °F to °C, subtract 32 and multiply by .55

Length/Distance & Area

	multiply by
inches to centimetres	2.54
centimetres to inches	0.39
feet to metres	0.03
metres to feet	3.28
yards to metres	0.91
metres to yards	1.09
miles to kilometres	1.61
kilometres to miles	0.62
acres to hectares	0.40
hectares to acres	2.47

Weight

	multiply by
ounces to grams	28.35
grams to ounces	0.035
pounds to kilograms	0.45
kilograms to pounds	2.2
British tons to kilograms	1016
US tons to kilograms	907

A British ton is 2240 lbs, a US ton is 2000 lbs

Volume

	multiply by
imperial gallons to litres	4.55
litres to imperial gallons	0.22
US gallons to litres	3.79
litres to US gallons	0.26

5 imperial gallons equals 6 US gallons

A litre is slightly more than a US quart, nearly the same as a British one

Guides to South-East Asia

South-East Asia on a shoestring

The well-known 'yellow bible' for travellers in South-East Asia contains detailed travel information on Brunei, Burma, Hong Kong, Indonesia, Macau, Malaysia, Papua New Guinea, the Philippines, Singapore, and Thailand.

Bali & Lombok – a travel survival kit

This guide will help travellers to experience the real magic of Bali's tropical paradise. Neighbouring Lombok is largely untouched by outside influences and has a special atmosphere of its own.

Burma – a travel survival kit

Burma is one of Asia's friendliest and most interesting countries. This book shows how to make the most of a trip around the main triangle route of Rangoon-Mandalay-Pagan, and explores many lesser-known places such as Pegu and Inle Lake.

Malaysia, Singapore and Brunei – a travel survival kit

These three nations offer amazing geographic and cultural variety – from the national parks and beaches of Peninsular Malaysia, the jungles and rivers of East Malaysia, the oil money of Brunei and the urban prosperity and diversity of Singapore.

441

The Philippines – a travel survival kit
The friendly Filipinos, colourful festivals, and superb natural scenery make the Philippines one of the most interesting countries in South-East Asia for adventurous travellers and sun-seekers alike.

Indonesia – a travel survival kit
Some of the most remarkable sights and sounds in South-East Asia can be found amongst the 7000 islands of Indonesia – this book covers the entire archipelago in detail.

Papua New Guinea – a travel survival kit
Papua New Guinea is the last inhabited place on earth to be explored by Europeans. From coastal cities to villages perched beside mighty rivers, palm fringed beaches and rushing mountain streams, Papua New Guinea promises memorable travel.

Also Available:
Thai phrasebook, *Burmese phrasebook*, *Pilipino phrasebook*, and *Indonesia phrasebook*

Lonely Planet Guidebooks

Lonely Planet guidebooks cover virtually every accessible part of Asia as well as Australia, the Pacific, Central and South America, Africa, the Middle East and parts of North America. There are four main series: 'travel survival kits', covering a single country for a range of budgets; 'shoestring' guides with compact information for low-budget travel in a major region; trekking guides; and 'phrasebooks'.

Australia & the Pacific
Australia
Bushwalking in Australia
Papua New Guinea
Papua New Guinea phrasebook
New Zealand
Tramping in New Zealand
Rarotonga & the Cook Islands
Solomon Islands
Tahiti & French Polynesia
Fiji
Micronesia
Tonga
Samoa

South-East Asia
South-East Asia on a shoestring
Malaysia, Singapore & Brunei
Indonesia
Bali & Lombok
Indonesia phrasebook
Burma
Burmese phrasebook
Thailand
Thai phrasebook
Philippines
Pilipino phrasebook

North-East Asia
North-East Asia on a shoestring
China
China phrasebook
Tibet
Tibet phrasebook
Japan
Japanese phrasebook
Korea
Korean phrasebook
Hong Kong, Macau & Canton
Taiwan

West Asia
West Asia on a shoestring
Trekking in Turkey
Turkey

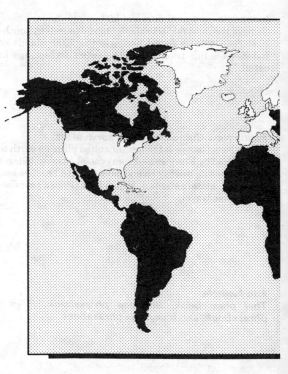

Indian Ocean
Madagascar & Comoros
Mauritius, Réunion & Seychelles
Maldives & Islands of the East Indian Ocean

Mail Order

Lonely Planet guidebooks are distributed worldwide and are sold by good bookshops everywhere. They are also available by mail order from Lonely Planet, so if you have difficulty finding a title please write to us. US and Canadian residents should write to Embarcadero West, 112 Linden St, Oakland CA 94607, USA and residents of other countries to PO Box 617, Hawthorn, Victoria 3122, Australia.

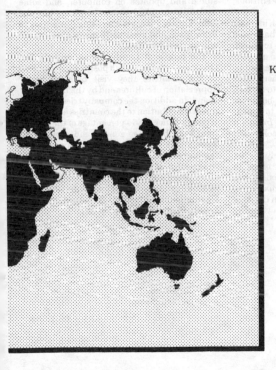

Eastern Europe
Eastern Europe

Indian Subcontinent
India
Hindi/Urdu phrasebook
Kashmir, Ladakh & Zanskar
Trekking in the Indian Himalaya
Pakistan
Kathmandu & the Kingdom of Nepal
Trekking in the Nepal Himalaya
Nepal phrasebook
Sri Lanka
Sri Lanka phrasebook
Bangladesh
Karakoram Highway

Africa
Africa on a shoestring
East Africa
Swahili phrasebook
West Africa
Central Africa
Morocco, Algeria & Tunisia

North America
Canada
Alaska

Mexico
Mexico
Baja California

South America
South America on a shoestring
Ecuador & the Galapagos Islands
Colombia
Chile & Easter Island
Bolivia
Brazil
Peru
Argentina
Quechua phrasebook

Middle East
Israel
Egypt & the Sudan
Jordan & Syria
Yemen

Lonely Planet

Lonely Planet published its first book in 1973. Tony and Maureen Wheeler had made a lengthy overland trip from England to Australia and, in response to numerous 'how do you do it?' questions, Tony wrote and they published *Across Asia on the Cheap*. It became an instant local best-seller and inspired thoughts of a second travel guide. A year and a half in South-East Asia resulted in their second book, *South-East Asia on a Shoestring*, which they put together in a backstreet Chinese hotel in Singapore in 1975. The 'yellow book', as it quickly became known, soon became *the* guide to the region and has gone through five editions, always with its familiar yellow cover.

Soon other writers came to them with ideas for similar books – books that went off the beaten track with an adventurous approach to travel, books that 'assumed you knew how to get your luggage off the carousel,' as one reviewer put it. Lonely Planet grew from a kitchen table operation to a spare room and then to its own office. Its international reputation began to grow as the Lonely Planet logo began to appear in more and more countries. In 1982 *India – a travel survival kit* won the Thomas Cook award for the best guidebook of the year.

These days there are over 70 Lonely Planet titles. Over 40 people work at our office in Melbourne, Australia and another half dozen at our US office in Oakland, California.

At first Lonely Planet specialised in the Asia region but these days we are also developing major ranges of guidebooks to the Pacific region, to South America and to Africa. The list of walking guides is growing and Lonely Planet now has a unique series of phrasebooks to 'unusual' languages. The emphasis continues to be on travel for travellers and Tony and Maureen still manage to fit in a number of trips each year and play a very active part in the writing and updating of Lonely Planet's guides.

Keeping guidebooks up to date is a constant battle which requires an ear to the ground and lots of walking, but technology also plays its part. All Lonely Planet guidebooks are now stored and updated on computer, and some authors even take lap-top computers into the field. Lonely Planet is also using computers to draw maps and eventually many of the maps will be stored on disk.

The people at Lonely Planet strongly feel that travellers can make a positive contribution to the countries they visit both by better appreciation of cultures and by the money they spend. In addition the company tries to make a direct contribution to the countries and regions it covers. Since 1986 a percentage of the income from each book has gone to aid groups and associations. This has included donations to famine relief in Africa, to aid projects in India, to agricultural projects in Central America, to Greenpeace's efforts to halt French nuclear testing in the Pacific and to Amnesty International. In 1989 $41,000 was donated by Lonely Planet to these projects.